History of Skye

Alexander Nicolson

Third Edition edited by Cailean Maclean

History of Skye, third edition
Published in 2012
by The Islands Book Trust

www.theislandsbooktrust.com

ISBN: 978-1-907443-14-5

Text © Alexander Nicolson
First edition published 1930. Second edition 1994.

British Library Cataloguing in Publication Data. A CIP record for
this book can be obtained from the British Library.

Front cover image © Mark Butterworth

Typeset by Prepress Projects Ltd, Perth (www.prepress-projects.co.uk)
Printed and bound by Martins the Printers Ltd, Berwick Upon Tweed
Cover design by Prepress Projects Ltd

The Islands Book Trust
Ravenspoint Centre
Kershader
South Lochs
Isle of Lewis
HS2 9QA

Tel: 01851 880737

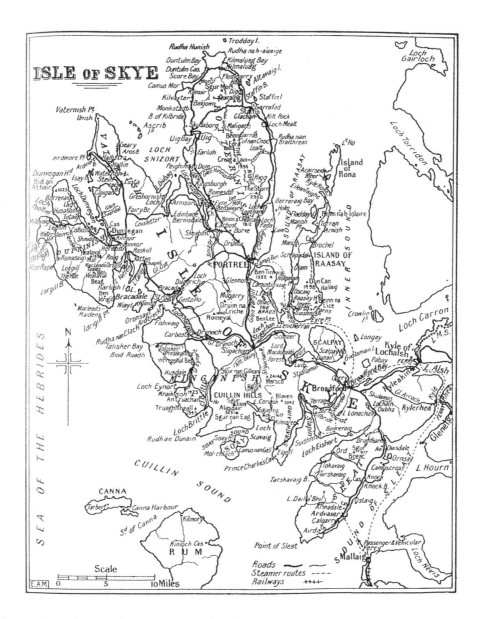

Map from Alexander Nicolson's own *Guidebook to Isle of Skye and Adjacent Islands*, circa 1931.

History of Skye

A Record of The Families, The Social Conditions
and The Literature of The Island

Alexander Nicolson, M.A

Second Edition edited by Dr Alasdair Maclean

It will be noticed that the traditional story, often unverified, and mayhap unverifiable, occupies a prominent place in this work; and its inclusion will no doubt be deplored by those who are severly historical. But, in treating of the history of a people whose lives have been influenced so profoundly by such tales, one feels that to ignore them wholly would be unpatriotic, apart altogether from their ethical implications, and their usefulness in illustrating certain phases in the evolution of our race. Through them, readers have been drawn into the pleasant by-paths of history. They certainly help to enliven its otherwise grave and monotonous aspect; and do they not often afford us more accurate glimpses of the manner of life and the aspirations of a people than those narratives which are founded on the most reliable records?

Alexander Nicolson.

GLASGOW 1930

CONTENTS

INTRODUCTION

That the Islands Book Trust resolved to publish this new edition of Alexander Nicolson's *History of Skye* is a testament to the enduring quality of the author's scholarship and the fact that, since it appeared first in 1930, no other has attempted such a detailed and comprehensive history of the island. Copies of the first edition of a *History of Skye* rarely appear in second-hand and antiquarian book shops' lists and, when they do, the books command prices which are hundreds of times greater than the original cover price of ten shillings and sixpence. A second, revised edition was published in 1994 and sold out quickly. Since then, there appears to have been a great deal of unsatisfied demand for this classic. Given this the decision of the Islands Book Trust to produce a third edition is most welcome.

This edition remains much the same as that produced in 1994 by Maclean Press. However, important changes in the design have been incorporated in this edition with a view to making text more accessible and the overall package more attractive to readers. It also includes, as one of the appendices, a fascinating biography of Alexander Nicolson, compiled by his grandson, Alasdair Beal. Another innovation in this edition is a glossary of places mentioned in the book along with their respective National Grid references. The latter's purpose is to be of help to readers who might not be so well acquainted with some of the smaller locations to which Alexander Nicolson referred in his text. Also it will be of help where his spelling of place-names departs from the versions accepted today.

Since the *History of Skye*'s publication in 1930 Gaelic orthography has changed, most notably as a result of work done at the end of last century to produce a standard orthography. This culminated in the publication of the Gaelic Orthographic Conventions or GOC as it is better known. Whereas it was tempting to 'modernise' the Gaelic appearing in this edition, a conscious decision was made not to, mainly in order to retain the charm and integrity of a book which was written early in the twentieth century.

As with the production 1994 edition, this one retains a close connection with Nicolson's family. My father, the late Alasdair Maclean, who edited the second edition for Maclean Press in 1994, was a nephew of Alexander Nicolson. At the time Maclean Press was a partnership involving Roger Miket, who contributed considerably to that edition, and me. Nicolson's close family, notably Alasdair Beal, also made a significant contribution to that publication. With the latter Alasdair, I have been involved in preparing this new edition for publication. That it is now available is in no small measure due to the efforts of Alayne Barton, John Randall and Donnie Morrison from the Islands Books

Trust, the organisation which took over many of Maclean Press's titles. A debt of gratitude is also owed to Nancy Gatz of Portree who, apart from performing a superb job at the proof-reading stage, made numerous useful suggestions. We also acknowledge the substantial work done by those who prepared the 1994 edition upon which this edition is largely based.

Cailean Maclean
Editor
January 2012

INTRODUCTION TO THE SECOND EDITION, 1994

The death took place at his Glasgow home on December 12 of Mr Alexander Nicolson, who was perhaps the greatest living authority on Scottish Gaelic and certainly the greatest authority on the island of Skye ...

(Oban Times, 15 December 1966).

It is a privilege to be able to offer this new and extended edition of the *History of Skye,* not only because of its intrinsic value, but also as a memorial to the remarkable man who wrote it.

Alexander Nicolson was born in 1884 in Achnahanaid in the Braes of Trotternish, the eldest son of Somhairle *Mór* Nicolson, son of John, son of Somhairle the Piper. His mother was Iseabail, daughter of Donald *Bàn* MacLeod, son of Alexander, son of John, son of *Ailean Ruadh.* Life was hard in the congested township of Achnahanaid, as Alexander Nicolson suggests, his people having been evicted from their ancestral land in Holm to make room for sheep and cattle on the extended farm of *Scorrybreck,* and having to find a foothold in the Braes overcrowded with the jetsam of that and other clearances on Skye.

It is unlikely that *Somhairle Mór,* literate only in his Gaelic Bible and the Oban Times and struggling to bring up his numerous family, would have had any academic ambitions for his eldest son but it is probable that Iseabail, herself deeply steeped in oral Gaelic culture, would have early recognised and nurtured his talents, and encouraged young Alexander Nicolson to qualify himself for University entrance as a primary school pupil and later a pupil teacher. Despite many difficulties, studying in a small house with poor lighting and crowded with several boisterous younger brothers, he succeeded in gaining entrance to Glasgow University.

The 'Obituary' continues,

At the university he gained medals and distinguished places in many of his classes, and he was a particularly able student in geology. After graduation, he was for many years a teacher in several Glasgow schools. He knew the island of Skye as no-one else did, having studied all there was to know of its geology and history and having been by foot to every village in the island. In 1930 he published a large history of Skye which he had been preparing for a second edition at the time of his death. For the past 40 years or so Mr Nicolson's main work was on Scottish Gaelic in particular, and to a lesser extent on Irish.

In an obituary elsewhere from the pen of the Rev TM Murchison, one time Moderator of the General Assembly of the Church of Scotland,

Perhaps even more important than his History of Skye is Alexander Nicolson's 'Modern Gaelic: A Basic Grammar', which appeared in 1936. There are many Gaelic grammars in existence, but Nicolson's has a place and authority of its own. Certainly few people had a better right to add to the number of Gaelic grammars, for he had many years' experience of teaching Gaelic, to young and old. Nicolson aimed in his Grammar at simplifying the somewhat complex intricacies of the declension of the Gaelic noun.

Among his other works, were books on Gaelic riddles, and children's games and rhymes (*Gaelic Riddles and Enigmas*, 1938 and *Oideas na Cloinne*, 1948). He was for more than 20 years Gaelic lecturer in the colleges of Jordanhill and Notre Dame, and during the war, in the absence of the late Professor Angus Matheson, he was lecturer in Celtic at Glasgow University.

Rev TM Murchison states that

Of the many lectures delivered by Alexander Nicolson to various societies at least two are in print - both in the published Transactions of the Gaelic Society of Glasgow. In Volume IV (The Active Gael), published in 1936, there is a paper on Mary Macleod, the poetess of Harris and Dunvegan in the 17th century, and in Volume V there is an excellent paper on The MacBeths, Hereditary Physicians of the Highlands.

Dr Alasdair Maclean

ACKNOWLEDGEMENTS FOR THE SECOND EDITION, 1994

The preparation of this new edition could not have been achieved without the help of the following individuals and institutions:

Firstly, thanks to Mrs Ishbel Beal, daughter of Alexander Nicolson, for permission to publish this second edition of her father's work, together with a specimen of his poetry. Secondly, to Alasdair Beal, who faithfully proofed his grandfather's annotations which had been prepared for a second edition prior to the latter's death. Thanks to Dr Sorley Maclean for advice in connection with oral and written source material, to Val Measham who painstakingly re-set the original text and to Sine Gillespie who proofed a number of the amendments and the bibliography.

Thanks are also due to Keith MacLennan who kindly provided the translation of Donald Roy MacDonald's Latin verses.

Our thanks are extended to the following libraries and institutions for their assistance in carrying out the research for this second edition – Clan Donald Library (Skye), Highland Regional Libraries (Portree and Inverness), Mitchell Library (Glasgow), National Library of Scotland (Edinburgh), and the library of *Sabhal Mor Ostaig* (Skye).

Finally, special thanks are due to Roger Miket who has been the mainspring of this second edition of Nicolson's *History of Skye*.

CHAPTER I

Prehistoric Remains

The wayfarer who strays through the silent glens, and over the lone moorlands of Skye, cannot fail to be impressed by the number and variety of the relics of antiquity that he everywhere encounters. He will notice that there, as elsewhere, these memorials of the past have suffered severely, through the years, at the hands of the utilitarian and the despoiler; but they still retain much of their original features, and they are of deep interest to us, for they represent the handiwork of our early ancestors.

The Burial Cairns

Examples of the chambered cairns are common. There is a cemetery at Eyre Point in Raasay, where the foundation of the cairn, the dolmen, and its rude stone cist, may still be seen, though the covering stones have been removed for building purposes. At Liveras, in Broadford, one was opened in 1832 and in its burial chamber were found a few stone implements, and some human bones. The traveller, Thomas Pennant, records that, in 1772, when he was in Skye, he was presented by Mrs MacDonald of Kingsburgh, the famous Flora MacDonald, with an urn found *"in a stone chest beneath an immense cairn"; and, he adds, "the urn was of excellent workmanship"*. It was probably to this relic that the Rev. Malcolm MacLeod, the father of Mr Roderick of Snizort, refers when he says, *"In the cairns are found urns wherein were deposited the ashes of renowned chiefs. One such was discovered recently in a cist 5 feet by 4½ feet, in which also was a sword and pin of compound metal. The urn was nicely carved"*.

Adamnan, in his account of the conversion of the chief, Artbranan, who came to Skye to be baptised by St. Columba, and died immediately after the ceremony, says, *"And his companions buried him, raising a heap of stones over his grave."*

Stone Circles

In view of the large number of stone-circles that are found in several of the islands of the Hebrides, it is surprising that so few have been preserved in Skye while, of those that are undoubted representatives of that type of construction, but a few isolated monoliths now remain to mark their site. Only three authentic examples are known, two of them in the parish of Strath and one in the district of Uig.

Duns and Brochs

Of these remains of a bygone age, the most common type is the dun, or the broch, and it is no exaggeration to say that, in the whole of Britain, there is no other region, of equal area, where so many of these ancient forms of fortifications are met with as in the island of Skye. On making a casual enumeration of them a list of eighty-three was compiled, and there are doubtless many more.

Some of them, it is true, are now represented merely by a few courses of masonry, and great heaps of dilapidation; but there are others, such as *Dun Beag* at Struan, Dun Borrodale in Raasay, and Dun Osdale in Duirinish, where a considerable portion of wall is still left standing; and where the general structure of 'balla nam fianntaichean' (wall of the Fingalians) may be studied with tolerable ease.

They are more numerous around the coast, especially in positions where no bold escarpments front the sea; but several are found far inland, as *Dun Bhuirbh* in Trotternish, Dun Arkaig in Glen Ullinish, and Dun Hallin in Waternish.

All of them show a uniformity of construction, of plan, and of position, which is indeed wonderful; and they would seem to differ merely in magnitude, and in height. Thus all are broad-based, circular in plan, and are built of large rectangular blocks of local stone, well knit together in definite courses. There is always a double wall, the inner approximately perpendicular, the outer sloping gradually inwards, so that the width of the whole narrows according to the height. The basal portion of the wall is from 12 to 15 feet broad, and here are found two, and sometimes three, chambers opening towards the courtyard of the building. These niches are built after the manner of the beehive type of primitive dwellings, the upper course overlapping the lower, until the topmost layer may be covered by a single slab of stone.

Stairs lead from these chambers to intramural galleries covered by large lintels and a special feature of the structures is that the upper portion of the wall is hollow, the passages being arranged in tiers and covered with large flagstones, the roof of the lower being the floor of the one immediately above it.

There is only one doorway, about 3 feet high and 2 feet 9 inches wide, spanned by monster monoliths, and in this entrance there is invariably found a guard chamber, if not two, in the thickness of the wall. There are no other openings whatsoever in the outer wall, but it is noticeable that there are small apertures, which may have been 'peepholes' in certain of the passages and chambers in the upper storeys and looking into the courtyard of the building.

It is noteworthy that no trace of mortar has ever been found in these buildings, but where limestone, or other fusible rock prevails locally, recourse was sometimes had to vitrification – i.e., the melting of the outer face of the higher parts of the wall by the application of intense heat, so that the fused material flowed down the lower courses welding stone to stone, cooling into one solid mass. Evidences of this mysterious process are found in such duns as that of Skudaborg, near Uig and in the old fort on an island that lies off *Dun Sgathaich*, on the west of Sleat.

Though there is little now left to attest it, these brochs were originally of a considerable height. Many people now living (1930) remember the time when a good specimen of this structure, Dun Borrodale in the island of Raasay, was over 17 feet high, before the upper courses had been dislodged for the purpose of providing stone for an extension of the local school. And Pennant, who toured the Highlands in 1772, tells us that *Dun Beag* in Struan was then 18 feet in height; its walls are over 12 feet high, in places, at the present day.

The fact that there is no indication of windows in the outer wall suggests the conclusion that these buildings were places of defence and of refuge to which the population of the region might retreat when beset by an invading foe. And well they would serve their purpose, for they must have been well-nigh impregnable, so far as primitive weapons could do them any damage. They could not be set on fire and, owing to the very constricted nature of their only doorway, entrance could never have been effected, so long as the defenders offered any resistance.

That these forts could provide a safe sanctuary for a large community is shown by the extent even of the floor space, without taking cognisance of the accommodation afforded by the chambers and passages, within the walls. Thus the diameter of *Dun Beag* in Struan is 60 feet, giving the court inside an area of over 310 square yards.

It was popularly believed that these buildings were used as sites for beacons, a view upheld both by tradition and by the early writers who make reference to them. Thus Martin Martin, in his account of the Western Isles, says of the duns of Skye:

All these forts stand upon eminences and are so disposed that there is not one of them which is not in view of some other; and by this means, when a fire is made on any one fort, it is in a few moments afterwards communicated to all the rest and this has always been observed upon sight of any number of foreign vessels, or boats, approaching the coasts.

(Martin, M, 1716, p. 153).

Again, in the First Statistical Account, published in 1795, the Rev. William Bethune, minister of the Parish of Duirinish, speaks of them thus: "Duns seem not to have been roofed and were probably intended for places to make signals from by smoke and fire."

All, of course, agree that the beacon usually served the purpose of the telegram to primitive man when alarms were to be communicated to his tribe, but it is highly improbable, if not impossible, that the site of the fire was the dun. The fire could be lit only in the courtyard of the building, and it would require to be a mighty conflagration to show flames above the topmost course when that was, in some cases, at least 40 feet high, apart altogether from the obvious contingency that a fire of such magnitude would render the fort untenable for a considerable period of time after it had died out. Indeed, all the evidence seems to force the conclusion upon us that the beacon was raised on the lofty mound so often found in close proximity to these ancient forts, and that may be suggested as an explanation of the problem of the higher knoll that invariably overlooks the site of the dun – a problem that has so long puzzled archæologists.

Naturally enough, toll has been taken of the masonry of these buildings for the construction of dwelling-houses and dykes, with the result that most of them are now merely chaotic masses of dilapidation. Where excavation has been carried out, as at *Dun Beag* in Struan, numerous specimens of primitive weapons and implements have been discovered. There were stone implements by the hundred, beautifully fashioned and polished, axes, hammers, and arrowheads, so many, indeed, that one chamber was piled high with these arms of the past, and their computation in hundreds is no exaggeration. Implements of horn and of bone such as combs and bodkins, were also found, and vessels made of baked clay were represented. Amid the heterogeneous collection of these ancient relics, one noticed a large mass of the slag of iron, showing that the fort was occupied at least as late as the 'Iron Age'.

Despite the numerous examples we have of the duns, their origin is still enshrouded in mystery. Tradition says they were built by the *Feinn*, mythical warriors of old, while the early records declare that they were erected by the Norse during their occupation of the Western Isles, but from the nature of the relics found in them, it may safely be averred that these towers were hoary with the moss and the lichens of the ages long before the first Norse galleys made their appearance in the western seas.

Beehive Dwellings

The formation of the chambers in the walls of the duns suggests other structures one meets with in Skye, namely, the beehive type of dwelling. These buildings are huddled closely together, circular in form, and roughly cone-shaped in plan so that the topmost course can be covered by one large slab. The best examples of such dwellings are found at *Lon Fearn,* on the east of Trotternish where they are called *Tighean nan Druinich,* or 'Druids' Houses'; and in the 'island' in the drained St. Columba's Lake at Monkstadt. From their restricted accommodation, and especially their location at the latter place, it has been suggested that they were used by the monks as places for contemplation and prayer. There can be no doubt they were, and Dr. Petrie has characterised these ruins in St. Columba's Lake as *"one of the best examples of a monastic establishment in the kingdom".* From the nature of the remains discovered in buildings of this type, however, some at least were constructed long before the Christian era.

The Erd Houses

Constructions of a different type, the earth houses, or 'Picts' Houses', as they are often called, also occur in Skye. These are long, narrow tunnels flanked and roofed with stone, penetrating the side of a hill, sometimes to a distance of 60 feet, and widening at their inmost end into a circular chamber which is so low that one cannot stand upright in it. Structures of this type have been discovered, among other places, at Ben Tianivaig, Scorrybreck, Ullinish and Claigean, at Loch Duagraich, Raasay and at Vatten, where is found perhaps the most elaborate of them all, with its offsets from the main passage and its large inner chamber. Their purpose remains unclear, but Martin Martin, who wrote an account of the Western Isles in 1716, believed that *"They served to hide a few people, and their goods in time of war".*

Miscellaneous Discoveries

Among other discoveries of the work of early man in Skye it may be recalled that during the operation of draining St. Columba's Lake, two canoes, shaped and hollowed out of a single tree-trunk, were found but they have been lost.

A party engaged in cutting peat in Braes, in the year 1910, happened to alight on what seems to have been the site of a 'factory' of Neolithic times. There were whole mounds of the 'flakes' of flint, and of other cherty rocks, rough rejected shapes they were, with only two specimens of the finished article procurable among the debris.

On the same moss in 1946 a socketed axe and gouge were unearthed from the blue clay at the bottom of the peat bank and, at Roisgil, another socketed axe was discovered with a goodly portion of its wooden handle discernible, preserved by the surrounding peat. Numerous spearheads in a wonderful state of preservation have been unearthed in many parts.

In the summer of 1913, the writer discovered a bloomery, or ancient furnace, in the island of Raasay. It lay in close proximity to that outcrop of ironstone where the winning of the ore was first begun by Messrs. Baird of Coatbridge. The hearth was roughly circular in form and about 8 feet in diameter. Like the sides of the building, it was constructed of the refractory Torridonian sandstone stained deep red by many a fire. All around and within the enclosure lay heaps of the slag of iron, incorporating fragments of undigested limestone that had evidently been employed as a flux.

It was with keen regret that one learned, after the turmoil of the World War had subsided, that the materials of this interesting relic of antiquity had been used in the repairing of an adjoining roadway, so that scarcely a trace of it now remains.

Amongst a great mass of other interesting matter, only a passing reference can be made to the discovery of such relics as sculptured stones, the famous symbolic stones of Raasay, Fiskavaig, Snizort, and *Tobar nam Maor* at the head of Dunvegan Loch, stone coffins, and weapons of bronze. When, however, we turn from a study of the prehistoric relics to consider the written records of the island in early times, we are confronted with such meagre and unsubstantial materials that the greatest difficulty is experienced in constructing a clear and coherent narrative of the whole. Indeed, so dim is our knowledge of Skye in the remote past, that there is much truth in the dictum that its early history is as misty as its mountains. A few facts do emerge from the pervading darkness, but they scarcely avail to allow us to fix our bearings with any degree of certainty.

Early Recorded History

One of the first to mention the island was Ptolemy of Alexandria, who flourished in the year 120 A.D. He included Skye in his famous map, but placed it midway between Caithness and Norway, and called it *Sketies*. Stray references to the island are found in the works of the Irish monks, as the statement in the *Annals of Ulster* to the effect that the people of Skye paid tribute to Badeun, son of Carril, who died in 581. *Tighernac*, too, writes of Skye as, when he adverts to the secession of the Scots clergy from the domination of Rome, he says they went to Ireland accompanied by the sons of Gartnaidh, and they took with them the Columban clergy of Skye, *"navigatio filiorum Gartnaidh ad Hiberniam cum plebe Scith"*.

These are cited as a few of the uncertain echoes that reach us down the years from that distant past, but so indefinite are they that one can make but little of their jumbled sounds.

We are not clear who the occupants of the island were in that faint dawn of history; whether they were Goths from Scandinavia, or Goidels from Europe's central plains.

Nor does the evidence from place-names help us much in our enquiry. The word Skye, itself, is most obdurate in yielding to derivation, and while some philologists advocate a Gaelic origin, others are as insistent on tracing it to the language of the Norse. Thus, MacBain says the root is Celtic, and is *sci*, which means cut, and it is noteworthy that in the *Annals of Ulster* it is called *Scith*. Following his lead, Henderson also holds that the word is pre-Norse.

On the other hand, the Rev. Dr. John MacPherson of Sleat was of the opinion that it was derivable from the Norse *sky* ('cloud') and *ey* ('island'), the Misty Island, and this interpretation is supported by the references made to Skye in early song and saga. Apart from the fact that it is frequently styled by James MacPherson, of Ossianic fame, *'The Isle of Mist'*, there is the supposition that this feature is such as to impress its early inhabitants much more powerfully than its indented coastline in the days when cartography was in its infancy; and one is lured to that view by the fact that the most prominent topographical features on the island have names of Norse origin.

But when we reflect that the term for island in Norse (-*ay* or -*ey*) invariably takes the form -*aidh* in Gaelic, that it is persistent, and that the name of Skye shows no trace whatsoever of that ending, we are forced to abandon this position.

Now the folk derivation is from Sgiath ('a wing'); and Dean Munro, who wrote in 1549, thus refers to the island: "This ile is callit by the Erishe, Ellan Skyane, that is, in English, the Wingitt ile, be reason it has maney wyngs and points lyand furth frae it through the devyding of the loches"; and Martin Martin, writing in about 1685, says "Skie, in the ancient language, Skianach, that is winged, is so called because the two opposite northern promontories – Waternish lying N.W., and Trotternish lying N.E., resemble wings". It may be added that several of our bards, notably Morison, *An Clàrsair Dall*, and Mackay, *Am Pìobaire Dall*, often called the island *Clar Sgith*, and the Minch *Cuan Sgith*.

The earliest form of the word we know is *Sketis*, in Ptolemy's map, and one is inclined to equate this name with the Celtic form, *Skeitos*, which means 'wing'. We have seen that *Tighernac* calls the island *Sgith*; while Adamnan, in his 'Life of St. Columba' (*c.* 700), refers to it as *Scia*. One is strongly persuaded to call this the Gaelic equivalent for wing, and to do so with the greater confidence in view of the suggestion in that book that the language spoken in Skye at that time was Gaelic. In narrating the advent of the heathen chief, Artbranan, to the island of Skye, he says that the converted chief was baptised in the water called *Dobur Artbranani*: '*Fluvius que ejusdem loci in quo idem baptisma acceperat ex nomine ejus Dobur Artbranani usque in hodiernum nominatus diem ab accolis vocitatus*' ('And the river of the same place in which he had received baptism is to this very day called by the inhabitants from his name, Dobur Artbrani') [Huyshe, W, 1922, p. 57] : water or well of Artbranan; *Dobar* is old Gaelic for modern *dobhar* as we have it in *dobhar chu* or *dobhran* for English otter.

These facts would therefore seem to postulate a Gaelic origin for the word 'Skye', and inferentially that the inhabitants of the island were Goidelic Celts, kindred with the Irish and the people of the Isle of Man. In view, however, of the prevalence in Skye of place-names of truly Norse origin, it may, with safety, be averred that Gaelic had received a severe set-back during the Norwegian regime; but that in no way warrants the conclusion that it had altogether ceased to be the spoken language of the people during the long period of foreign domination that extended to close on 400 years.

The Coming of the Norse

The freehold system of tenure, whereby the land was inalienably vested in a particular family, and the eldest succeeded to the whole property, continued to exist in Scandinavia until the middle of the ninth century. It had many disadvantages. As the estate was indivisible, the younger members of the family had no means of maintenance at home and were constrained by economic necessity to fend for themselves elsewhere. Believing that plundering was a virtue, they harried, among other lands, the Western Isles of Scotland. Their depredations were confined to the summer months, the winter being spent at home. Their first recorded descent on the Hebrides was in 794, and in that year, according to the Irish annalists, Skye was devastated from end to end, and we may conclude that, like other places, that unhappy isle was seldom free from their attentions for the next ninety years. Indeed the *Annals of Ulster* for 794 record, "*Devastation of all the islands of Britain by the Gentiles*", and for the year 795, "*Burning of Rathlin by the Gentiles and Skye was pillaged and devastated.*" (Hennesey, W, 1887, pp. 274–5).

About 875, however, their incursions assumed a new phase. They then came not as invaders, but as immigrants, who wished to flee from the effects of the revolution at home. Their country had long been convulsed by internal strife, and when Harald the 'Fair-haired' had finally emerged as supreme ruler, a new order was superimposed on his country. The old odal system was abolished; and in its place was established a sort of feudal ownership which the freedom-loving Norseman could never abide. Rather than relinquish the conception of absolute right to the soil which they cultivated, bands of them left their native shores and took up their abode on islands off the North and West of Scotland.

Using these as their base, they returned in hordes to plunder their old homes and, according to the *Ynglinga Saga*, written about 1200, "*they infested the coasts of Norway during the summer months, doing considerable damage to the country."* Their depredations had become so frequent, and disastrous that Harald *"went out with an army every summer but when the Vikings perceived his army they always fled, and took refuge in the open sea. The King, becoming dissatisfied with these expeditions, followed the Vikings one summer with his army westwards over the sea. He fought many battles in most of which he was victorious. He put to death the chiefs of the pirates and he made indiscriminate slaughter of their followers."*

It would seem, however, that the effects of this conquest were but short-lived for no sooner had he returned home than fresh incursions took place and, having despatched Ketill Flatnose to quell the insurgents, it appears that the viceroy revolted and made common cause with the men of the isles. They made him their king, *"and during his life he was master of the Hebrides."* This would seem to point to an amalgamation of the Norsemen with the native race and the suggestion is supported by the record which says that, in 907, *"the men of Lochlann had many a Goidelic foster son."* This mixed race, the *Gallgael,* as they were called, are described as *"a restless and ungovernable people"* in the Norse sagas, but they must have been reconciled to the Norwegian sway again, for, according to an Irish account of the Battle of Clontarf, in 1014, men from Skye (*Sgithidh*) fought in the ranks of the Norse against Brian Boru, the Irish King. The *Annals of Ulster* speak of *"a levy of fierce men, senseless, uncontrollable, unbiddable of the foreigners of Orkney, Man, Skye, Lewis, Kintyre and Argyll"* (Skene, WF, 1847, p. 271) while the *Annals of Innisfallen* mention the same tribes.

According to the *Orkneyinga Saga* Thorfinn and Ronald collected their forces in 1039 and plundered the Hebrides: *"They had a great battle at Vatnsfiórd (Skye) and were victorious"*: could this perhaps be Westerfiord (Loch Bracadale)? (Dasent, W, 1894, p. 42).

Less than 100 years after this, however, their old disaffection broke out afresh, culminating in the killing of Ingemund, the Norse viceroy. A terrible revenge was exacted of the Hebrideans by Magnus Barelegs, King of Norway. In *Magnus' Saga,* it is stated that as soon as the King came to the Hebrides, *"he commenced to burn their habitations – he killed the people and pillaged wherever he went ... Then he made war on Skidi,"* and his *skald* thus recounts his prowess:

> *The peasant lost his land and life*
> *Who dared to bide the Norseman's strife.*
> *The hungry battle-birds were filled*
> *In Skye, with blood of foemen killed;*
> *And wolves on Tiree's lonely shore*
> *Dyed red their hairy jaws in gore.*
>
> (Laing, S, 1844, III, p. 130)

This was in 1098, according to the Sagas.

Having completed his conquest, Magnus appointed Olave the Red as his viceroy and he is designated in history, 'King of Man'. During his reign, an insurrection broke out in Skye in 1140 but, with the support of the great Somerled, who in that year married his daughter, Olave succeeded in restoring order. In the *'MS History'* of Clan Donald, by Hugh MacDonald, the sennachie (the recorder and reciter of stories) of Sleat, we read:

> *Olay and Somerled killed MacLier, who possessed Strath in the Isle of Skye. They killed Godfrey Du by putting out his eyes, which was done by the hermit MacPoke, because Godfrey Du had killed his father formerly. Olay, surnamed the Red, killed MacNicoll in Uist likewise.*
>
> (Skene, WF, 1847, p. 284).

On the death of Olave, Somerled appears to have established himself as independent ruler over all the isles of the Hebrides, from Lewis to Man, together with the mainland of Argyll and he maintained sway over his scattered domains for about six years until he was murdered, in 1164, at Inchinnan in Renfrewshire. Then his brother-in-law, Godfrey *Dubh*, or 'the Black', who had been forced to flee to Norway during the rule of Somerled, returned, and he resumed possession of Skye and the other isles of the west as the vassal of the Norse king. From that time, for about a century, very few facts are found in the records which throw light on the history of Skye until the fateful year 1263.

End of Norse Sway

As might be expected, the inhabitants of *Innsegall*, as the Hebrides were called, were then seldom at peace with their neighbours on the mainland of Scotland; and the rulers of the latter were pleased to connive at the ruthless methods of retaliation which their vassals practised on the 'foreigners'.

Now there arose in Scotland an ardent patriot and loyal supporter of the king, in the person of Ferchar Macintaggart of Ross, the son of the Red Priest of Applecross. This man, of restless energy and abounding resource, had already proved himself of great value to the Scottish king, Alexander II, in quelling dangerous tumults, both in Moray and in Galloway and he seems to have been a veritable, 'thorn in the flesh' to the men of Skye. He was assisted by Kermac MacMaghan (? Matheson), so says an old account, *"against the Norse, especially those of Skie."* His depredations on that unhappy isle were frequent and ruthless for, according to the Norse sagas, *"he sacked villages, desecrated churches and his men, in wanton fury, raised the children on the point of their spears and shook them until they fell to the ground"* (Dasent, W, 1894, p. 340). At length Olave the Black, King of Man and the Isles, appealed to his superior and on 15th July,

1263, Haco, King of Norway, sailed from Bergen with a fleet of 120 ships, *'bent on the conquest of the whole of Scotland'*. The great Armada anchored at Kyleakin ('Haco's Strait') and there was joined by the barons of the isles and almost all the princes of the house of Somerled (Dasent, W, 1894, p. 340). Resuming the voyage, they sailed southwards by the isles to their defeat at Largs, in August, 1263, when the Hebrides were finally lost to Norway. In 1266 they were ceded to Scotland by the treaty of Perth and Skye was added to the territory of the Lord of the Isles.

In the North of Skye there is current a tradition to the effect that some years after this an extensive raid was made by the Norsemen on the district of Trotternish. Their fleet was anchored in Score Bay, but so resolutely did the natives acquit themselves that at the battle of *Blar na Buailte* the invaders betook themselves to their galleys, with the exception of one leader, *Arco Bronmhor* and a contingent who, in the stress of pursuit, made for the island in *Loch Chaluim Chille*, where they defied all efforts to dislodge them. In order to rid the land of such unwelcome intruders, the Lord of the Isles commissioned a certain MacSween, a man of prowess and acumen, to go against *Arco* and he promised him the district of Braes as his reward, if successful. So skillfully, however, had the Norseman fortified his position that MacSween's assaults were easily repulsed and, as his best laid stratagems proved unavailing, the Skyeman resorted to other forms of artifice. Disguising himself as a bard, he obtained access to the isle, and was entertained by *Arco*, as was due to a member of that privileged order. He regaled his host with song and story, a fare that seems at length to have sated the adipose *Arco*, for the sennachie says that *"he fell fast asleep"* and MacSween saw to it that he never woke again. He carried the foreigner's head in the folds of his plaid to his patron at Duntulm and was duly rewarded by being made tacksman of the Braes of Trotternish.

CHAPTER II

Social History

Religion and Culture

The Druidic forms of worship prevailed in Skye, as elsewhere, before the advent of Christianity and, although certain aspects of it were naturally repugnant to the new faith, such was the beauty of its ethic, relevant to particular lines of conduct, that much of it was retained and cherished by the early Christian Church. We catch faint echoes of the lofty morality of the ancient race in various accounts, as in the reference to the conversion of Artbranan in Adamnan's *'Life of St. Columba'* where we read: *"A pagan, an ancient man, whose conduct has been blameless throughout life"* (Huyshe, W, 1922, p. 58). Again, in *'The Dialogues of the Ancients'*, a compilation of the eleventh century and characterised, mayhap, by a reaction against the strict monastic code and methods of thought that were then in vogue, there is a scene where St. Patrick interviews Ossian. The former declares that the *Feinn* must be in Hell as they died without knowledge of Christ – a statement which Ossian, with impressive pathos and splendid piety, counters thus:

Fionn, King of the Feinne, the generous one, was without blemish! All the qualities that you and your clerics say are according to the rule of the King of the stars, Fionn's Feinne had them all and, if they are in pain, great would be the shame, for if God Himself would be in bonds, my chief would fight on his behalf. Fionn never suffered any one to be in pain or difficulty and can his doom be in Hell, in the house of cold?

Here are no notions of vindictiveness towards their fellow-men: nothing but the thought of sympathy and ready helpfulness. *"O Oscar, bend the strong in arms but spare the feeble hand,"* is a characteristic injunction and whether we believe in the authenticity of Ossian or not, we are forced to admit that there is a genuine feature of the race embodied in the saying ascribed to him: *"Within this bosom there is a voice. It bids Ossian help the helpless in their hour of need."* The readiness with which they went to the aid of those in distress is exemplified in the proverb, *"Ge fagus clach do'n làr, is faisge na sin cobhair Choibhe"* (Though near is stone to earth, nearer than that is the help of the Druid): (see *Nicolson's Proverbs*) and even the writers of Greece and Rome who mention them, are constrained to pay deference to their sense of chivalry and their practice of hospitality. The stranger was always welcome to partake of whatever entertainment they could afford, and they never closed the door at night without looking around in expectation of a visitor.

The red oak is ablaze; the spire of its flame is on high. The traveller sees its light on the dusky heath, as night spreads around him her raven wings. He sees it, and is glad. 'There,' says he, to his companion, 'we shall pass the night. The door of Fionn is always open, and the name of his hall is the stranger's home'.

And the classic writers were also careful to ascribe to them the qualities of display and of pugnacity; but if the sublimated ideals of the age, transmitted to us in their proverbs mean anything, their tenor seems to attest quite the contrary. *"Fuil mo naimh cha d' iarras riamh nam bu mhiann leis triall an sìth"* ('Blood of foeman ne'er was sought if he chose to part in peace'); and *"Cha deachaidh neach riamh dubhach bho Fhionn"* ('None ever went sad from Fingal'). These, and many others of similar import, show that that ancient race was fully imbued with the best ideals of a noble culture; and if the individuals did, on occasion, fall short in their ordinary conduct, there was surely hope for a people that could apprehend such lofty inspirations. *"If the Celt were made of the same materials as the Greek or the Roman"*, once declared a famous writer, *"his moral code should certainly have made him a better man, and a greater hero."* And there can be no doubt it was because of the clean soil it found ready to its hand that the Columban Church was able to nurture an ideal of Christian perfection which is not paralleled by any other branch of that faith.

St. Columba visited Skye about 585, and, according to Adamnan, *"he stayed for some days there"* (Huyshe, W, 1922, p. 58). He was the patron saint of the northern part of the island and his influence is manifest in the prevalence of places that bear his name. The Rev. Donald MacQueen, the cicerone of Dr. Johnson, says there were thirty places of worship in Trotternish, *"besides many monasteries,"* dedicated to the saint. It is noteworthy that Portree Bay was anciently called St. Columba's Loch, and a tidal island in the inner bay, off the shore of the township of Penifiler, is still called *Eilean Chaluim Chille*; and on it are found indications of an ancient building, which is held to have been a chapel of the early Church.

In the north of Skye, at Monkstadt (Monk's Steading), there is another *Loch Chaluim Chille*, which was drained, after two previous attempts, in the year 1824. Here are found the remains of a hamlet of Columban *coenobium*, consisting of beehive dwellings of dry stone, and a 'chapel,' which, from the fact that it is built with mortar, may belong to a later period. A writer of the seventeenth century describes these ruins as consisting of a *"tower and a town"*.

Again, on St. Columba's island at the head of Loch Snizort are the ruins of another church, which the Rev. Malcolm MacLeod, who wrote the *First Statistical Account* for the parish, says *"had in all probability once been the metropolitan church of Skye"* (see Appendix 4) and, among other places, chapels on Troday, and on *Fladda Chuain*, were dedicated to St. Columba.

There is an Annait (principal church of an area) a mile north of Fairy Bridge. This is the 'Temple of Anaitis' so called by Rev. Donald MacQueen, who conducted Boswell to it and is mentioned in the *'Tour...'* by the latter (Boswell, J, 1955, p. 153).

In the *'Life of St. Columba'*, by Adamnan, there occur two passages which refer to the sojourn of the saint in Skye. In one, mention is made of an encounter with a *"huge wild boar pursued by hounds,"* (Huyshe, W, 1922, p. 136) and the miraculous killing of the animal *"by the efficacy of the words"* of the saint. In the other, which is worthy of being quoted in full, Adamnan says:

One day, as the saint was staying for some days in the island of Skye, he struck the seashore with his staff and said to his attendants,

'Strange, my children, this day a pagan, an ancient man, whose conduct has been blameless throughout life, will receive baptism, die and be buried on this spot'; and, lo! about an hour after, a boat came into the harbour, on whose prow sat a decrepit old man the chief of the Geona Cohort. Two young men took him out of the boat and brought him before the Saint. After being instructed by the Saint through an interpreter the old man believed, and was baptised; and when the sacrament was administered, he died on the same spot after the saint's prediction: and his companions buried him there, raising a heap of stones over his grave (congesto lapidum acervo). The cairn may still be seen on the sea coast, and the river, in which he was baptised, is called to this day by the inhabitants, Dobur Artbranani.

(Huyshe, W, 1922, pp. 58–9)

Just as Columba was the patron saint of the north of Skye, so Maelruba was of the southern and central portions of the island. According to *Tighernac,* he founded a church at Applecross in 673, and thence he carried the torch of Christianity throughout the Highlands and the Isles as place-names show. There are sites of chapels dedicated to him at Ashaig, Kilmaree, and Eynort, and the 25th of August was observed at Broadford for many centuries as the festival of *Maol Ruadh.* Although there appears to be no record of it, we cannot doubt that he carried his proselytizing zeal in person to Skye, as elsewhere, during his long ministry of forty-nine years.

The other representatives of the early church whose names are commemorated in Skye are: – *Mo Luag,* the Bishop of Lismore, where he died in 592, and to whom chapels have been dedicated both in the north of Trotternish and in the island of Raasay; St. Congan, Coan or Comghan, has his name enshrined in ruined chapels in Glendale, in Strath and at Trumpan in Waternish, whilst other names are Talorgan, whose 'cell' was in Beal, near Portree, of old Kiltalorgan, and now corrupted into Kiltaraglen;

St. Martin, in Kilmartin; St. Donan, in Kildonan; St. Assynt, the patron saint of Bracadale, in the chapel at Caroy. St. Turos' Chapel was on Isle Altavaig, in Staffin, which Martin describes as *"a little old chapel".* St. Clement's name is perpetuated in *Tobar Chliamain,* a chalybeate well, in the district of Strath. St. Bride is commemorated in many a *Cill* and 'Kil' in Skye and St. Francis in *Teampul Frangaig* in Borreraig and Scalpay.

Many incidents go to show that the Columban clergy looked to Ireland for guidance and support, and it is interesting to note that when that keen controversy was raging, which culminated at the Synod of Whitby in 664, in rending the early church in twain, it is said Colman and the Scots clergy left the Roman section and removed to Ireland, *"accompanied by the sons of Gartnaidh, who took with them the Columban clergy of Skye and returned two years afterwards"* (Cameron, A, 1871, p. 12).

The coming of the Norse administered a severe blow to Christianity. Many of the monasteries were pillaged, their manuscripts scattered far and wide wherever the guardian monks could find refuge and, in the dispersal, numerous priceless records must have been for ever lost. In the *'Book of Leinster'* it is stated, in effect, that the writings of the *"few men of learning"* who had survived the Norse invasions were burned by the plunderers, while Keating says that neither bard nor musician pursued his wonted calling in the land during the sway of the Norsemen. But there is ample evidence to show that the accounts of atrocities which have come down to us have, in many cases, been exaggerated by the monks and that the Norse were not altogether the blood-thirsty ghouls the former would have us believe them to be. For we must not forget that the Norse themselves possessed numerous sagas and wonderful *eddas,* which, for sublimity of conception, chastity of taste, and wealth of imagery, mark them out as clearly no less inferior in culture to any other contemporary race in Europe. They were intensely fond of the *eddas,* which their *skalds* composed and sang, and their runic form of writing is supposed by some to date back to within a century of the opening of the Christian era.

Those of the Norse who came in 875 would, of course, be too eager to solicit the help of their hosts in the isles to interfere much in the internal affairs of the latter. It is true that widespread plunderings were committed during the expeditions of Harald 'The Fairhaired' and Magnus 'Barelegs', but in the *Magnus' Saga*, written, it must be admitted, when the Norse had become Christian, we find that the writer is very careful to mention that no sacrilege was done by the Norse King, especially when he came to Holy Isle (Iona). *"Magnus gave quarter and peace to all men that were there, and to the property of everybody"* and, again, when in 1263 an appeal was sent to the Norse King, Hacon, to succour the islanders from the cruelty of the men of the mainland of Scotland, it is imputed that the latter *"desecrated churches."*

Indeed, it would seem that the new religion had early made many converts among the Norse who had settled in the Isles, for we are told that the more recalcitrant spirits among them had grown so disgusted with the tenets of the Christian faith that they left the Western Isles and went to reside in Iceland, for the writer of the saga says: *"Ketill, son of Bjorn, would not abide there (the Western Isles), because he saw they had another troth and no wise manly it seemed to him that they had cast off the faith that their kin had held."*

There can be no doubt that the Norse had made some contribution to the Christian faith, and many suggest, with much justification, that it is probably through this channel that we have the conception of a *cold* hell in the oldest stratum of that belief.

> 'S mairg a roghnaicheas ifrinn fhuar
> > Pity him who chooses cold Hell
> Is gur h-i uamh nan draigheann geur.
> > As it is the cave of sharp thorns.

> Is beag orm ifrinn fhuar fhliuch
> > I abhor cold wet Hell,
> Aite bithbhuan is searbha deoch.
> > A lasting place of bitterest drink.
> > > (MacBain, A, & Kennedy, J, 1894, p. 401)

The word *ifrinn* is, of course, the Latin *infernum*, showing it to have been introduced by the early Christians and, indeed, it was held by such an eminent authority as Dr. George Henderson that a belief in hell is wholly absent from the religion of the Gaels in pre-Christian times.

Customs

At early dawn on *Latha Bealltuinn* (May Day) every community was in commotion, and cattle and sheep were rounded up and driven to the vicinity of the homes. Before noon all domestic fires were extinguished, according to the time-honoured custom, and care was taken that no one carried iron about his person. Thereafter bands of men, and animals, might be seen converging on some conspicuous hill in the neighbourhood where two heaps of wood lay piled in close proximity to one another.

When the company arrived there, a bull was sacrificed and portions of the carcase were placed on each pile. At the same time relays of men might be observed vigorously engaged in rubbing together two pieces of sacred hazel (*calltuinn*) until the friction should generate fire. The new flame was immediately applied to the heaps of wood and when it had taken a firm hold, cattle, sheep, and other domesticated animals were driven between the fires so that the whiffs of sacred smoke, which they inhaled, might cure those affected with disease and confer immunity on all, during the ensuing year.

After the performance of that rite several youths, carrying flambeaux of dried sage, encircled sunwise the herds, to ensure fertility and procure freedom from the evils of witchcraft. Finally, with torches still burning, they approached their homes and, after they had walked round the fields of growing crops once, and three times engirdled their dwellings, they entered and, with the consecrated brand, kindled a fire on their own hearths, which was not allowed to die out until the ceremony was to be repeated in the following year.

Meanwhile the elders of the tribe remained behind and on the hill-top offerings were made to the enemies of the flocks – the foxes, the eagles, and the storms – in order to induce them to desist their ravages. One of the fathers reverently placed such foods as butter, cheese, eggs, and milk on a hollow stone at the scene of the celebration and, uttering an incantation, he threw pieces of bread over his left shoulder invoking the floods and the storms to be favourable to corn and pasture and the beasts and birds of prey to spare the lambs and the kids.

According to Martin Martin, the 'need fire', or *tein eigin*, as the sacred fire was called, was withheld from the heads of families until tithes had been paid and other ecclesiastical obligations had been duly discharged; and he adds that male-factors suffered for their crimes by being burned in the fires of Beltane (Martin, M, 1716, p. 113).

Land (tenure and divisions)

The Celtic system of land tenure was entirely different from the Teutonic in that, in the latter, all rights in the land were vested in a superior whereas, in the former, the *tuath,* or the clan, was the virtual owner. It has been observed that this, indeed, was one of the outstanding features of the law that governed property in the early Celtic tribe and another was the principle of gavelkind, whereby the privilege of proprietorship was divided equally among all the male offspring, even the illegitimates having their claims sustained but females were stringently precluded from the rights of succession.

Now, it has already been shown that the laws governing the possession of land in Scandinavia were closely allied to those that obtained in the north and west of Scotland so that when the Norseman migrated to the west, taking with him his infixed notions of *odal,* or freehold, occupancy of land, his presence helped but to intensify the belief of the aboriginal inhabitant that the soil he cultivated was his own by absolute right; and the late Professor Mackinnon of Edinburgh was wont to point to this concept as the reason why the modern Hebridean crofter considers the plot whereon he resides as inalienably his own.

It is thus clear that the coming of the Norse to the Isles did nothing to upset the system of land tenure that prevailed there in the earliest times. The ownership lay with the community as a whole, and certain divisions were made when a family desired to have its own portion separated from that of another.

The Administration of Justice

In addition to his other functions, the Druid of Celtic times executed the offices both of a law-giver and of judge. Under the regime of the Norse, his authority was transferred to the jarl who was responsible for maintenance of order in his own domain. The jurisdiction of that nobleman was itself later delegated to another functionary, a sheriff, and about the beginning of the thirteenth century we find that a certain Paul Balkeson was acting in that capacity in Skye. He was a man of very great influence, owning Harris, North Uist, Sleat, Trotternish, Waternish, and Snizort; and it was probably he who is mentioned as one of the chief opponents of the great Somerled, when the latter sought, with the connivance of Thorfinn, to establish his son Dugall as King of the Isles in opposition to the tyrant Godfrey *Dubh,* or

Godred 'the Black'. Although Paul was virtually a petty ruler in Skye, he was nominally responsible to the King of Norway. He seems to have lived to a great age, for, according to the sagas, he was murdered about the year 1231, some say by putting him first to the torture, then commonly practised in the case of criminals, of gouging out his eyes. The *Chronicle of Man* recounts how the wife of Reginald, Olaf's brother, moved by bitterness at the separation of her sister from Olaf and his marrying the daughter of the Earl of Ross, prompted her son Godfrey to kill Olaf. Olaf fled to Ross where he was joined by Balkeson who also repaired there for refusing to be party to the murder of Olaf. Godfrey sheltered in Skye with a few men in the Island of St. Columba. Olaf and Balkeson, in the dead of night, dragged five boats from the nearest shore of the sea, which was at a distance of two furlongs from the island which was surrounded. Battle at dawn continued to the ninth hour of the day. Olaf and Sheriff Paul landed on the island and slew all found outside the enclosure of the Church, seized Godfrey, blinded and emasculated him.

> *Olaf did not consent to it but could not oppose it because of Balke's son, the Sheriff aforesaid. This was done in the year of Grace 1223.*
> (Goss, D, 1774, p. 89).

In *Hakon Hakonsson's Saga*, it is said that Paul was murdered in the Hebrides by 'Godfrey the Black', son of King Reginald.

In 1231 in the *Chronicles of Man* he is called "Vice Comites de Ski – Pol filius Boke" (Goss, D, 1774, p. 81).

General Conditions (dress, etc.)

As one might expect of such a race, we find that they were adventurous sailors, even in early times completing long voyages to places as remote as the Mediterranean. They imported weapons, richly ornamented, costly cloth, and jewellery, *"for they were inordinately fond of display"*.

Their women folk were highly skilled in the use of vegetable dyes and were thus able to produce that picturesque apparel whose gorgeous colourings so readily won the admiration of foreigners. The *Breacan-feile* (tartan kilt and upper garment combined) was apparently the dress worn by the men, for we read in the *Magnus' Saga* (*c.* 1093):

> *When King Magnus came from his western expedition he adopted those manners in dress which were in use in the western countries, and likewise many of his followers, so that they went about barelegged, having short kyrtles and upper garments and therefore many men called him 'Barelegged'.*

CHAPTER III

Family History

The MacLeods

Their Origin

There appears to be as much uncertainty about the origin of the MacLeods as there is about the early history of the island on which that clan has shed so brilliant a lustre. There are those who would go so far as to suggest that their reputed ancestor, Leot, or Leod, was not even an historical personage but merely the eponym of the tribe, while among those who maintain his actual existence there is much diversity of opinion regarding his parentage and the place of his nativity.

Some would have him to be one of the many sons of Thorfinn, that unscrupulous and able leader who was viceroy when the Norse sway was at the apex of its power in the Highlands; but the main trend of opinion follows the traditional account, which states that Leot was the son of Olaf the Black, King of Man, and Canon R.C. MacLeod of MacLeod, and Alexander MacKenzie, 'The Clans' Historian', hold the same view.

As is well known, that indefatigable worker, William F. Skene, would seem to discredit the belief in the Norse origin of the MacLeods for he declares that *"the accepted authority for this, namely, the Chronicle of Man, makes no mention of their Norse origin,"* but in this he is opposed by a powerful consensus of opinion. Though the ancient records do not help us much in our search for the place of origin of this clan, the name itself, the traditions of the race, and above all, the bards, point to Norway as its ancestral home. Thus *Màiri ni'n Alasdair Ruaidh* often alludes to it. In one of her numerous pæans in praise of her illustrious patron, Sir Norman of Bernera, she says:

> *Fuil dhìreach Rìgh Lochluinn*
> *B'e sud toiseach do sheanachais.*

which, in its literal rendering is:

> The direct blood of the Norse king,
> That was the beginning of your lineage.

(Watson, JC, 1934, p. 39)

And, again:

> *Lochlannaich threun, toiseach do sgeuil,*
>> Puissant Norseman you derive your line,
> *Sliochd solta bho fhreumh Mhànuis.*
>> Lush seed from the stock of Magnus.
>>> (Watson, JC, 1934, p. 48)

while in *The Fairy Lullaby* we have the couplet:

> *Siol nan Leodach, nan lann, 's nan lùireach,*
>> Seed of Leod, of the weapons, and coats of mail,
> *B'e Lochluinn dùthchas do shinnsir.*
>> Norway was the native land of your ancestry.
>>> (MacKay, JG, 1924, p. 133)

Further, we find the MacLeods referred to as:

> *Sliochd Olghair is Ochraidh,*
>> Seed of Olghar and Ochray
> *O bhaile na Boirbhe.*
>> From the city of Bergen.
>>> (Watson, JC, 1934, p. 58)

And in an elegy by another to Sir Norman of Bernera, he is referred to as *"Ua Mhanuis o' mhúr Manuinn,"* or 'The offspring of Magnus from the walls of Man.'

Donald MacLeod (*Do'ull nan Oran*), in his *Smeòrach*, in reference to their origin, says:

> *Cha b'i crionach liath no mosgan,*
>> It was not from hoary or dead wood
> *Bho'n a shiolaich treud an fhortainn*
>> That the fortunate tribe derived

> *Ach fiodh miath, gun mhiar, gun socadh,*
>> But from healthy timber without knot or water-logging,
> *Geal mar ghrian, bho bhian Rìgh Lochluinn.*
>> A kindred white like the Sun from the lustre of the king of Norway.
>>> (MacLeòid, D, 1811, p. 123)

Leod

The accredited progenitor of the MacLeods was the son of Olave the Black, who, by the help of Paul Balkeson, Sheriff of Skye, succeeded to Man, and the Western Isles, in 1223. Olave was married to Christina, daughter of Farquhar, Earl of Ross. He died about 1237 (Saccheverell, W, 1859, p. 45); and is probably the *"Olaghar nan lann, thogadh sròlaibh ri crann"* ('Olav of the spears who would hoist satin [flags] to the mast'), referred to by *Màiri ni'n Alasdair Ruaidh*, the bardess of Dunvegan (Watson, JC, 1934, p. 66). His son Leod, who was born about the beginning of the thirteenth century, entered the bonds of fosterage in his early youth with Balkeson, the kinglet of the northern isles, and on the latter's death in 1231 fell heir to all his lands. We read that,

> *Paul, who was lord of Skye as well as Sheriff, and a man of the greatest power and authority of any in those parts, had been a constant friend of Leod in all his dangers and distresses.*

Hence it happened that Leod was destined to come into possession of an extensive domain, embracing Uist and Harris, ceded to him on the death of Paul, the sheriff; Lewis, from his father; Glenelg, from his grandfather, the Earl of Ross; while, by his marriage, about 1220, with the only daughter of a Norse potentate named MacHarold (MacRaild), he secured Duirinish, Bracadale, Minginish, Lyndale, and much of Trotternish. Whether he came into possession of this portion of Skye by right of dowry or, as some say, by treachery, is not clearly known.

Leod died about 1280, and he was buried in Iona, where six successive chiefs of the clan found a last resting-place after him.

Leod's father-in-law, MacRaild, was a Norse noble, whose seat is traditionally said to have been on the site of the present castle of Dunvegan. He is referred to in the older writings as MacRaild Armunn, the cognomen signifying his office of chamberlain or tax-gatherer to the Norse jarl.

By his marriage with the daughter of MacRaild, Leod had two sons, Norman (*Tormad*) and Torquil (*Torcull*). From the latter, the Lewis branch of the MacLeods derive the patronymic *Siol Thorcuil*, while the descendants of the former, despite Gregory's averment, are seldom referred to as *Siol Thormaid*, but *Siol Leòid*. The appellation, *Siol Thormaid*, occurs once in the works of the bards, when *Màiri ni'n Alasdair Ruaidh* calls them *"Siol Thormaid nan sgiath"* (Watson, JC, 1934, p. 72).

When the patrimony was divided between the brothers, Norman was the older. In most charters granted by the Lords of the Isles the signature of the Skye MacLeods takes precedence over that of the Lewis MacLeods. According to Canon MacLeod, that part of Skye called Waternish was, for some reason or other, granted by Norman to his brother Torquil, and it remained in the family of the latter for several centuries. Torquil held the islands of Raasay and Rona, but not by cession from Norman.

Norman (Tormad), Second Chief

Norman, the 2nd chief of the MacLeods of Skye, assumed power about the year 1280. It would appear that he held part of his lands under the Earl of Ross, for we find that King Robert the Bruce assigned the island of Skye to that nobleman, as part of his dominion, in the year 1309, while Glenelg was ceded to Randolf, Earl of Moray, and it was held by him from 1307 until 1314.

During the chiefship of Norman, Scotland was engaged in a life-and-death struggle with England in order to preserve her freedom. As is well known, most of the Highland clans took part in the Battle of Bannockburn, and it has been stated that between 5,000 and 10,000 islesmen fought on that fateful day. Originally placed in the rear of the Scottish army, they were sent at the very commencement of the battle to reinforce Edward Bruce on the right.

It has not been specifically mentioned that the MacLeods of Skye were present and, accordingly, many writers have concluded that they did not take part in that epoch-making event. We find, however, that it is definitely stated in the *MS, History of the MacLeods* that their chief was at Bannockburn; and Canon MacLeod unhesitatingly adopts that view.

By all accounts, Norman seems to have been a man of great prowess, tall, of fine address, and picturesque appearance. His bushy beard swept his ample breast and it was so long that it was ordinarily *"tucked under his girdle"*.

In the *MS, History of the MacLeods* he is said to have been married to Christina, daughter of Lovat, whereas Mackenzie, in his *History of the MacLeods*, says his wife was Fingula MacCrotan, the daughter of an Irish chief (Mackenzie, A, 1889, p. 11). He had three sons, Malcolm, his successor; Leod, who followed Edward Bruce to Ireland, where he was killed, and Godfrey, who was dedicated to the church and became a monk.

For some time this chief held the office of Sheriff of Skye. He died at Pabbay, his seat in Harris, about the year 1320, and he was buried in Iona. It is noteworthy that he is the 'Torquil' who figures in Scott's *Lord of the Isles*.

Malcolm, Third Chief

Malcolm succeeded his father as chief about the year 1320, and it appears he was not yet reinstated in the family patrimony of Glenelg, as that land was then held by the Bissets. During his suzerainty, Scotland was convulsed by civil strife between the faction of Edward Balliol and that of David Bruce and the subtlest artifices and intrigues were practised by both parties in order to win the adherence of prominent Highland chiefs.

Hence it happened that, in 1335, Skye was conferred by Balliol on John, Lord of the Isles and, in the following year, the charter was confirmed by Edward III, of England who championed the cause of Balliol for his own ends. But when David Bruce had been once more restored to his kingdom, he annulled the charter of Edward and he gave the island to the Earl of Ross. This was in 1344 but by his marriage with the daughter of the Earl of Ross, the Lord of the Isles succeeded in adding Skye to his dominions (Gregory, D, 1881, pp. 25–7).

In order to secure the allegiance of Malcolm, the Chief of the MacLeods, David granted him two-thirds of Glenelg in the year 1343. In the deed is a clause to the effect that he was to hold that portion of Glenelg subject to his provision of a galley of twenty-six oars, to be maintained by him, for the king's service whenever it was required (MacLeod, RC, 1938, p. 275).

This chief is reputed to have been one of the most famous heroes of his age and the so-called, *Drinking Horn of Rory Mór* is still preserved in Dunvegan as a memento to his daring and his great strength. The traditionary accounts of the origin of this interesting relic are many and varied but the one that commands the principal place in popular favour is perhaps the following:

As Malcolm was one day passing alone through the wilds of Ratagan, in Glenelg, on his way home from the district of Beauly, he was assailed by a wild bull, *"the terror and the scourge of the inhabitants"*. The plucky chief grappled with the ferocious brute and so fierce was the combat that one of the horns of the animal was wrenched clean off in the unyielding grip of the puissant chief. Hence, it is said, are derived the crest of the MacLeods, which is a bull's head and their motto, *"Hold Fast"*.

In later years this athletic chief became very corpulent; and, being a man of kindly disposition, he is often referred to as *Calum Reamhar Math* ('Malcolm, the fat, and the good'). He died in the castle of Stornoway about the year 1360 and was buried in Iona. He was married to a daughter of the Earl of Mar, by whom he had several sons and, at least, one daughter. The last, whose name was Margaret, was married to John Bethune, an ancestor of the famous physicians of Skye. His third son, Murdo, was the progenitor of the MacLeods of Gesto, whence the name of this branch is *Clann 'ic Mhurchaidh*. This Murdo was married to the daughter of a noted warrior in Skye, named Gillies, and he acquired the lands of Gesto as part of his wife's dowry.

It is about this time that a man of forceful personality begins to attract our attention for the prominent part he played on the stage of Scottish history. He is John of Islay, the son of Angus *Og*, who had rendered such effective aid to Bruce during the struggle for national freedom. *The Lord of the Isles*, as John was now called, had greatly enhanced his power by his marriage with the heiress, Amie Macruairi, but his unbridled ambition continued to soar and, having attained his object by this marriage, he sought a divorce in order that he might marry the daughter of the High Steward of Scotland and his aims were ultimately realised. The Steward soon afterwards ascended the throne as King Robert II.

An infirm and vacilating king gave a man of John's disposition just the opportunity he desired. So arrogant and defiant had he shown himself in the reign of David II, that the king, after many rebuffs, had at length succeeded in persuading his unruly subject to appear at Inverness, there to tender his allegiance and give hostages for his future behaviour. This was in the year 1369. John acceded to the royal demands. Skye was surrendered to the king, only to be granted anew to the aspiring lord who, on the death of David, took every advantage of his prestige to consolidate his power and extend his dominions. From henceforth, the

Lords of the Isles began to regard themselves as independent kinglets who had inherited the rights of the Norse jarls. Accordingly, while they were willing to do homage to the Scottish king for their possessions on the mainland, they persistently refused to own allegiance for their dominions in the Isles. Thus it happened that, according to the power of the central authority, the Western Isles suffered many vicissitudes, and we find that Skye experienced several changes in ownership. We have seen that it had been granted to John, Lord of the Isles, in 1369, while, in 1382, it was given to Alexander Stewart, Earl of Buchan, by King Robert II.

John (Iain), Fourth Chief

Throughout this troublous time, the chiefship of the MacLeods was vested in John, the fourth of his line. He succeeded his father in 1360 and was the leader of his clan until his death in 1392.

He was a man of uncontrollable temper and tales of his fiendish ferocity are often related. Having heard that two of his daughters were about to be married to two brothers, sons of one of his vassals, MacSwan of Roag, he sought to nullify the betrothals but finding the contracting parties still defiant, he ordered the daughters to be buried alive in the dungeon of the castle, and, having seized the MacSwans, he had them flogged so savagely, *"that there was scarcely a spark of life left in them"* when they were hurled from a precipice to be drowned in a stormy sea (MacLeod, RC, 1927, p. 51).

On another occasion, during a hunt in Harris, he noticed that an albino stag, which he wished to be reserved for his own bow and hounds, had been killed by one of his retainers. He commanded the hapless huntsman to be brought before him, to be disembowelled on the spot by the antlers of the very deer that he had so unwittingly slain. Such an atrocious act could not be allowed to go unavenged and the sept of the murdered man stealthily attacked the MacLeods as they were returning to Skye. As the chief was stepping aboard his galley an arrow sped through the air, striking him in the back of the head and mortally wounding him, so that he fell between the boat and the landing stage. In the confusion that ensued, the boat, occupied by his wife and daughters, was left untended, and it began to drift before a strong westerly wind. It was driven eastwards across the Minch until it reached Idrigil, in Duirinish, where it was pounded to pieces on 'The Maidens' and all its occupants were drowned. (See map for MacLeods Maidens, tall skerries off Idrigil in Durinish) (MacLeod, RC, 1927, p. 53).

Long before that time the MacLeods had succeeded in staying the onslaught of their assailants whom they eventually overwhelmed. Their victory was due, primarily, to the gallantry and the leadership of the second son of the chief, a man named William, who, as he had been educated for the Church, is, in consequence, known as William *'Cléireach'*, or "The Cleric".

William Cléireach, Fifth Chief

William's older brother, Malcolm, was killed in Lewis where he had gone to seek the hand of a daughter of the chief of that island. He quarrelled with a brother of the young lady and in the fray both combatants were mortally wounded.

Although he had been bred for the Church, William proved himself to be a mighty warrior, who by his prowess and his generalship, had raised the name of his clan to a position of high prestige. He had no sooner been appointed chief than he gathered his men and set off for Easter Ross in order, it is said, that he might repay an insult he had received there from the Frasers in his youth. Having wreaked his vengeance on that clan in several successful encounters, he raided their lands far and near and drove an immense booty to Skye. At Harlosh, in the district of Vatten, the cattle were slaughtered and the place is known to this day as '*Bun an Sgamhaidh*', or 'the place of refuse'. This was in the year 1393 (MacLeod, RC, 1927, p. 56).

Two years later an incident occurred in which he was destined further to enhance his own fame and the name of his clan. At that time a powerful personality was dominating the north and the west, where he was endeavouring to establish a Celtic dynasty. This was Donald, the son of John, Lord of the Isles, and of Margaret Stewart, the daughter of Robert II. In order to placate his older half-brothers, whose power and possessions he had usurped, Donald conspired, among other designs, to wrench his lands in Skye from the chief of the MacLeods and to confer them on one of his own brothers. At that time the island of Skye formed part of the earldom of Ross and Donald could now assert his claims with the greater confidence, in that he had become affianced to Lady Mary Lesley, who was Countess of Ross in her own right.

But the Chief of MacLeod was not the man to surrender tamely to an usurping lord and he determined to resist this attempt at dispossession by every means in his power.

Meanwhile Donald despatched a strong force under his brother – the redoubtable *Alasdair Carrach*, to invade Skye. Having evaded the vigilance of MacAskill of *Rubh' an Dunain*, constable of *Dun Sgathaich* and hereditary coast-watcher of the MacLeods, the invaders effected a landing at Eynort in Minginish. Thence they rapidly made for the east, by Carbost and Drynoch, leaving a wide trail of devastation behind them.

Their progress was soon, however, to suffer an abrupt setback, for, at the head of Loch Sligachan, they were encountered by a powerful body of the MacLeods. Here a furious battle was waged and the natives acquitted themselves with such bravery and skill, that their opponents were thrown into hopeless confusion which soon developed into a rout. The pursuit was ruthlessly maintained by the stout-hearted islanders all the way back to the shores of Loch Eynort where a cruel fate awaited the

panic-stricken fugitives. On their arrival there, they discovered that their galleys had been taken possession of by the Macaskills, who had them moored some distance out to sea. Seeing that escape was now impossible they fled hither and thither in utter despair, only to be cut to pieces by their relentless foes. It is said that not a soul of them escaped that day of carnage and, according to the *MS, History of the MacLeods of Dunvegan*, the heads of the slain were collected, numbered, and despatched as trophies to be retained in the custody of the warder of Dunvegan Castle. It is stated by the same authority that the spoil was divided at *Creag an Fheannaidh*, or The Rock of the Flaying, which some identify with the 'Bloody Stone' in Harta Corrie (MacLeod, RC, 1927, pp. 57–8).

Now, although the victory is rightly attributed to the MacLeods, it is questionable if the defeat was such a signal one as the *MS, History* of that clan and the traditions of the island would have us believe. The Battle of Sligachan was fought in 1395, and we know that the leader of the invading army, *Alasdair Carrach*, was living in 1398 for, in the chartulary of Moray is a document of that date wherein he is described as, "*Magnificus vir et potens Alexander Dominus de Lochaber*" (Gregory, D, 1881, p. 63). He was present at Harlaw in 1411 and he must have been living in 1431, for, in that year, his estates were forfeited for the part he took in the insurrection of Donald Balloch.

And what is more, it is clear that the creatures of Donald of the Isles had succeeded about this time in obtaining a temporary footing in Skye, whether forcibly or by agreement cannot now be said. In any case, Godfrey an older half-brother of Donald, occupied Sleat, and lived in *Dun Sgathaich* from 1389 until 1401. According to Hugh MacDonald, the sennachie of Sleat, "*the country of Trotternish in Skye*" was refused by *Alasdair Carrach*, as, "*he preferred to it the forest lands of Lochaber*". Here we have the beginning of the suzerainty of the MacDonalds in Skye, a suzerainty that sixty years hence was to become permanent in the island and was destined to be the cause of never-ending disputes and feuds with the MacLeods who for several centuries continued to assert their right over the lands which the MacDonalds came to occupy.

After the Battle of Sligachan, the puissant and amiable chief of the MacLeods seems to have lived in peace for the rest of his days and it seems like the irony of a frolicsome fate that this warrior chief, who had been snatched from a life of celibacy by the accident of an older brother's death, should have left behind him a numerous progeny of illegitimate children.

Of his sons by wedlock, with Janet daughter of Maclaine of Lochbuy, the records tell of three, namely: – John, his heir; Norman, whose son, *Alasdair Ruadh*, was styled of St. Kilda (of which branch the most illustrious scion was the bardess *Màiri ni'n Alasdair Ruaidh*) and George, who settled in France. The chief died suddenly while yet a comparatively young man, at Castle *Camus* in Sleat in the year 1402, leaving as his heir a lad of the tender age of ten. That was *Iain Borb* ('John the Truculent'), the sixth chief.

Iain Borb, Sixth Chief

Owing to the youth of the chief, a 'tutor', or regent, had to be appointed to direct the affairs of the clan. The choice was a most unhappy one, for it fell upon a thowless relative who so discredited the trust reposed in him that he is known to tradition as *Iain Mishealbhach*, or John, 'the ill-fated'. Under him the clan fell from the honourable place to which the late chief, William *Cléireach*, had raised it and signs were not awanting of the baleful elements of disunion among the leading men of MacLeod. The MacDonalds were not slow to take advantage of this situation. They gathered a large army with which they invaded Sleat and took both Castle *Camus* and *Dun Sgathaich* by storm. Fired by these successes, they pushed northwards, according to the

MS, *History of the MacLeods,* to attack the castle of Dunvegan but, at Feorlig, they were met, and repelled, by a strong force of the MacLeods of Skye, and of Lewis, and led by the chief of the latter clan (MacLeod, RC, 1927, p. 62). That chief took young Iain of Dunvegan with him to Lewis, became his sponsor and, before long, had him proclaimed chief of the MacLeods at Rodel in Harris.

Meanwhile the MacDonalds had other designs in hand and Donald of the Isles, who had enormously aggrandised his position by his marriage with the daughter of the Earl of Ross, began to make overtures to the young chief of MacLeod in order that he might win his allegiance. Now, since the MacLeods had hitherto held their lands as vassals of the Earl of Ross, and since Donald had then assumed that dignity, the MacLeods had no alternative but to comply with the wishes of their superior.

That John was a loyal subject of the Lord of the Isles is shown by the fact that, when the latter rose in rebellion against the government of Albany, he had no more eager supporter than the chief of the MacLeods. Hugh MacDonald, Sennachie of Sleat, says that Donald commanded the centre at the Battle of Harlaw with John Macleod of Harris and Roderick MacLeod of Lewis (Skene, WF, 1847, p. 301). John was placed in the centre of the Highland army, but, as it is stated in the MS, *History of the MacLeods,* he resented the position accorded to him; and even refused to fight until he was given 'the post of honour' on the right. The authors of *Clan Donald* aver that the name of the MacLeod chief of that day was 'Norman' (Macdonald, A & A, 1896, p. 162), and we read in the MS, *History of the MacLeods* that, in the course of the battle, the chief was wounded by an arrow in the forehead and that, owing to the primitive surgical skill of his age, the wound had never healed, so that, when blood-pressure happened to be in any way increased the scar opened, and he bled profusely.

This disablement would, indeed, seem to have been the cause

of his death which took place in 1442. According to the *MS, History of the MacLeods*, whilst he was engaged in a friendly fencing bout with one of his men at his castle of Pabbay, in Harris, he became so incensed at being bested that, flinging aside his sword, he grappled in wrestling with his opponent, and, owing to the strain of the contest, the scar burst open, and he bled to death.

His fiery temper had earned for him the nickname of *Borb*, or 'The Truculent', but he had proved himself a good chief and a warrior of renown. That the dignity of the clan did not decline under his regime, is shown by the fact that two of his daughters were married, one to the chief of Lewis, and another to MacLean of Duart while his wife was a grand-daughter of the Earl of Douglas. His oldest son and heir was named William and his second son, Norman, whom some held to have been the older, was killed in Lochaber in 1429, in that terrible defeat that James I, in person, inflicted on Alexander, son of Donald, Lord of the Isles. On hearing of her husband's death, MacLeod's wife gave birth to a son prematurely. The child lived and in his youth he was placed under the protection of his uncle, MacLeod of Lewis, who conferred the district of Waternish on him. This man was the ancestor of the MacLeods of Meadle, Balmeanach, and Glendale and was the grandfather of John of Waternish, *Iain a' Chùil Bhàin*, who, for five or six years, gave such able service in that unhappy time that overtook his clan during the early days of The Heiress of the Isles.

In 1431 a new insurrection against the government broke out, headed by Donald Balloch, a cousin of the Earl of Ross. It was suppressed with relentless severity by the king, James I, whose troops overran Sleat, and took possession of its principal castle-forts, *Camus* and *Dun Sgathaich* (MacLeod, RC, 1927, p. 65). The MacLeods had, of course, always asserted their claims over that portion of Skye, although they possessed no legal title to it. Indeed the only part of their lands that they held by right of charter was, as we have already seen, the district of Glenelg, which had been granted to them in 1343.

William Dubh, Seventh Chief

The seventh chief of the MacLeods of Glenelg, as the clan was then styled, was named William *Dubh*, or 'the Black', and he assumed power about the year 1441. It is noteworthy that it was during his administration that the MacDonalds succeeded in obtaining in Skye a footing that they were never again to lose. Thus we find that John, Lord of the Isles in 1469, conferred a grant of 28 marklands of Sleat together with lands in Uist and Benbecula, to his brother, Hugh, whose descendants have held these lands in unbroken succession down the ages. It is significant that the charter conveying these lands to Hugh of Sleat was confirmed by William, the chief of MacLeod, showing the amicable relations that then existed between these clans (Munro, J & RW, 1986, p. 153).

And further evidence of the friendly feelings that animated the clans at that time is afforded by their joint action in a raiding expedition into Orkney. According to the Sleat sennachie, and also to *The Book of Clan Ranald*, the Earl of Orkney had made certain disparaging insinuations about Hugh of Sleat, as the latter was on a visit in Edinburgh. On his return home, Hugh got together a large fleet, and, reinforced by the MacLeods, under their chief, he made for Orkney. There, as the Sleat sennachie has it,

having routed the enemy, Austin (Hugh) and his party began to ravage the country, that being the only reward they had for their pains and fatigue, with which, having loaded their galleys, they returned home.

(Skene, WF, 1847, p. 307).

This was in 1460. In the year 1476 an event happened that was to have very far-reaching consequences, not only for the Western Isles, but also for Scotland as a whole. That was the surrender by John, Lord of the Isles, of all his lands to the king so that, for all practical purposes, this important dynasty has henceforth ceased to trouble the peace of the nation. Many of his closest relatives were incensed at this act of submission on the part of their superior but chiefly were they alienated from him by his action in conferring lands, somewhat lavishly, as they thought, on such of his vassals as the MacLeans, the MacNeills, and the MacLeods. His most bitter accuser was his own son, Angus *Og*, a man blessed with great vigour of body and mind, but cursed with an all-consuming ambition. The disaffected chieftains hoped to find in the undutiful son a leader who would help them to redress their wrongs and they hoped not in vain. Soon civil war was raging in the isles. The old lord was supported, among others, by the MacLeods while another Skye chieftain, Donald *Gallach*, son of Hugh of Sleat, ranged himself and his clan on the side of Angus *Og* (Gregory, D, 1881, pp. 51–2).

The associates of the opposing factions met in battle off the coast of Mull, at a place called Bloody Bay to the west of Tobermory, in the year 1480. According to the sennachie of Sleat, Ronald Bain, son of the laird of Moidart bore down upon MacLeod's galley and, fixing it to his grappling irons, a stalwart Irishman *"thrust the blade of an oar below the stern post of MacLeod's galley, between it and the rudder, thus preventing the galley from being steered"* (Skene, WF, 1847, p. 317).

It would appear that the battle was waged with great ferocity and determination, and it is said that when the issue was going against them the MacLeods displayed the Fairy Flag, but the effect was unavailing.

One after another of the dozen guardians of the clan's palladium was struck down in the terrible carnage and mention is made of one of these in particular. This was a certain *Murchadh*

Breac or 'Murdo, the Pock-marked', who, pierced by a spear, collapsed on the deck but the stout warrior unflinchingly held the flag aloft sticking the pole in the gaping hole in his side until a comrade relieved him of his charge.

In *The MacLeods of Dunvegan* it is said that the chief was killed early in the fight (MacLeod, RC, 1927, p. 70), while the authors of *Clan Donald* state that he was wounded so severely that he died on his return to Dunvegan; but in the most reliable account we possess of that engagement, namely, *The MS History of the MacDonalds*, written about 1664 by Hugh MacDonald, the sennachie of Sleat, it is stated that *"Angus Og and Allan, Laird of Moidart, attacked MacLeod and took him prisoner"* (Skene, WF, 1847, p. 317).

However, it happened, it seems that William did not long survive the affair of Bloody Bay. He was buried in Iona, the last of the MacLeod chiefs to be committed to the dust of that sacred isle.

Owing to the part the MacLeods had taken on the side of the Lord of the Isles, the MacDonalds sent an army to invade their territory in Skye. Having effected a landing at Aird Bay in Duirinish, they at once began their work of devastation. The chief of the MacLeods is said to have been from home, but the affairs of the clan did not suffer in the hands of his redoubtable son, Alexander, who acquitted himself with such bravery and skill that the invaders were routed. In the encounter, the young heir of MacLeod was severely wounded between the shoulders by the stroke of an opponent's axe. The severed tendons had never been brought to cohere again, so that he sustained a lasting deformity, and he is accordingly known to history and tradition as *Alasdair Crotach*, or 'the Hunchback'.

Two years after the Battle of Bloody Bay – i.e., in 1482 – it is recorded that Angus *Og* was styled Lord of Trotternish, and in *The MacLeods of Dunvegan* mention is made of his invasion of that district and his seizure of Duntulm castle, then, but never again, the property of the MacLeods. On the death of Angus, in 1490, the peninsula of Trotternish was claimed by his uncle, Hugh of Sleat, and for over two centuries that region was the cause of sore contention between the MacDonalds and the MacLeods (MacLeod, RC, 1927, p. 72).

Hitherto neither of these clans possessed any feudal title to the estates which they occupied in Skye, beyond the fact that their lands had been granted to them by an Earl of Ross, or a Lord of the Isles, each on his own authority. Thus, as we have already seen, lands of Uist and of Sleat had been conferred by John, Lord of the Isles, in 1469, on his brother, Hugh of Sleat and it is significant that this deed of gift was confirmed by King James IV, at Stirling in 1495 (Munro, J & RW, 1986, p. 226). In the charter Hugh is referred to as 'of Sleat' ('*carissimo nostri fratri Hugoni Alexandri de Slete*').

The MacDonalds

Hugh (Uisdean), First Chief

Hugh, the first chief of the MacDonalds of Sleat, was the third son of Alexander, the third Lord of the Isles, and the second Earl of Ross, *frater carnalis* to John, Earl of Ross and it is from him that the MacDonalds of Skye derive their patronymic, *Clann Uisdein*. We have already referred to the part which this warrior played in the invasion of Orkney in 1460, and to his inheriting of Uist and Sleat from his brother, Celestine of Lochalsh.

Like many another man of mark in his time, Hugh had a numerous family, legitimate and otherwise. Of these, the most noted were: (1) John, his heir, whose mother was Finvola of Ardnamurchan; (2) Donald *Gallach*, the successor of John as chief, the son of a daughter of the Crowner of Caithness, and whose association with Hugh is thus quaintly recorded by the sennachie of Sleat:

> *On his return from the expedition to Orkney, Austin, having halted at Caithness, he got a son by the Crowner of Caithness' daughter of the name of Gun, which at that time was a very flourishing name there, descended from the Danes.*
>
> (Skene, WF, 1847, p. 307).

(3) Donald Herrach, by a daughter of MacLeod; (4) Gillespie *Dubh* (black in person and in deed); and several others, all of whom are mentioned in the *Black Book of Clan Ranald*. Hugh died in 1498 at a very advanced age, and he was buried in Sand in North Uist.

As this brings us to the end of a century, the social conditions prevailing at that time now fall to be dealt with.

CHAPTER IV

Social Conditions, 1263–1500

The Clan System

By the end of the fifteenth century a new era had opened in the West Highlands of Scotland. On the extinction of the dignity of the Lordship of the Isles in 1493, the outlook of the chiefs underwent a material change. Hitherto they looked to the *reguli,* or the kinglets of the Isles, as their sole superiors and to these they owed whatever titles they held for their possessions; but from then onwards a new principle is imposed upon them whereby they were obliged to produce royal charters for any lands that they occupied.

The clan system, as we know it, had already come into existence about the middle of the thirteenth century and, during the intervening years, had come to be firmly established as a social organism that was to play an important role in the history of the Highlands. Neither at this stage, nor afterwards, were the units of the clan all of the same name. Indeed, none who placed himself under a chief was excluded from patronage, provided he was prepared to conform to the regulations governing the particular clan in which he sought protection. Those who wished to place themselves under some powerful chief were obliged to observe an agreement called Bond of Manrent and, for the privilege such a relationship entailed, they were bound to serve him, *"as their master, by land and sea"*. On the other hand, the superior was duty-bound to protect his protégé and *"maintain and defend him"* as he would do in the case of any of his own kin.

A predominating feature in the government of the clan was the method that was followed in connection with the succession to the chiefship. The law of primogeniture had not made its appearance, nor yet for many years to come and even the principle of hereditary succession was not observed with any rigidity. The individual raised to the dignity of chief owed his appointment to special qualities that commended themselves to the members of his clan; for it was not an uncommon occurrence to pass over the son of the last chief if unfit by age, or other constitutional disability and to choose some individual, a brother perhaps, or even, as sometimes happened, a more remote relative, strict attention being paid to the essential that he belonged to the reigning line. The choice sometimes fell on illegitimates, as when *Gillespic Dubh* was chief of *Clann Uisdein,* but females were stringently excluded.

The clan was divided into two classes – *Saoi* and *Daoi*. The former were the warriors, whose duty it was to defend the tribe, and, being thus honoured, were absolved from all manner of manual toil. The latter comprised the despised weaklings, men who, unfitted physically or mentally for military service, were destined to pass their days in tending the flocks or in cultivating the soil.

Law and Order

Although John Balliol had, in 1292, erected Skye into a sheriff-dom, as part of a wide district comprising Wester Ross, Glenelg, the Small Isles, and the Long Island, the powers of judge were vested virtually in the chief. Certain perquisites were allowed him in virtue of his office, such as rebatement in dues and one tenth of the fine imposed for convictions. There were then in Skye as for many decades thereafter, people who were members of no particular clan and, accordingly, were not readily amena-ble to the discipline that prevailed in the territory in which they sojourned. These men were included in the wide term, 'broken men', and were a source of serious perplexity to established authority. It is said that they haunted the inlets and the straits of Raasay and Rona, and they were a constant menace to trade especially to the fishing industry that was then beginning to attract the men of the east coast of Scotland and even those of the Netherlands (Munro, RW, 1961, p. 70).

Trade and Industry

Consequent on the far-seeing policy of James I in endeavouring to foster national trade, the fishing industry of the Highlands began to experience a period of great prosperity during the fifteenth century. Large numbers of cattle were reared, but few were then exported and for these, when bartering was not the practice, the prices were 2/- for a sheep, 13/4 for a cow, and 26/8 for a horse.

A Spaniard named Don Pedro de Ayala, who visited the court of James IV in 1498 and had compiled a useful record of his impressions, speaks of the numerous flocks of the Western Isles, and of the great quantity of barley that was raised there.

Manner of Living

People in those days lived almost wholly on what they them-selves could produce. Their wants were few and they were satisfied with a diet consisting of barley in varied forms, together with flesh and fish, both of which were plentiful. They were very abstemious and the vogue for foreign wines, which became so alarmingly prevalent in the succeeding century, had not then been introduced. The principal drink of the commonalty, and even of those in the higher rank of society, was a beverage called bland, produced from whisked whey and preserved in cogs of wood for weeks, and even months, until it was strongly fer-mented. It was highly relished for its stimulating, salutary, and sustaining properties.

They were a hardy race, who, even on a little barley and cold water (*fuarag eorna*) and with the *breacan* (plaid) to cover them at night, could, in their rough campaignings, subsist for days without other form of food and without seeking the shelter of a roof.

Despite the acts of lawlessness that at times disturbed the community, culture was not neglected among them. Indeed, it is questionable if Celtic art had ever touched the high place it then attained and, although their religion was permeated by much superstition and was corrupted by the worship of saints, it was a time of true devotion, and the influence of the Church was felt even by the most hardened warriors.

CHAPTER V

Family History, 1500–1600

Ever since the early part of the reign of James I, the influence of the central authority was slowly but steadily penetrating the Highlands and Western Isles of Scotland, until, by the end of the fifteenth century, all the chiefs had been tamed into submission to the king. Driven to the conclusion, often attained by bitter experience, that insubordination to the national government would not redound to their interests, they seemed to tumble over one another in their eagerness to meet the wishes of their king; and a monarch then ruled who was strong enough, and was sufficiently discreet to direct the new attitude into a channel that might benefit the nation as a whole. The chiefs had, at length, been convinced that their only security for the lands they held lay in their possession of a royal charter, and James IV saw to it that charters were not lavishly bestowed until he had assured himself of the loyalty of each grantee, and his beneficiaries were often reduced to a state of perplexing disquiet by his practice of conferring the same territory on different persons, even in the course of a single year.

But some of the chiefs, with whom he dealt in the Highlands, had displayed an astuteness under the circumstances that was truly marvellous, so that the cleverest artifices that the government of the day could bring to bear on the situation were often met by diplomatic strategy on the part of the chiefs that was every whit as nimble and as subtle as any that the central authority could devise. To the new conditions, few were able to adjust themselves so adroitly as the chief of the MacLeods of Skye, the celebrated *Alasdair Crotach*, whose prowess on the field of battle was equalled by his skill in the more difficult art of diplomacy.

The Macleods

Alexander (Alasdair Crotach), Eighth Chief
In *'The MacLeods of Dunvegan'* (MacLeod, RC, 1927, p. 73) there is mention of a battle which, if accepted as authentic, must have happened early in the chiefship of *Alasdair Crotach*. According to that account, the MacDonalds, under their chief Donald *Gruamach*, landed at Loch Eynort and made for Dunvegan, wasting Minginish, Bracadale and most of Duirinish on the way.

The chief of the MacLeods was in Harris at the time but he returned thence and, with a band of his own men reinforced by a strong body of the MacLeods of Lewis, he landed at the head of Loch Pooltiel. He arrayed his force on the brow of a hill, with a river in front and in this position he awaited the gathering of his own clan, which was being summoned to arms by Donald *Mór* of Meadle.

As soon as this cadet arrived with his contingent the battle began and for some time the MacDonalds were winning. Their success was, however, but shortlived, for *Alasdair Crotach's* mother – a MacLaine of Lochbuy – who is said to have repaired to the scene of combat with the Fairy Flag, had the wonder-working banner displayed, and immediately the tide of battle turned in favour of the MacLeods. Donald *Gruamach* was cut down by one of *Alasdair Crotach's* lieutenants, a Murdo MacAskill. This warrior raised the head of the slain chief on the point of his spear and the pipers of MacLeod immediately struck up a lament. The MacDonalds understood the situation and they fled from the field in confusion. In the pursuit, they were mercilessly cut down by the exultant MacLeods and, so terrible was the carnage, that the ravens of *Creag an Fhithich* gorged themselves full for many a week. In the account that has been quoted, the battle is said to have been fought *"about 1490"*. Now the chief of the MacDonalds of Sleat at that time, and for eight years thereafter, was Hugh, the first of his line, and not Donald *Gruamach* who was the fifth chief in order of succession, and he lived until 1537 (Cameron, A, 1871, p. 22).

On the forfeiture of the Lordship of the Isles in 1493 the lands of Skye, as of the other islands comprising that dignity, came to be vested in the crown. *Alasdair Crotach* craved, and secured, royal charters for his possession in Harris as well as for Duirinish, Bracadale, Minginish and Lyndale in Skye in 1498 (MacLeod, RC, 1938, p. 1). The family already possessed a charter for Glenelg, since David II conferred two-thirds of that district on Malcolm, the third chief, in 1343 (MacLeod, RC, 1938, p. 275).

In addition to these territories, *Alasdair Crotach* now sought to obtain a claim over Sleat and Trotternish – districts that were held by his family under the Earls of Ross, but he was successful only to the extent that he was recognised as holder of two unciates of Trotternish, together with the bailiary, or stewardship, of the whole district. That concession was obtained in the month of June 1498 and, in October of the same year, a grant was made by the king of the self-same region of Trotternish together with four marks of the tirunga of Duntulm and four of Airdviceolain, to Torquil MacLeod of Lewis (Innes, C, 1854, p. 351).

In return for these grants, the chief of Skye was enjoined to provide and maintain one galley of twenty-six oars and two of sixteen oars to be used in the service of the crown whenever desired, and the grantee was further obliged to preserve the nests of falcons on his domains for the king. (*ibid.*).

When the lands that had formerly pertained to the Lords of the Isles had been annexed to the crown, certain chiefs of the west became insubordinate and were a source of much perplexity to the government of the day. The disaffection had become so acute that the king resolved to dispossess some of the more recalcitrant offenders and substitute loyal subjects or *"true men"*. The effect of the royal resolution was to intensify the prevailing discontent, and at that time an event happened that was to precipitate matters for a general rising. Donald *Dubh*, whom all looked upon as the heir of the last Lord of the Isles, had escaped from prison and the disaffected chiefs gathered around him in rebellion. This happened in 1502 and the insurrection had soon assumed such formidable proportions that the king in person had to go north with an army before the hostile alliance was finally disrupted in the year 1506.

All this time *Alasdair Crotach* had remained loyal to the king and he was entrusted with the good government of the isles during those troublous years. His kinsman of Lewis was the last of the rebels to submit, and he was solemnly forfeited in Parliament. Thus it happened that Waternish in Skye, a district then belonging to the MacLeods of Lewis, was temporarily transferred to *Alasdair Crotach*. He was commissioned to let it to tenants but his brief period of possession came to an end in 1511, when Waternish was once again restored to *Siol Torcuil* (Innes, C, 1854, p. 360).

Once, however, the magnetic influence of James IV was gone the loyalty of *Alasdair Crotach* did not long remain true to the government. When the clans returned from the tragic field of Flodden, and a new insurrection was raised on behalf of the old House of the Isles, the chief of the MacLeods was one of the most active participants in the rebellion.

A meeting of the rebel chiefs was convened in Dun Akin, or Castle Moil, in Kyleakin, in 1513, and it was there resolved, with acclamation, to raise Sir Donald MacDonald of Lochalsh who had been knighted by the late king on Flodden, to the dignity of Lord of the Isles. With this end in view, *Alasdair Crotach* stormed *Dun Sgàthaich* and, after effecting much damage, he captured that stronghold (Gregory, D, 1881, p. 114). It was probably in the same cause that he launched an assault against Castle *Camus* at Knock but so obstinate was the defence opposed to him there, as tradition avers, by a lady called 'Mary of the Castle', that he was compelled to raise the siege, after a prolonged struggle (Innes, C, 1854, p. 343).

But, like several others of his associates, *Alasdair Crotach* soon became dissatisfied with the conduct of Sir Donald Mac-Donald and it appears the estrangement had become so acute that a conspiracy was afoot to seize the leader's person and to hand him over to the regent. He was, however, warned of the plot and was able to make good his escape; but so great was the pressure exerted by Argyle, both by threats and by entreaty, that *Alasdair Crotach* and his accomplice, MacLean of Duart, apprehended two of Sir Donald's brothers and offered them to the government in the hope of mitigating their own crimes. Remission was withheld for a considerable time and when at length safe conduct had been granted him, *Alasdair Crotach*

proceeded to Edinburgh where he was pardoned. The record of the incident is as follows:

> *In 1515 John, Duke of Albany, granted remission to Alasdair Crotach, his servants, landed men, gentlemen, and yeomen, for past crimes, especially for besieging and taking the Castle of Dunskaich and holding it against the regent, and assisting Sir Donald of Lochalsh and his accomplices.*
>
> (MacKenzie, A, 1889, p. 18).

The leniency accorded to him by the government emboldened him to plead for a grant of Trotternish. In that, however, he was unsuccessful, although a promise had been made that he would not be disturbed in his occupancy of it for eleven years (Gregory, D, 1881, p. 122).

On this occasion, as on many another, his consummate skill as a diplomat served him well, but he, like many another Highland chief, was fortunate that the country was at the time distracted by the rivalries of men like Angus, Arran, and Albany – place-seekers who made the office of government a farce. It was thus to gain his allegiance that the Earl of Angus, during his brief period in power, conferred on *Alasdair Crotach* a charter for the lands of Sleat, and of North Uist, a grant that was fated to arouse the bitterest hostility between him and his able contemporary, Donald *Gruamach*, the young chief of *Clann Uisdein*. His relations from now onwards with that family entail a brief retrospect, in order to bring the history of the latter to date.

The Macdonalds

As we have already seen, the first chief of the MacDonalds of Sleat, Hugh, son of Alexander, Earl of Ross, and Lord of the Isles, died in 1498. He left a large family of sons whose rival claims were to bring much misery on the House of Sleat.

John, Second Chief

John, the eldest son of Hugh, and of his first wife, Finvola of Ardnamurchan, succeeded his father in 1498.

On the final forfeiture of the Lordship of the Isles, in 1495, King James IV went north, and held his court in the Castle of Mingarry, whither many of the Highland chiefs repaired in order to tender their submission. As the Chief of Sleat was then very advanced in years, he sent his son John, as his representative, to offer allegiance to the king.

There is little to record of this chief but the sennachies always advert to his lack of patriotism and his unnatural antipathy to his many half-brothers. As he had no children of his own he tried to alienate the patrimony by resigning it to the king who granted it, in the year 1505, to Ronald Alanson of Moidart (Gregory, D, 1881, pp. 103–4). In the same year we find, in the *'Register of Crown Rentals',* that

> the 80 merklands of Trouterness were let by the commissioners of the crown for three years to Ronald Bane Alanson of Moidart, the Earl of Huntly being surety for the payment of rent by the latter.

In that year also died the feckless chief of Sleat, mourned by few and respected by none.

Donald Gallach, Third Chief

In spite of all the machinations of the late chief and even the granting of a charter to the Clan Ranald, the direct line was preserved in Sleat in the person of Hugh's second son, Donald *Gallach.* His cognomen was derived, as we have already seen, from the fact that his mother was a daughter of the Gunns of Caithness. Donald had fought at Bloody Bay on the side of

Angus *Og* and he took a very active part in the insurrection of Donald *Dubh* in 1503.

According to the sennachie of Sleat, *"he was a moderate man, inclined to peace, black-haired, and fair-skinned"* and he seems to have been of a different disposition from his older brother, for, according to the same authority, he granted lands to one of his half-brothers, Donald Herrach, to wit, *"the upper davoch of Sleat, the davoch of Dunsgathaich, with four merklands in the west of Trotternish".* This transaction is, however, of doubtful authenticity.

However it was, it would appear that Donald Herrach, third son of Hugh, the first Chief of Sleat, and of a daughter of MacLeod of Dunvegan (then styled of Harris), was in possession of lands in Uist. Now there was another son of Hugh, by a daughter of Torquil MacLeod of Lewis, one of the name *Gilleasbuig Dubh,* a man of outstanding ability but of unrestrained ambition and fierce temper, and who resented the neglect shown to him in the allocation of the patrimonial estates. Egged on by another half-brother, Angus *Collach,* whose mother was a MacLean of Coll and whose share of lands had also been stinted, *Gilleasbuig* determined to acquire by force what had presumably been denied him because of his illegitimacy.

With that end in view this dark schemer proceeded to Uist where he paid an ostensibly friendly visit to his brother – Donald Herrach – who received him with great cordiality. Festivities over, the party repaired, according to the custom of the age, to indulge in feats of strength and, as the weather was wet, the venue chosen for the games was a barn. This part of the entertainment was done at the instigation of the chief guest and, by suggesting it he was playing on the vanity of his unsuspecting brother, for Donald was known to be the most accomplished athlete in the whole island. *"Aon bhuille na's leor bho Dho'ull Hearach: cha robh feum riamh air a dhà"* ('One blow was enough from Donald

Herrach: never was need of a second'), the story-teller says of him.

After Donald had overcome all his opponents in wrestling and beaten them in leaping and in sword play, a novel competition was proposed, the aim in which was to touch with the chin, by taking a running leap, a noose that was projected over the top of a partition in the barn. This could easily be accomplished by Donald Herrach but the crafty *Gilleasbuig* had a man ensconced in the adjoining room holding an end of the rope, with the intention of pulling it tight when the victim's neck was in line with the loop. *Pòl na h-éille* ('Paul of the thong'), as the hired assassin was called, succeeded only too well in carrying out his part of the dark deed and as the athlete's body dangled from the rope, red-hot irons were thrust through the bowels and the nefarious work was over.

Having removed the obstacle in the way of his advancement, *Gilleasbuig* next hastened to Sleat where he arrived before the news of the murder of his brother. At *Dun Sgathaich*, he was kindly received by the chief. The latter, at the time, had under construction a galley of which he was very proud and he led his brother to the shore to inspect it. After expressing his admiration of the craftsmanship of the builders and feigning keen interest in every detail, *Gilleasbuig* suddenly drew his brother's attention to an alleged defect in the ship's stern-post, low down at the keel. His surprised host stooped to examine the supposed flaw and in that posture he was stabbed by his inhuman brother. The wound was not immediately fatal and in a prayerful attitude the dying chief implored his murderer to spare his infant son (see Gregory, D, 1881, p. 107, & Cameron, A, 1871, pp. 25–6).

Whether this blood-stained monster was at length stung with remorse for his deed of foul shame cannot now be said, but it is stated that he took his nephew together with the oldest son of the murdered Donald Herrach under his protection and that he treated them with fatherly care until they had attained manhood.

Gilleasbuig Dubh, Fourth Chief

This notorious fratricide succeeded in establishing himself in Sleat for a time but his sway was short-lived. It would appear that his clansmen hounded him out of the district and, escaping to Uist he was expelled thence also by Ronald Alanson of Moidart whom John, the second chief of Sleat, had nominated as his heir.

Gilleasbuig thereupon took to a life of piracy and for three years he carried on his work of rapine and evaded capture. At length the government's net was circling so closely around him that he saw the only way to purchase his own safety lay in betraying his associates and, like the unscrupulous man he was, he carried out his resolve and obtained the king's pardon. This was in 1509 and in the following year we find that he was granted the bailiary of Trotternish, hitherto held by *Alasdair Crotach*, and a royal letter of protection was given to him,

> *enjoining the lieges, especially the tenants of Troutarness, that they should not disturb him, his factors or servants, in their persons, or their goods, in the peaceable possession of their leases, which Gillespic had of the king in Troutarness, especially in the execution of his office of bailie.*
>
> (see Gregory, D, 1881, p. 108 & Cameron, A, 1871, p. 26).

This appears to have been his reward for delivering his fellow-pirates to justice and, in the decree granting him remission for his crimes, one is astonished to find no mention made of the murders of his brothers.

It seems that he was the tutor or leader of his clan, if not even its chief, for about eight years and the siege and capture of *Dun Sgathaich* by *Alasdair Crotach*, in the insurrection in favour of Sir Donald of Lochalsh, would therefore have happened during his regime.

According to Hugh MacDonald, the sennachie of Sleat, he was killed by his nephews whilst hunting on Ben Lee, in Uist, in the year 1518. The traditional account is that these young men, who were still his protégés, determined to despatch their guardian and their fathers' murderer.

In consonance with the preconceived arrangement to pick a quarrel with him, one of the youths, who was afterwards the famous warrior and diplomat, *Do'ull Gruamach* ('Donald the Surly') let slip his own hound on the first view of the deer and, being severely rebuked by the enraged chief for his act of presumption, the impetuous youth dealt his uncle such a blow as stretched him low on the heather.

Having recovered, the discomfited chief requested his other nephew Ronald Herrach to lend him a sword he carried, whereupon Donald *Gruamach* said, *"Give it to him, and let him who murdered your father, and mine, try to kill me also"*. Galled by the recollection, Ronald made a savage thrust and drove the weapon right through the body of the chief.

The young men then returned to the house of their slain uncle, and entering, with seeming unconcern, were asked by the widowed lady if they had enjoyed much sport that day. The elder answered that they had grassed the rarest stag that had ever fallen to huntsman in a forest and, interpreting the phrase of dark import aright, she wailed:

> *'S truagh nach mise bha 'sa ghleann,*
>   Pity I was not in the glen,
> *Far 'n d'rinneadh feòil 's na dhòirteadh fuil;*
>   When flesh was made and blood was shed
> *Far 'n leagadh an damh dualach, donn,*

Where the curly dun stag was grassed
Mo chreach lom nach robh mi muigh.
My disaster is that I was not out.

(Cameron, A, 1871, p. 26)

Donald (Do'ull Gruamach), Fifth Chief

Donald *Gruamach*, son of Donald *Gallach*, and of Agnes, widow of Torquil MacLeod of Lewis, succeeded to the chiefship of the MacDonalds of Sleat about 1518. For twenty long years the fortunes of his clan had been at a very low ebb; and it was a lucky stroke of fate that had raised a man of such ability, resource and determination as Donald *Gruamach* to the headship of the clan. In order to strengthen his position, he entered into a bond of manrent with Campbell of Cawdor, brother of the Earl of Argyle and this alliance obliged him to accompany the vacillating Scottish lords in their abortive incursion into England in 1523.

It was shortly before that time that a transaction was effected which was to invoke the bitterest animosity between the MacDonalds and the MacLeods and to involve these rival clans in internecine strife for many a year. This was all caused by a grant made during the regency of the Earl of Angus, who had married the queen-mother, to Alexander of Dunvegan, of the lands of North Uist and of Sleat – possessions which the MacDonalds considered as essentially their own – and the young chief of *Clann Uisdein* was not the man to allow such an action to go unchallenged (Gregory, D, 1881, p. 131).

He accordingly mobilised a vast army in Skye and in Uist and, aided by a considerable force of the MacLeods of Lewis under John MacLeod, whom he afterwards helped to become chief of the *Siol Torquil*, a descent was made on MacLeod's lands, the first objective being the expulsion of that clan and all their kin from the district of Trotternish. The allies landed on the northern shores of the peninsula, and they proceeded systematically to drive the MacLeods out of the whole region. Terrible atrocities were committed. No quarter was given and the panic-stricken inhabitants, leaving all their effects behind them, were in headlong flight. After having undergone intense suffering, the main body of the fugitives at length arrived at Skeabost. There they sent forward the survivors of their women and children, closed their ranks, and determined to arrest the pursuit at the ford of the river. Maddened by the cruelties they had endured, they swore an oath that each would exact the uttermost vengeance on the MacDonalds and, having chosen the most favourable position, they wrought terrible execution on their foes as the latter were endeavouring to cross the flooded river. But by sheer pressure of numbers the stubborn gallantry of the MacLeods was ultimately overcome and the much-reduced band was once more in full flight for the west. So great was the carnage that it is said the scene of the fight was in consequence called *Achadh na Fala*, or the 'Field of Blood'; and, as the heads of the slain combatants were carried down by the river, they accumulated in a deep pool near the estuary, since known as "*Coire nan Ceann*, or 'the Cauldron of Heads'" (MacKenzie, A, 1889, p. 22).

The MacDonalds then decided to discontinue the pursuit and they proceeded to plunder the lands of the MacLeods. This was carried out on a vast scale and, after several days of foraging, an enormous booty came into their possession. On the way home the lonely echoes of the Cuillin were stirred into unwonted activity by the lowing of herds and the lusty shouts of exultant warriors making for *Dun Sgathaich*.

All this happened in the year 1528 and it would appear that *Alasdair Crotach* had appraised the government of the devastation that was wrought by the MacDonalds, for we find that the Lords of Council had decreed that year that,

Donald Gruamach and John MacTorquil MacLeod pay the said MacLeods for the spulzie – To MacLeod, four score marks, as compensation for 100 cows; to Talisker, compensation for 300 cows, 100 horses, 2000 sheep and an equal number of goats; to Donald Roy, for the share of his loss in Carbost, 200 cows, 80 horses, 500 sheep, and an equal number of goats; to Ferchar Liath, 100 cows, 60 horses, 200 sheep, and 400 goats, to John MacAngus of Borroraig, 120 cows, 100 sheep, and the same number of goats; to Donald Glas, 80 cows, 100 sheep, 100 goats, and 100 horses.

(Mackenzie, A, 1889, p. 23).

No record has hitherto been found to show that the MacLeods had been compensated for the plunder and it is almost safe to conclude, in view of subsequent events, that the injunction of the Council had not been obeyed.

In order to answer for his inruption into the district of Trotternish, and perhaps also in view of the rebellious attitude of the island chiefs, when an effort was made by the young king to annul all grants of crown lands made during his nonage, Donald *Gruamach* was cited to appear before the Privy Council in 1530, but he refused to comply. In the following year, when a new summons was served on him, and on his neighbour, Ewen MacKinnon of Strath, he again flouted the royal command, and no measures were taken to compel him to obey it (Cameron, A, 1871, p. 32).

Henceforth, for all we know, the remainder of his short life was uneventful; but one incident falls to be recorded here. On one occasion a visit was paid to *Dun Sgathaich* by the chief's favourite cousin, Ronald Herrach, who, as we have seen, was his coadjutor in the murder of Gillespic *Dubh*. There was a large company at the castle, among whom the relatives of the chief's wife, Catherine of Clan Ranald, were accorded a high place at table. Their haughty bearing, the deference shown to them and especially the liberties which they took in the halls of his fathers, so roused Ronald's resentment that he resolved to despatch them *en bloc*. His opportunity came at night, when he massacred twelve of them and it is said he slung their bodies to the outside of the castle wall in full view of the bedroom of their patroness.

Early next morning he intimated his intention of leaving *Dun Sgathaich* forthwith and his astonished kinsmen pleaded with him to prolong his stay. Finding that all entreaties were futile, the chief finally begged him, at least, to delay his departure until the lady of the castle should be ready to bid him farewell. "No", answered Ronald, "*I must leave instantly, for she will not bless me when she looks out of her window and views my morning's work;*" and he judged aright, for this daughter of the Clan Ranalds had her revenge shortly afterwards when Ronald was murdered in Griminish, in North Uist, by an assassin of the name of Mackinnon whom she had hired for the purpose (Cameron, A, 1871, p. 33).

Ronald had spent the early part of his life in Ireland, where he greatly distinguished himself in the wars of that country. He afterwards returned, wounded, to Skye, whither he was accompanied by a faithful physician of the name of MacLean, on whom lands were conferred at Cuidreach. From this notable man was descended a succession of doctors, famous for their knowledge of botany and of the medicinal virtues of herbs. The best known of them was the learned Dr. John MacLean, who occupied Shulista and acted in the dual capacity of physician and factor both to Sir Alexander and to Sir James MacDonald of Sleat. He died about 1780.

Ronald Herrach passed the latter part of his life in North Uist and was the progenitor of the MacDonalds of Balranald.

Although he had never succeeded in securing royal charters for his lands, Donald *Gruamach* raised the prestige of his clan to a position of high eminence. According to the account already quoted from '*The MacLeods of Dunvegan*', he is said to have been killed at the 'Battle of Glendale'; but this is probably apochryphal (MacLeod, RC, 1927, p. 73). The persistent tradition in Sleat and in Strath is that he was found dead on *Druim nan Cleòc* at the spring, since called '*Tobar Dho'uill Ghruamaich*'. He died in 1537. An example of piobaireachd *Spaisdearachd Dho'ill Ghruamaich* ('Donald Gruamach's March') is extant.

He was twice married, first to Catherine, the daughter of Alexander MacDonald of Clan Ranald, and, secondly, to Margaret, daughter of MacLeod of Lewis. By the latter he had three sons, John Og, who married a daughter of *Alasdair Crotach*; Archibald 'the clerk', the father of the infamous Hugh ('*Uisdean MacGhilleasbuig Chleirich*'); and James *Gruamach* of Castle Camus, who also was married to a daughter of *Alasdair Crotach* and was captain of the clan during the minority of Donald Gormson. By his first wife Donald *Gruamach* had one son, his successor, Donald, who is distinguished by the agnomen, '*Gorm*', ('Blue') probably from a birthmark but it also meant 'noble' or 'stately' in Old Gaelic.

It is interesting to note that Donald *Gruamach* was the first of a succession of five chiefs, all of whom were called Donald. They were Donald *Gruamach*, Donald *Gorm*, Donald Gormson (*Sasunnach*), Donald *Gorm Mór*, and Donald *Gorm Og* (*MacGhilleasbuig Chlèirich*).

Donald *Gorm*, *Sixth Chief*

Donald *Gorm*, the young chief of Sleat, was a man of great promise, and one of the most able and ambitious of his line. He early aspired to the Lordship of the Isles for he was the direct heir to the dignity, as is shown by the fact that he received the support of all the branches of Clan Donald. But two important Highland chiefs opposed his pretensions, namely, MacKenzie of Kintail and Alexander MacLeod of Dunvegan.

Despite the severity with which the latter's clan had been expelled from Trotternish in 1528, it seems that they had returned to the district some time during the intervening years. Soon, however, it was permanently to be wrenched from them by the MacDonalds. The young chief of that clan had greatly strengthened his position by his marriage with his cousin, the heiress of Lewis, and, in May, 1539, he invaded Trotternish, aided, as was his father eleven years previously, by a formidable force of *Siol* Torquil (Gregory, D, 1881, p. 145). On this, the final expulsion of the MacLeods from Trotternish the family seat of the MacDonalds was changed to Duntulm which was to remain their principal residence until a few years after the Rebellion of 1715.

Duntulm Castle

The date 1539, which is given as the year the MacDonalds left *Dun Sgathaich* and removed to Duntulm, is tentative but, in the light of all the available evidence, it seems to be approximately correct. We know that this was their principal seat when James V paid his memorable visit to the Isles in 1540, and it is said that the king was impressed by its commodiousness and its strength, and well he might.

The castle of Duntulm occupies a formidable position on an imposing promontory to the north of Score Bay in Kilmuir. It is inaccessible from the sea that surrounds its foundations of pillared basalt on all sides, except at a narrow isthmus that joins its site to the mainland. There are, even still, so many traces of outworks here, of walls, of trenches and perhaps a moat, that this stronghold was well nigh impregnable in its day.

Local tradition declares that a fort occupied this site from very early times and that it was demolished to provide material for the erection of the castle. After the Norse sway had come to an end in 1263, the castle of Duntulm frequently changed hands – now in the possession of the vassals of the Earls of Ross, then of those of the Lords of the Isles, but, for the most part, it was held by the MacLeods of Dunvegan. It is said that nothing was spared to make it a residence worthy of a great chief, and in order to ensure fertility the soil of seven kingdoms was brought to its policies.

When *Iain Lom,* the bard, visited Duntulm in 1663, in order to exhort Sir James MacDonald to avenge the murder of the Children of Keppoch, he thus alludes to the castle:

> *Gu Dunthuilm nam fear fallain,*
> To Duntulm of the vigorous men,
> *Far 'n greadhnach luchd eallaidh,*
> Where merry are the music makers
> *Gabhail fàilte le caithream,*
> Bidding welcome with joyful sound
> As *na clàrsaichean glana,*
> Of the pure harps
> *Do mhnaoi òig nan teud banala binn.*
> To the young woman of the sweet maidenly voice.
>
> (Mackenzie, J, 1877, p. 37)

But little now remains to attest the pristine glory of, *'Dun Thuilm nam baideal àrda'* ('Duntulm of the high towers'). Two lofty, but ruinous, pieces of masonry represent all that is left of the keep and a dark vault or two may still be seen. The wall facing the Minch is well preserved and, as one looks from its giddy height, one is reminded of the tragedy alleged by tradition to have befallen the family of Donald *Gorm,* when a child, taking a sudden jerk in the arms of its nurse, fell from the awesome heights of the battlements to be dashed to death upon the cruel rocks below. Indeed, some writers aver that this was the reason why the MacDonalds left Duntulm altogether – while the credulous nurse another tradition, characteristically embellished, that what induced their removal was the disturbing frequency with which the ghost of *Donald Gorm Mór* sought to revisit his earthly mansion!

He often returned with two companions from the other world, for it would appear that they scorned the ambrosial liquour of the gods. They clearly preferred the native bree, on which he and his consorting shades oftentimes became hilariously rude, much to the annoyance, and the awe, of the mortal occupants of the castle. They could be seen and heard, but would not speak to any one; and lockfast doors offered them no resistance.

The bacchanalian visitations of the ghosts were becoming so alarming and frequent, that the tenants of Duntulm sought the advice of a saintly man who advised them to supply each of seven stalwart fellows with a spill of burning bog-pine and, equipped with these as torches, and as charms, they were to enter the chamber of the supernatural roysterers and try to drive them out.

This was done, and the ghosts were so influenced by the sacred lights that they were no longer formidable. Donald *Gorm Mór* addressed the human intruders and, bewailing his sudden transformation, said:

> *If it were not for thy slender lace of fire,*
> *This would have been to thy hurt, young Donald* Gorm.

He then went on to tell his nephew and heir the location of important documents relative to his estates; for he felt he must conciliate mortals in order to be released from the spell which now so strongly bound him:

> *I was in Edinburgh last night;*
> *I am in my own mansion this night;*
> *And worth of mote in the sunbeam,*

I have not in me of might.

(MacKay, JG, 1924, p. 19)

We are as ignorant of the exact date the MacDonalds left Duntulm as we are of the time they entered it. It is traditionally said that the last festivity that took place there was held just before the MacDonalds set out in the Rebellion of 1715 but according to the evidence of the Commissioners of Forfeited Estates, Sir Donald MacDonald was living there in 1716 and, in an account of the Highland clans, written in the year 1725, the MacDonalds had not even then evacuated this stronghold; for there it is said, *"the principal residence of the MacDonalds is Duntulm"*.

But to return. "Some days subsequent to the invasion of Trotternish in 1539," according to the Rev. Alexander MacGregor, the scholarly minister of Kilmuir, "Donald Gorm passed over from Trotternish to Kintail, to be avenged of the MacKenzies, owing to their hostility to his pretensions." The MacLeods of Lewis did not follow him then, but in their place he had the assistance of a goodly band of the MacKinnons of Strath and it is said that a fleet of fifty galleys bore the allies over to Applecross. After ravaging Torridon and Kinlochewe, Donald proceeded to take MacKenzie's stronghold, the castle of Eilean Donain and he concluded this would be an easy matter as the garrison that defended it consisted of only three men. He surrounded the castle but the brave triumviri put up a stout resistance for an hour or so, and then their arrows came less frequently. Concluding that their ammunition was at the point of exhaustion, Donald Gorm unwittingly exposed himself in his endeavours to find a place that might prove the best approach to the castle. Immediately an arrow whizzed through the air, the last, it is said, in the fort, and buried its barb deep in the thigh of the chief of Clan Donald. More annoyed than hurt by this mischance, he seized the galling shaft and, wrenching it recklessly out of his flesh, he severed an artery, so that, in spite of all his men could do, he bled to death. He was carried to an islet nearby, and the site of the rude hut in which the brave Donald Gorm died is still pointed out, according to Gregory as Làrach Tigh Mhic Dho'uill. His enraged followers took a terrible revenge before they returned home, and it is said that they burned every house and boat in the district (Gregory, D, 1881, pp. 145–6).

Thus ended an insurrection that might have had grave consequences but for the untimely death of an able and aspiring leader.

Meanwhile the king had fully gauged the seriousness of the disaffection that had shown itself in the West Highlands and he resolved to take effective measures to stamp it out. Great preparations were made. By the end of May, 1540, a large fleet, well-equipped with men and munitions, set sail from the Firth of Forth. On board were such notable men as Cardinal Beaton and the Earls of Arran and Huntly.

After it had called at several places on the way, the fleet sailed from Lewis to Harris. Thence it made for Skye and although some authorities, among whom are the authors of *Clan Donald*, aver that *Alasdair Crotach* was arrested here and made a prisoner, one is strongly tempted to doubt this. Lesley, Bishop of Ross, who wrote of a period of Scottish history in 1578, does not say that he was imprisoned: he states, merely, that the king sent, *"ane cumpanye to Mc Clewde Hariche, quha come furth of his Ile to the king's presens alsua."* Indeed, the chief of MacLeod had very strong reasons for dissociating himself with the cause of Donald *Gorm* in view of the raid made by the latter on his lands in the previous year. Besides, it would appear that *Alasdair Crotach* was a royal favourite for, in 1539, his charter for Glenelg was confirmed and, in 1542, he actually received a charter for the districts of Uist and of Sleat, while in the following year Trotternish was conferred on him in life-rent to the extent of 80

merklands. It is therefore highly improbable that, if he had been a prisoner in 1540, he should have been so generously dealt with in 1542. It is a fact, however that he was obliged to give hostages as a guarantee of his allegiance in future and to that end his third son, Norman, accompanied the king's entourage on its way to the south (Gregory, D, 1881, p. 147).

Resuming its voyage, the royal convoy made for Duntulm; and the king was greatly impressed by the natural strength of that imposing castle-fort. Thence rounding *Rubha* Hunish, the fleet proceeded by the east coast of Skye and it entered *Loch Chaluim Chille*, the name, until then, of the Bay of Portree. Here a stay was made of several days' duration; and so impressive was the spectacle that the name of the district came to be changed from Kiltaraglen, the chapel of Talorgan (the Culdee who had a cell at Beil), to Port an Righ, or the King's Harbour. See *Oran Mór Chloinn Neacail* ('Great Song of the Nicolsons')

> *Gu taigh Mór Mhic Neacail shuas ud*
> To the great house of the Nicolsons up yonder
> *Far 'm bu tric a shuidh na h-uaislean*
> Where the nobles often sat
> *Righ Seumas a Coig 's a shluagh ann*
> King James the Fifth and his host
> *Le chuirtearean glana suairce.*
> With his magnificent urbane courtiers.

(Oral tradition)

Thither went many of the mainland lairds, ostensibly to do obeisance to their king, but virtually to crave the royal favour, now that they were made aware of the measures he was taking against their brother chiefs. Bishop Lesley mentions, *"the laird of Clan Ranald and John Moydert"*, the captain of Clan Ranald whose haughty bearing so offended his sovereign that an order was given for his immediate arrest.

In view of the part the MacDonalds of Skye had played in the late uprising, one is inclined to conclude that the captain of *Clann Uisdein*, Archibald the clerk, was among the prisoners, but on this there is no evidence, and the authors of *Clan Donald* declared that he was free. The period of his detention could not, in any case, have been of long duration, for it is on record that, *"Archibald Ilis, alias Archibald the Clerk, and Alexander Mac-Connell Gallich had been granted remission on 22nd March, 1541, for their treasonable fire raising and burning of boats at Ellandonan, and for the heirchip* (plundering) *of Kinlochewe and Trouterness"* (Cameron, A, 1871, p. 34).

The fleet once more set sail, this time to loyal Kintail, whence passing through the Sound of Sleat, it steered south as far as Kintyre. There it was commanded to retrace its course and to take the captive chiefs and the hostages by the north of Scotland to the port of Leith. Lindsay of Pittescottie thus comments on the expedition to the Isles:

> *The king passed through the isles, and there held justice-courts, and punished both chiefs and traitors according to their deserts; syne brought many of the great men of the isles captive with him, such as the MacDonalds and the MacLeods of Lewis, etc. Some he put in ward, and some he had in courts, and some he put in pledges for true faith in time coming. So he brought the isles in good rule and peace, whereby he had great profitable service and obedience of people a long time thereafter.*
>
> (Cameron, A, 1871, p. 37).

But peace was not permitted long to reign undisturbed in the Isles, for the untimely death of the king in 1542, and especially the dominant position of England, encouraged the chiefs of the West Highlands to raise a new rebellion. The direct heir of the Lord of the Isles had at that time been granted his freedom. This was Donald *Dubh*, the son of the undutiful Angus *Og* and he was enthusiastically supported by most of the Highland chiefs, despite their pledges of loyalty of the previous year. *Alasdair Crotach*, Ewen MacKinnon of Strath, and *Gilleasbuig Cléireach*, the captain of the MacDonalds, joined the rebel Donald with all their men, and a formidable array was soon in the field. Cognisant of the weakness of the rule of Albany and confident in their own powers, they bade defiance to the government, and entered into overt alliance with England. The name of *Gilleasbuig Cléireach* is found about this time as signatory to a commission sent to Henry VIII. In 1545 an army, about 4000 strong, went to Ireland – men of splendid physique they were, by all account – and they took the oath of allegiance to the king of England, turning traitors, it must be confessed, for the sake of that country's gold. But Donald *Dubh* died shortly after this, and, as the next heir to the dignity of Lord of the Isles was Mac-Donald of Sleat, the position of the representative of that house as a minor and the loss of prestige under which his clan seems to have been suffering at the time, left him out of account. Besides, the MacDonalds were far from easy, owing to the machinations of *Alasdair Crotach*, and they had real cause for perturbation, as he was then in actual possession of a charter for the lands which they occupied (Gregory, D, 1881, pp. 170–7).

Alasdair Crotach was one of the ablest chiefs of his age. He combined in himself the powers of the warrior with the talents of the diplomat in a remarkable manner, and he must also have been endowed with a culture of high degree. He encouraged the bards by conferring lands on them free of all ordinary burdens, and the earliest of the MacCrimmons found in him a most helpful patron. In order to endow their college, he allocated to them the district of Borreraig and these lands remained in the possession of the family of the MacCrimmons until the year 1770.

Yet in the marriage contract between his son, William and Agnes Fraser of Lovat, in 1541, (according to *Wardlaw Manuscript;* Mackay, W, 1905, p. 131) his signature appears as *"Alister Mc.Leod of Dounveggan with my hand led at the pen by a notar underwritten because I could naucht writ myselfe."* (MacLeod, RC, 1938, pp. 26, 30).

He built one of the towers of his castle at Dunvegan, where he lived magnificently. A story is told of him when once in Edinburgh at the King's palace. Certain lowland nobles who were present were somewhat piqued at the graceful ease with which this 'uncultivated' Highlander conducted himself at the royal table. Sly comments were made on the munificence of the entertainment in order to induce him to evince surprise, but he remained imperturbable. Finally, one nobleman, more insistent than the rest, pointedly remarked,

Now MacLeod, I wonder if you have ever seen in Skye, halls so spacious as these, a roof so lofty, a table as ample and so richly laden, and candelabra so ornate, as those around us here to-night
(cf MacLeod, RC, 1927, p. 81).

These halls are certainly grand, and the plenishing is truly magnificent,

returned the Highland chief,

but in our country we could show you a roof that is even more impressive, a table greater and grander than this by far, and candelabra that are more wonderful than those gorgeous ones that support the lights of our chamber to-night.

I shall go all the way to Skye to prove that you are both vainglorious and false,

returned the Lowlander, with venom in his voice.

No one ever, with impunity, dared to ascribe such opprobrious terms to me,

replied Alexander, with unruffled dignity,

and it would have gone hard with you but for the deference that is your due as my prospective guest; but, after you have partaken of the hospitality I can provide, I hope you are man enough to give a true report to this august company of all you have seen and enjoyed.

The Highland chief returned home, and notice soon arrived of the approach of the Lowland earl, and preparations, on a grand scale were made for his reception.

He happened to arrive at Dunvegan in the late afternoon, but instead of being conducted with his retinue to the castle, they were led to the hills in the direction of *Healabhal Mhór* (one of the MacLeod's Tables). The sun had already sunk in the west when they gained the summit of that noble hill, around which stalwart clansmen stood, bearing flambeaux aloft to light the scene. The mountain's flat top was covered over its whole extent with viands of all kinds, and a copious supply of wine.

Turning to his guests, the chief ceremoniously invited them to sit down and partake of his cheer. After all had enjoyed the *al fresco* banquet, he turned to his detractor and, pointing to the star-spangled skies, he quietly remarked:

Truly, sir, this is a roof grander than was ever made by human hands; this table, you must confess, is more commodious than any that can be shown even in the royal court; while those faithful vassals of mine are more precious by far than any metallic contrivances, however costly and ornate the latter may be.

The Lowland earl humbly begged for mercy for his having been so rash and so unjust and his apology was accepted by the Highlander with his customary graciousness of demeanour. Thereafter the party proceeded to the castle where they were entertained for several days with the greatest cordiality and when they departed, there was no disposition amongst them to jeer at the Highland chief or at his manner of living.

Alasdair Crotach, the chief of Dunvegan, was now advanced in years and it appears he abdicated the chiefship in November 1540 in favour of his son, William, having already resigned to the latter certain lands in Easter and Wester Lyndale, and in Bracadale, of which the following are specially mentioned: "*Vngcladdach, Vngroak, Sagerry, Voagyne, Penyzegeyn, Stapok, Grobane, Layglane, and Oysestill in Braikodell*" (MacLeod, RC, 1938, p. 3). He went to live at the monastery of St. Clement's in Rodel of Harris, a church which he himself had generously endowed with lands. He rebuilt the church and in it he prepared for himself, nineteen years before his death, a tomb that is perhaps the most beautiful work of sculpture in the Western Isles. There he was buried in 1547, the first of the chiefs of MacLeod to be laid in Rodel, all his predecessors, from Leod down, having found a last resting-place in the Island of Iona.

It has been related that he established two chapels in Harris, one at Scarista, the other at Toe Head and that, in his retirement, he was engaged in translating the psalms into Gaelic (MacLeod, RC, 1927 pp. 83–4).

He was married to a daughter of Allan XII of Lochiel, and he had a family of three sons and two daughters. Of the latter, one was married to a half-brother of Donald *Gorm* of Sleat, namely, James *Gruamach* of Castle *Camus*, a man who was the captain of Clan *Uisdein* during the minority of *Do'ull Gorm Mór*.

The Macleods

William, (Uilleam na h-Uamha), Ninth Chief

Alasdair Crotach was succeeded, in 1547, by his eldest son, William, who, as we have already seen, had acted as regent during the latter years of his father's life. This chief is sometimes called *Uilleam na h-uamha*, or 'William of the Cave', and many take it for granted that he owes the latter designation to his being the perpetrator of the Massacre of Eigg, but as the date now given to that event, following the authority of Skene, is 1577, the guilt cannot be laid to the account of this chief, who was dead in 1551 (Skene, WF, 1902, p. 354).

He married Agnes Fraser, daughter of the fifth Lord Lovat in 1540, a union entered upon as part of the agreement that terminated the long-continued dispute between the MacLeods and Frasers over the possession of Glenelg (see *Wardlaw Manuscript*, Mackay, W, 1905, p. 131 for contract of marriage). There was but one child of this marriage, a daughter, and as William was old before he assumed the chiefship, he was naturally uneasy about the succession.

At his father's funeral in Rodel, he endeavoured to sense the feelings of the principal men of his clan and his worst fears were realised when most of them declared their aversion to the principle of female succession (MacLeod, RC, 1927, p. 90). He allowed this discovery to affect his whole attitude towards the cadets of the clan, with the result that he alienated their goodwill, so that few were disposed to support his daughter, Mary, at his death in 1551. The poem on him recounts:

'Se mac so a dh fhag Alasdair
   This son Alexander left,
Glac gheal a mhalairt òir
   White hand that dealt in gold,

'N t Uillam so a chuala sibh
    This William you have heard about
Air am bheil na buaidhean còr.
    Who has the plenteous talents.

               (Turner, P, 1809, p. 320)

'The Heiress of The Isles'

The heiress was then only nine years of age but for many years she was to remain a personage of note in the politics of Scotland. Her great wealth attracted the attention alike of chiefs and nobles who contended and intrigued for the rights of her wardship.

The first person to secure the coveted honour was the Chancellor of the realm, the Earl of Huntly and, in order to understand the significance of the transaction, it may be appropriate to give the gist of this deed of gift. It comprised control of *"all the dewties, males, ferms, of all the lands underwritten – Areth (Harris), Dunnevagane, Trouterness, Slaitt, North Oist, Duryness, Brakadell, Megynes (Minginish), and Glenelg, and all other lands and annual rents which perteined to the umquhile William Mac Cleoid, with the castles, towers, fortalices, mylnis, multures, woods, fishings"*, etc., all of which were conferred on Huntly in 1552 (Mackenzie, A, 1889, p. 27).

Three years later we find that Huntly transferred the rights of wardship to the Earl of Argyle for the sum of 1200 marks, but this transaction was soon to be declared null and void.

At this time disturbances had arisen in the Isles and the Western Highlands and the chiefs who were responsible for the feuds were said to have been Donald Gormson of Sleat, MacLeod of Lewis, and MacKenzie of Kintail. The Queen Regent, Mary of Guise, issued a commission to Huntly, and to Argyle, to proceed against these unruly vassals, and compel them to tender hostages as a guarantee of their good behaviour in future (Gregory, D, 1881, p. 186).

Huntly failed utterly to carry out his obligations, alleging general insubordination among his troops and incompatibility of action between the Highland and the Lowland sections of his army. His pretexts did not, however, commend him to the Queen Regent. She deprived him of all his honours annulling, at the same time, his contract with Argyle in connection with the wardship of Mary MacLeod which she reserved to herself.

The new faith was then making rapid headway in Scotland and, in order to stem its advance into the Highlands, the regent was eager to win to her side those who might support her against the bold activities of the new Protestant noble, the fifth Earl of Argyle. Accordingly, in the year 1559, she conferred the wardship of the young heiress of MacLeod on James MacDonald of Dunneyveg in Islay but she soon had cause to regret her choice, for the ingrate MacDonald doubly disappointed her by turning Protestant and marrying the sister of Argyle (Gregory, D, 1881, p. 187).

Meanwhile, by some stratagem that has never been explained, the heiress came into the custody of MacKenzie of Kintail who refused to deliver her up when enjoined to do so. In 1562, however, he was compelled, by an act of the Privy Council, to surrender her to the young queen who had lately returned from France. She seems to have been engaged as a maid of honour at the royal court from that time until about 1565 for, in notices from the accounts of the Lord High Treasurer of Scotland, there are such items as the following: *"XXIII, day of Decr., be the Quenis' grace, Precept to Marie MacCloid-Ane elne, 1 quarter, of black welvot to the hude, musell, and turet, the elne, Vij lib."*

Also, on *"XVj day of Marche, 1565"*, there appears another item of expenditure on behalf of *"Marie MacCloid, in her Grace's chamber"* (MacLeod, RC, 1938, p. 91), where we shall leave her meantime and survey affairs at home. She married Duncan Campbell of Auchinbreck (Gregory, D, 1881, p. 206).

We have already seen that the late chief had dealt harshly

with the principal men of his clan for their refusal to support the claims of his daughter to the headship of the clan and, in his exasperation, he also turned against his brothers, Donald and Norman, whom he drove out of Skye. It is said that the former betook himself to England where he remained until five or six years after the death of the chief.

John (Iain a' Chùil Bhàin or Iain Og), Tenth Chief

As this Donald and his brother were abroad at the time of William's death, the clan hailed as their chief the head of the family called *Sliochd Mhic Iain 'ic Leòid*, a man named *Iain a' Chùil Bhàin*, who was a great-grandson of Norman, twin-brother of William *Dubh*, the sixth chief, who fought at the battle of Bloody Bay in 1480. Indeed, this family had all along contended that their ancestor, Norman (who, as we have seen was killed in Lochaber in 1429 while fighting with Alexander, son of Donald, Lord of the Isles, against King James I), was the older of the two sons of *Iain Borb*. This branch now came into its own and their representative, John, 'The Fair Haired', proved himself to be an efficient chief, who guided the affairs of his clan to the entire satisfaction of all.

His popularity and worth were shown in a significant way when, towards the end of his reign, Donald, the exiled brother of the late chief, returned to Dunvegan apparently to press his claims to the chiefship. A meeting of the clan was held at Lyndale in the month of March 1557 in order to consider the situation, and, after a lengthy discussion, it was there decided to leave *Iain a' Chùil Bhàin* in undisturbed possession, but that, on his death, the estates were to revert to the original line, in the person of Donald MacLeod or of his heir (MacLeod, RC, 1927, p. 95).

The latter part of the contract roused to action the second son of *Iain a' Chùil Bhàin*, one variously called *Iain Og* and *Iain Dubh*, and the latter epithet is justly attributed to this man of "dark" deeds. That very night, while the company was still at Lyndale, he conspired to remove that relative who stood between him and his ambition and, when all had retired to rest, he burst into Donald's tent and murdered him in his sleep. For this outrage he was expelled by the clan, but he sought the protection of the notorious pirate, *Uisdean MacGhilleasbuig Chléirich*, who befriended him for a time (*ibid.*).

A few months after this incident the chief, *Iain a' Chùil Bhàin*, died, and he was buried in Rodel. After the ceremony of interment was over, it was resolved by the leading men of the clan to raise to the chiefship the grandson of *Iain a' Chùil Bhàin*, Norman, who was a minor and to confer the dignity of tutor on a younger brother of *Iain Dubh*, a man called Donald *Breac* (Mackenzie, A, 1889, p. 32).

John (Iain Dubh or Iain Og), Eleventh Chief (de facto)

When the cadets of his clan were in Harris, *Iain Dubh*, by a *coup de main*, succeeded in taking Dunvegan Castle and establishing himself there. On the return of his clansmen from his father's funeral, he laid a trap for his own brother, Donald who had been appointed regent, and for his two nephews, Norman and Donald. As soon as these men had passed through the 'sea-gate', they were set upon, and foully murdered by *Iain Dubh* and his associates. By maintaining a powerful garrison in the castle, and holding as hostages the sons or daughters of the chief men of the clan, he was able to enforce obedience to his will and to secure his hold on the estates for a period of about three years (MacLeod, RC, 1927, pp. 95–96).

Relative to his usurpation, there is extant a document that was sent, in 1557, by Mary of Guise, the Regent, to Rose, the 'Black Baron' of Kilravock. The latter chief is informed that forces are to be sent by land and sea to repress the tyrant of Dunvegan and it proceeds thus:

Forasmuch as it is not unknown to you how John Og MacLeod of Minginish, in the month of March last, cruelly murdered the umquhile Donald MacLeod, brother german to the umquhile William MacLeod, and took the house of Dunvegan, and withholds the same contrary to our dearest daughter's authority, etc.

(Mackenzie, A, 1889, p. 35).

Despite this threat, *Iain Dubh* was able to maintain his position as chief until his death in 1559, and it is said that, during the years he was in power, he had never ceased to plot against the life of Norman, the brother of that Donald he had murdered at Lyndale and now the male heir to the chiefship. In this, however, he was foiled by the vigilance and the self-interest of Argyle (Mackenzie, A, 1889, p. 37).

We have already seen that the latter nobleman had succeeded in investing himself with the rights of feudal guardianship of the Heiress of the Isles and, in order that he might translate that empty privilege into practical benefit to himself, he sought to marry her to a Campbell. Thus he was led to send some of the principal men of his clan with a strong force to Skye, in order to ascertain the attitude of the MacLeods to his project. The men of Argyle landed in Roag where they sought the hospitality of MacSwan, MacLeod's vassal in that district. MacSwan communicated the news to his chief who forwarded a cordial invitation to the strangers to pay a visit to Dunvegan Castle.

Eleven leading men of the contingent, accompanied by servants, set off, under the guidance of their host, and it was arranged they were to confer with *Iain Dubh* and his counsellors in the church of Kilmuir, near Dunvegan. There Iain feigned a sympathetic interest in their mission, which was that he should

abdicate in favour of Mary, the rightful heiress, and he in return would be richly rewarded by the Earl of Argyle. Iain expressed his willingness to subscribe to these overtures and an undertaking was ratified, there and then, whereby the Campbells were to be allowed to garrison the castle of Pabbay in Harris forthwith, and the whole of the estates were to be ceded to them on Iain's death and hence the persistence of the name Campbell in Harris and Skye.

The meeting was then adjourned and the party repaired to the castle where a sumptuous banquet awaited them. Each of the Campbells was sandwiched at table between two stalwart MacLeods and, at a certain stage in the proceedings, the attendants simultaneously placed before each of the guests a cup of blood. This was the preconcerted signal for action by their hosts and, in a flash, every Campbell fell forward and collapsed, a lifeless mass, under the table. Some of their servants succeeded in making their escape, and, when news of the massacre reached the main body of the Campbells at Roag, a general scramble was made for their boats and many fled from the shores of Skye (MacLeod, RC, 1927, p. 96).

Having failed in this project, Argyle now tried other means in order to attain his end. He had for some time been in communication with Norman, brother of that Donald who had been killed at Lyndale by *Iain Dubh,* and now the oldest surviving son of *Alasdair Crotach.* His protegé was then most likely to make an endeavour to claim the chiefship and, under the circumstances, he was sure to succeed. It would appear that this Norman had been a prisoner of war and that, through the instrumentality of Argyle, he had been set at liberty. It was thus an easy matter for Argyle to win the favour of Norman and it was but natural for the latter to consider the expediency of seeking the friendship of such an influential baron as Argyle. Hence it was that he entered into a bond of manrent with Argyle. It was written and confirmed at Dunune (Dunoon) on *"1st Mar., year of God, 1559"*, and is as follows:

> *It is accorded … between ane noble and potent Lord, Archibald, Earl of Argyll, and Tormoid MacCleoid, sone to umquhile Alexander MacCleoid of Herre, as principal in this contract, and Hector Maklane of Doward, as principal favourar and Tutour to the said Tormod, in maner, forme, and effect, as after follows: Forsamakle as said Earle has redeemit the said Norman out of captivity, and enemies hands, wherein he was with Frenchmen (under Mary of Guise), yet, the said Earle obliges him to fortify, help, and set forward the said Tormod to wyne and jois the heritage and rowmis that pertenit to his fader and brother of Herre with the pertinentis, Tewedes, and Glenelg and all other bounds whereof they have auld titill of heritage, and sail be ane good lord and master to said Tormod in all his actiounes, and just causes, and to the effect that the same may come the better forward has delivered the said Tormod to the said Hector to be helpit, and fortefeit for the which causis, the said Tormod presentis, giffis, and grants his band of manrent, his faithful and true service with all his kin, and friends, and his heirs, and successors of the Herre, to the said Earle, and his heirs, and successors perpetually. He sall not marry but by the consent of the said earle whose avyss he sall tak in marrying ane wife, and being established in his rowmis and the Herre Tewedes sall pay the valour or the estimation of the availe of the wards, marriage of the Herre, and the laboures, and the travellis of the said earle to him, and to the said Hector to be divided as the said earle thinks cause between him and the said Hector, and it follows that if MacCleoid does not honour this band he will be content to be perpetualie defamed, etc.* (see Innes, C, 1854, Vol. .2, part 1, p. 378).

Having succeeded in binding Norman MacLeod to his allegiance, Argyle then sought to wheedle the chief of the Clan Donald of Skye into his obligation likewise. This was to prove an easy matter for him, for MacDonald had no legal claims on the lands he occupied, either in Uist or in Skye. Indeed, as we have already seen, these possessions had been conferred on *Alasdair Crotach* in 1542, so that the chief of the MacDonalds was prepared to go far to meet the powerful lord of Argyle, who had promised to obtain the necessary charters for him. With all the cunning cleverness of which he was capable, Argyle induced Norman MacLeod to renounce his claims on the lands of the MacDonalds in his own favour and he made good use of this advantage at a later period.

Meanwhile Norman, the third son of *Alasdair Crotach*, had returned to Dunvegan to claim the chiefship of the clan. He had powerful supporters in the Earl of Argyle, MacLean of Duart, who was his father-in-law, and Lord Lovat; and the most influential members of his own clan soon gathered around him.

As soon as the regnant chief heard of Norman's arrival, he shut himself up in his castle whence it would not be an easy matter to dislodge him if his associates only remained true. But that was not to be, for his principal warder, Torquil MacSwan, was early in league with Norman, and he promised to admit him and his men on their arrival.

Iain Dubh discovered, too late, that most of his men had turned traitors so that, when Norman appeared before the castle and the gates were opened by MacSwan, he would assuredly have been captured but for the vigilance and the agility of four foster-brothers who, by a secret passage conducted him to his galley and conveyed him to Harris. The fugitives made for the castle of Pabbay but there they were refused admission and were driven out of the island. Thence they resumed their sail south and, after many vicissitudes, Iain made his way to Ireland where, it is said, he became a lone wanderer and, falling foul of one of the chiefs of O'Donnell, he was cruelly tortured to death by the latter's agents, who put red-hot irons through his bowels (MacLeod, RC, 1927, p. 97).

Norman (Tormad), Twelfth Chief

We have already seen that, when James V made his memorable expedition to the Western Isles in 1540, the chief of the MacLeods, *Alasdair Crotach*, rendered as hostage his son, Norman. It has also been mentioned that the latter suffered exile with his brother, Donald, during the chiefship of William, the ninth chief, and that he had been a prisoner with the French. In some accounts it is stated that he had been a student at Glasgow University and that it was then the blood-thirsty chief, *Iain Dubh*, had plotted against his life but that the dark schemer had been circumvented by the vigilance of Argyle, who had then interested himself in Norman's affairs (Mackenzie, A, 1889, p. 37).

As soon as the latter had established himself as chief, Argyle was once again in negotiation with him. Norman had owned the Earl as his superior in 1559, and in 1566 MacDonald of Dunnyveg, on whom the wardship of Mary MacLeod had been conferred, surrendered his right to Argyle on his marrying that nobleman's sister.

In return for services rendered, Argyle induced Norman MacLeod to promise to pay him £1000 on the marriage of Mary and the Skye chief was to benefit by an undertaking on the part of Argyle to cause "the Heiress" to surrender her claims on the estates to Norman who was to receive a royal charter by the help of his patron. Thus it happened that, in 1572, James VI, acting on the advice of Argyle, granted a charter for the estates of the MacLeods, together with a portion of Trotternish, and the bailliary of the whole of it, to Mary MacLeod, who, in the same year, acting no doubt on the advice of Argyle, conveyed her claim to Norman the chief. This agreement did not, however, receive the impress of royal sanction until the year 1579 (*ibid.*, pp. 43–4).

Some years previously, in 1573 Argyle had succeeded in bringing about a marriage between Mary MacLeod and a kinsman of his own, a Duncan Campbell, heir apparent of Achinbreck, and,

apart from the unsuccessful attempts made by her descendants to have it recognised that the contract for the conveyance of the estates to Norman was invalid, Mary MacLeod, 'the Heiress of the Isles', passes finally out of the history of Skye. She was alive in 1602 when she married MacNeil of Barra as her second husband (*ibid.*).

In view of the obligations under which he had placed his clan with respect to his patron Argyle, but especially on account of a foul deed he perpetrated shortly after his accession, Norman estranged the allegiance of a large section of his people. With the view to render his position secure, he resolved to massacre all who might have a claim on the chiefship, attention to be directed principally on the male representatives of his own nearest relatives and on all the descendants of *Iain a' Chuil Bhàin*.

To carry out the atrocious work, certain leading men of the clan were sworn to secrecy, each allotted his victim, and enjoined, on pain of death, to murder him on an appointed day. That a terrible carnage must have ensued is shown by the fact that *Iain a' Chùil Bhàin* alone had a family of twelve sons and four daughters, all of whose descendants, with one exception, were put to death. This was Norman, a nephew of the last chief, *Iain Dubh*, a young lad who was being fostered at the time in Harris by a cadet of his clan. The story is well told in *'The MacLeods of Dunvegan'*, by Canon R.C. MacLeod of MacLeod (1927, p. 102) and its main features fall to be narrated here. Such was the attachment between the foster-father and his protégé, and the reverence shown to the ancient obligations of fosterage that, despite the fealty he owed his chief and the oath he had solemnly sworn to carry out his command, he found it impossible to steel his heart to murder the boy. He had been anxious and unsettled all that day and, going into his house, sat down disconsolately, when the foster-son climbed on his knees and kissed him. This action by the innocent child forced the god-father to give way to convulsive sobs. On being asked by his astonished wife what ailed him, the only answer she could obtain was, *"Teich, is teasairg e, teich is teasairg e"* ("Fly and save him"). She, interpreting the advice aright, left Harris, and succeeded in reaching Duntulm, where she placed the lad under the protection of his relative, Donald Gormson, the chief of the MacDonalds. There the boy was brought up and, when he attained to manhood, the lands of Kingsborough were conferred on him and the district remained in the possession of his descendants until it was given to the famous warrior, *Do'ull Mac Iain 'ic Sheumuis*, during the chiefship of Sir James *Mór* of Sleat (MacLeod, RC, 1927, pp. 101–2).

It was probably in consequence of this massacre that the relations between the chief and his clan became so severely strained that, fearing assassination, he formed a bodyguard of twelve picked men who watched over him day and night. The tests of eligibility for inclusion in this band were alike severe and searching. They had to excel in leaping, wrestling, throwing the stone and in caber-tossing and, if they showed their proficiency in these feats they qualified for the final test, which was to wrench off with one hand a bull's leg at the knee. If they succeeded in this, they were admitted into the chief's circle, the *'Buannachan'* or 'Bullies'.

These warriors had many privileges, and were accorded a great amount of licence, for they were feared by all and, being imbued with that arrogance that comes of untutored strength, they harassed the people by their extravagant exactions.

According to *The MS, History of the MacLeods* (The Bannatyne Manuscript), the organisation soon came to be disbanded, a happy consummation due to the activities of a herculean member of the clan called *Fionnlagh na Plaide Baine*, or 'Finlay of the White Blanket'. This odd personage was invariably clad in a web of undyed cloth rudely girded around him as the *breacanfeile*, or the kilt as worn by his contemporaries.

As Finlay was one day engaged in his customary pursuit of 'rock'-fishing, the *buannachan* visited his house and they began to make free with whatsoever they could find. Not content with the food with which they had been provided they killed his best cow and, having slashed off the choicest parts of it, they ordered his wife to prepare their dinner.

The bullying gargantuans were partaking of their meal just as Finlay returned from fishing and, realising the situation, he proceeded, without ado, to the barn, whence he brought in a good ash-flail with which he put an abrupt termination to the banquet. He wielded the implement with such telling effect that he terrorised the *buannachan* into abject submission. He drove them before him into an outhouse where he stood threateningly over them, while his wife bound them by the method known in Gaelic as *'Ceangal nan coig caol'* – i.e. the ankles, wrists and neck of each individual were brought together and bound with one rope, and thus they were left to spend the night.

Early the following morning he deposited them severally in his boat, ferried them across Dunvegan Loch and, after he had unbound them, he led them to the castle. As he was a *persona grata* with his chief, owing both to his eccentricity and his great brute strength, Finlay was admitted into the presence of his superior without any preliminary ceremonies. Being full of bitter feeling against the presumptuous parasites, he descanted vehemently on their malpractices, with the result that this institution of mercenary warriors was forthwith abolished (MacLeod, RC, 1927, pp. 100–1).

And if all tales be true, the ghoulish nature of this cruel chief was not yet satiated, for another crime, as terrible in its barbarity as the slaughter of his relatives, must be imputed to him. That was the Massacre of Eigg.

Several of the chiefs of MacLeod have been accused by historians of that atrocious deed – *Alastair Crotach*; William, his son (by Canon R.C. MacLeod), *Iain Dubh*, the usurper (by Alexander MacKenzie, The Clans' Historian) but as the date now generally assigned to the event is 1577, it must have been perpetrated during the suzerainty of the present chief and, from what we know of his character, we are forced to conclude that he was quite capable of committing it.

It is a surprising fact that there is no allusion to the Massacre of Eigg in the works of contemporary writers, and that, so far, no reference to is has been found in the government archives; but, relative to this event, a document, *"which has all the appearance of being authentic"*, was discovered by Skene and it is quoted by Mackenzie (Mackenzie, A, 1889, pp. 44–5). In it occurs a statement to the effect that there are many caves under the earth in this isle (Eigg) which country folk use as strongholds, hiding themselves and their gear there. It happened that in March, anno 1577, war and enmity existed between the Clan Ranald and MacLeod of Harris in consequence of ill-treatment meted out to a daughter of Macleod's who was married to the Captain of Clanranald (*ibid.*, p. 25). The people, with one, Angus John MacMurdoson, their captain, fled to one of the said caves taking with them their wives, bairns and gear and MacLeod, apprised of it, landed with a great army, came to the cave, put fire thereto, and *"smoorit the haile people thairin to the number of 395 persons"* (*ibid.*, p. 45).

The Tragedy of Trumpan

In the township of Trumpan, in Waternish, there are the ruins of an ancient chapel, which is surrounded by the burial-ground of the district, probably 'Kilmory in Watternes' mentioned in 1501 as a vicarage of the parsonage of Snizort (Innes, C, 1854, Vol. 2, p. 358). The east gable and north wall are still standing; and in the latter is the doorway which is a rudely pointed Gothic arch. There also may be seen the windows, which are of the loophole variety, and about two feet in height, but only four inches in width on the outside of the wall. The chapel is situated on a windswept plateau that terminates abruptly towards the west in a long steep escarpment above the shore of the Bay of Ardmore. It was dedicated to one of the early saints, and is accordingly called Kilconan. In it was enacted one of the most gruesome tragedies of which there is record in our island story.

Ever since the Massacre of Eigg had been committed by the MacLeods, the Clan Ranald, to which the MacDonalds of Eigg belonged, had been secretly planning revenge. Hence it happened that, on a Sunday in the beginning of May, 1578, the MacDonalds of Uist put into the Bay of Ardmore, in Waternish, in a fleet of eight ships and, under cover of a dense fog, landed there unobserved. This was all the easier for them, as most of the people of the district were worshipping at the time in the church at Trumpan and when the MacDonalds discovered this their hearts were filled with savage glee at the prospect of exacting the full meed of vengeance on the murderers of their kin in Eigg.

After they had beached their galleys, the invaders stealthily climbed the slope above the shore and, once they had attained the edge of the plateau, they made a dash in grim silence for the church. A detachment was detailed to guard the doorway with strict injunction to allow none to escape alive, while the rest of the party began the dastard work of setting the sacred building on fire. This was no difficult task and the thatch-covered roof was soon ablaze. The song of praise was abruptly hushed for, in a moment, the doomed worshippers had realised their position. Soon the fire reached the timbers of the roof and its crackling was drowned by the blood-curdling shrieks of deep despair which came from that house of woe. Prayers for succour to God were mixed with pleadings for mercy to men, only to be answered by the besiegers with such taunts as, *"You have taught us how to smother a people"* and, *"Remember the Cave of Eigg"*.

Before the roof had fallen in, a woman made a frantic effort to escape and she succeeded in breaking through the cordon of men at the door but, in doing so, it is said that one of her breasts was cut clean off by the swipe of a MacDonald sword. Concluding that she was mortally wounded, the destroyers paid no further heed to her, with the result that she managed to reach the nearest house, where she raised the alarm; and then she made for her own home but succumbed to her injuries on the way at a place still pointed out as *"'Sloc Mairearaid'*, or 'Margaret's Hollow'.

By this time the rising wind had cleared the fog and the venue of the sacrilege could easily be located. All able-bodied men in the neighbourhood hurriedly made for the scene of desecration, only to be worsted in the fight by the invaders. But, as we say in Gaelic, *"News of woe are borne on the wings of the wind"*, so that the whole countryside was soon ringing with tales of the deed of shame. When the chief heard of it in Dunvegan, his galleys were hastily unmoored and manned by bands of eager and determined men.

It is, however, a far cry to Trumpan and time lags tardily when men are impelled by a consuming desire to revenge a cruel wrong; but a strong following breeze sped the birlinns onward and, in a short time, they arrived at the place of conflict. The triumphant MacDonalds had, by this time, overcome the weak resistance offered them by the natives and they were engaged in rounding up the cattle of the district when the reinforcements arrived from Dunvegan.

The chief had ordered the Fairy Flag to be taken out of its iron chest and, as soon as the MacLeods encountered the forces of the enemy, the latter fled in panic towards the shore for, as the story-teller puts it, *"the very grass blades were changed to armed men as soon as the folds of the magic banner were unfurled to the breeze!"*

When they reached the escarpment overlooking the shore the discomfited invaders discovered, to their horror, that the ebbing tide had left their boats high and dry and that a contingent of the MacLeods had already taken possession of them. As a last resort,

they sought shelter behind a dry-stone wall which had been built along the shore as a protection to the crops against the spray of the sea. Here they made a stand. Stimulated by that courage which is born of despair, they put up a brave, if ineffectual, resistance. But nothing short of annihilation would satisfy the avengers' lust for blood and, with the exception of a small band which had succeeded in launching a boat, the MacDonalds were butchered to a man. Their bodies were laid in a row along the base of the wall, which was tumbled over them to obviate the necessity for burial. This battle is accordingly called, *Blar Milleadh Gàraidh*, or The Battle of the Destruction of a Dyke; and it is said that during spring tides, when great billows are driven shorewards across the stormy Minch, breaches are made in the site of the old wall and human bones are often exposed to view (see Appendix 5) (Mackenzie, A, 1889, pp. 47–8).

Our main difficulty in connection with this narrative is that Waternish then pertained to the MacLeods of Lewis, and that it had not come into the possession of the MacLeods of Skye until over thirty years after the date assigned here to the massacre.

We hear no more of Norman, the chief of MacLeod, until 1580, when he is in trouble with the government for his remissness in paying the teinds due to the Bishop of the Isles and, in conjunction with several other landholders of Skye, he was, "put to the horn" in the following year, and his lands were declared forfeited.

It is noteworthy that this chief, who is reputed to have been a student at Glasgow University, declares, in the numerous signatures in his name that are extant, that his *"hand is leid at the pen by the notar, … at my command"* (Gregory, D, 1881, p. 204).

He was twice married: first, to Julia of Duart, and, secondly, to Janet of Argyle. By the former he had three sons, William, Roderick, and Alexander, designated of Minginish; and two daughters – Margaret, the famous *Cailleach Cham*, the divorced wife of *Do'ull Gorm Mór* of Sleat and Christina, who married

Torquil MacLeod of Lewis. The chief died in 1585, and was succeeded by his son, William.

The Macleods

William (Uilleam), Thirteenth Chief and John, Fourteenth Chief

The chief was a man possessed of a singularly attractive personality and was a capable ruler. He had just entered upon the responsibilities of his office when a feud occurred between the MacDonalds of Skye and the MacLeans of Duart, which was to involve almost all the clans of the West Highlands for a decade in internecine strife. As William's mother was of the MacLeans, his clan was allied with the latter against the MacDonalds (MacLeod, RC, 1927, p. 117).

In 1586 he was 'ordained' rebel, along with the other chiefs of Skye, for maliciously interfering with the Lowland fishermen who plied their trade around his shores.

On the 15th January, 1588, he entered into a bond of manrent with MacIntosh of Dunachton, whose daughter, Janet, he married and in it he engages to aid his father-in-law against all his enemies. This is a significant undertaking, in view of the fact that in the previous year MacIntosh had concluded a contract with Donald *Gorm* of Sleat to help the latter against such chiefs as MacKenzie of Kintail and MacLeod of Harris! It is interesting to note that in his contact with Dunachton, he signs his own name, calling himself *'Wm. M'Lloyd offe Dunvegane'*, thus showing that he was able to write (Mackenzie, A, 1889, p. 57).

The period of his chiefship was a short one, for he died in 1590. He left as his heir a young lad named John who was of delicate constitution, and died in 1595. In that year Roderick, known to history as *Ruairi Mór* and who had acted as tutor, or regent, during the previous five years, became chief of the clan,

and, as most of his life was spent in wars and feuds with the neighbouring house of MacDonald, it is necessary to bring the family history of that clan to date.

The Macdonalds

Donald Gormson (Sassunach), Seventh Chief

The heir to the chiefship of *Clann Uisdein* was a youth of tender years when his father was killed at the siege of the castle of *Eilean Donain* in 1539 and the government of the clan devolved on his uncle, Archibald, who, from the fact that he had been educated for the church, is designated, *Cléireach*. Yet this cleric signs his name with his *'hand at pen'*, a significant conceit, illustrating perhaps the fact that the art of writing was considered contemptible then by warriors and men of affairs (MacDonald, DJ, 1978, p. 405). Archibald was murdered, it is said, by a nephew of the name of John *Og*.

At that time the young chief was absent from Skye. It seems that the government, for some reason or another, was eager to secure his person and, in order to obviate that contingency, his uncle took him to Lewis. Thereafter he was not heard of for several years, some surmising that he had been for a part of that time at the court of Mary I, of England and hence his cognomen of *'Sassunach'*.

As the clan was then leaderless, the crafty Earl of Argyle began to interest himself in its affairs. He had already considerably aggrandised his position by his dealings with the MacLeods, whose claims over Uist, Sleat, and Trotternish he had induced their chief to transfer to himself. These lands were then occupied by the MacDonalds, but they had failed hitherto to procure a crown charter for them. Hence it was that, on the return of Donald Gormson as chief of the clan, Argyle immediately entered into negotiations with him, premising the offer that he would secure for him that heritable infeftment for his lands which was now coming to be considered in the Isles the essential requirement of tenure.

Under the circumstances there was nothing for MacDonald but to yield to the machinations of Argyle. He gave him his bond of manrent, agreed to pay him 1000 marks immediately and 500 on the marriage of his ward, Mary MacLeod, with the proviso that Argyle had by that time succeeded in securing the necessary title-deeds for him. Donald Gormson signs this contract in 1567 *"with hand at the pen led by the notar"* (Gregory, D, 1881, p. 206).

At that time the MacDonalds were engaged in a bitter feud with the MacKenzies of Kintail, the cause of the enmity lying in the relationship between the heads of these respective families to the House of Lewis. Roderick MacLeod, the chief of that island, had renounced the claims of his alleged heir, Torquil *Connanach*, the son of his first and undutiful wife, Janet MacKenzie of Kintail, who had eloped with MacLeod of Raasay; and her clan was determined to uphold the cause of their kinsman (Gregory, D, 1881, p. 208).

For a generation, and more, a state of war existed between the MacDonalds and the MacKenzies, owing principally to the opposition offered by the latter to the pretensions of the Mac-Donalds to the dignity of 'Lord of the Isles', and the antagonism between the clans had been bitterly intensified by the fall of Donald *Gorm* before the walls of *Eilean Donain* Castle in 1539 (Cameron, A, 1871, p. 44).

Even in 1553 we find that Donald Gormson is carrying war into their territory, harassing their friends, and helping their enemies. So fierce and frequent were his incursions that the government was at length induced to interpose. He was declared an outlaw and the injunction was given to take steps to prevent *"MacGorme, ane broken Hielandman, from taking timbers for*

long-faddis (galleys) out of MacKenzie's territory" (MacDonald, A & A, 1904, p. 22)

He seems, however, to have persisted in his forays, in spite of threats and warnings for, again in 1554, his conduct and that of his ally, MacLeod of Lewis, had become so outrageous that a commission was issued to Argyle and Huntly to proceed to the Isles, *"to the utter extermination of Donald Gormeson"*, for his failure to preserve the peace and to present hostages for his good behaviour. Eleven years later, however, he was restored to royal favour, when, in the abortive rising that took place on the marriage of Mary to Darnley, MacDonald took the side of the queen, and he helped to stamp out the rebellion.

Meanwhile the war between the MacKenzies and the MacLeods of Lewis went intermittingly on. When, however, the protégé of the latter, *Torcul Oighre* (Torquil the Heir), was drowned in 1566, on his way to Skye, Donald Gormson sought the succession to the lands of Lewis in virtue of the claims of his mother who was of *Siol Torcuil*. It would, indeed, appear that he had actually succeeded in securing his own recognition as heir from the chief of Lewis, for there is in the Dunvegan charter chest a document, dated 22nd of August, 1566, containing a strongly worded statement protesting against the claim of MacDonald to the lands of Lewis (MacLeod, RC, 1938, pp. 33–4).

Once again the quarrel attracted the attention of the government and, through the mediation of the regent, Murray, a reconciliation was effected. The contending chiefs of MacDonald and MacKenzie were persuaded to present themselves before the regent at Perth when, on the 1st of August, 1569, they submitted their dissensions to arbitration. They agreed to refrain in future from attacking one another's lands and Donald Gormson undertook to, *"cause Rory MacAllan, alias Nevynach, and all othirs the said MacDonaldis kyn, desist fra trubbling, or invasion* of the said Lord of *Garlauchis landis, rowmeis, possessiones, in ony tyme cumin*" (Gregory, D, 1881, p. 209).

It is noteworthy that this agreement continued to be honoured (an unusual occurrence in the West Highlands), so far at least as the contracting parties were concerned.

Donald Gormson then joined the Protestant party and he was held in high estimation at court. *"For his good and faithful service,"* the government conferred on him a yearly pension of 1000 marks, together with the 'fruits' of the vacant bishopric of Aberdeen (Cameron, A, 1871, p. 49).

But he was not to enjoy these privileges long, for he died in 1573 and he was mourned as a chief whose ability had raised his clan to a position of high honour and great prosperity.

He left two sons, Donald *Gorm Mór,* his heir, and Archibald Clerk, whose son, *Donald Gorm Og MacGhilleasba' Chléirich,* the first baronet of Sleat, succeeded to the estates in 1617.

Donald Gorm Mór, Eighth Chief

Donald *Gorm Mór* was only six or seven years old when his father died and, during his minority, the clan was placed under the captaincy of James *Gruamach,* the youngest son of Donald *Gruamach* and his second wife, a daughter of MacLeod of Lewis. The regent is sometimes called *Seumas a' Chaisteil,* or 'James of the Castle', from the fact that he resided at Castle *Camus,* in Sleat. He is reputed to have been a man of great common sense, an able soldier and administrator; but it would appear that, early in his career, the amicable relations that had existed between his predecessor and the government had been intermitted, and that the zeal for the Protestant cause, that had characterised the late chief, was now permitted to grow cold.

Thus we find that, at the very inception of his regime, he was in trouble with the government for his failure to observe his obligations to the church. In 1575 he was induced to sign a bond wherein he promised to remit to the Bishop of the Isles the teinds due for the lands of Sleat and of Trotternish, the gist of the contract being as follows:

"Obligation by James MacDonald of Castle Cames to John Bishop of Isles to pay teinds", among other items, "for the parsonage of Kilmoir in Slait, 17 marks; and for the Bishop's third part of said kirk, 15 marks." It was agreed that payment was to be made yearly and that arrears were to be paid at any time between then and midsummer upon fifteen days' notice. The captain was to be exempt from payment when his lands happened to be, "laid waste by enemies". "The payment of the males and dewties of the said landis and kirks in tyme cuming to be yeirly maid in Ycolmkyll, betwixt Petermess and Beltane; and, further, gif it happinnis the lands of Trouterness or any part thairof cum in my handis, oblisses us in lik maner to satisfie the said reverend fader and his factouris of his males and dewties within the samin, in so far as I sall have intromission therwith.

At Dounsceiche, Sic scribitur, I James MacConill growmeicht, with my hand at the pen, led by W. Cuming, notar publick, be speciale desirit thairto, because I cud not writ myself.

(Skene, WF, 1847, pp. 9–12).

Some commentators have interpreted this document as signifying that the MacDonalds were then recognised by the government as the legal possessors of Sleat but, in spite of the promises made by Argyle in 1566, they had not yet been awarded a crown charter for that district. It is actually stated in the contract that Trotternish also was not theirs by infeftment.

Despite the solemn promise he had given in 1575, James *Gruamach* is reprimanded by the government in 1580 for his remissness in paying dues to the church; and, again, in the following year, the government was forced to take drastic action against him, and several other landholders in Skye, for failing to honour their obligations to support the church. These men were: *"McConneill McNicoll of Trouterness; Donald MacGilles-pic Cleriche, bailie of Trouterness; Hugh, his brother; Ronnal Calvoch thair, MacGilliechallum of Raesay, Tormoid MacCloid of Herreis, Donald MacDonald Gormoche."*

In 1581 the government declared that the lands *"that per-tained to umquhile Donald MacGillespic Cleriche, bailie of Trouterness, Huchone MacGillespic, his brother; MacConeill Maknicoll, officar of Trouterness; Nicol, his bruther; … James MacDonald, Gromiche of Castel Cames, are escheat, through being of the said persons ordourlie denunceit our said sovereign lord's rebels, and put to horn for non-payment of their fermes, mailles, teinds, and dewties which thai have intrometit with respectivelie"* (Cameron, A, 1871, p. 49, and Brown, PH, 1911, Vol. 5, p. 69).

In the year 1585 Donald *Gorm Mór* assumed the chiefship and, shortly after his accession, he was involved in a life and death struggle with the MacLeans owing to the conduct of a relative of his own, who was destined to bring many a woe on the clans of the west. This sinister personage was *Uisdean Mac Ghilleasba' Chléirich*. He was a son of a former captain of *Clann Uisdein*, Archibald, the brother of the first Donald *Gorm*.

Donald *Gorm Mór* had a young brother also named Archibald, 'The Clerk', and that fact has led many historians to assert that Hugh was the son of this man, and therefore the chief's nephew, but since, as we have already seen, this *Uisdean Mac Ghilleasba' Chléirich* was in actual possession of lands in Trotternish in 1580, five years before his reputed father's older brother, Donald *Gorm Mór*, became chief, it is apparent that the latter view regarding Hugh's paternity is untenable.

Hugh had a brother named Donald whom some declare to have been a younger brother, but there are two documents extant in which mention is made of them both and, in each case, the name of Donald takes precedence, signifying his seniority. This Donald was bailie of Trotternish in 1580, and was reprimanded by the government for his remissness in paying church dues. It seems that he died in the course of that year for, in 1581 refer-ence is made to *"lands which pertained to the umquhile Donald MacGillespic Chléirich"* (Donaldson, G, 1982, p. 69).

Shortly after this Hugh was commissioned by his uncle, James *Gruamach*, with the factorship of North Uist and, for a time, he discharged his duties there with equity and fidelity. But before many years had run their course, an event happened that was destined to show him in his true colours and to make him for-ever afterwards a marked man in the Highlands.

According to Alexander Cameron, there was situated near his residence a davoch of land that was at once the most fertile and the best cultivated farm on the whole island of North Uist. It was occupied by four brothers, *Clann a' Bhiocair Mhóir* ('Children of the Big Vicar'), and the covetous Hugh had fixed longing eyes on it for many a month.

He approached the MacVicars with the allegation that the land originally belonged to his ancestry and that therefore they should vacate it for him, the rightful owner. The brothers stoutly repudiated his claim, asserting that the land had been in the pos-session of their family for generations. Finding this ploy was of little avail, Hugh had recourse to other action.

At the end of harvest, when the corn of the last of the MacVic-ars had been gathered in, and all were met in the house of the oldest to celebrate the *Deir' Bhuana*, or 'Harvest-home', Hugh surrounded the place of festival with armed men and, after a desperate struggle, succeeded in effecting an entry. The brothers were killed, and the ruthless usurper took possession of their farm.

But his occupancy of it was peremptorily terminated for, as

soon as Donald *Gorm Mór,* the young chief, heard of the dastard deed, he sallied forth and drove the murderer out of Uist.

Thereupon Hugh entered into league with another native of Skye, a man named Donald *Hearach,* and together they launched upon a life of piracy in the Hebrides (Cameron, A, 1871, p. 54).

In the course of their depredations they were once forced by stress of weather to seek the shelter of a cove in the north of the island of Jura. By a strange combination of circumstances, Donald *Gorm Mór* happened to make for an adjacent inlet that same night, as he was on his way to Islay with a large company of his leading men to visit his kinsman, Angus MacDonald of Dunnyveg.

That portion of the island to which the MacDonalds had betaken themselves belonged to MacLean of Duart, and the wily Hugh saw, in his chief's advent, material that would make a first-class plot. Accordingly, he raided a considerable number of cattle, shipped them on board his galleys, slipped his moorings and before daybreak was well on his way for the north.

From Hugh's point of view the ruse was highly successful for, on the following day, when the MacLeans heard of the foray, they naturally associated the depredation with the presence of the MacDonalds on their island and, mustering a strong body of men, they attacked the strangers in the night and, taking them unawares, slew sixty of them in cold blood. It is said that the chief himself would have shared the fate of his clansmen had he not been sleeping that night on board his galley. On his hearing in the morning of the atrocity that had been committed, Donald *Gorm Mór* left the island and returned to Skye, vowing vengeance on the MacLeans of Jura and all of their tribe (Gregory, D, 1881, pp. 230–1).

Internecine feuds, conducted with fiendish bitterness, followed and in a short time most of the clans of the West Highlands were embroiled in the strife. The MacKinnons of Skye and the MacLeods took the side of the MacLeans: the MacLeods, perhaps, because the mother of their chief was of Duart (MacLeod, RC, 1927, p. 117), but they were confirmed in their resolve in consequence of a special royal command issued to their chief on the 18th of September, 1585, urging him to supply the MacLeans with all his friends and force, *"in resisting the violence and the persecution of Clan Donald"* (Mackenzie, A, 1889, p. 35).

Through the intermediary of the Campbells, a temporary cessation of hostilities was effected in 1586 and it is worthy of note that, among the hostages given to MacDonald of Islay by MacLean of Duart, mention is made of Alexander MacLeod, afterwards styled 'of Minginish', and of two sons of Lachland MacKinnon of Strathordell, namely, Lachlan and Neil (Gregory, D, 1881, p. 234, note).

The truce was, however, but short-lived for MacLean, who now considered MacDonald of Dunnyveg his principal opponent, took advantage of the absence of the latter to devastate his lands, irrespective of the fate of the hostages.

The king thereupon took measures to end the turmoil. Huntly was commissioned to effect a settlement, and a law was passed, called 'The General Band', forbidding the chiefs from calling their men to arms without the royal prerogative and imposing on the leaders of clans, and the bailies of districts, the onus of compensating those whom their vassals should have injured in property or in person (Mackenzie, A, 1889, p. 51). This was in 1587 and in that same year, despite the edict, Donald *Gorm Mór* marshalled his clan to the number of 2500, according to the MacLean sennachie, and, landing in Mull, defeated the MacLeans at Cranalich but, taken unawares on the following day by a determined force of the local clan, MacDonald was signally routed at *Leac Li* leaving many among the slain and more as prisoners (MacDonald, A & A, 1904, p. 33).

The frequency of these destructive incursions was giving much concern to the government of the day, but they were averse to the use of armed force to stop them; and if duplicity and extreme deceit had been features of the contest between the Highland chiefs, the example set by the government, when an attempt was finally made to end it, was even more reprehensible still.

Messages were sent to the protagonists in the strife offering them instant remission and requesting them to proceed to Edinburgh for the alleged purpose of devising measures for the better governance of the Highlands.

Confiding in the good faith of the government, several of the Highland chiefs unhesitatingly responded to the summons. Donald *Gorm Mór* of Sleat set off with the others but no sooner had they arrived in the capital than they were cast in prison without a word of explanation. They remained under arrest until February, 1591, when they were liberated on payment of heavy fines and an undertaking that they would provide hostages. The chief of the MacDonalds was mulcted to the extent of £4000 to cover arrears of rent and provide a fund for the reimbursement of those who might suffer loss at the hands of his clansmen. In addition, he had to procure a surety, the person whom he nominated being John Campbell of Calder, who was then acting as guardian to the young Earl of Argyle (Gregory, D, 1881, p. 243–4).

It could scarcely be expected that a lasting settlement would be based on an undertaking such as that which we have recounted and we need not wonder that the Highland chiefs soon made light of the bonds to which they had subscribed as the price of their liberty. Hence it happened that, in the following year, when his sponsor, Campbell of Cawdor, was assassinated, Donald *Gorm Mór* considered himself free from further obligation to observe his contract and it was known to the government that he was making extensive preparations for an expedition to Ireland, to aid the rebellious subjects of that country.

In order to test his fealty he was cited to appear before the Privy Council but he disregarded the royal behest and a summons of treason was procured against him. At the same time, '*Rory Mak Cloyd, tutor of Harrich*', was commanded to find surety to the extent of 10,000 marks for the good conduct of his vassals, but the answer that the bold island-men made to these requests was to proceed, the following year, with a large armament into the North of Ireland to the assistance of Red Hugh O'Donnell who was then in rebellion against Queen Elizabeth (Mackenzie, A, 1889, p. 59).

The expeditionary force consisted of 1000 stalwart warriors of the MacDonalds and the MacLeods but their activities in Ulster were uneventful. After a stay there of only three days, Donald *Gorm Mór* returned to Skye, leaving his force behind him under the command of his brother, Archibald, 'The Clerk'. Rory *Mór* remained in Ireland for some time longer; but it is clear that the Irish chiefs were not enthusiastic about the presence of the Islesmen in their midst. We gather so much from an undertaking by the Earl of Tyrone to the Lieutenant General of Ireland, that the men of Skye would be dismissed his service and, when that had been effected, King James VI once again breathed happily, for his fears were growing that the action of his contumacious subjects might jeopardise his claim on the succession to the English throne (Gregory, D, 1881, pp. 261–2).

In 1596, both Donald *Gorm Mór* and Rory *Mór*, who had then assumed the chiefship of the MacLeods, made their submission to the king and were immediately restored to royal favour. Taking advantage, apparently, of the king's clemency, the chief of Sleat presented a petition for the heritable rights of the lands he occupied and he succeeded in securing a charter for them all, except certain parts of Uist and about eight merklands of Trotternish which the king reserved for the avowed purpose of placing Lowland tenants thereon, failing which Donald was to retain undisturbed possession of the whole peninsula. In return for these prerogatives, it was enjoined that he was to maintain

Castle *Camus* in future for the reception of the king, or his representative, whenever they might be sojourning in Skye and that *"Hugh MacGillespic Chleirich should be pledge, and none other"* (MacDonald, A & A, 1904, p. 47).

The government was eager to secure the person of that arch reiver whose ruthless plundering was doing such damage to the trade of the West Highlands. The local lieges had often to complain of his activities, while the fishers of Fife who then plied their trade in the Hebrides, were seldom safe from his violent sallies. Even as late as 1600, a complaint was lodged against him by one *"Thomas Inglis, merchant burgess of Edinburgh"*, for boarding one of his ships in Loch Shell in Lewis, and, *"wrongously, violently, and masterfully, against all order of law or justice, reft, spuilzeit, intromettit with, and away took them from the said ship, with the whole merchandise, goods, and gear"*. Hugh is then designated as of 'Waternes' (ibid; loc. cit.).

Some time after this Hugh succeeded in inveigling himself into the good graces of his chief; and, to all appearance, he became once again a man of consequence in his native island. It was probably then that he began to build that imposing pile that is named after him as *Caisteal Uisdein*, or, 'Hugh's Castle'. The main shell of this unique building still stands, stark and solitary, upon a commanding promontory on the shore at Cuidreach. It is a roughly rectangular tower, 54 feet long, and 36 feet broad. Its walls are 7 feet 6 inches in thickness. There are no windows in the lower storey, save that in each of three walls is a mere loophole, about 4 inches wide on the outside and about 2 feet high. The most striking feature of this grim structure is that the only doorway, which is situated in the north wall, is placed at a height of 8 feet 6 inches from the ground. Entrance could thus be effected only by means of ladders which would be pulled up inside the fortress when not in use. Leading upwards from the side of the doorway there is a stone stair in the thickness of the wall, after the pattern of those in the passages associated with the duns.

The building of this fort was one of the last acts in the life of that man of dark intrigues. When the work was near completion, Hugh repaired in his birlinn to Uist, there to seek out all who might be ill-disposed towards their chief. Soon there gathered around him a band of considerable strength that he meant to take to Skye. The ceremony of 'house-warming' was soon due, but the ultimate purpose of the entertainment was known only to two, namely, Hugh himself and a shifty pander of the name of Martin from the east side of Skye who had been hired to carry out the foul deed of murdering his chief on the night of the festival.

To conclude the final arrangements that pertained to the conspiracy, Hugh wrote two letters – one to his chief, inviting him to the 'house warming' and the other to Martin, with instructions as to how he was to play his part in a role of deathless shame. But, as a frolicsome fate would have it, the traitor was hoist with his own petard, for the chief's letter was enclosed in an envelope addressed to Martin, and Martin's was despatched to the chief and a courier sent with them to Skye.

Being now convinced beyond question of the malevolence and the treachery of his kinsman, the chief commissioned that warrior of renown, *Do'ull Mac Iain 'ic Sheumais*, to apprehend the conspirator and to bring him to Duntulm dead or alive.

Having been apprised of his danger, Hugh betook himself to a fort called *Dun an Sticir*, situated in a lake in North Uist, and accessible only by a secret ford. Though closely besieged by *Do'ull Mac Iain* and his men, he held out there for several weeks and he and his band suffered terrible privations. They were dependent for food on the devotion of a neighbourly crone who, with her sack of unground corn, repaired to their stronghold only on the darkest nights.

She had, however, gone to the relief of the starving garrison once too often for, having stayed one night later than usual, she was noticed at daybreak in the company of Hugh who, with a chivalry that seems strange in one so ruthless, was conducting her by the stepping stones to the shore of the lake. The position of the ford was thus marked and *Do'ull Mac Iain* despatched some of his men to the attack of the fort while he himself remained with the main contingent.

After all the ammunition in the fort had been exhausted, an entry was affected by the besiegers who seized and bound all its occupants except one tall person in female garb who, with seeming unconcern, was busily engaged in the operation of grinding corn by means of the quern. This individual was questioned as to the whereabouts of Hugh but so skilfully were the questions evaded and so clever was the banter with which the men were entertained, that they delayed so long that their impatient leader was constrained to cross the ford and he roundly scolded them for their untoward remissness in the discharge of their duty. His eagle eye soon caught sight of the wily Hugh in the feminine attire and, closing with him, a titanic struggle ensued, for these were two of the most powerful men of their age. *"b' eutrom a cheum, bu trom a bhuille"* ('light his step, heavy his blow'), the sennachie says of Hugh but the combat ended in his being overpowered and, securely bound after the ancient manner of *"Ceangal nan cóig caol"*, he was not loosened until he was brought before his chief at Duntulm.

With galling irony, the latter commended him for the ceremony of 'house warming' at Cuidreach but especially for the thoughtfulness and care with which he had laid his plans for his chief's entertainment on that momentous night and he informed him that, as a reward for all his trouble, he would now remain as guest at Duntulm for the remainder of his days.

Without more ado, the warders carried Hugh down to one of the castle vaults and the rusty bars were carefully driven home to make his incarceration sure. When his eye had grown accustomed to the livid light of his surroundings, he noticed in a corner of his cell a platter with a lump of beef upon it and a pewter jug beside it. After the terrible fasts he had endured in *Dun an Sticir*, this kind of meat was welcome fare. He found it very palatable if inordinately saltish and, having partaken of a goodly portion of it, he stooped for the jug to slake his thirst. What was his horror when he discovered that it was empty! and to add to his despair, were not those sounds he now heard made by masons in the act of building up the door of his prison? His surmise was only too well founded and when, years afterwards this vault was re-opened, there was discovered in it the skeleton of a mighty man, whose bony hand and lifeless jaw still firmly clasped a pewter jug, from which pieces had been crunched in the agony of a maddening thirst by one who has deservedly been called *'MacMallachd Chloinn Uisdein'* (the arch-demon of Clan Donald) (Cameron, A, 1871, pp. 54–5)

The Rev. Alexander MacGregor, who wrote *The Second Statistical Account* for Kilmuir, in 1841, says that the skull and thigh bones of *Uisdean MacGhilleasba' Chleirich* were preserved in a window of the parish church there and that, owing to their extraordinary size, they were objects of curiosity for many an age, until *"they were committed to the dust"* in the year 1827.

In spite of the consideration that had been extended by the king to the chiefs of Skye at Edinburgh in 1596 and the concessions that they had there obtained, they proved themselves to be as troublesome as ever once they set foot upon their native heath. They cast their promises to the winds and during that, and the following, year they had to be reminded frequently that they had failed to pay the royal dues. A final notice was sent to Rory *Mór* of Dunvegan, commanding him to appear before the king in Islay within two days, *"on pain of treason and forfeiture"* and the reply of the island chief is worth quoting, as it helps to illustrate the character of that interesting personality. The letter was sent from Marvak, Harris, on the 22nd of September, 1596. He begins by telling the king how impossible it would be for him to go to Islay from Harris on two days' notice when his men are scattered and he is at the mercy of winds and broken seas. But, as evidence of his loyalty to his king, he is prepared to meet *"any your Grace will command me to fight hand to hand in your Grace's sight and I shall prove my pith on him. Beseeching your Grace favourably to let not use me with letters of treason, or traitory, I being in mind to serve your Grace under God, as my native king and master, to the uttermost of my life."* (Mackenzie, A, 1889, pp. 61–2).

Despite these protestations of loyalty, Rory *Mór* was again in trouble with the government in less than two years after this. In 1597 an act was passed enjoining the Highland chiefs to repair to Edinburgh by the 15th of May, 1598 and there show their title deeds. This edict was issued because of the remissness of the chiefs in paying their yearly rents for, it is stated in the Act, *"they had made the Highlands and Islands, naturally so valuable from the fertility of the soil and the richness of its fisheries, altogether unprofitable either to themselves or to their fellowmen"*.

It would appear that many of the chiefs had either lost their charters, or were chary of producing them for fear of being deprived of them by the government and when Rory *Mór* went to Edinburgh, in order to present his case before the Privy Council, he was subjected to such rancorous raillery, and irritating innuendoes, by Sir Roderick MacKenzie, Tutor of Kintail, that the Skyeman dealt him such a blow as stretched him low on the floor of the council chamber. The words that brought *"Roderick's vengeance on his foe"* were prompted by the assistance the men of Skye had given MacLeod of Lewis who was fighting against the MacKenzies and their protégé, Torquil *Connanach*. The punishment for such an outrage in the *"regent's court and*

sight" was death, but Rory *Mór* succeeded in making good his escape to Skye (Mackenzie, A, 1889, pp. 63–4).

The upshot of this was that all his estates were declared forfeited – Glenelg, Harris, Bracadale, Duirinish, and Lyndale. A similar sentence was passed on Lewis, Waternish, and Trotternish; and King James resolved to "plant colonists" from the Lowlands on these crown lands.

Accordingly, a company, called by historians the 'Fife Adventurers' was formed, with the avowed object of 'colonising' the forfeited regions of the Western Isles, on the same principle as was to be effected in Ulster a few years later.

The Gentlemen Adventurers were ten in number, namely, The Duke of Lennox; Patrick, Commendator of Lindores; William of Pittenweem; Sir James Anstruther; Sir James Sandilands of Slamanno; James Learmonth of Balcolmy; James Spens; John Forret of Fingask; David Home and Captain William Murray. The stipulation with the government was to the effect that the company was to hold its lands rent free for the first seven years of occupancy, and thereafter they were to pay a fixed rent. It is interesting to note that the valuation of Trotternish, for the purposes of rent, was estimated at 400 marks.

Great preparations were afoot for the 'plantation'. A beginning was made at Stornoway where a town was being built but, after many attempts to establish itself there, the company was finally forced to evacuate the island, owing to the persistent harassment administered by the natives, backed, as they were, by the MacKenzies of Kintail and by the MacLeods and the MacDonalds of Skye. No attempt was made by the company to establish settlements in Harris, Glenelg, Trotternish or in Waternish (Gregory, D, 1881, pp. 278–80).

Towards the end of the century, Donald *Gorm Mór* was busy in his endeavours to interest Queen Elizabeth in his project to unite all the Highland chiefs in her service and to revive the title of Lord of the Isles in himself. He declared that all the chieftains of Clan Donald were sworn to follow him and that he was pre-pared to throw off his allegiance to King James VI whenever she should consider the time opportune; that he would raise a rebellion, *"to fasche King James"*, and that he would keep her informed of the movements of her enemy, and his own late ally, the Earl of Tyrone; and, further, that he would acquaint her with the activities of the Jesuit priests in the isles *"in their pestiferous and un-Christian practices"* (Cameron, A, 1871, p. 50).

Elizabeth was not at the moment disposed to entertain these intrigues, but Donald *Gorm Mór* continued in his state of disaffection with the government for many years after that.

Rory *Mór* of Dunvegan was still under sentence of forfeiture, as seems to be indicated by a complaint he forwarded to the Lords of Council in June, 1599. In it he states that some of his vassals on the way to the Lowland markets, had been waylaid in Glenorchy and robbed of their cattle and that at the market of Glamis two of his clansmen, *"Duncan Mac Ean Mac Gillechallum and Donald Mac Hucheon Vc Coneil, had been reft of twenty-four fat cows"*, the robbers having forged letters saying the *"king had ordained they were to rob Rory's clansmen"* (Mackenzie, A, 1889, p. 64).

The close of the year did not see the end of these troubles but, as the sequel belongs to the following century, we shall meantime leave them and survey the social conditions on the island during the last hundred years.

CHAPTER VI

Social Conditions, 1500–1600

The Church

James IV was indefatigable in his efforts to establish law and order among the Scottish Highlanders and, in view of the numbers of these that followed him to Flodden, there is no reason to doubt that he won their allegiance and their respect. That he considered the church an efficacious means of reforming the lieges is shown by the large number of 'presentations' he made to churches in Skye during the early years of the century.

Thus, in the year 1501, he conferred the church of St. Columba, at the head of Loch Snizort, and then the cathedral-church of the island, on one Sir Nichol Berchame who was also made responsible for the administration of *"the annexes and vicaragis of the same viz., Kilmalowakin in Raasay, and Kilmory in Watternes"*. The ruins of the former are still to be seen surrounded by the old churchyard in Clachan of Raasay – the latter is possibly the church of Kilmuir in Dunvegan. The successor of Berchame appears to have been 'Sir Tormot MacFarsane', (probably MacPherson) on whose decease, in 1526, the king presented Sir Donald Monro to the vacant seat (Innes, C, 1854, p. 355).

In Kilmuir of Trotternish there officiated a *'Master Mertyne M'Gillemertyne'* who was rector of that parish from 1507 until 1536; and in the first year of his ministry we find that a letter

of protection was granted to him by the king against such as might lay violent hands on his chattels, a significant precaution indicative of the lawlessness that then prevailed. On the death of *'Master Mertyne'*, in 1536, the succession devolved on Mr. *'Rodoric Farquhar Hectorissone'*, and the roll of appointments is continued in *'Rodoric Mac Clane, Elect of the isles'*, on whose demission Queen Mary presented the rectory to Sir Archd. McGillevray. After an interval of ten years, it was filled by Sir David Lawsoun who, in 1575, was followed by John Fearquhayrson and he in turn by John MacLane.

The site of the rectory of this district was on Kilmaluag Bay, on the north-east of Trotternish, and it was dedicated to Moluac, the patron saint of Argyll. After the Reformation the parish church was built on the declivity above Score Bay where the burial ground that once surrounded it yet remains; and as the new church was dedicated to the Virgin Mary, it was henceforth to be known as Kilmuir.

There was a chapel at Kilmartin and another at Kilvaxter, the latter of which seems to have belonged to the nuns of Iona. In this connection we find that, in 1561, the abbot of Iona held one-half tirunga (*tir-unga* or ounce land) of land in Trotternish, called *'Keilbakster'* and in 1574 the Prioress of Iona granted

Hector MacLean of Duart the nunnery lands, including ten penny-lands of Kilvaxter (*ibid.*, p. 349).

About the beginning of the sixteenth century the rectory of Uig was served by Sir Nicolas Brachan, who demitted his charge in 1512, when James IV presented Sir Donald Rede to the vacancy. After the last, a certain Sir John MacCrummey held the church, and on his decease, in 1552, Sir Donald Monro was elected as his successor. The church stood on the land now known as Clachan (*ibid.*, p. 354).

The rectory at the head of Loch Eynort, in Minginish, was conferred at the beginning of the century on Sir Neil Monro, on whose death, in 1511, James IV presented *"Master John Monro to the rectory of Mygnes, in the diocese of the Isles"* (*ibid.*, p. 357).

The church of Kilchrist, in Strath, the successor of Ashaig, was settled on a Sir Kenneth Adamson in the year 1505 (*ibid.*, p. 343).

In 1546 one, Sir Allan Macintosh, was the parson of '*Wattyrnys*' and in 1566 a certain Malcolm MacPherson was granted the vicarage of '*Durynthas*', rendered vacant by the death of 'Finlay Tormotsoun', who had been presented to the charge by the Earl of Argyle, then acting as the guardian of the Heiress of the Isles. There was a chapel also at Trumpan (Kilconan or Kilcoan), and another at St. Congan's in Glendale. This last is referred to in the *Calendar of Papal Petitions* as early as 1406, as held *"by Mac Kermath, rector of St. Congan's in Durenys"* (*ibid.*, pp. 358–9).

Sir Donald Monro, the Dean of the Isles, says that, in the middle of this century, there were twelve *"paroche kirkes in Sky inhabit and manurit"* but in order to save expenses, the number was reduced to seven in 1574 (Munro, RW, 1961, p. 68): thus Snizort, Uig, Kiltaraglen and Raasay were united as one. The church at *Cill Mhór* in Sleat is said to have been founded by a stunted and deformed son born to the wife of Logan, named *Crotach*, who was educated by the monks of Beauly, took holy orders and fathered several children, one of whom became a devotee of St. Finnan and was the eponymous ancestor of the Maclennans.

Very little is known of the state of religion in Skye after the troublesome times that succeeded Flodden and it would appear that no great regard was paid for many years to the needs of the church.

On several occasions it is evident that chiefs and bailies alike made light of their ecclesiastical obligations and stern warnings were issued by those in authority reminding them of their remissness in paying church dues. Thus, in 1575, an injunction was served on James MacDonald of Castle *Camus*, the captain of the MacDonalds of Skye, to pay as follows: For the *"Personage of Kilmoir in Sleit, 18 marks and for one-third part of the said kirk 15 marks, payment to be made yearly"*. In the same note he is enjoined to pay arrears of taxes to the Bishop of the Isles. No attention seems, however, to have been paid to this request and we find that in 1580 a summons had been raised against the captain, at the instance of John, Bishop of the Isles, for his failure to pay dues, and a similar citation is served on several other occupiers of land in Skye, e.g., Norman McLeod of Harris, *Mac Gille Chaluim* of Raasay, MacConneill MacNicol of Trotternish; Donald *Mac Ghilleasba' Chléirich*, bailie of Trotternish; Hugh, his brother; and *"Ronald Calvoch thair"*. All these persons were *"orderlie denunceit and put to the horn"*, the lands of some of them were declared forfeited to the king and, in 1581, 'made over' to John, Bishop of the Isles (Donaldson, G, 1982, p. 69).

It is worthy of note that, in the proclamation of escheat of 1581, no mention is made of the lands of the MacLeods of Dunvegan or of those of the MacLeods of Raasay, the surmise being that these chiefs had paid their dues and the arrears earlier in that year.

It may be interesting to mention certain of the districts that were set aside for the support of the church. They were the two Armadales in Sleat, one half the tirunga of Kilvaxter in Trotternish, a portion of Snizort and the islands of Raasay and Rona. The following churches and their lands were looked upon as belonging to the abbot of Iona, namely, *Cill Mhór* in Sleat, Kilchrist in Strath and St. Columba's Church in Snizort.

We have already adverted to the loyalty of Donald Gormson, the chief of the MacDonalds of Skye, and the favours that he had received for his faithful service to the government. This has led many to suppose that the chief had joined the Protestant party and, as he died in 1573, the Reformation must have reached Skye, through him, before that year. From the negligence that was shown to the church during the following decade, it would seem, however, that the new religion had not made much headway in the island. However, its lack of progress then may quite conceivably be attributed to the transition stage through which people's minds were then passing, when the lords of Skye were probably imitating the example set them by the Lowland barons, and were encroaching on the lands of the church in order to add them to their own domains. There can be no doubt, however, but that the Protestant faith had established itself there before 1590, for in that year Donald Gormson's successor, Donald *Gorm Mór*, was commanded by King James VI, and the Scottish Parliament, to suppress Jesuit activities in Skye and *"to punish those adversaries of the true religion presently professed within this realm"*. And when, at the very close of the century, the chief of Sleat was making traitorous overtures to the Queen of England and was professing his readiness to repudiate his allegiance to his king, he, at the same time, exhibits his zeal for Protestantism by declaring his intention to keep her informed of the *"pestiferous and un-Christian practices"* of the Jesuits in the Isles (MacDonald, A & A, 1904, p. 37; see also MacDonald, DJ, 1978, p. 411).

Education and Culture

Several instances have already been cited of the professions by chiefs of the inability to write their own names and it is a noteworthy fact that, on their own recognisances, none of the seventeen chiefs who supported the rebellious Donald *Dubh*, in 1545, could write. Even men such as *Gilleasbuig Cléireach*, who was being trained for the church until he was called upon to act as regent for his clan on the death of his brother, Donald *Gorm*, and Norman, the twelfth chief of MacLeod, who, according to some, had been a student of the University of Glasgow (though it is impossible now to verify that statement, as the extant roll of students of that institution does not go further back than 1590) – these men, when they had occasion to append their signatures to documents, required to have their *'hand leid at the pen'*. It has been explained that this was but a vain conceit in these men who may have considered calligraphy an art unbecoming in a warrior, but although the art of writing may not have been practised by the chiefs and may even have been despised by them, the surmise does not warrant the conclusion that these men were untutored, or illiterate, in the ordinary sense. Indeed, the evidence is far otherwise, for it can be shown that many of our island chiefs were men of noble culture who genuinely loved the arts.

Thus, the eighth chief of the MacLeods, *Alasdair Crotach*, evinced his interest in things spiritual by his generosity towards the church of St. Clement's in Rodel of Harris. He repaired it, endowed it with fertile lands, and he abdicated the chiefship several years before his death in order that he might devote the remaining portion of his life to meditation in the sacred precincts of that church. In that seclusion he is reputed to have produced a Gaelic translation of the psalms (Mackenzie, A, 1889, p. 24). Out of his regard for music, he allocated a large tract of land at Borreraig, in Duirinish, to endow the college of pipers there, over which the MacCrimmons presided for fully 200 years (MacLeod, RC, 1927, p. 84).

The chiefs also had their bards, who were held in the highest esteem. These men made it their duty, and considered it their privilege, to preserve and to popularise the poetry and the lore of the past. That a great body of poetry existed then goes without question, though only stray pieces have come down to us in writing, chiefly through the compilation by the Dean of Lismore. The sennachie, as well as the bard, told and retold his tales of *"the brave days of old"*, embellishing them, mayhap, according to the height of his own ideals, but contributing withal to the edification of his audience, and illustrating a marked trait in the psychology of the race. In his day, Bishop Carswell deplored the fact that such ancient tales as referred to the *Tuatha de Danaan*, the Milesians, and the Fingalian heroes, had a far greater influence on the imagination and the mind of the people than was exerted by the Bible.

The early chroniclers and historians paid little attention to the Highlands and when they did advert to the conditions then prevailing there, their judgement was so warped by prejudice that their accounts are often worthless. *"These writers"*, it has been said, *"never spoke a favourable word of the Highlanders, much less of the Islanders"*, and the misrepresentations from which the latter suffered for many an age were simply due to the fact that they spoke a language that was not intelligible to the Lowland writer. Indeed, the existence of that language was considered to be the cause of all the actual and alleged disorders in the Hebrides. Thus a contemporary writer says of James IV, probably the last king who knew the Gaelic language: *"He speaks the language of the savages who live in some parts of Scotland and on the islands"* (Mackie, JD, 1972, p. 120). In the reign of James VI a determined onslaught was made on that ancient tongue with the avowed object of discontinuing its use as the speech of the people; for, according to the royal edict, *"it is one of the chief causes of barbarity and incivility among the inhabitants of the isles"* (Gregory, D, 1881, p. 332).

Law and Order

The administration of justice was then vested in the chief of the clan, provided he were loyally disposed to the government. If, however, as was often the case during that century, he was in a state of rebellion against the central authority, the government appointed bailies. One of their duties was the preservation of order in their own districts, and these functionaries were sometimes engaged by the chiefs themselves for the execution of that office in certain portions of the island.

As we have already seen, King James IV took a real and practical interest in the Highlands; and he was ever ready with useful schemes for the betterment of that part of his dominions. As an illustration of his aims for the restoration and the maintenance of good government in Skye, we have it on record that, in the year 1508, he decreed that the rents of certain parts of Trotternish, namely, the tirunga of Kilmartin, and one half of the tirunga of 'Baronsmore', which were then crown lands, should be earmarked for the purpose of defraying the expenses incidental to the education of a certain Kenneth, son of William, in the study of law and it was stipulated that the beneficiary should afterwards *"exercise and use the samyn (administration of justice) within the bounds of the Isles"* (ibid., p. 104).

According to the *MS, History of the MacLeods*, this lawyer did return to Skye where, among his other duties, he acted in the capacity of chamberlain for the whole of Trotternish and he was remembered for many an age because of the severity of his exactions.

Following the death of James IV on Flodden, the administration of justice became lax in Scotland generally, and particularly so in the Western Isles. Indeed, during the three succeeding reigns, one is struck by the utter disregard that prevailed for the mandates of the government. Acts of brigandage and of piracy on the seas were rife, and the perpetrators of outrages such as these were subjected to no other penalty than the formal one of being 'put to the horn', a procedure that seemed to have no terrors for them whatsoever. If they were in danger of arrest, they had merely to migrate elsewhere and their safety was assured. The islands of Pabay and Rona were then notorious as the rendezvous and the inviolable sanctuaries of the criminal and the unruly. The former is described by Dean Munro in 1549 as

full of woods, good for fishing, and a main shelter for thieves and cutthroats;

while of the latter he says:

It is full of wood and heddir, with ane havin for hieland galeys in the middis of it, and the same havin is guyed for the fostering of thieves, ruggairs, and reivairs, till await, upon the peilling and spulzeing of poure pepill.

(Munro, RW, 1961, p. 70).

Statements such as these by men of responsibility, would no doubt convey exaggerated notions of the disorderliness that prevailed in the Isles, and they explain the extravagant accounts that were subsequently written by writers who knew of the Highlands only by repute. Thus, in *A History of King James VI*, written probably by a John Colbin, we find the following highly coloured invective against the inhabitants of the isles:

True it is that the islandish men are of nature very proud, suspicious, avaricious, full of deceit and evil invention, each against his neighbour by what way soever he may circumvent him. Beside all this, they are so cruel in taking of revenge that neither have they regard to person, age, time, or cause, so are they all addicted to their own tyrannical opinion that in all respects they exceed in cruelty

the most barbarous people that has been since the beginning of the world.

(Gregory, D, 1881, p. 232).

It cannot, of course, be gainsaid but that there was some justification for the violent accusations that were brought against the Islesmen of those times. Those strangers who came to prosecute the fishing industry, then so profitable in the Isles, were often subjected to grievous molestation, and were considered legitimate prey for unscrupulous demands. Anent the last, there exists an interesting document, dated 1586, in which a complaint is made by the Burghs of the Realm against the inordinate tariffs imposed on those engaged in the fishing industry by the leading men of Skye. They refer to fines for anchorage, dues on stances for huts and barrels and the frequent thefts of nets and boats (Mackenzie, A, 1889, p. 56).

Those whose names are cited as guilty of these misdemeanours are "Donald Gorme in the Sky, MacLeoud of Harris thair, John MacKinnon of Loch Slabin, Rory MacAllan of Gairloch, Hugh MacGillespic Chleirich of Troternish, and Duncan Rawsay of that ilk." All were summoned to appear before the Privy Council to answer the charges brought against them; and, when none obeyed, the usual ineffectual procedure followed, whereby they were "denounced as rebels and put to the horn". Again, in 1600, the proceedings before the Privy Council refer to a complaint, already quoted, by one Thomas Inglis, "merchant Burgess of Edinburgh, and Robert Sinclair, shipper in Leith,", against "Hugh MacGillespic in Waternes and others". It was then stated that, "Hugh MacGillespic, and others his accomplices, boding in fear of weir, came to the said ship, boarded it per force, and wrongously, violently, and masterfully, against all order of law and justice, rept, spulzeit, intromittit with, and away took from them the said ship, with the whole merchandise, goods, and gear". As usual, the accused failed to answer the charges, and they were 'put to the horn'.

In 1587 a very important law was passed, which made a real attempt at the pacification of the Highlands. This Act is commonly called the 'General Band'. It placed on the chiefs the onus of holding themselves responsible for the conduct of their vassals; and they were obliged to produce large sums of money as sureties, and out of this fund compensation would be made to such as were wrongously injured by their clansmen. Among other names appended to this document are *"William MacLeod of Dunvegan, Harris, and Glenelg; Malcolm MacLeod of Raasay; and Lachlan MacKinnon of Strathaird"* (*ibid.*, p. 57).

Agriculture

In that age, and for several generations thereafter, all the activities of the clan were carried on purely on a communal basis, so that while one section of the people was detailed for the purposes of defence, the other, and the larger portion, was engaged in the cultivation of the soil and in tending the flocks. There were then, of course, no farms as we know them later and fewer animals were reared, the number being determined by the needs of the people themselves for, as yet, there was no market for the surplus stock. Owing, however, to the wide range of its pastures and the reputed fertility of the soil, more cattle were maintained then in Skye than in any other area of similar extent.

The cultivated land was not then divided from the common pastures by any manner of protective boundary and men had to guard the growing crops from marauding animals by turns. The chief cereal grown then, as now, was oats and, according to a statement by Dean Monro, Skye was famous both for the abundance and the excellence of that particular crop.

The operation of tilling was done by means of the spade, although an occasional plough, of very primitive design, was utilised. As a matter of fact, two ploughs, of different form and purpose, were then pressed into service for the work that was later done by one. These were the *crann ruslaidh*, which merely cut a strip of soil perpendicularly of the required breadth; and the *crann rusgaidh*, whose function was to cut the ground horizontally and turn it over. The combination of the two implements was effected later.

The method of reaping that then obtained, and was continued in certain parts for two centuries afterwards, was to uproot the stalks of grain when ripe. The ears were then burned off the sheaves, and the straw was used as thatch to cover the roof of the dwelling-house so that, after it had been saturated with the peat-smoke of winter fires, it might be used to manure the soil in the following spring.

In addition to oats, barley was also grown, though not in equal quantity, while good crops of flax were produced. The linen was woven in the homes of the people, as was also the silky wool of the indigenous sheep, *a` chaora bheag*, which was so small as seldom to exceed 30 lb. in weight. Its delicious mutton was consumed locally, for few of them were exported.

Both sheep and cattle were, however, used in whole or part-payment of rent, that of *fearann peighinn*, or penny-land, being as follows: 6 sts. meal, 6 sts. cheese, 1 cow, and eke in money 4s 2d; the total value being estimated at £1 4s 2d. Twenty penny lands comprised the tirunga. Sub-divisions of the penny land were the *lephin*, or halfpenny land; and *feorling*, or farthing land, with its impost of 3 sts. of meal and an equal quantity of cheese. The farthing land was commensurate with the lot called cowland. It is not easy to define the measure called 'merkland', but it would seem to be co-extensive with the quarter land or four penny lands. In an account written in 1577 for the information of King James VI, it is stated that the rental for a merkland in Trotternish was: *"2 bolls of meal, 2 bolls of malt (i.e. barley),*

4 mairtes (cows), 16 wedders, and 16 dozen poultry" (Skene, WF, 1890, Vol. III, p. 432).

In this document there appears a reference to the district of Sleat, of which it is asserted that

> it is occupied for the most part by gentlemen; therefore it pays the old duties – that is, of victual butter, cheese, wine, ale, and aquavitæ, as much as their master may be able to spend any night on each merkland, although he had a company of 600 men.

This last exaction refers, of course, to the practice, then in vogue, of supplying the chief with food and shelter for himself and his retinue without compensation when on a tour of his estates and it was called '*cuid oidhche*', or night's portion.

Finally, we find in this account the statement: "There is many woods in all parts of Skye, specially birkis (birch) and orne (oak), but the most wood is in Slait and Trotternish. There is ane wood in Slait 8 miles long, with many deir and roe, and it is very fertil in all kinds of bestial and corns" (*ibid.*, p. 433).

The assertion concerning the extensive 'woods' of Skye is probably an exaggeration, for there is abundant evidence that the amount of timber produced on our island was never sufficient for local needs and that, in order to supply the deficiency, it was necessary to make frequent descents on the mainland. Thus, about the middle of the century, an injunction was served on Donald Gormson, to restrain him from taking timber *"for long faddis* (galleys) *from the MacKenzie's territories"* (MacDonald, A & A, 1904, p. 22).

Trade

Communication with the outside world for the purposes of commerce was then in its infancy, so far as Skye was concerned and, as has already been shown, there was scarcely any endeavour

made to dispose of the surplus stock outside the island. A few commodities were, however, exported, and these consisted principally of fish, hides, and wool. Of the first, it is said in the account of Skye, written in 1577, and from which we have already quoted, *"There is plenty of salmon and herring"*; and Dutch and Lowland fishermen reaped lucrative harvests out of the abundance of the herring around our shores (Skene, WF, 1890, p. 433).

About 1580 a licence was obtained from the crown for the institution of a fair at Portree. The market was held there twice a year, from Wednesday until the Saturday, when the varied products of the island were exposed for sale – meal, butter, cheese, poultry, sheep, cattle and horses, hides, wool, linen, and dried fish, especially herrings and salmon. Of the latter there was great abundance, for Dean Monro says:

> There is gud tak of salmont upon five watters principally, to wit, the water of Sneisfort, Sligachan, Strathwardill, Ranlagallan, and Kilmartin.
>
> (Munro, RW, 1961, p. 68).

The commodities brought to the market were bartered almost wholly among the natives themselves, for it was seldom then that a stranger came to make purchases. The money equivalent of a milch cow was estimated at 10/–; while a stone of oatmeal cost 8d, and an equal quantity of cheese was valued at 1/–.

Towards the end of the century a tentative beginning was made in the exportation of the native black cattle, but nothing of note was yet accomplished until, towards the middle of the following century, *Do'ull Mac Iain ic Sheamuis*, the first of the MacDonalds of Kingsburgh, set the vogue in this trade that was to prove so lucrative to the island for close on two hundred years.

Habits, Pastimes and Manner of Living

The people were then fond of hunting, and game was free to all, and was plentiful. Writing about 1543, John Elder says that the principal animals then hunted in the Highlands were deer, grouse, foxes and wolves; while, as has already been shown, mention is made of the deer and the roe as being plentiful in Sleat and elsewhere in Skye about the year 1577.

There were then two sections in the community, namely, the overbearing warriors, who defended the clan and fought its battles, and the despised peasants, whose duty it was to till the soil and tend the stock. When they were not engaged in raiding or in war, the former spent their time in idleness as it was beneath them to engage in the menial labour of cultivating the ground, while the latter, who were the weaklings of the clan, for the most part aped the warriors and, in their counterfeit manner of life, were aided and abetted by their wives who, for the sake of appearance, did all the drudgery, while their husbands, if they were allowed to take part in work at all, did light labour only but most often they dallied their time in idleness, or joined the privileged clansmen in their trials of strength and skill.

These contests took many forms. There was wrestling, swimming, leaping, running, casting the stone, and archery. Canon R.C. MacLeod of MacLeod tells of an occasion when, in the chiefship of Norman, twelfth of his line, many of the Highland chiefs, with a tail composed of their best athletes, assembled at Dunvegan, there to hold high carnival. After the contestants had displayed their prowess, it was noticed that no athletes from Dunvegan had taken part in the competitions. The MacLeod chief was twitted on his neglect of manly sports and he excused himself on the ground, as he alleged, that as the host it would not be seemly that any of his men should eclipse the other sportsmen, but now that aspersions had been cast on him, and on his clan, he would show what his men could do. His best, however, he would reserve until he had discovered how his meanest would acquit themselves. He accordingly brought forward a deformed tatterdemalion, one of the name of *Pòl Crubach*, a short, thick-set fellow with thews like an auroch bull, and he was pitted against the best of the strangers. The marvellous versatility of this diminutive giant was soon apparent, and at the end of the day it transpired that he had overcome the best of his opponents singlehanded (MacLeod, RC, 1927, p. 107).

Now we know of a *Pòl Crubach*, the son of a MacLeod of Lyndale, and a poet of great merit; but he flourished about the middle of the following century (Watson, WJ, 1932, p. 201). His best known work is *Iorram na Truaighe*, composed on the death of John, the son of Sir Rory *Mór*, in 1649; and tales are still told in Skye of his abnormal strength.

Dress

The *breacan-feile*, or tartan plaid and kilt combined, was then worn by the men. It was belted by a leather girdle around the waist, and was plaited to the knees. Under it they wore a saffron shirt (*leine chroich*). That part of the *breacan* that covered the upper portion of the body was secured at the breast by a pin of bone or silver, according to the rank. In the year 1594, when a force of 500 MacDonalds and an equal number of MacLeods set off on an expedition to Ulster to aid Red Hugh O'Donnell, who was then in rebellion against England, mention is made of the splendid physique of the men, and their garb is described as follows:

The outward clothing they wore was a mottled garment with numerous colours, hanging in folds to the calf of the leg. with a girdle round the loins over the garment.

(Gregory, D, 1881, p. 261).

Figure 1.1 Edmund Burt was sent to Scotland to work as a contractor for the government and for most of the time he was based in Inverness. In the period 1724–25 he wrote regularly to an acquaintance in London about his experiences. His letters were published much later as 'Letters from a Gentleman in the North of Scotland'. This image from Burt's book depicts 18th century Hebridean dress.

Figure 1.2 Dùn Beag near Struan, as depicted by Moses Griffiths, Thomas Pennant's illustrator. Pennant was a Welsh naturalist who visited Scotland in 1769 and again in 1774. The books based on his visit proved hugely popular. Dùn Beag itself is the best preserved and the most accessible broch on Skye. Dating from the Iron Age, it has massive walls which in places are over three metres in height.

Figure 1.3 At one time the residence of a Norse chief, Duntulm Castle was occupied by the MacDonald chiefs during the 16th century and one of them, Dòmhnall Gorm, effected alterations and improvements to the structure. The celebrated 17th century poet, Mary MacLeod, (Màiri Ni'n Alasdair Ruaidh) wrote of Duntulm 'wherein waxen candles blaze and wine is drunk right freely from these wan and gleaming cups of silver in a mansion wide and joyous and full of music'. Duntulm was abandoned by the MacDonalds in the 1730s. Much of the castle remained when it was sketched by Moses Griffiths later in the century for Thomas Pennant's book.

Figure 1.4 Dunvegan is thought to mean 'the Fort of Began', Began being a Norse personal name. Dunvegan Castle is thought to be the oldest continuously inhabited residence in Scotland and has been the stronghold of the chiefs of the MacLeod clan for nearly 800 years. This is Moses Griffiths' depiction of the castle in the late 18th century.

Figure 1.5 George and Ashley Abraham were brother climbers and photographers who lived in Keswick in the English Lake District. Amongst other places where they made a photographic record of climbing exploits, the Abrahams spent time in the Cuillin. Ashley was to write *Rock Climbing in Skye* which was published by Longmans, Green and Co., of London in 1908. This is an Abraham postcard view of the Cuillin from Bruach na Frithe.

Figure 1.6 Valentines of Dundee were, by the end of the 19th century, among the most commercially successful postcard producers. This is one of their postcard views of Dunvegan Castle.

Figure 1.7 This postcard view of Duntulm Castle features the tall upstand which collapsed in a gale in January 1990.

Figure 1.8 Another postcard view of Dunvegan Castle.

Figure 1.9 Waulking (or fulling) was an essential part of tweed manufacture in which the cloth was shrunk. Waulking served to rid the woven cloth of oils, dirt and other impurities, and making it thicker. In the past the cloth was pounded by the feet of waulkers, as shown in Moses Griffiths' depiction of a waulking at Talisker. In more recent times, waulkers used their hands to shrink the cloth.

Figure 1.10 Quern-stones are stone tools for hand grinding a wide variety of materials. They were used in pairs, the lower, stationary, stone being called a 'quern', whilst the upper, mobile, stone is called a 'handstone'. The quern stone shown is featured in Burt's 'Letters from a Gentleman in the North of Scotland'.

Figure 1.11 Spinning wheel. ©Mark Butterworth – George Washington Wilson Archive

Figure 1.12 Washing Day. ©Mark Butterworth – George Washington Wilson Archive

Figure 1.13 The cas-chrom in use near Portree. Edward Dwelly's celebrated Gaelic dictionary tells us that the cas-chrom is 'an implement of tillage peculiar to the Highlands, used for turning the ground where a plough cannot work on account of the stony ground.' ©Mark Butterworth – George Washington Wilson Archive

The women wore a cloak called the *"earasaid"*, which extended to the heels. It was white, with narrow bands of diverse colours, and, like the garment worn by the men, was fastened by a buckle of silver or of brass. It was drawn in at the waist, around which a leather belt was worn and the latter was often gaily decorated with precious metals or stones. The women wore also a bodice-like garment of scarlet, with long flowing sleeves that were closely fitted at the wrists. They were very fond of ornament and, when, on the days of the fair, they cast aside their working clothes and went to Portree in their gayest attire, they presented a picturesque sight. Over her hair the maiden wore the snood, while the married lady covered her head with a kerchief of fine linen.

Weapons

In the account of the expedition of the Skyemen to Ulster, to which reference has previously been made, there occurs an interesting description of the weapons that were then in use. Of these it says:

Some had horn-hafted swords, large and military, over their shoulders. When a man did strike with them he was obliged to apply both hands to the haft. Others were equipped with bows, well-polished, strong, and serviceable, with long twanging hempen strings.

The common soldier was, of course, equipped with the bow as his principal weapon while in his belt he carried a large dagger, sharpened on one side only. When they were engaged in battle, the fighters wore a covering of linen, well daubed with pitch, and over it a chest-protector of raw hide.

In the account of the conditions that prevailed in Skye in 1577, it is stated that, *"Slait could raise 700 men and Trotternish 500"*; and on the 20 merklands of Waternish, MacLeod of Lewis could muster a force of 200 able-bodied men.

CHAPTER VII

Family History, 1600–1650

The beginning of the seventeenth century in Skye saw the two great clans of the island engaged in a war that was marked by intense bitterness. It is traditionally called '*Cogadh na Cailliche Caime*', or the War of the One-eyed Woman, and the cause of it is said to have been as follows:

Donald *Gorm Mór*, the chief of the MacDonalds, had contracted a conjugal agreement, called hand-fasting, or trial marriage, with Margaret, the sister of Rory *Mór*, the chief of the MacLeods of Dunvegan. This lady, having sustained damage to an eye, seems, in consequence, to have lost her sight and the favour of her partner who determined to be quit of her. Accordingly, when the contractual period of a year and a day had expired, MacDonald callously drove his mistress from Duntulm, and, heaping insult on the injury, had her mounted on a one-eyed nag, escorted by a one-eyed groom, and followed by a one-eyed mongrel dog.

The arrival of this pathetic band at Dunvegan naturally aroused the bitterest passions in the heart of MacLeod, but for the time being he wisely curbed his surging rage and despatched a courier to MacDonald demanding an explanation of his repellant conduct, and requesting him to take his wife back again. This the latter blankly refused to do and, having succeeded in securing a divorce, he married a sister of MacKenzie of Kintail, thus forming an alliance with Roderick's most bitter foe (Cameron, A, 1871, p. 58).

There could, of course, be but one consequence of an action such as this, and Rory *Mór* observed, with vengeance in his voice, that although the making of a bonfire had been overlooked in celebration of the union, he would take very good care that a mighty conflagration would mark its dissolution. He promptly carried his threat into execution, with the result that a ruthless and calamitous war was waged between these clans for a period of almost two years.

Raids and counter-raids were made into each other's territories; mercy was shown to none, and, according to Sir Robert Gordon,

their peoples were reduced to such dire extremities that they were forced to eat horses, dogs, cats and filthy vermin in order to sustain life.

(Gregory, D, 1881, p. 296).

Rory *Mór* carried a raiding expedition into Trotternish, burning and slaying wherever he went. The MacDonalds retaliated by attacking MacLeod's lands in Harris and, having sated their desire for revenge, returned to Skye just when Rory *Mór* had set off for MacDonald's lands in North Uist. On hearing of the invasion, the natives of that island collected as much of their stock as they could and, with their goods and their families, sought sanctuary in the church called Cilltrionaid, in Carinish. Rory *Mór* made Rodel his base of operations and thence he despatched his cousin, Donald *Glas*, the second of the family of Drynoch and a man of great bodily strength and vigour of mind, to raid the island with a godly band of determined men. An extensive round-up of the whole island was made, so that scarcely a hoof remained on mountain or on machair. The spoilers finally approached Carinish and, after having over-powered the weak resistance offered them and taken possession of all the cattle and the gear, they decided to rest there for a few days before they returned with their booty to Harris.

But that they were fated never to do, for a young cadet of the MacDonalds, by name *Do'ull Mac Iain 'ic Sheamuis,* who then farmed the Island of Eriskay, heard of the depredation that was being wrought on his kin, and he resolved to put an end to it. This man played such a notable part in this incident, and its sequel, that a brief sketch of his life, is necessary here.

Do'ull Mac Iain 'ic Sheamuis was the grandson of James *Gruamach,* who was captain of *Clann Uisdein* during the minority of Donald *Gorm Mór.* He was born in Moidart, his mother being a MacDonald of that district, his father, 'John of the Castle', being at the time a hostage in Edinburgh. At the age of four or five years, young Donald was brought to Castle *Camus,* his ancestral home, where he lived till he was about eighteen years of age. He was then invited by his godmother, a lady named *Nic Coiseam,* who was very fond of him, to take possession of her farm, which was on the island of Eriskay in the Kyle of Barra.

There he grew up to be an industrious man, of exemplary character and of noted strength. None in the adjacent isles could cast the stone so far as he or vie with him in the race or in the leap and worthily he deserved the compliment paid him by the sennachie; 'A neart mar dharag na coille, a chumadh cho direach ri giuthas na beinne, 's a chorp cho subailte ri cuilc nan lòn' ('His strength like the oak of the forest, his form straight as the mountain pine, and his body lithe as the reed of the marshland'). Few could shoot the arrow with such dexterity as he. He was a fencer of skill and his '*Lainnire Riabhach*', as he termed his sword, had often taken a terrible toll of the foe in many a hard-fought fight.

It was this young Achilles, then, who heard of the plight of his clansmen in Uist and set off from Eriskay early one morning with twelve manly fellows and made for the north. A wayfarer who met them at a ford was accosted by *Do'ull Mac Iain* with the words: "*Tha latha buana foghair agam ort*" ('You owe me a day's harvesting'). "*Ma ta*" ("Okay,"), returned the other, "*chan fhada bhitheas*" ("it will not be for long"), and he turned on his heel and joined them. Shortly afterwards they overtook another man, who was carrying peats for a neighbouring farmer. "*What wage do you get?*" asked MacDonald. "*Five pence*", was the answer. "*Join us*", said his questioner, "*and you will win a better wage, and honour forbye.*" The peat-carrier became a recruit and soon another was added to the band so that it now numbered sixteen men.

When they arrived at Carinish, at dawn the following day, the 'Children of the Mare', as the MacLeods were called, were partaking of a meal preparatory to their leaving for Harris. Mac-Donald divided his men into three companies. Five he stationed behind a hill about a mile from the church, five others about half a mile nearer it and he enjoined the remainder to proceed to within arrow-range of the sanctuary, to take steady aim, and to make sure that each brought down one of the foe. They were then rapidly to retreat to the point where the second company was stationed, make a stand there, discharge their arrows run to the hill occupied by the band that was farthest from the church, where all were to make a determined stand together.

The ruse worked admirably for, when the MacLeods noticed the despicable company that had dared to attack them, they made a sortie without caution or order, like sheep from a fold, and five of their foremost were soon brought to earth. Twice as many were despatched when the MacDonalds halted with the second party and over thirty of them had already fallen when they came within range of the full force of the MacDonalds now posted on the hill.

There the MacDonalds discovered that their bows shot farther than those of the enemy, and the advantage was quickly put to good account for, while the arrows of the latter were falling harmlessly short, those of the MacDonalds were doing dreadful execution in the opposing ranks.

The slaughter of the MacLeods had soon assumed such proportions that the two parties was almost equal in number and, confident that victory now lay within their grasp, the exultant MacDonalds pressed closer on the foe. But they paid dearly for their rashness for an arrow was sunk in *MacIain's* thigh and he was incapacitated from taking further part in the contest. The mishap did not, however, daunt his men who now set upon the foe with redoubled vim, and the MacLeods were soon in hopeless flight. Their leader, Donald *Glas*, and those who fled with him, were killed on the shore at Baleshare, at a place called *Oitir Mhic Dhòmhnuill Ghlais* to this day. The battle is also called *Blar na Feithe* or the Battle of the Ditch (Cameron, A, 1871, pp. 58–9).

Meanwhile his wound was causing *Do'ull Mac Iain* great pain, despite the care of one of his comrades. It is said that his godmother had no sooner ascertained the reason why he left home than she followed him and she arrived on the north shore of the island of Grimsay just as the fray was ending. She shouted loudly at the ford. Her godson heard and knew her voice and he immediately ordered the man who was attending him to ferry her across to the main island, and right worthily she repaid the trouble.

It is said that it was she who extracted the arrow from the flesh and, as she was performing the operation, she caused a band of young women who had gathered around her to sing the chorus of a lilt she was composing, in order to divert the attention of the young warrior from the pain of his wound. A portion of the extemporised song is as follows:

Mhic Dho'uill, a laoigh mo chéille,
　　MacDonald, love of my reason,
Hi ri ri ri ho u;
　　(line of chorus);
Gur moch a chuala tu m' éigheach,
　　Early you heard my call,
Ho ro ho hi ri;
　　(2 lines of chorus);
Chall eile bhó hi o ro ho,
Fhreagair thu 'n tràigh 's an là a' glasadh;
　　You negotiated the ford at daybreak;
Hi ri ri ri ho u;
　　(line of chorus and so on);
Bhuail thu maidhm air Siol a' Chapuill,
　　You struck terror into the seed of the horse,
Ho ro ho hi ri;
Chall eile bhó hi o ro ho,
Siol na làire, blàire, bacaich, etc.
　　Seed of the mare, white faced and lame.
　　　　　　　　　　　　(MacDonald, A & A, 1911, p. 31)

A poem on the same subject appears in the *Oranaiche* (Mac na Ceardaich, G, 1879, p. 131) but is called *"Do Iain Dòmhnallach, Mac Iain Mhic Sheumais le Mhuime Nic Coiseam"* ('to John

MacDonald, son of John, son of James by his foster mother Nic Coiseam') a fine song set to an attractive air recounts his prowess at the Battle of Carinish: *A Mhic Iain 'ic Sheumais, tha do sgeul air m'aire*. Its tune first appears in the *Pìobaireachd* Collection of Donald McDonald of Glenhinnisdale (MacDonald, D, *c.* 1820, pp. 116–7), our earliest collection of the kind. He intended to publish the words in Vol. 2.

It seems that *Nic Coiseam* was as skilled in the art of the surgeon as she was in that of the bard for, within three weeks of the fight, her patient set sail for Duntulm to acquaint his chief with the affair at Carinish and to enlist in his service. The galley was half-way across the Minch when it encountered a violent gale, with blinding snow-showers from the south-east, so that no course remained but to slacken sail and run before the wind until, as fate would have it, they landed at Rodel in Harris.

The storm-stricken voyagers were now literally between the devil and the deep sea, for they learned that Rory *Mór* was still at Rodel, with a strong body of his clan. It happened that the Chief of the MacLeods had as his page a pert and prying youth of the name of MacCrimmon who was in the relation of foster son to *Do'ull Mac Iain* and the attachment between the two was consequently stronger than any other bond of relationship could be. As soon as MacCrimmon heard that his foster-father had been driven on the coast of Harris, he was at his wits' end to devise means for his safety. As the storm was wildly raging, Rory *Mór* had occasion to look outside; but he soon recoiled from the open door as the freezing gust swept wisps of crisp snow into the warm chamber he had left. *"Pity"*, said he, *"those who have not the shelter of a roof on such a night as this. It is so wild and cold that I would extend the hand of hospitality even to my most bitter foe were he in need to-night"*.

"I take you at your word", broke in the forward page. *"Do'ull Maclain 'ic Sheamuis is in a cave by the shore of Rodel and great is his need of shelter"*.

"Invite him hither", said the magnanimous chief, *"and let none put a finger on him, or on any of his men, so long as they are under my roof"*.

Thereupon MacCrimmon bounded to the shore. When he returned with the MacDonalds, the MacLeods had just sat down to supper. A place was made for the strangers at the table, and threatening looks were often exchanged between those who sat below the salt.

At last his feelings got the better of one of the MacLeods, and he remarked: *"Three weeks to-day happened the affair of Carinish"*. Instantly every man was on his feet and dirks flashed in the flickering light of the candles. Rory *Mór* jumped up at the head of the table and, with shame in his countenance and rage in his voice, commanded his men to sit down. He was at once obeyed, and he roundly scolded them for their disgraceful breach of hospitality.

His action created a lull for the time being and, when calm reigned once again he facetiously asked MacDonald whom he had intended to strike first had the parties come to blows. *"Had any of my men been struck in your house"*, replied MacDonald, *"I would have sought the best bird in the covey and that is you"*.

When it was time to repair to rest for the night, pallets were laid in a large barn for the MacDonalds, but their leader was invited to sleep in a room adjoining that of the chief. He, however, declined the offer, remarking that it had never been his custom to separate himself from his men in a hostile country and he was not disposed to change his habit then, especially after what had transpired earlier in the night. He proceeded, therefore, with his men to the barn and the company lay down to rest.

Some time before daybreak, MacDonald was suddenly awakened and, looking up, he saw MacCrimmon bending over his bed. The boy hurriedly told him that a conspiracy was afoot to set the barn on fire and that, as the weather was now favourable, they should resume their voyage (Cameron, A, 1871, pp. 59–61).

Without further ado, the MacDonalds made for the shore where their galley was soon on trim and a course was set for Skye. They had barely left the land when they noticed, in the grey light of the morning, that the barn where they had spent the night was in flames. Whereupon one of the crew tuned up his pipes and played that challenging air, *'Tha an Dubh-thuil air Mac Leòid'*. 'Macleod now has diarrhoea!' (Mackenzie, A, 1889, p. 70).

It would appear that Rory *Mór* did not remain long in Harris after this episode, but that he went to Argyll to seek counsel, it is said and, what is more probable, to obtain help against the Mac-Donalds. In any case, he was away from home when an extensive raid was made by his enemies over his lands of Minginish and Bracadale. Great destruction was done to houses and crops and a large number of cattle was rounded up. The *creach* was gathered in that awesome corrie on the western slopes of the Cuillin Range where a halt was made until all the raiders should reach the rendezvous before they began to drive the booty home.

The locality has since been known as *'Coire na Creiche'*, or the 'Corry of the Foray', and there the MacDonalds were set upon by a large body of the MacLeods with reinforcements from the MacLeods of Lewis. The pursuers were led by a brother of Rory *Mór*, *Alasdair Og* of Minginish, who had been left in charge of the affairs of the clan and it is on record that he was clad in mail.

It was late in the afternoon when the issue was joined and during that night the lonely echoes of the surrounding peaks were in constant agitation as the triumphant yells of lusty conquerors mixed with the death-shrieks of vanquished foes.

After the tide of battle had swirled this way and that for some considerable time, it was noticed that the ranks of the MacLeods had been severely thinned in the course of the combat. Many of the MacDonalds also had fallen, but the leader of the MacLeods, together with thirty of the most prominent members of the clan, were taken prisoners. The MacLeods were routed. The battle of *Coire na Creiche* is memorable as being the last clan-fight that was fought in Skye. It took place in the year 1601 (Cameron, A, 1871, p. 61).

Among the victorious MacDonalds, tradition avers that none could compare in prowess with *Do'ull Mac Iain 'ic Sheamuis*. The fight was just commencing, it is said, when he joined the ranks of his clansmen, and his *'Lainnire Riabhach'* wrought terrible havoc among his foes. He was a bard of merit, as well as a warrior of note, and in an *'iorram'*, or boat-song, that is attributed to him, he sings of the victory of *Coire na Creiche*, which literally translated is:

Latha dhomh 's a' Chuilitheann chreagach;
    One day I happed in rocky Cuillin;
Chuala mi phiob mhòr 'ga spreigeadh;
    I heard the great warpipe astrumming;
Nuallan a' chruidh laoigh 'ga freagairt;
    Lowing of milch kine responding,
Bha beul-sios air luchd an leadain,
    Ill-luck befell the men of (long locks),
Bha làrach am bròg 'san eabar;
    The imprints of their brogues in mire;
'S iad Clann Dho-uill rinn an leagadh, etc.
    Clan Donald was responsible for their whelming.
        (MacDonald, A & A, 1911, p. 32)

Though the subsequent history of this hero belongs to a later period, it may be as well to narrate it here.

He was married to a daughter of MacDonald of Keppoch, and it seems that he was a member of that gallant band that went under the command of another warrior of Skye, equally famous, and a bard of even greater renown, Archibald MacDonald (*An Ciaran Mabach*), to avenge the murder of the 'Children of Keppoch'.

His wife died young leaving him with two sons and one daughter, named Mary, who was married to John MacLeod, VI of Gesto. After he had quitted Eriskay, he went to live with his daughter in Gesto and while he was there he engaged in the trade of cattle-dealing – an industry that was fated to bring a large measure of prosperity to Skye. It is said that he was the first man from Skye to drive a herd to the markets of Crieff and Falkirk – an achievement then rightly considered a distinct feat, when robber bands on the mainland were so daring as to defy even the government itself.

It was then considered an indignity for a man with pretensions to rank to take part in any occupation other than war, raiding, or hunting so that Donald's proud son-in-law was never tired of casting aspersions, and slinging innuendoes at *'Aireach liath nam bó'* ('the grey-haired cattle-keeper'), as he disparagingly called him (Cameron, A, 1871, pp. 66–7).

It may easily be inferred then that he was far from happy in the house of Gesto, a surmise strengthened by the evidence afforded by another composition of his called '*Oran Bràthann*', or 'Quern Song'. As two maidservants were one day grinding corn in an outhouse at Gesto, he noticed that the song did not, as was the custom, accompany the rotation of the quern-stone. He chid them for their neglect of the time-honoured practice and, when they observed they could not remember an appropriate refrain, he lifted his grandchild on his knee and composed the following song as the maidens in rhythm whirled the quern and ground the corn.

Hu o hi ri ibh o,
  (Chorus: Ho o hi ri ibh o).

Cia mar tha thu fhir an taighe? Hu o hi, (etc.)
  How are you today goodman?
Tha mi mar a bha mi roimhe,
  I am as before
Gun mhire, gun cheòl, gun aighear.
  Without mirth, music or joy
'S mi thug na tri seòid do t' athair,
  It was I gave the three heroes to your father,
Lùireach is clogad is claidheamh.
  Coat of mail, helmet and sword.
Thug mi sin dha is deagh bhean taighe,
  That I gave him and a splendid house wife,
Bean a riaraicheadh na maithean.
  A wife to entertain the nobles,
Mhic nan gormshuilean á Mùideart,
  Son of the blue eyes from Moidart
Cha b' e deatach dhubh an dùdain
  It was not the black fume of the milldust
Chleachd thusa bhi 'n tùrlach t'athar,
  That you experienced in your father's house
Ach fir òga losgadh fùdair,
  But young men burning gun-powder,
Ri mire, ri mùirn 's ri aighear.
  With mirth, joy and festivity.
                    (MacDonald, A & A, 1911, p. 34)

Despite the indignities that he had so often heaped upon him, his pompous son-in-law was obliged to beg a favour of his despised relative on one memorable occasion, if the tale following be true.

A sister of MacLeod of Gesto was married to a MacAskill of Ebost, and, on a daughter being born to the latter, MacLeod went to congratulate him. The brothers-in-law, having imbibed somewhat freely of the liquor provided, quarrelled, and swords were drawn. It is recorded that the point of MacAskill's weapon stuck in a rafter and MacLeod, throwing chivalry aside, stabbed him so that he was mortally wounded. MacLeod hurried home in grave anxiety, knowing well that the MacAskills would be after him. He asked his wife's advice as to what he should do and she suggested that he should seek the protection of *'Aireach Liath nam Bó'*! Though hurt at the insinuation, he concluded that that would be the wisest course under the circumstances and he repaired to Cuidreach, where his father-in-law then resided.

Early the following morning a party of the MacAskills was seen approaching MacDonald's house but when they saw the grey-haired Achilles perambulating in front of his door and brandishing his great sword the while, they halted. As a discretionary measure, it was decided that one of their number should go forward and ask for the surrender of 'Gesto'. This was done, but the messenger was so terror-struck by the attitude of the grizzly giant he encountered, that he fled ingloriously to his comrades who, considering it hazardous to join issue with the best fencer of the age, turned about and returned to Ebost (Cameron, A, 1871, pp. 67–8).

As we have already seen, it was *Do'ull Mac Iain 'ic Sheamuis* who was commissioned by his chief to secure the person of the traitorous *Uisdean MacGhilleasbá Chléirich*, but, in spite of all he had done for his clan, he had been so neglected that, as has been previously said, he was constrained to live in another man's house. His plight so touched his brother bard, *Iain Lom*, who visited him on one occasion at Gesto, that the Gaelic Laureate went straight to Duntulm and, playing on the privilege due to his caste, roundly rated his chief, Sir James *Mór*, for the disregard that was shown to one who had always been the most eminent protagonist of his clan. Finding that Sir James was somewhat dilatory in making any proposal, the satirist began to compose a scathing lampoon on him and, after he had inveighed against his chief to a considerable length, the latter demanded him to

desist. *"I shall"*, said the bard, *"on condition that you do as I advise and settle a competent portion of land on Do'ull Mac Iain 'ic Sheamuis"*. The chief now readily concurred and he implemented his promise by conferring the district of Cuidreach on MacDonald (MacDonald, A & A, 1904, p. 67). He died there about 1680. His descendants occupied Kingsborough for many generations, and one of them was the notable lawyer, Sir J.H.A. Macdonald who, until recently, was Lord Justice Clerk to the Court of Session.

Cessation of Clan Warfare

The battle of *Coire na Creiche* marks the commencement of a new epoch in the history of Skye, for with it ended the age-long feuds between the MacDonalds and the MacLeods whose relationship to each other during the previous centuries has been waggishly described as *"putting rings on each other's fingers and dirks in each other's hearts"*

The authors of 'Clan Donald', and Sir Robert Gordon in his *History of Sutherland*, declare that the battle of Carinish was fought after, and not before, *Coire na Creiche*, but the traditions in Skye are consistent in placing the former anterior to the latter. *Coire na Creiche* was fought in 1601 and the Scottish king, James VI, who was now most anxious to impress the English with his good government, was in a state of consternation lest news of the trouble among the clans of the Western Isles should get abroad and prejudice his claims to the English throne.

He, accordingly, commanded MacLeod to surrender himself to Argyle, and MacDonald to Huntly, and remain with these noblemen until their quarrels should be settled by arbitration. Through the intermediary of MacDonald of Dunnyveg, MacLean of Coll, and other Highland chieftains, a reconciliation was effected and, in accordance with its terms, those who were made prisoners at *Coire na Creiche* were set free (Mackenzie, A, 1889, p. 71).

In celebration of the peace, a great festival was held at Dunvegan. Donald *Gorm*, and the principal cadets of the clan, with all his train, attended; and a magnificent gathering took place. MacLeod's renowned piper, Donald *Mór* MacCrimmon, struck up the famous *pìobaireachd*, '*Fàilte nan Leòdach*', (MacLeods' Welcome), as the MacDonalds were approaching the castle; and when he was finished, MacArthur, the piper of MacDonald, reciprocated the friendly greetings by playing that favourite tune, 'MacDonald's Salute'.

For six days the festivities were continued. There were athletic contests, piping competitions, composition exercises by the bards, and trials of wit between the jesters. Food and drink were provided on that generous scale that has always been a feature of the hospitable halls of Dunvegan, where, as *Màiri ni'n Alasdair Ruaidh* says:

> *Bu tric aoidh chàirdean,*
> > Frequent was the welcome to friends,
> *Gu d' Dhùn àghmhor,*
> > to your splendid fort,
> *Suilbhir, fàilteach,*
> > Cheerful, welcoming,
> *Cuilm-mhor, stàiteil,*
> > festive, stately,
> *Gun bhuirb, gun àrdan,*
> > Without cruelty or pride
> *Gun diultadh air màl dhéirceach.*
> > Ready with alms for the needy.
>
> (Watson, JC, 1934, p. 92)

From a reference made to this memorable occasion by one of the bards namely, Neil Mac Vurich, we gather that there was no stinting then of "*the generous wine which would overcome the hardiest heroes*", for he confesses:

> *Fiche misge lin g'laoi;*
> *Nochar leisge lin no le.*

which means:

> Twenty times drunk we were each day,
> Nor did we rebel against it any more than he.
>
> (MacBain, A, & Kennedy, J, 1894, p. 286)

An incident that is said to have happened during one of these carousals is worthy of mention. MacMhuirich, the bard of MacDonald, overcome with wine, was stretched full-length in a lobby, surrounded by a pack of licking hounds. MacLeod's bard, noticing the comical posture of his rival, observed:

> *Tha bàrd Mhic Dho'uill air a dhruim,*
> > MacDonald's bard is on his back,
> *'S e cur os a chionn a chòrr*
> > Throwing up his excess
> *'S am fear thug dhàsan a dhiol,*
> > And he who gave him his burden
> *Thug e biadh do choin 'ic Leòid.*
> > Gave food to MacLeod's dogs."

To which, with lively wit, the prostrate bard retorted:

> *An sgeula dh' aithriseadh air MacLeòid,*
> > The tale that could be told of MacLeod,

'S ann bu chòir a bhith 'ga chleith;

    Which ought to be denied;

Nach faigheadh a chuid chon ri òl,

    That his dogs only get to drink,

Ach na dheanadh a luchd òil a sgeith.

    What his drinking friends vomit.

                  (compare Matheson, A, 1953, p. 325)

As an interlude in the proceedings, the fools of the respective chiefs were one day pitted against one another, in order to discover which was the wiser. They were led to the shore, for the tide had ebbed, and were told to busy themselves in collecting shellfish. A gold piece had previously been placed in a conspicuous position on a boulder that lay in the course the *'amadain'* were enjoined to take, while the chiefs hid themselves behind a rock hard by, closely watching their behaviour. Mac-Donald's fool, who was the first to observe the coin, shouted aloud: *"Oh, see the gold"*. *"Never mind it"*, said the other, with well-feigned nonchalance, " *'nuair bhitheas sinn ri òrach, bitheamaid ri òrach; 's 'nuair a bhitheas sinn ri maorach, bitheamaid ri maorach"* ("when we are collecting gold let us collect gold and when we are collecting shellfish let us collect shellfish"). They left the gold and resumed their work. Soon, however, it was noticed that MacDonald's simpleton had been sent on a quest farther along the shore, while he who had so lately given him such a magnificent homily on the virtue of concentration on the *"duty that lies nearest"*, slunk hastily back and pocketed the precious metal.

We *"ask not proud philosophy to teach"* us which of the fools showed the higher wisdom.

Later, in that same year, an order was issued by the king and his Council, requesting Rory *Mór* to attend at Falkland Castle, or at any other venue that the king might afterwards decide on, by the 10th day of August and should he fail to obey the summons,

he was to be held guilty of treason and his estates were to be forfeited. Rory *Mór* refused to comply, as is evidenced by a fresh command, dated 11th August, 1601, in which he is denounced as a rebel.

So far as is known, no such summons was served on Donald *Gorm Mór* but, shortly before the first royal command was despatched to Rory *Mór,* an injunction was given to each of the chiefs of Skye to give assurances that they would in future refrain from invading each other's lands, and to find sureties for their behaviour.

The MacLeods

Sir Rory Mór, *Fifteenth Chief*

But Rory *Mór* continued on his career of defiance so that in the year 1605 the host".government issued an edict ordering him to quit Dunvegan and all the other forts he occupied, within twenty-four hours, and surrender them to his majesty's representatives who were to be despatched to deliver the charge (Mackenzie, A, 1889, p. 72). But on this occasion, again, no attempt was made to carry out the threat of eviction and the net result of all these warnings was to make the chief more insubordinate than ever. Thus we find that, in 1607, he set out on an expedition to harass the 'Gentlemen Venturers' at Stornoway. He stormed the castle of that town, took possession of it, and refused to surrender. Again there is issued a command wherein he is ordered to deliver the castle over to the king's bailiffs within six hours, *"under penalty of treason"*. In the same year the Privy Council commissioned Argyle to seize Rory *Mór* and present him at court to answer for his conduct and, whether Argyle was successful or not, we find that a bond of friendship was drawn up in 1609 between the Skye chiefs who pledge themselves

to forget, forgive and abstain from quarrelling in future, being
certainly persuaded of their dread sovereign's clemency and to live
hereafter in Christian society and peace.

It is interesting to note that the witnesses to this contract are
Lachlan MacKinnon of Strath ('*Lachlan mise Mac Fingon*') and
"*Allan O'Colgan, minister of Duirinish*". (MacLeod, RC, 1938,
pp. 47–8.

The change of attitude presented by the chiefs is attributed
to an event, of far-reaching consequence, that happened in the
previous year. In 1608, the king sent Lord Ochiltree, accompanied by a large armed force, on a mission to the Western Isles to
ascertain, and report on, the conduct of the recalcitrant chiefs
and, if possible, to tame "*the wicked blood of the Isles*". A ship,
called the '*Moon*', was placed at the disposal of the commissioners of whom Andrew Knox, Bishop of the Isles, was president.
At the same time a royal command was issued, warning certain
chiefs to present themselves, with their principal followers, at
the Castle of Aros, in Mull.

All the chiefs who had been notified seem to have obeyed the
summons; and the following regulations were read to them and
they were asked to promise, in writing, that they would obey
them:

1 They were to find security for the payment of His Majesty's
rents.
2 The chiefs and vassals were strictly to observe the laws of
the realm.
3 They were to surrender to the king all garrisoned houses.
4 They were to renounce the heritable jurisdiction and submit
to sheriffs or other officers appointed by the Crown.
5 All galleys were to be burned, except such as were to be used
for essential services – *e.g.* the conveyance to the mainland,

or from island to island, of the rents (then, of course, paid
in kind).
6 Children to be sent to school in the South and to learn
to speak and read English as a condition of succeeding to
estates.
7 The use of two-handed swords, guns and bows and arrows
to be prohibited.

Most of the chiefs demurred to subscribe their names to
these conditions; and then was enacted a plot as discreditable
to the government authorities as several others that were practised on the Highlanders. On Sunday morning an invitation was
extended by Lord Ochiltree to the chiefs asking them to go on
board the "*Moon*" for the alleged purpose of attending divine
service, to be conducted by Bishop Knox and, after that, to discuss affairs at dinner. All the chiefs obeyed, save Rory *Mór* who
suspected a conspiracy, and they were immediately told they
were the prisoners of among their pursuers, and then the king.
The ship sailed south to Ayr and, while others were imprisoned
in Stirling, Donald *Gorm Mór* was placed in Blackness Castle
(Gregory, D, 1881, pp. 323–4). Here he was detained for a
time, and was liberated on his promising to respect the following conditions:

1 He was to find security for his appearance yearly at Stirling
at a fixed date;
2 He was to declare his adhesion to Protestantism;
3 He was to maintain order in his dominions; and
4 He was to give his help in surveying the Isles (a work which
he undertook and was completed in 1609).

In that year Bishop Knox was authorised by the government
to summon the chiefs, this time to Iona, and it is significant that
he earnestly requests to be relieved of the duty, as his "*credit*

has gone of late", referring no doubt to the part he played the previous year in kidnapping the men of the Isles. Most of the chiefs obeyed the command and among the names of those who attended we find that of Rory *Mór*, Donald *Gorm Mór*, and Lachlan MacKinnon of Strath.

The famous Bond and Statutes of Icolmkill were drawn up and the chiefs subscribed to them without a single dissentient. Rory *Mór's* name was appended to the 'Bond' and it is noteworthy that, from that time until his death, his loyalty suffered no lapse. Until then he had, of course, been in disgrace with the government and a new grant of his lands, which is still in the charter chest at Dunvegan, had been made to Lord Balmerino, Sir Patrick Spens, and Sir George Hay and the districts that were alienated are mentioned as Harris, Dunvegan and Duntulm, the last of which had uninterruptedly been in the possession of the MacDonalds since 1538. But, as had happened so often before, the gift was not taken over by the southroners (MacLeod, RC, 1927, p. 132).

From the time he had agreed to the 'Statutes of Iona', Rory *Mór* was steadily growing in royal favour. In May, 1610, he received a pardon for all his crimes and, in the following month, in compliance with the promise made in Iona, he presented himself at Holyrood. With him then were Donald *Gorm Mór* of Sleat and Lachlan MacKinnon of Strath; and the island chiefs pledged themselves to help to restore order, to maintain justice, to refrain from attacking each other and to submit all differences to arbitration (Mackenzie, A, 1889, pp. 79–81).

Henceforth Rory *Mór* concerned himself chiefly with the consolidation of his estates. In 1610 he acquired from Lord Kintail, who in the previous year had purchased from the 'Gentlemen Venturers' the rights of the forfeited lands of Lewis and Skye, the district of Waternish, in exchange for the portion of Trotternish, namely, the two unciates at Uig, which he claimed as his own; and in August of the following year he received a royal charter for his lands which, as we have already seen, had been forfeited ten years previously. In the grant there is included the estate of Waternish (MacLeod, RC, 1938, pp. 78–81).

In November 1611, a royal order is made in favour of Andrew, Bishop of the Isles, probably for his services in connection with the settlement effected in the Hebrides, of "*all, and whatsoever sums of money shall be resting owing to his Majesty by Roderick MacLeod of Dunvegan*" (Mackenzie, A, 1889, p. 82), and whether the bishop benefited by such a grant or not cannot now be said; but we find a significant minute in the records of the Privy Council for the year 1613, to the effect that Rory *Mór* and Donald *Gorm Mór* had each reached a settlement with the Exchequer in regard to their arrears of rent and that these chiefs were continuing to obey the laws (Mackenzie, A, 1889, p. 83).

It is obvious that Rory was now rapidly becoming a royal favourite and the culmination of his preferment was attained in 1613, when he visited London, and was fêted by the king who honoured him with the order of knighthood. This was James' wise method of "*taming the wild blood of the Isles*" for, "*being allured by our good usage, he may in time coming be so much the more allured to manifest his good-will to our service*", and His Majesty guessed aright (*ibid.*, pp. 82–3).

The indulgent treatment accorded to Sir Rory *Mór* no doubt induced his brother chief, Donald *Gorm Mór*, to endeavour to find out how he stood in the good graces of his sovereign. He, therefore, craved confirmation of the charter granted him in 1594, and his plea was readily assented to. This was in 1614.

In a letter to Lord Binning, dated April 15th 1615, Sir Roderick complains that, returning from Glasgow where he had been visiting his children who went to school there, he had been thrown off his horse by Lord Fleming who had collided with him in Stirling, and that two of his ribs were broken and that he had to stay for 15 days in Perth for treatment. During his absence *Coll Mac Ghilleasbuig* had attacked his Island of St. Kilda and had slaughtered all the cattle there and had made south for Islay. He commends that powers be given him to follow them up and avenge the incident (MacLeod, RC, 1938, p. 53).

In the following year Sir Rory *Mór* wrote a letter of protest to the Privy Council against the granting to MacDonald of a charter for Sleat, Uist and Trotternish from which the Clan Donald had, he declares, *"most violently detruded my forbears"*. He adverts to the changed conditions in the Highlands, when appeal is no longer made to war but to arbitration, for the settlement of disputes and he craves that justice be done to him (MacLeod, RC, 1927, p. 121).

He was granted his wish in 1616 when a court of arbitration was held and judgement was given to the effect that the lands over which the MacLeods claimed a *de jure* right were to be assigned to the MacDonalds. The latter were, however, ordered to pay a sum of money to MacLeod by way of compensation and, for that purpose, Sir Rory *Mór* was to draw the rent for Sleat for a period of years. That this contract was carried out is shown by the fact that during the years 1618, 1619 and 1622, the taxes for Sleat were paid by Sir Rory *Mór* (MacLeod, RC, 1927, pp. 123–4).

It was on his return journey from Edinburgh, after his successful interview with the Privy Council, that Donald *Gorm Mór* was persuaded by the Bishop of the Isles to join the expedition that was set on foot to proceed against Sir James MacDonald of Islay who was then in revolt. The Skye chief had only a small retinue with him at the time but he joined the Bishop, though the mission proved wholly ineffectual to induce the men of Islay to surrender Dunnyveg.

According to the Statutes of Iona, which decreed the chiefs were to present themselves once a year before the Privy Council in Edinburgh, Sir Rory *Mór* and MacKinnon of Strath appeared there in July, 1616, but, owing to illness, Donald *Gorm* was unable to attend. The rebellion of Sir James MacDonald of Islay, in which many of the vassals of Donald *Gorm* took part, still convulsed the Western Isles, and the Privy Council felt it to be incumbent on them to enforce the 'Statutes' with greater stringency than they had hitherto done. It was with that aim that they added new clauses to the 'Statutes', ratified the old ones, and presented 'The Regulations for Chiefs' to those whom they concerned. All the chiefs agreed to be bound by these 'Regulations', and they duly observed them until 1622 (Gregory, D, 1881, p. 396).

The necessity for passing these 'Regulations' affords such an interesting insight into conditions that prevailed in our island at that time that some of them will be quoted:

1   At their annual appearance before the Privy Council, MacDonald and MacLeod were each to present three of their principal cadets, while MacKinnon was enjoined to exhibit one. (The last chief gave the names of five members of his clan for whose conduct he declined to be answerable.)

2   In their households, Donald *Gorm Mór* and Sir Rory *Mór* were not to maintain more than six gentlemen each, and MacKinnon three.

3   MacDonald was to reside at Duntulm, MacLeod at Dunvegan, and MacKinnon at Kilmaree. They were to add to the amenities of their policies by planting trees, and they were to cultivate home farms, so that they might thereby *"be exercised, and eschew idleness."*

4   No chief was to maintain more than one *birlinn*.

5   They were to send all their children above the age of nine to the Lowlands to be instructed in English, a knowledge of which was to be held an essential condition for any who might claim the succession to an estate. Under this head

there occurs a lengthy statement in which it is averred that the principal reason

> *for the barbarity, impiety, and incivility within the Isles has proceeded from the neglect of the education of the children who see nothing in their tender years but the barbarous and ancient forms of the country. They are, thereby, made to apprehend that there is no other form of duty or civility kept in any other part of the country; … whereas, if they had been trained in virtue and the English tongue, they would have been the better prepared to reduce their country to godliness, obedience and civility.*

6   Finally, a regulation was imposed on the chiefs with a view to restricting the consumption of wine:

> *The great and extraordinary excess of drinking commonly used among the commons and tenants of the Isles is not only one occasion of the beastly and barbarous cruelties and inhumanities that fall out among them, … but it draws numbers of them to miserable necessity and poverty.*

7   While MacKinnon's allowance was fixed at one tun per annum, MacDonald and MacLeod were each permitted a ration of four tuns of wine (Gregory, D, 1881, pp. 393–6).

That the last regulation was most necessary is shown by the carousals that took place during the celebration of the peace that ended the war called *Cogadh na Cailliche Caime*; but that the regulation was more *"honoured in the breach than the observance"* is amply proved by the accounts we have of the inordinate drinking of wine at Dunvegan in spite of the enactment that sought to restrict such excesses. Canon R.C. MacLeod of MacLeod refers to letters of horning in the charter-chest at Dunvegan, issued against Sir Rory *Mór* and in one of these, for the year 1625, just before his death, the amount of debt charged against him for wine alone, was £500! (MacLeod, RC, 1927, p. 139).

In the year 1616, when the epoch-making 'Statutes of Iona' were formulated, there died the chief of Sleat, Donald *Gorm Mór*. He had been in failing health for some time previously and, as we have already seen, he had been prevented by illness from attending the conference of chiefs with the Bishop of the Isles in Iona. He was thrice married – (1) To Margaret of Dunvegan, the famous '*Cailleach Cham*', whom he divorced; (2) to Mary, the sister of MacKenzie of Kintail; and (3) to Marjory, a sister of Macintosh of Dunachton. He died childless and was succeeded by the oldest son of his brother, Archibald the Clerk, and the heir is therefore known to history as '*Do'ull Gorm Og, MacGhilleasba' Chlérich*'.

The young chief of the MacDonalds became early apprehensive of the power of Sir Rory *Mór* who, as we have already seen, was to hold Sleat, the best part of his patrimony, until the instalments of compensation agreed on early in 1616 had been duly paid. In the summer of 1616 young *Donald Gorm* went to Edinburgh, primarily with the object of seeking protection from the king against the chief of Dunvegan. He was graciously received and made such a favourable impression on his sovereign that he was invested with the insignia of knighthood, and he was confirmed in his title to all his estates with the exception of Trotternish. A promise was given him, however, that, as soon as all the arrears of compensation had been duly paid to Sir Rory *Mór*, this territory also would revert inalienably to his clan (Cameron, A, 1871, p. 69).

About this time there was much disquiet in the Western Isles, caused by piratical bands composed chiefly of men belonging to Clan Ian of Ardnamurchan. It seems that this clan had been goaded into rebellion through the stratagem of Argyle who sought to extend his sway over their territory. In that he succeeded and on their detrusion the MacIans launched upon a life of wholesale plundering. They carried on their nefarious work for several years, until their confederacy was broken up in 1625. In the summer of that year they had been extraordinarily bold. They had been harassing ships off the coast of Skye, and Sir Rory *Mór* determined to put an end to their depredations. He collected his clansmen and, having encountered the pirates, he defeated them in a short and sharp struggle. He closely pursued them to their fastnesses in Ardnamurchan where, in conjunction with Lord Lorne, he succeeded in rounding them up. Their leaders were either killed or banished and from that time the Clan Ian of Ardnamurchan ceased to exist as a separate entity (Mackenzie, A, 1889, p. 89).

In the year 1623 the freedom of the City of Edinburgh was conferred on Sir Rory *Mór*, a significant honour, indicating the change in his conduct, and a recognition of the important services that this erstwhile rebel was now rendering to his country.

Sir Rory *Mór* was married to Isabella of Glengarry, whose effigy in stone may still be seen in the Castle of Dunvegan. By her he had a large family of sons and daughters. These were John, his successor, Sir Roderick of Talisker, Sir Norman of Bernera (who both graduated at Glasgow University), William of Hamara, and Donald of Greshornish; Janet, who married Iain *Garbh Mac Gille Chaluim* of Raasay; Florence, who was the wife of Donald MacSwan of Roag. Margaret who married Sir Eachann *Mór* of Duart; Mary who married Sir Lachlan, brother of the former, and Marion who married John MacDonald of Clanranald in 1613 (*ibid.*, p. 92). It has been said that, if he was not a Catholic, he favoured that persuasion. His wife was a Clanranald and his daughter Marion was married into that family.

In the year 1626 the chief had occasion to pay a visit to Fortrose and while there he became suddenly ill and died and he was buried in the cathedral of that town where his epitaph, on the recumbent stone, is still visible.

He was a man possessed of great vigour of body and of mind, of quick decision and clear discernment and as able a diplomat as his renowned grandfather, *Alasdair Crotach*. Like the latter, he succeeded in raising his clan to a position of high honour and it was for that reason that he earned the cognomen '*Mór*', or 'Great', that succeeding generations have rightly conferred upon him.

He was highly revered in life and in death he was sincerely mourned by every member of his clan. His famous piper, *Pàdruig Mór* MacCrimmon, could no longer bear to play the pipes that had so often delighted his large-hearted patron and he left Dunvegan's hospitable halls and went to live on his farm in Borreraig. It was then he composed the melting melody of '*Tog Orm Mo phìob*':

Tog orm mo phìob is théid mi dhachaigh;
> Put my pipes on my shoulder and I will go home

Mo thruaighe mi, mo léir mar thachair.
> My wretchedness and my distress at what has happened,

Tog orm mo phìob 's mi air mo chràdh
> Put on my pipe I am in pain

Mu Ruairidh Mór mu Ruairidh Mór.
> About Rory Mór about Rory Mór

Tog orm mo phìob, tha mi sgìth,
> Put on my pipe I am tired

'S mur faigh mi i, theid mi dhachaigh:
> And if I do not get it I shall go home

Clàrsach no pìob cha thog mo chrìdh,
> Harp or pipe will not raise my spirits

Cha bheò fear mo ghràidh Ruairidh Mór.
> My beloved is no longer alive, my Rory Mór.

(Mackenzie, A, 1889, p. 90)

In '*Luinneag Mhic Leòid,*' which she composed to Sir Norman of *Bernera, Mairi ni'n Alasdair Ruaidh,* the far-famed bardess of Skye, thus sang the praises of Sir Rory *Mór:*

> *(A mhic an) fhir chliùitich*
>> (Son of the) worthy man,
> *Bha gu fiùghantach, ainmeil;*
>> Who was generous, famous
> *Thug barrachd an gliocas*
>> Who showed more wisdom
> *Air gach ridir' bha'n Albainn,*
>> Than any knight in Scotland
> *Ann an cogadh, 's an sìochainnt,*
>> In war and in peace
> *'S ann an dìoladh air airgiod.*
>> And in paying of money.
>
>> (Watson, JC, 1934, p. 38)

An unpublished elegy on *Ruaraidh Mór,* found in Munster, composed by *Eoin O'Murgheasoin* and containing 65 stanzas, is found in *Scottish Gaelic Studies* Vol. 5, '*Creach Gaoidhal i Reilig Rois*' (O'Rahilly, TF, 1942, pp. 102–3).

Niàll Mór MacMhuirich praises his hospitality:

> *Se hoidhce dhamsa san dun*
>> Six nights I had been in the Dun,
> *Nior bhe an coinmhe fallsa fhuar*
>> It was not a fallacious entertainment I received,
> *Cuirm lionmhur ga hibhe ahor*
>> Plenty of ale was drunk at the board
> *Fionbhrugh mor is lionmhur sluagh.*
>> There was a large wine hall and a numerous host.
>
>> (MacBain, A, & Kennedy, J, 1894, p. 284)

Iain Mór, Sixteenth Chief

Sir Rory *Mór* was succeeded by his oldest son, John, a man who, from his enormous physique, was called *Iain Mór,* or Big John. He is mentioned as a student of the University of Glasgow in 1624, and reference is made a few years afterwards (1630) to a grant of 100 marks he made towards *"the building of the college and the library"*. He was cautioner for his cousin Angus of Glengarry for several thousand marks. The policy of peace and retrenchment, so well advanced by his father in his later years, was continued by him. The direct result of this was the amassing of vast wealth but great encroachments were fated to be made on his hoard by his indigent relatives, especially by his numerous brothers-in-law for whom he had often to stand surety and to lose his guarantee. In addition, he was mulcted to the extent of 20,000 marks by Argyle, who, in 1606, had promised Rory *Mór* he would intercede for him with the king for a charter for Glenelg on condition that the Chief of Dunvegan would acknowledge him as his overlord for that portion of his lands. In 1633 John was induced to do homage to Argyle and to pay him the fine above mentioned as well. Thus it was that the MacLeods held Glenelg as the vassals of Argyle until 1811, when that estate was sold out of the family (MacLeod, RC, 1927, pp. 146–7).

It was probably the relationship he bore to the Duke of Argyle that prevented the Chief of MacLeod from throwing in his lot with Montrose during the Great Civil War, just as it was the inherent hatred of that House that sent many another Highland chief to the side of the Stuarts. As we shall see later, his neighbour, Sir James *Mór* of Sleat, though not himself very active in the Stuart cause, sent a contingent of some 400 men under his brother, Donald of Castleton, to join the ranks of Montrose but John of Dunvegan gave his support neither to the King nor to the Covenanters. It is on record that, as Charles was on the way north in 1639, on that futile expedition of his to force

Episcopacy on Scotland, he addressed a letter to the Chief of MacLeod, soliciting his support, but the latter made no response to the royal appeal (Mackenzie, A, 1889, p. 98). Nor did he take part in the marvellous campaigns of Montrose. He seems, indeed, to have had no inclination for war, for his mind was set on far higher things. He was a pious man, endued with pure and altruistic purposes and intensely eager to improve the morals of his age (Mackay, W, 1905, p. 244). In the *Bannatyne Manuscript*, he is said to have been assiduous in the endeavour to convert his people from the Roman to the Protestant form of worship. In 1617 Lord Lovat sold Glenelg to MacLeod.

In addition to his lofty aims, he was also famous for his princely generosity, and, in spite of all the calls made upon him for financial aid he had much to spare, if all accounts be true. According to Canon MacLeod of MacLeod, when his treasure-chest was opened after his death, it was found to contain many a bulging leather bag and well-filled stocking, a *"yellow woollen sark"* covering a hoard and several catskin purses that the careful chief had used as repositories for his cash (MacLeod, RC, 1927, p. 148).

He was married to Sibella, daughter of MacKenzie, first Lord of Kintail, and he had a family of three sons and five daughters. Of the former, two, namely Rory ('the Witty') and John (*Iain Breac*), were chiefs, while one of his daughters, Sibella, was married to Thomas Fraser of Beaufort. That nobleman died at Dunvegan in 1699 and he was buried there at his own request:

> For the great love he bore the family of MacLeod, he desired to be buried near his wife's relations, in the place where two of his uncles lay.

Such is an extract from the inscription on an obelisk of free-stone erected to his memory in the churchyard of Kilmuir by the notorious Simon Fraser, who was beheaded on Towerhill in 1747 (Cameron, A, 1871, p. 82).

John's oldest daughter, Mary, was married to Sir James *Mór*, the Chief of Sleat; and it was probably to her that Roderick Morison, the harper and bard of Dunvegan, referred when, in his lament for *Iain Breac*, *"Creach nan Ciadan"*, he says:

> *Gheibh gach neach de na dh' fhàg thu,*
> All you have left behind,
> *Rud an àite na bh' aca,*
> Will get something for what they have lost,
> *Ach mis' agus Màiri*
> But I and Mary
> *Chuir a bràthair an tasgadh.*
> Who has lost her brother.
>
> (Matheson, W, 1970, p. 53)

There is extant another lament which is a worthy tribute to this generous chief. It is called *'Iorram na Truaighe'*, and is the composition of a cadet of the clan, one known as *Pòl Crùbach*, the son of a MacLeod of Lyndale. Apart from its historical interest, it deserves to be quoted because of its high poetic merit and its genuine ring:

> *Ach a' ghnùis na féile,*
> But oh generous face,
> *Nach do bhreugnaich riamh t'fhacal aon uair,*
> That never once belied your word,
> *Ceann-uidhe nan deòraidh,*
> Who gave respite to the destitute,
> *Nan aircleach gun treòir is nan truagh.*
> The feeble cripple and the poor.
> *A chearraich na tice,*

Thou player of dice,

Aig am bu tric bhiodh àireamh sluaigh;

 Who ever entertained hosts of people;

An fhéile dhùbailt

 The full hospitality

Nach iarradh an cùnntas cruaidh.

 That would not press for the hard bargain.

(Turner, P, 1809, p. 29)

The Macdonalds

Sir Donald Gorm Og (Mac Gilleasba' Chléirich), Ninth Chief and First Baronet

Speaking of the chiefs who lived in his own time, MacMhuirich, in the 'Black Book of Clan Ranald', mentions, among others, "John, son of Rory MacLeod of Harris; Lachlan, son of John Balbh MacKinnon; John Garbh MacGillechallum of Raasay; and Sir Donald Gorm, son of Gilleasbuig MacDonald, Lord of Sleat and Trotternish" – and the last he characterises as "a great courtier with King Charles" (MacBain, A & Kennedy, J, 1894, p. 175). Iain Lom, the Gaelic poet-laureate of Charles II, also mentions the estimation in which Sir Donald was held by royalty:

Do'ull Gorm bu ghlan gnùis,

 Donald Gorm of fair countenance,

Fear bu mhìn bha de 'n triùir,

 The smoothest of the three,

Cha bu chorr-cheann thu 'n cùirt,

 No dolt were you in court

Rìgh Tearlach.

 Of King Charles.

(Mackenzie, J, 1877, p. 52)

Sir Donald had been knighted, as we have seen, by James I in 1617, and such was the favour with which the king regarded him that he was raised to the rank of baronet in the year 1625, being designated 'of Nova Scotia' (Cameron, A, 1871, p. 72). As he was an ardent supporter of the Stuart line, and the bitter foe of Argyle, who led the Covenanters, he early showed his bias in the struggle of King Charles. Such was the trust reposed in him that, in 1639, he was made the king's Lieutenant in the Isles, with authority to suppress all those who might be disloyal to the crown. About this time he paid a visit to London and he made a highly favourable impression on the king.

In consequence of his loyalty to the Stuart cause, he was summoned before the Scottish Parliament in 1641 and was accused of treason to his country (*ibid.*, pp. 12–13). After suffering imprisonment for a short space, he was at length set at liberty; but he did not long enjoy his freedom, for he died in 1643.

At the time of his death, big things were adumbrated in the Highlands. From the commencement of the Civil War, King Charles had been in communication with the Earl of Antrim, who was himself a MacDonald, on the advisability of raising a large force of Irish that would act in conjunction with the Highlanders on the west coast of Scotland. After much deliberation, that project was agreed to and an army of at least 10,000 Irishmen was to be transported to the district of Morvern. There the command was to be assumed by Sir Donald of Sleat who was to raise his own men and as many of the other Highland clans as he could influence to join (*ibid.*, p. 73).

There was much enthusiasm in Skye about the coming of this force but, after many months of weary waiting, the expected army had not arrived, so that the war-ardour of the Skyemen began to cool.

At length, in 1644, the Irish contingent set sail. But instead of 10,000 it consisted of only 1500 men – a ruffianly band that, according to Patrick Gordon, himself a strong supporter of the Stuarts, was so degraded that, *"to them, there was no distinction between a man and a beast"*. This auxiliary force was under the command of Alexander MacDonald, better known as *'Alasdair MacCholla Chiotaich'* – a man of herculean proportions and of paramount courage, whose exploits made a deep impression on the imagination of his age. The contemporary bards, *Iain Lom* and Dorothy Brown, the poetess of Luing, sing his praises; the latter composed a meritorious panegyric on him.

The most reliable account we have of this expedition is to be found in the *'Black Book of Clan Ranald'*, where it is stated that the Irishmen landed in Morvern and, after they had seized the castles of Kinlochaline and of Mingarry, they made for Bernera of Kylerhea by the very difficult terrain that intervenes. Their ships sailed to *"Loch Eishort in the Strath, to Sir Donald Mac-Donald; for the King's and the Marquis of Antrim's orders were for him to take the command of the army and to take every man who would rise with him: but Sir Donald died half a year before that. Alasdair then offered the command to Sir James, the son of Sir Donald, but he refused it, for he thought the army too small since the whole kingdom was against him, he having only 1500 men, so that Alasdair came to the resolution of returning to Ireland."*

He was just weighing anchor in Loch Eishort, preparatory to quitting Scotland, when his small fleet was beset by three ships of war, sent by the 'Covenanting Parliament' to watch affairs in Skye. A short, sharp struggle ensued and the superior equipment of the Covenanting frigates soon gave them the advantage, so that the Irish force had no option but to ground their ships at the head of Loch Eishort in order to avoid capture. Thus, as *Mac-Mhuirich* naïvely puts it, *"MacDonald was obliged to remain in the kingdom into which he had come, whether he liked it or not."*

Concluding that it would be dangerous to remain any longer in Skye, MacDonald made for Kylerhea by Bealach Udal and, having crossed the narrows to the mainland, he succeeded at length in joining Glengarry. Thereafter his career is well known. His unique military skill won for him the rank of Major-General under Montrose, and his important services were recognised by the king, who raised him to the order of knighthood (MacBain, A & Kennedy, J, 1894, pp. 178–9). Of him, *Iain Lom* enthusiastically sings:

> *Cha b'e suid an siubhal cearbach*
> That was not the awkward expedition
> *A thug Alasdair do dh' Albainn;*
> That brought Alasdair to Scotland;
> *Creachadh, losgadh, agus marbhadh;*
> Foraying, burning and slaughter;
> *'S leagadh leis coileach Strathbhalgaidh.*
> And by him fell the Cock of Strathbogie.
>
> (Mackenzie, J, 1877, pp. 37–41)

Although Sir James MacDonald of Sleat declined to accept the command of the Irish troops, many of his clansmen fought under Montrose. They were present at Inverlochy, and also at Auldearn, where such a notable victory was won as a result of the brilliant leadership of Montrose and the bravery of *MacCholla Chiotach*, not to mention the treachery of the Convenanting leaders. The contingent from Skye, numbering about 400 men, and commanded by the chief's brother, Donald of Castleton, and Alexander MacDonald of Skerinish, remained with Montrose until the close of his brilliant career at Philiphaugh in the year 1645 (MacBain, A, & Kennedy, J, 1894, pp. 181–203).

CHAPTER VIII

Social Conditions, 1600–1650

Law and Order

The seventeenth century was ushered in to the accompaniment of great changes in the Isle of Skye and of these the most noteworthy was the cessation of clan warfare. A new outlook supervenes. Instead of having recourse to arms to settle their disagreements, the chiefs now submit their differences to courts of arbitration. The will to plunder and destroy had, to a large extent, subsided; and it must be admitted that much of that reformation in conduct was due to the exertions of King James I. It is a strange fact that that monarch was never so solicitous about the behaviour of the men of the Isles as when he crossed the Scottish border into England. Hitherto, his laxity in enforcing his commands had emboldened the more recalcitrant chiefs to disregard the royal authority, so that feuds and rebellions were frequent. Henceforth the establishment of order in the 'peccant region' of the Isles was, without a doubt, the object nearest his heart; and he set about its attainment in no uncertain manner.

The necessity of possessing charters for their lands had been driven home on the chiefs, and they had at length been persuaded that they could no longer afford to hold themselves aloof from, or act in independence of, the central authority of the state. Their change of attitude is seen in their eagerness to cut a figure at court – Sir Rory *Mór* of Dunvegan and Sir Donald MacDonald of Sleat go all the way to Edinburgh, and even to London, to visit their king and place their pleas before him. It is of interest to record that the former was given a licence by the king to travel out of Scotland and proceed to the English court whenever he chose, *"and none was to challenge him or pursue him"* (MacLeod, RC, 1938, p. 141).

The new viewpoint was induced principally through the 'Statutes of Iona' that had been approved of in 1608, and amended and confirmed in 1616, under the title of 'Regulations for Chiefs'. Many years were to elapse, however, before people had become accustomed to the new conditions and the 'Regulations' were often broken. This was to be expected, for, owing to the state of lawlessness that had previously existed in Skye as elsewhere in the Highlands, malcontents and criminals from all parts of Scotland made for the Western Isles and, when they failed to attach themselves to a chief, they formed piratical bands that were the scourge and the terror of the west. Vagabonds also, taking advantage of the spirit of hospitality that prevailed, flocked to the Isles, and proved to be a heavy drain on the resources of the people. By the Statutes of Iona, such 'sorners' were ordered to be placed in the stocks and, after that punishment, to be expelled the country.

These ruffianly idlers were, no doubt, responsible for much of the molestation to which fishermen who resorted to the coasts of Skye were subjected; but it must be added that the natives themselves were not wholly free from blame for many an outrage. Thus, in 1635, complaints were made by *"those of His Majesty's subjects who were engaged in fishing"* that the natives stole their fish, gear, victual, and "furniture", and letters of inhibition were issued against Sir Donald MacDonald of Sleat, John MacLeod of Dunvegan and others, warning these chiefs that it was incumbent on them to supply warrants to any that entered the lochs where fish was being pursued, unless they were prepared to hold themselves responsible for the conduct of such persons (Mackenzie, A, 1889, pp. 96–8).

A letter was written in 1631 by Charles I to the Privy Council in Scotland enquiring about the state of government in the Hebrides and the answer by John, Bishop of the Isles, is a document of great significance. The Bishop complains that there is no respect for the law among the inhabitants and that therefore it is impossible to make any headway either in religious or civil administration among them. He also adverts to the manner in which they flout the recent 'Regulations' and he points out that, despite numerous infringements, *"no punishment is ever inflicted on them"*.

Of the 'Statutes', that one which suffered most was the fifth. It aimed at the curtailment of the consumption of strong drink and we find that, in 1622, the Privy Council inserted a new regulation in that code, prohibiting masters of ships from selling wines to the peoples of the Western Isles in excess of the allowance fixed by law.

For the insatiable desire whereof the said Islanders are so far possessed that, when there arrives any ship there with wines, they spend both days and nights in their excess of drinking, so long as there is any of the wine left; so that, being overcome with drink, there falls out many inconveniences among them, to the break of His Majesty's peace.

(*ibid.*, p. 88).

The Church

We have already seen that the Protestant faith was professed in Skye as early as 1573 but, as a result of the transitionary phase that succeeded the Reformation, the Church and its affairs were much neglected. For many a year the fire of the new faith burned but low in Skye as in the rest of the Highlands, for none had arisen there with the enthusiasm of Hamilton, of Knox and the other Reformers, to fan it into a flame. No martyrs had been called upon to seal their beliefs with their blood and nothing, indeed, had been done to arouse the imagination of the people, who had been actuated in their conversion more by policy than by principle. They had discarded the old faith, but they failed to be influenced by the new. The churches were allowed to fall into a state of disrepair. Stipends were not regularly paid to the incumbents – were, indeed, sometimes withheld altogether – and there supervened a callous indifference to sacred things, so that we need not wonder at the prayer of Bishop Knox to the king to establish order among *"folk devoid of the true knowledge of God"*. Again in 1622, the same three chiefs, among others, are enjoined to build and repair their parish churches *"at the sicht of the Bishop of the Iles"* (Skene, WF, 1847, p. 122).

In this connection, the preface to the 'Statutes of Iona' furnishes a significant commentary on the position of the Church in the Isles at the beginning of the seventeenth century. It proceeds to state that

> *the great ignorance to which the chiefs, for the most part, themselves, but also the whole commonalty, have been, and are, subject to which is the cause of the neglect of all duty to God, to the great growth of all kinds of vice, proceeds partly from the lack of pastors and partly from the contempt for those already planted there. Now they agree that the pastors to be planted there are to be reverently obeyed, their stipends dutifully paid, the ruinous kirks, with reasonable diligence, to be repaired, the Sabbaths solemnly kept, adulteries and such vile slanders to be severely punished.*

That was in 1608 (Gregory, D, 1881, pp. 330–1).

In the following year a bond was signed by Donald *Gorm Mór*, Rory *Mór*, and Lachlan MacKinnon, among others, wherein they declare that they are to *"profess the true religion publicly taught within the realm of Scotland, and embraced by His Majesty and his estates, as the only and undoubted truth of God"* (Mackenzie, A, 1889, pp. 77–9).

Although the religion then *"publicly taught within the realm of Scotland"* was Presbyterianism, most, if not all, of the ministers of Skye belonged to the Episcopalian Church. One of the most notable of the clergy of that time was Rev. Neil MacKinnon, who, in 1627, had been presented to the parish of Strath. He was a nephew of Sir Lachlan MacKinnon, chief of his clan, and he was a graduate in Arts of the University of Glasgow, having been laureated there in the year 1625. He is said to have been the first minister in the island to dispense the sacrament according to the rites of the Protestant faith. His principal church was at Kilchrist in Strath, the successor of Ashaig, which was then in a ruinous condition. It is said that he was always dressed in the kilt, wearing that garb even when he was officiating in the pulpit, and carrying a sword. It appears that one Kenneth MacKenzie

ministered in the district of Sleat and the Small Isles, to which charge he had been presented by Andrew, Bishop of the Isles, in the year 1609. These two clergymen of Skye declared, in the year 1627, that they would surrender all the Papists in the Isles to the Clerk of the Council. When, about the year 1641, the church of Sleat became vacant, the Rev. Neil MacKinnon was presented to it, and he laboured there until 1661. In that year the parishes of Strath and Sleat were conjoined, and they continued as one charge until the year 1726, when Skye was divided into the seven parochial districts that have persisted to the present day. Mr MacKinnon was succeeded by Rev. Farquhar MacLennan, who had been translated thither from the district of Loch Broom, and he ministered in Strath until 1675 (Lamont, D, 1913, pp. 90–1).

In the year 1642 a notable event happened in the extensive parish of Snizort that then comprised the present parish of Portree. This was the induction of the Rev. Archibald MacQueen mentioned in the Presbytery Records of Dingwall in 1649, the first of a succession of ministers, son succeeding father without a break to the fourth generation, over a period of 145 years (Mackay, W, 1896, p. 155).

In the year 1609, one 'Allan O'Colgan', who is described as *"minister of Diurinish"*, was a witness to a contract of friendship entered into by Donald *Gorm Mór* and Rory *Mór* of Dunvegan (MacLeod, RC, 1938, pp. 47–8). The Rev. Hew MacSween, a graduate of Glasgow in 1597, was admitted minister to this district in 1626, and he was still there in 1643. He witnessed the contract of fosterage of Sir Norman of Bernera in October 1614 as *"Mr Eoghan Mac Suibhne, Ministear Dhiurinish"* (Skene, WF, 1890, p. 222). He had, as assistant, a *"reidar"* named "John MacCorkill", who officiated in the districts of Minginish and Bracadale also.

In the year 1632 the Rev. John MacKinnon who graduated in Glasgow University in 1620 was ordained by John Lesley, Bishop of the Isles, minister in Bracadale and Minginish. He officiated in the chapel of St. *"Assind"* near the head of Loch Caroy in the former, and in the latter, in the *"Kirk of Oynort in Menynes, dedicated to St. Malrube, called Kilmulruy"* (Innes, C, 1854, p. 357). He was succeeded by Lachlan Fraser.

In the report concerning the state of his diocese in 1626, by Thomas Knox, Bishop of the Isles, the amounts contributed by the chiefs of Skye towards the support of the church are given. The levy on Sir Donald MacDonald was 200 marks per annum; Sir Lachlan MacKinnon paid £50, while from the Chief of Dunvegan nothing had been received towards the funds of the church.

The Presbytery of Skye is mentioned for the first time in August 1642, when it was joined by the Assembly to the Synod of Argyll.

Education and Culture

As has already been said, we are dependent for almost all the facts we possess concerning the conditions of life in the Isles on the writings of Lowlanders. As these people did not understand the Gaelic language, and were out of sympathy with the manner of life then prevailing in the north, it is evident that we cannot derive much authentic information from their records to enable us to form an estimate of the true state of affairs. As is well known, George Buchanan described the Highlanders as *'Fures et latrones'* (thieves and robbers), while James I, in his *'Basilikon Doron'*, counsels his son, afterwards Charles I, to consider the Highlanders as *"mere wolves and bears"*. Again, in 1608, Bishop Knox, who was the president of Lord Ochiltree's Council, reports to the King that *"the Islemen are void of the true knowledge of God and are ignorant of your Majesty's laws"*. In the 'Regulations for Chiefs' occurs the statement:

The principal cause of barbarity, impiety, and incivility in the Isles has proceeded from the small care the chiefs and principal clansmen have had in the education and the upbringing of their children in virtue and learning. Careless of other duties, they keep their children still at home with them, where they see nothing in their tender years but the barbarous and ancient forms of the country; so that, when they come to years of maturity, they cannot be reclaimed, for incivility has been bred and settled in them, whereas, if they had been sent to the inland in their youth and trained in virtue and learning, and the English tongue, they would be the better prepared to reform their countries and reduce the same to godliness and civility.

(Gregory, D, 1881, pp. 304–5).

It is manifest that these observations are a travesty on the manner of life that obtained in the Highlands at that time; for the Lowlander, who was out of sympathy with the life of the people, and was ignorant of their language, concluded that the inhabitants of the north and west were wholly devoid of culture merely because they spoke a tongue other than English. Those in authority, therefore, were endued with the settled conviction that the cause of all the trouble in the Isles could be traced to the Gaelic speech and, accordingly, everything possible was done to uproot the offending tongue. In the 'Regulations for Chiefs' of 1616, it was enacted that

the vulgar Erse (Gaelic) language, which is one of the chief causes of the continuance of barbarity and incivility amongst the inhabitants of the isles, be abolished and removed.

(Gregory, D, 1881, pp. 394–5).

But proscribed tongues, like persecuted peoples, often thrive under duress; and that such was the case with Gaelic at this time we shall see when we come to deal with the poetry of the second portion of this century in Skye. Then a brilliant galaxy of bards arises, among whom may be mentioned Archibald MacDonald (*An Ciaran Mabach*), *Màiri ni'n Alasdair Ruaidh*, Roderick Morison (*An Clàrsair Dall*), and Lachlan MacKinnon (*Lachlainn Mac Thearlaich Oig*) .

That culture was not neglected is evident from the patronage that was extended to the bards. The MacBeathaigs, as bards to the MacDonalds, were succeeded by the MacRurys, otherwise *Clann a Bhàird,* who flourished about this time and, in virtue of their office, they possessed the district of *Achadh nam Bàrd*, in Trotternish. The works of these bards have practically all been lost, with the exception of some stray pieces by one, Duncan, of that name, that survive in the *Fernaig MS* (MacBain, A & Kennedy, J, 1894, p. 74). *Clann Mhic 'ille Riabhaich* are also said to have been hereditary bards to the MacDonalds in Kilmuir. Instance *Baile Mhic 'ille Riabhaich* ('farm town of the tribe of the Bridled Lad') held by them (see Adams, F, 1970, p. 313).

That the bards exerted a powerful influence on the minds of the people at that time is attested by the enactment in the 'Regulations for Chiefs', forbidding the encouragement of bards, who were included in the class of 'sorners'. It was decreed that they were to be punished in the stocks and after that, if they did not cease from composing, they were to be banished, for *"they defylit the haill isles"*. The reason for this was probably the custom of going on bardic rounds, from time to time, to the houses of the Great, a practice which had been in vogue from early times and continued, with much acceptance for many generations after that (Gregory, D, 1881, p. 393).

The bards sang the praises of those who won distinction in war and they extolled the virtues of courage and of chivalry. They were thus a potent moral force in the community, where they kept the lamp of learning alight, for they were the living repositories of the literature of the race. Knowing that their deeds would be extolled in song, men gave of their best and, fired with the hope of glory, they fought in deadly earnest in order to attract the attention of the bard and to win his approbation. We can imagine what pride Sir James MacDonald of Sleat would have taken in *Iain Lom's* panegyric, *A Bhean Leasaich an Stòp Dhuinn*, for the part he took in bringing to justice the murderers of the 'Children of Keppoch'; and what an incentive to emulate the prowess of their fathers the same author's *Latha Inbhir Lòchaidh* would be to the youth who listened to its triumphant notes in praise of the MacDonalds and its scathing ridicule of the vanquished men of Argyll! (Mackenzie, J, 1877, pp. 37 & 41).

The office of bard was hereditary and it was the duty of the father to dedicate and train one of his sons who showed the greatest talent, but preferably the oldest, to his own calling. There was thus often a long succession of poets who acted in the capacity of bard to a chief. We can at once perceive how such a practice would affect culture, for the bards made the poetry and the lore of their predecessors their province and they transmitted their knowledge to the following generation. When the Highland Society was engaged, towards the end of the eighteenth century, in its researches to discover how much of the Ossianic poetry then existed in the Highlands, there is in the report they issued a declaration by one, Lachlan *MacMhuirich*, son of Neil *MacMhuirich*, the last hereditary bard of that name to Clan Ranald, that he believed his father was the seventeenth in direct descent from *Muireach*, the first of his line (Watson, WJ, 1929, p. 139).

Like that of bard, the office of physician also was a hereditary one and the earliest members of that profession, of whom we have any record in Skye, were the MacBeths, or Beatons, or Bethunes. They are said by Cathelus *MacMhuirich* to have been a native race and nothing has arisen anent their history to confute that statement. There seems to be no doubt that they practised their calling under the regime of the Lords of the Isles. There was a long succession of them in Sleat where they acted as physicians to the MacDonalds. The family was held in high esteem both for the culture that distinguished it and for the marvellous proficiency they displayed in the practice of their profession (MacBain, A & Kennedy, J, 1894, p. 301).

This feature of their character has been crystallised into a proverb, for they are still referred to as:

> *Clann 'ic Bheatha a' ghnàth ghrinn,*
> MacBeths of the polished ways,
> *Luchd snaidheadh chnàmh is chuislean.*
> Men who slit bones and veins.

Further references will be made to this illustrious family when we come to deal with the septs of the island.

Mention should here be made of another race of physicians that arose in Skye at this time and was destined to bear a distinguished name through many generations. They were the MacLeans, the first of whom is said to have been brought from Ireland by Ronald *Hearach*, a cousin of Donald *Gruamach*, the fifth chief of the MacDonalds of Sleat. Lands were assigned to this family at Cuidreach on the west side of Trotternish, but their descendants were afterwards removed to Shulista and they held that township rent-free when they became physicians to the MacDonalds. Like the Beatons, they were noted for their wide and deep knowledge of botany and especially of the medicinal property of herbs. They wrote voluminously on the various branches of their profession and the last of them, Dr. John MacLean, was a highly accomplished man, as is attested by many a contemporary writer. He died in the year 1790 and, in addition to his having occupied the office of physician to the

MacDonalds, he acted also, for some time, in the capacity of chamberlain to that family for the district of Trotternish.

Music

From earliest times the harp held sway as the principal musical instrument. Commentators from those early times make frequent reference to the Highlanders' love of the Arts. Thus in the *Spottiswoode Miscellany* they are mentioned as *"great lovers of all manner of music and they have a good ear. They treat strangers with great civility"* (Maidment, J, 1845, p. 348). In the household of every chief the harper occupied an honourable place, while itinerant minstrels received as much patronage as was accorded to them elsewhere in Scotland at that time. They came even from Ireland, whither the chiefs sent their own musicians to be trained, and were often heard in the halls of the chiefs of Skye. In 'Cumha Mhic Leòid', Màiri ni'n Alasdair Ruaidh makes mention of these wandering harpers when she sings of Dunvegan, where:

> *Bu bhinn caismeachd sgeòil,*
> Sweet was the progress,
> *Aig luchd astair,*
> Of the travelling people,
> *Is ceòil na h-Eireann.*
> And the music of Ireland.
>
> (Watson, JC, 1934, p. 88)

The office of harper was continued in Skye until about the beginning of the eighteenth century, when the last, and certainly the most versatile of all our island harpists, Roderick Morison (*An Clàrsair Dall*) left Dunvegan for his native Lewis.

Towards the beginning of the sixteenth century, a serious rival to the harp, and one that was destined to supersede it, was introduced into Skye. This was the bagpipe and although few of the old bards make mention of it, there can be no doubt that it was in use even earlier than this time. Thus, one of the famous succession of family bards to the Clan Ranald, namely, *Niàll Mór Mac Mhuirich*, the son of Lachlan *Mór*, who exhorted the Highlanders with his war-songs on the field of Harlaw, has left a metrical account of the pipe that has fortunately been preserved. It is called by him *"Seannachas Sloinnidh na Pioba Bho Thùs"*, or *'History of the Descent of the Bagpipes from the Earliest Times'*, and it was composed about the middle of the fifteenth century. He traces the development of the instrument from the time when it consisted only of a chanter, mouthpiece, and one drone:

A' cheud mhàla nach robh binn,
    The first bag(pipe), that was not sweet,
Thainig bho thùs na Dilinn.
    Came from the beginning of the Flood.

⚜ ✸ ⚜

Cha robh 'nuair sin anns a' phiob,
    In the pipe there was only,
Ach sionnsair, agus aon liop,
    The chanter and one mouth-piece,
Agus maide, chumadh nam fonn,
    With a rod that harmonised with the music,
Do 'm b' ainm an sumaire.
    And was called the drone.
Tamull dhaibh na dheidh sin
    Some time thereafter
Do fhuair as-innleachd innleachd,
    A crude artifice led to an invention,
Agus chinnich na tri chroinn innt',
    And three drones developed,

Fear dhiubh fada, leobhar, garbh,
    One of them long, clumsy and rough,
Ri durdan reamhar ro shearbh.
    Droning coarsely and harsh.

(Mackenzie, J, 1877, p. 67)

It may be interesting here to record the bequest by Mr. R. Glen, F.S.A. (Scot.) of a set of Highland bagpipes to the Society of Antiquaries of Scotland, in the year 1911. The instrument, which bore the date 1409, consisted of a chanter, mouthpiece and the two small drones which were inserted in one stock, thus showing that the large drone had not then been introduced.

The MacCrimmons early rose to pre-eminence in the Highlands as exponents of this noble instrument but, since a sketch of the family is to be given at the end of this century, farther reference to them will be reserved till then.

What the MacCrimmons were to the MacLeods so, though in a lesser degree, were the MacArthurs in Trotternish, and the Macintyres in Sleat, to the MacDonalds. The MacArthurs claimed to have been pipers to the Lords of the Isles but although such an assertion is difficult to substantiate, as there is no record to show that the Lords of the Isles had ever employed bagpipe players, there may be something in the claim, in view of the facts that have been stated above.

Like the MacCrimmons, the MacArthurs also conducted a musical college but, in spite of professional jealousy and the pride of race, they did not consider it an indignity to seek from their great rivals the secret whereby the latter drew their magic music from the pipes. We know that Charles MacArthur, who is described by the traveller and author, Thomas Pennant, as a *"master of his instrument"*, had studied under *Padruig Og Mac Crimmon*. This family occupied Hungladder in Kilmuir rent free until the end of the eighteenth century; and it is noteworthy that in 1733 their holding was valued at 84 marks *"of silver duty"*.

Customs

Fosterage

One of the most interesting customs then, and during several succeeding ages, was that of fosterage. In effect, this practice meant that the child of a superior was handed over to a man of inferior rank to be maintained by the latter till the age of fourteen years in the case of a girl and seventeen in that of a boy. It was an honour that was assiduously coveted; for many a privilege accrued to the fosterer in virtue of his office, and principally that of protection both for himself and for his kindred. In the *National Manuscripts of Scotland*, No.84, part 3, 1872, there occurs a contract of fosterage for Sir Roderick *Mór* MacLeod dated 1614. His son Norman is contracted to John Mackenzie (John, son of Kenneth): the foster father to give four mares and the father to give three, the keeping of the mares to be with the foster father to put to increase for Norman. Witnesses Ewen MacSween, Minister of Durinish, Donald, son of Black Paul, John O'Colgan, Minister of Bracadale and Turlough O'Morisay (Skene, WF, 1890, p. 222).

In return for such advantages, the fosterparent had to provide some money, or its equivalent in stock, as soon as the contract was initiated; and this, *"with its increase"*, was to become the property of the foster-child on the expiry of his term of fosterage.

This bond of relation seems to have been stronger even than that of blood, as our Gaelic proverbs bear eloquent testimony, e.g., *"Is caomh le fear a charaid, ach is smior a chnàimh a chod-halta"* ('Beloved by a man is his friend, but as the marrow of his bone his foster–brother'), and *"Codhaltas gu ceud, 's càirdeas gu fichead"* ('Fosterage to a hundred, friendship to twenty degrees'). Of the services mutually rendered by persons in the relation of fosterage, we have numerous instances in the historical records of Skye and they all attest the fidelity and devotion that that relationship entailed. There is extant a notice of fosterage between John MacLeod of Dunvegan (*Iain Mór*) and the Rev. Neil MacKinnon, who was minister of Strath and Sleat. The fosterling was afterwards the famous *Iain Breac* MacLeod, the patron of the arts, and the generous chief. The date of the contract is 1638. By it MacLeod engages to lay aside a sum of 600 merks, the amount of which is to be his son's portion when the fosterage ends, while MacKinnon undertakes to *"foster, maintain, and upbring the said John in the fear of God and with God's assistance to save him from fire, water and all such accidents which may ensue"* (MacLeod, RC, 1938, p. 120).

Manrent

There was another custom that bore a certain resemblance to fosterage, and it was termed 'manrent'. This was an undertaking between two parties, one of whom sought the protection of another more powerful than himself, and, in return for that privilege, the inferior promised to serve his protector with the full strength of his clan by land and sea. The contract entered into by the former was the true Bond of Manrent while the obligation binding the latter was distinguished as the Bond of Maintenance. Out of many such documents that are concerned with Skye, the following is singled out. It was drawn up in the year 1601 between Archibald, the seventh Earl of Argyle, and Lachlan MacKinnon of Strath. It begins by commenting on the age-long friendship that had existed between Argyle and the MacKinnons and it proceeds to state that those party to the contract henceforth wish to continue in a state of friendship. Accordingly, Argyle promises *"to protect, maintain and defend the said Lachlan MacKinnon and his dependents"*, as he would those of his own kindred; and, in return, MacKinnon binds himself to serve Argyle *"as his master and protector"*.

Calpa (In Scots; Herezeld)

Calpa was the name given to the exaction demanded of a vassal by his superior for the privilege of protection for himself and his family. It was the custom, on the death of his vassal, for the chief to take his choice of the horses or of the cows of the deceased. The practice naturally lent itself to great abuse, for it was no uncommon thing for more than one superior to lay claim to calpa and to take it willy-nilly from the dead man's relatives. The custom had been abolished in the south of Scotland as early as 1510 by King James IV, but it lingered on in the Highlands until, by the 'Regulations for Chiefs' of 1616, it was decreed that it was to end. The clause is as follows:

> *His Majesty's lieges have sustained great skayth these many years by the chiefs of clans within the Highlands and Isles of his kingdom, by taking from them, their children and executors, after their decease, under the name of caulpes, of their best aucht whether it be ane mare or horse, or cow, alleging their predecessors to have been in possession thereof for maintaining and defending them against their enemies.*

(Gregory, D, 1881, p. 397).

In spite of this regulation, the practice was continued in Skye for many generations after this. The Rev. John MacKinnon, who wrote *The Second Statistical Account for Strath'* in 1841, says that *"until recently the custom of the laird to take the best horse from a tenant's farm, on the death of the occupier, was observed"* and an account is given of the reason why the custom was abolished. On the death of a tenant in Strath, the ground officer went, as was usual in such circumstances, to the widow's house and demanded the best horse. The widow vainly resisted and was roughly treated by the proprietor's functionary. She pronounced a curse on him and vowed vengeance through her infant son who was then but a year old. Seventeen years had elapsed, when the same official had occasion to perform a similar service in a neighbouring township where he also maltreated the defenceless widow. News of the outrage came to the ears of *Dunnachadh Mór*, the son of that widow who had suffered at the hands of the laird's instrument seventeen years previously; and the young giant rose, pursued the officer, and, when he overtook him, battered him so savagely that he killed the man. He then cut off his head, washed it in *Tobar a' Chinn*, and presented it at the laird's gate. When the whole story was told the young man was pardoned and it is said that he was appointed ground-officer for the district in succession to the man he had killed.

Another imposition on tenants, holding more than one eighth of a davoch, was the exaction by the chief of a horse or a cow on succession to property. This was called Herezeld and was in practice until about 1710 (see *Regulations of the Privy Council*, viii, 334).

The customs observed at birth and at baptism deserve mention here. The belief prevailed in that age, and even for many generations after it that a child left unattended was always in danger of being kidnapped by fairies, who left one of their own kind in the cradle in its place. The changeling invariably proved to be most refractory in behaviour and troublesome in every way; so that the utmost precaution was taken to guard the human offspring and to carry out the customary rites that would ensure its immunity from the attention of the 'little folk'. It was therefore considered necessary to walk round the mother and the babe with a burning peat or a piece of flaming pine seven times in the morning and as often in the evening, until the child was baptised.

On the way to the church for the ceremony of baptism, cakes of bread were taken ('*bonnaich Bhaistidh*'), pieces of which were served to all who might be met on the way. If several children were to be baptised at the same time, precedence was always given to the boys, for it was held that if a girl were baptised before all the boys had been attended to, she would grow a beard when she attained womanhood. After the baptism was over and the parents had returned home, the ceremony of purification was performed. In this, the practice was to fill a basket with bread, hang it to the pot-chain and transfer the child over it seven times from the arms of the parents, who stood on opposite sides of the fire-place (Henderson, G, 1911, pp. 208–11).

Marriages

Records of marriage contracts, as we know them now, are very rare in the Western Isles until after the middle of this century. The form of marriage commonly in vogue before that time was that termed 'Handfast', or left-handed marriage. It was purely a probationary union in which a couple agreed to cohabit for a year and a day; and, if during that time they discovered they were not suited to one another by temperament or otherwise, they were free to dissolve the contract at the expiry of the customary period, with this obligation, however, that the man was to maintain any offspring of the union and return whatever portion the 'trial' wife might have brought him. Should the partners, however, decide to continue in wedlock beyond the prescribed period, the marriage was held to be legally binding, and any children born previous to the final agreement were to be considered legitimate.

Martin, a Skyeman, who wrote about 1693, makes mention of this form of marriage, as follows:

> It was an ancient custom in the Isles that a man take a maid to his wife and keep her for the space of a year without marrying her; and if she pleased him all the while, he married her at the end of the year and legitimatised her children; but if he did not love her, he returned her to her parents.

(Martin, M, 1716, p. 114).

We have already seen that this manner of union led to one of the most disastrous wars ever fought between the MacLeods and the MacDonalds of Skye, when Donald *Gorm Mór* who handfasted with Margaret MacLeod, a sister of Rory *Mór* of Dunvegan, expelled his mistress so ignominiously from Duntulm. It is, indeed, not improbable that it was as a result of this war that Lord Ochiltree's Committee was induced to insert a clause in the Statutes of Iona by which *"marriages contracted for several years"* were prohibited; and any who might disregard this regulation were to be *"punished as fornicators"* (Gregory, D, 1881, p. 331).

It is not easy to say how soon after this the practice of handfasting fell into desuetude in Skye, but from our knowledge of the way the other sections of the Statutes were infringed, we are led to conclude that this one also was *"more honoured in the breach than the observance"*.

Manner of Living and Habits of the People

So far as food was concerned, enough could be raised locally to supply the ordinary needs of the people. Indeed, the only article they did import was wine and a brisk trade it then proved to be in the Western Isles. The trafficking in the wines of France and Spain began about the middle of the sixteenth century; but until its last decade the people of Skye were fairly temperate. Soon, however, the love of strong drink was to seize gentle and semple alike, and great excesses were the result. In the 'Regulations for Chiefs' issued in 1616, mention is made of the lawlessness and the misery that followed from this inordinate indulgence in intoxicating liquors. It asserts that

> The great and extraordinary excesses in drinking wines, commonly used among the commons and tenants of the Isles, is not only one

occasion of the beastly and barbarous cruelties and inhumanities that fall out among them, to the offence and the displeasure of God and the contempt of law and justice, but with that it draws numbers of them to miserable necessity and poverty.

(*ibid.*, p. 395).

If the voice of tradition and the written records speak true, we are forced to the conclusion that this account of the state of affairs is not overdrawn. We have already referred to the drunken orgies that marked the close of the war known as '*Cogadh na Cailliche Caime*', and also to the large amount of debt incurred by Sir Rory *Mór* solely for strong drink. We need not wonder at the enactment, passed in 1616, restricting the consumption of wine in his household to "*four tuns per annum to be bought from the south*"; but this regulation was never observed and a similar disregard was paid to the edict, passed in 1622, by the Privy Council, aimed at those masters of ships who smuggled wines into the Western Isles.

In an interesting song said to have been composed by his nurse to Donald *Gorm Mór*, in praise of a *birlinn* or galley the chief had constructed, she extolls the luxurious equipment of that noble ship (*Bards of Clan Donald*).

Tha stiuir òir oirr',
> She has a golden rudder,
Tri cruinn sheilich,
> Three masts of willow,
Gu'm bheil tobar fiona,
> A well of wine
Shios 'na deireadh;
> Down in the stern
'S tobar fior-uisg',
> And a well of pure water

'S a' cheann eile.
> In the other end.

(Watson, WJ, 1932, p. 247)

It is a lengthy poem; and in it references are made to the recreations that were then in vogue, throwing a flood of light on the home life of that age. The poetess adverts to the practice of tale-telling, the music of the pipe and the harp, the joy of the dance, indoor games with draughts, dice, and cards; outdoor sports, such as leaping, wrestling, football, etc. but there is no mention of shinty:

Gu'm bi mire, cluich is gàire,
> There will be mirth, sport and laughter,
Bualadh bhrog, leòis air deàrnaibh,
> Tapping of feet and raising blisters on hands,
Bidh sud is iomairt, hò! air tàileasg,
> There will be there, hò! playing draughts,
Air na cairtean breaca, bàna,
> And playing white speckled cards,
'S air na disnean geala, cnàmha.
> And on the white bone dice.

Bidh sud mar ghnàths ann, ceòl, is seanchas,
> The practice of music and of recitation,
Piòb, 's clàrsach, àbhachd, is dannsa.
> The pipe, the harp, jollity and dancing.

Bidh deanamh chleasa leat, da chiad diag;
> At sport there, will be twelve hundred with you;

Bidh iomairt a' bhuill choise leat, da chiad
And a like number at football.

diag.
(ibid.)

In the *Duanaire*, p. 140, there is a poem, *Pòsadh MhicLeòid*, 'Macleod's Marriage', (wrongly ascribed to *Màiri n'in Alasdair Ruaidh*) which has much in common with the foregoing, even whole couplets being identical. In it reference is made to Marjory MacIntosh, third wife of *Do'ull Gorm Mór*: *'Mairearad chrìdhe Nic an Toisich, is bliadhna an seachdain 'on a phòs thu'* ('Beloved Margaret MacIntosh the week since your wedding seems a year'), and also to the incarceration of Donald *Gorm Mór* in the Castle of Blackness:

> *gun do thriall a mod air*
>> that the court went against him
> *... 's gun do ghlas na Gaoill e 'n seomar*
>> and the Lowlanders imprisoned him

(MacMhuirich, D, 1868, p. 140)

Trade

In the early part of the seventeenth century there was great abundance of fish around the shores of Skye, especially herring, cod and ling. The natives, however, derived little benefit from this source of wealth, for the enterprising among them cared little for the industry and, in any case, their methods of catching the fish were inadequate and crude. A rich harvest was, however, garnered from our sea lochs by fishers who hailed from the east coast of Scotland and even from Holland and it seems they made enormous profits during the period from 1620 until 1640.

If we are to take the numerous proclamations issued by the Privy Council at their face value, there can be no doubt that those engaged in the fishing industry were often subjected to grievous molestation by the men of Skye. In 1622 the three chiefs, Rory *Mór*, Donald *Gorm Og* and Lachlan MacKinnon, were sternly warned by the Privy Council to cease from troubling the strangers who fished around their shores and, in 1634, a Commission was appointed, under Lord Lorne and the Bishop of the Isles, to inquire into the allegations made regarding the heavy duties that were exacted from fishermen – *"to the great prejudice of the king's subjects when fishing in the Isles"*.

This Commission seems to have done its work very thoroughly and, among others, the chiefs of Skye were cited to present themselves at Inverarary, in order to give evidence. All obeyed, except MacKinnon, for whom deputised Lachlan Mac-Charles MacFingon.

They were severally questioned by what authority they imposed fines on fishermen who plied their trade in Skye and their answer was that they were within their rights, as heritors of land, to exact ground-leave and anchorage, *"it being the ancient custom, and in use to be done past the memory of man"*. They further state that the amount of the dues exacted before 1620 for specified items was as follows: For every anchor laid on shore they charged 6s 8d; for ground-leave they demanded one barrel of ale or of meal, according to the occupier's option, and £3 for every last (12 barrels) of herrings taken, together with the whole of Saturday's fishing.

After the year 1620, however, in accordance with a contract concluded with the fishermen themselves, the contribution agreed upon was 36s per boat employed during the whole year, and 20s if they were engaged in winter fishing only.

Still, the relation between the fishermen and the natives was seldom very cordial. A proclamation was issued in 1635 drawing the attention of the chiefs of Skye to the *"great insolences committed on fishers by the islanders in bands who go to the lochs where the fishing is carried on and rob the men of fish, victual, and gear, break shoals of herrings and hinder them in their industry"* (Mackenzie, A, 1889, pp. 96–8).

It was about the end of this period that the traffic in cattle-dealing was established in Skye. It had been initiated by the enterprise of the warrior-bard, *Do'ull Mac Iain 'ic Sheamuis*. This pioneer of an important industry took numerous droves to Falkirk and to Crieff, and thus was established a trade that was destined to be the principal source of wealth in the island for many generations.

Indeed, it seems that Skye was then in the enjoyment of a remarkable measure of prosperity. Clan warfare had ceased and its attendant evils, such as reiving and the burning of crops, were no longer to be dreaded. The peasant could now cultivate the soil in the confidence that nothing but adverse weather conditions could interfere with the garnering of his crops and the industry of cattle-rearing could be safely developed, for there was no longer any fear of the creach (foray).

Agriculture

No great change falls to be recorded in the methods of tillage or in the nature of the crops that were then reared in Skye. Root crops had not yet made their appearance and only cereals, such as oats, barley and rye were grown. Arable land was still held on the communal basis and the runrig system was the vogue. By it each individual in a *tuath* or community, had to take whatever plot was allotted to him by the maor or ground officer who apportioned the fields once a year.

Tillage was effected by means of the spade and although many have declared that the caschrom, or the crooked spade, was not introduced until the advent of the potato, there can be no doubt that it was in use at this time, however long before. In the poem, *B' annsa Cadal air Fraoch*, by '*An Ciaran Mabach*', the brother

of Sir James MacDonald of Sleat, and who lived in this period, reference is made to the implement:

> …*Uiginnis riabhach,*
> > Brindled Uiginish,
> *An tric a dh'iarr mi 'n damh-donn,*
> > Where often I sought the dun stag,
> *'S a bhi triall thun nam bodach,*
> > And visited old men,
> *Dha'm bu chosnadh chaschrom.*
> > Who plied the crooked spade.

(Mackenzie, J, 1877, p. 53)

In order to replenish the soil, the chief manures in use were the smoke-saturated thatch, cattle bedding and the ashes of the peat fires. The last was considered of great potency, especially on peaty soil, and the method by which it was spread on the land was comical in its primitiveness. According to the authors of '*Clan Donald*', a creel filled with ashes was carried pick-a-back by a woman, while her husband, travelling light, walked leisurely behind her, hitting the laden creel the while with a stout cudgel and sending clouds of dust around with every vigorous stroke.

The comedy of this method of manuring, which seems to have been confined to the west side of Trotternish, roused the satirical faculty of a native of the east side, who derisively described the custom in the following quatrain:

> *Am fasan a bh'ac' ann an Uige,*
> > The habit they practised in Uig,
> *Chan fhaca' mi riamh am dhùthaich,*
> > I never saw in my country,
> *Gabhail le bat' air mo chulaibh,*
> > Striking at my back with a stick,

'*S smùid as a' chliabh luatha.*
　And clouds from the ash creel.

(oral tradition)

Owing to the boom in cattle-dealing that had then set in, the native black cattle were reared in large numbers on the straths and the hills of Skye. As an indication of the magnitude of the herds, we may instance a dowry conferred by Sir Rory *Mór* of Dunvegan on one of his daughters, *Moire*, who was married to John MacDonald of Moidart. It consisted of *"nine score good ky, with twenty others, if the said John shall desire them and a galley of 24 oars and three sets of oars and sails"* (MacLeod, RC, 1938, p. 53).

Large droves of cattle from Skye were sold every year in the markets of the Lowlands and more money then circulated in the island than ever before. As a result of the enhanced price of cattle, the value of land appreciated in proportion, so that tacksmen had to pay a higher rental for the land they occupied.

It may be mentioned that there were notable tacksmen then in Skye, as the MacAskills of *Rubh' an Dunain*, the MacDonalds of Kingsburgh, of Skerinish and of Castleton of Sleat, the MacLeods of Talisker, of Drynoch, of Gesto, etc.; the Nicolsons of Scorrybreck; the MacQueens of Garrafad; the Martins of Bealach and the MacSwans of Roag.

Weapons

The commonest weapon was still the bow. Numerous references are made to it by the poets of this period, and it continued in use for a considerable time after this. In the exhortation by *Iain Lom* addressed to Sir James MacDonald of Sleat on the murder of the 'Children of Keppoch', that famous poet says:

Bidh an t-iubhar 'ga lùbadh,
　The bows will be bent,
Aig do fhleasgaichean ùra,
　By your fresh youths,
Dol a shiubhal nan stùc-bheann,
　As they traverse the mountain peaks,

(Mackenzie, J, 1877, p. 37)

the bows being made of yew.

The sword and the lance, or pike, were also in use, while a crude sort of arquebuse had then found its way to Skye, and would seem to have been fairly common. In a quern-song composed by *Do'ull Mac Iain 'ic Sheamuis,* we find the verse:

Cha b'e deatach dhubh 'n dùdain,
　It was not the fume of the mill dust,
Chleachd thusa bhi 'n tùrlach t' athar;
　That you were accustomed to in your father's establishment
Ach fir òga losgadh fùdair,
　But young men burning gun-powder,
Ri mire, ri mùirn, 's ri aighear;
　With merriment, joy and gaiety;

(MacDonald A & A, 1911, p. 34)

and the Uist bard, '*An Ciaran Mabach*', says:

Cha leig mi mo ghaothar,
　I shall not release my hound,
Ri faoghaid an tuim bhàin,
　To hunt the white hill,
'*S cha sgaoil mi mo luaidhe,*
　And I shall never again spread lead,

An Gleann Ruathain gu bràth,
   In Glen Ruathan,

                   (Mackenzie, J, 1877, p. 53)

thus showing clearly that firearms were then in use in Skye.

And we have corroborative evidence in the record of a meeting held at Duntulm in the year 1628, when the island chiefs, John MacLeod of Dunvegan, Sir Donald MacDonald of Sleat, Sir Lachlan MacKinnon of Strath and Alexander *Mac Gille Chaluim* of Raasay, together with the Earl of Seaforth, assembled there, in order to devise means for preventing poaching on their respective estates. An order was issued that no one was to hunt with hound, bow or hagbut, unless he was in possession of a licence from his chief; and it is interesting to note that the game to be preserved were the hart, hind, roe, and doe *"and any other beasts in the forest"*. Anyone found trespassing was to surrender his weapons to the forester and was to be, *"punished in his body as his superior pleases"*. That the chiefs took a serious view of poaching and were determined to stamp it out is shown by the severity of the punishment they decreed for the first offence. A fine of 100 marks was to be imposed on any who was caught 'in the act', and his weapons and his hounds were to be forfeited. Witnesses to the order were, among others, William MacLeod of Talisker, John MacKenzie of Fairburn and John Nicolson and John Ros, notars (Skene, WF, 1847, pp. 190–3).

Such weapons as swords and guns were made by the hereditary armourers of the chiefs. The MacRurys of *Baile Ghobhain*, in Kilmuir, acted in that capacity to the MacDonalds while the MacLeods of Suardal performed similar services to the chiefs of Dunvegan. The work of these armourers was of a very high order and the designs they engraved on the weapons showed great artistic skill.

CHAPTER IX

Family History, 1650–1700

The MacDonalds

Sir James Mór, Tenth Chief and Second Baronet

We have seen that a large contingent of the MacDonalds were fighting under Montrose during the Great Civil War. After the defeat of the Royalists on the field of Philiphaugh, in 1645, a large part of the Highland army deserted. In the following year Charles, the son of the late king, was crowned at Scone and he received the enthusiastic support of the Scottish Convenanters. Sir James MacDonald was forthwith commanded to raise his men, as were the other chiefs of Skye and he readily responded to the summons; but it would appear that he himself took no active part in the affair and, like the MacLeods, the MacDonalds marched into England with the Covenanting army, but without their chief. At Worcester, on the 3rd of September, 1651, the Highland Brigade had to bear the full brunt of the onslaught of Cromwell's forces and the clans were severely cut up and scattered in hopeless flight. In small bands and by devious ways the fugitive Skyemen made their way home, after having endured months of terrible hardship. Those who were taken prisoners in the battle were consigned as slaves to the plantations of America.

When once the disaffection to his government had somewhat subsided, Cromwell displayed a great amount of forbearance towards the Highlanders who had taken up arms against him; and whether it was the magnanimous spirit shown by the Protector that appealed to him, or the fear of reprisals that actuated him, Sir James was soon busy trying to win favour with the Commonwealth. In this he succeeded; and we find that in 1653 he went so far as to write a letter from Duntulm apprising Colonel Fitch, the governor of the Castle at Inverness, of the activities of Glengarry and other Highland chiefs to coerce him to rise in rebellion and he received the commendation of the government for his loyalty at a time when many of the Highland chiefs were still in open revolt.

In view of his compliance with the Republican party, it was but natural that he should be moved with deep concern when the Restoration took place and it says much for his acumen and ingratiating ways that he succeeded so well with the Royalist government as he did. Within a year of the accession of Charles II he had managed to secure confirmation of the charter that had been granted to his grand-uncle, Donald *Gorm Mór*, in 1614 while in 1665 the Royalist government armed him with a *"commission of fire and sword"* against the murderers of the heir of Keppoch and his brother. He carried out this behest with alacrity, though at first he was loth to take action, as is indicated in several places in the works of the bard, *Iain Lom, e.g.:*

> *Sir Seumas nan tùr 's nam baideal,*
>> Sir James of the towers and battlements,
> *Gheibh luchd mùirne cuirm 'na d'aitreabh;*
>> Joyful people will feast in your halls;
> *Ged a rinn thu 'n dùsal cadail,*
>> Though you showed drowsiness of sleep,
> *'S éibhinn leam do dhùsgadh maduinn.*
>> A delight to me was your morning awakening.
>>> (Mackenzie, J, 1877, p. 39)

A strong force of the MacDonalds, under the command of the versatile Archibald MacDonald (*'An Ciaran Mabach'*), the chief's half-brother, and the redoubtable *Do'ull Mac Iain 'ic Sheamuis*, was despatched to Inverlaraich in Lochaber, where they soon brought the usurpers to justice. A special letter of thanks was sent to Sir James by the Privy Council acknowledging *'the singular service he had done to his country, and assuring him that it would not pass unrewarded'*, with many other clauses much to Sir James' honour.

Sir James added the supporting leopards to the family coat-of-arms that *Iain Lom* has so skilfully described in verse:

> *B'e do shuaicheantas taitneach,*
>> Your fitting armorial is,
> *Long is leomhann is bradan,*
>> The ship, the lion and the salmon,
> *Air cuan liobharra 'n aigeal;*
>> On the smooth waves of the sea,
> *'S an crann figuis gun ghaiseadh,*
>> And the fig tree without blemish,
> *Chuireadh fion dheth le pailteas;*
>> Yielding wine in plenty,
> *Làmh dhearg roimh 'n ghaisgeach nach tiom.*
>> The Red Hand before the stout hearted hero.
>>> (Mackenzie, J, 1877, p. 37)

This chief was noted for his prudence – *"a man of very great ability and judgment"*, he was characterised by the government of Cromwell; and for a time the affairs of the clan, under his peaceful rule, were in a flourishing condition. In later life, however, he began to frequent the cities of the south and there he entertained on a lavish scale. Numerous guests visited at Duntulm, and at Armadale, where all was gaiety and unfailing generosity:

> *'Nàm gluasad bho tir dhuinn,*
>> When moving from land,
> *Bu neomhiodhoir ar lòistean,*
>> Not mean would be our hospitality,
> *Cornach, cupanach, fionach,*
>> Drinking horns and cups of wine,
> *Glaineach, liontaidh a stòpaibh,*
>> Filled from flagons,

(Mackenzie, J, 1877, p. 56)

sings *'An Ciaran Mabach'* of his brother's munificence.

In 1834 he was a student of Glasgow University – *'Jacobus Primogenitus Donaldii MacDonaldi de Sleatt'* and, in the previous year his father, Sir Donald, gave £100 towards the funding of the University and Library.

It seems, however, that this extraordinary liberality had plunged the estate deeply in debt and it led to domestic troubles that caused much anxiety to the clan. Quarrels between the chief and his oldest son became so acute as to induce the wadsetters to threaten the deposition of the one and to refuse to recognise the other as heir. The execution of this decision was, however, obviated by the death of Sir James in 1678.

He was married, first, to Margaret MacKenzie of Tarbat. By her he had a large family, of whom the following are known to history: Donald, his successor; Hugh of Glenmore, John of Bernisdale, Somerled of Sartil, and James of Aird, in Sleat. The chief's second wife was Mary, the sister of *Iain Breac* MacLeod of Dunvegan; and by her he had a son, John of Balconie, whose daughter, Elizabeth, became the wife of the Rev. Hugh MacDonald, the first minister of the parish of Portree.

Three very touching elegies were composed on his death – one by the Lochaber bard, *Iain Lom*, and two others by his own devoted brother, Archibald, *'An Ciaran Mabach'*. One verse from the lament of the latter is quoted because of the mellifluence of its diction, the genuineness of its feeling, and its elegant and beautifully fashioned phrase:

> *O na chaill mi mo fhradharc*
> > Since I lost my eyesight
> *Is nach tadhail mi 'n ard-bheinn,*
> > And I cannot frequent the high ben,
> *Chuir mi cul ris an fhiadhach,*

> I abandoned the deer hunt
> *Pong cha'n iarr mi air clàrsaich;*
> > And I do not wish a tune on the harp,
> *Mo cheol laighe, is éirigh,*
> > My music at lying and rising
> *'M osnadh gheur air bheag tàbhachd,*
> > My wakeful bitter sigh,
> *Fad mo ré bi mi 'g acain*
> > All my days I shall be mourning,
> *Mheud 's a chleachd mi de d'-àilgheas.*
> > All I tasted of your pleasure.

(Mackenzie, J, 1877, p. 55)

It may be of interest to note here the statement made by the Sleat sennachie, Hugh MacDonald, who flourished at this time, and has left on record a useful and reliable history of Clan Donald, that *"the family of Sleat can produce a paper signed by all the principal men of the name* (MacDonald), *wherein they acknowledge, as head of the family, MacDonald of Sleat"*.

In the Regulations of the Great Seal occurs the note: "charter to John Earl of Middletoun, Lord Clearmont and Fettercairn and his heirs and assignees, the twenty pound lands of the old extent in Slait … the two mark lands of Armydillis in Slait, the ten penny lands of Kilibaxter in Trouterness and all the other lands in Trouterness which belonged to James MacDonald of Slait and Donald, his eldest son, and all the manor places, buildings, mills, woods etc. similarly the lands of Leuduct, Chylis, Yle Ornsay, Castle Chanish, Kilmure in Slait, Tinshell, the little and meikle Crosswaik, the Ord of Slait, the Aird of Slait, Dunskaith, Glenroy, Ostaik, Altva all in the £20 lands of the old extent or in other of the above mentioned lands; the town and lands of Kilmalive and Scousorie, Messoun, Camastinanake, Portray, Hoall, Belnaskittach, Kilmuir, Knockbay, Laybost, Coudroch and Erask, Coulinknock, Scourabrek and Duntallan, Findfort, the small towns and shielings thereof, Grunstatt, Kyllest, Glentininstone, Glenronisle, Glenhalthin and Rig with all the manors, grassums, woods and fishings, patronage of churches, which tiends and other subjects belonging to James Macdonald and his eldest son and, on the 15th of February last, apprised from them at the instance of John, Lord Middletoune for payment to him of 85,785 marks of principal and 4289 marks of Sheriff's fees, one sasine being sufficient at the manor place of Duntallin or elsewhere" (Stevenson, JH, 1984, p. 453).

The MacLeods

In order to record the contemporary history of the MacLeods, it is necessary to go back to the year 1649, when John (*Iain Mór*) the chief of Dunvegan, died and left as his heir a minor who was afterwards known as Roderick, 'the Witty'. The office of tutor, or regent, devolved on the late chief's oldest brother, Roderick of Talisker.

We have seen that Charles Stuart was crowned at Scone in 1650, and that the Covenanting Parliament called all Scotland to his support. The MacLeods answered the call with enthusiasm; over 700 of the men of Skye were marshalled on the gathering ground of the clan, *Lag Buidhe*, in Balmeanach. Thence they marched south, exhilarated by the stirring strains of the *piobaireachd* of *Pàdruig Og* MacCrimmon. They were joined by 300 of the men of Harris, under the leadership of Norman of Bernera and the combined force, now 1000 strong, followed the young king in the disastrous march into England. At Worcester no clan suffered so severely as the MacLeods, and so great were their casualties that it was agreed to exempt them from military service for several years, in order that the clan might be able to recuperate. It is said that about 700 of them were slain, among whom were two of the sons of MacLeod of Meadle, namely, William and Alexander (MacLeod, RC, 1927, pp. 153–4). Many of those

taken prisoner were shipped to servitude in the West Indies, and an interesting letter of discharge, for Angus MacQueen, from a prison in Barbados is preserved in the Muniments at Dunvegan (MacLeod, RC, 1938, p. 112). *Màiri ni'n Alasdair Ruaidh* refers to the part the MacLeods played in one of her songs, *Fuaim an t-Taibh*, when she says:

> *Bha fios cò sibh,*
> > It was known who you were,
> *Ann an iomartas rìgh,*
> > In the King's conflicts most tragic,
> *'Nuair bu mhuladach strì Theàrlaich.*
> > When Charles' struggle was most bitter.
> > > (Watson, JC, 1934, *p. 48*)

Roderick of Talisker who was knighted before the battle, succeeded, after many hardships and romantic adventures, in making his escape to Skye, but his brother, Norman, was captured, tried for his life but acquitted owing to a technical error in the indictment. After an incarceration of eighteen months, he managed to make good his escape but the harshness of his treatment helped only to intensify his ardour for the Royalist cause. He served on several dangerous embassies, to Prince Charles in Paris, to the King of Denmark and to the Dutch Government, which entrusted him with the commission of taking to Scotland a large consignment of much-needed arms and ammunition and he successfully carried out the project. These exploits of his no doubt led his panegyrist to refer to him as:

> *...Sealgair na frìth*
> > Hunter of the forest
> *Nach bu chearbach do'n righ,*
> > Who was invaluable to the King,
> *Agus seirbhiseach dìleas a' chrùin.*

And a fruitful servant of the Crown.

(Watson, JC, 1934, p. 98)

The Highlanders rose once again in 1654, but, owing to the incapacity of their generals, they could not entertain much hope of victory.

The end of the insurrection came when, on 26th July, 1654, the clans, under General Middleton, were signally defeated by General Morgan at Loch Garry. Thence many of the chiefs repaired to Dunvegan, whither they were escorted by Norman of Bernera (Mackenzie, A, 1889, p. 101).

Norman of Bernera

It was to this romantic personage that *Màiri ni'n Alasdair Ruaidh* composed most of her songs, and not to a chief of MacLeod, as has been erroneously stated by MacKenzie in *The Beauties of Gaelic Poetry*. It is worthy of notice that the bardess often styles her hero 'Sir'; but, as is well known, no chief of Dunvegan was ever knighted with the exception of Sir Rory *Mór*, who died in 1626. Such of her poems as *Fuaim an t-Taibh, An Talla 'm bu Ghnàth le MacLeòid, Cumha Mhic Leòid*, and *Luinneag Mhic Leòid* – all have as their subject Sir Norman of Bernera.

Sir Norman was the kind of man that was bound to impress an unsophisticated race. He was blessed with great personal beauty, princely generosity, a gallant bearing and he was endowed with a lofty purpose and a staunch integrity of conduct – qualities to which admirable expression is given by the poetess of Dunvegan:

Fear do chéille, 's do ghliocais,
    One of thy prudence, thy wisdom
Do mhisneach, 's do mheanmain,
    Thy courage and thy spirit,
Do chruadail, 's do ghaisge,

One of thy hardihood and valour,
Do dhreach, is do dhealbha,
    Thy mien and thy mould
Agus t'-fholachd, is t'-uaisle,
    Thy courage and thy nobility,
Cha bu shuarach ri leanmhuinn.
    Were no trifle to trace.

(Watson, JC, 1934, p. 36)

Along with his brother, William, afterwards of Hamara, Norman was a student of Glasgow University in the year 1622. He was married first to Margaret MacKenzie of Kintail, by whom he had a son, John (of Contullich), who has been immortalised in a *Luinneag* by *Màiri ni'n Alasdair Ruaidh*.

On the death of his first wife, Norman married Catherine, the eldest daughter of Sir James MacDonald of Sleat:

Fhuair thu fortan bho Dhia
    From God thou didst receive a dower
Bean bu schocraiche cial
    A wife most steadfast of sense
'S i gu foisteannach, fial, nàrach.
    Sedate, shamefast and hospitable.

'S tric a riaraich thu cuilm,
    Often has thou dispensed a banquet,
Gun fhiabhras gun tuilg,
    Without confusion or pomp,
Nighean oighre Dhun Thuilm, slan dhut.
    Thou daughter of Duntulm's heir; Hail to thee.

(Watson, JC, 1934, p. 48)

In the *Book of Clan Ranald* there occurs an elegy, written to Sir Norman, probably by one of the *MacMhuirichs*. In it the date of his death is definitely stated:

> *Seacht cced deg sa do re riom*
>> Seventeen hundred and two to be reckoned
> *'Stri bliadhna aois a nairdriogh*
>> And three years the age of the supreme King
> *Orslat budh cneasda do chi*
>> A gold wand of the purest to be seen
> *Go teasda romhac Ruaidhri.*
>> To the death of the excellent son of Rory.
>>> (MacBain, A, & Kennedy, J, 1894, p. 274)

He died on the 3rd March, 1705, and a touching lament was composed to him by *Màiri ni'n Alasdair Ruaidh.*

> *An treas latha de'n Mhart,*
>> On the third day of March,
> *Dh'fhalbh m' aighear gu bràth:*
>> My joy left me forever.
> *Be sud saighead mo chràidh*
>> Was the arrow that wounded me
> *Bhi 'g amharc do bhàis,*
>> To behold thee dead,
> *A' ghnuis fhlathasaidh àillt, etc.*
>> Thou princely noble countenance, (etc.)
>>> (Watson, JC, 1934, p. 90)

It may be of interest to note that the sword of Sir Norman, now hanging on the wall in a lobby in the castle of Dunvegan, was gifted to the chief by the late Captain Norman MacLeod of Orbost.

As has been already stated, the principal leaders of the Royalist army went to Dunvegan after their defeat at Loch Garry and in those hospitable halls they passed the winter of 1654–55. There they deliberated in earnest conferences as to the course they should then pursue and it was at length decided that, as they were so lacking in money, munitions and men, they should strive to make the best terms possible with the Commonwealth and, owing to the tolerant spirit the government had displayed to the rebels, this was an easy matter. Long before this time they had been assured that, if they submitted, the sentences of forfeiture on their estates would be abrogated.

Through the influence of General Monk, who had been left by Cromwell in charge of the affairs of Scotland, a basis of agreement was effected. By it the Chief of MacLeod was to be pardoned but he was enjoined to arrest his uncles, *"if he can"*, and surrender them to the government. He was to find security in £6000 for his future behaviour and Sir James MacDonald of Sleat became his surety. That sum was to be refunded to the guarantor when a fine of £2500 had been paid by MacLeod and a full payment was made in 1656 (MacLeod, RC, 1938, pp. 85–8).

Roderick 'the Witty' (Ruairidh Mir), Seventeenth Chief

Shortly after the Restoration, Roderick, the young chief of MacLeod, went to London to visit the king. In view of what his clan had done, and had lost, for the Stuart cause, it was but natural that he should have set off with high hopes of preferment. But he was sadly disillusioned when he interviewed the ingrate king in Whitehall, for there was not even a mention of the sacrifices the chief's clan had made for his sake. Roderick returned home a disappointed man, vowing, it is said, that, so far as he was able, his clansmen would never again raise a finger on behalf of the Stuarts; and it is a noteworthy fact that his descendants honoured this vow, if ever made, to the very letter.

His visit to London took place in 1661, and from that year until his early death in 1665, most of his time was passed in the cities of the south, where he led a life of great extravagance. *"This summer, 1665, died Rory, Laird of MacLeod, a vitious spendthrift, and his brother, John, succeeded, a most hopeful, excellent and wise youth"* (*Wardlaw Manuscript* in Mackay, W, 1905, p. 456).

He was married to Margaret, daughter of Sir John Mackenzie, tutor of Tarbat, and by her he had a son and a daughter. His son, Norman, died young, and, in a lament, 'Cumha do Mhac Leòid', written by *Màiri ni'n Alasdair Ruaidh,* on the death of Roderick, she says:

> *Ach a Ruairidh Mhic Iain,*
>> Thou son of Iain,
> *'S goirt leam faighinn an sgeul ort,*
>> It is sore to hear the news of thee,
> *'S e mo chreachsa mac t-athar*
>> My grief that thy father's son
> *Bhi 'na laighe gun éirigh;*
>> Be lying still never to rise;
> *Agus Tormad a mhac san,*
>> And Norman thy son,
> *A thasgaidh mo cheille,*
>> Oh, treasure of my heart,
> *Gur h-e aobhar mo ghearain*
>> That they are lost together
> *Gu'n do chailleadh le chéil' iad.*
>> Is the burden of my plaint.
>
> (Watson, JC, 1934, p. 54)

The daughter was married to a Stewart of Appin; and as her brother, the heir, was dead, there was grave concern among the clan that her son might claim the succession to the estates. This feeling of disquiet is adverted to by the bardess in the lament already quoted:

> *C'uim a thigeadh fear coigreach,*
>> Why should a stranger,
> *A thagradh ar n' oighreachd,*
>> Come to impede thy heritage,
> *Ged nach eil e ro dhearbta,*
>> Though it be not well proven,
> *Gur searbh e ri eisdeachd;*
>> It is bitter to hear;
> *Ged tha sinn air ar creachadh,*
>> Though we are despoiled,
> *Mu chloinn mac an fhir fhéilidh,*
>> Of the sons of the generous one,
> *Sliochd Ruairi Mhóir allail,*
>> The race of Roderick great and renowned,
> *Is gur airidh iad féin oirr'.*
>> They alone are worthy of thee.
>
> (Watson, JC, 1934, p. 58)

Sir Roderick of Talisker, who had acted as captain to his clan from 1649 until 1656, lived to a good old age, and died in 1675. Beyond stray references to his liberality, the contemporary poets pay him no tribute in verse.

John (Iain Breac), Eighteenth Chief

At the time of the death of the late chief, the affairs of the Clan MacLeod were at a low ebb indeed. Many causes had contributed to this – the disasters of the late rebellion but, principally, the excesses of the chief. The estate was loaded with debt and it was fortunate for the clan that the successor was a man of unselfish motives, who was prepared to work unsparingly to redeem it from its financial embarrassments. This was the famous *Iain Breac*, who endeared himself to his people by his generosity, his culture and his great sagacity. Though he was often from home, he did not remain long away, but spent most of his life among his own people. He busied himself in projects for the development of the estate, and by wise organisation and prudent retrenchment he was able to free it of the burden of debt. In the *Book of Dunvegan* (MacLeod, RC, 1939, Vol. 2, p. 18), *Iain Breac* is said to have been the first Protestant chief.

The allurements of the cities, and of the court, failed to attract him and, as he was endowed with a highly refined mind himself, he was able to appreciate the value of the native culture and he nurtured it with sympathy and care. In his household were the bard, the harper, the piper and the jester, and he is said to have been the last of the Highland chiefs to maintain that complement of such functionaries in his retinue. Dunvegan Castle was then the hospitable haunt of the wandering bards, the musicians and the story-tellers, whose influence had been so potent in the moulding of Highland character. The generosity accorded to all who came within its walls inspired the bards to lofty flights in their enthusiastic praise. In one of her songs, *Cronan*, or 'A Crooning', composed by *Màiri ni'n Alasdair Ruaidh* on the recovery of Norman, the chief's second son, from a dangerous illness, she describes the castle and its cheer:

> *...Dun tuireideach, àrd,*
> > To the tall battlemented tower,
> *B'e sud innis nam bàrd,*
> > That was often the resting place of bards,
> *'S nam filidh ri dàin,*
> > And the makers of songs,
> *Far 'm bu mhinig an tàmh,*

> It was a place where they often reposed,
> *Cha b' ionad gun bhlàthas dhaibh sud;*
> > It was a place that lacked not warmth;
> > > (Watson, JC, 1934, p. 62)

Roderick Morison, the blind harper of the family, bemoaning the changes that had taken place in Dunvegan on the death of *Iain Breac*, impersonates the echo, once so lustily activated by the sounds of mirth and the expression of good cheer, as saying:

> *'S mi mactalla bha uair*
> > I am the echo who once
> *'G éisdeachd faram nan duan gu tiugh;*
> > Listened to the carroling of songs in rich profusion;
> *Far 'm bu mhuirneach am beus*
> > Accompanied by a ground base pleasing to the ear
> *An am cromadh do'n ghrein 's an t-sruth.*
> > What time the sun was becoming dim in the ocean flood.
> *Far am b' fhoirmeil na seòid,*
> > It was a place where the gallants might be found in high glee,
> *'S iad gu h-òrganach, ceòlmhor, cluth,*
> > Enjoying the music of organs at their ease,
> *Ged nach fhaichte mo ghnùis*
> > Though my face could not be seen
> *Chluinnt' aca 'san Dùn mo ghuth.*
> > My voice could be heard by them in the Castle.
> > > (Matheson, W, 1970, p. 60)

And when *Iain Breac*, the chief of Dunvegan, was engaged in his efforts to retrieve the fallen fortunes of his clan and in extending his patronage to the arts, the rest of the Highlands was torn asunder by the cruel hands of war. The Revolution had occurred in England and the last Stuart king had been expelled from the country by a people who were determined to end absolute monarchy. While many of the clans rallied to the support of the fallen House of Stuart, the MacLeods held aloof from the struggle, although a considerable amount of pressure was brought to bear on their chief, both by the other chiefs of the north and by the late king himself. In 1689, Melfort, who was then acting as Secretary of State to James II, wrote to *Iain Breac* from Dublin Castle, commanding him to muster his men and join the Royalists, and threatening him with condign penalties should he refuse to obey the summons (MacLeod, RC, 1938, p. 142). Shortly afterwards another letter was addressed to *Iain Breac*, this time from Viscount Dundee; but it also failed to move him from his state of neutrality (MacLeod, RC, 1938, pp. 143–4). A second note from Dundee, a short time before the Battle of Killiecrankie, was despatched to *Iain Breac*, apprising him of the fact that most of the Highland chiefs had already joined the Royalist forces and recommending him, if he wished to share the glory of playing a part in the restoration of the House of Stuart, to throw in his lot with them immediately. Again he declined to rise and, finally, on the 29th of May, 1690, King James himself wrote from Dublin Castle a letter, which was sent to Sir Donald MacDonald of Sleat and in which he hints that the Chief of Dunvegan had promised to join the Stuart cause if the king landed in Scotland. This letter is marked by a haughty tone and a feeling of irritation at the delay on the part of *Iain Breac*. It proceeds: *"This is not the time for any man to make conditions for himself, or to consult barely his own private interests … We are sure you wish your country and posterity too well not to contribute all you can to its liberty"*. A note of such ungraciousness as that could scarcely have the desired effect upon a proud Highland chief and, in any case, James' hopes of success were shattered about a month afterwards, when he was so ingloriously defeated at the Battle of the Boyne on the 1st of July, 1690 (*ibid.*, pp. 142–3).

Nor did *Iain Breac* show any ardour for the cause of King William. Whether it was from antagonism to his government, or, what is more probable, that he was taking advantage of the conditions of uncertainty that prevailed in the Highlands after the Revolution, he seems to have withheld the royal rates for a few years and, by way of intimidation and punishment, troops were quartered on his estate, whence they were not withdrawn until 1692, when he had made the necessary reimbursement to the national exchequer (MacLeod, RC, 1938, p. 46).

After he had stabilised the affairs of the clan, *Iain Breac* busied himself in improving the amenities of his estates. He effected much-needed repairs on the castle and, having completed these, he commenced in 1685 to make additions to it. In token of his work there, a stone above one of the lower windows bears a Latin inscription: *'Joannes MacLeod, Beganoduni, Dominus gentis suae, Philarchus Diurinisiae, Haraiae, Vaternisiae, etc. Baro D. Florae MacDonald matrimoniali vinculo conjugatus, turrem hanc Beganodunensem, proavorum habitaculum longe vetustissimum, diu penitus labefactatam. Anno aerae vulgaris MDCLXXXVI instauravit'*. ('John MacLeod, Lord of Dunvegan; Harris; Waternish etc. United in marriage to Flora MacDonald restored in the year of the Vulgar era, 1686, his tower of Dunvegan, long the ancient abode of his ancestors, which had fallen utterly into decay) (Cameron A, 1871, p. 81).

From this time until his death in 1693, there is little to record of this chief; but the sennachies of Skye fill the blank by means of an interesting tale, the theme of which is the exploit of a family fool.

Macleod's Fool And The Highwayman

To the south-west of Loch Garve, in Ross-shire, lies a district called Tarvie, which was once densely wooded *Coille Tharbhaidh*, but has sorely been depleted of its timber to meet the exigencies of a nation at war. Through it, in the past, stretched the main thoroughfare to the west from the town of Inverness and much business was done in olden times by the men of the isles in that city. These woods afforded an effectual harbourage to bands of ruffianly highwaymen, who intercepted travellers and robbed them of whatever money or means they might have in their possession.

Iain Breac had occasion to send his chamberlain, accompanied by two stalwart clansmen to Inverness, in order to obtain money to pay for the cost of the extensive additions he was making to the castle. On the return journey, by Tarvie Wood, MacLeod's men were waylaid by robbers, who, pointing pistols to their breasts, peremptorily commanded them to deliver up whatsoever monies they possessed. The small band of messengers had no alternative but to comply. The money-bag was handed over in its entirety and sadly they trudged on their way home to Dunvegan, whither they brought but the report of their loss. As there was pressing need of funds to carry on the new schemes, MacLeod sent another steward; but a similar act of depredation was committed against this man and he, too, was sent home empty-handed. This considerable loss of ready cash greatly worried the chief, so that his harper, his piper, or his bard (and he had all these in his household), had not the art to raise his mind from out of the morass of depression into which it had been plunged by his heavy loss. The family fool was quick enough to notice his master's changed frame of mind and he asked him, in his customary privileged manner, what it was that troubled him. On being told the reason, he announced that he would go to Inverness and would guarantee that whatever sums were entrusted to him there would be safely delivered to his chief in Dunvegan.

Naturally enough, the chief refused to countenance his fool's embarking on an adventure in which his two most trusted servants had already so signally been foiled. The fool was, however,

so very persistent in his solicitation that the chief finally agreed to let him have his way. Preparations were accordingly made and the best horse in the stable brought out and saddled; but, to the amazement of all, the jester refused to take it and he demanded instead a superannuated grey mare that was maintained by the chief for sentimental reasons and had not been on the road for years. The chief now demurred more than ever to the project, but such was the insistence of his retainer that he was prevailed upon to let him go and away the fool ambled on the ancient nag, followed by the derisive jeers of the bystanders. Many a traveller he met and all wondered and laughingly passed him by. After trudging wearily onwards for several days, the messenger at length approached the thief-infested Wood of Tarvie. Here he was stopped short by a lithe robber on a high-stepping steed and was asked whither he was going, and what was his errand. The fool answered blankly that he had been commissioned by the Chief of Dunvegan to go to Inverness for the purpose of conveying home some money. Thereupon the robber asked him if he were to have any escort on his return and, on being told that none was expected, the thief said that he would be pleased to convoy him a part of the way, as the road he was now on was a very dangerous one. He then asked him on which day he was likely to return, and on the simpleton telling him, the thief wished him good luck and returned to his retreat.

Eventually the fool reached Inverness, and, having obtained the amount of money asked for, he deposited it in a bag, filling another with sea-shells. He then repaired to his lodging, saddled the old mare and began the return journey. He tied the bags to his waist-belt, one on each side of him, and, concealing them under his cloak, made for the west.

On the very day he had appointed, he came once again in sight of the Wood of Tarvie, and his would-be benefactor darted out of a coppice by the wayside and rode for some distance beside him. Suddenly the thief whipped out a pistol and, presenting it to the fool's breast, demanded his money. The latter protested, but he was sternly told to deliver all without further talk. Thereupon the fool took a bag from under his cloak, slung it well down a steep declivity, at the same time saying it would never be imputed to him that he had handed over his master's property to any robber. The highwayman sprang sprightly from the saddle and ran down the slope to recover the bag and the seemingly lethargic fool leapt as lightly from his own saddle, mounted the thief's gallant steed and rode off at full speed, leaving to the robber the old mare, to follow in hopeless pursuit.

A few days afterwards the *gocaman*, or watcher, on the battlements of Dunvegan marked a rider, on a well-appointed steed, approaching the castle. On coming nearer, the jaunty horseman was seen to be none other than the family fool himself and all turned out in mock ceremony to welcome his return. But the spirit of derision was soon changed into one of wonder at the splendid horse the fool rode and their wonder developed into unbounded enthusiasm when it became known that his mission had been successful. In the courtyard of the castle the fool unsaddled the horse and, leaving it to the care of attendants, carried the saddle into the presence of his chief. On a table he deposited the bag of money he had been commissioned to deliver and thereupon began to examine the purses of the saddle which were found to contain, not only the amounts stolen from the two previous messengers, but much else besides.

We have already seen that *Iain Breac* was married to Florence, the second daughter of Sir James MacDonald of Sleat and the sister of the wife of his uncle, Sir Norman of Bernera. They had three sons, Roderick, Norman, and William, the two oldest of whom were successively chiefs, and the last died young. The daughters were Isabella and Janet. It is interesting to record that the tutor to the family was Martin Martin. He was a native of Trotternish, had qualified as a medical practitioner, but had never taken up the profession. He compiled an instructive account, descriptive and sociological, of the Western Isles in 1693 (Martin, M, 1693).

Iain Breac died in 1693.

> *Ann an seachdain na Ceusda,*
>> In Easter week,
> *Diciadaoin mo bhristidh,*
>> On the Wednesday that ruined me,
> *Chaill mi iuchair na Feudail',*
>> I lost the key to riches,
> *Cha mhi 'n aon neach as misd e,*
>> I am not the only one who is the worse of it,
>> (Matheson, W, 1970, p. 52)

laments the blind harper and bard, Roderick Morison.

The Rev. Canon R.C. MacLeod of MacLeod says he was buried at Inverness, *"where his tomb is still visible"*; but the poet Morison, in his lament for his chief, *Creach nan Ciadan*, seems to suggest that he was buried in Rodel of Harris, where so many of his predecessors had found a last resting-place:

> *Tha mo thaic anns na Hearadh*
>> My support is in Harris
> *'N deidh fhalach 'na aonar.*
>> Hidden (in the grave) and alone.
>> (Matheson, W, 1970, p. 50)

And again he refers to his body being carried across the sea:

> *'Is fhaide seachduinn na bliadhna,*
>> A week seems longer than a year,
> *Bho 'n thriall sibh thar linne,*
>> Since you set out across the seaway,

Le friamhachd na fialachd,
> With him who was the essence of liberality,

Bha 'san lion-bhrat air fhilleadh.
> Wrapped in a linen shroud.

> (Matheson, W, 1970, p. 50)

Gun phailteas ri daimh,
> Without liberality to men of learning,

Gun mhacnus, gun mhanran beòil.
> Without dalliance or voice raised in tuneful song.

> (Matheson, W, 1970, p. 58)

and:

Roderick (Ruairidh), Nineteenth Chief

And the venerable harper had good cause to mourn the departure of his benevolent chief, on whose death another arose, who saw no virtue in the arts. This was Roderick, the nineteenth chief, by whom *"Dunvegan Castle was neglected, and the services of bard, harper, and piper were dispensed with to make room for grooms, gamekeepers, factors, dogs and the various etceteras of a fashionable English establishment"*. Nor need we wonder that the sudden reversal of conditions should have wounded the feelings of those who valued the native culture; and the harper-bard thus deplores it, contrasting the changed ways with the hospitable days of old:

Tha mactalla fo ghruaim
> Echo is dejected

Anns an talla 'm biodh fuaim a' cheòil:
> In the hall where music was wont to sound:

'S ionad tathaich nan clear
> In the place resorted to by poet bands

Gun aighear, gun mhiadh, gun phòit,
> Now without mirth, pleasure or drinking,

Gun mhire, gun mhùirn,
> Without companions and without joy,

Gun iomrachadh dlùth nan còrn,
> Without passing round of drinking horn in quick succession, without feasting,

Lean an dualchas bu t-Athair,
> Follow the tradition that was a birthright,

A mhic an athar a chraidh sinn,
> Son of the father who left me grief stricken,

Na bi ud chrionach gun duillich,
> Do not be a withered stock without foliage,

Anns an ionad 'n do thamh thu.
> In the place where you have gone to dwell.

> (Matheson, W, 1970, p. 56)

The bards have nothing to record in praise of this chief. To them he was *crionach gun duilleach* ('a barren tree without fruit or foliage'). The traditions of his race and its culture were alike insipid and uninspiring to him, for his artificial mind assiduously aped the manners of the South.

No event of importance happened during his regime, which lasted six years. He was married to Lady Isabel Mackenzie, the daughter of the third Earl of Seaforth, and his family consisted of an only daughter, named Anne, who was married to the notable warrior, Donald MacLeod of Bernera, better known by the agnomen of 'The Old Trojan'. The chief died in the last year of the century, and, as he had no male issue, the succession devolved on his brother, Norman. Since the period of the chiefship of the latter falls in the subsequent century, we shall meantime defer its narration in order to bring the story of the MacDonalds to date.

The MacDonalds

Sir Donald, Eleventh Chief And Third Baronet

We remember that the affairs of this clan were in a perplexing state during the latter days of the chief, Sir James, owing to domestic dissensions between him and his heir, and that the discord was occasioned by the financial difficulties in which they were embroiled. We have seen that the wadsetters threatened the deposition of the chief and the exclusion of the heir from the succession; but an unpleasant situation was averted by the sudden death of Sir James, in 1678 (MacDonald, A & A, 1904, pp. 68–9). His oldest son, Donald, succeeded to the estates. It seems, from a reference made to the latter by the bard, *Iain Lom,* that, like many another of that age, his face was disfigured by the marks of smallpox.

> *Og mhisneachail treun thu,*
>> Young, strong and straight are you,
> *'S blàth na bric ort 'san eudann,*
>> And the stigma of small pox on your face,
> *Mur misd thu ro mheud 's tha de nàir innt'.*
>> If you are not too much embarrassed by it.
>>> (Mackenzie, AM, 1964, p. 104)

Sir Donald had never been in robust health, and for many years after his accession he was constrained to lead a very quiet life; but he was unwearied in his endeavour to raise the low fortunes of his clan. Like his father and especially his grandfather, he was an ardent Loyalist. This was seen, as on other occasions, when the Duke of Argyll was in rebellion against King James in 1685. Sir Donald was asked by the Privy Council to raise his men and, with about 300 of his clan, he marched to the head of Loch Ness, where he joined the other Highland chiefs, who had mustered in force in opposition to *MacCailean Mór* of Argyll.

And, again, in 1689, when the Highland chiefs rose on behalf of King James, under Viscount Dundee, Sir Donald was not lagging in his support of the Stuarts. In the MacDonald charter-chest is a letter, sent by Dundee to Sir Donald, who was enjoined to forward it to *Iain Breac* MacLeod of Dunvegan, beseeching the latter to be in Lochaber by the 10th of June, 1689, and adding: *"I am persuaded that Sir Donald of Sleat will be there by this time"* (MacLeod, RC, 1938, p. 144). In that surmise Dundee was not mistaken, for Sir Donald was there, and with 500 of his clansmen. He did not, however, remain long with Dundee, for, on account of the impaired state of his health, he was not then fit for rough campaigning and so was compelled to return home. The command of the clan he deputed to his son, Donald, afterwards known to history as *Do'ull a Chogaidh,* or 'Donald of the War'.

From Lochaber, Dundee set off for Blair Castle. He had only 2500 men and they could hardly be said to be disciplined. Against him was sent a royalist force 4000 strong, under the command of a brave and magnanimous Highlander, Mackay of Scourie. The latter marched north from Dunkeld to attack Dundee at Blair Atholl, but, on the way, in the wild gorge of Killiecrankie, or *Raon Ruairi,* he was beset by the Highland army. It was a gloomy morning that succeeded a night of rain when Dundee's men saw Mackay's troops winding their way by the swollen waters of the Garry. The MacDonalds were placed by Dundee on the extreme left of his army, where they were opposed to the best of King William's men. There were no cavillings about posts of honour that day, as, with a yell far louder than the roar of the turbulent torrent of the Garry, the clansmen dashed to the onset. Though met by a disciplined phalanx, the charge of the Highlanders was that day irresistible and the opposing forces were swept clean off the field in less than fifteen minutes (MacDonald, A & A, 1904, p. 71).

But the Highlanders, and especially the Skye men, paid a heavy price for their glorious victory. Many of the leading men of the House of Sleat were left on the field:

> *Air Raon Ruairidh nan stràc,*
>> At Killiecrankie of the blows,
> *Far 'na bhuannaich thu blàr,*
>> Where you won the victory,
> *Chaill thu t'uaislean, 's t'armuinn ghleusda.*
>> You lost your nobles and your competent officers.
>>> (Mackenzie, J, 1877, p. 52)

and:

> *A Dho' ill nan Do'ull*
>> Donald of the Donalds
> *'S og a fhuair do dheuchainn*
>> Though young you were sore tried
> *'Sioma bean a bha bronach eadar Trodairn'*
>> Many wives between Trotternish
> *is Sleibhte*
>> and Sleat were sorrowful
> *Mu chinneadh mor t-athar is iad na laighe*
>> About the noble kin of your father lying
> *gun eiridh;*
>> in eternal rest;
> *Luchd bhualadh na buillean air fuireach*
>> Men who could strike blows falling
> *'san teugmhail.*
>> in the conflict.
>>> (Gillies, E, 1786, pp. 145 & 271)

and:

> *Oran Raon Ruairi' le Do'ull mac Alasdair Ruaidh a Gleann na Comhain*

> *'S ann dhiu Dòmhnull is Seumas*
>> There were of them Donald and James
> *'S iad gun eirigh on chumasg*
>> Who fell in the struggle
> *Mu chreach leir mar a dh' eirich*
>> My sorrow what happened
> *A chuid bu leithe bu duilich*
>> Those most hoary were the saddest
> *Dhoibh bu dual a bhi' treubhach*
>> Their destiny was to be brave
> *O'n athar fein thar gach duine*
>> From their own father above all men
> *Sgeul bu donna na dheigh sud*
>> The bitterest tale to be told is
> *Ri lighes leigh cha do dh' fhuirich.*
>> That they did not remain for a surgeon's healing.
>>> (Song of Killiecrankie, composed by Donald, son of Red Alasdair from Glencoe. Gillies, E, 1786, p. 145)

Iain Lom in *Air Cath Raon Ruairi* says;

> *Mo ghaol Do'ull Gorm Og on Tur*
>> My love, Young Donald Gorm, from the tower
> *Sleibhteach is an Ord*
>> of Sleat and from Ord
> *Fhuair thu deuchainn is bu mhor an sgeul e.*
>> You were sore tired and a great tale it is.
>>> (Gillies, E, 1786, p. 154)

After Killiecrankie, the Highland army was leaderless, for Cannon and Buchan were both incompetent, and although there were men of commanding personality among the Highland chiefs, the difficulty was that few of them were disposed to serve under one of their own order. That spirit of independence inevitably induced disintegration, and young Donald and his men went home to Skye. With them went General Buchan and the Earl of Seaforth, but they did not remain there long. A new force was raised, about 1500 strong and it made for the east. But its campaign was cut short when it was defeated by Sir Thomas Livingston at the battle of Cromdale on Speyside.

The broken force repaired to Skye, where it was joined by General Cannon. He remained there for about nine months; but he did little during that time for the cause of the Stuarts, being mainly concerned in negotiations with the king for the purpose of securing advantageous terms for himself. In that he succeeded and he slunk away from Skye in a French trading-vessel to join the exiled James at St. Germains (Cameron, A, 1871, p. 78).

Meanwhile, what of the affairs of Sir Donald? The ever chivalrous MacKay did all that was possible to persuade him to make his peace with King William, but the indomitable old warrior treated those friendly overtures with scorn. His answer was that nothing would ever induce him to recognise William as his king. It is small wonder, then, that sentence of forfeiture was passed on the estates of the family in the month of June, 1690 and that two frigates were despatched by the government to Skye in order to intimidate the chief from pursuing the paths of treason.

The government vessels *Dartmouth* and *Lark* were commanded by Captains Pottinger and Douglas respectively, and strict injunctions were given to these officers to have recourse to force only when they found that all the possible avenues to conciliation were barred against them. Numerous messages were sent by Captain Pottinger to Sir Donald, but their effect on the chief was nugatory. Nothing then remained to the emissaries of the government but to use force after a bombardment of about half an hour. A party was accordingly landed at *Creag a' Chaim*, in Armadale, and an attack was made on Sir Donald's residence. On the approach of the invaders, the garrison took to the hills but, seeing their chief's mansion and one of his galleys aflame, the natives returned, and fell on the Southerners with such determination that they overcame them and scattered them in all directions.

One section of the landing party made for the north, and succeeded in gaining Castle *Camus* in Knock, which was then unoccupied. There, owing to their advantageous position, they put up an effective resistance for a time; but they were finally forced to surrender. Tripods were made of oars, and to these rude gallows the whole band was strung by the enraged islanders.

Another section of the party was pursued along the shore to the south, until it made a stand on *Dun Flò*, a mound on the shore in front of the lodge of Tormore. Here twenty-six of them took refuge in a cleft, the approach to which was so well guarded by a powerful Royalist with his sword, that for some considerable time he was able to maintain a clear area in front of him. According to the local tradition, one of his assailants at length clambered up the mound on the shore-side and, with an axe fixed to the end of a fishing-rod, swung a blow at the gladiator from above and mortally wounded him. On the death of their leader, the party yielded and they suffered a fate similar to that of their comrades who had betaken themselves to Castle *Camus* (MacDonald, A & A, 1904, p. 73). The Rev. Martin MacPherson who wrote *The First Statistical Account* for the parish of Sleat, about one hundred years after the incident, states that twenty-six of the invaders were buried on the top of *Dun Flò*.

This episode served but to stiffen Sir Donald's resistance and he treated with contempt all the efforts of the government to effect his reconciliation. Indeed, one cannot but marvel at the forbearance of William in his attitude towards his unruly subject and especially so when, in 1691, four French ships-of-war arrived in Skye with arms and ammunition, in order to support a new rising. This project came to nothing, however, for the dour Jacobite, with unaccountable suddenness, took advantage of the amnesty that was to be extended to the Highland chiefs who offered their allegiance to King William before the end of the year. He thus perhaps escaped the fate of his kinsmen of Glencoe.

From this time onwards, Sir Donald was a loyal subject of King William, if one may judge from the correspondence that so frequently passed between him and Colonel Hill of Inverness, who was the king's representative in the Highlands. The remainder of his life was uneventful, and this chief of outstanding wisdom and fortitude, according to the bards, died at Armadale on the 5th of February, 1695, and was buried in Kilmore.

The poet *Iain Lom*, who wrote so much about the contemporary chiefs of Clan Donald, has immortalised the name of Sir Donald in a *cumha*, or 'lament', he composed on the occasion of his death. He characterises him as:

> *Leomhann fhireachail, àigh,*
>> Proud mountain lion,
>
> *Muinnte, spioradail, àrd,*
>> Erudite, spirited, noble,
>
> *Umhail, iriosal, feardha, treubhach,*
>> Scrupulous, humble, manly and brave,
>
> *Léigh nan arm, is nan each,*
>> Skilled in arms and horsemanship,
>
> *Reumail, aireil, gun airc,*
>> Authoritative, watchful without anxiety,
>
> *Dh'eug thu 'n Armadal ghlas nan déideag.*
>> You died in Armadale of the jewels.
>
> (Mackenzie, J, 1877, p. 51)

Sir Donald was married to Margaret Douglas, daughter of the Earl of Morton and three of their sons are known to fame, namely, Donald, the heir; James of Oransay, who also was chief; and William.

This takes the political history of the island to the end of the seventeenth century, and we shall now treat of the social conditions that appertain to that time.

CHAPTER X

Social Conditions, 1650–1700

The Church

There was then, and for many generations after that, much superstition rampant in Skye. Yet the preaching of the true religion was by no means neglected, for there were many zealous members of the clergy in the island during the latter half of the seventeenth century.

We have seen that the Rev. Neil Mackinnnon was minister of Sleat, to which he was translated in 1641 from the district of Strath, where he had ministered previously for seventeen years. His successor in Strath was the Rev. Farquhar MacLennan, a native of Lochbroom, who continued there until 1675. In that year the Rev. Donald MacKinnon, a graduate in Arts of the University of Glasgow, was presented to Strath by Charles II. He was succeeded in 1696 by the Rev. Martin MacPherson, M.A., who held this charge until 1712, when he died at the early age of 40 years. This noted scholar is described as "a mild, good-natured and well-bred gentleman" (Lamont, D, 1913, pp. 90–1). He was the grandson of Rev. Martin MacPherson, who was minister of Duirinish until his death in 1661.

This latter clergyman had a romantic career. He had been forced to relinquish his charge in South Uist and, having fled to Skye under threat of assassination, he was taken under the protection of *Iain Breac* MacLeod and nominated to the parish of Duirinish by that famous chief. All his property in Uist was confiscated and he thus sustained great loss. As a result of the damage he suffered, the Captain of Clan Ranald was excommunicated by the Church and it was ordained by parliament that the injured clergyman should be reimbursed to the extent of £150 out of the 'vacant Stipends' in his own and adjoining parishes, but the Rev. Martin waived his claim, in spite of the promptings of his brethren to take advantage of it.

He was succeeded by his son, Dugald, a graduate in Arts of Glasgow, who was admitted to this charge before 1689 and who died in 1717, at the age of 76 years. He is said to have "strenuously opposed popery. He possessed a fine poetical vein and was exemplary in the discharge of his duties". Of his large family, the most noted were the Rev. Martin MacPherson, who was minister of Sleat and Strath and John, who was one of the most outstanding schoolmasters in Skye in his age. The latter conducted a school in Orbost, and was a famous student of the classics.

The large parish of Snizort was served by the Rev. Archibald MacQueen, M.A. of the University of Glasgow at which he graduated in 1636. In the year 1656 he was deposed by the Synod for his grievous breach of discipline in marrying the Captain of

Clan Ranald, who had been excommunicated for the injuries he had inflicted on the Rev. Martin MacPherson, the minister of Duirinish. Further depredations were brought on the Reverend Martin for, when Colonel Cobbet's troops left Lewis after they had subdued the Rising there, by the young Earl of Seaforth, against the Commonwealth, they would seem to have landed on Skye. There is an account extant of the spoiling committed there, especially on the Minister of Duirinish, the Rev. Martin MacPherson, who applied to King Charles II, after the Restoration for compensation for the plundering.

The Rev. Archibald was succeeded by Rev. George Monro who in about 1656 was translated to the Church of Snizort and Raasay, from Urquhart. He died within a year of his appointment, and the expelled minister was reinstated. He retired, however, in 1658, and was succeeded by his son, Rev. Donald MacQueen, M.A. of Edinburgh. This incumbent was deprived of his charge for non-jurancy but is said to have continued in possession until 1710.

In the parish of Kilmuir, the Rev. Donald Nicolson, who was also chief of the family of Nicolson of Scorrybreck, was the minister from about 1663 until 1696, when, on account of his zeal for Episcopalianism, he relinquished his charge rather than conform to Presbyterianism. He died in the following year.

His son, Alexander, was Episcopalian minister at Stenschol, where he intruded in 1715. He was the last of the line of ministers who, after the Restoration, had been established in Skye by Charles II.

The Rev. John Mackinnon was admitted to Bracadale in 1632, and he continued there until 1662, when he was succeeded by Rev. Lachlan Fraser, who gave place to Rev John Bethune, M.A. The last was the oldest son of the famous physician, Angus Bethune, and is described as *"a learned divine, and an able physician"*. He is said to have been the first minister in the island to have dispensed the sacrament according to the rites of the Presbyterian Church. He was married to Marion MacLeod of Drynoch, and one of his sons, Kenneth, was minister of the parish of Kilmuir.

The Rev. Angus MacQueen is mentioned in the records of the Synod of Argyll as minister of Sleat as early was 1653. He was an accomplished scholar, showing special talents in his mastery of Gaelic. In the year 1694, it was ordained that he be deprived of his charge, probably because he was a non-juror but it seems he continued there until the year 1709.

Before the Restoration, Presbyterianism had been instituted, and Skye was joined to the Synod of Argyll. When that council was engaged, in 1649, on the translation of the Shorter Catechism into Gaelic, two representatives of the clergy of Skye paid a visit to the conference of their Argyllshire brethren, who met in Inveraray. They were Rev. Angus MacQueen of Sleat and Rev. Neil MacKinnon of Strath. They were heartily welcomed, and each of them submitted Gaelic translations of the Catechism they had rendered independently. The quality of the work they presented so impressed the men of Argyll that they unanimously resolved to make use of their versions in the effort to evolve a true and worthy translation. The work of Neil MacKinnon was especially commended, both on account of its faithfulness to the original and for its terse, idiomatic constructions, *"for he is a man able in that language"*.

The approved version of the Catechism in Gaelic appeared in 1651, and a strong recommendation was made to the people to commit it to memory. In order to effect this, it was proposed that schoolmasters should teach the Catechism to their pupils, and that as soon as the latter had acquired a reasonable proficiency in the reading of it, they were to go from house to house and teach those of their neighbours who could not themselves read the Catechism in Gaelic.

It is not known how far this commendable project was pursued, but there is no reason to believe that it was permitted to fall into abeyance through neglect. The clergy of Skye in these days were earnest men, who carried out their duties with faithfulness and often in face of great privations. Many of them suffered even from the want of the bare necessaries of life. The Synod of Argyll, already referred to in connection with the translation of the Shorter Catechism, were so impressed by the indigence of the worthy cleric of Skye, Rev. John MacKinnon of Bracadale, that they decided to confer on him *"twelve bolls of victual out of the vacant parishes of Kintyre"*, in order to relieve his immediate wants. These men did not, however, labour in vain. In a poem by Iain Lom, called *A Bhean Leasaich an Stòp Dhuinn*, in praise of Sir James MacDonald of Sleat, we find the following significant verse:

> *Nuair bu sgìth de luchd theud e,*
>> When he tired of stringed instruments,
> *Gheibhte Biobull 'ga leughadh*
>> The Bible would be read
> *Le fìor chreidheamh, is céille,*
>> With earnest belief and wisdom,
> *Mar a dh' òrduich Mac Dhè dhuibh;*
>> As the Son of God decreed for you;
> *'S gheibhte teagasg na cléir uaith le sith;*
>> And the teaching of the Clergy would be got from him
>> with peace;
>>
>> (MacKenzie, J, 1877, p. 38)

and the same author shows that those in authority were not neglectful of the affairs of the Church when, in his *Cumha*, or lament for Sir Donald, the successor of Sir James MacDonald, he says:

> *Eaglais Shléibhte nan stuadh,*
>> The gabled church of Sleat,

> *Chosg thu féin ri cur suas,*
>> You, yourself paid for its building,
> *Ged nach d' fhuirich thu buan ri sgleutadh.*
>> Although you were not spared to see it slated.
>>
>> (MacKenzie, J, 1877, p. 51)

The church of Kilmore referred to here was erected in 1681 according to the Rev. Martin Macpherson in the *First Statistical Account* but given as 1631 in the *Second Statistical Account*. Sir Donald died in 1695. About the same time a new church, the successor of the ancient church of St. Columba at Skeabost, was built at Loch Snizort *Beag*.

Immediately after the Restoration in 1660, efforts were made to re-establish Episcopacy in the island and that a large measure of success attended the king's endeavours in this direction is indicated by an asseveration by the Rev. Donald Nicholson, minister of Kilmuir, to the Privy Council in 1666, to the effect that there were only six Non-conformists in the whole of Skye at that time. In 1662 the parishes of Sleat and Strath, then conjoined, were assigned by the king to the Archdeacon of the Isles, as one of his 'proper kirkes'; and at the same time the churches of Snizort and of 'Lendell' (Lyndale) were conferred on that cleric also. The latter church was probably the chapel mentioned then as situated at 'Kildoren' (now Kildonan) in Lyndale.

On the accession of William and Mary, it appears that the majority of the clergy of Skye took the oath of allegiance to the new rulers. When the extrusion of the non-jurors took place in 1689, we have record of only two of the ministers of Skye who were threatened with deprivation. These were Rev. Donald Nicolson of Kilmuir and the Rev. Angus MacQueen of Sleat; and even they were allowed to continue in the enjoyment of their livings for a considerable time.

The Church itself was held in high veneration by the people; and so prevalent was this attitude that, in many cases, as the congregation approached the building, they might be seen kneeling down at various points on the way and offering prayers. The sacred edifice impressed them with profound devotion and it actuated them with becoming decorum, so that, no matter what their conduct might have been during the week, their minds sensed something of spiritual moment at last when they were inside the church.

That they were capable of lofty ideals there can be no doubt; and if, as has been suggested, that wonderful prayer in verse, called *Beannachadh Beothaidh*, or 'Blessing the Kindling' (of the fire), belongs to this period, we have, in essence, the aspirations of our race. True, *Beannachadh Beothaidh* shows internal evidence of its having been composed by a Catholic, perhaps of the Outer Hebrides; but we may take it as expressive of the moral ideals that prevailed in Skye at that time as well. It is as follows, and there is perhaps nothing in the Beatitudes to transcend its ethos:

> *Dhé fadaidh thusa am chrìdhe steach*
>> God kindle within my heart
> *Aiteal gràidh dom' choimhearsnach;*
>> A flame of love to my neighbour;
> *Dom' nàmh, dom' dhaimh, dom' charaide,*
>> To my foe, my friend and my kindred all,
> *Do'n t-saoi, do'n daoi, do'n tràille;*
>> To the brave, to the knave, to the slave;
> *O Mhic na Muire minghile,*
>> A son of smooth, white Mary,
> *Bho 'n ni is isle crannachaire,*
>> From the lowest one,
> *Gu ruig an t-ainm is àirde.*
>> To the name of the highest.
>>> (Carmichael, A, 1928, Vol. 1, p. 230)

Their most ardent wish in life was that, in death, they might find a last resting-place within the precincts of the church, with the result that, at this time, numerous burials were carried out even in its floor. The graves were dug dangerously shallow, so that the stench was noisome and often overpowering. Bones and skulls sometimes littered the floor and were placed in niches in the walls, in order that the worshippers might be constantly reminded of their latter end.

Education

Although the inhabitants of Skye, during the latter portion of the seventeenth century, might fail to approach the standards in education that we moderns attain to, there is no warrant to conclude that they were a whit behind us in real culture. They were imbued with a passionate love for poetry, music and the traditional tale, the pipe and the *seannachie*, and no one occupied so high a place in their minds as the bard. He possessed privileges that none other could hope to enjoy, for he comported himself as freely in the presence of the chief himself as he did in that of the lowest vassal.

At the 'ceilidhs', the practice of composing impromptu verse was extremely popular and all present were expected to make their contribution to this form of intellectual entertainment. The story-teller, too, was held in high estimation and the ancient tales and the poetry of the *Feinne* were told and retold to eager listeners. Nor were these pastimes despised in the homes of the great, for our bards make frequent reference to the institution, especially in:

> *Dunbheagain nan steud,*
>> Dunvegan of the steeds,
> *'Sam faighear luchd-theud,*
>> Where harpers would be found,

Bheir greis air gach sgeul
    Who would long recite
Buaidh-ghlòrach,
    Each choice worded tale,

                      (Watson, JC, 1934, p. 74)

as *Màiri ni'n Alasdair Ruaidh* has it; and according to the same authority:

Gu'm bu chleachdadh 'na dhéidh sin
    It was the custom thereafter
Greis air ursgeul na Feinne.
    To devote time to the romance of the Feinne.

                      (Watson, JC, 1934, p. 24)

Competitions were eagerly entered into for the purpose of ascertaining the individual in the company who was capable of quoting the largest number of proverbs. This was done by a process of elimination. Each contestant was expected to repeat a proverb that had not been mentioned in the course of the evening and if one failed, they were debarred from farther participation in the game, which went on until there was only one survivor. Such an exercise, entailing the constant enunciation of the concentrated wisdom of the past, was bound to have had an enormous influence on the morals and the intelligence of the race. Riddles, too, were propounded in the same fashion, with the incidental effect of stimulating the powers of observation and whetting the intellect.

They had a wide knowledge of field botany and took great pride in their ability to name the plants of the countryside. And this learning had for them a practical bearing, in that it helped them to know those herbs that possessed medicinal or dyeing properties.

They had skilled musicians, acknowledged masters of the harp and of the pipe and they were able to appreciate the best that these matchless musicians could produce; so that, on the whole, the sum of their culture must have been a notable quantity.

And they did not neglect to pay attention to the advancement of education. Tacksmen, and others who could afford it, formed themselves into organisations in order to employ teachers to educate their children. They were often able to secure the services of men of ability for this purpose, with the result that such a love of the classics was then inculcated and maintained during the following century, that the name of Skye was honoured wherever such culture was appreciated.

The most noted schoolmaster of that time in the island was John MacPherson, the son of Rev. Dugald MacPherson, minister of Diurinish. He conducted a school in Orbost, where many a pupil got the benefit of his profound knowledge of Latin and Greek. At that time a noted student of the Classics, and a man of outstanding talents, was Martin Martin, who was tutor to the family of *Iain Breac,* the Chief of Dunvegan. In Sleat, the schoolmaster was James Beverley. According to the *Old Statistical Account,* he taught Latin and most branches of learning. His salary was about £24. In Strath the salary was £22 and there were 60 on the roll, and Latin was taught.

Recreations

During the latter part of the seventeenth century the art of music was widely cultivated and generously patronised in Skye. We know that *Iain Breac* MacLeod maintained a piper, a fiddler, and a harper in his establishment and numerous references are made by contemporary poets to the inspiring artistry of these instrumentalists. *Màiri ni'n Alasdair Ruaidh* sings of:

Piòb nuallanach mhòr,
 Great strumming pipe,
Bheir buaidh air gach ceòl,
 Surpassing all music,

        (Watson, JC, 1934, p. 44)

and *Gàirich nam piòb, 's nan clàrsach a rìs,* "Throbbing of the pipes and the harp thereafter", while Roderick Morison, the blind harper and bard, makes mention of the pipe, the harp, and the fiddle as being played daily in Dunvegan in his own time; and to each he pays a tribute, which, for graphic description of the instruments and their music, has rarely been equalled in our poetry. Of the bagpipes, he says:

'Nam eirigh gu moch
 When early awake
Anns an teaghlach gun sproc, gun ghruaim,
 In the household without dejection or gloom,
Chluinnte gleadhraich nan dos,
 The clamour of the pipe would be heard,
'S an céile 'na cois bho'n t-suain;
 With her partner awakened from sleep;
'N trath ghabhadh i làn,
 Once she was filled,
'S i gu'n cuireadh os 'n aird na fhuair,
 She would express all she got,
Le meoir fhileanta bhinn
 With able, sweet fingering
'S iad gu drithleannach, dianach, luath.
 Flickering, tight fitting and swift.

       (Matheson, W, 1970, p. 60)

His genius finds expression no less happily in his account of his own instrument, the harp:

'Nuair a chuirt i 'na tàmh (*i.e.,* the bagpipe)
 Once she (the bagpipe) was set at rest
Le furtachd na fàrdaich féin,
 Comfortably in her own quarters,
Dhòmhsa b' fhurasd' a ràdh
 It would be easy for me to speak
Is gum bu chuireideach gàir nan teud;
 Of the skilful playing of the harp;
Le iomairt da làmh
 With double-handed movement
A cur binneas do chàch an céill,
 Evolving sweet music for all,
'S gu' bu shiubhlach am chluais
 And flowing to my ear
'Moghunn lùghmhor le luasgan mheur.
 The stirring of swift fingers.

       (Matheson, W, 1970, p. 62)

In another stanza he mentions the fact that singers were accompanied by the music of the violin:

Gheibhte fleasgaich gun ghràin
 Young men would be found without hate
'Na d' thalla gun sgrath, gun fhuath.
 In your hall without dread or gloom.
Mnai fhionna 'n fhuilt réidh,
 Fair women with well groomed hair,
Cur binneas an céill le stuaim;
 Modestly making music;
Le ceilearadh beòil,
 With trilling voices,

Bhiodh gu h-ealanta, òrdail, suaire,
> Music that is talented, well performed and urbane,

Bhiodh fear bogha 'nan còir,
> A violinist nearby,

Ri cur meoghair a mheòir 'nan cluais.
> Keeping them in tune with skillful fingers.

> (Matheson, W, 1970, p. 62)

We gather from a verse in the works of *Màiri ni'n Alasdair Ruaidh* that the organ, or rather the spinet, was in use in Dunvegan at this time:

Sliochd Ollaghair...
> Stock of Olver...

⊰ ✸ ⊱

Nan còrn gormghlas
> Of the blue drinking horns

'S nan ceol òrghain.
> And the music of spinets.

> (Watson, JC, 1934, p. 93)

Nor was music neglected at Duntulm, the seat of the MacDonalds of Skye; but, after a perusal of the works of *Iain Lom*, and of '*An Ciaran Mabach*', one concludes that the pipes held then a subordinate place there to the harp and the fiddle.

These recreations were varied by the telling of tales, the enunciation of proverbs, and the propounding of riddles. Their other indoor diversions did not differ materially from those that were practised in the early portion of the century. They consisted of games with backgammon, dice, cards, etc.; and of them '*An Ciaran Mabach*' says:

'Nàm gluasad bho thir dhuinn,
> When we sailed from shore,

Bu neo-mhiodhair ar lòistean;
> Unstinted would be our provision;

Còrnach, cupanach, fionach,
> Drinking horns and cups of wine,

Glaineach, liontaidh a stòpaibh;
> Glasses filled from flagons;

Gu cairteach, taileasgach, dìsneach,
> Card games, backgammon and dice,

'S tailc air uidh nam fòirnibh;
> Keen in their eagerness for chess men;

Dhòmhsa b' fhurasd sud innseadh,
> It would be easy for me to say,

Bu chuid de m ghniomh 'o m' aois òige.
> That that was my activity in the days of my youth.

> (MacKenzie, J, 1877, p. 56)

Their outdoor sports, too, had suffered no change – putting the stone, wrestling, leaping; and they were passionately fond of hunting:

'S e bu mhiannach lem' leanabh
> It would be my dear one's pleasure

Bhith am beannaibh na seilge;
> To be hunting in the peaks;

Gabhail aighear na frithe,
> Taking joy of the forest,

'S a direadh nan garbh-ghlac:
> And ascending the rough dells:

A' leigeil nan cuilean,
> Letting slip the young hounds,

'S a furan nan seanna chon,
> And inciting the old ones,

'*S e bu dheireadh do'n fhiuran*
    Of that incitement it would come
Ud fuil thoirt air calgaibh,
    That blood would flow on the bristles,
O luchd nan céir geala,
    Of the folk with the white flanks,
'*S nam falluinnean dearga.*
    And the russet mantles.

                    (Watson, JC, 1934, p. 42)

Weapons

The weapons in use were bows and arrows, dirks, swords, carbines, and fowling-pieces. In one of her songs, *Màiri n'in Alasdair Ruaidh* gives an interesting account of the arms in the 'gun-room' of Sir Norman of Bernera:

Gheibhte sud ann ad fhàrdaich,
    In thy dwelling would be found,
An càradh air ealachainn,
    Ranged upon the weapon rack,
Miosair, is adharc, is rogha gach armachd,
    Powder horn and shot horn and the choice of every armoury,
Agus lanntainean tana,
    And sword blades slender,
'*O 'n ceanaibh gu 'm barra dheis;*
    Tapering from the hilt to the tip,
Gheibhte sud air gach slios dhiubh,
    And would be found on each side of them,
Isneach, is cairbinn,
    Rifle and carbine,
Agus iubhar chruaidh fhallain,
    And bows tough and sound,
Le'n taifeidean cainbe.

With their bow strings of hemp.
Agus iubhar chruaidh fhallain,
    And bows tough and sound,
Le'n taifeidean cainbe,
    With their bow strings of hemp,
Agus cuilbhearan caola,
    And narrow culverins,
Air an daoiread gu'n ceannaicht' iad,
    That would be bought although dear;
Glac nan ceann liobhte,
    A handful of polished arrows,
Air chur sios ann am balgaibh,
    Thrust down into quivers,
'*O iteach an fhir-eoin,*
    Fledged with the plumage of the eagle,
'*S o shioda na Gaillebhein.*
    And the silk of Galway.

                    (Watson, JC, 1934, p. 40)

The Chiefs

There is noticeable, towards the end of this period, a marked change in the attitude of the chiefs towards the clan. No longer satisfied with the old ways of life at home, they sought the cities of the south where they often spent their means in extravagance. We have seen this, especially, in the case of Sir James *Mór*, the Chief of the MacDonalds and of Roderick, the son and successor of *Iain Breac*, the celebrated chief of the MacLeods.

In order to meet the increasing demands of an artificial mode of life, they began to exact higher dues from their people but what pained the latter more than anything else was that the chiefs were losing interest in the culture of their own race.

In spite of all this, the chief still continued to be revered by his clan. So strong was the bond that held them to him that his wants were ungrudgingly supplied. He could act, if he chose, as the autocrat, for he had power of life and death over his clan. Invested with the privilege of heritable jurisdiction, he made a circuit of his estates, holding courts for the trial of those guilty of misdemeanours, and settling disputes. Near the ruin of Duntulm Castle is a round knoll called the 'Hill of Pleas', where the Chief of the MacDonalds dispensed justice in that portion of Trotternish; and there is a similar site in the vicinity of Ullinish House which, as the Rev. Donald MacQueen informed Boswell, was known as *"the Hill of Strife, for justice was of old administered there"* (Boswell, J, 1955, p. 167).

In their itinerary, the chiefs were accompanied by a large body of their cadets and others of the principal members of the clan. They were still entitled to those privileges of 'Bonnacht' and 'Coshering' – tributes covered by the term, *cuid-oidhche* or 'night-portion', referred to in a previous section, the former being an obligation to provide free lodging for the chief and his retinue, the latter an exaction for the victualling of the party.

Firm as was their loyalty to their chief, and genuine as was their reverence for his person, it was, however, always clear that his interests were subordinate to those of his clan whenever these should fail to harmonise. We have seen this in an acute form when domestic dissensions between Sir James *Mór* and his son, Donald, threatened trouble to the House of Sleat. Then the leaders of the clan met in conclave, and, in no uncertain voice, informed the disputants that, unless they composed their differences, the chief would be summarily deposed, and the heir would be prevented from the succession.

The Commissioners of Clan Grant, at the beginning of the eighteenth century, had the young Laird of Grant imprisoned, for his prodigality that endangered the welfare of the Clan lands (Stewart, D, 1885, pp. 68–9 note) and, in 1522, at the insistence of the principal kinsmen, the Laird of Innes was consigned to Garringoe Castle for *"wasting his landis and guidis"* (Forbes, D,

1698, pp. 98–9). See also MacFarlane's *Genealogical Collections* (Mitchell, A, 1906, p. 182) where the resignation of Ferquherd MacIntosh of MacIntosh is effected by the clansmen in favour of his uncle.

The Land

Cultivation and Tenure

We have seen, in the Regulations for Chiefs of 1616, that it was enacted, among other precepts, that the chiefs were to let any land they themselves could not cultivate, that they were to set up home-farms, and make 'planting' about their houses, in order to add to the amenities of their estates.

Tacks

Some difficulty was naturally experienced by the chiefs in collecting rents for the lands they had thus let, and they were accordingly led to dispose of large tracts of it on tack – i.e., by a lease granted for a specified period. The tacks were often of large extent, the stock of one of average size being 40 cows, 40 followers, 36 horses and about 120 sheep. The arable land of such a holding produced 70 bolls of barley, 20 of oats and an equal quantity of rye.

The obligations imposed on the tacksmen were:

1 Grassum, which was a premium paid by the tenant to his superior on his entering on a lease; and, for a large holding, it might be as much as 300 merks, or its equivalent in cattle.
2 Rental – This usually took two forms, namely, that paid in kind and made up of cattle, poultry, butter, cheese, fish, and blankets or that of money rent, which was designated 'tack-duty'.

3   The rendering of military service.

When Donald *Gorm Mór* of Sleat received a charter for his lands in 1596 from James VI, he was also given a 'letter of tack' for Trotternish.

Wadset

The chief, or other superior, sometimes disposed of an extent of land to a tenant on mortgage and such tenure was termed 'wadset'. The occupier of such a holding was obliged to pay the crown dues and the ecclesiastical duties that fell on his portion. He was at liberty to sub-let, or to sub-divide, his land; but he laboured under the disadvantage that his superior could displace him, or his sub-tenants, whenever the amount of the security could be paid.

This form of land tenure became very common in Skye when the chiefs sought the luxury of the cities and were always in need of money. It appears to have been instituted under the regime of Sir James *Mór* of Sleat, and of Roderick MacLeod, the predecessor of *Iain Breac*. Then numerous wadsetters sprang up all at once on the island. They consisted of the principal men of the clan and in many cases they held other lands on 'tack', in addition to those that were leased to them on 'wadset' by the chief. The wadsetters became so numerous in Skye during the eighteenth century and held their lands so long, that it is difficult to distinguish them from the tacksmen. Among many similar contracts, there is extant a notice of the bestowal of a wadset of land in Bornaskitaig on Archibald MacDonald by his brother, the chief, Sir James *Mór*, in 1667.

The larger tenants sub-let portions of their holdings and they assigned plots to workers in return for labour. The latter built houses on their land, while a souming of cattle and sheep was also allotted to them. The arable land of these sub-tenants was held on the runrig system, and was apportioned usually by lot. The principal crops that were grown consisted of barley, oats, rye, and flax.

An indication of the relative extent of the estates of the three great chiefs of Skye at the end of the seventeenth century is afforded by the amount of rental for each, being £7000 for MacLeod, £6200 for MacDonald, and £2400 for MacKinnon (Cameron, A, 1871, p. 74).

Trade

The selling of the black cattle of the island, begun by *Do'ull Mac Iain 'ic Sheumais* before 1650, was continued by him into the latter portion of the seventeenth century. Others, by his example, now took part in that profitable industry. So prosperous had this trade proved to be, that the higher ranks no longer considered it an indignity to engage in this and other pursuits. *"Trade"*, says Fletcher of Saltoun, *"is now become the golden ball for which all nations in the world are contending"*, and, as inter-clan warfare had then ceased, the men of Skye were not averse to participate in the benefits that accrued from this industry.

Fishing still continued to be profitable around our shores, and large quantities of herring and salmon were secured. The natives were now less disinclined to engage in it; but they were lacking in resource, so that the major portion of the gains went to the Lowland crews, and especially to the Dutchmen, who were on very friendly terms with the islanders. It has been said that, about the beginning of the following century, as many as 700 Dutch vessels were employed annually in fishing in Scotland. They had obtained an enormous advantage over the native fishers, in that they had introduced the method of barrelling the herring for transmission to the continental markets.

The wool of the native sheep was sold to manufacturers in the eastern counties of Scotland, and some of it was woven locally into a coarse woollen cloth called 'plaiding', that was exported to Denmark, and to the Netherlands; but the trade in this commodity was never very active.

During the major portion of this period, there was a state of great disquiet in the Highlands, so that trade sustained a serious set-back. Skye suffered much because of the part many of the clansmen took in the campaigns of Montrose, of Charles II and of Dundee; and we saw that Sir Donald of Sleat remained in opposition to the government until late in the year 1691. There were so many in arms all over the Highlands that robberies were rife, with the result that those who drove their cattle to the Lowland markets were often deprived of whole herds. It required men of the resolution and the prowess of *Do'ull Mac Iain 'ic Sheumais* to run the gauntlet of these marauders successfully. In a letter written by Fraser of Beaufort to *Iain Breac* MacLeod of Dunvegan, in 1691, there is a statement to the effect that *"the letter may not reach you owing to robbers"*, while in another epistle, written to that chief also, this time by his oldest son and heir, Roderick, who was a student at the University of Edinburgh in 1690, it is stated that he could not enter college that year, for all the *"masters"* and professors were to be displaced and *"no man can lay his mind to his book for reason of the tumult and confusion"* (Mackenzie, A, 1889, p. 167).

Industry

Some of the principal industries, such as agriculture, fishing, cattle-dealing, and the manufacture of cloth, have already been dealt with. There were meal mills in several districts and people were ordered to send their grain to these places to be ground. In exchange for his labour, the miller received a modicum, consisting usually of one-thirteenth part of the meal produced and it would appear that he exacted a toll from every householder, whether the grain was sent to him or not. This claim was

called 'multure'; and there is a distinct reference to it in a song composed by *Màiri ni'n Alasdair Ruaidh*, to John, the son of Sir Norman of Bernera:

> *Ged theid mi dom' leabaidh,*
>> Though I go to my bed,
> *Chan e cadal is miannach leam,*
>> It is not sleep I desire,
> *Aig ro mheud na tuile,*
>> For the flood is so great,
> *'S mo mhuileann gun iarunn air:*
>> And my mill is unshod:
> *Tha mholltair ri pàigheadh,*
>> The multure is to be paid,
> *Mur cailltear am bliadhna mi,*
>> If this year is not to ruin me,
> *'S gur feumail dhomh faighinn,*
>> And get it I must,
> *Ge do ghabhainn an iasad i.*
>> Though it be that I borrow it.

(Watson, JC, 1934, p. 82)

Private milling had been prohibited by a law passed in the year 1284. By it the miller was empowered to seize and break all the querns in his district but it is improbable that this regulation was enforced with much rigour in the islands and we know that in Skye there were querns in most households then, and that grinding was a daily exercise.

There were three methods of preparing the grain for the milling. These were:

1 *Ealachaidh*, in which the corn was parched in a kiln;
2 *Earraraidh*, when it was slowly parched in a pot over the fire before grinding, and

3   *Gradaning*, in which sheaves of corn were, in turn, held over a flame and the ears were separated from the straw and partially parched before the grinding.

The meal produced by the last operation was considered to possess greater palatability than that yielded by either of the other processes. The details of its production are as follows: splints of burning wood were held under a sheaf of corn, and the ears thus separated were allowed to fall on a piece of cloth, or a dried skin. The corn was then winnowed, parched in a pot, ground with the quern and winnowed again, to produce the meal. It is said that the whole operation, including the baking of the bread, could be accomplished in the space of one hour. The work of gradaning corn was carried on, as we shall see later, far into the succeeding century.

The three methods of preparing the corn are referred to in a stanza of an old poem:

> *Ma 's ealachaidh a th'agad, no gradan,*
> > Whether the grain be parched in a pot or by flame,
> *Ma 's earraraidh e, thoir dhomh màm;*
> > Whether in the kiln, give me a bag;
> *'S ma's acras, gu'r manadh 'ga chasgadh,*
> > If you suffer from hunger the means of arresting it,
> *Fideagann blasda mhin bhàin.*
> > Are the tasty crumbs of white meal.

In grinding, two circular slabs of stone were used, the convex face of the upper stone fitting into the concave surface of the lower one. Two persons generally attended to the grinding, one feeding the quern and the other rotating the upper stone. It was, of course, held to be beneath the dignity of a man to engage in this work, as in many another form of manual labour, and the old hunter-bard of Lochaber, *Do'ull MacFhionnlaigh nan Dàn*, pointedly adverts to this prejudice in his magnificent poem, *A' Chomhachag*:

> *B' annsa leam na dùrdan bodaich*
> > I would prefer to the humming of the carle (old man)
> *Os cionn lic ag earraradh sil,*
> > Over the quern grinding corn,
> *Bùirean an daimh am bi ghne dhuinnead*
> > The belling of the stag, by nature dun (brown)
> *Air leacainn beinne 's e ri sin'.*
> > In flight on the mountain slope.
> > > (Mackenzie, J, 1877, p. 18)

The work of grinding was accompanied, as were most forms of labour, by an appropriate song. *"The island lassies"*, says Pennant, speaking of his tour through Skye in 1770, *"the island lassies, as in the days of Aristophanes 'warbled as they ground their parched corn' "*. We have numerous examples of this type of 'labour'-song and the following is given, as its rhythm so well illustrates the movement of the quern; and it shows the prevalence of superstitious beliefs among the people of that time:

> *Cuir 'n car deiseal am feasda de'n bhràth,*
> > At all times turn the quern sunwise,
> *Ma's math leat min bhàin bhith torrach dhut,*
> > If you would wish white meal to be nourishing,
> *Mu'n cuairt i na stìll, le luinneagan binn,*
> > Round with it gushing, with merry verses,
> *'S cha toirear do'n t-sìthean deannal dhith.*
> > And not a pinch of it to be taken to the fairy knoll.

Quern stones were usually made of the gneiss of the mainland, the district of Lochaber being long noted for their manufacture; and they cost then about 14/– per set. The production of these, later to become such an important industry there, had not yet begun in the island of Raasay.

Diet

The food of the people does not seem to have changed to any appreciable extent during this century, though the steak of seal, and of the stranded whale, was sometimes added to the menu. Beyond this, however, they made much use of shellfish, of which there was an abundance in every sea loch, according to writers of that time. In Macfarlane's *Geographical Collections,* (Mitchell, A, 1906, p. 220) mention is made, among other molluscs, of *"an infinite number of oysters"*. The poor had little else in late winter and spring except bread and brochan or skilly, but on that scanty fare they were able to toil all day. Their powers of endurance were marvellous, aided it must be said, by a magnificent fund of fortitude. One has only to refer to the campaigns of Montrose in illustration of this characteristic, when long distances were covered in such a short time as to excite the surprise and the admiration of all who ever heard of their exploits; and yet these hardy warriors had often to subsist, for days together, on nothing else save a little oatmeal mixed in cold water.

There is extant a very interesting account of the people of the Western Isles, written by a certain William Sacheverell, who, in 1688, had been commissioned to salve the '*Florida*', a ship of the Spanish Armada, which had been sunk 100 years previously in the bay of Tobermory. Of the people, he says: *"They appear in all their actions to have a certain air of freedom and contempt of those trifles, luxury and ambition which we so servilely creep after. They bind their appetites by their necessities, and their*

happiness consists, not in having much, but in coveting little" (Sacchaverel, W, 1859, p. 19).

In the *Spottiswoode Miscellany*, we find reference to *"men of good stature, strong and nimble"* in Skye at that time (Maidment, J, 1845, p. 348).

Yet in that same year the people of Skye were in sore straits. Owing to the fact that very little food was imported, terrible privations were endured when, from climatic or other causes, the staple crops failed. The Rev. Donald Martin, who wrote the *First Statistical Account* for Kilmuir, makes mention of that memorable year as follows: *"In 1688 the seasons were so eminently unfavourable, and corn was so deficient in quantity and quality, that the poor actually perished on the highways for want of aliment"*. Such contingencies were of frequent occurrence in those days.

The people were less intemperate during the latter portion of the seventeenth century than they had been during its earlier part. Indeed, it is no exaggeration to say that not one-third of the amount of wine consumed previously was now used but it is noteworthy that other liquors had made their appearance; whisky, brandy and ale being introduced about 1650. The bards refer to these intoxicants then for the first time. In his poem, *B'annsa Cadal air Fraoch*, Archibald MacDonald, 'An Ciaran Mabach', sings thus of the red deer, incidentally mentioning whisky and ale:

> *B'e mo ghràdhsa fear buidhe,*
> My love is the yellow one (stag),
> *Nach dean suidhe mu'n bhòrd;*
> Who sits not at table;
> *Nach iarradh ri cheannach*
> That will not seek to buy
> *Pinnt leanna no beòir;*
> A pint of ale or beer,

Uisge beatha math dùbailt
> Good whisky, twice distilled

Cha b'e b' fhiu leat ri òl;
> You would not consider worth drinking;

B' fhearr leat biolair an fhuarain,
> You would prefer the watercress of the spring,

A's uisge luaineach nan lòn;
> And the restless water of the streams;

> (MacKenzie, J, 1877, p. 54)

while *Iain Lom*, in a lament written on the death of Sir James MacDonald, the brother of *An Ciaran Mabach*, in 1678, describes the entertainments that were wont to be held in the castle of Duntulm during the life-time of the dead chief:

Bhiodh do ghillean mu seach
> Your attendants would in turn

'Lionadh dibhe b' fhearr blas
> Be filling liquour of best taste

Fion Spàinteach dearg ac', agus beòir;
> Red Spanish wine and beer of the best,

Uisge beatha nam pios,
> Whisky in cups,

Rachadh 'n t' airgead ga dhiol,
> That would be bought with money,

Gheibhte 'n glain' e mar ghriog de'n òr.
> Found in the glass like a bead of gold.

> (Mackenzie, J, 1877, p. 48)

Most of the whisky was brewed locally from the surplus grain, and all partook of it, in order, as they thought, to counteract the baleful influence of the moist climate on their constitution; but the inordinate indulgences that were so marked a feature of the early part of the century were now almost unknown.

They had a craving for snuff, and would work contentedly in the hope of getting a pinch of that stimulant at the end of the day. In the works of the bard, *Iain Lom,* we find a reference to this also, as:

'S ann leam nach bu chruaidh an ghaoir ud
> I regretted not the cry

Bh' aig mnaibh galach nam falt sgaoilteach,
> Of weeping women with dishevelled hair,

Bhi 'gan tarruinn mar bheul snaoisean,
> Snorting like a snuff taker,

Sealg nam boc, mu dhos nam maoilseach.
> The quest of the buck at the rump of the doe.

And *Mairi ni'n Alasdair Ruaidh* composed a poem to John MacLeod, son of Norman of Bernera, on receiving a snuff mull from him as a present (Watson, JC, 1934, p. 82).

Manner of Living

The homes of the people consisted of rude hovels, some constructed of dry stone with very thick walls, others had walls made of earth. The former were thatched with the straw of oats, of barley, or of rye, which was used in the spring as manure for the fields; the latter were often covered only with divots and, as the grassy side was outermost, the whole structure soon assumed the appearance of a mound of green earth. The dwelling-houses of the more prosperous tacksmen were constructed of stone and lime and were partitioned into rooms, in many instances by means of thick stone walls; but the vast majority had no divisions whatsoever.

Some of the cattle were housed during the winter months under the same roof as their owners, even in the more pretentious houses, and the poultry were freely admitted all the year round.

During the day the house was lit by the door, the smoke hole and, in warm weather, by a slit in the wall that did duty for a window. The last was closed by clods of earth, or a bag of straw, when weather conditions were unfavourable. At night the partitionless interior was lighted by the fire that was placed in the middle of the floor, helped sometimes by the smoky and foul-smelling cruisie, with its bath of oil prepared from the seal, the whale, or fish offal and its wick of the pith of the bullrush.

In the homes of the chiefs, and the more affluent tacksmen, candles were in use in Skye, a fact illustrated by a reference to them in the lament by *Iain Lom* on the death of Sir James Mac-Donald of Sleat, in 1678:

> *Coinnlean geala de'n chéir,*
>> White candles of wax,
> *'S iad a' lasadh gu geur,*
>> Burning keenly,
> *Urlar farsuinn mu'n eight' an t-òl.*
>> Wide floor where drink would be offered.
>>> (Mackenzie, J, 1877, p. 48)

During the day the women were engaged in the industries of digging, harrowing and reaping, in their season; and at night they were busy in the home, grinding, spinning and weaving. For them there was no time for leisure. The woman was still the slave of the tribe, always employed on the heaviest and the most irksome toil. The men folk were comparatively idle, for labour in the field was still dishonourable to men with pretensions and the only occupation in which they would deign to take part was the rearing of cattle.

The people were hospitable to a fault, and they would give the best they could afford to the stranger, no matter what his station might be; for after his circumstances they never enquired and they considered it an honour to entertain him. Despite the advantage that was so frequently taken of this noble characteristic, they never grew weary of providing for the wayfarer and, on his departure, they supplied him with a stock of necessaries for his journey. We need not wonder at the fact that, as a result of this spirit of kindliness, homeless vagabonds and worthless idlers continued to prey upon them. Hence we find that, at the beginning of his chiefship, Sir Donald of Sleat granted a commission to the Chief of the MacKinnons in 1679, enjoining him to bring to justice all 'sorners' in the district of Strath (MacDonald, A & A, 1904, p. 70).

There were then, of course, no institutions for those who were incapacitated by age, by physical infirmity or mental deficiency from providing for themselves. Still, these unfortunates never lacked the necessaries of life and, no matter how cantankerous their nature might be, they were never turned away from the door at which they called for food and shelter.

On account of the primitive conditions of sanitation that then prevailed, epidemics took a terrible toll of life. The ravages of such diseases as smallpox and fevers were truly appalling and were responsible for the fact that the population did not appreciably increase on the cessation of the clan wars at the beginning of this century.

Although they had physicians like the Beatons and the MacLeans, skilful practitioners in their day and generation, most of the people were their own physicians; and superstitious cures were believed to have far greater potency than the most carefully prepared remedies. An incantation muttered over the sufferer, a special flower carried on the person, the movements, sunwise or the opposite, of a vessel placed on the surface of a sacred well, were firmly held to possess properties that could counteract the

most diverse ailments and who can say but that their faith had sometimes made them whole!

Marriage Customs

Although some contracts were still carried out, according to the ancient custom of 'handfasting', the institution of marriage was then in a large measure under the auspices of the Church. When a young man desired a woman's hand, he went to her home with a few of his friends, among whom his father took a prominent part. The company stood in the doorway, where the oldest of them intimated that they had come to ascertain if one of the daughters of the house, who was, of course, mentioned by name, would marry him who had come in quest of a wife. If her people consented, the party was invited to enter and, after they had partaken of refreshments, they departed. This stage in the preparation for the nuptials was called *'An Còrdadh Beag'*, or 'The Little Agreement'.

A fortnight or so, thereafter, a more important ceremony took place. This was *An Reiteach Mór*, or 'The Great Contract', when, after much discussion, such matters as the amount of the dowry, and the date of the wedding day, were fixed. Great care was exercised in the choice of the latter, for no day of the week was considered to be auspicious except Tuesday or Thursday and no time except a period of waxing moon.

About a week before the nuptials were to be celebrated, the young couple perambulated the district together, inviting their neighbours to the marriage feast. All those who attended the wedding brought presents in kind, but only of such articles as might be of use at the function. The duration of the ceremony was determined by the amount of the commissariat that had been collected, so that, as a rule, it lasted for a few days and on occasion even as long as a week. Much healthy fun was then indulged in. At night, songs of interminable length were sung, accompanied by the sweet notes of the harp; while the exhilarating strains of the pipe roused even the most lethargic to take part in the dance. During the day the young men vied with one another in athletic feats; but on that occasion it was obvious that their aim was to display their prowess rather than to exercise the body.

On the conclusion of the entertainment, a procession was formed, and the bridal party conveyed to their new home. This used to be a picturesque spectacle, as men and women in couples swung along the road, arm in arm, to the accompaniment of a chorus of songs, or the playing of pipes. On their arrival at their destination, the concluding item in the round of ceremonies was performed. The oldest member of the party, who was deputed to receive the young bride, broke a bannock over her head just as she stepped across the threshold. She entered, and immediately a boisterous scrimmage ensued to secure a piece of the lucky bread.

These marriage customs were upheld for many generations after the period with which we are now dealing and a few of them cannot be said to have fallen into desuetude, even in our own day.

In accordance with his rights as superior, the chief demanded a fine from the father of the bride. The exaction then was in kind, consisting of some animal, such as a horse, cow, or sheep. But later it took the form of money, the amount of which depended on the station of the young wife (Henderson, G, 1911, pp. 247–52).

Death Customs

When a death took place in a district, all work was suspended until after the interment, as a mark of respect for the deceased. If there was any food that was immediately perishable in the house in which the corpse lay, a piece of iron was inserted in the substance, as otherwise they believed it would degenerate synchronously with the corruption of the dead body. All the fires were extinguished, and were not rekindled until the burial took place. The body was placed on deal boards, with two vessels on its chest, one containing earth and the other salt – symbols of the mortal body and the imperishable soul.

Neighbours watched the body by turns, and their duty was called a 'Wake'. Much food and drink were then consumed, so that it often happened that the relatives of the dead person were impoverished for years as a result of the drain on their resources. The bard, too, officiated there, when he recited his song of praise, the *Moladh Mairbh*, for which he never failed to get a substantial reward (Guthrie, EJ, 1885, pp. 211–12).

On the day of interment, which was never a Friday, the body was carried to the churchyard in solemn procession and women followed the cortege wailing their eerie dirges, which were supposed to ensure rest for the soul.

In the case of the poor, the body was enclosed in a coffin of wickerwork that belonged to the parish. The bottom of this receptacle was hinged so that, after the body had been lowered into the grave, this crate could be used again when required. It was called *caisil chrò*.

After the burial, the neighbours continued their 'wakes' at the grave until the next interment, sheltering in small rude huts, called *bothain caithris*.

Superstitions

All their movements were carried out, so far as possible, in strict accordance with the direction of the apparent motion of the sun. An instance of this observance has already been given in the stanza quoted from the 'quern song'. When putting to sea, they rowed the boat sunwise at first, the contrary course being supposed to be the prelude to certain disaster.

In order that they might bring auspicious weather conditions, they poured libations into the sea, or on sacred stone in their chapels, and a similar rite was performed when fish had forsaken the coasts, for thereby they sought to conciliate the spirit that presided over the produce of the sea.

The being that controlled the yield of the flocks was called *Gruagach* – a long-haired woman, whose malicious interference with the cattle could be counteracted only by weekly offerings of milk poured into the hollow of the *gruagach* stone of the district. These liberations offered were made on Mondays before sunrise, and it was significant of the attitude to the practice that three such stones are known in Skye. Of the practice, Martin Martin observes, *"there were scarce any, the least village in which this superstitious custom could not prevail. I have enquired the reason for it from several well-meaning people who, until of late had practised it, and they told me that it had been transmitted to them by their ancestors who believed it was attended with great fortune"*. (Martin, M, 1716, p. 110). The evil-eye was also considered to be responsible for charming the milk away from the cows; and in order to defeat its machinations people had recourse to various practices. The person whose stock was affected sometimes perambulated the district in which the individual suspected of possessing the evil influence resided and, going from house to house, he exhibited the milk whose quality had been impaired, in order that the eye that charmed its essence away might behold it and thereby restore its stolen property. These sinister persons were invariably witches, who, in the shape of cat or hare, carried out their nefarious work in the stillness of the night. In their assumed appearance they were sometimes maimed by dogs and the injury persisting, even after they had reverted to the human form, they were thus identified! (Henderson, G, 1911, pp. 294–5).

The belief in the existence of second-sight held then a strong grip on the imagination of the people. They were persuaded that it was wholly an involuntary power, that even pained its unfortunate possessor. It is on record that a servant of the Rev. Dugald MacPherson, who was minister of Duirinish at this time, was endowed with this faculty, and that he warned his master that the corn the latter was about to parch in a kiln would be consumed by fire; and, notwithstanding every precaution, the whole consignment was destroyed as foretold. On the repetition of the process, and a similar premonition having been given, a like result ensued.

As in previous centuries and for many succeeding years, the time for commencing any labour was determined by the phases of the moon. Certain operations were entered upon when the moon was waning; others again were to be begun only when the moon was new. And certain days of the week were considered to be unpropitious for specified undertakings, the most lucky being Monday; the least favourable, Saturday. The following quatrain illustrates this quaint notion:

> *Imrich Sathurna mu thuath,*
>> Move on Saturday to the North,
> *Imrich Diluain mu dheas.*
>> On Monday to the South.
> *Ged nach biodh agam ach an t-uan*
>> But if I had but a lamb,
> *Is ann Diluain a dh' fhalbhainn leis.*
>> On Monday I would go with it.
>>> (Henderson, G, 1911, p. 293 fn)

Dress

The men wore the tartan kilt and plaid, each district having its own fancy in the manner of colouring and design, so that, according to Martin, it was possible to tell the place of residence of a man by the pattern of his dress. The trews also, was then an article of clothing. Thus, in his description of the grandeur of the castle of Duntulm, during the chiefship of Sir Donald, the first baronet of Sleat, who died in 1643, *Iain Lom* makes mention of the fact that:

> *Gur lionmhor triubhas saothrach seang ann.*
>> With many trews, slender and well-filled.

The *earasaid* was worn by the women, and was a white plaid with a few stripes of blue, black, and red colours, and it extended to the heels. It was constricted around the waist by a belt that was tied by a buckle of silver, or brass, according to the station of its wearer. Some of these buckles were of extravagant size, being, according to Martin, as large as *"a pewter plate"*. They were set in the centre with a large crystal, while the circumference was studded with smaller stones. Some wore a leathern belt adorned with pieces of silver.

The matron was distinguished from the maiden by having her hair covered by the *breid*, or 'coif'; while the latter wore the *stiom*, or 'snood'.

All the materials for clothing were manufactured in the home; and natural dyes, locally prepared, were used in the colouring of the apparel.

The Bards

Archibald MacDonald (An Ciaran Mabach)
This poet and warrior was a son of *Do'ull Gorm Og MacGhilleasbuig Chléirich*, the first baronet of Sleat. He was not, as is erroneously stated by MacKenzie, (Mackenzie, J, 1877, p. 53), the *"son of Sir Alexander MacDonald, sixteenth baronet of Slate"*, for that step has not even yet been reached in the baronetcy of

that house, as the present holder of the dignity (1930) is only the fourteenth in descent from Sir Donald, the father of our bard.

The bard's name was Archibald; *Gilleasbuig Ruadh*, he was sometimes called and is so named by *Iain Lom* in one of his songs. In view of that designation, it is difficult to account for the nickname *Ciaran*, or 'Dusky One', that is more commonly assigned to him (although in a poem in the *Eigg Collection*, *Marbhrann do Shir Seumas Mór*, 'Elegy to Sir James *Mór*', he is called, *'Gilleasbuig Dubh MacDhòmhnuill'* (Turner, P, 1809, p. 35). The epithet, *Mabach*, having probably been applied because of an impediment in speech.

We first hear of him in 1654, when he secured a wadset for the district of Bornaskitaig, in Trotternish and it would appear that he also occupied lands in North Uist. He was resident in the latter island when the chief, Sir James *Mór*, received from the Privy Council a commission of *"fire and sword"* against the murderers of the Children of Keppoch. The chief delegated the duty to his brother and the latter, with thirty trusty warriors, set off for Inverlair, under the guidance of *Iain Lom* and soon brought the usurpers to justice.

So expeditiously and effectively had they executed the work entrusted to them, that Sir James received the thanks of the government, and *Iain Lom* paid the following tribute in verse to his brother bard:

Slàn fod' thriall a Chiarain Mhabaich
    Fortune favour your journey Ciaran Mabach
Shiubhladh sliabh gun bhiadh, gun chadal;
    Who would traverse the moor without food or sleep;
Beul gun ghò, gun bhòsd, gun bhagradh,
    Lips without guile, vaunting or threat,
Chuir thu ceò fo 'n ròiseil bhradaich.
    You smoked out that pilfering rabble.

                (Mackenzie, J, 1877, p. 39)

But it is from his fame as a bard, rather than his exploits as a soldier, that *An Ciaran Mabach* is now remembered. Of his works, only three pieces are extant, one, *B'annsa Cadal air Fraoch*, written during an enforced sojourn in Edinburgh owing to a sprained foot. It is full of a poet's longing for the scenes and the pursuits he loved and is characterised by a pleasing imagery and a deep feeling for nature. How ecstatically he sings of the stag:

'Nuair a thigeadh am foghar,
    When autumn comes round,
Bu bhinn leam gleadhar do chléibh;
    Sweet to me the bellow of your chest;
Dol a ghabhail a' chrònain
    Going a-roaring
Air a' mhòintich bhuig, réidh;
    On the soft peaty moor;
Dol an coinneamh do leannain,
    Going to meet your lover;
Bu ghile feaman is céir;
    Of whitest tail and quarters,
Gur h-i 'n eilid bu bhòidhche,
    The hind is the prettiest,
'S bu bhrisge, lògh-mhora, ceum.
    With its brisk majestic tread.

                (Mackenzie, J, 1877, p. 54)

There is no straining after effect in the efforts of this bard. His diction flows unforced with a quiet, yet stately naturalness that is markedly pleasing to the fancy. His skilful vowel-play, the sweet harmony of his finely-filed phrase, its polish, its chastity, and its noble sentiment, all make one regret that so little of his work has been preserved; while these qualities force the conclusion on us that he had written much more that has been irretrievably lost.

As an example of perfect assonance, and the expression of genuine pathos, there is little in Gaelic poetry to surpass the following stanza from *Marbhrann*, or the lament he composed on the death of his brother, Sir James, in 1678:

Fàth m' acain, 's mo thùrsa,
   The source of my moaning and sorrow,
Nach dùisgear le teud thu,
   That you cannot be wakened by the harp,
No le toraghan na fidhle,
   Or the murmuring of the violin,
Mo dhiobhuill, 's mo léir-chreach:
   My loss and my utter devastation:
Fhir a chumadh i dionach,
   He who would keep her (galley) dry,
Dh' aindheoin siantan 'gan éiread,
   In spite of the surging tempest,
'N diugh fo leacann na h-ùrach,
   Is today beneath the flags of the grave,
Gun mo dhùil s' ri thu éirigh.
   Without hope of rising again.
                              (Mackenzie, J, 1877, p. 54)

Very few facts are known of the life of this poet. He died about the year 1688.

Mary Macleod (*Màiri n'in Alasdair Ruaidh*)

That assonantal property, which is so characteristic a feature of the works of *An Ciaran Mabach*, has been brought to the acme of expression by *Màiri ni'n Alasdair Ruaidh*, the bardess of Dunvegan.

Much has been written about this poetic genius, but we know very little that is really authentic concerning the facts of her life.

Most authors draw their information from *The Beauties of Gaelic Poetry*, though the account given there is, in many instances, wholly unreliable (Mackenzie, J, 1877, pp. 20–1). The date of her birth, given by MacKenzie as 1569, is obviously wrong, for we know that she was writing her best poetry over a century after that time. It is clear that the verse:

Bha fios co sibh
   It was known who you were
Ann an iomartas rìgh,
   In the Royalist cause,
'Nuair bu mhuladach strì Theàrlaich,
   When Charles' struggle was at its direst,
                              (Watson, JC, 1934, p. 48)

refers to the part the MacLeods played on the side of the Stuarts at Worcester, and after; while her poem, *Cumha Do Mhac Leòid*, was written on the death of the chief, Roderick, 'The Witty', an event that happened in 1664.

And there is as much uncertainty concerning the date of her death, for if, as is generally stated, it took place in 1693, she would then have attained the phenomenal age of 124 years. Then, again, her *Cumha Mhic Leòid* was written by her as a lament, on the death of her patron, Sir Norman of Bernera, the warrior son of Sir Rory *Mór* and as he died in 1705, she must have lived to the age of 136 years at least, if 1569 was the date of her birth.

Furthermore, MacKenzie declares that he heard a poem composed by her, but never published, in which she averred she had nursed five lairds of the MacLeods and two of Applecross; and, the song ends with an address to *'Tormad nan tri Tormaid'*. Now this "third successive Norman" was the heir of the chief, General MacLeod, and, as he was killed on board the 'Queen Charlotte' about 1790, it is evident that *Màiri ni'n Alasdair Ruaidh* could not have been the author of that composition.

MacKenzie affirms, in addition, that most of her poetry was written in praise of a chief whom he calls 'Sir Norman'. Now, of the chiefs of the name of Norman who approach nearest to her time, the first died in 1585, and the next assumed the chiefship in 1699 and it is noteworthy that, of all the chiefs of the name of Norman in the House of Dunvegan, none had ever received the honour of knighthood.

In his efforts to explain the reason for her banishment, Mac-Kenzie makes the extraordinary statement (exhibiting a woeful lack of understanding of the psychology of that time) that the chief so resented the songs his panegyrist composed in his praise, that he drove her into exile to the Isle of Mull! (Mackenzie, J, 1877, pp. 20–1).

The subject of the poems of *Màiri ni'n Alasdair Ruaidh* was none other than the famous Sir Norman of Bernera, the third son of Sir Rory *Mór* and it has been suggested that it was because she extolled the praises of a cadet of the clan that the chief, out of pique, had banished her.

In all, ten pieces of her works have been preserved; and of these it is apparent, from internal evidence, that five were composed to Sir Norman. These are *Fuaim an t-Taibh, An Talla am bu Ghnàth, Luinneag Mhic Leòid, Sàth-Ghal Mhàiri ni'n Alasdair Ruaidh,* and *Cumha Mhic Leòid;* while one of her poems, namely, *Oran,* was written for Sir Norman's son, John of Contullich.

Of the remaining poems, one named *Cumha Do MhacLeòid,* was composed on the death of the chief, Roderick, 'The Witty'; and to his son, Norman, who was always in delicate health and who predeceased his father, she sang her *An Crònan* on his recovery from an illness. *Cumha Iain Ghairbh* was her lament on the occasion of the drowning of the young laird of Raasay, with all his crew, off the rocky shore of Staffin in 1671 and her

first composition was a lament on the death of another of her patrons, MacKenzie of Applecross, who died in 1646.

One of her poems requires special treatment, for there has been much misunderstanding concerning its theme. This is the lament, *Cumha Mhic Leòid;* and all who have written about the bardess maintain that it was composed on the death of the chief, *Iain Breac,* an event that happened in 1693. There is much in the poem to support that view. The bardess makes frequent mention of the princely generosity of her patron; and we know that *Iain Breac* was perhaps the most hospitable chief of his age. Another item in this evidence, that has been thought to place that theory beyond doubt, is the fact that the chief was married to Florence, the daughter of Sir James MacDonald of Sleat; and it has been supposed that the poetess refers to her in the verse:

> *Nighinn Sheumais nan crùn,*
> > Daughter of James of the Crowns,
> *Bean chéile ghlan ùr, etc.*
> > A wife radiant and young.

> (Watson, JC, 1934, p. 48)

But a closer investigation easily disposes of the supposition that *Iain Breac* was the subject of her verse. Thus we know that at least three of the poems of *Màiri ni'n Alasdair Ruaidh* are in praise of Sir Norman of Bernera, and, in all of these, she records his generosity, his friendliness, and his patronage of the bards, the musicians, and the story-tellers. In the poems *Fuaim an t-Taibh, An Talla 'm bu Ghnàth,* and *Luinneag Mhic Leòid,* Sir Norman is definitely mentioned by name. Among the many qualities she ascribes to him in the last, she praises him who is, "*Fiughanta* (liberal); *fial* (generous); *farsuinn* (open-handed); *measail* (worthy); *cuilmeach* (hospitable); *gibhteail* (gift-giving)", – epithets that are practically synonymous with the foregoing. But what disposes of the main prop of the generally accepted theory, that *Iain Breac* is referred to in the poem, is the fact that Sir Norman, too, was married to a daughter of Sir James MacDonald. In *Fuaim an t-Taibh*, she is mentioned as *"Nighean Oighre Dhuin Thuilm"* ('daughter of Duntulm's heir'), and in the poem under review as *"Nighinn Sheumais Nan Crun"* ('daughter of James of the Crowns').

On pressing the inquiry further, other facts emerge that immediately rule out the notion that *Iain Breac* is the subject of the lament. For example, she calls her hero, *"Mac Ruairi reachdmhor"* ('son of vigorous Rory'), clearly pointing to Sir Norman's father, the capable chief, Sir Rory *Mór*, while the father of *Iain Breac* was called John *Mór*.

Again, *Iain Breac* was a man of peace, who, during the troublous times that prevailed in the period of the Revolution, held aloof from any participation in the various risings, despite the pressure brought to bear on him, both by his brother chiefs and the deposed king himself. But the person mentioned in this poem is a warrior of renown, one who is at all times accoutred in the soldier's panoply. He is mounted on

> *"Each cruidheach ceannard*
> > ...a horse, shod, with high carried head
> *Is lann ùr than' ort,*
> > And carrying a slender blade,
>
> > > (*ibid.*, p. 92)

and he is –

> *Sàr mhac 'ic Leòid*
> > Excellent son of MacLeod
> *Nam bratach sròil,*
> > Of the banners and pennants,
>
> > > (*ibid.*, p. 88)

referring no doubt, to the part Sir Norman played on behalf of Charles II at Worcester, and after it.

In a poem by the Clàrsair Dall, called Creach nan Ciadan, lamenting the death of Iain Breac, that chief is said to have died in Easter Week:

> *Chaill mi 'n ùr ghibt' a chreach mi,*
> > I lost the splendid gift which destroyed me,
> *Ann an seachduin na Ceusda,*
> > In Easter week,
>
> > > (Matheson, W, 1970, p. 50)

while the person referred to in *Cumha Mhic Leòid* died on the 3rd of March:

> *An treas latha de'n Mhàrt*
> > On the third day of March
> *Dh' fhalbh m' aighear gu bràth,*
> > My joy departed forever,
>
> > > (Watson, JC, 1934, p. 90)

and it is obvious that Easter Week could not in any year fall so early as the 3rd of March. That, in itself, proves that the subject of *Cumha Mhic Leòid* is not *Iain Breac*; and much more could be adduced to show that the lament was composed on the death of Sir Norman of Bernera.

Roderick Morison (An Clàrsair Dall)

Roderick Morison, the famous harper of Dunvegan, was a native of the Island of Lewis, where he was born in the year 1646. He was thus a contemporary of *Màiri ni'n Alasdair Ruaidh*. His father was a clergyman, and it was decided to educate young Roderick for the Church also.

Whilst he was pursuing his education in Inverness, he was seized with the dread malady of smallpox, and so severe was its incidence that it deprived him of his eyesight, and he was forced to relinquish his studies for the ministry.

Like many another who had been similarly afflicted, he took up the study of music, and he evinced such a wonderful aptitude for the art that he soon came to be reckoned the most skilful performer of his age. The excellence of his gifts so captivated MacLeod's generous chief, *Iain Breac*, that he was appointed to the post of family harper in the castle of Dunvegan.

In addition to his having been an outstanding exponent of the music of the harp, he was also a composer of renown; but it appears that his works in this connection have been lost, if they had, indeed, ever been committed to writing. Now he is chiefly remembered for his poetry, which has secured for him an abiding niche in the hall of Celtic fame.

Of his poetical works, only five pieces have been preserved and it is noteworthy that all of them, with one exception, were written in praise of his chief, *Iain Breac* MacLeod. His verse is characterised by an engaging diction, a pleasing harmony, and a lofty style, features that are no doubt traceable, at least in part, to his highly cultivated taste in music. His rare artistry is perhaps best exemplified in *Oran Mór Mhic Leòid,* a composition in which he mourns the change that has come over the hospitable halls of Dunvegan since the death of the munificent chief, *Iain Breac*, and the accession of the son and heir, Roderick, who cares nothing for the traditions and the arts of his own people (Matheson, W, 1970, pp. xxi-xxvi).

A few personages of historic importance, referred to in his poems, deserve special mention. For example, in his *Oran*, he addresses Norman, the second son of *Iain Breac*, as follows:

> *Ma thuirt iad ogha Thormoid riut,*
>> If they called you the grandson of Norman,

> *B'i sud an fhoirm-fhuil ghlan;*
>> That was the noble unsullied blood;

> *Ma thuirt iad iar-ogha Ruairi riut,*
>> If they called you Rory's great grandson,

> *B'i 'n àrd-fhuil uaibhreach, mhear.*
>> That was the highborn, proud, swiftly coursing blood.

> *'S ogha 'n Eoin gun truailleadh,*
>> And the grandson of the honour unblemished John,

> *Thug suairceas air gach neach,*
>> That gave joy to everyone,

> *Mac an fhir nach b' fhuathach leam,*
>> The son of the man I did not dislike,

> *An nochd thog suas mo ghean.*
>> Tonight lifted my spirit.

(*ibid.*, p. 10)

Although the relationship attributed to him in the first line is obscure, there can be no doubt that the person referred to is Norman, the son of *Alasdair Crotach*, and the twelfth chief of MacLeod, who was the great-great-grandfather of the subject of this poem. The chief mentioned in the third line is Sir Rory *Mór*, whose son, John *Mór*, is spoken of in the fifth line; while in the seventh line he extols his patron, *Iain Breac*.

In that meritorious composition of his, *Creach nan Ciadan*, written on the death of the last-mentioned chief, the poet exhorts young Roderick, the heir, to uphold the honour of the name he bears, and preserve it from any slur:

> *Ma's tusa rinn suas*
>> If you reckon you are

> *An ceathramh Ruairi, na dearmaid,*
>> The fourth Rory, do not fail,

> *Lean ri sinnsireachd d' aiteam,*
>> To follow the ancestry of your line,

'S na toir masladh do 'n ainm sin.

> And do not bring scandal on the name.

> (*ibid.*, p. 56)

He then speaks of his namesakes as follows:

Ruairi reachdmhor, run-meanmnach,

> Roderick, resolute and bustling,

Tartach, toirbheartach, teannshath,

> Open handed and acute,

Do shi-seanair 'o 'n tàinig,

> Your great-grandfather from whom you are
> sprung,

Cha b' ion do nàmhaid dol teann air,

> It was not wise of his enemy to press him,

'S Ruairi gasda na dhéidh,

> And goodly Roderick who came after him,

Cha b' e roghainn bu tàire,

> He was not the meaner choice,

'S an treas Ruairi fa dheireadh,

> While the third Roderick, the last one,

Cha b' e 'n gainneanach fàs e.

> Was no empty handed miser.

> (*ibid.*, p. 54)

The three persons of the name of Roderick mentioned in this verse are, respectively, Sir Rory *Mór*, Sir Roderick of Talisker, and Roderick the Witty.

Under the regime of that Roderick to whom this exhortation was addressed, a new dispensation was observed in Dunvegan, so that those members of the last chief's retinue who cultivated the muses were treated with cold indifference; and, knowing that *"their date was fled"*, this last minstrel left Skye for his native Lewis, where he died about 1725, and was buried in the churchyard of his fathers at Eye, near Stornoway.

Lachlan MacKinnon (*Lachlainn Mac Thearlaich Oig*)

This fine poet was one of the MacKinnons of Strath, his father being *Tearlach Og*, the second son of the chief, *Lachlainn Dubh*, and his mother, Marion MacLeod of Drynoch. He was born about the year 1665 in Scalpay, of which island his father was then tacksman. Young Lachlan was liberally educated, as became one who was a cadet of the House of MacKinnon. When he attained manhood, he farmed the Island of Pabay, together with that portion of the adjacent mainland known as Ardnish.

He was twice married. First to a Flora Campbell, daughter of Campbell of Strond, a lady of elegant ways and amiable demeanour, who died within a year after marriage. His second marriage was a very unhappy one, for his lot fell on a widow, a Xantippe, who despised his talents and whose termagancy made his old age a misery. He had a daughter, a love-child, who was greatly attached to him and who, inheriting his own poetical gifts, was the solace of his later years.

One of the best known of his works is *Latha Siubhal Sléibhe*, an allegorical composition after the theme of *Oran Mór Mhic Leòid*, by *An Clàrsair Dall*, in which he regrets the changes that had supervened in the Highlands, when the chiefs neglected the native arts and sought the allurements of the south instead. It occurs, *inter alia*, in *The Eigg Collection* (Turner, P, 1809, p. 117). He composed a moving tribute to John MacLeod, second of Talisker, *Cumha Mhic Leòid Thalascar*, and it appears in *The Gaelic Bards*. His *Oran*, to the daughter of MacKinnon of Gemball, is marked by very superior artistry. It is characterised by a faultless rhyme and untrammelled rhythm; so that, although the whole piece moves at a high speed, there are no impediments to its graceful and smoothly-flowing diction. It is one of the earliest love-songs extant in our language, and it ranks high among compositions of that order. One stanza is quoted in illustration of its ease of movement and the unforced harmony of its verse:

Ach òigh na mais', is òrbhuidh falt,
  But winsome maiden of golden hair,
'S do ghruaidh air dhreach an neòinean;
  With cheeks of the bloom of the flower;
Tha éideadh grinn, mu dheud do chinn,
  Your teeth are prettily formed,
'S do bheul bho'm binn thig òran.
  As is your sweet singing mouth.
Ruisg thana, chaoin, fo-d' mhala chaoil,
  Delicate eye-lashes under a slender brow,
'S do mheallshuil mhin 'ga seòladh;
  And your bewitching eyes lighting them;
'S i 'n t-seirc tha t'eudann, ghreas gu eug mi,
  The beauty of your face hastens me to the grave,
Mur toir a' chléir dhomh còir ort.
  If the clergy do not give a right to you.

(Mackenzie, J, 1877, p. 83)

The poet died in 1734 at the age of 69 years, and was buried in the churchyard of Kilchrist, in Strath. It is noteworthy that the first of the famous succession of MacKinnon ministers in Strath, viz., Rev. Donald MacKinnon, was the great-grandson of the bard, *Lachlainn Mac Thearlaich Oig.*

The MacCrimmons

As the MacCrimmons were at the height of their fame during the latter part of the seventeenth century, it is appropriate that a brief sketch of that celebrated family should be given here.

The early history of their race is shrouded in obscurity and, as always happens in such a case, wild conjectures have been framed about their origin and still wilder surmises formed as to the derivation of their family name.

Some have gone as far as to postulate that Cremona, in the Plain of Lombardy, is the place whence they sprang, and derived their name. Some, like the late Dr. George Henderson, suggest they may belong to a Norse stock and he, accordingly, derives their name from Hromunder, meaning 'noted protector'. Others, again, point to Ireland as the original home of the family, and, from what we know of the barderie and the music of that country, that opinion is not an untenable one.

It is possible that the name MacCrimmon may be associated with *crimthan* ('wolf') which was the original name of St. Columba, but was changed to *Columba* ('dove') because of the simplicity and innocence of his life (Connellan, O, 1860, p. 20).

In *The MS History of the MacLeods of Dunvegan*, it is averred that they can be traced to the south of Harris, where they owned a considerable portion of land under the rule of the Norse, and, later, under Paul Balkeson. It is not known when they came to Skye, nor whence, with any degree of certitude; nor are we sure who was the first of them to become an exponent of *pìobaireachd*.

The earliest of them is said to have been *Iain Odhar* (John, 'the Dun'), probably from his sallow complexion; and he was a piper of such skill, and was endowed with such high culture, that it is safe to conclude that many exponents of his art went before him.

Iain Odhar lived about the beginning of the sixteenth century and we know that the bagpipes had not been introduced into the Highlands long before that time. It is quite possible, however, that the MacCrimmons were skilful players of the harp, and may have been composers of its music, before they began to cultivate the other and more romantic instrument.

The first of the MacLeods who is said to have patronised the MacCrimmons was the famous warrior, *Alasdair Crotach*; and *Iain Odhar* flourished during his chiefship. He assigned to the family the district of Borreraig, where they lived, free of all feudal impositions, their only obligation being to train at least one son for the office of piper to the chief. During the reign of *Iain Breac* they occupied Galtrigill as well.

At Borreraig they founded a college of piping that was destined to become the most famous of its kind in the world. The tuition that was given there was of such a high order that it became a custom with most of the chiefs of the Highlands to send their young pipers thither in order to complete their training. Even the MacArthurs of Skye, who conducted a minor institution of their own, did not consider it an indignity to study under the MacCrimmons. The famous piper-bard, John Mackay (*Am Pìobaire Dall*) (The Blind Piper) of Gairloch, was perhaps their most notable student.

There seems to be no doubt now that what raised the Mac-Crimmons to such a position of pre-eminence as masters of their instrument was their unique system of notation. It is called *canntaireachd* , or 'vocalising'; and it consisted in expressing the notes by means of syllables, the roots of which were definite vowels. Thus the highest note was *i* (ee) and the lowers *u* (o). By all accounts, this system of notation made piping easy, and it suited the scale of the chanter more effectively than any other method of recording musical signs (Mackay, A, 1838).

The MacArthurs, who were hereditary pipers to the MacDonalds in Trotternish, seem to have invented a system of notation of their own; but the vocables they employed were entirely different from those that made the MacCrimmon *canntaireachd* so famous.

In addition to their unrivalled technical skill, the MacCrimmons were the most noted composers of pipe music; and it seems to be true that it was they who gave its peculiar structure to *pìobaireachd*, or the classical music of the bagpipes. This major branch of pipe music (*ceòl mór*, or 'the great music', as it is sometimes called, to distinguish it from *ceol aotrom*, or 'the light music', that is concerned with reels, strathspeys, etc. and is considered by all pipers as inferior to the *pìobaireachd*) consists of two main parts, namely, the *urlar* and the *siubhal*. Every *pìobaireachd* is founded on these. There are subsidiary components, called *taorluath* and *crunluath*, with rapid offsets to each, which go under the specific name of *breabach*. Most of the world's greatest *pìobaireachds* were composed by the MacCrimmons.

Some of the most famous of these compositions are *Maol Donn*, or 'MacCrimmon's Sweetheart', produced by *Iain Odhar*, the first of the line, in praise of the bag of his pipes. *Failte nan Leòdach* or 'MacLeod's Welcome', was composed by Donald *Mór* MacCrimmon in 1601, when the reconcilement was effected between Rory *Mór* and Donald *Gorm Mór*, after the war called *Cogadh na Cailliche Caime* ('The War of the One-Eyed Woman).

The son of Donald *Mór* was called *Pàdruig Mór*; and he is perhaps the most famous of the race. He was the author of several *pìobaireachds*, the best known of which are *Cumha na Cloinne* ('Lament for the Children'), composed on the death of seven of his children during the course of a single year; and *Thug mi Pòg do Laimh an Rìgh* ('I Kissed the King's Hand'), which he composed when he received that honour at the camp of Torwood, the Royalist rendezvous before King Charles II was crowned at Scone after the Restoration (Mackay, W, 1905, p. 379):

> *Thug mi pòg, is pòg, is pòg,*
>   I gave a kiss, a kiss, a kiss,
> *Thug mi pòg do laimh a' rìgh,*
>   I gave a kiss to the King's hand,

Cha d' chuir gaoth 'n craicionn caorach
  No one who blew into a sheepskin
Fhuair 'n fhaoilt ud ach mi.
  Got that honour but myself.

On the death of his generous patron, Sir Rory *Mór*, he composed that melting melody, *Cumha Ceann-Cinnidh nan Leòdach*. Other compositions of his are *Cumha an Aona Mhic* and 'Lament for MacDonald of Glengarry'. The wife of Sir Rory *Mór* was Isabella *Mhòr* of Glengarry, and it is said that she was lulled to sleep every night of her life by the playing of that last plaintive *pìobaireachd* by *Padruig Mór* MacCrimmon.

Padruig Mór was succeeded in the profession by *Padruig Og*, whose son, Malcolm, carried on the succession, and the last of this illustrious race to maintain the college in its position of pre-eminence was John *Dubh*.

Donald *Bàn* MacCrimmon was killed at the Rout of Moy in 1746, and about thirty years after this that chief of MacLeod, Norman, 'The Wicked Man', owing to the enhanced value of land, decided to take half of the farm of Borreraig from the Mac-Crimmons, saying he considered the remaining portion ample patronage for the office of piper. The chief's action so galled the retainer, that he left Borreraig altogether and, according to the Rev. Archd. Clark, who wrote the *Second Statistical Account for Duirinish*, the family renounced the pipes when they relinquished the farm in 1770. In the early days of the eighteenth century, payments were made to the pipers in each district: twenty-six pounds, six and eightpence (Scots) to each, but the MacCrimmons received one hundred and sixty six pounds, thirteen and four pence. As late as 1791, there is an account of four pounds being paid as wages to MacCrimmon (MacLeod, RC, 1939, Vol. 2, p. 92).

Pipers, however, continued in the family, for the Rev. Dr. Norman MacLeod, 'Caraid nan Gàidheal', says that on the homecoming of General Norman MacLeod of MacLeod from India, he heard Captain Donald MacCrimmon, who had served in the American War of Independence, play *Fàilte Ruairi Mhóir* on the battlements of Dunvegan Castle, and he concludes, *"I can never forget the impression the whole scene made on my youthful mind."* Another member of the family was Captain Peter Mac-Crimmon, who also had distinguished himself in the American War of Independence and is reputed to have been a man of gigantic stature, and enormous strength.

Two of the pipes of the MacCrimmons are preserved in Dunvegan Castle; and one of them, designated *An Oinnseach* ('the idiot'), is still playable.

Owing to the magic art that this family possessed, we need not marvel at the gorgeous webs of fancy that tradition has woven around them. In order to account for their unique skill, it is said that one of the first of them received the gift of music from the fairies, who were held to be masters of the chanter. This member of the family, by name *'Iain Og'* (who may have been *Iain Odhar*), was playing in *Sloc nam Pìobairean* one calm evening, so the story runs, when a full moon was shining in the sky. On such a night an inspired piper can charm the best music from his instrument, and, as happens under such conditions, creatures of the night crowded around to listen to the enchanting strains of the pipe of *Iain Og*. The fairies were there in force, spellbound by the sweetness of the music. After they had been regaled for some time, one of them, the queen, it is said, approached the young piper, and thus accosted him:

Young man, your matchless playing has moved me to confer on you your choice of two gifts which it is in my power to bestow. Tell me, then, which you prefer, Ealain gun rath, no rath gun ealain. ('Skill without fame, or fame without skill'.)

Unhesitatingly the young piper replied:

Give me skill to play this music, and let prosperity and fame go to those who love not art for art's sake.

Few mortals would have chosen as you do, fair youth, said the fairy, *and your ideals therefore entitle you to more than falls to the lot of ordinary men. You shall not only have skill transcending that of any of your predecessors, but you shall also have fame that will make your posterity proud of the name they bear.*

Having said so, she handed him the silver chanter, *A chachalaidh dhubh*, and she departed with her train.

Thug do mhaise 's ceòl do phiòba
    Your beauty and the music of your pipe
Leannan sìthe air do thòir,
    Have attracted a fairy lover to you,
Sineam dhuit an sionnsair airgid
    Let me hand you the silver chanter
A bhios binn gun chearb fo d' mheòir.
    That will be sweet and faultless in your fingers.

In due time *Iain Og* became the most skilled of pipers, and his genius was perpetuated in his race down the ages. This, of course, is not history – but what of that!

Fuirbidh, tailceant, 's cumta pearsa
    A steadfast hero of shapely body

Treun Laoch, spraiceil, dòid-gheal;
    Strong, confident, white-handed;
Pìòb 'ga spalpadh suas 'na achlais
    A pipe stuck up on his armpit
Mhosglas lasan gleòis duinn.
    That would strike a flame of daring in us.
Caismeachd bhrasbhinn, bhrodadh aigne
    A stirring rally swift and sweet that would
Gu dian chasgairt slòigh leis,
    Stimulate one's spirit to fierce slaughter of hosts,
Chiureadh toraghan a' phuirt bhaisgeil
    The strumming of the fierce tune would
Spiorad bras 'nar pòraibh.
    Rouse an impetuous zest in our persons.

In his book on *Pìobaireachd*, Angus MacKay states that in 1838 there were eighteen families on the farm of Borreraig paying a rent of £100. The MacCrimmons, he declares, held this land rent free and, he continues,

the College houses still remain displaying thick walls and mossy cabers or rafters. The house is in two parts at right angles, one a class room; the other sleeping apartments. There is a hollow on the top of the brae near the college where they practised. Near the rock called the 'Lady' there is a place called 'Uamha nam Pìobairean' ('The Pipers' Cave') to which the pipers resorted. To 'Uamha nan Calamain' ('Cave of the Pigeons'), the women who could play betook themselves with the Oinnseach.

        (MacKay, A, 1838, p. 5).

Figure 2.1 The original Raasay House that was home to the MacLeod chiefs of Raasay was razed by Hanoverian troops in 1746 after the Battle of Culloden, along with the homes of MacLeod clansfolk, as an act of retribution for the Raasay MacLeods' support of Prince Charles Edward Stuart. It was rebuilt in time to receive diarist James Boswell and essayist Samuel Johnson during their celebrated Tour of the Hebrides in 1773. Dr Johnson, the great man of English letters, described it as 'a neat, modern fabrick'.

Figure 2.2 A hairpin bend in the road above Uig as depicted in an early postcard.

Figure 2.3 Staffin Bay from Glasphein as captured by an early 20th century photographer.

ELGOL SCHOOL AND SCHOOLHOUSE, ISLE OF SKYE.

Figure 2.4 The Strathaird peninsula, which includes Elgol, was historically the heartland of the Mackinnon Clan. In July 1746, Prince Charles Edward Stuart, the so-called Young Pretender, found sanctuary at Elgol whilst fleeing from his Hanoverian pursuers. The cave where he is said to have waited for a boat to the mainland, 'Uamh a' Phrionnsa', can still be visited today. The photograph is of the village school and schoolhouse at Elgol.

Figure 2.5 The tower in Uig was built in the 19th century for the notorious Capt. Fraser who owned the local estate. While it is considered to be a folly, the tower was used as a family home for many decades. Uig pier is seen in the background. Now substantially improved, it is a major ferry-port for the Western Isles.

Portree Pier with Quay Street.

Figure 2.6 Portree's Gaelic name, *Port Righ*, tends to be translated as 'king's harbour', purportedly because of a visit by King James V of Scotland in 1540. However this etymology has been contested with many now preferring the older name, *Port Ruighe(adh)*, 'harbour of the slope '. Prior to the sixteenth century, the settlement's name was Kiltaraglen from the Gaelic *Cill Targhlain* (the church of St. Talorgan). This image shows a 'steamer' at Portree Pier.

BROADFORD HOTEL AND BEINN-NA-CAILLICH, SKYE.   B.2421.

Figure 2.7 In Nicolson's *Handbook to the Isle of Skye*, published in the 1930s, a 'tariff and particulars' could be got for this hotel by phoning Broadford 5. *Beinn na Caillich* (the hill of the old lady) is in the background.

Figure 2.8 An estate which included Portnalong was bought by the Board of Agriculture and broken up into smallholdings. Of the 68 such units which became available in 1923, 43 went to migrant families from Harris, 20 to families from Lewis and five were taken over by Skye families. The lady in this picture spinning wool at Portnalong is likely to have been from one of the families to benefit from these new tenancies.

Figure 2.9 For many centuries peat was the principal domestic fuel in Skye and other parts of the Highlands and Islands. Much less peat is harvested today than in Nicolson's day. In the days before tractors and other mechanised transport, creels were the preferred way to carry peat.

Figure 2.10 'Portree is a convenient centre for touring Skye', according to Nicolson's *Handbook to the Isle of Skye*, 'and there are cars in plenty to whisk the tourist, who may not be fit for much exercise, over roads constructed long before the urge of modern life was thought of'. This image depicts Somerled Square in Portree on a quiet day.

CHAPTER XI

Family History, 1700–1746

The MacLeods

The opening of the eighteenth century saw the installation of a new chief in Dunvegan. This was Norman, the second son of *Iain Breac*, who succeeded his brother, Roderick, in the year 1699.

In manners and bearing Norman was the exact antithesis of his brother, the late chief, for he was the patron of the bards and the musicians, a lover of learning, who aimed at the restoration of the ancient customs of his race. The minstrels and the singers were once again made welcome in the hospitable halls of Dunvegan and they failed not to record their appreciation of his noble conduct. The poets sang his praises. In that remarkable composition, *Latha Siubhal Sléibhe*, by *Lachlainn Mac Thearlaich Oig*, the bard allegorically recounts his meeting with three of the native virtues – Clemency, Love and Generosity, which were now homeless wanderers among the hills of Skye. They tell him their sad plight is due to the passing of the large-hearted Chief of MacLeod:

> *Tormad fial an t-sùgraidh*
> Norman of the generous entertainment

Nach d' fhàs m'a chùineadh cruaidh;
> Who has not been niggardly with his means;

A bha gu fearail, fiùghantach,
> Who was manly and worthy,

'S a chum a dhùthchas suas.
> And maintained his heritage.

'S ann air bha ar tathaich
> It was our wont to visit him

On thugadh Iain bhuain
> Since Iain was taken from us

'S beag m' fharmad ris na feumaich
> I envy not the needy since

On a bheum na cluig gu truagh.
> The bells have sadly tolled.

(Mackenzie, J, 1877, p. 81)

There is little else to record of the brief career of this chief. In 1703 he married his cousin, Ann Fraser, daughter of Hugh, eleventh Lord Lovat, and by her he had two sons, John: who succeeded him but died in the same year (1706) and Norman who succeeded his brother in infancy (MacKinnon, D, & Morrison, A, 1968, p. 28).

Norman ('The Wicked Man'), Twenty-second Chief

During the nonage of the heir, the management of affairs was confided in a small body of the principal men of the clan and, such was the skill and the devotion with which they carried out their trust, that a vast fortune was accumulated. To it the young chief automatically fell heir on the attainment of his majority. His inheritance must have been an enormous one for, in addition to a patrimony already considerable and consisting of the estates of Glenelg, Harris and the various portions of Skye that belonged to the family, a new capital of about £60,000 accrued to him. He was thus rightly considered to be one of the wealthiest chiefs of his time. In an account of the Highland clans, written in 1725, it is stated that *"this chief"*, viz., Macleod, *"possesses the greatest estate of any in the Highlands … In Skye, where most of his clan reside, there are a great number of gentlemen of good account"*.

But he, whose prestige had been raised to such a pitch by the ability and the care of his guardians, was a man who was fated to give nothing but disappointment in return. Inordinately vain of display, he lent untrammelled rein to a spirit of reckless extravagance, so that he early gave cause for real alarm to those who had the welfare of their clan at heart. Like his uncle, Roderick, he found little to interest him in the concerns of the clan beyond the contribution it might make towards the satisfaction of unnatural yearnings after a riotous life. He had aspirations after parliamentary honours and, in 1732, when he was twenty-six years of age, he contested his native county but was unsuccessful. Nine years later, however, he succeeded in his candidature, after much intrigue and bribery, and represented Inverness-shire from 1741–1754, a period of thirteen years.

During that time many matters, some of which were of great moment, fall to be recorded. The chief had already been married in 1726 to Janet, the youngest daughter of Sir Donald of Sleat ('Do'ull a' Chogaidh'), a lady whom he treated with heartless cruelty. She early lost his love and was forced to leave him, as he was shamelessly consorting with other women.

MacLeod and his first wife agreed to separate in 1733. In a letter to MacLeod in June of that year, Sir Alexander Mac-Donald writes that it has been represented to him that she was being kept a prisoner in Skye. She went to Edinburgh, MacLeod having been granted an inhibition freeing him from her debts. In 1738 there were negotiations for her return to Dunvegan and, in 1740, she did return and died about a year afterwards (MacLeod, RC, 1939, p. 19).

That incident, by the way, gave rise to dark hints. It is said that, after a separation of several years, he sent a courier to Mogstadt, where his wife then lived, imploring her to return to Dunvegan and promising that he was prepared for a full reconciliation. The unsuspecting lady was persuaded to comply, but shortly after her return she was reported to have died under mysterious circumstances and some have gone so far as to aver that she had been starved to death in the dungeon of the castle. He married Anne Martin, a beautiful girl who dwelt in the neighbourhood, shortly after Janet's death. There is a magnificent portrait of her by Allan Ramsay in Dunvegan Castle.

Meanwhile the chief continued on his career of extravagance. The family wealth, vast as it was, began to show signs of sore depletion and it was apparent to all that the estate was swiftly heading towards bankruptcy. For the capital that had accrued to him through the careful husbanding of resources by the *curatores boni* during the period of his minority was now all gone, and many thousands more, but he continued to squander and to gamble the patrimony away as though that were to him the chief end of life. Need we marvel, then, that this chief had earned for himself the unenviable title of *'An Droch Dhuine'*, or 'The Wicked Man'?

Lady Grange

He was implicated in still another transaction that does not serve to redeem his name. That was the abduction of the ill-starred Lady Grange. His guilt in connection with that affair was not, be it said, any deeper than that of many another Highland chief, but, during the years she had been hidden from the world he had more to do with her custody than anyone else.

"The true story of this lady", as Boswell says in the *Journal* of his tour, *"is as frightfully romantic as if it had been the fiction of a gloomy fancy"*. Ann Chiesley, as was her maiden name, was married to James Erskine, Lord Grange, a senator of the College of Justice and a brother of 'Bobbing' John, Earl of Mar, who raised the Jacobite Rebellion of 1715. She was cursed with a congenital irascibility of temper, bordering at times on insanity, which strained the relations, never very cordial, between herself and her husband. The latter was an ardent Jacobite; she a devoted Hanoverian; and some have even suggested that she was a government spy. In any case, Jacobite intrigues were then afoot and, about the year 1730, Lord Grange was deeply embroiled in some of these. His home in Edinburgh was the rendezvous of those who favoured the 'King Across the Water' and conclaves were held there with such frequency that his lady became suspicious and, having secured certain papers belonging to her husband, threatened to disclose his activities and those of his associates, among whom were Simon Fraser of Lovat, Sir Alexander MacDonald of Sleat and Norman MacLeod of Dunvegan.

In 1731 an assemblage of conspirators was gathered at the home of Lord Grange and, after some had gone away, a few of the prime movers in the plot remained behind to discuss momentous affairs. All this time Lady Grange had been a spy on the proceedings, having esconced herself beneath a sofa. A sneeze, however, betrayed her presence and, on her being challenged, she bluntly declared that she would show no hesitation in revealing the plot to the authorities. Without further ado,

those present decided, with the connivance of her husband, to spirit her away to some remote spot in the Highlands, where she could no longer interfere with those who were interested in the Jacobite cause.

Horses were got ready and, under the cloak of night, she was blindfolded, while her hands were tied behind her back. She cursed, kicked and bit her kidnappers in the struggle and, we are told, she lost two of her front teeth. Strong arms, however, soon forced her into the saddle and she was hastened into the fastnesses of the North, under the escort of John MacLeod of Bernera, a cadet of the House of Dunvegan and a MacDonald of Morar.

Next morning a report was spread about to the effect that Lady Grange had suddenly died and people were asked to her funeral. Many attended the ceremony, when a coffin, filled with sods, was solemnly interred in the churchyard of Greyfriars in Edinburgh.

By this time the person who had been accorded the mock-burial was being hurried by unfrequented ways into the Highlands. A halt was made for the first time at Castle Tioram but, as no place on the mainland was considered to be safe, she was forthwith conveyed to Idrigil, in MacLeod's country in Skye (Mackenzie, A, 1889, pp. 125–6).

According to the Rev. A. Clark, who wrote the '*Second Statistical Account for the Parish of Duirinish,*' it was from this place and not from St. Kilda, as is generally supposed, she sent intelligence to her friends of her whereabouts. This was effected by means of a note, cleverly concealed in a clew of woollen yarn; but her custodians soon learned of the intention of her relatives to make an attempt at her recovery and immediately they took steps to have her removed once again – this time to an island called Heisker, on the wild west of North Uist.

A boat was manned and one of the crew sat beside the hapless prisoner, holding a rope, with a large stone attached to one end of it and a running noose formed on the other, so that, if the government sloop should be encountered on the way, the captive was to be raised over the side of the boat and as expeditiously and as quietly as possible consigned to the deep. But she was destined to *"dree her weird"* for many a year to come, for that boat that might have mercifully saved her from the miseries that were in store was never sighted. On Heisker she was kept in close captivity for two long years, under the care of the local tacksman, a cadet of Sir Alexander MacDonald.

Information concerning the activities of her friends once more raised alarm in the minds of her gaolers, who determined to transfer her to lonely St. Kilda, where she was to suffer further torments. There she was detained for seven years among a people who understood not a word of her language and whose speech was utterly foreign to her. Her sufferings during that time must have been bitter in the extreme; and we need not marvel at her description of the place of her imprisonment as a, *"neasty, stinking, poor isle"*.

Once again her friends got information of her place of confinement and her captors despatched her to the wilds of Assynt. Her detention there was but brief and she was finally removed to Skye, where she was concealed in a cave near the point of Idrigil, in Duirinish. After some time, she was accorded a certain measure of freedom; but her faculties were now beginning to fail and she was allowed to wander about among the kindly-disposed people, a wrecked mind in a restless body, until death put an end to her chequered career in the year 1745 (*ibid.*, pp. 126–7).

She died in a cottar's hut in Waternish and once again her burial was made a mockery, for, while a coffin weighted with sods was consigned to a grave in Duirinish, her body was taken to Trumpan and was secretly buried in the ancient churchyard, situated on the bare and wind-swept plateau above the bay of Ardmore. A few feet from the north wall of the ruined chapel there, a grey rectangular slab marks her grave. In the hall of the castle of Dunvegan is still shown the cruisie she used in St. Kilda, whilst certain documents, yellow with age, attest that the cost of her board was defrayed by MacLeod and that it amounted to £30 per annum. This shows that, in so far at least as the creature comforts were concerned, she was amply provided for; and it is a strange coincidence that the amount spent yearly on her maintenance was practically equivalent to the expenses of her funeral. The liberality of the former sum may have to be accounted for as being partly 'hush money', for MacLeod, now a M.P., was no doubt anxiously concerned about his part in the sequestration and he would go to any length to prevent its gaining publicity. That attempts were made to take advantage of his state of anxiety in this connection is shown by another document in Dunvegan Castle. It is a letter, addressed to the Chief, by the man who was entrusted with the removal of Lady Grange from St. Kilda; and therein is a threat, intimating that if he were not given a larger sum of money than was offered him, he would reveal the location of the captive. It is not known whether or not this extortioner was ever accorded any satisfaction (MacLeod, RC, 1939, p. 172).

The stirring times of 'The '45' were now arriving in the Highlands, and it is necessary for us to take a brief retrospect, in order to bring forward the story of the MacDonalds. Their history has been carried to the time of the death of the redoubtable warrior, Sir Donald MacDonald, the third baronet, who died in 1695.

The MacDonalds

Sir Donald (Do'ull a' Chogaidh), Twelfth Chief and Fourth Baronet

Sir Donald was succeeded by his eldest son, Donald, a man who, as we have already seen, had greatly distinguished himself at the Battle of Killiecrankie in 1689; and, in consequence of his warlike exploits then and subsequently, he is known to history as *Do'ull a' Chogaidh*, or 'Donald of the War'. The young chief was a man of great stature, fine appearance and of a most engaging and commanding personality.

> *Sir Dòmhnull a' Sleit'*
>> Sir Donald of Sleat
> *Ceannard nan ceud*
>> A chieftain of hundreds
> *Ceansgallach treun ro-ghlic.*
>> Masterful, mighty and exceedingly wise.
>
> (Watson, JC, 1934, p. 66)

Like his father, he was always active in the Stuart cause and he was privy to all the intrigues of the Jacobites.

During the early years of his chiefship he was often from home. In 1714 he bought an estate at Culross. He was at that time deeply embroiled in treasonable activities with many other Highland lairds but, like them, he signed the address of welcome to King George I. Those in authority knew that such signatures were not worth the paper they were written on and it was undoubtedly for that reason that Sir Donald was commanded by the then Lord Advocate to make a declaration of allegiance to King George and, on his refusal to sign such an undertaking, he was immediately put into prison in the city of Glasgow (MacDonald, A, & A, 1904, p. 80).

> *Bhon tha Sir Iain air fogradh*
>> Since Sir John (Maclean) is a fugitive
> *Sir Dòmhnull an Glaschu na thamh*
>> And Sir Donald is inactive in Glasgow
> *'S gun oighre MhicLeòid*
>> And Macleod's heir
> *Ach ag òl a bhrochain le spain.*

> Is only able to sup porridge from a spoon.
>
> (Maclean-Sinclair, A, 1898, p. 109)

Such high-handed action served but to accentuate his bias and, on his release, he returned to Skye with bitterness in his heart against the government. He had no sooner arrived home than he was visited in Duntulm by other Jacobite leaders, among whom was Simon Fraser, the Earl of Lovat. Many earnest conferences were held there and the cause of the House of Stuart was always uppermost as a topic of discussion. From the preparations that were afoot it was soon evident that Sir Donald had resolved on a momentous undertaking. His charter-chest, with other precious possessions of the family, he sent, under the care of a trusted vassal, to the islet called *Bòrd Cruinn*, or MacDonald's Table, a flat-topped rocky isle, with precipitous cliffs fronting the sea and swept by such powerful currents that it would be impossible for a stranger, however great his skill, to gain access to it. The clan was summoned to arms and a memorable festivity was held in Duntulm Castle on the eve of setting out in the rebellion. It has been said that this was the last ceremony of its kind that took place within those historic walls and that Duntulm was then finally abandoned by the clan but, as we shall see later, the MacDonalds remained in residence there for some time after this date.

The MacDonalds of Skye and Uist had meanwhile mustered to the number of about 800 men, who, with a piper, MacArthur at their head, presented a gallant array as they marched towards Kyleakin. Not being in time for the gathering on Braemar, they joined forces with the Earl of Seaforth at Brahan Castle.

> *Bu leat Sir Do'ull Shléibhte 'nuair dh 'éireadh do chabar ort,*
>> Sir Donald of Sleat would be with you, when your antlers are raised,

sings Matheson, the bard of Seaforth. Their first taste of fighting was in an encounter with several of the clans of Sutherland and of Ross, whom they sent to their homes, scattered in hopeless flight:

Theich iad uile 's cha do dh' fhuirich
  They all ran and did not remain
An treas duine bh' aca san,
  A third of their men,
An t-Iarla Catach ruith e dhachaigh,
  The Earl of Sutherland ran home,
'S cha do las e dhagaichean;
  And did not fire his pistols;
Mac Aoidh nan creach, gun thàr e as,
  Mackay of the forays took to his heels,
'S ann dh' éigh e 'n t-each a b'aigeannaich,
  And called for the most spirited horse,
Ri gabhail an ratreuta,
  Taking safety in retreat,
'Nuair dh' éirich do chabar ort.
  When your antlers were raised.

(Mackenzie, J, 1877, p. 359)

That classic epic, *Moladh Cabar Féidh*, by the *Aosdana Mac-Mhathain*, MacKenzie's family bard, clearly commemorates this affair, though the editor of *The Beauties of Gaelic Poetry* erroneously postulates another theme for it. In the poem, as given in *The Beauties*, verses 6 to 9 are evidently interpolations and may form part of the satire on the occasion of the invasion of the shielings, as stated by MacKenzie (Mackenzie, J, 1877, p. 361, fn).

Flushed with their success, the Islesmen made for the south, overtaking the Earl of Mar at Perth. The Hanoverian forces, under the Earl of Argyle, were sent north to stem the activities of the insurgents and they took up their position on Sheriffmuir, a few miles from the village of Dunblane. There they were attacked by the Jacobite army on the 14th of November, 1715. The MacDonalds, with about 150 MacKinnons, were marshalled on the right of Mar's forces, together with other clans of the west. Opposed to them were the veterans of Marlborough, disciplined and experienced warriors, who had harried the French eagles on Blenheim and Oudenarde and who were commanded by a tried soldier named General Whethman.

When the command was given to begin the battle, the Highlanders, in the traditional fashion, having discharged their muskets, threw these weapons away, together with their bonnets and plaids, as mere impediments. Carrying swords and dirks only, they rushed with wild yells on the foe. Nothing human could withstand that furious onset and Argyle's left was broken under the strain and thrown into wild confusion. The flight became a rout. Nor was it stayed until the vanquished reached safety, within the walls of Stirling, five miles away from the field of battle.

But the brilliant achievement of the men of the West was rendered nugatory by the utter incompetence of Mar. When the victors returned from the pursuit, they discovered, to their chagrin, that the whole left wing of their army had given way to the Hanoverian forces and had been driven beyond the Allan Water, a distance of two miles. Damped in their hopes, the Islesmen took up a strong position on a hill and, although they still outnumbered the army of Argyle by over two to one, they had lost faith in their leader and heart for the enterprise. For a few weeks longer they continued in the field with Mar.

It is noteworthy that this was the last occasion on which the MacDonalds of Skye fought as a clan. At Sheriffmuir they were commanded by two of the chief's brothers, namely, James of Oransay and William, the former of whom afterwards succeeded to the chiefship. In *Oran do fheachd Mhorair Mhair le Sileas*

Nighean 'ic Raonuill ('Song to the forces of the Earl of Mar by Cecilia Macdonald') we have:

> *Bheir soiridh bhuam gu Dòmhnull 'on Dun*
>> Send my greetings to Donald of the Dun
>
> *Gu Seumas 's gu Uilleam an triùir*
>> To James, to William, the three
>
> *Nuair a chruinneachas uaislean do chinnidhmun cuairt dhut*
>> When the nobles of your kin gather round you
>
> *Glac an t-urram a fhuair thu le cliu.*
>> Grasp the honour you won with distinction.
>
>> (O'Baoill, C, 1972, p. 20)

Sir Donald himself had become ill on the way south to Perth and had to be carried all the way back to Skye. There he was joined early in the following year by his clansmen, who returned disappointed at the treatment they had received at the hands of the Old Pretender and of Mar. As Sir Donald had not complied with the overtures made to him by the government for unconditional surrender, Hanoverian troops, under General Clayton, were sent to Skye. On their arrival, Sir Donald's men were disbanded and he himself fled to his lands in Uist (MacDonald, A, & A, 1904, p. 87).

At this time General Cadogan, who was stationed at Inverness, was the government officer responsible for the pacification of the Highlands. By him the insurgent chiefs were commanded to present themselves at the castle of Inverlochy, before the 1st of June 1716, on pain of attainder and the forfeiture of their lands. Sir Donald answered by a letter, written in April, offering surrender and acknowledging allegiance to the king, but craving exemption from the obligation of being personally present at Inverlochy on the ground of his continued state of indisposition. His plea was, however, rejected by the government and, in

June, 1716, he was declared guilty of treason, his estates being forfeited.

According to the Commissioners of Forfeited Estates, it would seem that Sir Donald had left Uist for Skye some time between April and the following June and they used this information in defence of their sentence of forfeiture, saying that, as it had been possible to remove him to Duntulm, it was as easy to take him to Inverlochy and the argument was upheld in the House of Lords. The matter is interesting, apart altogether from other considerations, in that it shows that the castle of Duntulm had not yet been evacuated by the MacDonalds; indeed, in an account of the Highland clans, written in 1725, we find the statement, *"The principal residence of the MacDonalds is Duntulm. They have also another place of residence, adorned with stately edifices, pleasant gardens and other regular policies, called Armodel".*

Sir Donald did not long survive these anxious times, for he died in March, 1718. It is said that it was he who revived the pattern of the tartan cloth worn by Donald of Harlaw, obtaining the scheme from a detailed description in verse that was sung by a woman weaver in the castle during the festivity that was held there on the night before the clan set off to join the rebellion of 1715.

Do'ull a' Chogaidh was married to Mary MacDonald of Castleton, in Sleat, and he had one son, Donald, who became chief in 1718.

Sir Donald, Thirteenth Chief and Fifth Baronet

The chiefship of young Sir Donald fell on inauspicious times. His estates were still under sentence of forfeiture and the rents were being collected and paid to the Commissioners of Forfeited Estates, through a factor they had appointed for that purpose. This agent was one of the MacLeods of Hamara and his office made him the most hated man in Skye, despite the fact that he was a man of acumen who exercised the utmost prudence in the execution of his duties. A story told of him is worth recording. MacLeod was in the habit of travelling to Inverness with the king's rent and accompanied only by one man as escort. This servant, weak in intellect but abnormally strong in body, proved himself to be a brave and faithful guardian, if at times somewhat slow in action. On one occasion, as they were resting in a wood, they were set upon by three highwaymen, who demanded money. The thieves, being offered a crown, rejected it with scorn and became uproarious. MacLeod was now alarmed and, as his escort was still soundly asleep, he was in an extremity of anxiety as to how to arouse him. Addressing one of the ruffians, he told him he would reward him well if he administered a thwack to his lethargic servant. The advice was no sooner given than acted upon and the sleeping giant was on his feet at a bound. He wrenched the gun from the robber nearest to him, shot down one, battered out the brains of another, while the person who was first disarmed fled and was brought down by MacLeod himself. Thereafter the factor considered it prudent to go to Inverness with an armed escort.

Sir Donald appealed again and again against the sentence of forfeiture; and, although the government was prepared to abrogate it, the House of Lords refused to sanction its removal. Owing to adverse weather conditions in the year 1718, crops had failed and large numbers of cattle and sheep succumbed to the rigours of that wild winter, so that much poverty prevailed in Skye. Sir Donald did all that was possible to alleviate the terrible distress among his own people; for he was a man who had their welfare close to his heart (MacDonald, A & A, 1904, p. 83).

And testing times had come to him shortly after his accession to the chiefship. Great expectations were then abroad of a formidable invasion of England by the joint armies of Sweden and Spain and Sir Donald was eager to lend his aid to the cause of the fallen House of Stuart. One misfortune after another,

however, befell the efforts of the Jacobite champions, Charles XII of Sweden and Alberonie the puissant cardinal of Spain and all that came of the threatened invasion was the abortive affair of Glenshiel in 1719.

Gladly would Sir Donald and his men have joined the insurrection, but the wiser counsels of a few of the elders of the clan prevailed. Foremost among the latter was the chief's uncle and successor, James of Oransay and, fortunately for themselves, the clan took no action this time against the government (*ibid.*, pp. 83–4).

In the following year – i.e., 1720 – the young Chief of the MacDonalds died in the prime of life, when eagerly engaged in his efforts to retrieve the fortunes of his people. He was a man of great promise, a born leader of men and endowed with scholarly parts. He had been educated at the University of Glasgow. In the roll of students for the year 1712, he is entered as a 4th year student: '*Donaldus McDonaldius, filius unicus Domini Donaldii MacDonaldius de Sleit Equites Baronette*'.

In the *Caledonian Mercury* of June 2nd, 1720 is reported a petition by Margaret, widow of the late Sir Donald, on behalf of her four infants, Mary, Margaret, Isobel and Janet, praying that the House of Lords should make a settlement on them from the Forfeited Estates as though they had not been attained. His Majesty ordered that a committee be set up to see to their relief.

Sir James of Oransay, Fourteenth Chief and Sixth Baronet

Sir Donald died leaving four daughters but no son in 1720 and the succession devolved on his uncle, Sir James, who, as we have already seen, had distinguished himself both at Killiecrankie and at Sheriffmuir. He also had been instrumental in preventing the late chief from throwing in his lot with the hopeless affair that ended in the debacle of Glenshiel. Sir James lived only a few weeks after his accession and the Clan Donald of Skye were once again mourning the loss of a good chief – a frequent occurrence during the last forty-two years, for no fewer than five chiefs had died in that period.

> *Chaill sinn ionnan agus comhla'*
>> We lost them similarly and together
> *Sir Domhnull, a mhac 's a bhrathair.*
>> Sir Donald, his son and brother.
>>> (Cecily Macdonald, in Mackenzie, J, 1877, p. 58)

In a poem of condolence, written on the occasion of the death of the young wife of Sir James' son, Sir Alexander, *Am Pìobaire Dall,* the famous poet-piper, avers that he himself had been personally acquainted with six chiefs of the MacDonalds of Sleat.

> *B' aithne dhomh Sir Seumas Mór,* (Second Baronet, died 1678)
> *'S b` eòl dhomh Do'ull a mhac;* (Third Baronet, died 1695)
> *B' eòl dhomh Do'ull eile ris,* (Do'ull a' chogaidh, died 1718)
> *Chumadh fo chis na slòigh ceart.*
> *B' eòl dhomh Do'ull nan tri Do'ull,* (Fifth Baronet, died 1720)
> *Ge b' òg e, bu mhór a chliu;*
> *Bhiodh fearaibh Alb' agus Eirinn,*
> *Ag éirigh leis anns gach cùis;*
> *B' eòl dhomh Sir Seumas nan rùn*
> *D' athair-sa mhic chliùtich féin;* (Sir James of Oransay, died 1720)
> *'S tus a nis an siathamh glùn,*
> *Dh'òrduich Rìgh nan Dùl 'nan déidh.* (Sir Alexander, Seventh Baronet)
>> I knew Sir James Mór,
>> And I knew Donald his son;
>> I knew the other Donald,
>> Who would ably discipline the hosts.
>> I knew Donald of the three Donalds,

> Though he was young, his fame was great.
> The men of Scotland and Ireland,
> Would rise with him on all occasions;
> I knew the respected Sir James
> Your own father – renowned son;
> And you are the sixth generation,
> That God ordained to follow them.
>> (Mackenzie, J, 1877, p. 96)

Sir James was married to Janet MacLeod of Greshornish. Two of their children were Sir Alexander, the heir, and a daughter, Margaret, who married Sir Robert Douglas of Glenbervie, the author of the famous *Baronage.*

During the minority of the young heir, five notable men were appointed to act as regents. They were Alexander MacDonald of Glen Haultin, William MacDonald of Bornaskitaig, Donald MacDonald of Sartil, Norman MacLeod of Greshornish and Donald MacLeod of Talisker who is eulogised in the *Maclean Bards,* (Maclean-Sinclair, A, 1898, Vol. 1, p. 128). All of them were grieviously handicapped, in that the Commissioners of the Forfeited Estates still held their grip on the lands of the clan and now advertised them for sale. It looked, indeed, as though the family patrimony would be alienated from the House of Sleat but such a catastrophe was happily averted by the loyalty of the cadets of the clan and by other gentlemen who were zealous in its cause. Thus it happened that when the MacDonald's estates were brought under the hammer at Edinburgh, in 1723, instructions were sent by the wadsetters to a lawyer named William MacKenzie, to act as their agent and to buy the estates. This transaction was duly carried out and the lands were restored to the clan for a sum of £21,000 (MacDonald, A & A, 1904, p. 84).

The tutors now exerted themselves to develop the resources of the estates and, under their care, matters soon began to prosper. They also saw to it that their ward was accorded the best education that could be procured. After attending school for some time in Edinburgh, he proceeded to the University of St. Andrews, where his society was eagerly cultivated by the neighbouring nobility and he himself entertained on a princely scale.

For several years, after he had attained his majority, the estates continued to be held by Sir Alexander on mortgage from his principal tenants but, after much careful organisation, he was finally able to clear himself of all pecuniary obligations. Even before that result had been achieved, the chief had been granted a royal charter for all his possessions in Sleat, Trotternish and in Uist. It is in reference to this occurrence that the blind piper of Reay says:

> 'S ait le fearaibh an Taobh tuath,
>> A delight to the people of the North
> Gun bhuannaich thu mar bu chòir.
>> That you gained, as was right
> Tròtarnis uile, agus Sleibht',
>> The whole of Trotternish and Sleat
> Uibhist nan eun, is nan ròn.
>> Uist of the birds and seals.

(MacKenzie, J, 1877, p. 96)

The stanza is from the poem of condolence by the piper-bard to Sir Alexander on the death of his wife, Ann Erskine, who lived only a year after her marriage.

The chief's second wife was Lady Margaret Montgomery, the accomplished daughter of the Earl of Eglinton and one of the most beautiful and cultured women of her day. Such qualities alone would have endeared her to a people endowed even with less of the romantic temperament than her vassals in Skye but when to these virtues were added a humility of bearing and a kindliness of disposition, we need not wonder that she became the idol of all. In his *Journal*, Boswell says that he had been told by Mrs MacKinnon of Corry that such was the respect Lady Margaret enjoyed, that when she went about among her people the latter could often be seen running along the road in front of her, picking stones from off the track, *"lest she should be hurt by the stumbling of her horse"* (Boswell, J, 1955, p. 181).

'Soitheach nan Daoine'

Now an event happened in 1739 that roused the people of the West Highlands to indignation and the greatest alarm. A party of men, acting under the leadership of Norman MacLeod of Unish, the son of Donald, the 'Old Trojan', had been engaged in the kidnapping of young men and women, in Skye and elsewhere, with the intention of selling them as slaves in the American colonies. Anyone found alone was forcibly arrested and pressed on board their ship so that consternation reigned in many parts of the island because of the large number of people who were going amissing, mysteriously and unaccountably. The secret leaked out by an accident. A ship laden with people, and bound for America, put in at the port of Donaghadee, Co. Down. Some escaped and they revealed what had hitherto been a problem. Many declared that Sir Alexander MacDonald had been privy to the dark business and some clergy of Skye accused him of having commissioned MacLeod and his reckless confreres, to rid the island of its surplus population and felons by instituting this method of forcible emigration. Lady Margaret was keenly aggrieved at the insinuations levelled against her husband and she stoutly maintained that he knew nothing whatever about the project. Despite the hints that were being thrown out, no one had come forward to incriminate Sir Alexander, so that the duty of vindicating her husband's honour in a court of justice had not been vouchsafed to Lady Margaret.

It has been suggested that it was in anticipation of the institution of an official inquiry into the whole affair that she was prompted to write to the Lord Justice Clerk of the time a letter, in which she observed,

In harvest last we were pretty much alarmed with accounts from different corners of this and the neighbouring isles, of persons being seized and carried off aboard of a ship which put in to different places on this coast. Sir Alexander is both angry and concerned that some of his own people were taken in this manner, but could not learn who were the actors in this wicked scrape till the ship was gone.

(Forbes, D, 1815, p. 154).

Norman MacLeod himself always maintained that he trafficked solely in such as were known thieves and he never charged Sir Alexander with being accessory to the act (Mackenzie, A, 1889, p. 250). After his misadventure, he would not, of course, dare to return to Skye, and he resided for some time in the North of Ireland. He left that country, however, when his chief was mobilising the clan, in support of the government, during the rebellion of 1745. He was commissioned with the rank of captain and it is alleged that none was so zealous as he in the pursuit of his father, who was a rebel (Cameron, A, 1871, p. 104).

After 'The '45', MacLeod settled down to farming and he became a noted breeder of Highland cattle but, what especially commends him to fame, is the fact that it was he who was one of the pioneers in the manufacture of kelp – an industry that was to prove such a lucrative one for a generation or two in the Highlands of Scotland (Mackenzie, A, 1889, p. 257).

There were some in Skye who declared that MacLeod had succeeded in the shipment of a considerable number of people to America previous to the incident at Donaghadee and a pathetic tale is told, replete with circumstantial detail, of a wayfarer in Canada, who one day accosted a maid at a roadside house and asked her the time of day. The question, put in English, elicited no response. Thinking she might be of French stock, the traveller asked her the same question in the language of that people but still received no reply. He then tried her in German, but that also was of no avail. Finally he plied her with Gaelic. Instantly her face beamed with intelligence and she quaintly answered, *"Tha e àm cròdhadh chaorach mu dhà thaobh Beinn Duagraich."* As the questioner happened to hail from Skye, his interest was kindled and he asked her what she knew of Ben Duagraich. She replied by quoting a rhymed list of place-names in its neighbourhood, *"Grùla, is Brunnal, da Chnoc Scarail, Airigh nam Bó, Da chnoc na Ho, Lag nan Aighean, Beinn Thotaig Ghormshuil nam fear' sgiamhach, Mineam 's mo chiall Beinn Duagraich"* ("Grule and Brunnal, the two hillocks called 'Sgarral', the shieling of the cows, the two hillocks of Ho, Gormul's Stackyard Hill of the handsome men, My treasure and my reason, Ben Duagraich."); and the story ends by the assertion that she had been seized by the kidnappers as she was one day collecting dulse on the shore at Gesto (oral tradition).

Whether or not Sir Alexander had any part in the episode of *'Soitheach nan Daoine'* may at this time be impossible to determine; and it should be observed that he was never so concerned to absolve his name of the imputation as was his devoted wife. He had a good friend in court who, he felt, would not press charges against him. In alleviation of his behaviour in this connection, those disposed to *'kindly scan their brother man'* declare that other matters engrossed his attention at this time.

He was enthusiastic in the work of developing all the resources of his estates to their utmost capacity. He was a good chief, eager to do all he could for the benefit of his people and he showed his concern for the mass of his vassals when, on several occasions, he administered stern rebuke to his tacksmen for the heavy burdens they imposed on their sub-tenants. He showed himself to be possessed of great ability and industry and all acclaimed him for his straightforward dealings. He well deserved the encomiums bestowed on him by those who knew him well. John MacLeod of Drynoch, an intimate friend and admirer, composed a noble eulogy to him, in which he declares this chief was:

A model for the human kind;
A body faultless and a faultless mind.

⚜

Great, good and regular his every part;
His form majestic, Godlike was his heart.

Another describes him as "a downright honest man, true to his friend and firm to his word", while the Gaelic bard, *Am Pìobaire Dall*, sings of his disinterested motives and his transparent honesty:

Deagh MhacDhò'uill nan rùn réidh.
    Worthy MacDonald of the clear intentions.
(Mackenzie, J, 1877, p. 96)

Indeed, but for the fortuitous supervention of the incident of 'The '45', the fame of Sir Alexander would have gone down to history as one of the most distinguished chiefs of his clan. As it happens, all his virtues have been masked by his conduct in that affair, so that his name has come to be considered by all as a slur on his illustrious race. During his latter days members of his own clan were frankly ashamed of him; and what deeper degradation could have befallen a chief? By others he was execrated as an apostate, because of the dishonourable part he played in what they considered to have been the most glorious event in the history of the Highlands. The epitaph written for him by a Jacobite wag, and quoted in *The Lyon in Mourning*, in no way

exaggerates the opinion in which Sir Alexander was held at the time of his death:

If Heaven be pleased, when sinners cease to sin,
If Hell be pleased, when sinners enter in,
If earth be pleased, to loose a truckling knave,
Then all be pleased; MacDonald's in his grave.
(Forbes, R, 1975, Vol. 1, p. 239)

Dugald Roy Cameron, who shot Munro of Culcairn in mistake for Captain Grant of Knockando for whom he was lying in wait, praised Lochiel, who supported Charles although he had not promised to do so. He goes on:

Cha b' ionnan 's MacLeòid
    Not so did MacLeod
A tha' n drasd aig Rìgh Deors'
    Who is now with King George
Na fhogarrach soilleir
    A manifest outlaw
Fo choibhreadh 'n da chleoc.
    Beneath the shade of two cloaks
A Mhic Dho' ill gun sgoinn
    MacDonald without strength
'S ann a chomhdaich thu 'n fhoill
    Guile sheltered you
Ged a gheall thu bhi' dileas
    Though you promised to be faithful
'S ann a dhiobair thu 'n groim
    You let go your grip
Tha ball dubh ort 's an t-stròin
    There is a blemish on your nose
Is misd' thu ri d' bheò
    That will mark you for life

'S chan fheàrr thu nam baigear
> You are no better than a beggar

'S a bhata 'n a dhorn.
> With his staff in his hand.

(Campbell, JL, 1984, p. 267)

The '45 Rebellion

In view of the intense loyalty of his predecessors, it is difficult for us to-day to understand the vacillating attitude of Sir Alexander towards the cause of the Prince. There were, of course, strong reasons why he should not have joined the rebellion. There was the seeming hopelessness of the adventure, the strong influence of President Forbes, the persuasive power of MacLeod and the risk he would run of losing his estates, for which he had so recently acquired title-deeds; but with the possible exception of his father, Sir James, any one of his immediate ancestors would have thrown all these prudent considerations to the four winds and would unhesitatingly have declared for the cause of Prince Charlie. He himself was a Jacobite at heart; his wife, Lady Margaret, a strong, though secret, supporter of the cause; while staunch clansmen, like Donald Roy MacDonald, MacDonald of Kingsborough and Hugh MacDonald of Armadale, would sacrifice much on behalf of the 'Young Pretender'. Indeed, there was only one man, of all the cadets of the House of Sleat, who can be said to have been truly a Hanoverian and that was Allan Mac-Donald of Knock, the captor of Prince Charlie's guide, Donald MacLeod of Galtrigil.

The rank and file of the clan were enthusiastic for the Prince. Writing to Forbes of Culloden, Sir Alexander says, *"The men are as devoted to the young gentleman* (Prince Charlie) *as their wives and their daughters are"* (Warrand, D, 1929, p. 63). He had very good reasons for making that assertion for, when he called out the clan and reviewed them at Portree, we have it on the declaration of Hugh MacDonald of Baleshare, as given in *The Lyon in Mourning*, that

> *the people denied rising in arms if Sir Alexander did not go and join the Prince; upon which the people all dispersed. I told Sir Alexander I was vexed at the disobedience shown by the people to their chief. He told me to keep silence. It was all by his private orders, as it did not lay in his way to do him* (the Prince) *good, he had no inclination to do him hurt.*

(Forbes, R, 1975, Vol. 2, pp. 101–2)

and this affirmation is amplified by a statement in an interesting MS by Sir John MacGregor Murray of Lanrick, in which we find,

> *When Sir Alexander had resolved not to join the Prince, he desired Kingsborough, then his factor, to speak to the people, of whom 400 had assembled, to advise them not to go to the Prince. Kingsborough made no impression on the MacDonalds, who exclaimed they would join the Prince. One of the gentlemen, Iain MacAlister Bhàin of Peinfeiler, asked Kingsborough if he would not go with his own company and, on his answering in the negative, that gentleman insulted him with a slap in the face, reproaching him with being unmanly and unlike his predecessors. The factor then returned to Sir Alexander, told him he could not prevail on the people and had even been insulted for the proposition. Sir Alexander then went out, conversed with the gentlemen and the people who were assembled and asked them whether they would not remain with him to defend the country, or follow the Prince. They all exclaimed that they would join the Prince, observing that he had also promised to do so and that to fail would be dishonourable. He desired such as were with him to separate from those who were resolved to join the Prince. None of them separated, but stood firm with the Prince. Sir Alexander then said that, if they deserted him, the country would be exposed very*

soon to fire and plunder by the king's troops and that the family of MacDonald, as well as their own, would be ruined. Upon which they repeated that the discredit would be his own if he flinched but that, if he was resolved, they would follow him to the devil.

The spirit of the people towards the rebellion may be illustrated by another incident. On the retreat of the Highland army from England, Donald Roy MacDonald was despatched once more to solicit Sir Alexander and MacLeod to join the Jacobites. The emissary spent three days, on his return from Skye, at Kyleakin, where his brother, Hugh MacDonald of Baleshare, was stationed as captain in the Hanoverian Militia; and with him and his men Donald Roy made merry,

eating plenteously of King George's beef and provisions with the white cockade in his bonnet, his several friends of the militia heartily wishing and drinking success to the Prince's cause.

(Forbes, R, 1975, Vol. 2, p. 35).

In the maze of the wildly conflicting pronouncements (often the creations of intensely biased minds) that have been made regarding the real attitude of Sir Alexander to the rebellion, certain facts emerge that make it reasonable to conclude that he had been enthusiastic enough in support of the project of rising with the Prince, but that his zeal was severely damped when he discovered that the latter had not brought with him a following commensurate with the undertaking. Thus, when a letter, written by Sir Alexander to Lord President Forbes and intercepted by the Jacobites, was shown to the Prince, it is said that he evinced great disappointment and that he declared *"it was on their advice he came, as their letters would show"* (Mackenzie, A, 1889, p. 131). In that reliable account of the Rebellion, *The Lyon in Mourning*, there is an asseveration by Captain Malcolm

MacLeod of Raasay to the effect that Sir Alexander MacDonald had apprised MacDonald of Boisdale of the Prince's intention to come to the Highlands and that, as the first landing was to be made on the lands of Boisdale, the latter was to advise the Prince to return immediately to France, if he had not a large following, and await a more favourable opportunity (Forbes, R, 1975, Vol. 1, p. 147).

In the same compilation there is another statement by Captain Malcolm respecting a conference held in *"a publick-house in Sconsary"*, at which Sir Alexander, Kingsborough, MacLeod of Raasay and Captain Malcolm were present. A man from Glenelg had come with news of Gladesmuir (Prestonpans) and *"Sir Alexander was so impressed, he doubted not now of the Prince's succeeding in his attempt and that therefore every one should raise men to assist him"*. Sir Alexander is reported to have observed to Raasay, *"'Tis true you cannot raise many men, but those you have are good. You can easily raise 100 and I resolve to have 900, making a good 1000 stout fellows betwixt us"*. Captain Malcolm goes on to say Sir Alexander expressed his intention of dividing this force into two battalions, making Raasay colonel of 500 men. The latter were to proceed to join the rebellion as soon as possible after the necessary preparations had been completed, while Sir Alexander was to follow with his detachment a day's march behind him. Detailed arrangements were made for the setting out, even to the number of cattle they were to take with them as part of the commissariat, *"till they should come to the Low Country, where they would get plenty"*. They spent the night at the inn and were a merry company.

Next morning, however, it was noticed that the disposition of the Chief of the MacDonalds had undergone a pronounced change. A courier had arrived bearing letters, one from Forbes and another from MacLeod, who was then in Inverness. *"Sir Alexander went aside to read them and he left the inn"*. Captain

Malcolm asked Kingsborough if he could account for the sudden departure of the chief and his change of demeanour. Kingsborough answered that he could only surmise that his chief had changed his mind about the project to join the Prince (Forbes, R, 1975, Vol. 1, pp. 146–7). There can be no doubt that it was Forbes and MacLeod who were instrumental in determining Sir Alexander's subsequent course of action in regard to the rebellion. His defection gave grave disappointment to those who were zealous in the Jacobite cause and occasioned John Roy Stuart, the bard, to lament:

A chlann Dhòmhnuill mo ghaoil,
    Beloved Clan Donald
Do'm bu shuaicheantas fraoch,
    Whose emblem is heather
Mo chreach uile nach d' fhaod
    My utter destruction is that
Sibh éirigh.
    You were not allowed to rise.

(Mackenzie, J, 1877, p. 267)

And the same tale may be related of the MacLeods. While the semple of the clan were unanimously for the Prince and the great majority of the gentle were similarly minded, the chief actually fought on the side of the Royalists, though he was on principle a Jacobite. When one of the cadets of the House of MacLeod, Donald of Bernera, the 'Old Trojan', as he has been called, was ordered by his chief to bring his men to Dunvegan, he readily complied with the request; and, presenting his company, he thus addressed the chief,

I place at your disposal the twenty men of your tribe who are under my immediate command and, in any other quarrel, I would not fail

to be at their head, but in the present juncture I must go where a more imperious duty calls me,

and with that he joined the Highland army (Mackenzie, A, 1889, p. 250). It is said that MacDonald of Heisker, in North Uist, acted in the same manner towards Sir Alexander MacDonald, when the latter had decided to throw in his lot with the government.

It is reasonable to conclude, from the assertions so often made in affirmation of it, that very few of the rank and file of the MacLeods would have been prevailed upon to leave Skye but for the fact that they had been deluded into the belief that they were going to fight for Prince Charlie. *"It is well known"*, declares Bishop Forbes, in *The Lyon in Mourning,*

that the Laird of MacLeod used this dissembling art to raise his own men in so much that the MacLeods had white cockades in their bonnets at their rising and, in passing from Skye to the continent (mainland), which I, Robert Forbes, have had affirmed to me by several persons from Skye who had access to know this affair well.

(Forbes, R, 1975, Vol. 2, p. 85).

There are some, indeed, who aver that MacLeod's eldest son had actually set off from Skye at the head of his clan, with the intention of joining the Prince but that on the way he had been prevailed upon to reconsider the position and so abandoned the enterprise. In a letter by his factor to John Grant of Grant, in October 1745, is a statement to the effect that Lovat called MacLeod a *'perjured villain'*, for his failure to supplement a solemn oath he had given at Castle Dounie, that he would hasten home, mobilise his men and join the Master of Lovat at the Pass of Corrieyairack.

And just as the charge has been made that Sir Alexander MacDonald had encouraged the Prince to come to Scotland and that he deserted him when he did arrive and even joined his enemies, a similar imputation has been made against MacLeod; for MacKenzie, 'The Clans' Historian', has left it on record that *"Miss MacLeod of MacLeod remembers having seen in the family chest a correspondence, which has since disappeared, showing, without doubt, that MacLeod had encouraged Charlie to come over"* (Mackenzie, A, 1889, p. 129).

Notwithstanding, it was MacLeod who, on the 2nd of August, conveyed to the government the first intimation of the arrival of the Prince. Prudent considerations undoubtedly constrained him to act in that way, when he heard that the Prince had but one ship, *"mounting sixteen or eighteen guns"*, and only *"about thirty Irish, or French, officers"* (Forbes, D, 1815, p. 203). As M.P. for the County of Inverness, he felt it was his duty to give intelligence of the insurrection and he exerted himself to prevent his own men from joining the outbreak. On 17th August, 1745, he wrote a letter to President Forbes from Sconser, as he was on his way *"in great haste"* to his property in Glenelg, in order to dissuade his people there *"from being prevailed upon by their neighbours to join the Prince"* (ibid., p. 208).

Prince Charles despatched an emissary to MacLeod, as he had to MacDonald, soliciting his aid; and that fact probably explains the letter MacLeod sent Forbes and in which he says,

We not only gave no countenance to these people but we use all the interest we have with our neighbours to follow the same prudent method; and we are persuaded we have done it with such success that not one man of any consequence north of the Grampians will give any sort of assistance to this mad, rebellious attempt. How far you think we have acted properly I shall long to know but of this I am certain, we did it as our duty and for the best; for, in the present situation in Europe, I should be very sorry to see anything like disaffection to the government appear, though ever so trivial. Sir Alexander is here and has seen this scrawl.

Shortly afterwards Forbes wrote Sir Alexander, advising him that either he or MacLeod should proceed to Inverness with as large a force as they could muster while the other was to remain in Skye, in order to suppress any risings in the island and *"to keep proper countenance in the country"*.

The chiefs of Skye were quite prepared to obey this command but they declared they were woefully lacking in equipment. MacLeod describes the situation thus: *"Sir Alexander and I can easily raise from 1500 to 2000 men for the king's service but we require arms, else 1800 staves, with about 200 swords, would make but a foolish picture"* (ibid., loc. cit.).

It is not known whether the necessary arms were forthcoming or not; but, in any case, the MacLeods were marshalled on *Lag Buidhe*, at the head of Loch Caroy, about the end of October. The detachment consisting of between 400 and 500 men with their piper, Donald *Bàn* MacCrimmon at their head, they made for Kyleakin. Tradition has it that the piper was far from easy, probably because he knew that the true purpose of the expedition was not to join the Prince, but to oppose him. He was very depressed and fears began to develop in his mind that he would never return. In accordance with the superstition of the age, the story goes, he went to consult a witch, who lived hard by, in order to ascertain his chances in the campaign. This was on the morning of the day they were to set out.

The banshee informed him that everything would depend on the attitude of his wife towards him before the expedition started. If she helped cheerfully and of her own accord, then all would go well but, should she display no anxiety to attend to his needs, disaster was sure to be his portion. Now the condition would be impaired if he were compelled to ask her for anything. All he was to do was to show he was preparing to leave home on an important enterprise.

In a state of intense anxiety he went home wondering how it would fare with him, for his wife's aversion to work was known far and near and she earned the censure of all her neighbours by her habitual neglect of her respected husband. When he entered the house, he found her, as usual, lying down on a bench, with the room untidy and the fire unkindled. She took no notice of him as he bustled about, making as much stir as he possibly could to attract her attention. The time for his departure was drawing distressingly near. Yet she had not bestirred herself! He was all the time in deep meditation as to the most effective way of bringing his desires to her notice. He would take up his pipe, try to tune it and lay it down again, only to repeat the operation. His hose required adjustment, his brogues seemed to give him no end of trouble! With much ado, he would take them off; with ostentation quite as great, he would fasten them on again. Still the condition so fateful for him seemed to be no nearer its fulfillment. At last the tumult outside announced the hour of departure! As a final effort to rouse his lethargic spouse he undid one of his brogues and threw it down on the floor with much clatter but this also failed to produce the desired result. He tied it on again and, with a heavy heart, lifted up his pipe. As he crossed the threshold he gave utterance to the saying that has since become a proverb: '*Cha ghluais bròg, no bruidheann, droch bhean tighe*' ('Neither boot nor speech will move a bad housewife').

It is with him also, that the island tradition associates the ballad called *MacCrimmon's Lament*, the assertion being that, as he marched at the head of the clan on the way to the mainland, he composed the soul-subduing lament extempore and, so deftly did he play, that the pipes seemed to enunciate the words:

Mo chùl, mo chùl, mo chùl ri tilleadh
    My despair, my despair, my despair of returning
Mo chùl ris an Dùn gun mo dhùil ri tilleadh.
    My back to Dunvegan without hope of returning.

The melody of this haunting strain, so often on the lips of sorrowing emigrants during the subsequent century, was first published in Patrick MacDonald's *Highland Vocal Airs* (MacDonald, P, 1784, p. 19) and it was afterwards made more widely known when the words appeared in the pages of *Cuairtear nan Gleann*, when that paper was under the editorship of Rev. Dr. Norman MacLeod, *Caraid nan Gàidheal*. Some have attributed their composition to that famous author himself.

The contingent of the MacLeods arrived at Inverness about the middle of November, when they were immediately commanded to proceed to the region of Moray, in order to check the exactions that were there being raised on behalf of Prince Charlie. They formed part of the force that, on the 23rd of December, encountered a superior body of Jacobites, under Lord Lewis Gordon, at the village of Inverurie. The skirmish lasted but a few minutes; but that was ample time in which to drive the Islesmen from their position, whence they were pursued in utter confusion beyond the Spey. In the rollicking Jacobite ballad, '*MacLeod's Defeat at Inverurie*', the denouement is thus described:

MacLeod that nicht got sic a fricht,
Rade aff ere brak o' day, man.
He lost his bridle in the fecht,
Rade aff wi' ane o' strae, man.

Large numbers of the MacLeods then deserted, going home to Skye; but it is said that about 150 of them were later brought back to Inverness by MacLeod of Talisker. The rest were rallied and were amalgamated with the force that held Inverness for a time under the Earl of Loudon. They were involved with that army, which also included a considerable body of the MacDonalds of Skye, in the famous *Rout of Moy*.

On the evening of Sunday, the 16th of February, Loudon planned an attack on Moyhall, where the Prince's headquarters then were and great precautions were taken to prevent knowledge of the intended coup from getting abroad. A cordon of soldiers was drawn round the town and none was to be allowed to pass through on any condition. Despite these measures, a messenger was despatched, it is said, by Macintosh himself, who was an officer with Loudon, in order to warn the Jacobites; and he succeeded in the attempt.

Preparations were immediately made by the Prince to repel the attack, the duty of providing outposts being allotted to the men of Clan Ranald, among whom were the MacLeods of Raasay. A smith named Fraser and four men went along the road from Moy in order to *reconnoitre*. When they were about two miles from the castle they heard the Hanoverians approaching. In the pitch darkness orders were given by the dauntless blacksmith to imaginary clans and shots were fired. The Dunvegan men formed the van of Loudon's army and, it is said that, fearing, or feigning that an ambush had been laid, they were seized with panic and retreated helter-skelter towards the town of Inverness. The first shot, some say the only one, fired by *"the merry men of Moy Castle"*, killed the piper of the MacLeods, Donald *Bàn* MacCrimmon.

On the following Tuesday the Prince's army marched on Inverness. At its approach the Hanoverian forces vacated the town and made for the North. They were pursued by the Earl of Cromarty into Sutherland, where they were dispersed. The MacLeods, whose heart was never in the affair, readily availed themselves of the opportunity to cease opposing the Prince and made for Skye, whither the chief followed them, with Loudon and President Forbes in his company.

Soon afterwards the fate of the Stuart cause was decided on the field of Culloden. The scattered remnants of the Highland army, broken in spirit and in headlong flight, made as best they could for the mountain fastnesses of the West. Terrible hardships were endured by these gallant men and every ruse was adopted in order to avoid capture. Their sense of despair and the poignancy of their sufferings, are epitomised by the bard, John Roy Stuart, who himself played such a notable part in the rising:

> *Tha ar cinn fon a choille,*
>> We are outlawed,
> *'S fheudar gleanntan is beanntan thoirt oirnn;*
>> We must take to the glens and bens;
> *Sinn gun sùgradh, gun mhacnus,*
>> Without diversion or sport,
> *Gun aoibhneas, gun aiteas, gun cheòl,*
>> Without joy, delight or music,
> *Air bheag bidhe no teine,*
>> With little food or fire,
> *Air na stùcann mu'n laigheadh an ceò,*
>> We are like the feathered owl,
> *Sinn mar chomhachaig eite,*
>> On the peaks whereon the mist lies,
> *Ag èisdeachd ri deireas gach lò.*
>> Listening to the calamity of each day.
>>> (Campbell, JL, 1984, p. 174)

With the wanderings of Prince Charlie on the mainland and subsequently in the Long Island, we are not here concerned. But there are two persons connected with Skye who played such a prominent part in association with him in these places and have, in consequence, acquired such fame in history, that it is necessary, at this stage, to give a brief sketch of their lives. They were Donald MacLeod and Flora MacDonald.

Donald MacLeod

The 'Faithful Palinurus', as he was called by Walkingshaw, the patron of the condemned Jacobites during their sojourn in London, was a tacksman, in fairly comfortable circumstances, in Galtrigill, and a trader of note in his day. He happened to be in Inverness, whither he had gone for a cargo of meal, when his clan was stationed there after the debacle of Inverurie. Urgent appeals were frequently made to him by his chief to show his loyalty to his clan and the government, but Donald stoutly refused to be swayed from his resolve. It says much for his sense of independence that he should thus have defied tradition, which held the clan spirit in such reverent awe. If he did, at times, think that obedience to his chief should have been his first considera-tion, though there is no evidence of that, the events that now supervened left no room in his mind for uncertainty. The Jaco-bite army had entered Inverness in triumph and the Hanoverian forces were retreating abjectly to the north, after the Rout of Moy. It appears that Donald joined in the celebrations that fol-lowed and he thus became acquainted with some of the Jacobite officers. Owing to his wide experience, as a trader among the Western Isles, he was commissioned by the Prince and his council to convey one, Aeneas MacDonald of Kinlochmoidart, to Barra, in order to bring to the mainland a sum of £380 in gold that had been lodged there for safety. In spite of many difficulties the adventure was successful, and the money was safely deposited in the district of Moidart.

A few days after the disaster of Culloden, the Prince met Donald at Borrodale, on *Loch nan Uamh*, in Arisaig and he asked him to proceed to Skye with letters to his chief and to Sir Alexander MacDonald. Donald reasoned against the practicabil-ity of such a project; and he succeeded in convincing the Prince of its futility. Thereupon the latter asked to be taken to the Long Island, throwing himself unreservedly on Donald's responsibil-ity. An eight-oared boat was procured, one of the crew being Donald's young son, Murdoch, who had been attending school in Inverness, but whose ardour for the Jacobite cause had led him to quit his books and, although only 15 years of age, he had joined the Highland army and had fought on Culloden. This brave youth followed the general trend of the fugitives towards the west and had arrived at Borrodale in time to accompany the Prince across the Minch.

It was a wild night of thunder and rain when, in deep dark-ness, the Prince and his party left the Scottish mainland. Donald was a man of 68 years of age, but such was his skill and daring as a seaman, that, notwithstanding the very adverse weather they encountered, those on board had implicit faith in the man at the helm. After enduring much hardship, they effected a landing at Rossinish on the following morning. Clanranald who came there, at the Prince's command, dvised that they should go on to Stornoway, where they might be able to secure a ship capable of carrying the Prince back to France and accordingly they set sail and landed on the Island of Scalpay. From there it was decided that Donald MacLeod should continue to Stornoway in order to negotiate the charter of a ship. With his customary devotion, Donald set off but his mission was thwarted by the action of two ministers of the name of MacAulay, father and son, who advised another member of the clergy, the Rev. Coll Mackenzie, to incite the people against the Prince by the allegation that he was approaching the town with a strong force, in order to put the inhabitants under tribute and to seize a ship forcibly to take him to France (Forbes, R, 1975, Vol. 1, pp. 158–168).

The people of Stornoway were thus roused to such antago-nism to his venture that Donald was forced to leave the town. He rejoined the Prince's party once more and, in their own boat, they retraced their course to South Uist. On the way they were beset with constant danger for the ships of the govern-ment were everywhere in the Minch. Twice they were sighted and on one occasion followed for some nine miles; but by skilful manœuvring and hard rowing they succeeded in eluding their pursuers.

After the fugitives had been consigned to temporary safety in the house of Ranald MacEachain, a tacksman in lone Glen Corrodale, Donald was commissioned to proceed on another adventure; this time to Loch Arkaig, where Lochiel and other Jacobite leaders were in hiding, in order to bring back some of the gold that had been hoarded there and also a supply of brandy – stuff that was then becoming a first necessity with the Prince. Again Donald was successful in his perilous enterprise; the Prince's spirits were high, though it was becoming daily clearer that they must evacuate the Long Island if they were to evade capture.

Through the loyalty of Hugh MacDonald of Armadale, who was an officer in the Skye Militia, passports were supplied to Flora MacDonald and the Prince for proceeding to Skye. It was considered unwise that Donald should form one of the escort; and at Loch Boisdale he parted with his Prince, who had been under his care from the 21st of April until the 21st of June – a period that must have been one of intense anxiety to a person of such deep loyalty and lofty sense of duty as Donald MacLeod.

A thorough combing out of the Long Island was now initiated by the Militia and, a fortnight after his parting with the Prince, Donald was captured in Benbecula by a fellow Skyeman, Lieut. Allan MacDonald of Knock in Sleat. This man has the questionable distinction of having been the only cadet of his house who was whole-heartedly a Hanoverian and he has left behind him a reputation that, for cruelty and mean dealing, places him very low among the many dastards of that unhappy time.

As General Campbell, the chief officer commanding in the Western Isles, was then supposed to be in Barra, Donald was sent thither to be tried. It was, however, discovered that the General had proceeded to Skye and Donald was sent there after him. At Portree he was joined by other captives, chief of whom was Captain Malcolm MacLeod, the cousin of 'Raasay'. It was ascertained that the government ship, *'Furnace'*, commanded by the notorious Captain Ferguson, lay in Applecross Bay at that time, whither the prisoners were despatched. A court was immediately convened, presided over by the gentlemanly General Campbell. During the inquiry the General observed that Donald might have secured £30,000 if he had acted wisely and betrayed the Prince. The retort made by Donald is so characteristic of this gallant and true-hearted son of Skye that it is worthy of being quoted in full:

£30,000! Though I had got it, I could not have enjoyed it eight and forty hours. This conscience of mine would have got up upon me and that money would not have kept it down. Though I had got all England and Scotland for my pains, I would not allow a hair of his body to be touched, if I could help it.

The *'Furnace'* cruised about the Western Isles for several weeks and the poor prisoners suffered extreme privations. There was no attempt at sanitation, the food was scanty and inferior and their clothes were worn to rags. Ten long months he endured these hardships in the prison ships and his health was being sorely tried. Yet such was the magnanimity of his nature that, on no occasion, did he show any bitterness towards his tormentors.

God forgive them, he used to say, *but God let them never die till we have them in the same condition they had us, and we are sure we would not treat them as they treated us. We would show them the difference between a good and a bad cause.*

(Forbes, R, 1975, Vol. 1, pp. 158–82).

He was released on the 10th of July 1747 and arrived home in Skye about the middle of October. His health was broken owing to the ill-treatment he had received but what aggrieved him most of all was the manner in which he was despised by his chief. The latter slighted him, *"because it was thought that that was the proper way to be popular with the government"*.

Donald did not long enjoy his freedom. He died at Galtrigill on the 8th of September 1749. His name will be remembered with pardonable pride so long as loyalty, fortitude and a disinterested regard for those in distress awaken the admiration of mankind, for his was a noble role, in what Lord Rosebery once called *"the last burst of chivalry"* (*ibid.*, Vol. 2, p. 359).

Flora MacDonald

The other person associated with the Prince in this episode of his life was Flora MacDonald. Although she cannot be claimed as a native of Skye, so much of her romantic career was run in that island that it is necessary to include a brief biography of her also.

She was the daughter of Ranald MacDonald of Milton, South Uist, where she was born in 1722. When she was but a child, her father died and her mother married again, this time a notable scion of the House of Sleat, Hugh MacDonald of Armadale, one who is reputed to have been the strongest man of his time in Skye.

Flora was brought up in Skye and was educated in the local school in Sleat. She was a prime favourite with Sir Alexander and Lady Margaret MacDonald, at whose mansion in Mogstadt she was often a guest.

Flora developed into a lady of great versatility and resourcefulness. She was a good English scholar, an accomplished musician, but what attracted her especially to her acquaintances was her engaging personality for she had *"a great sprightliness in looks, abounded with good sense and modesty, gentleness and humanity"*. In *The Lyon in Mourning* her personal appearance and her manners are thus naively described by Bishop Forbes, *"Of low stature, of fair complexion and well enough shaped; and no lady, Edinburgh-bred, can acquit herself better at the tea-table than she did in Leith Road"* (Forbes, R, 1975, Vol. 1, p. 117) and among others who have left interesting accounts of her, Boswell refers to her in his *Journal* as *"a little woman of genteel appearance, uncommonly mild and well-bred"* (Boswell, J, 1955, p. 129).

Just when the pursuit of the Prince was becoming keenest, Flora MacDonald had occasion to go to Uist, ostensibly to pay a visit to her brother, who was tacksman at Milton but, probably, as the agent of Lady Margaret to aid in the escape of the Prince. For weeks previously, Lady Margaret had been unwearied in her efforts to obtain information and to acquaint the Prince's friends of the movements and the intentions of the enemy's forces. This was an easy, albeit a hazardous matter for her, as her house at Mogstadt was the daily rendezvous of the officers of the crown. Her help was so much appreciated by the Prince that he sent her a special letter of thanks, with the enjoinment that it was to be burned immediately after perusal. Lady Margaret, however, treasured the royal epistle, despite its serious implications, with such regard, that she resolved to preserve it as an heirloom; but she was ultimately persuaded, on the urgent representations of Donald Roy MacDonald and other friends, to destroy it when news came of Captain Ferguson's arrival at Mogstadt (*ibid.*, Vol. 2, p. 8).

Simultaneously with Flora's departure from Skye, Lady Margaret sent a communication to Uist, acquainting those in league with her there, namely, Hugh MacDonald of Baleshare and his namesake of Armadale, that a minute search of the Long Island was contemplated by the troops of the government.

Meanwhile, things were stirring in the Island of Skye. Rumours were abroad that, as the pursuit in the Outer Isles was becoming too close for him, the Prince and his party were planning a flight to Skye. Every vantage point along the western shores of that island was occupied by troops in order to intercept the royal fugitive, and these activities on the part of his enemies kindled feelings of harassing solicitude in the minds of those who had the safety of the Prince at heart.

Lady Margaret, together with her faithful ally, Donald Roy MacDonald, had been making extensive preparations to receive the Prince on his coming to Skye. Her agent was untiring in his efforts to elicit information about the movements of the Hanoverian troops. This hero was the son of Ronald MacDonald, a natural son of Sir James *Mór*, Baronet of Sleat. He had been wounded in the foot on Culloden but he had managed to hirple home to Skye, practically on one leg, enduring great agony the while. Owing to neglect, the wound festered; yet he was seldom at rest, being constantly on the move as Lady Margaret's emissary on behalf of the Prince.

Towards the end of June, it was anticipated that the Prince might arrive in Skye at any moment. It was thought that he would betake himself to *Fladda Chuain*, an island to the north of Trotternish, then occupied by a single tenant. Thither, it was proposed that Donald Roy should go, in order to receive him. Every precaution was taken to prevent anyone from ascertaining the purpose of this outing and the principal movers in it gave it out that Donald was going to the island to fish and also to procure shells for the making of lime. As he meant to pass a few days on the island, a considerable stock of provisions was taken, together with a bundle of *"six shirts belonging to her husband and a sum of twenty guineas, sent by Lady Margaret for the use of the Prince"*.

Donald Roy remained on the island for a whole day and night, vainly awaiting the arrival of Prince Charlie. Losing patience and concluding that the latter might have repaired to *Bòrd Cruinn*,

Donald Roy proceeded to that rocky islet of powerful currents and difficult approach. As he did not wish the oarsmen to land, in case the Prince and his party were concealed in the ruin on the top of the island, Donald effected a landing alone by jumping out of the boat on to a ledge, whence, in spite of his injured foot, he climbed to the highest point; but, finding no on there, he returned to the mainland and paid a visit to Dr. John MacLean, the chief's physician, who then occupied Shulista (*ibid.*, Vol. 2, p. 12).

During these events in Skye, Flora MacDonald met Captain O'Neill, one of the Prince's retinue, *"by a lucky accident"*, as is the account of it in *The Lyon in Mourning*, *"and he got her to promise to take Prince Charlie to Skye."*

While preparations for the flight were proceeding, Flora was one day on her way to visit the Lady of Clan Ranald, when she was apprehended by members of the Militia. She protested against such interference and demanded to be brought before their commanding officer. After much hesitation, her wish was granted and she was ushered into the presence of her step-father!

Whether Hugh MacDonald knew of the projected adventure or not has never been divulged though General Campbell, on more than one occasion, accused him of cozenage in the escape of the Prince. The fact remains, he supplied Flora and a young student, named Neil MacEachain, with passports for Skye, while another was drawn up for one 'Betty Burke', who was alleged to be her maid. In a letter which he despatched by Flora to his wife, MacDonald wrote,

I have sent your daughter from this country, lest she should in any way be frightened with the troops lying here. She has got one, Betty Burke, an Irish girl, who, as she tells me, is a grand spinster. If her spinning pleases you, you may keep her till she spins all your lint or, if you have any wool to spin, you may employ her.

Armed with the visas, the party made for Rossinish, in Benbecula, where an open boat was procured and a crew of five to man her.

It was a clear and calm evening when, about 8 p.m. on Saturday, the 28th of June, the fugitives put to sea. They had only been an hour afloat when a freshening westerly wind developed into a tempest and heavy rain began to fall. Contrary to the assertion in the popular ballad, *'Over the sea to Skye'*, it was Flora who slept, while the Prince sang songs.

They rowed on all night and, early next morning, as they were approaching the Point of Waternish, it was proposed to land in order to rest the oarsmen. On drawing closer to the shore, however, it was noticed that it was occupied by soldiers and they rowed off as fast as they could. They were fired upon, but no one was hit and, after they had rounded the promontory, they sought safety in a creek nearby, for ships-of-war were then in sight. There they hid for a short time and partook of food and much-needed rest. As delay was dangerous, they resumed their journey, and shortly after noon, on Sunday 29th June, they landed at a place called *Allt a' Chuain* in Kilbride Bay, about half a mile to the south-west of Mogstadt House. Thither Flora proceeded with MacEachain, leaving the Prince to conceal himself as best he could among the rocks of the shore (*ibid.,* Vol. 1, pp. 71–3).

When she arrived at Mogstadt, a party of soldiers was idling without, while some officers were inside dining with Lady Margaret. Among the latter was Lieutenant Alexander MacLeod of Balmeanach. Flora accepted the invitation to sit down with the company; and she soon found she had to exercise all the wit and all the resource she possessed, in order to parry the very pointed questions that were addressed to her. *"She afterwards"*, Boswell says *"often laughed in good humour with these gentlemen on her having so well deceived them"*.

Notwithstanding the difficulty of the situation, she succeeded in informing Lady Margaret of the circumstances and the latter lost no time in coming to a decision. She sent MacDonald of Kingsborough, Sir Alexander's factor, who chanced that day to be at Mogstadt, to the Prince with victuals and to acquaint him with the plans that had been concerted for his safety. After searching about for some considerable time, Kingsborough succeeded in locating the Prince, to whom he communicated the designs of his friends. These were that he was to spend the night in Kingsborough House and proceed next day to the Island of Raasay, which was then free of the soldiers of the government.

In the late afternoon the Prince and Kingsborough set off for the south on foot. The old road which they followed may still be traced, particularly at Cuidreach and beyond Glen Hinnisdale, where, at *Lòn Ruadh*, slightly to the west of the present highway, a *'Tobar a' Phrionnsa'*, or Prince's Well, is still pointed out.

It was about eleven o'clock at night when the party arrived, to the great surprise of the household at Kingsborough for, it is said, the ladies of that establishment were intensely curious as to the identity of the raw-boned female, with the uncouth gait, who accompanied their father. Mrs MacDonald alone was brought into the secret and, after partaking of her good cheer, the happy company, among whom were Flora and MacEachain, repaired to rest for the night.

Next morning, preparations were made for continuing the journey but great difficulty was experienced in rousing the Prince from *"a most refreshing sleep"*. And the utmost haste was now necessary for, as Mrs MacDonald of Kingsborough had conjectured, the crew that ferried the royal party across the Minch were arrested immediately on their return and forced to confess all.

After his experience of the Prince's deportment in female garb on the previous day, when he had on several occasions mildly to remind him that it was necessary to his safety to observe the feminine conventions with greater care ("*s tu dh'fhàs mi-bhanail bho'n uiridh*" – 'you have become unwomanly since last year.'), Kingsborough concluded that it would be prudent to dress his charge in male attire. In a *MS.*, said to have been written by Neil MacEachain himself and published in *The New Monthly Magazine* in 1840, there appears a statement to the effect that people going home from church watched Kingsborough and his companion. It proceeds:

> *They continued to speak of the ignorance and the assurance of Miss Burke, who was not ashamed to walk and keep company with Kingsborough. But what they most took notice of was, when Kingsborough and his companion came to a rivulet, about knee-deep, which crossed the high road, to see Burke take up her petticoats so high when she entered the water. The poor fellows were quite confounded at this last sight!*
>
> (Blaikie, WB, 1916, pp. 263–5).

Though the Prince, as Kingsborough puts it, *"was very bad at acting the part of dissembler"*, it was deemed essential that he should leave the house in the clothes in which he had come, lest the suspicion of the servants should be aroused. This was done and, in a wood a short distance from Kingsborough House, the Prince donned a suit belonging to his protector, from whom he parted here and, in the company of Neil MacEachain and a boy, named MacQueen, who acted as guide, the party proceeded to Portree. Past Eyre, Annishader, Borve and Drumuie, they went and, in the evening, they arrived at MacNab's Inn, now the Royal Hotel, in Portree. There they were joined by Flora MacDonald and, after feelingly bidding each other farewell, the heroine parted with her Prince and, with Neil MacEachain, set off to her home in Armadale, where we shall meanwhile leave her, while we follow the Prince in his itinerary in Raasay and in Skye (Forbes, R, 1975, Vol. 1, p. 73).

While the party was resting in the inn, Donald Roy Mac-Donald was active in his preparations for taking the Prince to Raasay. He discovered that young *Mac Ghille Chaluim*, the heir of Raasay, was then at Totterome, for all the houses on his island had been burned down and he had gone to live with a sister who was married to MacQueen, the tacksman of that part of Scorrybreck. Having apprised 'Raasay' of the adventure and enlisted his support, Donald Roy hastened back to Portree, where he rejoined the Prince.

In the meantime, young 'Raasay' was not idle. He managed to drag a boat from Loch Leathan, one of the lochs of Storr, down the steep declivity to the shore at Berreraig and in this crazy cobble he rowed across the sound to Raasay. There he procured a larger boat, one of the two on his island that had been saved from the general destruction and with Dr. Murdo, his brother, Captain Malcolm, his cousin and two others, namely, John Mackenzie, who had been a sergeant in the Jacobite army, and a Donald MacFriar, they put to sea and sailed to Portree Loch (*ibid.*, Vol. 2, pp. 72–3).

In the early hours of the morning of Tuesday, 1st July, they brought the boat round to a place called *Sgeir Mhòr*, where the Prince embarked, and they made for a rocky and secluded cove immediately below the district of Glam, in Raasay.

In a shepherd's shieling, so low that they could scarce sit upright in it, these five devoted men tried to make their Prince as comfortable as they could. Great difficulty was experienced in procuring food and they had to exercise extreme caution lest the natives should apprehend any unusual occurrence. Young 'Raasay' went in search of victuals and, we are told, "*he brought back a kid in the fold of his plaid*".

That day the sentries noticed a stranger on the track that led past their hut. A council was at once convened and all, except the Prince, advocated the shooting of the man there and then. He alone opposed such action, remarking, "*God forbid that we should take any poor man's life while we can save our own"*. John MacKenzie, who was keeping watch at the door, overheard the royal observation and he muttered in Gaelic,

Feumar an gùnna a chur ris. Ged is esan an rìgh, is sinne a' chomhairle, agus is e an ni a their sinne, is còir a dheanamh. 'He must be shot. Although he (the Prince) is king, we are the counsellors and, what we say, is what ought to be done.' (John was a thorough-going Parliamentarian as well as a good Jacobite.)

Luckily, the man passed the hut unconcernedly and it was afterwards discovered that he was one of the fugitives of the Highland army lurking in Raasay and posing the while as a vendor of tobacco (Cameron, A, 1871, p. 125).

Before he left Portree, the Prince had secretly arranged with Donald Roy MacDonald to meet him on the following Sunday in Braes, in the house of a certain Peter MacQueen in Camustianavaig. In the interval, however, he had changed his plans for, on Wednesday morning, he intimated that he was anxious to leave Raasay, in order to consult with 'Donald Roy MacDonald in Trotternish'. He was so firmly fixed in his resolution, that it was seen to be futile to oppose him; and, about 7 p.m. on Wednesday, 2nd July, they left Raasay and made for Scorrybreck.

A gale from the north was blowing at the time and so fierce did it become that all except the Prince wanted to return to Glam. He urged them to proceed and on the way he whiled the time *'by singing Highland songs'*, for he had by this time acquired a smattering of the Gaelic language.

Between 9 and 10 o'clock at night, they landed near Nicolson's Rock, in Scorrybreck, at a place called *Lag na Bàthaich* ('Byre Hollow'), where they sought the shelter of a cowhouse, 'situated about two miles from Scorrybreck House'. Though drenched to the skin, the Prince was in good humour on the way. When Malcolm MacLeod requested to be allowed to carry part of the Prince's luggage, the latter seemed piqued at the implication of fatigue, for he remarked he should be as fit as any in

the company to carry his own equipage. When they arrived at the byre they partook of food, consisting of 'a little bread and cheese'. The Prince then sent Raasay's heir in quest of Donald Roy MacDonald, a man in whom he had the most implicit faith.

He had slept but little during the night; and next morning he seemed to be in a very unsettled state of mind. It was early apparent to Captain Malcolm MacLeod, who was then his sole guardian, that he was projecting another move but its purport had not been broached. Having matured his plans, it is said that *"he lifted up his baggage and walked out of the byre at 7 o'clock that evening, telling Malcolm to guide him to the district of Strathaird"*. The latter was greatly perturbed at this request, for he was aware that a contingent of the Militia was then stationed at the head of Loch Sligachan and *"he was most anxious that nothing should befall the Prince in his company"*. When Malcolm observed there was great danger in the undertaking, the Prince replied, *"There is nothing now to be done without danger"*. Seeing the Prince was resolved, Malcolm suggested, as the safer course, that they should go by sea. This proposal was also waived, and they made for the south by land.

It was decided that the Prince was to travel as Malcolm's servant and that he was to assume the name of 'Lewie Caw', after a Jacobite student who was then known to be hiding in Skye, *"where he had some relations"*. As they went on their way, it was arranged that the Prince was to act the part of servant with circumspection, that if anyone should be met on the way he was to stand aside, as became one in his station, and feign a lack of interest in whatever conversation should take place.

Through Glen Vargill they trudged, the Prince a splendid walker for, as he told Malcolm, he had prepared himself on the continent for the hardships of rough campaigning by going long distances barefooted. On the way they discussed many things. The conduct of Lord George Murray was subjected to criticism, the Prince going so far as to suggest that he suspected him of treachery; for, as he told Malcolm, *"he disobeyed all orders two or three days before Culloden"*.

As they passed in the darkness through the marshlands of Coireach and Caipleach, the Prince sank to the armpits in a bog and Malcolm suffered a similar mischance in his efforts to extricate him. Having wiped off as much of the peaty ooze as they could and put the brandy bottle under contribution, they resumed their march. They were now approaching the government station at Sligachan, where extreme caution was essential and Malcolm was anxious to pass it in the night.

Their effort was successful and when they had cleared the zone of danger the Prince was in a merry mood and glancing at his soiled garments, said he would one day yet walk the streets of London in the kilt he was then wearing. This fortitude was characteristic of him and it failed not to inspire the admiration of all who were ever associated with him; as one account has it, *'He always made light of his discomforts'* (Forbes, R, 1975, Vol. 1, pp. 130–7).

Here it should be noted that the late W.B. Blaikie, a historian who is justly acclaimed as one of our most reliable authorities on the Rebellion of '45, asserts that the route followed by the Prince and his guide was by Sconser, over *Druim nan Cleòc*, by the head of Loch Ainort, to Luib, thence through Strath *Mór*, by Loch Slapin side, to Kilmaree and finally to Elgol, their destination. Many have written of this phase of the rebellion and it is note-worthy that no one has ever called that authority in question. That fact strikes us as strange, when we consider the circumstances of the case and especially when we remember the position of the centres of population in that part of Skye at that time. Had they followed that route they would perforce have had to pass, in broad daylight, through several districts that were then inhabited, namely Torra Michaig, Kinlochainort, Aricharnach and Luib, not to mention the very populous region of

Kilmaree before they could arrive at Elgol, where their journey was to end.

Let it be said at once, that in none of the existing records of the event is there any item of evidence to show that this was the itinerary they followed. Indeed, apart altogether from the manifest needlessness for making such a detour, the data that are available point to a route at once as easy for men on foot, obviously more direct and certainly more secure. That way was through Glen Sligachan and Strath na Créithich. Thus, in a statement made to Bishop Forbes by Captain Malcolm himself and quoted in *The Lyon in Mourning*, we find this sentence:

> *The Captain remarked to the Prince that it was proper they shall pass the road that leads into the Laird of MacLeod's country in the night-time, for fear of parties spying them.*
>
> (*ibid.*, p. 137).

This had been Malcolm's chief concern ever since they left Scorrybreck, for he knew they would be out of danger once they had negotiated that point in their journey. The road he was so anxious to cross was that track that leaves the present highway on the declivity a few hundred yards to the north of Sligachan Inn and by *Carnan Thormaid* wends westwards through Crossal to *Dùthaich 'ic Leòid*.

The narrative continues:

> *They succeeded in crossing it by break of day and the Prince, looking about him and seeing nothing but hills all around them, said: 'I am sure the Devil himself cannot find us now'.*

That description of their surroundings at once suggested Glen Sligachan; and the sense of security it exhibits rules out the possibility of a journey through the populous townships that have been mentioned – a journey that would of necessity have had to be made, in its major portion, in the light of broad day. Moreover, in a testimony given by Captain Malcolm MacLeod, *Iain Dubh*, the old Chief of Mackinnon and others, the total length of the itinerary from Scorrybreck to Elgol is given as 24 miles. It is actually 22, if the traverse is made through Glen Sligachan; while it is over 30 miles if we follow it by Blaikie's route.

Again, in several accounts that are extant of this part of the Prince's wanderings, it is stated that they had barely crossed the head of Loch Sligachan before the break of day; while in the narration of the event given by Captain Malcolm to Boswell, it is said that Elgol was reached *"pretty early in the morning"*. Such a time for their arrival is consistent only with the shorter route through this difficult terrain, for, allowing for delays and bearing in mind the time at which daybreak occurs at the beginning of July, they could have accomplished the journey through Glen Sligachan by 6 o'clock in the morning, whereas the course through Strath *Mór,* which is over 20 miles, could not have been covered before 10 o'clock in the forenoon.

But what is perhaps the strongest link of all in this chain of evidence, is the presence, at the base of Marsco, in Glen Sligachan, of a well known as *'Tobar a' Phrionnsa',* or the Prince's Well; and here we have a striking instance of the value of a knowledge of place-names as a handmaiden to history.

The day was now advancing as the wanderers trod the rough ways through Glen Sligachan, Strath na Créithich, past Camusfhionary, along the shore by the steep slopes of Leacach and Ben Cleitt; and here a fresh cause for anxiety supervened (but see Appendix 8).

Owing to the fact that such a large number of the men of Strathaird had served in the Jacobite army, Malcolm was afraid that the Prince's identity might be here disclosed. He busied himself, thereto, in perfecting the latter's disguise. He tore the ruffles from off his shirt, the buckles from his shoes, which he tied instead with strings; but, as Malcolm used to assert with enthusiasm, *"There was something about him not ordinary, something of the stately and grand"*.

It happened, however, just as Malcolm had feared for, on approaching the township of Elgol, they met two men who had been 'out' in the Rebellion. These at once recognised the Prince and we are told, *"They lifted up their hands and wept bitterly at seeing him in such a sad pickle"*. Malcolm cautioned them against such demonstrations and made them swear on the naked dirk that they would not divulge they had seen the Prince until his escape had been made public.

One of Malcolm's sisters was married in Elgol to a tacksman named John Mackinnon. This man had been a captain in the Highland army and, as Malcolm had no cause to suspect his loyalty, he made for the house of his brother-in-law. He entered, leaving the Prince outside and after the customary greetings had been exchanged, he informed his sister that he had come to Strathaird in the hope that it was safer than Raasay. He asked her if any redcoats had come to the district and he was assured that none had been seen there so far but, she added, he would get more definite information from her husband, who was that morning from home, but was expected to return at any moment.

While she was preparing the normal fare for travellers in those days, namely, bread, cheese and milk, Malcolm announced that he had left a servant outside and he would go and call him in. This was done and the Prince entered. With seeming diffidence he deposited the baggage he carried in a corner, took of his bonnet and made a low bow to his master. There was something in the deportment of the servant that greatly attracted Mrs. Mackinnon. She asked Malcolm where he had got such a fine type of 'man', for said she, *"there is something about the lad that I like"* (ibid., p. 139).

They were now asked to partake of food but 'Lewie', preserving his deferential demeanour, held back in order to make it appear that it was not his habit to sit at the same table as his 'master'. The latter, however, commanded him to go forward and then only did he obey, 'still keeping off his bonnet'.

When the Prince and Malcolm were partaking of food, the lady of the house, who had been watching outside, returned with the news that her husband was coming. Desiring to be excused for leaving the table with such informal haste, Malcolm hurried out to meet his relative, in order that he might assure himself of his continued attachment to the Jacobite cause.

After the customary salutations, Malcolm commented on the large number of government ships that were then cruising along the coast and remarked he hoped the Prince was not on board any of them. Mackinnon said he hoped likewise, at the same time expressing the wish that the Prince were then in his keeping, *"for"*, said he, *"we would take care of him"*. Convinced now beyond doubt of the loyalty of his brother-in-law, Malcolm said, *"Well, then, he is in your house"* and on hearing this, Mackinnon was so transported with joy that Malcolm had to remind him he must preserve his customary composure, lest the curiosity of the servants should be stirred. They entered the house and found the Prince playing with the young son of Mackinnon.

After he had made obeisance to the Prince with becoming restraint, Mackinnon sent his servants on different errands to get them out of the way, while he and his guests discussed their next course of action. Among other things, the propriety of acquainting the old chief with the presence of the Prince in his territory came under review and the story is variously told as to how he became a party to the escape of Prince Charlie from Skye.

By some it is said that the Prince was averse to tell Mackinnon, owing to the advanced age of the latter but that his clansman, on going to the shore to prepare a boat for the passage to the mainland, had accidentally met his chief and that he could not refrain from telling him what had transpired. The chief was overjoyed to hear his Prince was still free and that he could be of service to him once again. His galley was brought from Kilmaree round *Rudha na h-Easgainne* and it put into a cove near Prince Charlie's Cave there, where the refugees awaited its coming.

Captain Malcolm now proposed that he should be allowed to relinquish his charge, 'to honest Mackinnon', for he was afraid that his absence from home might be noticed and that questions would be asked. The Prince commended this as a prudent step and, after receiving a souvenir, in the form of a 'silver stock buckle', in addition to a present of ten guineas, which he accepted much against his will, for *"the royal purse did not appear to contain above forty"*, Malcolm performed his last service to his Prince by lighting the latter's *'short cutty pipe with a tow'*, inadvertently singeing the royal cheek the while!

As they were preparing to embark, Malcolm was given a letter by the Prince, in which he subscribed his name as 'James Thomson'. It was addressed to Donald Roy MacDonald, thanking all in Skye and in Raasay, for what they had done on his behalf (Forbes, R, 1975, Vol. 1, pp. 139–142).

After a sojourn of six days, Prince Charlie left the shores of Skye, shortly after 8 o'clock, on the evening of Friday 4th July, 1746. And while he is being conveyed across the Sound of Sleat to the mainland, we turn for a moment to consider the fate of some of those who had been instrumental in effecting his escape.

We have seen that Flora MacDonald had parted with the Prince at the inn in Portree, whence, in the company of Neil MacEachain, she set off to her home in Sleat and, it is said, she never even hinted to her mother the reason for her speedy return from Uist. About the ninth day after her arrival, she was made a prisoner by soldiers who served under MacLeod of Talisker, an officer who made himself odious by his assiduity in tracking down the Jacobite loyalists of Skye.

She was unceremoniously hurried on board the *'Furnace'*, from which she was fortunately transferred, after two days' confinement, to the *'Eltham'*, then commanded by the 'polite and generous' Commodore Smith. As his ship was passing down the Sound of Sleat, the commander of the *'Eltham'* allowed Flora to go ashore for two hours to acquaint her mother with what had happened and she was allowed to take with her from home one Kate MacDonald as her maid.

In the month of November she was transferred from her 'honourable captivity' on board the *'Eltham'* to the *'Royal Sovereign'*, by which she was taken to London. There she was consigned to the custody of a man named William Dick, in whose house she remained a prisoner until the passing of the Indemnity Act in 1747.

On her release she found herself immediately famous and perhaps the chief person of interest in the Metropolis. People vied with one another in fêting her. She was visited, among others, by Frederick, Prince of Wales, who asked her why she had been persuaded to give such service to one who was a rebel. Her reply was that she would have acted in a similar manner towards anyone else, irrespective of station, had she found him in the same sad plight in which she had found Prince Charlie. It is said that Prince Frederick was so charmed with her ingenuous answer that he filled her hand with gold.

Several influential persons, chief of whom was Lady Primrose, organised a subscription on her behalf, and a sum, amounting to a few hundred pounds, was thereby collected. This gift enabled her to hire a post-chaise for Edinburgh, whither she travelled in the company of Captain Malcolm MacLeod of Raasay, as Miss Robertson, *'in order to avoid too much attention on the way'*. She stayed for a few days in Edinburgh, after which she resumed her journey for Skye (*ibid.*, Vol. 1, pp. 110–124).

Three years after this, at the age of 28, she married Allan MacDonald, the eldest son of MacDonald of Kingsborough. For twenty-two years they resided in Flodigarry, whence they removed, in 1772, to Kingsborough, when Allan succeeded to the patrimony on the death of his father.

There they were visited among other notable travellers, by Dr. Johnson and Boswell and, as the former notes, *"we were entertained with the usual hospitality by Mr. MacDonald and his lady, Flora Macdonald"*. Boswell makes the very pertinent observation that the family of Kingsborough was in straitened circumstances and he attributed the fact to the exorbitant rents that were then exacted from tacksmen generally in Skye (Boswell, J, 1955, p. 129). These burdens led many representatives of good families to emigrate to the colonies and the MacDonalds left Kingsborough in 1774 for America.

The MacDonalds had just purchased a small estate in North Carolina when the American War of Independence broke out and Allan of Kingsborough joined the Royal Emigrant Regiment with the commission of captain. This force suffered a severe reverse and MacDonald was made prisoner.

Thereupon Flora, after a short sojourn in Nova Scotia, decided to leave America. On the voyage home, the ship was attacked by a French privateer and, when she was hurrying below deck, her arm was broken. She landed in London and made her way north by easy stages. On the conclusion of the war, her husband came back from America and, after a period in South Uist, they returned to Skye.

They had a family of seven children, five sons and two daughters, one of the latter being the wife of a reputable Skyeman, Major Alexander MacLeod of Lochbay.

Flora died in the year 1790, in the township of Peinduin. She was buried in the churchyard of Kilmuir and it is said the concourse of people at her funeral was the largest ever seen in Skye at such a ceremony, for it was estimated that over 3000 persons attended. Her grave is marked by a noble Celtic cross, on which is inscribed as epitaph the eulogy once paid her by Dr. Johnson: *"A name that will be mentioned in history and, if courage and fidelity be virtues, mentioned with honour"* (Johnson, S, 1984, p. 80).

Nadur fiachail, fialaidh, finealt
    A nature dignified, generous and gentle
Ann am pearsa chuimir dhirich
    In a shapely erect frame
Crìdhe blath, le gràdh a liònadh
    A warm heart filled with love
Is caoimhneas tlath do àrd 's do iosal.
    And tender sympathy to high and low.

MacDonald of Kingsborough

As has already been mentioned, the crew of the vessel that conveyed the Prince and his party across the Minch to Skye, was arrested immediately on their return to Uist and they were forced to confess all they knew of the Prince's wanderings. Five or six days after that, the '*Furnace*' sailed into Loch Snizort and made for the shore below Kingsborough House. Captain Ferguson himself, with some of his men, went ashore to reconnoitre and they met one of the factor's servants, a dairy-maid, with whom they entered into conversation.

They asked her to accompany them on board their ship and, flattered by the invitation, she innocently consented. She was entertained so well that, it is said, she let slip the remark that she had not enjoyed such fun since the night the Prince had been in Kingsborough House. This was, of course, all that Ferguson wanted to know and he immediately proceeded to arrest Kingsborough. This was done but, on the intercession of General Campbell, the prisoner was allowed to go on parole to Fort Augustus, where his chief, Sir Alexander, then was, at the headquarters of the army of the government.

On his arrival there, Kingsborough was instantly ordered to be put in chains. Owing to an inadvertence, he was soon afterwards released and was just preparing to return to Skye when the mistake was discovered and peremptory orders were issued for his immediate arrest. He was brought before Lord Albemarle, the commander-in-chief of the forces in Scotland, who, on hearing of the charge preferred against him, gruffly ordered his subordinates to "*throw the dog into irons*" (Chambers, R, 1934, p. 370).

From Fort Augustus, MacDonald was transferred to Edinburgh Castle. There he occupied the same quarters as Major MacDonell, Leckie and other Jacobite prisoners but, from the fact that he narrated the Prince's wanderings with such glowing enthusiasm and extolled his virtues in such a convincing manner to those who visited him in prison, his jailers thought it prudent to consign him to solitary confinement for, as Bishop Forbes naively remarks,

> *truth, though never so glaring, when it runs cross to the partial notions and inclinations of poor frail mortals, grates very hard and becomes a very uneasy and painful thing.*
>
> (Forbes, R, 1975, Vol. 1, p. 128).

It was characteristic of Kingsborough that he never complained of the treatment he received while in prison. He was a man of such marvellous fortitude and forbearance, that even his jailers were constrained to express their admiration of him for these qualities. Strong representations had frequently been made for his release by people of influence and especial emphasis was laid on the fact that, as he had acted in the capacity of manager of the estate of his chief for several years, it would be an act of grace to the widow of the latter were MacDonald set free to resume his duties as factor. It was not, however, until the general amnesty had been extended to all Jacobite offenders that 'Honest Kingsborough' was released after having, as Bishop Forbes expresses it, "*suffered twelve long months' imprisonment for one night's lodging*" (Forbes, R, 1975, Vol. 1, p. 82).

On his return to Skye, he resumed the management of the

estates of the clan and he continued in the execution of that office until his death, in 1772, at the age of 83 years. He was noted for his business acumen, his probity in all transactions and his capacity for hard work. All who knew him spoke highly of his character and Bishop Forbes pronounced on him the now famous and well-merited encomium, *"So long as a spark of honesty remains, the name of MacDonald of Kingsborough will ever have a mark of veneration put upon it"* (Forbes, R, 1975, Vol. 1, p. 186).

Captain Allan MacDonald of Kingsborough

'Kingsborough' was succeeded by his oldest son, Allan. He served as a Lieutenant in a MacDonald Independent Company, one of the units raised by President Forbes of Culloden in defence of the Hanoverian regime. We have seen that he was married to Flora MacDonald in 1750 and that for a time they lived in Flodigarry, whence they removed to Kingsborough in 1772.

Allan was a man of splendid physique and extraordinary strength. Few men of his age could hope to vie with him. On many an occasion he was the conqueror even of the redoubtable Martin of Bealach in those trials of strength that were then in vogue. Boswell, who visited him in the company of Dr. Johnson, describes him as *"completely the figure of a gallant Highlander, exhibiting the graceful mien and manly looks which our popular Scotch song has attributed to that character"* (Boswell, J, 1955, p. 129).

The portraits of him that are extant show him to have been a man of great force of character. His leonine countenance, the very prominent bridge of his shapely Roman nose, his firm mouth, straightly cut, are the outward expressions of a powerful personality.

He was reputed to have been the best judge of cattle in the Highlands in his day and, during his father's tenure of the post of factor for the estate, the services of Allan were in frequent demand as valuator of the cattle that then composed the major portion of the rent. Many a herd he drove to the trysts of Falkirk and thus he earned for himself the name of *'Ailean nam mile mart'*, or 'Allan of the thousand kine'. He died in 1792 and was buried beside his wife in the churchyard of Kilmuir.

Donald Roy MacDonald

Among all those who had rendered such faithful service to the Prince in his wanderings, few were more active than Donald Roy Macdonald. A reference has already been made to the assiduous care he showed in preparing for the Prince's safety in Skye. When the latter left the island he asked Captain Malcolm MacLeod of Raasay to convey a letter to his home; he sent a man with the Prince's note to the district of Braes, to the house of a certain Peter MacQueen, in the township of Camustianavaig. Thither Donald Roy had been advised by the Prince to proceed on Sunday after their parting at the inn in Portree; for it would seem that it had then been the Prince's intention to stay longer in Raasay than he did and to cross from that island to Braes and not to Scorrybreck, as he had actually done.

Donald Roy arrived in Camustianavaig on the night appointed and, in spite of the agony he endured from his wounded foot, he had been wandering all over Trotternish during the whole of the previous week in order to obtain information on the movements of the Prince's pursuers. On his receiving the royal letter from Captain Malcolm's servant, Donald Roy left Braes and made for the north of Trotternish.

There he spent most of his time hiding in the shore caves of Skye, frequently changing his place of concealment. When circumstances allowed it, he indulged in the strange recreation of the composition of Latin verse! He was an accomplished classical scholar and two poems by him are extant, one *A Lament*

for *Culloden* and the other an *Ode to his Wounded Foot*. They exhibit pleasing examples of poetic imagery and are consummate productions so far as the technique of Latin versification is concerned. They were published in *The Lyon in Mourning* but, as they appear there, they have been marred by very careless editing. Selections from these works will be given when we come to deal with the state of education during the period that ended with 'The '45'.

Though he constantly exposed himself to great dangers and the pursuit of him was often perplexingly close, it says much for his coolness and his resource that he alone, of those who had aided the Prince, succeeded so cleverly in evading capture (Forbes, R, 1975, Vol. 1, pp. 30–1).

The Mackinnons

A different tale remains to be told of those devoted men who sailed with the Prince from Strathaird to the district of Morar. Mackinnon was shunned by his brother chiefs of the mainland, who impugned his action in bringing the Prince back in no mistaken terms for they dreaded another visitation by the government troops and the consequent devastation of their estates. The old chief was captured before he left the mainland, while the rest of the crew were arrested by the Militia on their return to Skye. The brave Captain John Mackinnon, whose house the Prince had visited in Elgol, was threatened by Ferguson with irons if he would not turn informer and, when he refused, his tormentor swore bloodily, according to the account in *The Lyon in Mourning*, *"that when he got him on board, the barrisdale and the cat-o'-nine-tails would make him squeal"*.

Another of the crew, by name John MacInnes, was examined by Captain Ferguson himself. Despite the acts of intimidation to which he was subjected this loyal fellow declined to disclose anything. Thereupon it was ordered that he be stripped naked, strung to the yardarm and given five hundred lashes with the cat-o'-nine-tails, in instalments of fifty – a cowardly proceeding, designed to give the victim an opportunity of turning traitor in the intervals of his punishment. The stout fellow, however, endured to the bitter end, *"till the blood gushed out at both his sides"* and he was thrown into the ship's hold more dead than alive (Forbes, R, 1975, Vol. 2, p. 253). The Rev. John Mackinnon, who wrote the *Second Statistical Account of the Parish of Strath* in 1841, says that this man died about 1811 and that he himself remembered *"seeing the marks of the cat-o'-nine-tails on his back"*; while Bishop Forbes says, *"Kingsborough witnessed this scene of cruelty, as he himself frequently declared to me"*.

Among others who played a part, noble or otherwise, according to one's point of view, in the rebellion of 1745, were Colonel John MacLeod of Talisker and Major Allan MacDonald of Knock.

John MacLeod of Talisker

Just as the foregoing were all whole-hearted supporters of the Jacobite cause, so John IV of Talisker, was as enthusiastic on behalf of the government. At the time the Rebellion broke out, he was studying for the medical profession. He relinquished his studies, joined the body of 'Independent Companies' raised by his chief and was commissioned with the rank of captain. After the defeat at Inverurie, he brought from Skye to Inverness many of those who then deserted and he was present both at the Rout of Moy and in the retreat in which his clan, with several others, played such an inglorious role when the Prince entered the town of Inverness.

After Culloden, none was more eager than he in tracking down the Jacobite loyalists; and it was mainly through his activities that such notable persons as Flora MacDonald and Captain Malcolm MacLeod of Raasay were captured and delivered over to the vindictive Captain Ferguson. Talisker was nothing if not true to his trust; in this respect, differing widely from those other gentlemen from Skye who were officers in the Hanoverian Army.

Shortly after 'The '45', he joined the Scots Brigade in the Netherlands and he retired from that service with the rank of Colonel. He was a cultured man; so learned, indeed, that he deeply impressed Dr. Johnson, who visited him in 1772. The great lexicographer also pays a compliment to Talisker's wife, a daughter of MacLean of Coll, as one who was *"skilful in several languages"*. The Colonel was visited by Thomas Pennant, by Dr. Johnson and also, in 1780, by the traveller John Knox, who says of him that he was then *"extremely corpulent"* and he refers to Talisker House as *"the seat of plenty, hospitality and good nature"*.

Colonel MacLeod died without issue in 1798, in his 80th year. Donald MacDonald, a grieve in Minginish, composed his lament and it is a song of touching beauty:

> *'S fada chaidh do bhiuthas*
>> Far went your reputation
> *An dreach 's an cliù, 's an uaisle*
>> For appearance for fame and nobility
> *An céill 'an inbh' 's an gàirdeachas*
>> For common sense, for dignity and triumph
> *An àilleachd is ann an uabhar.*
>> For beauty and haughty bearing
> *B' fhionan air a' chinneadh*
>> A vine generated
> *Ann an lionsgaradh na fine thu*
>> Within your widespread kin
> *Bho 'n chiad la riamh a ghineadh thu*
>> Since your first creation

> *Bu chinneachail air buaidh thu.*
>> Certain you were of success.

(MacLeòid, D, 1811, p. 22)

It may be mentioned that the last of the family of Talisker was Major Donald MacLeod, who sold the estate in 1821, when he emigrated to Tasmania.

Major Allan MacDonald of Knock

While several members of the family of MacLeod were zealous supporters of the government in this rebellion, it is true that there was only one gentleman of the MacDonalds of Skye of whom it can be said that he devoted himself whole-heartedly to the cause of the Hanoverians. This was Lieutenant Allan MacDonald of Knock. It was he, as we have seen, who arrested Donald MacLeod of Gartrigill and he is said to have treated those Jacobites whom he took prisoner with great severity. After the rebellion had been quelled, it was alleged that he informed Captain Ferguson of the presence of a stock of arms in Mogstadt House, probably in order to gain favour with his confidant. In consequence of this, Sir Alexander, fearing that a search would be made, consigned all weapons to the sea off Kilbride.

In 1753 we find that a Royal Warrant was issued, authorising payment of the sum of £100 out of the forfeited estates to Major Allan MacDonald *"for good and faithful services rendered"*. He was heartily hated in his native island and it was for that reason, probably, that he was induced to leave Skye and spend the later part of his life in Ayr (MacDonald, A & A, 1904, p. 535).

> *Tha dubh thuil air Ailean a' Chnuic*
>> The flux affects Allan of Knock
> *Is ait leam a chluinntinn air Ailean a' Chnuic*
>> And it cheers me to hear it of Allan of Knock

Gu bheil an dubh thuil air a sparadh gu grin
And that he is well packed with flux
'S gur h-ait leam a chluinntinn air Ailean a Chnuic.
It cheers me to hear it of Allan of Knock.

In the *Edinburgh Evening Courant* of 22nd February 1773, there is an advertisement to the effect that there was to be a sale of cattle owned by Allan Macdonald of Knock, *"order to be sent to William Tolmie, Merchant, Dunvegan, Isle of Sky"*. One of his sons, Donald, had a distinguished military career, attaining the rank of general. He fought in Holland where he was wounded in 1799 and he died later in London.

A few minor incidents fall to be narrated before this record of the first portion of the eighteenth century is complete. As soon as it became known that Prince Charlie had betaken himself to Skye, the Militia concentrated its attentions on that island and the search became intense. Captain Ferguson thereupon established the headquarters for the ships of war in *Loch na Dàil*, at the head of which inlet the Earl of Loudon pitched his camp. Then the work of repression and devastation began. Practically all the houses in Raasay were burned down, while all the boats, with two exceptions, it is said, were either confiscated or given to the flames. Tortures were inflicted, often on innocent people, in the attempt to extract information. Yet all suffered in Skye, as in other parts of the Highlands, with a will, rather than turn traitors and the unholy bribe of £30,000 failed to induce anyone to swerve from the paths of loyalty!

We have seen that Sir Alexander MacDonald was with Cumberland's army at Fort Augustus at the time his factor, MacDonald of Kingsborough, was taken there as a prisoner. When Sir Alexander appeared in his camp, Cumberland accosted him in his customary gruff manner, blurting out tactlessly, when the chief was presented to him, *"And is this the great rebel of the isles?"* Galled by such hauteur and the implied insult, Sir Alexander retorted, *"Had I been a rebel, you would never have crossed the Spey"* (Cameron, A, 1871, p. 111).

When the last embers of the rebellion were still smouldering, Sir Alexander died. He was on his way to London, in order to interview the Duke of Cumberland and had barely left Skye when he contracted a severe chill. Acute pneumonia supervened and he died in the barracks at Glenelg, in November 1746. He was buried in the parish churchyard of Kilmore in Sleat, where he was accorded what was perhaps one of the most sumptuous funerals ever witnessed in our island. All the pipers of note were there and a mighty concourse of mourners gathered from far and near. Such, indeed, was the magnificence of the ceremony and so great was the consequent expenditure, that it is said to have cost the estate about £2,645 – truly an enormous sum of money for those days. Strong drink was dispensed with such a lavish hand that acts of riotous revelry ensued (MacDonald, A & A, 1904, p. 42). In the fights that took place, many were grievously injured and a MacDonald of Ord, referring to a similar carouse years afterwards, said,

There has not been a funeral like it since that of Sir Alexander MacDonald, when three men were killed and fifty were taken out of the churchyard with the breath just left in them.

CHAPTER XII

Social History, 1700–1750

Radical changes in the social life of the people of the Highlands followed the rebellion of 1745. These will be dealt with in greater detail under appropriate heads, and may now be merely hinted at in passing.

The power of the chiefs was considerably weakened and, by a strange irony, no distinction was made between those who had been loyal and the others who had been disloyal to the government. No longer could the chiefs call out their clansmen in arms at their own behest. The heritable jurisdiction which they had exercised for centuries was abolished; the administration of justice was henceforth to be vested in men who were duly qualified for the practice of the law and were to be appointed for that purpose by the crown.

The Disarming Act forbade the possession of any weapons whatsoever, though we know that this clause was often cleverly evaded.

Ged tha bacadh air na h-armaibh,
> The weapons are banned,

Chùm mi Spàinnteach thun na seilge,
> I have retained a Spanish gun for the hunt,

> (MacLeod, A, 1978, p. 156)

the hunter-bard, Duncan *Bàn* Macintyre, confesses in one of his songs. Even the bagpipe was held to be an 'instrument of war', and was accordingly proscribed!

Dress

But what injured the feelings of the Highlanders most, because it sought to deal a blow at what they considered to be a distinctive feature of their race, was the prohibition of the Highland dress. The galling nature of this imposition, when they were concussed into the wearing of the tightly-fitting trousers, is well exemplified in the poem, *Oran na Briogais*, by Duncan *Bàn*; while Lachlan MacPherson, the bard of Strathmassie, and John MacCodrum, the family bard of the MacDonalds of Sleat, have each composed a satire on the same theme. The first mentioned anathematises the new costume, thus:

On tha a' bhriogais liathghlas
　　As the hodden grey breeches
Am bliadhna cur mulaid oirnn
　　Are this year casting gloom on us
'S e 'n rud nach fhacas riamh oirnn,
　　It is a thing never seen on us,
'S nach miann leinn a chumail oirnn,
　　And we do not wish to wear it,
'S nam bitheamaid uile dìleas,
　　Had we but been faithful,
Do'n rìgh bha toirt cuiridh dhuinn,
　　To the King who appealed to us,
Chan fhaicte sinn gu dilinn
　　We would not, until Doomsday
A' striocadh do'n chulaidh sin,
　　Be submitting to this garb,

　　　　　　　　　　　　(MacLeod, A, 1978, p. 8)

and it is with evident relish that the same poet recounts the fact that this incommodation was inflicted on 'Hanoverian' and Royalist alike:

'S bha h-uile h-aon de'n pharlamaid
　　And every member of Parliament
Feallsail le' m fiosrachadh,
　　Were wittingly deceitful, When they forced the Campbells,
Teanntachd nam briogaisean
　　Into the confinement of breeches
'S gur h-iad a rinn am feum dhaibh
　　As it was they who backed them
A' bhliadhna thàin' an streupag,
　　The year the strife began,
A h-uile h-aon dhiubh éirigh
　　When they arose to a man

Gu léir am milisi dhaibh.
　　For service in the Militia.

　　　　　　　　　　　　(MacLeod, A, 1978, p. 12)

It should be stated here, however, as we have already pointed out, that long before the Highland dress had been placed under a ban, it had ceased to be the universal garb in the Isle of Skye. There are several references in the works of the bards to the wearing of trousers before 'The '45', and Martin Martin, a native of the island, who wrote at the end of the 17th century, although he mentions the kilt also, declares that this article of apparel was in common use in his day. In describing the clothing of the people, he says, *"The men wear a coat, waistcoat, and breeches, as elsewhere"* (Martin, M, 1716, p. 206).

There is also extant an interesting account of the conditions of life in the household of the tacksman of Ullinish at the beginning of the 18th century. Mention is made of the dress worn by the boys in that family and it may be taken as representing pretty closely the kind of clothes then generally in vogue among children of that quality. It consisted of a kilt, a waistcoat with sleeves buttoned at the wrists and a woollen shirt. Boys wore neither foot- nor head-gear, winter or summer, 'in rain or in snow', though some of the older lads had a pair of brogues, made of raw hide, 'more for ornament than for use'. The boys bathed in cold water every morning, in order to season themselves to the weather.

The dress of the women of the higher ranks in Skye was similar to that worn by those of the same station in life elsewhere in Scotland at that time. Among the so-called 'vulgar', the *earasaid* continued to be the common article of apparel; while around the head was still worn a kerchief of fine linen, closely fitting, with its loose ends tapering down the back. The women of this class went barefooted during the greater part of the year.

Customs

In accordance with their views on civility to strangers, doors were seldom closed and were never locked, for it was considered to be tantamount to lack of trust in one's fellows if the lock were used. The key was associated with meanness and that cardinal sin, inhospitality, so that *"cho mosach ris a' ghlais"* ('as mean as the key') had been raised by them to the status of a proverb.

When privacy was desired for a space, a whittled wand was fixed athwart the open door and care was taken to have it removed as soon as circumstances in the household permitted. We have it on the testimony of Martin that the practice of inserting the *"maide doicheallach"* ('the stick of churlishness') was a common custom in his own day. *"They treat the stranger with great civility"* is one of the many observations on their hospitality made in MacFarlane's *Geographical Collections* (Mitchell, A, 1907, p. 221).

The wayfarer was always welcomed at whatever house he called, and it was looked upon as a privilege to entertain him. His purpose was never enquired after and everything was done to make him comfortable. His feet were washed, for roads did not then exist and bogs abounded. The tracks that had been marked out by the treading of people and driven animals for ages showed small cairns at approximately equal distances. These heaps marked the places where the relays in the funeral procession laid down the corpse on the way to the burial. This custom was continued in Skye long after this and even to-day one may meet with the observance of the ancient usage in the numerous little mounds of stones to be found on the divide, along the branch-roads to Tarskavaig and to Ord, in Sleat.

The festival of St. Michael which was held among the Catholic community of the Long Island until recent times, was then celebrated in Skye with much ceremony. All the young men of the parish turned out, each on his best horse and, on a level sward by the shore they indulged in equestrian sports. It was a day of high holiday and the cavalcade, as it set off for the rendezvous, was followed and admired by young and old. When they arrived on the field of play, each contestant lifted his sweetheart behind him, and, with a tangle-stem, dried and hardened months before, he lashed his horse to full gallop (Martin, M, 1716, p. 80). After the games, they partook of cakes, which had been prepared for the occasion, and were called *Bonnaich Micheil* ('St. Michael's Bannocks') (Henderson, G, 1911, pp. 255–6).

The Church

During the first portion of the eighteenth century, there is little to record of the activities of the Church in Skye. To all intents and purposes it was a period of stagnation, marked by a lukewarmness towards religion that bordered almost on total indifference. And the causes of this state of unconcern for the Church, and its affairs, are not far to seek.

On account of their sympathy with the Stuart cause in 1715 and 1745, the people were strongly inclined to support Episcopalianism and the most ardent Jacobites among them could not be expected to view with disfavour even the faith of the Roman Catholics. It was with the aim of checking the popular leaning to the latter church that a law was passed in 1700 for the 'Prevention of the Growth of Popery in the Highlands'; but such an act could have but one result, and that was to urge the Catholics in a body to the side of the exiled House of Stuart and to give a bias to the less devout among the Protestants in the same political direction.

Again, owing to the extent of the parishes of Skye at the beginning of the century, and to the great difficulties experienced in travelling, it was impossible for the clergy, adequately, to minister to the needs of their scattered flocks. The ministers had splendid auxiliaries in the catechists and schoolmasters but their combined efforts were often of little avail in combating the growing unconcern for the Church. When it is remembered that people had often to walk a distance of over twenty miles in order to attend a religious service, and that ministers had to ride long distances across roadless moors and through dangerous mountain passes, or to sail the stormy intervening seas to adjacent islands that formed part of the parish, it becomes immediately apparent how difficult were the problems that confronted the church in those days. Indeed until after the '45, Puritanism and Sabbatarianism affected the people but little. They married and held other festivities on Sunday, buried and often deserted the pulpit for the entertainment that followed the funeral (see *Presbytery Records of Inverness and Dingwall* – Mackay, W, 1896, p. xxiv).

And the imputation has often been levelled against the incumbents that their evangelising spirit was then none too robust, while the firm belief of some in the general superstitions of the age may be cited as an index of their mentality. One cleric, Rev. John MacLeod who, in 1742, had been promoted from Uig to the Parish of Duirinish, believed he possessed the gift of second-sight; and Martin Martin makes mention of an incident, of the truth of which he says he was *"assured by the minister of the place"* (Sleat), that on the night of the Battle of Killiecrankie it was observed that, instead of milk, blood was given by the cows of 'James MacDonald of Capstil', who was killed in the battle (Martin, M, 1716, p. 156).

Beset by the prevailing indifference and the general difficulties of the situation, we need not marvel at the fact that some of the clergy lost heart for their work and allowed themselves to sink into the morass of apathy that surrounded them. From being indifferent ministers of the gospel, they naturally developed into assiduous cultivators of the soil and their good fat glebes soon came to absorb their whole attention.

The incongruous role played by these clerical farmers was bound to wound the sensibilities of the perfervid and to excite the wit of the satirical. Of the latter, none could apprehend so clearly the inconsistency of their profession with their practice as the poet, Rob *Donn* and, with that incisive raillery and good-natured banter of which he was master, he depicts them as follows:

Falbh 'nan cuideachd 's 'nan còmhradh,
    Move in their company and converse,
'S gheibh thu moran de'n ghràisg ud,
    And you will find that many of that rabble,
Dheanadh ceannaich no seòldair,
    Would make a merchant or a sailor,
Dheanadh dròbhair, no fàctor,
    A drover or a factor,
Dheanadh tuathannach sunndach,
    Would make a lively farmer,
Dheanadh stuibhard neo-chràbach,
    Or an impious land steward,
'S mach 'o'n cheaird air na mhionnaich iad
    And, apart from the calling to which they were dedicated,
Tha a h-uile ni gàsd' ac,
    They were experts at everything,

                     (Morrison, H, 1899, p. 75)

all of which means, that they were fitted by nature and for any and every calling except that sacred one that they chose as their life's work.

There were, however, some ministers in Skye at that time who were imbued with a strong zeal for their high office. The number of the incumbents had been increased in the island for, in the year 1726, new parishes were formed by the division of the large and unworkable old ones. In order to obtain a conception of the dimensions of these districts, it may be said that the Parish of the Small Isles then comprised Strath, Sleat, and the islands of Rum,

Eigg, Canna, and Muck; while the extensive Parish of Snizort stretched from Loch Sligachan on the south to Loch Greshornish on the north, whence, by a line drawn eastwards to Rona, it was divided from Kilmuir.

The newly-formed sub-division of Snizort, namely, the parish of Portree, was served by the Rev. Hugh McDonald as its first minister. He was a graduate in Arts of the University of Aberdeen, and a son of Hugh Macdonald of Glenmore. He married his first cousin, Elizabeth, they both being grandchildren of Sir James MacDonald, second baronet of Sleat, and Mary, the favourite sister of Iain Breac, the Chief of Dunvegan. A few years after his settlement there, a church, with a slated roof, was erected in the village of Portree. He served this parish for about thirty years until his death, in 1756, at the comparatively early age of 57 years (MacDonald, A & A, 1904, p. 524).

In the parish of Snizort which, in the early part of the century until 1726 also included Raasay and the parish of Portree, we have seen that Rev. Donald MacQueen was minister until 1710, when he was succeeded by his son, Archibald, who was a graduate of the university of Edinburgh. The latter is described as a *"person of uncommon abilities, distinguished as well by erudition and extensive knowledge as by his piety, zeal and other virtues"*. By his second wife, Florence MacDonald, he had a family of eight sons and one daughter. He died at the advanced age of 83, in the year 1754, when he was succeeded by his second son, William, who had been admitted to the charge of the reduced parish in 1753. Another of his sons was the famous Rev. Donald Mac-Queen, the cicerone of Dr. Johnson, and minister of the parish of Kilmuir, where he was ordained in the year 1740 as successor to Rev. Kenneth Bethune. At the beginning of the century, the Rev. Daniel MacAulay, a graduate in Arts of Edinburgh University, was the incumbent in Kilmuir. He was the first Presbyterian minister there and he remained only seven years, when he was translated to the parish of Bracadale. His successor was Rev.

Kenneth Bethune, a son of the scholarly minister of Bracadale, and he served the parish from 1718 until his death in 1739.

The parish of Bracadale was served, as we have already seen, in the early years of this century by Rev. John Bethune, and it has also been mentioned that he was succeeded on his death in 1708 by Rev. Daniel MacAulay, who came thither from Kilmuir. The latter continued as minister there until the year 1748, when he died, and was succeeded by Rev. William MacLeod, who came from a charge in Barra and remained in this parish until 1765.

At the beginning of the period under review, the minister of Duirinish was the talented Dugald MacPherson, on whose death, in 1717, the Rev. Norman MacLeod was appointed as successor. The latter had previously held the charge of Strath. In the year 1739, while he was crossing the Minch on a visit to Barra, the boat was lost and all aboard were drowned. He was succeeded by Rev. John MacLeod, M.A., who had been promoted to this parish from Uig in the year 1742. This minister entertained the belief that he was endowed with the gift of second-sight, and yet he is referred to as a man of great ability, 'equalled by few', and one who was most zealous in the interests of religion. He died in 1752 at the age of 50 years.

Towards the end of the previous century, the parish of Strath was served by Rev. Martin MacPherson, the son of the famous minister of Duirinish, Rev. Dugald MacPherson. He died in 1712 at the early age of 40 years and is reputed to have been a man of high refinement and wide scholarship. He was succeeded by Rev. Norman MacLeod who, five years afterwards, went to Duirinish. In 1717, the Rev. Donald MacLeod, a graduate of Aberdeen, was called to fill the vacant charge, and he served the parish until 1749, when he died at the age of 49 years.

In the adjacent district of Sleat, the Rev. Edmund MacQueen, M.A. was admitted minister of the newly-constituted parish in 1726 and continued there until 1741. In that year the noted minister, Rev. Dr. John MacPherson, was appointed his successor.

The new incumbent was a man of profound erudition, a monument to which remains in his famous *Dissertations*. He was a classical scholar of note, as well as a poet of no mean order. A paraphrase of the *Song of Moses* written by him in Latin, and shown to Dr. Johnson, so impressed that great author that he commented, *"It does him honour. He has a great deal of Latin, and good Latin"* (Boswell, J, 1955, p. 186). He was married to Janet, a daughter of Donald MacLeod of Bernera, and two of their sons were Rev. Martin MacPherson of Sleat and Sir John MacPherson, who was a Governor-general in India.

Education

In the year 1696 an Act was passed by the Scottish Parliament enjoining every parish to establish a school and to build a suitable house for a schoolmaster but, although it received a greater measure of attention than did previous enactments of a similar nature, its observance was left in abeyance, so far as Skye was concerned. No new schools were then erected in our island but education was not neglected in consequence of that. *The Society for the Propagation of Christian Knowledge* had been formed in 1709, and its beneficent influence had penetrated to Skye early in the century. In 1711, the *Society for the Propagation of Christian Knowledge* resolved to erect a school in the Presbytery of Skye, the teacher's salary to be 300 marks.

It was only during the winter months that any attempt at education was made. Then any kind of shelter was utilised as a schoolhouse; barns were convenient places for the purpose, and on their floors the young men squatted on rushes, or sat on improvised seats, while they were being taught. The system of education was, however, of a very desultory nature and only the very rudiments of knowledge were in most cases acquired.

As a result of the practice, instituted in the previous century, whereby tacksmen combined to secure the services of a schoolmaster for their children, men endowed with sound scholarship were often employed. Although these teachers were paid but a mere pittance, and were left to occupy the lowest rung in the social ladder, yet they gave unstinted service, being imbued with a perfervid urge to foster learning in those pupils who were under their charge.

One such schoolmaster in Skye at that time was John MacPherson, the son of Rev. Dugald MacPherson, minister of Duirinish, and brother of the Rev. Martin of Strath. He lived in Orbost, where he died about the year 1730. If we are to judge by results, this teacher must have been a man of wide learning and eminent ability. Mention has already been made of one of his pupils, namely, Donald Roy MacDonald, who figured so conspicuously as one of the guides of Prince Charlie. Two Latin poems by this man – one an ode composed to his wounded foot and the other a lament on the disaster of Culloden – are still extant. They exhibit such chastity of diction, and such skill in the construction of Latin verse, that they deserve a greater publicity than has yet been accorded to them. These productions are the more commendable when we remember that their author was a hunted loyalist, skulking in the caves of Skye, when he wrote them, in order to *"while away the time"*, as he himself declares. The work is of such a high order that one is tempted to quote a stanza or two in exemplification of the quality of these compositions. The first verse of the *'Lament'* is as follows:

> *Ah! quantam tulero solicitudinem*
>> What troubles shall I suffer
>
> *Per praerupta vagans culmina montium*
>> Straying among sheer mountaintops
>
> *Per saltus varios, per cava rupium*
>> Uneven glens, rocky caves
>
> *Ericeta per aspera,*
>> And stony heathlands,

and in the 'Ode' he says:

Cum peto lectum cupidus quietis

    When I go to bed, longing for a night's rest,

Nocte perrarus brevis atque somnus

    My eyes close in sleep which is both fitful and short

Prae pedis laesi nimio dolore

    For the agonizing pain

Lumina condit.

    In my damaged foot.

⊰ ✸ ⊱

Interim curat medicus mederi

    Meanwhile the busy doctor

Sedulus partem mihi vulneratam

    Is eager to relieve my wounded limb;

Et precor coeptis faveat benignus

    And may the world's Creator

Conditor orbis.

    Look kindly on his efforts.

              (Forbes, R, 1975, Vol. 2, pp. 37–8)

The *'medicus'* (physician) who is referred to here was Dr. John MacLean, whose ancestors had for many generations been hereditary doctors to the MacDonalds of Skye. He occupied Shulista rent free as perquisite of his office. He was a man of fine culture and one of the most noted botanists of the age, *"for he had skill in the virtues of all local shrubs and herbs"*. Travellers, such as Pennant and Johnson, were much impressed by his wide learning. It is noteworthy that with him the post of hereditary physician to a chief comes to an end.

The common people were much influenced by the culture that prevailed in the houses of the higher orders in the island for the association between the members of the clan was a very close one at that time. Besides, there was an eager desire for knowledge on the part of all, and they availed themselves of every opportunity to acquire some education. *"The unhappiness of their education, and their want of converse with foreign nations"*, says Martin, *"deprives them of the opportunities to cultivate and beautify their genius, which seems to have been formed by nature for great attainments"* (Martin, M, 1716, p. 200).

Then, again, certain customs which they delighted to observe were calculated to develop their faculties. Around the fire of the ceilidh-house, the choicest tales were still told to appreciative audiences and the works of the bards were held in high esteem. The practice of composing extempore verse was also sustained and, in this connection they indulged in a game at the ceilidh that was both entertaining and instructive. The conventional procedure was for a member of the party to go outside and, having secured the dried skin of some animal in an outhouse, he would cover himself with it and re-enter the dwelling-house. At his approach the inmates would feign fright and all rush outside. Once there, the outer door was closed, and none was re-admitted until he had composed a stanza or two on a theme suggested by the guisard. At Hallowe'en, and on other occasions of festivity, this custom was often observed so that people acquired wonderful skill in the art of versification. Adverting to this penchant of theirs, Martin remarks, *"Both sexes have a quick vein of poesy, and they compose pieces which powerfully affect the fancy"* (ibid., loc. cit.).

Music

The same author refers to their intense fondness of music and he even goes the length of asserting that he had observed that

several of their children, before they could speak, were capable of distinguishing one tune from another, and appeared uneasy until the tune they fancied best was played. Several of the people invent tunes, which are very taking in the south and elsewhere.

(*ibid.*, p. 199).

The playing of the harp was rapidly falling into desuetude during the early decades of the eighteenth century but another instrument, namely, the fiddle, was steadily rising in popular favour, and Boswell makes mention of a sister of Rev Martin Macpherson in Ostaig who played on the guitar (Boswell, J, 1955, p. 186). The bagpipe, however, continued still to hold a paramount place in the regard of the people and, although the MacCrimmons did not then possess the influence they formerly enjoyed, their college was still attended by many aspiring young pipers. The MacDonalds maintained a piper in each of their three baronies, namely, Sleat, Trotternish and North Uist. We knew that in the year 1723 the clan piper in the first was a Malcolm Macintyre who, like all his colleagues, was given a portion of land free in virtue of his office. In Trotternish lived the principal pipers of that clan, the MacArthurs, who maintained the hereditary succession here for several generations. They farmed as a freehold the district of Peingown, in Kilmuir, where a hillock, called *Cnoc Phàil*, is still pointed out as the rendezvous where these pipers and their pupils delighted to practise. An Angus MacArthur piped the MacDonalds of Skye to the onset of Sheriffmuir, while his son, Charles, practised his profession in the service of Sir Alexander MacDonald during the student days of the latter in St. Andrews, much to the entertainment of the lairds of Fife. In 1726, a salary of £66 13s 4d was paid to this piper, a perquisite that was additional to his tenure of Peingown (MacDonald, A & A, 1904, pp. 126–7).

Just as the language and the dress of the Gael were proscribed in 1746, so also was the bagpipe, it being held to be an 'instrument of war'. The mere fact that it was then placed under a ban was not, however, the reason for its decline; rather is that to be sought in the great changes that occurred in the Highlands after 'The '45', when the chiefs degenerated into landlords, and their cadets into mere farmers. The old order was changing and, in the new, the piper held but a very subordinate position compared to that which he had occupied in the past.

It is said that, about this time, one of the wandering pipers had called in his old age at a castle in Skye, where he was denied that place of honour which custom had always accorded him in the past. Instead of being ushered into the presence of his chief and his guests, as was formerly the wont, he was now relegated to the servants' hall in the basement of the mansion. The proud piper rankled under the indignity that was put on his profession and, when a liveried menial announced in English that the chief, who was dining in the room immediately above this hall, had expressed a request that a tune or two be played, the slighted musician answered in Gaelic,

Abair ris matà, gur h-ann a b'àbhaist dhòmhsa bhi toirt aoibhneis lem' cheòl do chluais athar anns an talla so; agus nach 'eil mi nise nam' sheann aois a dol a chur a leithid de dhimeas air a' phiobmhóir 's gu'n téid mi 'ga séideadh suas 'na dheireadh-san!

(Say to him then that I was in the habit of giving joy with my music to his father's ears in this hall, and that I, in my old age, am not going, so to demean my great pipe, as to go and blow it up his rear).

The tale had a more pointed sting than is here expressed.

The Chiefs

Long before the last Jacobite rebellion there was a marked incli-nation on the part of the Highland chiefs, and especially of those of Skye, to ape the customs and the manners of the South.

This tendency was always bemoaned by those who cherished the traditions of the past and wished to preserve the identity of the Highland race. Our bards were constantly voicing notes of warning to the chiefs who forsook the interests of their clan for the glamour of the court. Allusion has already been made to the works of Morison, the blind harper of Dunvegan, to *Lachlainn Mac Thearlaich Oig* and to others, where references are made to these changes in manners; and the strictures passed by men such as Rev. Dr. Donald MacQueen of Kilmuir, who valued the traditional ways and the native culture, on those chiefs who, "*at the instigation of luxury and the ambition of cutting an unmean-ing figure in the Lowlands, were altering the tones of society*", are highly justified (MacDonald, A & A, 1904, p. 142).

Still, among a primitive people, tradition dies hard and it was not until long after 'The '45' that the ancient attitude of venera-tion for the chiefs began to show signs of decline among their clansmen. The prerogative of heritable jurisdiction, which the chiefs exercised in their own dominions, vested them with the power of absolute sovereignty over their people and there can be no doubt that they lost much in prestige when they were deprived of that authority in the year 1747. It cannot, however, be said, with any show of fairness, that on the whole that power had been abused by the chiefs during the centuries they had pos-sessed it for, as General Stewart remarks,

> nothing can be more erroneous than the prevalent idea that a Highland chief was an ignorant and oppressive tyrant, who rewarded the object submission of his followers with relentless cruelty and vigorous oppression.
>
> (Stewart, D, 1885, p. 60).

Far from being an irresponsible autocrat, the chief was at all times expected to seek counsel from the cadets of the clan and he was invariably guided by their advice. His conduct was closely watched by these elders and, should he commit any action that might be construed as being derogatory to the good name of the clan or unworthy of his own high office, his people had no compunction in bringing him to book and even threatening him with deposition.

At the same time, if their chief should find himself in strait-ened circumstances, even on account of an extravagant manner of life, the members of the clan failed not to interest themselves in his affairs and even to impose on themselves a temporary increase in their rent, in order to mitigate, if possible, the pecu-niary embarrassments. Their regard for the chief bordered even on reverence, and Martin observes, "*The people conclude grace with a petition to God for his welfare and prosperity*".

And a close intimacy existed between the chief and his clans-men, even to the very lowest grade. When they were free from the presence of strangers, they mingled on terms of unrestrained familiarity, and, indeed, behaved towards one another like the members of one family. This relationship was all to the good for, since the chiefs and their tacksmen were often men of lofty character and fine culture, it was but natural that their influ-ence should permeate the tribe; and to it may be attributed the undoubted polish in speech and manner that distinguishes a Highlander from persons in the same station in other parts of the country. Anent this we find the observation in Dalrymple's *Memoirs*:

> The Highlanders, whom more savage nations call savage, carry, in the outward expression of their manner, the politeness of courts without their vices, and, in their bosoms, the high point of honour without its follies.
>
> (ibid. op. cit.).

Food, etc.

The common people then seldom partook of more than two meals a day and the regimen was characterised by little or no variety. The chief articles of their dietary consisted of bread made of oats, or of barley; *brochan*, which was a thin gruel, and often taken with bread; potatoes, which had been introduced towards the end of this period; colewort, butter, cheese, milk, and fish. The poorer people seldom tasted any kind of meat, despite the large herds that were reared for we have it on the testimony of Martin, himself a native of the island, that *"there is no place so well stored with such great quantities of good beef and mutton, where so little was consumed by eating"* (Martin, M, 1716, p. 202).

During the lean months of the winter and spring, bread and gruel formed the staple food of the vast majority in the community and, even in the houses of the tacksmen, bread, cheese, and milk were considered to be the choicest fare.

Some tasty dishes were produced from a varied treatment of milk. One of the commonest, and certainly the most favoured of these preparations, was called *Omhan,* which means 'froth'. In making this decoction, milk, or whey, was boiled and vigorously stirred with a crossed stick until it was converted into a frothy substance that was commended for its rare palatability and its sustaining qualities. When meal and potatoes had been exhausted, this *omhan* was for months their only article of food. And it then happened too often that even milk failed them, for, when the winter was severe and the small stock of provender had been used up, the emaciated cattle went dry. In such a contingency, the people had recourse to the bleeding of young and healthy animals and this blood was compounded and boiled with a pinch of meal.

On such occasions, also, they resorted frequently to the shore for shellfish, and it is no doubt from those times of extreme privation that the well-known proverb dates: *'Nuair a' bhitheas an crodh caol, bithidh a' maorach reamhar'* ('When the cattle are thin, the shellfish are fat'), – a saying which aptly enunciates a physiological law, and, at the same time, displays an abounding faith in an all-seeing Providence. In commenting on the shore-life of Skye, Martin observes,

Mussels abound in Bernisdale and this was a great support to many poor families in the neighbourhood in the late years of scarcity". In MacFarlane's *Geographical Collections* is a note that in the lochs of Skye are *"an infinite number of oysters"* (Mitchell, A, 1906, p. 220). They made a broth of limpets and milk, and it was held to be a savoury and sustaining food. The acuteness of the destitution of those times may be finally exemplified by a further quotation from Martin, who is the principal authority for the social conditions that prevailed in the early years of this century. Alluding to the wholesomeness of a well-known spring in Uig, he asserts, *"The waters of Tobir Telliebrek in Uig with dulse would serve as food for a considerable time, as was experienced in times of war"* (Martin, M, 1716, p. 141).

Owing to its exorbitant price, very little salt was used and what little was imported of that commodity was sedulously husbanded for the sole purpose of preserving the butter as, without it, that article of food could not be kept for any length of time. To inhibit putrefaction in cheese, they sometimes used the ashes of sea-ware but for other perishable foods they employed no preservative whatsoever. By special methods of curing they were able to season fish that was caught after the middle of September, for a period of eight months. According to Martin, *"they used no art in it, but take out their guts, and then, tying a rush about their necks, hang them by pairs, from a rope made of heather, across the house"* (ibid., p. 144).

There was one article, however, in the importation of which no sparingness was observed. This was the foreign brandy, the drinking of which, together with the native whisky, made for great intemperance. Their inordinate craving for these stimulants was fostered by the belief that it was necessary to partake of them in order to counteract the baleful effects on their health resulting from the moistness of the climate. This last was often made the pretext for excessive indulgence, with the usual repercussion on the morals of the people. Riotous scenes were too often a feature even of solemn assemblies and even funerals were made the occasion for renewing old feuds and originating new ones. We have already referred to the unseemly incidents witnessed at the funeral of Sir Alexander MacDonald of Sleat. The cost of the ceremony is stated to have been £2645 and it can be safely asserted that most of that amount was due to the single item of drink. Indeed, the quarrels that occurred among the people in those times were so frequent, and so fierce, that when a party set off in procession to a marriage, or a burial, the boys of the district would follow, in expectation of the fights that ensued before the company dispersed.

Their immoderate habits were no doubt due, to a certain extend, to the prevailing conceit that, if a vessel were once broached, it would be an insult to the host if it were not drained dry. It was considered to be the proper thing to continue drinking until all were quite intoxicated, for to refrain before that stage was attained was held to be unmanly. It is unlikely that Martin exaggerates the custom that ruled in his own day when a party of men once began drinking. He says that two men were detailed to attend at the door and their duty was to carry off the revellers, one by one, on a barrow, as they succumbed to inebriation and deposit them in some chamber, where they were left until they should become sober, and *"the carriers returned again and again to their posts, and so carried off the whole company!"* (*ibid.*, p. 106).

Their Daily Toils

Most of the agricultural labour, certainly that which entailed the greatest drudgery, was still done by the women. And it was a toil self-imposed and ungrudgingly performed, for, by their view of life, much of the work of cultivation, and the tending of crops, were held to be unworthy of a man, whose prerogative it was to guard his chief and the clan. Hence the digging of the soil, the reaping of the crops, the cutting of peats and the bearing of burdens, were the lot of women; nor did any one think of the cruelty or the shame of it. In addition, they plucked heather for the purpose of making ropes and, when thatch was required for the houses they had to cut rushes or sedge, which they carried home in large bales, often for long distances. At home, again, their work was never done – grinding with the quern; although, when much meal was to be ground, they went with the grain to the nearest water-mill, there being then several on the island. The women prepared the wool and the lint for cloth; they dyed and fashioned the fabrics and, in spite of all their toil, they not only sang at their work, but composed appropriate songs as well.

About the middle of the century a new industry was introduced that was to prove a great blessing to many people while it lasted. This was the manufacture of kelp by the calcining of the shore tangles, and all classes took part in the work. At first the price was less than £1 per ton, but by 1755 it had risen to £3 10s. The real boom in this industry set in after Culloden, when, towards the end of the century, the price rose to the phenomenal figure of £22 a ton (MacDonald, A & A, 1904, p. 142).

About the end of this period another industry had just reached Skye, and it was to prove of far-reaching consequence in the life of the people. There had sprung up in England, and especially on the continent of Europe, a brisk demand for Scotch wool, with the result that the whole outlook of farmers was radically changed. The effect of this phase of the evolution of society was, of course,

unfelt in any aggravated form until the latter part of this century, and its baneful influence on the lives of the people will be seen when we come to deal with the evictions of that period.

Trade

There were then no 'made' roads in Skye, the principal tracks that existed being due primarily to the treading of droves of cattle on the way to the Lowland markets. Large numbers of horses and black cattle were still sent south, and were exported from Skye by way of the narrows of Kyleakin, or Kylerhea. Across these straits the animals were made to swim and, as soon as 'slack' water supervened, the work of ferrying began. The animals were bound together in files of five, the tail of the one in front being tied by a rope of heather, or of straw, to the muzzle of the one behind and the first of the line was fastened to the stern of a boat that was rowed across the sound with its trail behind it. By this means, as many as 100 animals could be transferred to the mainland by one boat in the course of a single day.

The trek to the south was generally made in autumn, when animals were in the best condition. The markets to which they were brought were those of Crieff and of Falkirk; and we have it on record that, at the former place, in the year 1723, English dealers bought 30,000 black cattle for as many guineas, *'an amount of money the Highlanders had never seen before'*.

We have seen that local fairs had been instituted towards the end of the seventeenth century, and that they were held at Portree twice a year, namely, in May and in August. To these markets was brought the varied produce of the island, consisting for the most part of horses, cows, sheep, goats, hides, wool, butter, cheese, and dried fish. In the transactions that ensued, most of the business that was done between local dealers was by the system of bartering, there being then little circulation of specie in Skye. Indeed, such was the dearth of cash in the island

at that time, that people experienced the greatest difficulty in finding enough money to pay their servants' yearly wage, or to buy any article for which they could not give some other commodity in exchange. When, about fifteen years after this period ends, Boswell succeeded in securing twenty-one shillings in bullion in Portree, such a large amount of money in the possession of one person was *"thought to be a wonderful store"* (Boswell, J, 1955, p. 177).

There were, of course, no shops in the island then, for the need for such institutions had not yet arisen, as practically all the necessaries of life were produced on the island.

Agriculture

Although few changes fall to be recorded in agricultural methods during this period in the history of Skye, there are certain features that clearly mark it off from its predecessor. These are the institution of the crofting system and the first tentative beginnings in the payment of rent in money, and not in kind.

The crofting system, as now known, was introduced about the beginning of the eighteenth century, the first mention we find of it in Skye being in the year 1718. This was in the reign of Sir Donald MacDonald, the son and heir of *'Do'ull a' Chogaidh'* (See MacLeod, RC, 1939, Vol. 2, p. 118), who sub-divided some large tacks among a community of tenants. These paid their rent in kind, or by service, directly to the chief and, although these exactions were originally never enforced with any stringency, they were increased little by little, until, by the end of this period, the tenants were unable to discharge their obligations. There were cottars on the lands of the tacksmen and their lot was often worse than that of those who were directly under the chief. The service rendered to the tacksman by his tenants was called '*Caraiste*', in contra-distinction with '*Bòrlanachd*', which was the name given to the labour due to the chief.

These services often demanded so much of their time that tenants had little opportunity to attend to the cultivation of their own allotments. That work was not, however, neglected. It devolved, as a matter of course, on the women folk, who carried it on with their customary assiduity. So well indeed was it done that travellers to the Highlands at that time were greatly impressed by the amount of labour that was given to the fields and one, Captain Burt, who had lived a considerable time in the North, says, "*Every available patch was cultivated by the spade, and crops of oats and barley were grown*".

It would appear, too, that the soil was then fairly responsive to tillage. Martin observes that, in plentiful seasons, such large crops were produced in Skye that the natives were able to export considerable quantities to the mainland of Scotland and, he adds, "*I have an account that a small tract of ground in Scorrybreck yielded one hundredfold of barley*". But such periods of plenty were few and far between (Martin, M, 1716, p. 139).

As might be expected in an age when people were dependent solely on their own production, great privations were endured when weather conditions were unfavourable to growth. The years 1715 and 1717 are especially mentioned as seasons which were so very severe that the people could not secure what meagre crops did grow. During the winters of these years great losses were sustained in stock, for the practice of housing the cattle had not then been instituted and there was no provender to eke out what little the animals could cull for themselves. Consequently, the cattle that did survive became "*mere skeletons in the spring, when many of them were not able to rise from the ground without help*".

The damage wrought by the storms of these years was long remembered in Skye and its incidence was heaviest in the district of Trotternish, where, it is said, "*the sea overflowed parts of the country, breaking down many houses to the hazard of lives and the impairing of lands*". There is on record a plea by the tenants and the wadsetters of that area to their chief in 1721, beseeching him to lower the rent on account of the extreme poverty occasioned by an 'unusual murrain' in the year 1716, but more especially by a similar calamity in the spring of 1720, whereby they lost '485 horses, 1027 cows, and 4556 sheep' (MacDonald, A & A, 1904, pp. 81–2). The petition was drawn up and signed at '*Renedray*', by '*D. MacDonald, Sartil; J. MacDonald, Lachasay; D. Nicolson, Culnacnock; J. Nicolson, Scoudiborow; J. MacDonald, Rigg; J. Martin, Flodigarry; J. MacDonald, Valtos; A. MacDonald, Knockowe; A. MacDonald of Bornaskitag; D. MacLeod, Ormisgarry; N. MacDonald, Totscor; A. MacDonald, Glenmore; J. MacDonald, Cuidrach; Eugene MacDonald, Yr., of Glenmore; Aeneas MacQueen, Prabost; Allan MacQueen, Kingsborrow; An. MacDonald of Eskedle; Jo. Nicolson, Glenmore; J. MacDonald, Libost; H. MacLean, Gerich; A. MacQueen, Totarome; Margt. MacDonald, Mogstadt; J. MacDonald, Grealine; Rev. Archd. MacQueen, Snizort, Rev. K. Beaton, Kilmuir*' (MacDonald, A & A, 1904, p. 663).

In the attestation, the appellants proceed to observe that the factor of MacLeod had, for similar reasons, lowered rents to an aggregate of £110. Following this petition we find that, in the year 1719, the chief, Sir Donald MacDonald, wrote to his agent in Edinburgh, informing him that he had been constrained to grant a temporary rebatement in rents to his vassals in Trotternish, "*on account of their great poverty*", accruing from the phenomenal casualties in stock that they had recently sustained (*ibid.*, p. 83).

The runrig system of tenure was, of course, still generally the vogue and its continuation served, for a time, to check that process of the sub-division of land that was to become such a flagrant evil during the period the boom in the kelp industry prevailed.

Since most occupiers of land possessed no lease for their holdings, they could, of course, be displaced at any moment at the whim of their superior. The direct result of this state of insecurity was that land was seldom developed to its full capacity and among many of its other attendant evils may be cited the fact that no effort was made to improve the soil by drainage and no provision was made for the preservation of the growing crops. In some cases, however, when a new tenancy was entered upon, a contract was concluded according to the following custom: A withe and a wisp of straw were handed by the owner to the new occupier. The latter immediately returned the tokens; and we have it on the testimony of Martin that this agreement was as binding *"as if they had signed any deed"* (Martin, M, 1716, p. 115).

Implements

As an implement of tillage, the spade was held to be far superior to the plough for it was found by experience that the crop that followed the operation of ploughing was invariably lighter than that which grew on land that was dug by the spade. This was, of course, as might be expected, owing to the very crude construction of the ploughs of those days, when the marking implement and the moulding one had not yet been combined.

The harrow then in use was entirely of wood. The front portion was studded with two rows of wooden teeth behind which was fixed a line of rough heather or brushwood, for the purpose of smoothing the soil. In most cases the harrowing was done by human labour, frequently by women; but occasionally a horse was pressed into service, the method of yoking being to tie the implement to the animal's tail by means of a rope of hair or of rushes.

General Conditions of the People; Their Superstitions, etc.

Owing to the life they led, and the plain fare on which they lived, the people were then very healthy; and we find Martin stating that *"there is no place of the habitable globe where so few bodily imperfections are to be seen, or where the children go more early"*. In MacFarlane's *Geographical Collections* a note says *"...the people of Skye are of good stature, strong and nimble"* (Mitchell, A, 1906, p. 220). A terrible toll was, however, taken of the lives of the people by the dread epidemics of smallpox and fevers; of the latter, scarlet fever had made its advent to the island in the first years of the eighteenth century. Owing to the lack of medical skill and the want of adequate provision for the physically disabled, the span of life was, on the average, shorter than at present, while individual longevity was much the same as it is to-day.

The practice of empiricism by the Beatons was now on the decline, though, according to Martin, they still *"wrought many cures"*. People placed great faith in superstitious remedies; among other methods of treatment, the water of sacred wells was supposed to have great potency as an antidote to disease (Martin, W, 1716, pp. 197–8).

Of such places, the most frequented was Loch Siant, in Trotternish. Invalids bathed in it, and they drank of its waters that were held to be a panacea for all ills. It was, in truth, a Skye *'Siloam'* and those who stirred its waters, thereby, as they thought, drowning the spirit of their disease, made offerings in the form of strips of coloured cloth, pins, brooches, and other trinkets, to the presiding divinity of the place. It is mentioned in MacFarlane's *Geographical Collections* as being a place *"resorted to from all the airts"* (Mitchell, A, 1906, p. 222). The trout in this lake none would deign to touch; and the coppice, growing nearby, was held to be so sacred that no native would allow a branch of it to be broken. Among other wells that possessed healing virtues, one was reputed to be in Uig, and another in Kilbride, in the parish of Strath (Martin, M, 1716, p. 140–1).

The methods adopted for the treatment of certain diseases are so diverting as to merit some mention here. For those afflicted with 'depression of the spirits', recourse was had to two forms of 'cure', in each of which the principle was to impart sudden fear to the patient. In one case the prescription was to take him out to sea in a boat, throw him unawares into the water and expect the immersion to cure him. In the other, he was taken to a blacksmith in Kilmartin, at this time the thirteenth of his line, who claimed to possess the art of healing this trouble. Here the sufferer was laid on the anvil, face upwards, while the powerful son of Vulcan raised the sledge-hammer aloft and, bringing it down with tremendous force and a threatening grimace, stopped short when almost in contact with his client's brow, *"else"*, as Martin has it, *"he would be sure to cure the patient of all diseases!"* (*ibid.*, p. 183).

These empirics accompanied the practice of their art by appropriate incantations, numerous examples of which could be cited. Thus, in applying the recognised remedy for the cure of worms in the human body, they invariably recited the following stanza:

> *Mharbhainn dubhrag, 's mharbhainn doirbheag,*
>> I would kill a worm and a mite,
> *'S naoi naonar de a seòrsa;*
>> And nine nines of the species;
> *Is fiolan crion nan casan lionmhor,*
>> And the stunted centipede of the numerous feet,
> *Bu mhór pianadh air feadh féola.*
>> The source of much pain in flesh.
>
> (Watson, JC, 1941, p. 302)

Superstitious beliefs still exercised a powerful influence on the mind of the people, and it may help to throw some light on the psychology of our race at that time if a few instances are given. At least once a week a pilgrimage was still made to the *'Clach na Gruagaich'* of the district, into the hollow of which a libation of milk was poured, accompanied by an incantation to the female deity that presided over the yield of flocks and herds. This custom was continued long after 'The '45'. The Rev. Dr. Donald MacQueen informed Dr. Johnson in 1772 that he had succeeded in stamping it out in his own parish.

Other rites also were performed with a view to the safeguarding of the cattle from ill. They still encircled them with torches, and the ceremony was most efficacious, as they thought, at Whitsuntide, when a similar treatment was accorded the growing crops. Should an epidemic, such as *'murrain'*, break out among the cattle, a quaint rite was performed in order to produce an antidote. The men of the township, to the number of 81 (*naoi naonar*), worked, nine at a time, rubbing two planks of hazelwood together in the endeavour to generate fire. When they had succeeded, water was boiled over the flame and they sprinkled it on the herd, at the same time chanting an incantation, as follows:

> *Trath thréigeas buair am buabhal bhò,*
>> When cattle leave their stalls
> *Trath thréigeas cuanal an cual chrò,*
>> When sheep leave their folds
> *Trath dh' eireas ceigich ri beinn a' cheò,*
>> When goats ascend the misty mountain
> *Treòir na Trianaid bhi triall 'nan còir.*
>> May the power of the Trinity travel with them.
>
> (Carmichael, A, 1928, p. 184)

Even Martin believed in the efficacy of this form of quackery.

Two fossils that are very common in Skye and the adjacent

islands, namely, Ammonites and Belemnites, were much used in animal pharmacy. When cattle suffered from local pains, the part affected was vigorously massaged with water in which the 'crampstones', as the former were called, had been steeped for hours; while in the case of the latter, or the 'botstones', as they were termed, the water in which they were steeped, when drunk by horses suffering from worms, was held to be a safe and certain remedy.

People still believed that the *'toradh'*, or the essence of the milk, could be charmed away by various agencies – the 'evil eye', witches and also by bulls that sometimes swam across intervening seas and returned with the stolen virtue to their own pastures. As a preventative against contingencies of this kind, amulets were placed in the bottom of milk-vessels and one of the most potent was held to be the root of the groundsel. In order to suppress this superstition, the Rev. Dr. Donald MacQueen was wont to challenge any person in his congregation to charm the milk away from his cows; but he was forced to confess that even such a demonstration on his part was quite ineffectual in eliminating this strange belief.

Calves born with slits in the lobes of their ears, or with very minute organs of hearing, were believed to be the offspring of the *'corc'* or 'water bull', and were accordingly said to be *'corc-chluasach'* or *'torc-chluasach'*. Animals with such deformities were supposed to be ominous of disaster to the herd. They were, therefore, despatched at birth and their bodies were consigned to the sea, or to the nearest river. These are the cattle called *'corcyfyre'* by Martin in his *'Account of the Western Isles'*.

In commencing any work they held that, if the undertaking were to be successful, it was essential to turn sunwise, a procedure which was invariably observed. A tacksman, who then lived on *Fladda Chuain*, and who faithfully followed the ancient custom, was wont to justify his action by declaring that, on their first appearance there from their winter haunts, the *'coulter-nebs'*, or puffins, encircled the island three times *'deiseal'*, or sunwise; and on their departure again, in the early autumn, they performed similar evolutions.

Certain inanimate objects were supposed to possess oracular powers and were resorted to for the purpose of determining the course of future events. Thus, in a chapel dedicated to St. Columba, and situated on *Fladda-Chuain*, there was a stone in the altar that was held to possess the property of affecting the weather. Hence those who frequented the surrounding seas often resorted to it, in the hope of finding out the weather conditions that were likely to ensue. If storms persisted for some time, or winds were contrary, they repaired to the island and washed the stone. They believed that this formality would ensure auspicious weather. So great, indeed, was their veneration for this stone that Martin says *"they swear decisive oaths on it"*.

Oaths sworn on the naked dirk were held to be peculiarly binding. It is on record, for example, that when Donald Roy MacDonald wished to go to *Fladda-Chuain* from the island of Troday, in order to ascertain if the Prince had arrived there, he asked the tenant of the latter island, one Alexander Cameron, to accompany him. Cameron demurred, alleging as his reason his fear that the government might punish him by depriving him of his lands. Thereupon Donald Roy caused him to swear on the dirk that he would reveal to no one what he had been asked to do and, we have it on the testimony of him who administered the oath that *"it was kept with the utmost fidelity"*. In commenting on this incident, Bishop Forbes observes, *"The taking of an oath upon the holy iron is as sacred among them as swearing upon the Bible"*. Another means of binding people to secrecy, and concerted action, was to sip a drop of each other's blood taken from the little finger (Forbes, R, 1975, Vol. 2, pp. 9–10).

CHAPTER XIII

Family History, 1746–1800

The MacDonalds

We have brought the history of the MacDonalds to the death of Sir Alexander, in the year 1746. This chief was twice married, first to Ann Erskine, who was the daughter of a Senator of the College of Justice. She died within a year after marriage, and a notable poem was composed by the *'Pìobaire Dall'*, who happened to be at Armadale on Sir Alexander's return from London to learn of the death of his young wife. It is called *'Dàn Comhfhurtachd'*, or 'Song of Consolation', and it is written in the loftiest strain of the famous piper-bard. There was one child of the marriage, who died young (Mackenzie, J, 1877, pp. 96–7).

Sir Alexander's second wife, the handsome and accomplished Lady Margaret, was the daughter of the Earl of Eglinton. Apart altogether from the role she played in the adventure of 'The '45', she had other qualities that endeared her to her people. She was the mother of two sons, James and Alexander, both of whom were successively chiefs.

Sir James ('The Scottish Marcellus'), Sixteenth Chief And Eighth Baronet

Sir James, the elder, was born in 1741, so that he was only five years of age at the time of his father's death. During his minority the management of the affairs of the estate were in the capable hands of his mother, Lady Margaret, and her faithful steward, Alexander MacDonald of Kingsborough. It was at Kingsborough that the young heir, Sir James, received some of his early education. His father, Sir Alexander, in a letter to MacLeod of MacLeod declares that *"son Jamie (was) getting more Gaelick at Kingsburgh than tongue can tell"* (MacLeod, RC, 1939, Vol. II, p. 40). Thence he proceeded to Oxford, where he had a brilliant career in science, languages and in philosophy. Of him General Stewart of Garth says, *"He was one of the most accomplished men of our own or of any other country"*, and Sir Robert Douglas of Glenbervie, the compiler of *'The Scottish Baronage'*, asserts that, for 'knowledge of the liberal arts and sciences, he was inferior to none of his contemporaries'. Many of our own people bore witness to his high character and outstanding genius; chief of whom the bard, John MacCodrum, whom Sir James himself so generously maintained, composed a well-merited panegyric on him, a portion of which is as follows:

Gur h'-innealt' an connsmunn
　　A handsome warrior
Ceann-cinnidh Chloinn Dòmhnuill.
　　The chief of Clan Donald
Fear iriseal, stòlda,
　　Humble and sedate
Gun tòir air an àrdan:
　　Without tendency to haughtiness
Eireachdail, coimhlionta,
　　Beautiful and versatile
Soilleir an eòlas,
　　Clear in knowledge
Goirear dheth togbhail
　　In times of dissention
Bòcan mo làmhsa;
　　I wager he will be called a terror
Cùirtear na siobhaltachd,
　　Urbane Courtier
Tlusoil ri dilleachdain
　　Sympathetic with the orphan
'S cuimhneach air airidh.
　　Mindful of the deserving.

(MacMhathain, U, 1939, p. 53)

By way of illustrating his linguistic attainments a story is still told in Skye to the effect that, when Sir James was in Rome seeking health during his last and fatal illness, the Pope sent a cardinal to interview the young nobleman whose praises were on the lips of all who valued learning. The legate was commissioned to find out if the fame that had gone abroad of his extraordinary scholarship was in reality true. When interrogated on his return as to how the Highland chief had acquitted himself in the tests of learning, the deputy replied,

I addressed him in seven different languages, and he answered me in all with fluency and obvious familiarity; and when I was about to leave his room, he gave an order to his servant in a language that I am sure nobody in the world understood but themselves.

It need not be enquired what the language was!

His had never been a robust constitution. In his early adolescence the state of his health was such as to occasion grave concern to his friends. An accident, that happened to him on his estate in Uist, resulted in accentuating his infirmity. As he was one day hunting with a party that included Colonel MacLeod of Talisker, the rifle of the latter went off and the discharge lodged in the leg of Sir James. Firearms in those days had no guard and, in this instance, the unprotected trigger was moved by a sprig of heather that came in contact with it, thus accidentally firing the shot. It was, indeed, after this incident that the guard for the trigger was devised and it is accordingly termed in Gaelic, '*an t-iarunn fraoich*', or the 'heather-iron'.

The wounded chief was carried to the house of a tacksman, Ewen MacDonald, a noted piper, who, in order to beguile the time for the patient, played many a *pìobaireachd*, and even composed an ode called '*Cumha na Coise*, a quatrain from which is:

Mo ghaol, mo ghaol do chas threubhach,
　　My love, My love, your firm leg,
Do'n tig an t-osan 's am féile;
　　Comely with hose and kilt;
Bu leat toiseach nan ceudan,
　　You would be the first among hundreds,
'S na féidh bhith gan ruith.
　　When following the deer.

(Cameron, A, 1871, p. 142)

That night crowds of the Uist folk gathered around Valay House, where their wounded chief lay, demonstrating against Colonel MacLeod and even threatening reprisals for his supposed design on the life of Sir James. It required all the tact and powers of persuasion of which the tacksman was capable to convince them that the incident was quite accidental.

Shortly after he had left Oxford, Sir James travelled on the continent in the company of the versatile Topham Beauclerk, and that pioneer of the science of political economy, Adam Smith, who was then Professor of Moral Philosophy in the University of Glasgow. Such a distinguished company was bound to command respect wherever they went and the deference shown to the young Chief of Clan Donald was no whit less than that accorded to his illustrious associates.

On his return from the tour, he set himself to improve the amenities of the estate and to better the lot of his people for he had their welfare close to his heart. Among his many projects was the building of a large village at Portree, in order to stimulate local industries and to foster trade. As was natural in a man of such wide learning, he was eager to spread the influence of culture; and it was through his exertions that a large school was established at Portree, as the most convenient centre on the island for the education of the local youth. He was keenly interested in the 'Ossianic Controversy', and was a strong protagonist of the view that the spirit of the old traditional barderie had been faithfully preserved by MacPherson. *"I have"*, he once declared, while speaking of his family bard, John MacCodrum – *"I have heard him repeat, for hours together, poems which seemed to me to be the same with MacPherson's translations"* (Cameron, A, 1871, p. 143).

In the winter of 1765 the state of his health was again precarious and it was therefore proposed that he should make a tour of the Mediterranean countries in the course of the following summer. He set off with the intention of making Italy his headquarters but the change failing to produce any betterment in his health, he died in Rome about the middle of July, 1766, *"universally regretted"*, as the Rev. Donald Martin of Kilmuir put it in 1793, *"both by his countrymen and by foreigners, who contended with each other who should pay the greatest marks of respect to his merit and his virtue"*.

He was only twenty-five years of age. But such was the fame of his learning and the great respect in which he was held, that a public funeral was accorded him in Rome greater than any that had graced a Protestant before his time.

On hearing of his untimely death, David Hume, the philosopher, wrote to Adam Smith, *"We could not possibly have suffered a greater loss than that valuable young man"*; while Dr. John MacLean, the last of the famous line of physicians of the MacDonald chiefs, and himself a man of deep erudition, declared, *"The youngest of us will never see a person of warmer heart, better principles, or more inclined to do all the good in his power"*. Tributes to his name poured in from high and low. An anonymous bard composed a noble elegy, in which he laments the loss to the clan:

> *Craobh mhullaich a b' àirde,*
> > Top tree and the tallest,
> *Seo bh' oirse ri àireamh,*
> > This was related of you,
> *Chaidh a gearradh gu làr dhuibh;*
> > It was cut down to earth;
> *Och nan och! rug am bàs ort cho òg;*
> > Alas, alas, death overtook you so young;

and the family laureate, MacCodrum, sings with majestic power and genuine pathos of the passing of his great-hearted chief:

Ar toilinntinn, 's ar sòlas,
    Our comfort and solace,
Craobh a dhidean ar còrach,
    Hero to defend our rights,
Ann an cathair na Ròimh air a chàradh.
    In the city of Rome is buried.

          (MacMathain, U, 1939, p. 75)

Mrs Grant of Laggan wrote:

The gentle chieftain of the Misty Isle,
Snatched in the bloom of opening worth away
Thus lives in many a plaintive lay
Which still his honoured memory shall prolong
So young Marcellus lives in Virgil's song.

          (Grant, A, 1803, p. 25).

An elegant monument, executed in Rome, was placed by Lady Margaret, in 1768, in the church of Kilmore, in Sleat. The epitaph was composed by his college friend, Lord Lyttleton, and it is such a magnificent and well-merited encomium that a portion of it is quoted:

To the memory of
Sir JAMES MACDONALD, Bart.,
Who, in the flower of youth,
Had attained to so eminent a degree of knowledge,
In Mathematics, Philosophy, Languages,
And in every other branch of useful and polite learning,
As few have acquired in a long life
Wholly devoted to study.
Yet, to this erudition, he joined,
What can rarely be found with it,
Great talents for business,

Great propriety of behaviour,
Great politeness of manners.
His eloquence was sweet, correct, flowing;
His memory vast, and exact;
His judgment strong, and acute;
All which endowments, united
With the most amiable temper,
And every private virtue,
Procure him, not only in his own country,
But also from foreign nations,
The highest marks of esteem.

He died at Rome
Where, notwithstanding the difference of religion,
Such extraordinary honours were paid to his memory
As had never graced that of any other British subject
Since the death of Sir Philip Sydney
The fame he left behind him is the best consolation
To his afflicted family,
And to his countrymen in this isle
For whose benefit he had planned
Many useful improvements,
Which his fruitful genius suggested,
And his active spirit promoted,
Under the sober direction
Of a clear and enlightened understanding.

In accordance with his own expressed wish, that nothing he had written should be preserved, all his manuscripts were consigned to his coffin and buried with him, and the regret will grow with the years that we have no record of the works of this outstanding genius. The brilliance of his natural parts, together with the amiability of his nature and his untimely death, suggested to some the parallel history of the adopted son of Octavious Caesar; and hence his cognomen of *'The Scottish Marcellus'*. Sir James was succeeded by his brother.

Sir Alexander, Seventeenth Chief, Ninth Baronet and First Lord

This chief had been educated at Eton and St. Andrews, and he was a cultured man, widely read, and a genuine patron of learning. Boswell describes him as 'a gentleman of talents' and, as earnest of his ability, we have a Latin ode by him, written as a welcome to Dr. Johnson, which possesses considerable merit. He was also an accomplished musician, renowned alike for his taste and for his skill as a player of the violin. Two note-worthy compositions that will long remain among the prime favourites of fiddlers and pipers stand to his credit, namely, *'Lord MacDonald's Reel'* and *'Mrs. Mackinnon of Corry'*.

While one would not go so far as to agree with Dr. Johnson's observation that his education had unfitted him for the position of chief, yet it must be conceded that he was wholly devoid of sympathy either with the culture, or the manner of life, of his own people. In his dealings with them he stood purely in the role of landlord and he had no scruples about increasing their burdens when occasion presented itself. The demand for wool and the boom in kelp, had furnished him with ample pretexts for raising rents and he took the fullest advantage of the situation. Great resentment, therefore, prevailed against him and several of his tacksmen actually united, pledging themselves to resist the payment of what they looked upon as unwarrantable impositions. Many were constrained to emigrate.

Owing to certain animadversions cast upon his conduct by Boswell, Sir Alexander suffered for a time under the shadow of unpopularity and he smarted so bitterly under these strictures that, it is said, he even went so far as to threaten Boswell with physical violence. Caricatures appeared in the London press making humorous allusions to the relations between the inter-meddling litterateur and the offended chief. In one of these there was depicted a scribe, in a prayerful attitude, supplicating mercy from a resolute Highlander, who gripped him with one hand by the nape of the neck, while in the other he held a stout stick, with which he pointed to an unfinished manuscript. There can be no doubt that Sir Alexander fell far short of Dr. Johnson's conception of an ideal Highland chief and, in view of the facts already stated, no one need wonder; but, on the other hand, it cannot be gainsaid that Boswell had been eminently indiscreet in giving the publicity he did to the over-zealous sentiments of his great master.

As is well known, Sir Alexander and his wife were on their way to Edinburgh on business, and they had just reached Armadale on the way south, when they were apprised of the arrival of Johnson and Boswell in Skye. They did all that was possible under the circumstances to entertain the distinguished visitors, even delaying their journey for a few days with that end in view. When Johnson and Boswell returned to Sleat from the north of Skye, the chief and his lady were in Edinburgh but instructions had been left with their factor, James MacDonald, to attend to the convenience of the visitors, and they spent a cheerful night in the chief's house at Armadale, after they had left the manse of the Rev. Martin MacPherson in Ostaig.

This 'English-bred chieftain', as Boswell calls him, was raised to the peerage in 1776, as 'Lord MacDonald of Slate, Co. Antrim', a designation that has no territorial identity. Whether it was in return for his honour or not, he busied himself at that time with the raising of a regiment on his estates for fighting in the American War of Independence. This was, however, a more difficult task than he had anticipated; for the traditional antipathy to the House of Hanover still prevailed, and many left the island rather than be party to this unpopular enterprise.

Owing, however, to the effects of pressure and intimidation and the still potent, though waning influence of a chief, he succeeded in mustering over 700 men from his own estates. The regiment was reviewed at Inverness in 1778, and towards the end of the year it was despatched to America. 'The MacDonald Highlanders', as they were called, fought in several engagements, and, on their return to this country, they were disbanded at Stirling in the year 1784. Ten years later, when a real menace threatened the nation in the form of a French invasion, he helped to raise a defence corps, 'The MacDonald Fencibles', that was commanded by Major John MacDonald of Kingsborough, one of the many soldier-sons of Flora MacDonald.

While he was still comparatively a young man, Sir Alexander died, in September 1795. He was married to Miss Boswell of Gunthwaite, in Yorkshire, a lady of exceptional beauty. Of their family of ten children, the two older sons, Alexander and Godfrey, were chiefs, while a third, named Archibald, who was a posthumous child, rose to the now obsolete dignity of Lord Chief Baron of the Exchequer.

The MacLeods

The early chiefship of Norman has already been treated, and brought to the episode of 'The '45'. We have dealt with the role he played in that romantic adventure, and the effect it has had upon his name. He joined the Hanoverian forces and took an active, if inglorious, part against the Prince; but the deed of deepest shame was his letter to Kingsborough, previous to Prince Charlie's arrival in Skye, advising him to take advantage of the government's offer of £30,000, and to betray the royal fugitive:

For I am persuaded he will pay you a visit. It will then be in your

power (I hope you will use it) to aggrandise your family beyond many in Scotland.

(Forbes, R, 1975, Vol. 2, p. 1)

Such is the extract from it in *'The Lyon in Mourning'*. Despite numerous requests, Kingsborough persistently refused to show the original copy to Bishop Forbes, the editor of that monumental work; but, when the version quoted was read to Kingsborough he observed that it contained the substance of the text, *"though the original was still worse"* (Forbes, R, 1975, Vol. 3, p. 85). And when the whole history of this chief has been told, the conclusion will be inevitable that he was quite capable of work as debased as is suggested here.

We have followed the declination of his life to a state of prodigality and infidelity – his thirst for squandering, his utter recklessness in launching upon a life of gambling and riotous living. We have seen how he spent the vast fortune acquired by the industry and the devoted care of the faithful guardians of his nonage, and that his appellation, 'The Wicked Man', was not undeserved. In an interesting account of the affairs of the clan, written by his grandson, the General, we find it asserted that

he was the first of our family, who was led by the change of manners, to leave the patriarchal government of his clan and to mix in the pursuits and the ambitions of the world.

(Mackenzie, A, 1889, p. 150).

During the last years of his life the affairs of the estate were in dire straits. The burden of debt had amounted to the colossal figure of £50,000 and, in order to relieve the financial position, it was decided to raise the rents. Colonel MacLeod of Talisker and the chief's grandson and successor, Norman, were commissioned to lay before the principal tenants the critical position to which the estate had been brought and the necessity there existed for their aid to save the family name from ruin. They declared that disaster was to be averted only by a general raising of rents; but the promise to grant relief from the additional burdens was duly implemented some years after the young man who made it was raised to the chiefship.

'The Wicked Man' died in 1772, and was buried in St. Andrews. He was predeceased by his only legitimate son, John, whose mother is reputed to have suffered such cruel treatment that she was forced to leave him, while her death was associated with mysterious circumstances. He had three daughters by his second wife, Miss Anne Martin, and two natural sons – men who rose to fame, namely, Major Alexander MacLeod of Lochbay and Captain MacLeod of Cyprus. The latter were both distinguished officers in the American War of Independence; and Major Alexander was married to Anne, the oldest daughter of Flora MacDonald. During the time the young chief, General MacLeod, was engaged in the foreign wars in India, Major MacLeod occupied Dunvegan Castle; and he was held in the highest esteem because of his urbanity and his munificence.

Norman, ('The General'), Twenty-third Chief

In 1772 the old chief was dead and was succeeded by his grandson, who also was called Norman. This was a man of great vivacity of temperament, sturdy physique, and pronounced ability. He had been educated at Edinburgh and St. Andrews and before he had left these institutions he had given abundant evidence of a genuine desire for knowledge and of distinct natural talents. Indeed, so impressed was Dr. Johnson by this youthful chief that he says of him, *"I never met with a young man who had more desire to learn, or who had learned more"*. We have already seen that, out of regard to the confidence reposed in him, he had been delegated by his grandfather, when only eighteen years of age, to treat with his people in order to evolve ways and means

of extricating the estate from its financial embarrassments; and what was a more difficult and delicate task – to check the tide of emigration to the colonies that was then in full flood. We have alluded to his success in inducing his clansmen to accede to an increase in rent so that we do not wonder at the tribute paid him by the traveller, Thomas Pennant, who asserts,

> *To all the milkiness of human kindness, usually concomitant with his early age, is added the sense and firmness of more advanced years.*

He had compiled an interesting fragment of an autobiography dealing particularly with his early life and, while it displays the fine style of a highly cultivated writer, it, at the same time, furnishes us with evidence of a noble personality at once amiable and in deep sympathy with the lot of his own people. *"A man whose personal character"*, says Pennant, *"does him infinitely higher honour than the fortuitous distinction of his ancient and honourable descent"*.

That this chief was intent, heart and soul, on the promotion of the welfare of his people is shown by numerous sayings of his that are on record; and some are quoted in order to show the altruistic motives that activated him.

The government has deprived us of our ancient power", he once declared, *"but it cannot rob us of our domestic satisfaction"*; and, again, *"I would rather drink punch in the house of my people, than be enabled by their hardships to have claret in my own.*

Despite his lofty motives, and unselfish actions, matters were not progressing smoothly. The people groaned under the burden of rents and, as the demands of creditors were being insistently pressed, the prospect of relief for his tenants seemed very remote. In Boswell's *'Journal'* there occurs a significant statement that throws a flood of light on the relationship between the chief and his clan at that time. It is:

Talisker was grave and somewhat depressed by his anxious concern about MacLeod's affairs, and by finding some gentlemen of the clan by no means disposed to act a generous and affectionate part to their chief in his distress, but bargaining with him as with a stranger.

(Boswell, J, 1955, p. 151).

But a man imbued with such independent spirit and altruistic disposition as MacLeod could not long abide a life of inactivity in which he was to remain a parasite on his people. In order, therefore, to help to dispose of the debt that had accrued on the estate, he decided to join the army. The American War of Independence had just then begun, and such a demand for recruits had set in that emigration was temporarily stayed.

He was commissioned with the rank of captain, but his regiment preceded him to America, as he had sustained a severe injury by being thrown from his horse while he was training. When, at last, he did embark, he took with him his young bride, the daughter of Mackenzie of Suddie, who had nursed him so carefully after his accident. On their voyage out their ship was captured by the American Navy, and they became prisoners of war. During his captivity, MacLeod made the acquaintance of George Washington and a spirit of mutual affection and admiration was engendered in these great men that neither time nor distance could impair (Mackenzie, A, 1889, p. 166). It was during this time that certain parts of the estate, situated in the parish of Snizort, were sold to four different proprietors.

On the cessation of hostilities in America, Captain MacLeod, as he then was, returned home and in 1780 he was made lieutenant-colonel and given the command of the Black Watch, with which he was ordered to proceed to India. After a voyage of strange vicissitudes and misfortunes, he at length reached India towards the end of May, 1782 (*ibid.*, pp. 167–9).

The forces of Hyder Ali were causing trouble in Southern India, but his son, Tippo Sahib, with an army of 24,000 Hindus and two corps of Europeans under the French general, Lally, received an effective rebuff at Panniani, when Colonel MacLeod, with a small contingent of 380 Europeans and 2200 Sepoys, inflicted on them a telling defeat.

It was of this exploit that Sheriff Nicolson sings so exultantly in his battle-song, *'Agus ho Mhórag'*:

Many were their deeds of arms
'Gainst the swarms of Hyder Ali,
Leaguered close in Mangalore
Tippo and his hordes they baffled.

The following year brought him many moments of intense anxiety, as the army under his command was hopelessly inadequate to cope with the overwhelming forces that were then brought into the field against him by Hyder Ali. In 1783, MacLeod was raised to the rank of general and was given charge of the Malabar Coast. But the situation was becoming more and more critical for him. At Mangalore he was hemmed in so closely by the Hindoo hordes that he was practically besieged for a period of nine months. Numerous sallies were made and enormous losses were inflicted on the enemy, whose numbers seemed to be inexhaustible. The besieged suffered such privations, being forced to eat whatsoever came their way – dogs, cats, mice and even snakes – that they were finally forced to surrender. The contingent was deservedly commended for the gallant defence they had set up, *"one that has seldom been equalled, but never surpassed"*. Shortly after this a new army order came into force, establishing the principle of holding rank according to seniority with the result that MacLeod found himself unfavourably placed; for officers, who had hitherto been his subalterns, now became his superiors. He, therefore, resigned his command and returned home in the year 1789 (*ibid.*, pp. 177–9).

During the period of his service in India, he had succeeded in amassing an enormous fortune, as much, indeed, as £100,000, according to one very reliable authority. But this man of lofty principles allowed himself to fall from grace and, like his grandfather, he was caught by the pernicious lure of gambling, so that he soon lost the whole of his wealth.

In his absence, as we have already seen, his castle of Dunvegan was occupied by his natural uncle, Major Alexander MacLeod of Lochbay, and his wife, Anne, the daughter of Flora MacDonald. The utmost enthusiasm prevailed among the members of the clan when the news of the chief's home-coming became known, and elaborate preparations were made to celebrate the occasion with becoming ceremony. According to the *Edinburgh Courant* of February 1790, *"Col MacLeod of Tallisker, James MacLeod of Raasay and several others met at the ancient Castle of Dunvegan to do honour to Col MacLeod of MacLeod on his return from India."* All over his estates bonfires were lit on the most conspicuous eminences and as many of his clan as could avail themselves of the opportunity repaired to Dunvegan to accord in person their welcome to their chief.

The Rev. Dr. Norman MacLeod, *'Caraid nan Gaidheal'*, in one of his memoirs says that he himself was on a visit to the castle at the time and that the impressions then made on his youthful mind would remain indelibly imprinted there to the end of his days. And there was one feature of that memorable day that especially caught his fancy. That was the playing of a *pìobaireachd*, *'Failte Ruairidh Mhóir'* ('Rory Mór's Salute'), by way of salute, by a certain Captain Donald MacCrimmon, who, however, was not of Borreraig.

But this chief, who, in his early years had given such splendid promise and of whom Pennant has said,

> *He feels for the distresses of his people, and insensible of his own, with uncommon disinterestedness has relieved his tenants from oppressive rents, has received, instead of the trash of gold, the treasure of warm affections and unfeigned prayer.*

This chief now could see nothing in the affairs of his clan to induce him to stay at home and attend to their needs. His life abroad had unfitted him for the quiet conditions of existence in Skye, so that in the following year he entered the turmoil of politics. He continued to live beyond his means. The estate was sinking deeper and deeper in debt. While he was in America in 1779, his trustees sold Harris, Lyndale, etc.; and, in order to defray the electioneering expenses incurred in an unsuccessful contest during the year 1796, he was constrained to part with the district of Waternish, which had formed a portion of the family dominion since the time of Sir Rory Mór, Greshornish, Isay etc. In 1796, Orbost, Skinindiin, Colbost, Husabost and several lesser farms were sold. In referring to these alienations, his son, John Norman, in his appendix to the fragment of autobiography by his father, from which we have already quoted, says,

> *He was the first of his family to part with his inheritance and he was doubly grieved to find that he had impoverished his heirs without materially benefitting himself.*

(*ibid.*, p. 181).

His oldest son, Norman, *'Tormad nan tri Tormaid'*, was accidentally killed in 1799, on board the *'Queen Charlotte'*, on which he was a lieutenant. This was a great blow to the chief, who was then in a weak state of health. With a view to recuperate, he was invited to pay a visit to the Channel Islands. On the way there he became gradually worse and he had only arrived in Guernsey when he died at the early age of 47 years. He was succeeded, in the year 1801, by John Norman, the son of his second wife, Sarah Stackhouse, the daughter of a Member of the Council at Bombay. The portrait of him by Raeburn shows a full face, with eyes set widely apart, a long nose and the whole aspect cast in a melancholy mould.

As this brings the family history to a new century, it is now necessary to review the social conditions of the latter portion of the eighteenth century.

CHAPTER XIV

Social Conditions, 1746–1800

Transition Stage

The episode of 'The '45' has been taken to mark a period in our narrative but it must at once be stated that, in spite of its effect on our island, the shadows of changes crowding the horizon of history at that time are not to be attributed wholly to that untoward event. For the changes in the social conditions of that time we have to seek for other causes and these have been adumbrated in some of the previous sections. We have seen how the chiefs were being slowly, but surely, transformed from patriarchs to mere parasites on their clan. The old order was failing to interest them, for they were carried away by the glamour of the new.

But these revolutions did not immediately result from the unhappy hurly-burly of 1745 nor from its consequences, the confiscations, the Disarming Act, the ban on the Highland dress and especially the breaking up of the clan system. Indeed, the sense of clanship was too deeply rooted in the heart of the Highlander ever to be affected by acts of repression, or the rigours of governmental laws. The disintegration of that institution could never have been wrought from without. Rather are we to seek for the causes of its dissolution in the changed attitude of the chiefs to their clan. Those laws that deprived the Highlanders of their arms and garb and sought to abolish their language and their tribal institutions, would have gone far to destroy the feudal authority of the chiefs, but the fond attachment of the clan to its recognised head would have yielded to no laws. The chiefs themselves were the destroyers of that pleasing relationship. *"Sucked into the vortex of the nation"*, as MacLeod of MacLeod asserts regarding the chiefs, in the account he has left of the conditions of that time, *"and lured to the capitals, they degenerated from patriarchs and chieftains to landlords; and they became as anxious for the increasing of rents as the new-made lairds, the novi homines, the mercantile purchasers of the lowlands"* (MacKenzie, A, 1889, p. 151).

Mention has been made of the great demand in the south for the hardy black cattle of the north and much prosperity accrued to the Highlanders in consequence. One of the direct results of this trade was an appreciation in the value of such land as could conveniently be used for the purpose of pasture. Those with means clamoured for more land, so that the value of grazing districts soon soared high. The temptation to sell to the highest bidder was naturally too strong for most landlords to resist, with the result that lands were now rented at double, and in some cases at treble, their original amount; and, according to Pennant, that increase had taken place between the years 1750 and 1770.

The change in the attitude of the chief was poignantly felt by the members of his clan. Now they saw that those time-honoured bonds, that knit all members of the tribe so closely together, were being snapped on every side. A feeling of restiveness began to manifest itself and, rather than endure the new conditions, many were constrained to consider the painful alternative of emigration. In the *North Carolina Record*, June 1771, Vol. 8, p. 620, it is stated that,

> *James MacDonald, Merchant in Porterie, Norman MacDonald, Sleat, Hugh MacDonald, Edward MacQueen, John Beaton, Rev Alex MacQueen (Sleat), Rev William MacQueen and others had petitioned the Navy Council for 40,000 acres in North Carolina, but they were refused.*

That same year,

> *A large colony of the wealthiest and substantial people in Skye are preparing to go to the fertile and cheap lands in America. It is to be dreaded that these migrations prove hurtful to the Mother Country. The number was 370 and the reason for this emigration was rise in rents.*
>
> (*Scots Magazine*, 1771).

While the *Edinburgh Courant* of 1773 says,

> *800 persons from Skye have engaged a vessel at Greenock to take them to North Carolina. The fare to be £3.10/–.*

Mrs Grant of Laggan was no less forthright as to the source of the pressure which led to emigration:

> *The only cause of complaint in Scotland is the rage for sheep farming. The poor people have neither the language, money nor education to push their way anywhere else, though they possess feelings and principles that might reserve human nature from reproach, which false philosophy and false refinement have brought upon it.*

To crown all, a succession of bad seasons, from the year 1770, supervened and, so great were the losses in stock, that many were unable to pay their rent. From this time onwards, for about one hundred years, the emigrant ship, with its broken-hearted freight, was to be a common object in the lochs of Skye . "*That boat*", as Boswell says in referring to the ship '*Nestor*' in Portree Bay, when he and Dr. Johnson arrived there in 1772, "*that boat made a short settlement of the differences between a chief and his clan*" (Boswell, J, 1955, p. 126). According to the Rev. William Bethune, eight large transports sailed from Skye to America between the years 1771 and 1790, carrying away "*about 2000 souls*". The exodus on a large scale was at first confined to the district of Bracadale, whence 128 left between 1771 and 1774, 200 in 1788, and an equal number left for America two years later. Although Rev. Alexander Campbell declares that few had gone from the parish of Portree before 1791, it is known that several isolated families had emigrated from that district also. The youthful and the energetic among the emigrants were naturally stimulated to enthusiasm by their new environment, and the glowing accounts these men sent home, in many instances, induced others to follow.

Indeed, the depletion of the population had assumed such proportions that the government at length began to view the situation with alarm, especially after their experience of the value of Highlanders as combatants in the American War of Independence. At this time, also, the demand for black cattle began to show signs of waning in the south, and the chiefs began to see that a land without a peasantry would become valueless. Anent this there is a significant statement in *The Lyon in Mourning* (Forbes, R, 1975, Vol. III, p. 259), to the effect that 2000 emigrants were preparing for their departure to the colonies from Skye. It proceeds, *"They are all of the estate of Sir Alexander MacDonald, who may yet chance to be a proprietor without tenants. That they may go as a formed colony, a parochial preacher and a thorough-bred surgeon are to go with them;"* and he adds the comment, *"all this is due to the exorbitant rents for land"*.

That the burden of rent was the chief contributing cause to the evil of emigration cannot be gainsaid. Of that we have ample evidence. Johnson observes: *"That the immediate motives of the desertion of the clansmen must be imputed to their landlords, may be reasonably concluded, because some lairds of more prudence and less rapacity have kept their vassals undiminished"*. Thus, prior to 1774, only one person had emigrated from Raasay though a different tale remains to be told of that island during the succeeding century, when both there and in Skye the wholesale clearing of the people from the land was ruthlessly carried out.

> *When rents were nearly trebled in 1811, a number of the old tacksmen emigrated rather than pay rents which they thought were impossible. Among them were the MacLeods of Drynoch … and Talisker.*
>
> (MacLeod, RC, 1939, Vol. II, p. 113).

While the more enterprising, and especially those with some means, had been seized by the *"epidemic fury of emigration"*, as Dr. Johnson calls it, the poorest were not affected by it. When the clamour for land prevailed, and they were squeezed out, they went to swell the community of cottars by the shore. Among these a state of dire poverty prevailed till relief came to them by the advent of a new industry.

Trade and Industries

Kelp

The manufacture of alkalies by the incineration of sea-ware, made its first tentative appearance in Skye about the year 1758. The price was then about £2 10/– per ton; by 1772 it had risen to £25, and in that year there was exported from Skye some 400 tons of kelp. About the year 1790, the amount manufactured in certain of the parishes of Skye was: 100 tons in Duirinish, 80 in Bracadale, 50 in Portree, 35 in Snizort (an insignificant quantity owing to the inaccessibility of the seaboard to the east of Trotternish), and 100 tons in the parish of Strath.

Owing to the competition of Spanish barilla, kelp suffered a grievous decline in price and by 1793 it realised only between £4 and £5 per ton. This depression was but temporary, for, during the Peninsular War, the importation of barilla received a decided set-back and at the beginning of the following century kelp value had again appreciated, so that by 1810 it was as high as £22 per ton. On the termination of the Peninsular War, the trade in Spanish barilla was again revived and when, in 1817, the duty on salt was reduced, the kelp industry received another heavy blow. By the lowering of the import duty on barilla from £11 to £8 a ton in 1822, the manufacture of kelp was no longer a lucrative industry. True, it continued to linger on in a moribund state for many years after this but the industry was of little moment, so far as Skye was concerned (MacDonald, A & A, 1904, pp. 142–3).

Following, as it did, on the decline of the boom in the sale of black cattle, all were induced to participate in the occupation of kelp-making during the period of its prosperity, with the result that farming was sadly neglected. Even the tacksmen were not averse to engage in it and the landlords were not slow in asserting their rights to exact fat royalties from those engaged in its manufacture on the foreshores of their estates. The rents of maritime farms were raised, and these new impositions were strongly resented by the people, for, as Johnson has it, *"they considered the profits of the kelp as the mere product of personal labour, to which the landlord contributed nothing"* (Johnson, S, 1984, p. 91).

This new source of revenue led the landlord to set a higher value on those who helped to produce it and, as these in turn were assured a means of livelihood, the tide of emigration temporarily ceased to flow. Those engaged in the making of kelp could each earn from 1/6 to 3/– a week and that was considered a fair income in those days. Early marriages thus became the rule, for all that was necessary for the establishment of a new home was the site for a lowly cottage by the shore. A great increase in the population ensued and when, years afterwards, this source of subsistence failed, a state of terrible privation prevailed among those unfortunate people who were dependent upon it.

It should be noted that, where the industry of kelp manufacture was prosecuted, the elders of the district appointed a man, called *'buachaille cladaich'* ('shore-warden'), whose duty it was to report the presence of wrack on the shore. He did so by raising a bundle of tangle on the top of a perch and none was allowed to begin the gathering of the weed until all had assembled.

Fishing

The fishing industry was then, as it was often afterwards, prosecuted with indifferent success in Skye. Those who speak of the state of fishing at that time deplore its failure, as compared with its prosperity in the past. Thus, Thomas Fraser, who compiled the *'Old Statistical Account'* for Strath, remarks that *"herrings are not now in the lochs as formerly"*.

The truth is, however, that the industry was as inconstant then as it has proved to have been so often since that time for, during this same period, there were occasions when the lochs of Skye yielded a prolific supply of herring. Another authority of those times, namely, Rev. Martin MacPherson, who was parish minister of Sleat, declares that he saw as many as, *"one hundred sail in Isle Oransay"*, engaged in fishing and he adds that, among the herring 'busses', there were several that had come even from the Baltic; while the traveller, Thomas Pennant, states that, as he was crossing over to Skye, he saw a fleet of 'busses' at Kyle, *"waiting for the herring that was late that year"* (1774).

With the benevolent intention of fostering the fishing trade in Skye, the British Fisheries Society acquired land in Waternish in 1787 for the purpose of establishing a centre for the industry. The place chosen for the station was Stein, on Lochbay, where a quay was built, and stores and dwelling-houses were erected. A small plot of ground was allotted to each family, together with summer-grazing for a cow or two. This project, however, failing to answer the expectations of its promoters, owing principally to the high cost of salt, they were forced to abandon it in the following century at a loss of £1241. The houses of Stein were afterwards of use in providing accommodation for those who had suffered eviction during the clearances.

One of the chief reasons for the failure of the fishing industry then was the exorbitant price at which salt was retailed. Mr. Thomas Fraser, who wrote *'The Old Statistical Account'* for Strath, makes pointed references to the iniquitous salt-laws and he remarks that it often happened that little of the commodity was procurable *"at the very time the greatest shoals enter our lochs"*. The Rev. Alexander Campbell, afterwards parish minister of Portree, likewise inveighs against this impost, while the Rev. Malcolm MacLeod of Snizort declares:

There is much fish in Loch Snizort; but the country people, from the difficulty of procuring salt, have not reaped from it the advantages they might receive, were the Salt Laws such as to allow them to furnish themselves at an easier and cheaper rate.

The price of salt in Skye was then 10/– per barrel and an equal quantity of cured herring could seldom be bought at less than 19/– although, according to Rev. William Bethune of Duirinish, consignments were often exported from his parish at 16/– per barrel. The last authority tells us that a small trade also existed in the exportation of other fish and that about 20 tons of cured ling were annually sold from his own parish, at an average price of £13 per ton.

Cattle

The trade in the sale of black cattle attained its peak shortly after Culloden and it was maintained at its high level, with scarcely an intermission, until the beginning of the nineteenth century. The number despatched to the southern markets seldom fell below 4000 head in an ordinary year so that cattle-rearing may be said to have been the staple industry of the island at that time. In the best years the prices ranged from £2 to £3 per head, and Dr. Johnson mentions the fact that a cow was sold in Skye for the phenomenal sum of £5! (Johnson, S, 1984, p. 91).

In view of the large numbers that were annually disposed of by sale, enormous herds must have been reared at that time in Skye and on the adjacent islands. A herd of about 400 animals, that had never been under the shelter of a roof, was maintained on the islands of Raasay and Rona; and of these, 100 were annually sold. The latter island was then uninhabited, except for one cow-herd, who was placed there in charge of 160 cattle that were grazed on the island.

A considerable amount of trade was carried on in the sale of horses, of which about 250 were yearly exported. Pennant says that he saw four score horses at Kyle that were being transferred to the mainland, four at a time, and made fast to a boat by means of halters and withies. The price then obtaining averaged about £3 10/–, with individual sales that, in rare instances,

rose to £6 10/–. According to the *Caledonian Mercury*, '*the Sligachan Market, later to be transferred to Portree, was first held in 1753.*' Sheep were sold at from 4/– to 6/–. Few were ever exported.

Industries

In those days very little trade existed in the importation of goods, for most of the articles used in the home, and on the farm, were produced locally by amateurs. They tanned raw hide into leather by means of the bark of the oak, or the birch, or the roots of the tormentil, and most could fashion the simple brogues, the making of a pair of which was the work of an hour. This artless shoe was stitched with thongs so loosely that, although it defended the foot from injury, it did not exclude the water. The Rev. A. Campbell of Portree states that there were three 'brog-masters' in his parish about 1790; *"but"*, he adds, *"generally the people make their own brogues"*. The same authority tells us that the number of artisans who plied their trade in that parish was five carpenters, eight tailors, two weavers, twelve 'weaveresses' and two blacksmiths. The last-mentioned trade had now fallen from the honoured state it enjoyed prior to the episode of 'The '45'. Even for some time after that event it remained a hereditary occupation and a few members of the craft still occupied their lands free of all burdens in virtue of their office as armourers to their chief. The title had now, however, degenerated to that of smith. The ancestors of the MacLeods of Morvern acted in that capacity to the chiefs of Dunvegan, while the MacRurys performed similar services to, and enjoyed equal privileges from, the MacDonalds. The finely tempered blades they produced showed work of marvellous ingenuity, while their magnificently carved gunstocks with wonderfully fashioned and embellished locks, were the expressions of an art that was soon to be irretrievably lost.

There were water-mills in plenty – two, at least, in every parish, and in good seasons they were kept busy grinding the home-grown grain. That the amount of meal thus produced was insufficient for the needs of the community is attested by the observations of ministers, who deplored the large importation of foreign meal into Skye. The Rev. A. Campbell says there were *"five petty merchants in Portree"*; and the prices that ruled for exchangeable commodities were as follows: a boll of oatmeal cost from 17/– to £1 towards the end of this century, while potatoes were sold for 1/9d per barrel. Butter was 6d per lb., cheese 2½d, eggs 3d per dozen, a barrel of salt 10/–, and a pair of shoes cost 2/6.

It is of interest that practically all the gear used by fishermen was made in the homes of the people. Even the ropes in use were made from local materials and the purple melic grass (*Molinia varia*) was considered then to be one of the best substances for the making of cordage, because of its toughness and its durability. Such ropes were also used as halters for horses, though in rare instances, hair was used for the same purpose.

Bags were made of plaited rushes or of straw; and these were the receptacles for grain, etc. ('*plàta ghràin*'). The candle and the cruisies were manufactured locally and, while the art of making the former was generally known, the latter naturally presented greater difficulties, so that its production was confined to the few who had a mechanical bent. Hitherto the cruises had been brought from the south but, after 'The '45' they were made by the smiths, and soon amateurs came to practise the art. These vessels, with wicks of the pleated pith of the tufted rush, in a bath of fish-oil, afforded the principal means of lighting in the homes of the common people then and for some years thereafter.

Labour was then so cheap that a large staff of servants was employed by the more prosperous tacksmen of Skye. Pennant tells us that, in several houses, there were as many as twenty, and he was not slow in casting animadversions on their industry or,

rather, their lack of it, for they impressed him as *"the laziest of creatures, for not one will do the least thing that does not belong to his own department"*. This calumniation is perhaps unmerited and the character of the people is more justly described by one of our ministers, the Rev. William Bethune of Duirinish, who, writing in 1791, says, *"The people are very industrious when working for themselves, but are lazy and indifferent when they are employed by others."*

Wages

In some of the principal families of Skye, the wages of servants were still paid in kind, the women being given a sheep or two, whose wool they span and wove for their own clothing. In the wealthier households, however, a monetary payment was usually the rule. When hired for a year, men received from £2 10/– to £3 10/–, varying according to the extent of land allotted to them for their own exclusive use. The annual wage of a maid-servant ranged from 10/– to £1, *"besides three pairs of shoes"*, a not inconsiderable burden on the employer of those days for it was said by one of our parish ministers in 1791 that *"servants' shoes cost their masters as much as their wages, twenty or thirty years ago"*. The increase in wages was due to the fact that, even at that time, men and women went south to engage in harvesting in Stirlingshire and the Lothians, while, at home, men could earn from 1/6 to as much as 3/– a week at kelp-making. For casual labour in husbandry, the daily wage for men was 6d to 8d and half that amount for women, exclusive of victuals.

Numerous cottars then lived around, and on, certain farms and these people were obliged to give three days' work per week to the farmers in return for the grazing of a cow and a small extent of ground for tillage. For his services, a married man, who contracted to serve the tacksman for a year, was entitled to grazing for two cows, twelve sheep and two horses; on two days a week he was free to labour on his own plot. Those who did not render service in lieu of the land they occupied did so in kind – corn, cattle, sheep, poultry, and even peat being contributed as rent.

Specie was still very scarce, and Boswell tells us of the great difficulty he experienced in securing even 21/- in silver. When at last he did succeed in getting that amount in Portree, *"it was considered a great store"*. The Rev. Donald MacQueen, parish minister of Kilmuir, asserts that he often had great trouble to get enough money to pay the wages of his servants, or to buy such necessaries as food and clothing.

Dress

As has already been shown, the wearing of the Highland garb was prohibited in 1746 and it lay under proscription until the year 1782, when, owing primarily to the exertions of the Marquis of Graham, Parliament abrogated the Unclothing Act. The dissatisfaction that prevailed because of that mode this new was imposed upon them, was acute, and Dr. Johnson, and other travellers to Skye at that time, make frequent references to the resentment of the people. As was to be expected, the abolition of the detested measure was everywhere hailed with acclamation, and our bards gave expression to the general sense of relief in many a song. Chief among them Duncan *Bàn,* who thus refers to it:

Deich bliadhna fichead is còrr
    It is thirty years and more
Bha casag de'n chlò m'ar druim.
    Since the woollen cassock covered our backs.
Fhuair sinn ad, agus cleòc,
    We got a hat and a cloak,
Cha bhuineadh an seòrs' ud dhuinn.

    In style quite foreign to us.
Bucaill a' dùnadh ar bròg,
    Buckles to fasten our brogues,
'S e 'm barr-iall bu bhòidhche' leinn;
    The lace was considered more comely,
Rinn an droch fhasan a bh'òirnn,
    The abominable fashion we suffered,
Na bodaich de'r n-òigridh ghrinn.
    Made old men of our handsome youths.

                (MacLeod, A, 1978, p. 238)

Our own bard, William Ross, ardent Jacobite that he was, sings of the revocation of the ban with evident enthusiasm:

Thàinig fasan as an achd
    A fashion emerged from the Act
A dh òrduich pailt am féile,
    That put the kilt in favour,
Tha éirigh air na breacanan,
    There is a resurgeance of the tartan,
Le farum treun neo lapanach,
    With strong unfailing bustle,
Bi oighean tapaidh sniomh, 's a' dath,
    Smart maidens will be weaving and dyeing,
Gu h-éibhinn ait le uaill;
    Happy, glad and proud;
Gach aon dhiubh 'g éideadh a gaoil féin
    Each clothing her loved one
Mar 's réidh leo anns gach uair;
    As opportunity offers.;
                (MacCoinnich, (etc.), I, 1834, p. 26)

while Kenneth Mackenzie is ecstatic in his praise of the garb of the Gael:

'S e 'm feile preasach tlachd mo rùin,
> The joy of my love is the pleated kilt,

'S an osan nach ruig ach a' ghlùn
> The hose that reached but the knee

Is còta beag nam basan dlùth,
> The short coat of close stripes,

Is boineid dhù-ghorm thogarrach.
> And an attractive dark blue bonnet.

> (Mackenzie, J, 1877, p. 272)

The revival of the tartan so impressed the popular fancy that everyone was wearing it. The vogue had become so general that even the women wore it, and Ross sings of the Highland lass:

Gur h-ainnir shoighn i,
> A comely maiden,

Gun sgòd ri dhearc oirra;
> With no defect visible,

'Na h-earradh glé mhath
> In her excellent dress

De eudach breacanach.
> Of tartan cloth.

> (Mackenzie, J, 1877, p. 290)

Such household trappings as curtains for windows and covers for furniture were made of tartan. The craze became so strong as to overreach itself, with the result that, towards the end of the century, the fashion was suffering from a marked decline. It was, however, subsequently to be revived, on account of the exploits of the Highland regiments and the writings of Sir Walter Scott. Adverting to the use of the Highland dress in Skye about 1791, the Rev. Mr. Martin of Kilmuir says, *"The common people still wear the Highland garb; and they adhere more closely to the ancient customs and manners than their superiors"*. We know,

however, that those in better circumstances did wear it during the latter half of the century, albeit only on ceremonial occasions and on Sundays, and even long before the law against the garb had been repealed it was worn in Skye, especially by those who favoured the Jacobite cause. Boswell describes the dress of Allan of Kingsborough, the husband of Flora MacDonald, as follows: *"A large blue bonnet, short brown coat, a tartan waist-coat with gold buttons, a bluish phillibeg, and with tartan hose"* (Boswell, J, 1955, p. 129). Some wore waistcoats with red flaps, and embroidered with gold lace; neither coat nor shirt having a collar.

The women of the upper classes dressed then much as they did elsewhere in Scotland. Gowns of dark silk were much in favour. The hair was drawn up tightly from the forehead, and made into a top-knot on the crown of the head, and it was profusely powdered. They covered the head with caps of muslin, fringed with deep flapping frills, and they were very fond of ornaments. Men were then, as at all times, ready to expose feminine foibles in dress. The Rev. A. Campbell, parish minister of Portree, writing in 1793, says, *"The women of Skye are excessively fond of dress, so that servants lay out all their wages that way"*.

The maiden was still distinguished by the snood, while the badge of matrimony, the curch, was then, as previously, worn (*'ghiulaineadh bréid, uallach gu féill,* – 'who would wear the coif jauntily to market', William Ross sings of them). These linen kerchiefs were manufactured locally, there being then several fields of flax, and a few weavers of linen on the island.

Means of Communication

Despite the large amount of intercommunication that existed between Skye and the Scottish mainland during the latter portion of the eighteenth century, there were then no roads as we know them now. Dr. Johnson says that when he made his memorable tour in 1773 there was not even a mark by which a stranger might find his way and he comments on the very indifferent tracks that then existed, thus: *"The way is so narrow that only one at a time can travel; and you cannot indulge in meditation by yourself, because you must always be attending to the steps which your horse takes"*. It is true that Pennant, who travelled in Skye two years previously, states that there was then, *"a good horse road between Kingsborough and Uig"* but that track, traces of which are still quite clear in places, was not a constructed road, being merely the beaten way that had been trodden for many a decade by numerous droves of cattle from the fertile lands of the north of Trotternish to the southern markets.

The first road contemplated for Skye was not decided on until the year 1799, when surveyors marked out a highway from Kylerhea, by Broadford, Sconser, and Bracadale, to the recently established fishing village of Stein, but it was not completed until the succeeding century. We know it was under construction between 1811 and 1820. It cost about £40,000 of which the bridge at Drynoch took £2,000 (MacLeod, RC, 1938, p. 115).

Towards the end of the eighteenth century several of our ministers deplore the lack of roads in the island. According to Rev. Roderick MacLeod of Bracadale, neither a 'turnpike' road nor a bridge had been built in his parish, and in Kilmuir a similar state of affairs obtained.

In a place where the coastline is so deeply indented as in the Isle of Skye, the lack of roads was not a serious deterrent to communication; for the people being skilful boatmen, much traffic was accordingly carried on by sea.

As early as 1751 Lady Margaret MacDonald had proposed the siting of a Post Office at Sconser, where was an inn, in which a considerable amount of business was then transacted.

(MacLeod, RC, 1939, Vol. II, p. 48).

It was known as *Taigh a' Phuirt* (*House of the Port*). Walker, writing in 1812, mentions the establishment of a Post Office in Stornoway in 1754, the only one in the North West Highlands and that, shortly after that year, another was opened at Dunvegan, between which and Stornoway, a packet-boat plied once a fortnight. (Walker, J, 1812). There was a small inn at Kylerhea and a tolerable one at Portree, where Johnson and his travelling companion had "dinner and praeterea nihil" (beyond which nothing) (Boswell, J, 1955, p. 128).

Diet

The potato had been introduced into Skye shortly after 1750 and by 1770 it had already become the principal article of food. Travellers, who visited the island about that time, make frequent mention of the large quantity of it that was consumed and the dependence of the people on it as their staple diet. *Dòmhnall nan Oran,* (Donald MacLeod), the Skye Bard, among others, sings its praises:

Thàinig fortan an aigh ort
    The grace of fortune is on you
Ni thu arach 'is Dotair.
    You are an encouragement and a doctor.
(MacLeòid, D, 1811, p. 99)

Owing, however, to the defective drainage of the soil, the quality of the crop was very inferior.

Brochan, or gruel, with oaten bannocks, still held a large place in their bill of fare and, when the potato crop failed, or the supply had become exhausted, this constituted their chief food.

A certain amount of fish was consumed in its season but the writers of the period deplore the small place that meat found in the people's menu; and they attributed the low state of vitality, that so often prevailed among the poor, to the lack of carbo-hydrates in their daily food. The flesh of the native sheep was highly nutritious and of savoury taste, and it was preserved for the winter by drying, as was also the flesh of the goat, but of these very little was used. It is a significant fact that the flesh of the pig, and of the eel, were both held in abhorrence by the people of Skye at that time.

Butter and cheese they had in fair abundance. The milk of cows, sheep, and goats was plentiful and they had firm faith in the virtues of the last, as is indicated by the proverb, *'Bainne nan gòbhar fo chòbhar 's e blàth, sud a chuir spionnadh 's na daoine a bhà'* – 'Milk of goats frothy and warm, was what put energy in the people of yore.' (Oral tradition). Bland, or fermented whey, was still a favourite drink, and a barrel of this healthful beverage was stored in every house.

It need not be wondered at that a people so dependent on what they themselves could raise should suffer great privations when the harvest proved a failure. A succession of unfavour-able seasons, and that was a frequent occurrence, had terrible consequences for the community so that, in the lean time of the year, many were faced with the prospect of starvation. Then they were driven to the shores, in hungry bands, to search for the shellfish, which, together with dulse soup, formed their sole means of subsistence for several weeks. Pennant observes:

> *Hundreds thus annually drag through the season a wretched life, and numbers unknown, in all parts of the West Highlands, fall beneath the pressure, some of hunger, more of putrid fever, the epidemic of the coasts, originating from the unwholesome food, the dire effect of necessity.*

Thus, during the years 1768 and 1769, the weather had been so bad that the scanty crops the people grew could not be secured; and again, in 1772 and 1773, there was such scarcity in Skye that the government was constrained to act; as much as 44 bolls of oatmeal were assigned in the latter year to the parish of Duirinish alone. MacLeod of Ullinish to MacLeod of MacLeod, 21 April, 1772, *"Things are awful, cattle dying in their thou-sands, the Poor living on carcases, no bread, no seed"* (MacLeod, RC, 1939, Vol. II, p. 10).

In the years 1778, and again in 1782, great want prevailed. The last was remembered in Skye for many a generation as *'Bli-adhna na Peasraich'*, when pease meal alone was procurable. We find that strong appeals were made next year to the chief of the MacLeods, and also to MacDonald, to lower the rents they had recently raised for, on the lands of the former, the tenants had lost *"one third of their cattle, which constituted their substance"*, owing to the severity of the previous winter.

A significant statement is made by Pennant, the author already quoted, when commenting on the vicissitudes of existence in our island. *"Golden seasons"*, he says, *"have happened, when they had a superfluity, but the years of famine are as ten to one"*.

In the homes of the tacksmen the food was varied, including oaten and wheaten bread, flesh, fish and plenty of eggs, butter and cheese. It was the custom then to serve cheese at almost every meal. In commenting on their entertainment in Raasay Boswell observes:

> *There was, among a profusion of other things, what I cannot help disliking at breakfast – cheese. It is the custom all over the Highlands to have it.*
>
> (Boswell, J, 1955, p. 117).

That they considered it a delicacy is shown by the fact that the food commonly offered to the wayfarer was bread, cheese and milk. The testimony of many notable travellers who then visited Skye witnesses that a competent portion of the good things of this life was purveyed in the houses of the higher ranks of society. *"He that shall complain of his fare in the Hebrides"*, says Dr. Johnson, *"has improved his delicacy more than his manhood"*, and, elsewhere, he remarks, *"If his good fortune brings the traveller to the residence of a gentleman in Skye, he will be glad of a storm to prolong his stay"*; while he was so impressed by the hospitality he had received, and the good cheer he had enjoyed, in the house of the Laird of Raasay, that he observed one day to Boswell, *"I know not how we shall get away"* (Johnson, S, 1984, p. 71).

Until the beginning of the following century the drinking of tea had not become a fixed habit in Skye though, in the houses of the tacksmen, the delicate Lilliputian china was produced on occasion and tea was drunk more for the purposes of ostentation than for its need as a stimulant. A considerable quantity of brandy and whisky was consumed and the latter, imported from Ferintosh, was sold by the bottle in many a shebeen.

So far as the drinking of intoxicants, however, was concerned, the people were then more temperate by far than they had been in the early part of the century. Johnson observes, *"The people of Skye are not a drunken race; at least, I never was present at much intemperance"*; while his fellow traveller, speaking of an entertainment in Raasay, says, *"We had a company of thirty at supper, and all was good humour and gaiety without intemperance"*. Yet the punchbowl was much in favour, as it remained for many years after this time in Skye, and we have only to point to the condition of our last authority, on the night of his return to Corrichatachain, to indicate the extent to which the men of that age indulged this symposial habit (Boswell, J, 1955, p. 183).

Manners of the People

From what has already been said, it will be concluded that the virtue of hospitality, which had characterised our people throughout the ages, had not suffered a decline. Travellers who visited Skye during the period under review give unstinted praise to this feature of our race. One of these, John Stanhope, with apparent enthusiasm, makes the suggestion that

> *a statue of hospitality should be placed upon this shore, holding out her hands to welcome strangers as they arrive. Here we seemed suddenly to have become the near relatives, or intimate friends, of every individual we saw; while I almost began to fancy we must have recently succeeded to the whole island and were come to take possession.*

And Pennant declares, *"They were hospitable to a high degree, and full of generosity"*, and no opportunity fails him to express his sense of gratitude at the kindness shown him wherever he went in Skye.

Dr. Johnson was similarly impressed by the warmth of his reception. Of Raasay House he writes:

> *Such a seat of hospitality amid the winds and the waters fills the imagination with a delightful contrariety of images. Without is the rough ocean and the rocky land, the beating billows and the howling storm. Within is plenty and elegance, beauty and gaiety the song and the dance. In Raasay, if I could have found a Ulysses, I had fancied a Phaeacia.*
>
> (Johnson, S, 1984, p. 80).

The disinterested manner in which the people helped those in distress was another pleasing trait that struck the imagination of the stranger. *"They have in themselves"*, says Pennant, *"a natural politeness and address that flows from the meanest when least expected"*; and Dr. Johnson says of the people of Raasay: *"More gentleness of manners, or a more pleasing appearance of domestic society, is not found in the most polished countries"*. Elsewhere he observes, in speaking of the people of Skye: *"Their* conversation is decent and inoffensive. I never heard a health offered by a Highlander that might not have circulated with propriety within the precincts of the king's palace", and this is the testimony of one who was not disposed to flattery (*ibid.*, p. 109).

Law and Order

Among the numerous changes that followed the rebellion of 1745, there came the abolition of the prerogative of the chiefs to administer justice. Though they had exercised that authority for several centuries, there is nothing on record to show, so far as Skye is concerned, that the chiefs had not carried out their obligations with wisdom and impartiality. But the government had decided that their power was now to be curtailed, and one way of weakening it, they thought, was to deprive them of the right of heritable jurisdiction. The place of these legal amateurs was henceforth to be taken by duly qualified administrators, who were to be responsible for the dispensation of justice in the particular district allocated to them.

The island of Skye had been officially administered from Inverness for many years; now a sheriff-substitute was installed in the island, armed with powers to settle disputes about property and to punish those guilty of petty crimes. One of the first to officiate in that capacity in Skye was Sheriff Alexander MacLeod of Ullinish, whose name is so well known as one of the hosts of Dr. Johnson and of Boswell during their tour in the Hebrides. His son Norman, mentioned by Boswell as a student at Aberdeen in 1772, was dead by 1812; *vide, Stewart's Grammar,* (Stewart, A, 1812, p. xxii), where he is called Captain Norman MacLeod of Ullinish.

The duties that fell to such an officer in Skye were then by no means arduous, for, according to the records of the time, cases of dishonest dealing were very infrequent. Writing in 1793, the Rev. Donald Martin of Kilmuir declares that *"crimes are*

rarely committed". He relates a pathetic incident that happened twenty-five years previously, in which a man had been caught in the act of stealing sheep. The thief offered a reward to those who detected him if they would keep the matter secret but, on their declining to give such a promise *"the wretch was found next morning hung to the roof of his own house"*. One of the few instances of crime at that time is recorded by the Rev. William Bethune, minister of Duirinish. He states that the people of his parish were *"peaceable and gentle"*, but that, in the year 1785, two families had been banished thence *"for the crime of cow-stealing"*.

Quarrels between individuals were, of course, frequent enough then, as they have been since. Long-standing family feuds were renewed at markets, marriages, and burials, where drink was consumed, but such incidents seldom, or never, went so far as to place the participants within the ambit of the law. It is a notorious fact that people would then suffer much before they would deign to avail themselves of the official form of justice for the redress of wrongs. Was it not a Skyeman who, on hearing that the long arm of the law had then stretched as far as Ross-shire, exclaimed, *"It behoves Christians to be wary for, if the Lord Himself does not check it, it will soon touch us here!"*

Until 'The '45', all who could afford it went about armed and they carried their weapons even to church. When the prohibition was introduced, they found it most difficult to conform to a regulation that forbade the arbitrament of the sword for the adjustment of any and every grievance. Johnson adverts to the case of the tenant of Scalpay at this time, who refused to pay the increased rent imposed on him by his landlord and, when Sir Alexander talked of forcing payment, or evicting him from the island, the tacksman *"declared his resolution to keep his ground, and to drive all intruders from the island; and he continued to feed his cattle, as on his own land, until it became necessary for* the sheriff to dislodge him by violence" (Johnson, S, 1984, pp. 109–10).

Farming

We have already seen that the boom in the sale of black cattle had led to a considerable appreciation in the price of land. Taking advantage of this state of affairs, the chiefs or, rather, their chamberlains gave the land to the highest bidder. That provided his opportunity to the man of wealth, with the result that multiple-farming became an established fact in Skye.

As it happened, however, that the occupiers of land had no security of tenure, nothing was done to develop the land or to conserve its resources. No attempt was made to erect enclosures, to construct drains, or even to apply manure to the soil, for the danger was always present that such improvements would enhance the value of the holding, and induce the landlord either to demand a higher rent, or to place the land once more on the market.

Through the activities of Lord Advocate Grant a law was passed about the year 1753, which proved to have far-reaching consequences. By it the principle of lease-holding was established; and among the numerous benefits that flowed from this enactment was the practice of enclosing lands; and a real endeavour was made to improve the quality of the soil. It was no unusual custom in Skye, before this time, to work the same land for several years without contributing anything to its renewal, with the result that the cultivated patches rapidly deteriorated until they were rendered sterile. Adverting to this wasteful system, the Rev. Malcolm MacLeod of Snizort declares that the gradual impoverishment of the soil had proceeded so far that it would yield no produce unless it were "*laid over with a thick coat of manure*". On the other hand, Dr Walker, writing in 1764, says: "*Crops of oats and bere without any other assistance than*

a covering of seaweed once every two years; yet they produce mighty crops reasonably free of weeds" (McKay, MM, 1980, p. 205).

The more progressive farmers took immediate advantage of their new security to begin the work of enclosing the arable land, and contemporary writers have left on record the beneficial results of their enterprise. Towards the end of the century the larger farms of Skye were almost all enclosed. In Kilmuir this work had been completed, and, according to the Rev. Donald Martin, who wrote in 1793, "*it had advantages of which all were sensible*". On the other hand, the Rev. Martin MacPherson, minister of Sleat, states that many farms in that parish were still open, "*and the land suffers much from poor drainage*".

It should be added that the advantages of this statute did not extend to smaller occupiers of land, and that these 'tenants at will' were removed on the most flimsy pretext, often without any reason being given at all, if another person were found who was prepared to give a higher rent for the holding.

During the time that the cultivated land was left unprotected, the labour of saving the growing crop from roving animals was a very exacting one. It was especially difficult at night, when the men of the township watched, two by two, throughout the seasons of growth and they were obliged to tender compensation for any damage that might accrue owing to their negligence.

Such portions of the pasture-land as lent themselves to enclosing with ease, e.g., peninsulas and tongues of land between the forks of rivers, were walled off for the purpose of folding cattle by night. The designation of these spaces was determined by the kind of animals that were kept in them. There was the '*buaile*' for the cattle, '*crò*' for the sheep, '*mannir*' for the goats and the '*marclan*' for the horses.

Certain parts of the pasture-land were then marked off for special purposes. Of such was the '*fàsach*' ('wilderness'), an uncultivated district, whose site and soil made it a suitable place for grazing during the winter and spring. The duty of watching these 'winter parks' usually devolved on the '*àireach*', or cattleman, of the farm, who remained in the hills for most of the year. As some of his perquisites he was provided with a house, grazing for two or three cows, a few sheep, and, if arable land were available, he was supplied with seed. When the crop was secured, he was allowed to retain half of it, the other portion going to his master. If there were milch cows in the herd, he was obliged to give his employer two stones of butter and four of cheese for each one under his charge. These men led a very lonely life, consigned, as most of them were, to remote regions for the greater part of the year. The lot of *Mac Ghille Chaluim's* cattleman on the island of Rona, where he was the only human occupant, must have been a trying one in the extreme (Johnson, S, 1984, p. 75).

An analogous calling, and one that was in certain cases synonymous with that of '*àireach*', was the work of the '*buachaille fàsaich*'. The latter was usually employed by a township for the purpose of ranging the '*fàsachs*' and keeping them clear of horses, sheep, and the younger cattle. He was also expected to fend marauding animals from off the arable land in the day-time during the seasons of growth.

Shortly after the seed was sown, and before the braird had appeared above ground, sheep, goats, and horses, together with the young and the farrow cattle, were driven to the hills. The day of clearing the arable lands was observed with much ceremony. Men, women, and children were out in force, and all took part in the 'drive'. On the way songs were sung, often of an invocatory nature; and many a wish was expressed when they arrived at the summer pasture. Then they partook of bread and cheese from last year's making ('*féisd na h-imrich*' 'feast of the removal')*; and the elders of the township asked a blessing on the stock, hoping for:

Laoigh bhalgfhionn bhoireann air gach fireach,
　White bellied female calves on every hill,
Piseach crodh na h-àirigh.
　The increase of the shieling cattle.

(Oral tradition)

About the middle of June a new movement of animals took place, when the milch cows and their calves were driven to the shieling-land. The most fertile spots among the hills were chosen as grazing ground whereon rude huts were constructed, both for the housing of the calves and for the accommodation of the young women, who then tended the cattle. The period of their sojourn on the '*àirigh*' (shieling) varied from six to eight weeks and, during that time, a considerable quantity of butter and cheese was made, while the ordinary pasture-ground of the cattle was given an opportunity to recuperate. The time spent on the shieling ground was a picturesque episode in the life of the people, and it seemed to touch the deepest springs of sentiment in their being. Hence it happens that some of the sweetest lyrics in our language have the life of the shieling for their theme.

Souming

The amount of stock each member of the community was entitled to put to pasture was clearly defined and stringently regulated. A wide choice was given as to what animals were to be grazed, and the equating of the various classes for this purpose ('*coilpeachadh*') was as follows: One horse = 2 cows = 16 calves = 16 sheep = 16 goats = 24 hoggs (yearling sheep) = 32 lambs = 32 geese. Any member whose stock exceeded the stipulated number was obliged to make contribution to the common lot, and this was divided equitably among those whose portion fell short of the authorised souming.

A statement of the stock raised on the island at that time is reserved until we come to deal with the general fauna of the island; but here it may be added that, on the larger farms, the average number of cattle reared was, according to an accredited authority, 50 cows, 20 heifers fit for bull, 30 three-year-old heifers, 35 of two years, and 40 yearlings. Of these, about 20 head were sold annually, at a price of about £2 5/– each. Pennant states that the rent of such a farm was £16 at the time of the last Jacobite rebellion, but that in his own day it had risen to £50.

The time for the laying out of farms entirely for sheep-pasturing had not yet arrived, so that, at this time, the number of sheep on the island was only about two-thirds of the stock of cattle.

Tillage

The runrig system of land tenure still prevailed in every township. The apportioned patches were assigned by lot, and a fresh allocation was made every three years. When the land was being divided, care was always taken to set aside a portion for the landless, and such allotments were known as *'cionagan nam bochd'*, or the plots of the poor. (A *cionag* equalled ¼ *cliteag* which was ¼ feorling or 'farthing-land').

Owing to the neglect of drainage, cultivation was generally carried out in long narrow strips running parallel with the slope of the land. These 'beds' were about two yards in width, and they were divided from each other by a trough about a foot deep and two feet wide. They were termed *'feannagan taomaidh'*, a species of multiple lazy-bed, and such a disposition of the soil ensured a dry bed for the growing crop. Potatoes were invariably grown in this manner, but such precautions were not always taken in the cultivation of their other crops. These consisted of small oats, barley, rye, and flax. The district of Kilmuir was then the granary of Skye, raising in favourable seasons *"excellent crops of oats and barley"*, the surplus of which was sold in the neighbouring parishes and even to the adjacent mainland.

It should be noted that the turnip had been introduced just at the end of this century and, according to Stanhope, who toured Skye in 1805, the *"crop promised well"*. The same writer adds that he saw *"one field of wheat"* that was being grown in the island of Scalpay. During the latter years of the century vast quantities of potato were grown, and this formed the principal article of food for half the year. In one parish as much as 5000 barrels of potatoes were raised in one season, while the yield of oats in the same district amounted to 1600 bolls. Pennant declares that, for the whole island, the quantity of corn produced *"in tolerable seasons"* was estimated to be 9000 bolls.

The produce was, however, very precarious for, as Rev. Malcolm MacLeod of Snizort declared in 1793, *"the crops of corn and potatoes are ample when the seasons are favourable; but, as is oftenest the case, there is great demand for imported meal"*. Indeed, the ministers of the island deplored, with one voice, the change in conditions that necessitated the importation of such large quantities of foreign food.

Attempts at haymaking were made at that time. But they were seldom successful. *"Their hay, which is got at the same time as their corn, at the end of September, is thoroughly bad"*, is the observation of Stanhope; while Dr. Johnson says, *"it is often a collection of withered stalks, without taste or fragrance; it must be eaten by cattle that have nothing else; and by most English farmers it would be thrown away."*

The principal implement used in tilling the ground was still the crooked spade, though a cumbersome form of wooden plough was also pressed into service. Of the latter, there were twelve in Sleat in the year 1793, and fifteen in the parish of Strath, and these numbers are approximately representative for the other parishes as well. This method of husbandry was a very tedious one. The plough was drawn generally by four horses, sometimes six, yoked abreast, and four men were required to attend to each team. There was the man who guided the implement, the driver who led the horses, and did so walking backwards, and two other men who were busily engaged in laying the upturned ground and dressing it before it could be in a fit state to receive the seed. The results that followed this manner of tillage were usually inferior to those yielded by the operation of the spade, so that we need not wonder at the prejudice that long existed in Skye, as elsewhere, against the use of the plough.

> *Leigidh mi as an t-sheisearach*
> I shall unyoke the team of six horses
> *'S an fheasgar a tarruing driuchd.*
> As the dew of the evening is falling.
> (Said to be from a song of *c.* 1640, composed to Donald *Gorm Og* of Sleat, and his son, Sir James).

An improvement was, however, effected in this implement when Small's swing plough was invented and it is noteworthy that the first specimen of that type to come to Skye was introduced by MacDonald of Lyndale in the year 1791.

The harrowing of the ground was done chiefly by the women; though the horse was sometimes used, the harrow, according to Pennant, being tied to the animal's tail.

In cutting the ripened grain the sickle was used for the oats, and its strokes were timed to the measure of the reaping song. The barley was secured by being pulled up by the roots. The woman was still the uncomplaining slave of her lord and master, her husband, and what drudgery was to be attended to she had to undertake. She reaped the corn while the men bound it in sheaves. The husband filled creels of farmyard manure, or of seaware, on a convenient boulder, and she carried them away and spread the material on the fields with an appropriate song on her lips. She was resigned to that manner of life for she would rather work her fingers to the bone than see a man degraded to such base toil. *"Haughtily indolent"*, says Mrs. Grant of Laggan, in speaking of Highlanders, *"they thought no rural employment compatible with their dignity, except perhaps the plough"*. Any other work 'spoiled the man', their women believed; and it must be admitted that a sneaking regard for that primitive tenet is even still existent in some parts of Skye.

Customs

Marriage

The two betrothals were still observed – *'an reiteach beag'*, when the parties became engaged, and *'an reiteach mór'*, when a final settlement was made as to the amount of dowry to be given, and other particulars. The *'tocher'* usually consisted of so many cows, the number varying from two to twenty, or even more, according to the substance of the donor.

The ceremony of betrothal was usually attended with much hilarity; and not a little bickering was often indulged in as the parents or the guardians of the contracting parties haggled over the amount of the marriage portion. These cavillings often developed into bitter recriminations when old sores were re-opened and fierce fights in consequence ensued.

On the morning of the wedding-day people gathered from wide areas, and the custom still prevailed whereby the guests were expected to bring their own provisions. The friends of the bride met in her home, those of the groom in his, and they were entertained separately. After the wedding the parties joined. The duration of the festivity depended on the amount of the commissariat, such functions being carried on sometimes for as long as three days.

On the first morning after the marriage, the bride's mother, or, failing her, the groom's, entered the bed-chamber and bound the bride's hair in the *'breid beannach'*, the pointed linen coif, before she left her bed. When the bride arose, she was dressed by the young ladies present and on the completion of her toilet a procession was formed, and her attendants marched out of the chamber, led by the bride herself. The first man to accost her on leaving the room was obliged to address her in verse, the greeting being termed, *'Beannachadh Bàird'*, or the 'Poet's Blessing'. This custom was honoured with strict insistence and few would care to shun the obligation. It is related by the 'Clans' Historian', Alexander Mackenzie, that on the occasion of the marriage of the Rev. Donald MacLeod of Duirinish, who afterwards became the third laird of Greshornish, poetic inspiration so failed the guests that none was prepared to offer the bride the customary salutation. As none would venture, and the young bride's arrival was due, the duty of performing the time-honoured ceremony devolved on the bridegroom himself; and his composition, though somewhat lengthy, is worthy of being quoted, owing to the beauty of its sentiment and its lofty moral tone:

Mile fàilte dhuit led' bhréid;
> A thousand welcomes to you in your coif;

Fad' do ré gun robh thu slàn.
> May health be yours throughout your life

Móran làithean dhut le sìth,
> With many days in peace,

Led' mhaitheas, is le d` ni bhi fàs.
> And, in your goodness, growth in your means.

A' chulaidh cheutach a chaidh suas
> The splendid headdress you have donned

'S tric a tharruing buaidh air mnaoi;
> Has often brought prosperity to a wife;

Bi-sa subhailceach, ceutach,
> Be thou virtuous and pleasing,

A thionnsgain thu féin 's an strì.
> On entering upon your trial.

An tùs do còmhraidh is tu òg,
> At the beginning of your talk in your youth,

An tùs gach lò iarr Dia nan Dùl;
> And in the morning of your day, seek thy God;

'S chan eagal nach dean thu gu ceart
> And there will be no fear but you will do the right

Gach dearbh bheachd a bhios 'nad rùn.
> In each resolve in your regard.

Bi-sa fialaidh, ach bi glic,
> Be generous but be wise,

Bi misneachail, ach bi stòld.
> Be courageous but be calm.,

Na bi bruidhneach, 's na bi bàlbh,
> Be not talkative but be not dumb

Na bi mear, no marbh, 's tu òg.
> Be not wanton or vapid when young.

Bi gleidhteach air do dheagh rùn;
> Be guarded about your good intentions;

Ach na bi dùinte, 's na bi fuar,
> But be not silent or cold,

Na labhair air neach gu h-olc,
> Speak no ill of any one,

'S ged labhrar ort, na taisbein fuath.
> And though you be vilified show no anger.

Na bi gearanach fo chrois;
> Complain not of difficulties

Falbh socrach le cupan làn.
> Move steadily with a full cup.

Chaoidh do'n olc na tabhair spéis,
> Never show favour to wickedness,

'S le do bhréid ort – mìle fàilt.
> And with your coif a thousand welcomes.

(MacKenzie, A, 1889, pp. 226–7)
(See Carmichael, A, 1928, Vol. II, p. 214 for a
version bearing a close resemblance to this one).

Burials

Funeral ceremonies also were attended with much feasting and consumption of strong drink. The eve of the interment was often made the occasion of riotous merrymaking and, strange as it may appear, those attending the 'wake' indulged in such an unseemly practice as dancing, which they kept up till the morning.

As the body was being carried to the churchyard, the halting-places on the way were marked by those cairns that in the past were such common features along the beaten tracks. A concourse of women still followed the cortege, chanting the melting strains of the *coronach* – a poignant spectacle as the sad procession slowly wended its way across the moorlands to the 'everhouse' of the dead.

It was considered dishonourable to the deceased if the supply of food and drink were in any way stinted and, so great was the quantity of liquor and eatables consumed during the obsequies that the nearest relatives were often reduced to such poverty that they were not able to recover from it for several years. Immediately the interment was over, the mourners were formed into rows around the grave and drinking was resumed, *"so that"*, as the Rev. A. Clark of Duirinish observes in 1841, in speaking of the customs of the previous century, *"the people forgot the sacredness of the place and the solemnity of the occasion, and were soon engaged in renewing old feuds and fighting fiercely amid the graves of their ancestors"*.

Domestic Customs

The ceilidh was then one of the principal institutions in the island; and he who could best relate the heroic tale, or recite the ancient barderie, was the person most respected among those who frequented the meeting. People were then very fond of dancing, and the singing of the traditional song was an art in which all would wish to excel. Despite their trials they were a happy people and their songs helped to lighten their hard lot. Every form of labour was accompanied by its appropriate strain. Thus, *'iorrams'*, or rowing songs, were common and Pennant tells us that, when he was being taken to view *Stac an Fhùcadair*, the boatmen sang *"songs that are solemn and slow and have a religious turn consonant to that people"*. Likewise, as Dr. Johnson was crossing from Skye, mention is made of the *'iorram'* as being sung by the oarsmen on the way to Raasay. The same authority adverts to the pleasure it gave him, when he landed on the latter island, to hear the melodious voices of the reapers as they cut and bound the grain in a field by the shore.

For the operation of spreading the manure on the fields they had special songs, whose measures closely suited the action. They also had their quern songs, their churning songs, their milking songs, the numbers of which were respectively as numerous as those more persistent ones associated with the fulling of the cloth. That operation is not even yet wholly extinct in Skye, and in its modern form it consists of rubbing the cloth, that has been treated with ammoniated liquid, by a party of young maidens. The number varied from six to twelve, or, on rare occasions, even more, and they moved the cloth rhythmically forward and sideways, so that, by the latter movement, the whole piece was made to go interminably round a long platform close to which the women sat, an equal number on each side. For several generations the work was done solely by the hands; but during the period under review the feet were sometimes brought into action to relieve the hands temporarily of the labour. In a print in Pennant's *'Tour'*, depicting the work of fulling, we see a band of women, sitting along two sides of a table, on which they are engaged in fulling the cloth by their bare feet, and it deserves notice that the surface, on which the cloth is laid, is prominently corrugated after the manner of a washing-board, in order, presumably, to accelerate the operation of thickening the web. The maidens vied with one another in the singing and also in the extemporising of the waulking songs. Their labour over, after they had washed and dined, and the barn in which they had worked was cleared, they danced into the morning to the thrilling strains of the bagpipe.

The Bagpipe

That instrument was still in constant practice. On account, however, of the measures adopted after 'The '45', its influence was now appreciably on the wane. *"I have had my dinner exhilarated by the bagpipes at Armadale and at Dunvegan"*, says Dr. Johnson; and he elsewhere observes: *"The college of pipers under the direction of MacCrimmons is not quite extinct"* (Johnson, S, 1984, p. 107). There can be no doubt, however, that the playing of this instrument was even then showing signs of falling into desuetude and, as we have already seen, the long and illustrious succession of MacCrimmon pipers terminated about the year 1776, when their freehold was taken over by the chief. The MacArthurs, too, had fallen on evil days, and the last of the line, by name Angus, died in London about the beginning of the nineteenth century. In Raasay, however, the Mackays still continued in their office of pipers to *Clann 'ic 'ille Chaluim*, and their prestige was maintained at a high level. In 1792, John MacKay of Raasay won the Gold Medal of the Highland Society of London, the premier award for piping (Mackay, A, 1838, p. 16).

The Fixing of Boundaries

Before the days of dykes and fences a very curious and cruel custom was observed at this time in our island. When the work of delimiting the marches between the owners of neighbouring properties was in dispute, several representatives from both farms were gathered together and heaps of stones were raised at intervals to mark the boundaries, in accordance with the decision of two men who acted as umpires for the interested parties. When the exact position of the boundary had been fixed, two young lads were severely scourged with thongs, so that they should not forget the scene of the agreement! Pennant says that, when he travelled in Skye in 1770, *"the last thus used is now a pensioner of Sir Alexander MacDonald"*.

A pleasing custom, betokening friendship between the chiefs, is recounted by Dr. Johnson. The contracting parties to this observance were the Houses of Raasay and of Sleat, and it consisted in the bequeathing of the sword of the deceased chief of one clan to the keeping of the living chief of the other, and the practice had been honoured for about two hundred years. He further avers that the sword of Sir James MacDonald, who died in 1766, was thus conferred on John MacLeod, who was Chief of Raasay when Dr. Johnson visited the island.

Graddaning

This ruinous method of making meal prevailed in Skye until the very end of the nineteenth century. Several of the writers of the *'Old Statistical Account'* for the island declare it was practised in their parishes even as late as 1793, and the Rev. Archd. Clark, who in 1841 wrote the *'New Statistical Account'* for the parish of Duirinish, says *"it is not more than thirty years since graddaning was departed from"*. Most people deplored the continuance of the wasteful habit, and, apropos it, Dr. Johnson comments:

"With the genuine improvidence of savages, they destroy the fodder for the want of which their cattle perish". In corroboration of this observation, the Rev. A. Clark, whose allusion to the practice has already been quoted, states, "I have it on undoubted authority that a tacksman, who died a few years ago, a man of wealth and information, who used to quote the 'Georgics' and passages from 'Horace' over his wine, allowed, just thirty years ago, ten milch cows to die of starvation while he had six stacks of corn reserved in the barnyard for 'min ghradain' " (meal made from corn, parched by burning the straw in the sheaf). Sir James McDonald of Skye prohibited the making of meal by the process of 'gradanning' in 1765 and, according to Prof Walker, other proprietors followed suit. (Walker J, 1812, Vol. 2, p. 370).

Superstitions

The time for commencing any new undertaking was still determined by the phases of the moon. The seed they sow in the moon's increase; the reaping of the grain is begun only when it is in its wane. This superstition has been persistent down the years and it cannot be said to have died even yet.

Reference has been made to the 'gruagach' cult in preceding sections and it is a noteworthy fact that the superstition prevailed in Skye until the end of the nineteenth century. The Rev. Alex MacGregor, writing in the 'New Statistical Account for the Parish of Kilmuir', says that, even as late as the year 1770, dairymaids observed the rite of pouring libations of milk into the hollow of the 'gruagach' stone on the island of Troday on Mondays, in the hope that that genius would watch over their cattle, and ensure the milk supply from being filched away during the ensuing week.

Their system of therapeutics, in connection with the diseases of animals, is highly interesting, and, although it also has already been touched upon in earlier chapters, a few instances are given here to show the survival of strange beliefs among our people. Flint arrow-heads were carefully preserved, because of their alleged efficacy as a means of curing various diseases. They were believed to be bolts shot by fairies at the cattle and, acting on the principle of curing "by the hair of the dog that bit him", the animal was made to drink water in which these ancient weapons had been steeped, if the trouble was internal; while, if the injury was external, the affected part was rubbed with the arrow-head. Belemnites and ammonites, too, were used from their supposed curative properties, while the head of a snake was held to be a specific antidote against adder-stings. The last was placed in contact with the wound and it was supposed to abate the swelling and absorb the poison. So strong was the belief in this manner of treatment that we find, as late as the end of the eighteenth century, a parish minister, a scholar and a man of affairs, placing full credence in its virtue. It was still in use even towards the end of the succeeding century, and the writer was an eye-witness of its application to a young heifer, supposed to be suffering from snake-bite. After the traditional remedy had been applied for some time the swelling ultimately subsided, and the animal made a complete recovery. Post hoc et proper hoc!

People still made periodic pilgrimages to the ancient chapel on Fladda Chuain, which contained a round bluish stone that was held in deep veneration. Three times they walked round it sunwise, to procure a favourable wind, or a good catch of herring, and a drop or two of the water that exuded from it was supposed to cure all ills (Martin, M, 1716, pp. 166–7).

A form of divination, known as 'Taghairm', was then practised on rare occasions in Skye. Its purpose was to determine the course of future events, and even to shape them to the advantage of the diviners through the mediation of demons. Two persons, at least, were essential as participants in this repellent ceremony, the scene of which was usually a secluded cave in the rocks by the shore. According to Pennant, the rendezvous of the last rite of

EMIGRATION FROM THE ISLE OF SKYE.—"THE HERCULES" IN THE HARBOUR OF CAMPBELTON.

Figure 3.1 The ship *Hercules* left Campbeltown on 26 December 1852, carrying 756 emigrants from Skye, Harris and North Uist.

Figure 3.2 Angus Stewart from Peinachorrain, Braes was the author's great uncle. Stewart was the first person to give evidence to the Napier Commission of 1883. His evidence was heard in the church at Ollach in Braes.

MEETING OF CROFTERS: JOHN MACPHERSON SPEAKING.

Figure 3.3 The Illustrated London News of December 1884 depicted a meeting in Glendale which was addressed by John MacPherson, 'the Glendale Martyr'. This meeting contravened the Landlord's decree that an assembly of more than three people constituted a riot and those attending were liable to summary eviction.

Figure 3.4 Charles Reid of Wishaw took many wildlife photographs and he gave lectures to the Edinburgh Photographic Society on animal and bird photography in 1882, 1890 and 1896. He must have spent some time on Skye as a number of views, including this one, depict scenes of the island. This one shows the entrance to Portree harbour, the Sound of Raasay and a 'steamer' heading north.

"Crossing the Sea to Skye"

Figure 3.5 An early ferry crossing from Kyle of Lochalsh to Skye.

Figure 3.6 Mary MacPherson or *Màiri Mhòr nan Oran* (Big Mary of the Songs) was a celebrated bard particularly associated with the land struggle in Skye and elsewhere. She was born in Skeabost in 1821. Mary eventually moved to Glasgow where she trained as a nurse and worked until 1882. While living there, she regularly attended Highland Society ceilidhs and met leading advocates of Highland land reform. She became well known in these circles for her poetry and songs. When she returned to Skye, she was Bard of the Land League agitation of the 1880s. Her personal sense of injustice and empathy with the sufferings of her people gave a unique force to her poetry. She died in Portree in 1898.

Figure 3.7 This fine sandstone building stood on the site of the present Portree High School. Sadly it was demolished in the early 1970s when a new school was built. The latter building has since been demolished to make way for the present High School.

Figure 3.8 A 'Puffer' and a paddle streamer at Portree Pier. Puffers were traditional coastal trading boats that plied the west coast of Scotland. They had flat bottoms to allow them to be beached on islands with no quay. The Puffer would then be unloaded at low tide and re-floated at high tide to sail off to the next port of call.

Figure 3.9 A postcard of Portree viewed from the southern approaches to the village. The wooded area above the district now called Bayfield (originally, *An Sligneach*) is that of *Meall na h-Acarseid*, or the hill of the harbour, which hosts the annual Highland Games. More colloquially, *Am Meall* is called 'The Lump'.

Figure 3.10 Kyleakin was for many years the principal ferry port for Skye. Since the building of the Skye Bridge its former importance to the economy of the island has diminished.

Herring Fishing at Portree, Skye

J. G. Mackay, Portree.

Figure 3.11 Fishing boats alongside Portree Pier.

Figure 3.12 A George Washington Wilson image of Portree. This view is of the same general area as depicted in Fig 3.11 but taken from the other side of the bay. ©Mark Butterworth – George Washington Wilson Archive

this kind took place in the cave behind the waterfall at Berreraig, in Scorrybreck. There a fire was lit and, while one of the actors was busily engaged in roasting cats alive, one after another, until by their screaming, he should succeed in attracting a contingent of demons, the other, attired in a cow's hide, was obliged to try to coerce the evil spirits to propitiate the future for the partners in this nefarious act (Henderson, G, 1911, pp. 267–9).

The Church

During the latter half of the eighteenth century, the Presbyterian form of worship had succeeded in consolidating its position firmly in Skye. It is true that in those parishes, as, for example in Strath, where the Jacobite cause was strong, several of the leading families still adhered to Episcopacy; but, from about 1775, the Scottish Church began to make progress even there. Before the end of the century there remained but a few adherents of the English Church. Thus, in the whole of the parish of Bracadale, there were only two families of Episcopalians in the year 1791. There was about the same number then in the parish of Duirinish; while in Kilmuir, with the exception of two or three who belonged to the Roman Catholic Church, all were Presbyterians. In the parishes of Snizort and Portree all the people were of the latter persuasion and a similar situation obtained in Sleat.

The clergy of Skye at this time were men who were imbued with a genuine zeal for their lofty calling. Endowed with native ability of a very high order, their earnest desire for learning, and their ripe scholarship, excited at once the wonder and the admiration of all strangers who happened to sojourn in their midst. Such an astute observer and keen student of humanity as Dr. Johnson, ardent Episcopalian though he was, says of the ministers of Skye:

I saw no pastor there whom I had reason to think either deficient in learning or irregular in life; but I found several with whom I could not converse without wishing, as my respect, that they had not been Presbyterians.

Pre-eminent among these estimable men was Rev. Donald MacQueen, minister of the parish of Kilmuir, where he succeeded the Rev. Kenneth Bethune about the year 1740. This man of high character and wide learning, is reputed to have been one of the most cultured divines of his day. He was a stout protagonist of those who championed the authenticity of MacPherson's '*Ossian*' and, among his other works, he wrote '*A Dissertation on the Government of the People of the Western Isles*'. For the long period of forty-five years he ministered to the spiritual and moral needs of his parish and he was untiring in his efforts to uproot the prevailing superstitions. He will always be remembered as the constant associate of Dr. Johnson, when that great writer visited Skye. He died in Raasay in the year 1785, when he was succeeded by the saintly Donald Martin. The latter was of the family of Marishader and was educated at Aberdeen, of whose university he was a graduate in Arts. The Rev. Mr. Martin served this parish for about twenty-two years and he left Skye for Inverness in the first decade of the following century. His stipend was £80 a year. In 1770, the Presbytery of Skye threatened an action if stipends were not paid and among the Dunvegan papers, we read that the Minister of Glenelg '*was very angry that his stipend was unpaid*' (MacLeod, RC, 1939, Vol. II, p. 8). Towards the end of the eighteenth century, the old church of Kilmuir, built about 1600, was in a dilapidated condition, and in 1810 a new church, the present one, was built on an exposed position near the shore of Score Bay.

The Rev. Donald MacQueen of Kilmuir had a brother, William, who was minister of Snizort. The latter was the fourth

generation of the same family to serve this parish, where he became assistant to his father, the Rev. Archd. MacQueen, in the year 1747. He was ordained minister of the parish in 1754, the year before his father's death. Like his brother, Donald, he was a man of deep culture and outstanding gifts of oratory – qualities that, combined with a rich vein of humour, earned for him the high regard of his parishioners. He died in 1787, in the 69th year of his age and he was succeeded by the Rev. Malcolm MacLeod in 1788. *'Maighstear Calum'* was a son of *Mac Ghille Chaluim 'Camachasach'* (the MacLeod of Raasay of 'The '45') by a second marriage with a vassal's daughter, Janet MacLeod, better known as *Bantighearna Dhubh Osgaig*. He was a graduate of Aberdeen and is described in a contemporary record as, *"in breeding and in manners, as well as in descent, a gentleman of the old school"*.

The church of Snizort was in such a ruinous state in 1793 that it was no longer used as a place of worship and the minister was without a church or manse. When he married Mary, daughter of Donald MacLeod of Suardal, the hereditary armourer to the Chief of Dunvegan, he was constrained to rent a farm in order to provide a dwelling-house for his family. The ruins of his house in Glen Haultin may still be seen.

In fact, only two of the ministers of Skye at that time were supplied with manses and they were Rev. Donald Martin of Kilmuir and Rev. Roderick MacLeod of Bracadale. The manse of the latter was built in 1789; that of the former in 1778, and it was the first of its kind on the island. Among the Dunvegan papers is a letter from Talisker to MacLeod of MacLeod, saying that the appointment of Mr Rory MacLeod to Bracadale was very unpopular (MacLeod, RC, 1939, Vol. II, p. 7).

About the middle of the century, the Rev. William MacLeod was ordained minister of Bracadale. He was the brother of Sheriff Alexander MacLeod of Ullinish and he had been translated

hither from Barra. He left Skye in 1767, when he was called to Campbeltown. His successor was Rev. Roderick MacLeod, who came from Harris. The Rev. Roderick was a man of wide learning, a fact that was recognised by his university, which conferred on him the degree of Doctor of Divinity. He is described as *"eminently zealous in the work of his Master"* and did one know of him but his contribution to the *'Statistical Account'* for his parish, one would gather that he was a man imbued with lofty principles. On alternate Sundays he preached in Eynort, where a large community then resided. The old church, built on the ruins of the chapel there, was *"in a very ruinous state"* in 1791. The Rev. Dr. Roderick continued as minister of the parish until his death in 1812.

In 1752 died the Rev. John MacLeod, minister of Duirinish, a new incumbent being appointed two years afterwards, in the person of Rev. Donald MacLeod, M.A., who had been translated from North Uist. This was a man of lofty ideals and outstanding ability for, it was said of him, shortly after his death, that

he adorned his profession, not so much by his literary merit, of which he possessed a considerable share, as by the constant practice of the most useful and exalted virtues. To do good was the ruling passion of his heart, in composing differences and diffusing the spirit of peace and friendship.

He was a poet of outstanding power, though little has been preserved of his works beyond one piece, *'Beannachadh Bàird'*, to which allusion has already been made. This good Christian was succeeded, in 1762, by Rev. James Nicolson, M.A., who, after serving the parish for four years, went to Sutherland. In 1767 the Rev. William Bethune, of the famous family of physicians and divines, was appointed to the parish. He was a son of Rev. Kenneth Bethune, minister of Kilmuir, and the grandson of the Rev. John Bethune of Bracadale. The Rev. William was a man of scholarly parts and sterling character. As we have seen already, he formed one of the party that entertained Dr. Johnson and his companion during their memorable tour in 1772. It was he who compiled the *'Old Statistical Account'* for his parish, which he continued to serve until his retirement in 1810. He died in 1814 in his 76th year.

In a previous section we have seen that the first minister of the newly-constituted parish of Portree was Rev. Hugh MacDonald, who died in 1756 (MacDonald, A & A, 1904, p. 324). In that year he was succeeded by the Rev. John Nicolson, who was of the famous tacksmen of Scorrybreck. For the long period of forty-three years, 'Mr. John' continued to render faithful and ungrudging service to his flock, ministering to their spiritual and temporal needs with earnestness and zeal, enduring hazards and discomforts in a manner that shows him to have been a man possessed of a noble sense of duty and very high ideals.

A man of exemplary life, sincere, benevolent, of such untainted rectitude, and of such indefatigable perseverance in discharging his pastoral duties that, being appointed to preach in Raasay every month, and once a quarter in another part of Skye, he did not fail to do so above four times during his long incumbency, till the spring of 1795, when he met with an accident which dislocated his shoulder and confined him to his house.

He was a man of great independence of mind and anecdotes are still related in Skye by way of illustrating this phase of his character. By him gentle and semple were treated with equal respect and such a person was bound to give offence to those who expected to be favoured with special deference. Such, for example, was the regard then shown by ministers, especially to the chiefs, that Stanhope says:

The minister prayed for him (the chief) and recommended him to the care of the Almighty, less as a petition, than as though he were admonishing the Deity on no account to neglect a primary duty.

It would appear that 'Mr. John' paid little attention to this form of entreaty and, knowing well this characteristic of his minister, Alexander, the first Lord MacDonald, once banteringly pointed out, after a service in Portree, that he had omitted to make special mention of his chief in his prayers. The reminder brought no apologies from this stalwart divine, who, with his customary imperturbability, observed:

You, I have always in my thoughts, as I have other members of my flock and in my prayers I fail not to include Your Lordship in the great company of sinners.

This minister of powerful personality and striking appearance, died at the ripe age of ninety-two, in the last year of the century, when he was succeeded by Rev. Alexander Campbell, who had been schoolmaster and catechist in Portree since 1791.

In Strath, the Rev. Donald MacLeod died in 1749, and in the following year he was succeeded by Rev. Donald Nicolson, who, for twenty-nine years, served this parish with earnestness and wisdom. He has been described as a man of uncommon probity and goodness. His successor, who was presented to the charge by George III, was Rev. Donald Mackinnon, a graduate in Arts of the University of Aberdeen. For the phenomenal period of sixty-five years as an ordained clergyman this great and good man, the first of an illustrious line, dedicated 52 years of his life to the service of his native parish. At the age of ninety years he retired, in the full confidence that the work on which he had laboured so long would be faithfully continued by his second son, the Rev. John Mackinnon, who succeeded him in 1826. The

Rev. Donald died in 1831, in his ninety-sixth year, with all his faculties unimpaired.

The scholarly Dr. John MacPherson served the adjacent parish of Sleat until 1764 and in the following year his son, Martin, became the minister. The latter had been educated both at Aberdeen and Edinburgh. Like his father, he, too, was a man of ability and an earnest student of the classics. Boswell describes him as a man of intelligence and taste, while Dr. Johnson was delighted with the magnificent library in the farmhouse occupied by the minister at Ostaig. There the famous travellers were constrained to stay for five days, owing to unfavourable weather conditions, but such was the nature of their entertainment that they suffered never a moment of dulness until they left the island – on a Sunday! The ruins of his house may still be seen near the branch road to Tarskavaig, a short distance from the point where it leaves the main road of Sleat. The lady of the manse was a daughter of Mackinnon of Corrie. For the long period of forty-seven years the Rev. Martin MacPherson served this parish and, in recognition of his work there, and his ripe scholarship, the University of Aberdeen conferred on him the degree of Doctor of Divinity. He died in 1812, at the age of sixty-nine years.

Some quaint usages were still observed by the Church. Human bones were placed on window-sills, or in recesses in the walls of the church. Boswell states that in the church of Clachan, in Raasay, were to be seen *"human bones of an uncommon size"*, while Rev. Alexander MacGregor tells us that the skull and thigh bones of that man of hapless fame, *Uisdean MacGhilleasbuig Chléirich*, were preserved on view in the church of Kilmuir until the year 1827, *"when they were again consigned to the dust"*. From the comments made by unbiased observers on this custom, one is forced to the conclusion that it savoured rather of a foolish pride in the strength of their forbears than of a genuine desire to advance those matters that pertained to the glory of God.

That the Church wielded a powerful sway is shown by the disciplinary measures that were then put into practice against such as were guilty of breaches of the Moral Law. Among many other forms of punishment administered to those who fell from grace was the strange one of condemning an adulterer to stand in a barrel of cold water at the door of the church before and throughout the service. The severity of this amusing form of penance was sometimes tempered, when the culprit was allowed, instead, to stand on a seat, in full view of the congregation, dressed only in a wet canvas shirt!

Education

In a previous section mention was made of the high degree of culture that prevailed, especially among the upper classes of Skye, in the early part of the eighteenth century. During the remainder of that century the love of learning had suffered no decline; rather had it grown to such an extent that it was no uncommon incident during this period to hear conversations carried on in Latin in the houses of the tacksmen, when it was thought desirable, to keep the matter under discussion a secret from the servants. These accomplishments excited the wonder and the admiration of all such as appreciated learning for its own sake. *"I believe"*, said General Stewart of Garth, *"it is rather unique for the gentry of a remote corner to learn Latin, yet so it was in Skye"*. At Corriechatachain, Dr. Johnson observed to Boswell, *"one of the remarkable things of Skye is that there are so many books in it"*; but, what especially aroused his surprise was that in every house he found books in more languages than one. *"Literature"*, says he, *"is not neglected by the higher ranks of the Hebrideans"*; while one of our own ministers, the Rev. Donald Martin of Kilmuir, writing about 1790, remarks: *"The principal farmers are well educated and well informed"*.

Nor did they neglect the literature of their own race. The MacDonald chiefs still maintained the office of laureate, on whom they conferred, among other perquisites, lands free of all exactions. Thus, to one, Duncan MacRury, who held the post of family bard, they allotted 5 bolls of meal, 5 stones of cheese, and 25/- in wages for a year, in addition to his freehold. MacRury was succeeded in the laureateship by the renowned poet, John MacCodrum, who was the last to hold this position of privilege under the MacDonalds of Skye and North Uist (Watson, WJ, 1922, p. 197).

Such was the encouragement given to the native culture, in face of a bitter opposition that sought, by overt and covert means, to stamp out all that was distinctive of the people of the Highlands. Their language was assailed from all sides. Its use was forbidden as a means of instruction in the schools and many went so far even as to advocate the proscription of the Gaelic version of the Scriptures in order, as they thought, that no monument would remain of the ancient tongue.

In the year 1750, the Committee for the Management of the Royal Bounty allocated a sum of £25 per annum to an instructor who was to act in the dual capacity of teacher and catechist in the district of Trotternish. Sir James MacDonald, the scholarly chief, decided to erect a school in Portree; and, according to Rev. Alexander Campbell, who had been schoolmaster there before he became the minister of the parish, *"a large and commodious school was built"*. To it pupils were attracted from all parts of the island; and, when he wrote in 1793, he says *"three were ready for college"*. Those who were there as boarders paid from £3 to £4 10/- a quarter, and to that sum was added a fee of 2/6 for instruction. The number of pupils in attendance varied with the season, being often double in winter what it was in summer. Mr. Campbell, who was the son of a tacksman of Corlarach, near Dunvegan, was appointed schoolmaster in 1791.

In Sleat, the parochial schoolmaster during the major portion of this period was a certain James Beverley, a native of Aberdeen, and he was held in high repute in the district. The school population there varied from twenty-five to forty, and the teacher's salary amounted to £25 a year. It may be mentioned that a spring in that part of Skye is still known as *'Tobar Bheb-herli'* (*'Beverley's Well'*), after this famous dominie.

In the parish of Strath the number of children attending school towards the end of the century ranged from thirty in summer to sixty during the winter months, and the wage paid to the schoolmaster there was £22 a year. In Snizort there was no parish school at that time.

The Housing of the People

The housing of the people was then not much worse than it was even for a century after this time. It is true that there were still some of the turf dwellings, in which the walls were composed of blocks of earth, bound together by wattles, and the roof covered with divots and thatched with heath, fern, or rush. Such erections became grass-grown after a few years and, at a distance, could not be distinguished from the natural mounds that surrounded them. They were still to be seen in 1774, and they probably continued to be occupied until a later date.

The vast majority of dwelling-houses were, however, built of stone. They consisted really of two parallel walls, with a wide intervening space that was packed either by earth or by a mixture of earth and rubble, to make the walls draught-proof. The back wall was often single, as the house was built into the face of a declivity. The roof was made of couples and rafters covered with divots thatched after the manner of the turf-huts, and all bound by ropes of heather, with 'anchors' of stone attached as weights to their ends; so that the houses looked, as Boswell graphically observes, *"like a lady's hair in papers"*.

Owing to its thickness, a wide extent of the top of the wall was left uncovered, an architectural device calculated to deflect the wind's full force from the somewhat loose and light material of the roof. Such a plan was not, however, without many inconveniences, for this projecting portion acted as a catchment area for the drip from the roof so that runnels of water often percolated the walls and found their way into the inside of the house. Then, again, it soon came to be so overgrown with grass that animals, such as sheep, goats and even cattle, were tempted to graze there, because of the easy access from the back. In their perambulation they sometimes glissaded from the narrow ledge and broke their limbs or, as often happened, when the larger animals endeavoured to turn in such a narrow space they went right through the roof, to the danger of their own lives and those of the inmates of the house.

The houses were lit only by the door and the smoke-hole, the windows, if any existed, being filled with bags of straw or divots of earth, except in fine weather. The doorway was seldom placed in the middle of the wall but was much nearer one end of the house than the other. It is thus evident that ventilation was very defective and since, in the vast majority of cases, cattle occupied that portion of the house nearest the door, and were the first to use the ingoing air, the atmosphere breathed by the humans was dangerously vitiated before it reached their quarters.

In most of these houses there were no partitions of any kind. The floor of the portion occupied by the cattle was invariably hollowed to a depth of about two feet below that of the human occupants of the house, in order that the animal litter might there accumulate, ferment and mature, and thus have its fertilising virtues unimpaired by the rains of winter. Besides, this internal cesspool was the repository for all manner of domestic refuse, which added its noisomeness to that of cattle, horses, and poultry. Through this mushy waste lay the way to the quarters occupied by the people themselves!

This consisted of one long uninterrupted chamber, dim even by day, and darker by night when the cruisie shed its feeble ray and diffused its fishy smell throughout the gloomy hall. The fire was placed on a raised hearth in the middle of the floor and health was safeguarded by the all-pervading peat-reek, begriming everything, it is true, but, at the same time, effectually sterilising and deodorising the unwholesome atmosphere. As the floor consisted only of the bare earth, it was often softened to a mire in wet weather.

The more pretentious tacksmen lived in cottages, with walls cemented by lime, with glazed windows and boarded floors, but roofed with thatch for, according to Thomas Pennant, *"there was not above two or three slated houses"* in the island of Skye in the year 1770.

Population

During the half-century under review, the population of Skye had increased by leaps and bounds. No official records were, of course, kept in those days, but, on a careful computation of all the available data, it is no exaggeration to say that the increase was almost 30 per cent. during a period of thirty-five years, from 1755 to 1790. In the former year the total population of the island was about 11,200; in the latter it had risen to 14,400.

Appended is the population of the several parishes of Skye in 1755, 1764 and 1790, respectively:

Parish		1755 (Dr. A. Webster)	1764 (Prof. J. Walker)	1790 (Sinclair)		Percentage increase
Strath	...	943	1200	1579	...	67
Sleat	...	1250	1848	1788	...	43
Portree	...	1385	1466	1980	...	43
Kilmuir	...	1572	1900	2065	...	31
Duirinish	...	2568	3600	3000	...	17
Bracadale	...	1907	3333	2250	...	18
Snizort	...	1608	1700	1808	...	12
Total	...	11,233	15,047	14,470		

These figures are, of course, only rough approximations, and it is evident that there was no uniformity in the methods employed to arrive at an accurate estimate. Thus the Rev. Alexander Campbell states that the population, as given for the parish of Portree in 1790, and estimated *"after the exactest inquiry"*, represented the *"total number of souls"*; while in the parish of Strath the figures given for the same year are exclusive of children under *"nine years of age"*. All those who were responsible for the compilation of the Statistical Account, already quoted, advert to the remarkable increase in the population. The Rev. William Bethune of Duirinish affirms that the old men in his parish declare that lands *"which lay waste for lack of men to occupy them"* within their own recollection, were then densely populated; and it is noteworthy that the increase in the parish of Sleat was so very marked, despite the toll taken of its population by *"emigration and repeated drains to the army"*, according to the Rev. Martin MacPherson. All are unanimous in attributing the cause of the increase in the population to the preservation of life, consequent on the introduction of vaccination, that was universally practised in Skye since about 1760.

> *Here Mr MacAskill, surgeon, began the statutory practice of innoculation, anno 1763; between the 1.11.63 and 1.9.64, innoculating 287 of whom only 3 died. At the same time Mr Maclean, surgeon, innoculated 11 who all lived. Mr MacLeod, surgeon; 26 of whom 2 died … The last time smallpox visited Glenelg, of 220 who were ill, 140 died.*
>
> (McKay, MM, 1980, p. 203).

It would indeed appear that, until then, the ravages of the dread disease of smallpox were enormous *"almost whole families being swept away by it"*, declares the Rev. Malcolm MacLeod of Snizort, *"leaving one or two, or sometimes three, in a house"*; and the Rev. Donald Martin of Kilmuir states that, before the practice of inoculation had been adopted, this disease *"almost depopulated the district"*.

Stature

There existed then, and for several decades after that time, a preconception, the validity of which will not bear the test of close investigation. That was the notion that the men of former days were much bigger, and therefore stronger, than their descendants. This failing, which mayhap *"leaned to virtue's side"*, and was really a faint survival of ancestor-worship, was so far indulged that when bones of an exceptionally large size were brought to the surface in a graveyard, in the course of a new interment, they were preserved with great care and exhibited in the windows of the churches. They were pointed to as a monument of the great size and strength of the forebears, although, in referring to bones kept in the church in Raasay and alleged to have been those of a giant, traditionally called *'Faobairneach MacCuithean'*, the Rev. Alexander Campbell of Portree, writing near the close of the eighteenth century says *"the present generation is in that respect little superior to their neighbours"*.

We know that travellers, who have left on record their impressions, found no instance of extraordinary stature in Skye. Martin Martin does not say that the people there were in any way taller than others among whom he sojourned. Pennant saw none of outstanding physique; while Dr. Johnson observes:

> *The inhabitants of Skye are commonly of the middle stature; with fewer among them very tall, or very short, than are seen in England.*
>
> (Johnson, S, 1984, p. 92).

Indeed, the Rev. William Bethune of Duirinish, who wrote in 1793, says *"the men are of low stature, from 5ft 4ins to 5ft 8ins, and a very few are 6ft. in height"*; while his contemporary, the

Rev. A. Campbell, declares that no one in the parish of Portree exceeded 6ft., although there were *"five about that height"*. The Rev. Mr. Martin of Kilmuir corroborates these observations by his assertion that the height of his parishioners *"ranges from 5ft. 8ins to 5ft.; and the greatest height to which any has attained is 6ft. 4ins."*

Longevity

Nor was the span of life longer then than it is at the present time. *"I found no instances here"* (Skye), Dr. Johnson declares, *"of extraordinary longevity"* (Johnson, S, 1984, p. 93), and his statement is substantiated by a considerable body of evidence supplied by those who compiled the *'Old Statistical Account'*. Thus, in Sleat, there were then thirteen persons over 80 years of age and, of these, one had reached 98, while another had attained his 95th year. Of Strath it is said *"there are a few persons now living whose ages range from 80 to 90 years"*; and, concerning Portree, it was thought to be worthy of comment that *"two were over 90"*. The Rev. Malcolm MacLeod of Snizort states that *"five or six persons died within the last two years, whose ages ranged from 84 to 90"*. Of the adjacent parish of Kilmuir it is said *"there are some people above 90 years of age, but few reach 100"*, and in Duirinish there lived *"two men of 95 and 88, and two women of 97 and 93"*.

Hence we see that, although the average age has undoubtedly been raised down the years, the maximum life for the individual has remained fairly constant. It should be observed that, since the registration of births had not then become an institution in our island, it is possible that some of the figures quoted above are only approximately correct.

Climate

Despite the pronouncements of the aged, and the *laudatores temporis acti,* who always place the 'Golden Age' behind them, the climate of Skye was in the past neither better nor worse than it is at the present time. Indeed, an element of comedy appears when we collate the averments of the ministers of Skye who wrote the *'New Statistical Account'* of 1841 with those of their brethren who described the conditions prevailing in the same parishes fifty years previously. Thus the former speak of *"sensible changes in the seasons"* from what obtained in the days of their fathers, while the latter, in effect, declare that the climate of the island had appreciably deteriorated within living memory. And yet several of these writers make reference to periods of necessity brought about by inclement conditions of the weather in the past. The year 1688 was long remembered in Skye for its storms and its rains and, in adverting to it, towards the end of the following century, the Rev. Mr. Martin of Kilmuir says,

The seasons were so eminently unfavourable, and the corn so deficient in quantity and quality, that the poor actually perished on the highways from want of aliment.

Martin Martin, who, as we have already seen, has left on record a most illuminating account of the Western Isles, written at the end of the seventeenth century, says, *"The climate here* (Skye) *is uncommonly moist and cold"* (Martin, M, 1716, p. 171). Thomas Pennant, who toured our island in 1770, observes,

The farmer labours to remedy this distress (want of food); but the wetness of the land late in spring prevents him from putting into the ground the early seed of future crops;

and the same writer states elsewhere,

The difficulties the farmer undergoes in this bad climate are unknown in the south.

There is nothing so unfavourable to the crops raised by Tillage, as the autumnal rains which are heavy and sometimes uninterrupted during that season.

He also refers to the mildness of the winters (McKay, MM, 1980, p. 206). Such was the severity of the winter of 1771 that, according to MacLeod of MacLeod, afterwards the general, his tenants *"lost one-third of their stock"*; and so great was the destitution that the government was constrained to send food to the West Highlands, a cargo of meal being sent to Skye, of which the parish of Duirinish alone got 44 bolls. The spring of that year was remembered as the 'Black Spring', when the weather was so unseasonable that, as Dr. Johnson tell us, *"many of the roebucks perished"*. The observation made by that great author on our climate is worth quoting. He was in Skye in the autumn of 1773, and he says:

Their weather is not pleasing. Half the year is deluged with rain. From the autumnal to the vernal equinox, a dry day is hardly known, except when the showers are suspended by a tempest … Their winter overtakes their summer, and their harvest lies upon the ground drenched with rain.

(Johnson, S, 1984, p. 88).

On the 5th of November 1776, the *Edinburgh Courant* reported *'storms very severe in West Highlands, the thermometer sank to 10 degrees, ice 18 inches thick and water fowls frozen to death'*.

Owing to adverse weather conditions in 1778, and again in 1782, the crops proved a failure, many being left destitute. At the end of the century there was no marked change for the better. *"From the lateness, as well as the uncertainty of the seasons"*, says the Rev. Malcolm MacLeod of Snizort, *"this district, and, indeed, most of the island, seems calculated by nature more for grazing and green pasture than for raising corn"*. The Rev. William Bethune of Duirinish observes: *"The air here is moist and foggy – the west and south-west winds bring floods of rain"*; and the same authority informs us that in his parish *"the common distempers were rheumatics, sciatica colds, and nervous fevers, due to the wet climate"*.

The Maintenance of Paupers

No efforts were made in those days by the civil authorities for the maintenance of the indigent poor. These were wholly dependent for their sustenance on the community among whom they lived; and a serious burden they often proved to be. True, not much was required for keeping body and soul together but there were so many in a state of necessity, and so few were in affluent circumstances, that the little extra conferred on the needy often made for the donors all the difference between sufficiency and want.

In addition to those deficient in means, there were those whose mental powers were so defective as to preclude them from supporting themselves. They, too, lived on the charity of relatives and neighbours and, so refractory was their conduct on many an occasion, that they were a sore trial to the forbearance of their hosts. But no matter how intractable in behaviour, or ungrateful in demeanour these unfortunate individuals might be, it was considered a religious duty to give them a night's harbourage. They went from house to house, seldom remaining more than a single night with any one family; nor were they ever met with a closed door. Many of these half-witted people were endowed with a considerable fund of subtle cunning, that led them to trade on their own avowed weakness and the native generosity of their neighbours in order to lead a life of idleness.

The indigent made periodical wanderings and, when they had amassed enough provender, they retired to their hovels to renew their peregrinations when want, or inclination, prompted them. It is evident that, under such conditions, the less assertive were bound to suffer great privations as the funds raised locally for the relief of destitution were woefully inadequate for their purpose. These monies accrued principally from church collections, eked out by fines imposed on delinquents, but when we recollect that in a district like Skye, where crime was rare and Sunday collections seldom consisted of more than 'a few halfpence', the income from such sources could not be other than meagre. So small, indeed, was it, that the Rev. Donald Martin of Kilmuir states: *"The session cannot give above 3/–, or 3/6 at most, per annum a-piece, even to the most distressed, and still less to others"*. It is true that, in some parts of the Highlands, a few parishes were able to amplify this trifling sum through the munificence of wealthy philanthropists; but such means seldom came the way of the kirk-sessions of Skye, except in the notable instance of the parish of Sleat, where the famous diplomat, Sir John MacPherson, son of the Rev. Dr. John MacPherson of Sleat, and Governor-General of Bengal, made a substantial contribution to the funds of the poor of his native parish.

Well did this great-hearted man deserve the pæan pronounced on him by the wife of Major Alexander MacLeod of Stein, when she says:

> *Tha thu iriosal bàidheil*
> > You are humble and kindly
> *Tha thu measail air càirdean*
> > You prize friends
> *Gun dh' fhiosraich thu 'n-t àrdan*
> > You have acquired dignity

> *Tha feumail.*
> > Which is valuable.
> *Chunnaic mise as mo chadal*
> > I saw in my sleep
> *A' chraobh urail bu taitneach*
> > The flourishing tree most pleasant
> *'S a' duileach cur fasgadh air ceudan.*
> > Whose foliage gives shelter to hundreds.
> *Gur h-e 'n t-Iain Mòr alainn*
> > The great magnificent John
> *Sud a' chraobh tha mi gratainn*
> > Is the tree I am speaking of
> *Se mo dhùrachd s' blath bhi na dhèidh ort.*
> > It is my wish that bloom will persist on it.

> (MacLeòid, D, 1811, pp. 104–5)

The aggregate number of paupers in the seven parishes of Skye was between 500 and 600, a not inconsiderable proportion of the total population of the island. Towards the close of the period under review, there were as many as 170 in the parish of Bracadale alone. We need not wonder, therefore, at the agitation that was gaining ground, even in Skye, advocating the institution of Parochial Boards which should be responsible for attending to the welfare of the paupers of their districts.

Military

When the proscription against the carrying of arms was in force, the military ardour of the Highlanders found an outlet in the Continental wars. Thus many Skyemen enlisted in the Dutch service, in which the Scottish Brigade formed a formidable unit. Men like MacLeod of Talisker and MacLeod of Balmeanach, held high posts in the army of the Netherlands, the former being raised to the rank of colonel, the latter retiring in 1787 with the rank of major. When these officers were home on furlough, they recruited large numbers of young levies from Skye, chiefly from the parish of Bracadale.

A far-seeing statesman like Pitt was not long in a position of power before he felt the necessity of conciliating the estranged feelings of the Highlanders; and he conceived that the best way to achieve that object was to enlist them in the service of their country. The opportunity soon presented itself on the outbreak of the War of Independence in America, when Pitt was not slow to make use of the splendid qualities of the Highlanders for the rough campaigning that was a feature of that unfortunate event. The Highlanders readily responded to the call. Sir Alexander MacDonald of Sleat raised about 700 men, who were sent to America as a detachment of "The MacDonald Highlanders", men who as Dr Walker declared, *"every where supported the character of a noble and high spirited people"* (McKay, MM, 1980, p. 203). We have already seen that the young Chief of MacLeod had been commissioned with the rank of captain in the new army and that a large contingent was recruited from his clan.

Among other notable men from Skye who played a part in this war were Captain Allan MacDonald of Kingsborough; the courtly and clever Major Alexander MacLeod of Lochbay; Captain John MacLeod, afterwards of Ollach; his brother, Captain Norman of Camustianavaig, both of the family of Rigg and of Raasay; their uncle, Norman, who was a lieutenant, and another young officer, who afterwards became famous as Lieutenant-General Sir John MacLeod, the first Director-General of Artillery, a post created for him by the Duke of Wellington. As a young officer, William MacAskill, son of a tacksman of *Rubh' an Dùnain*, fought in the same war. This fine soldier rose to the rank of major-general, subsequently holding the post of Governor of Mauritius. Contemporary with these was Lieutenant Charles MacDonald of Ord, the father-in-law of the author, Alexander

Smith. This officer had seen much service and he took part in his last fight at Vinegar Hill, in 1798 (see MacInnes, J, 1899, p. 66).

It was the prowess of men such as these that inspired the Earl of Chatham to give expression to that memorable eulogy of his on the achievements of the Highlanders:

> *I sought for merit wherever it could be found. It is my proud boast that I was the first minister who looked for it, and found it in the mountains of the North. I called it forth, and drew it into your service, a hardy and intrepid race of men – men who, when left by your jealousy, became a prey to the artifices of your enemies. These men were brought to combat on your side. They served with fidelity, as they fought with valour and they conquered for you in every quarter of the globe.*
>
> (*ibid.*, p. 1).

On the completion of their term of service, the vast majority of these soldiers returned to Skye and, not only were they thus the means of bringing a considerable amount of wealth into the island, but they were also bound to have exerted a powerful influence on the manners of the people at that time. *"There are among us"*, says Rev. Donald Martin of Kilmuir, *"many officers of the army, who have retired on half-pay, after having bravely served their country – men who possess all those polite and elegant accomplishments by which their profession is distinguished"*.

Fauna

During the latter half of the eighteenth century the black cattle constituted by *far the most numerous group of animals on the island. Immense herds of them* were reared, huge droves being yearly driven to the Lowland markets. Pennant declared that the number sold from Skye, in a normal year, rarely fell below 4000 while, on a careful computation, based on the available evidence, it is found that, towards the end of the century, the stock considerably exceeded 17,000 head. They were hardy animals and, in describing them, Pennant states that in Skye was produced *"the largest breed of cattle in all the Highlands"*. The young and the farrow cattle were wintered in the open, the milch cows alone being housed during the colder seasons. According to the writers of that time, the yield of the best cows was about three quarts of milk daily.

Next to the cattle in order of number came the sheep, which were of the breed known as *'Caoraich Bheaga'*. This species was native to the island. They were characterised by their diminutive size, seldom exceeding 30 lbs. in weight, by the fine quality of their wool and the delicious flavour of their mutton *"which far surpasses that belonging to the best-fed of the larger breeds"* of the south. They were varicoloured, being white, black, grey, and brown, or with these colours intermingled. A long tuft of wool adorned the forehead; and they bore supernumerary horns, some of the rams of this breed having as many as six. That they enjoyed complete immunity from those disastrous diseases to which the genus is now subject, is attested, among other evidence, by the fact that we have no Gaelic names for the common ovine disorders. These troubles resulted from the crossing of the *'Caoraich Bheaga'* with the larger breed of the South, when the great demand for wool supervened about the beginning of the following century.

The small breed of sheep has long since become extinct in Skye, but a few persisted, notably in the parish of Duirinish, even as late as 1843. They were not exported, being reared merely for local consumption, since their mutton was noted for its delicacy. Their wool, which was of fine quality, was made into clothes of all kinds. So tame were they that they submitted to milking, the normal daily yield being one pint per head.

The total stock of sheep was less by one-third than the number of cattle on the island at this time and, although it was higher than this in certain of the parishes, as, for example, in Strath, where the number of sheep even exceeded that of the cattle, yet, in the contiguous parish of Sleat, the number was *"so few"*, according to the Rev. Martin MacPherson, who wrote in 1793, *"as to be hardly worth calculating"*.

In numerical order, the third place was taken by horses, the total number of which was about 3400. These animals were so hardy that they were never put under shelter, even in the most rigorous weather, but this virtue was neutralised by the fact that they were inclined to be restive and often intractable while at work.

The goat also existed then in large numbers, the rugged configuration of the island and especially the rocky coastline, offering an ideal habitat to these animals. They abounded on the eastern slopes of Ben Tianavaig, on Scorrybreck, the shore rocks of Duirinish, Minginish and Talisker, the hills of Strathaird and the island of Raasay. Owing to the injury they inflicted on trees, by stripping the bark, the maintenance of the goat was discouraged wherever attempts were made to set up plantations in any part of the island.

Numbers of them, however, tethered near the dwelling-houses, were kept for the sake of the large quantity of milk they yielded. This amounted, on the average, to a quart a day and it was held to be of a highly nutritious quality.

There were few or no hogs on the island, though Dr. Johnson observes he saw one pig at Dunvegan.

Of creatures in the feral state, there were deer, roe, hares, and several kinds of wild fowl but, on the island of Raasay, there were no deer, hares, or rabbits, although the hills abounded with feathered game. The fox was then very common, *"not withstanding a handsome premium given for every one killed"*, and the writers of that time deplore the havoc it wrought among sheep and lambs. Its depredations were so great that the *'brocair'*, or fox-hunter, was kept busy in every district. Walker reports that *in 1764 a fox hunting club was formed in Skye and three shillings was paid for every fox killed. In 1765, 112 were killed in Trotternish alone*

(Walker, J, 1812, Vol. 2, p. 360).

Johnson declares that there were neither rats nor mice in the island of Raasay in his own time, but that weasels were so common that they lived even in the walls of dwelling-houses, where *"they could be heard rattling behind chests and beds"*. The black rat did exist then, however, on the island of Skye (Johnson, S, 1984, p. 92).

The birds of prey, now met with on the island, are mentioned also at that time – eagles, hawks, and ravens; while game birds, such as grouse, partridge, blackcock, and ptarmigan, were common. The last lived principally on the Cuillin and the neighbouring hills, and flocks sometimes made their home on the great ridge of Trotternish.

Flora

The ancient forests of the island had long since disappeared, only a few scattered coppices of birch, hazel, oak and alder then remaining. *"This isle hath antiently been covered all over with woods"*, declares Martin Martin, *"as appears from the great trunks of fir trees, etc., dug out of the bog"*. It must be said that the Scotch pine, the only native conifer of Britain, is not widely distributed in the peat-bogs of Skye, the more prevalent logs discovered there being the birch, the hazel, and an occasional oak. In the adjacent island of Rona, however, the pine is present in abundance in the mosses, from which its huge boles still protrude, and large trunks of that tree are brought to the surface. Only a few years ago, a peat-cutter there unearthed a log that was 52ft 6ins long, and as *"straight as the mast of a ship"*. Dr Walker refers to *Coille Esketill* (Eskadale):

... an old wood occupying about 300 acres, birch, hazel, alder, hagberry and water elder, but now contains no good trees ... formerly it has been filled with wood of which there are still some considerable remains ... At Armadil ... is a garden of very good fruit trees ... The wood of Dunscaich in Sleat is also very considerable and thriving consisting of birch, oack, ash, alder, rowan, holly, hazel and the Grey Willow. Here I measured an alder which was 17 feet in circumference, at the height of 4 feet above the ground.

(McKay, MM, 1980, pp. 204–5).

Martin states that the most extensive wood in Skye in his own day was *"Lettir hurr (Letterfura, to the east of Kinloch in Sleat), and it exceeds not three miles in length"* (Martin, M, 1716, p. 142).

Literature

Whereas in other parts of the Highlands this period of history is characterised by a great outburst of song, scarcely a note was sounded in the island of Skye. It is, indeed, a remarkable fact that a place, so famed as the nurture-ground of military fervour, should have received so little inspiration from the stirring times of 'The '45'. That the romance of the movement had seized the imagination of the people, in no uncertain manner, has already been amply demonstrated; and the wonder therefore grows that its influence has found no expression in their poetry. The dilly-dallying attitude of the chiefs of Skye, in the first stages of the Rebellion, brought bitter disappointment to their clansmen, and when, later, the former joined the Hanoverian cause, the popular ardour glowed fitfully and low. Such conditions could only prove unfavourable to the cultivation of the muses, and the poetic night that then supervened reigned over the island for a long period. It was, however, to be illumined by one star, whose brilliant but brief ray shone towards the end of the century.

This solitary figure was William Ross, and it is noteworthy that, of his compositions that are extant, only three treat of the Jacobite movement and in none of them do we perceive those traits of genius so apparent in his other works. Only in his *'Oran do Mharcuis nan Greumach'* (Mackenzie, J, 1877, p. 279), written by him in 1784 on the revocation of the hated 'Unclothing Act', do we detect even a suggestion of that intense feeling that pulsates through his other productions; and, his stout Jacobitism notwithstanding, his *'Lament'* on the death of Prince Charlie, composed in the same year (1788), utterly fails to stir the sympathy of the reader (*ibid.*, p. 282). An earlier poem, written in 1782, on the occasion of the restoration of their estates to certain of the Highland chiefs, has neither depth of feeling nor conviction for he appears, even then, to have become reconciled to the Hanoverian regime.

Indeed, there can be no doubt that his name would have been long lost to fame had his reputation rested solely on those pieces that have been mentioned. There are, however, other compositions of his that will live as long as the language in which they are written, breathing, as they do, the true spirit of poetry. Nevertheless, it must be conceded that his themes are somewhat circumscribed, being confined chiefly to love, whisky and quiet pastoral scenes. In that last branch of the art of poetry he stands high, and those of his lyrics that treat of that theme communicate a peculiar charm to the mind. He delights in describing nature's quieter moods; the mazy windings of the shady glens, the gentle slopes where the lone shielings lie – scenes of those pastoral pursuits that poets have idealised and which seem to us like the last lingering phases of the 'Golden Age'.

He is at his best in *'Oran air Gaol na h-Oighe'*, composed during his sojourn in Perthshire, as well as in that other exquisite fragment, *'Oran a Rinn am Bàrd ann an Dun-eideann'*, where the most pleasing imagery is blended with sweetest sentiment:

O 's tric bha mi falbh leat,
  Often I strayed with you,
A gheala-bhean na féille,
  My kindly fair maid,
Ann an doire nan geug.
  In the branchy grove.
Is air reidhlean an driùchd;
  On meadows of dew;
'S air sraithibh a' ghlinne
  And on the floor of the glen
Far 'm bu bhinne guth smeòraich
  Where the mavis was sweetest
'S air iomair nan neòineinean
  And on the fields of daisies
Feòirneanach, chùr'.
  Grassy and fresh.

(Mackenzie, J, 1877, p. 287)

His diction is in keeping with this theme – gentle and chaste while the smooth glide of his metre, strong and free, is suggestive of the deeper waters of the lower hills. Take the following verse, with its arresting alliterative touches, its marvellous metrical interlaceries, like the ancient Celtic sculptural designs, so intricate, yet so seemingly simple:

'Nuair bhithinn 's mo mhin-mhal'
  When my fair browed love and I were wont to be
'N gleannan riomhach na cuaich,
  In the picturesque glen of the cuckoo,
No 'n doire fasgach na smeòraich
  In the sheltered grove of the mavis
Gabhail sòlais air chuairt,
  Taking pleasure in the stroll
Cha mhalairtinn m' éibhneas,

I would not barter my joy,

O bhith ga h-eugmhais car uair,

    In exchange for being ever without her for an hour,

Air son stòras fir stàta

    Though I'd get the riches of a statesman

Dh'aindeoin àirdead an uaill.

    Despite the greatness of the prestige.

          (MacCoinnich, I, 1834, p. 110)

In his delightful idyll, *'Moladh na h-Oighe Gaidhealaich'*, we have abundant illustration of the untrammelled movement of his harmonious cadences, and his delightful picture of the healthy joys of shieling life:

'Nuair thig a' Bhealltuinn,

    When Maytime comes,

'S an Samhradh lusanach,

    And the leafy summer,

Bidh sinn air àirigh

    We will be in the shieling

Air àird nan uchdanan;

    On the height of the braes;

Bidh cruit nan gleanntan,

    The lyre of the glens,

Gu cainntir, cuirteasach,

    Will be sweetest and dignified,

Gu tric 'gar dùsgadh

    Often rousing us

Le sùrd gu moch-eirigh.

    With the joy of early morning.

          (Mackenzie, J, 1877, p. 290)

Apart from his *Comhradh eadar am Bard agus Blabhein* (conversation between the Bard and Blaven) composed in a nostalgic

mood and declining health, as he rested on a hill in Gairloch and viewed from afar the mountain that dominated the land of his fathers in Skye, (MacCoinnich, I, 1834, p. 13) nature in her sterner moods has no place in his themes – the wild grandeur of his native land failed to inspire him, and even the pleasures of the chase, in which his contemporary bards delighted to revel, held out no attractions for him. In that poem of doubtful authorship, *'Bruthaichean Ghlinn Bhraoin'*, there are several verses attributed to him that are full of the true huntsman's passion for the sport of the wilds, but, in addition, to other matters, the reference in that exquisite song to the author's imprisonment in French hands, when the real struggle with France came after 1791, the year of the poet's death, suggests that some of the verses were added to the original by a soldier who had suffered during the Napoleonic Wars.

It should be observed that Ross occasionally introduces scenes from nature as a foil, in order to set off the graces of the woman he loves. He is pre-eminently the bard of love for none ever sang of the lady of his heart as William Ross did. The depth of his passion, his ability to express it in language as charming as his theme, and especially the purity of his thoughts, are all features that place him in an almost unrivalled position among the Gaelic bards. Though he is not wholly blind to 'lovely cheeks, or lips, or eyes', there is, for him, far greater beauty in the "gentle thoughts and calm desires" of her who first inspired his lay. Thus, in *'Cumha a' Bhàird'*, which he composed when unrequited love was shattering his delicate health,

…an aon rùn,

    …the one desire,

A bhuin mo ghaol gun ghaol da chionn.

    That engaged my love without love in return,

          (MacCoinnich, I, 1834, p. 67)

he delights in recording her spiritual as well as her physical attributes:

Gur gile mo leannan
> Whiter is my love
Na'n eal' air an t-snàmh,
> Than the swan as it swims,
Gur binn' i na smeòrach
> Sweeter than the mavis
Air barraibh ròchruinn 's a' Mhàigh.
> In the treetops in May.
Gur h-e geanmnachd a beusann
> It is the chastity of her nature
'S i gun eucoir 'na càil
> And the guilelessness of her ways
A lùb mise gu géilleadh
> That induced me to surrender
Air bheag éiginn 'na gràdh.
> Without difficulty to her love.
>> (MacCoinnich, I, 1834, p. 67)

'Love at first sight' rarely inspired bard to compose a nobler panegyric on the object of his affections than we find in the poem entitled *'Feasgar Luain'*:

Dhiuchd mar aingeal mu mo choinneamh
> There appeared like an angel before me
'N ainnir òg bu bhinne snuadh;
> The young maiden of the finest looks;
Seang slios fallain, air bhlàth canaich,
> Healthy, slender flanks, like the hue of bog cotton,
No mar eala air a' chuan.
> Or like the swan on the sea.

Sùil ghorm mheallach, fo caoil mhala,
> Winsome blue eyes, under fine eyebrows,
'S caoine sheallas 'g amharc uaith',
> Whose kindly gaze shines forth,
Beul tlàth tairis, gun ghné smalain,
> Tender, delicate mouth without haughtiness,
Do 'n gnàth carthannachd gun uaill.
> Used to friendliness, not pride;
>> (MacCoinnich, I, 1834, p. 63)

and love's fiery furnace never burned with fiercer flame than it did for this bard when he was constrained to compose *'Cuachag nan Craobh'*:

Thuit mi le d' ghath, mhill thu mo rath,
> I fell by your dart and destroyed my prospects,
Striochd mi le neart dòruinn.
> I have succumbed to the strength of torment.
Saighdean do ghaoil, sàbht anns gach taobh,
> The arrows of your love sunk in my sides,
Thug dhiom gach caoin còmhla.
> Have reft me of every pleasure.
Mhill thu mo mhais, ghoid thu mo dhreach,
> You have ruined my looks and stolen my grace,
Mheudaich thu gal bròin dhomh
> You have increased my cry of sorrow
'S mur fuasgail thu tràth, le d' fhuran, 's
> And if you do not soon relieve me with friendly
le d' fhàilt
> welcome
Is cuideachd am bàs dhòmhsa.
> Death will be my portion.
>> (Mackenzie, J, 1877, p. 286)

Yet, in spite of the depth and the intensity of his passion, how chaste are his thoughts and what noble feeling pervades his expression; while in that 'other song', *'Oran Eile'*, written when he heard of the marriage of Marion Ross, the poignancy of his grief has plunged him helplessly into the depths of dark despair. And, if the chief test of poetry be its power to arouse the emotions, then this sweet, sad last song of William Ross must take its place among the greatest lyrics in our language:

'Is fada tha m'aigne fo ghruaim,
    Long are my spirits in gloom,
Cha mhosgail mo chluain ri ceòl,
    My peace will not come with music,
Am breislich mar ànrach a' chuain,
    In a daze like one tossed on the ocean,
Air bharraibh nan stuadh ri ceò.
    On the wave crests in a fog.
'S e iondrainn t'àbhachd bhuam
    It is the loss of your dalliance
A chaochail air snuadh mo neòil,
    That has changed the face of my outlook,
Gun sùgradh, gun mhire, gun uaill,
    Without spirit or pleasure or pride,
Gun chaithream, gun bhuaidh, gun treòir.
    Hilarity, success or strength.

(Mackenzie, J, 1877, p. 297)

William Ross has been called the 'Burns of Gaelic Song'; and there is much to justify the title. Each stands out pre-eminently, in his own language, as the poet of love and, of the works of Ross, two pieces are extant in praise of strong drink, that make the parallel the more pronounced. In his treatment of this theme our bard is particularly happy. That rollicking tavern-song of his, *'Moladh an Uisge Bheatha'*, ('in praise of Whisky') furnishes many a brilliant burst of wit and humour, while underneath the surface a rich vein of satire permeates the whole composition. In extolling the virtues of whisky, Burns, at his best, has said nothing better than the following:

Chan eil cléireach, no pears' eaglais,
    There is no cleric or churchman,
Cràbhach, teallsanach, no sagart,
    Saint, philosopher or priest,
Do nach toir thu caochladh aigne
    Whose disposition you will not change
Sparradh céill 's an amhlair.
    Cramming sense into the dolt.

(Mackenzie, J, 1877, p. 289)

His other work, *'Mac na Braiche'* ('son of malt'), falls far below the foregoing in poetic merit and in it occurs a reference to Dr. Johnson's alleged lapse while he was travelling in the Highlands:

Dh'fhàg mac-na-braiche e gun lide
    The son of malt left him speechless
Mar amadan liotach dall;
    An idiot, lisping, blind;

(MacCoinnich, I, 1834, p. 90)

a mis-statement of fact that must appear egregiously strange to all who know of the great Englishman's abstemious habits.

Like Burns, again, Ross has a just conception of the correct use of satire. His is never of the bitter, vindictive kind that descends to the particular and the personal; rather is it the playful banter of the mind that can rise above the common-place conditions of life, and can send its stinging shafts to worry rather than to wound. By this method of treatment he makes the object of his scorn at once a despicable and ridiculous thing. In *'An Ladie Dubh'*, a satire he composed on a censorious cleric, who had himself not been over-scrupulous in keeping close to those paths of rectitude which he had so sanctimoniously urged his flock to follow, Ross exhibits his satirical powers in a conspicuous manner. His rapier-like thrusts are made with such masterly deftness, and with such apparent lack of acerbity, that no sympathy is felt for his opponent but rather we are forced to rejoice in his utter discomfiture. The poet's skill in the involved intertwinings of Gaelic rhyme is seldom better illustrated than in this poem:

> *Bha sagart 's na criochan,*
>> There was a priest in this district,
> *'S bu diadhaidh 'm fear-leughaidh,*
>> And godly was the reading man,
> *Air dùnadh le creideamh*
>> Packed full of faith
> *'S le eagnachd cho eudmhor.*
>> And jealous in prudence.
> *Is b' ann a cheann-eagair*
>> The theme of his sermons
> *A theagasg bhi beusach,*
>> Was to be chaste,
> *Gun ofrail a nasgadh*
>> And not to lay offerings
> *Air altaireann Bhénuis.*
>> On the altars of Venus.

(Mackenzie, J, 1877, p. 291)

One is forcibly struck by the numerous classical allusions in his works, but especially we are surprised by his unwarranted use of Anglicisms and although he errs less grievously, perhaps, than many of our other Gaelic bards, he is not wholly free from the sin of tautology. Indeed, several of his noblest efforts are marred in a marked degree by his tendency to employ redundant expressions. Thus, in one of his greatest compositions, *'Feasgar Luain'*, we are forced to wade through a purposeless plethora of epithets, *e.g.*:

> *Gur bachlach, dualach, casbhuidh, cuachadh,*
>> Curled, braided in yellow wreaths and whorls,
> *Càradh suaineas gruag do chinn.*
>> The plaited ringlets of your head of hair.
> *Gu h-àluinn, bòidheach, fàinneach, òrbhuidh',*
>> Most lovely, ringletted, golden yellow,
> *An caraibh soighn', 's an òrdugh grinn.*
>> In attractive dressing and fine array.
> *Gun chron a fàs riut a dh' fhaodt' aireamh*
>> Without a blemish that I could name in you
> *'O do bhàrr gu sàil do bhuinn;*
>> From your head to your heel;
> *Dhiuchd na buaidhean, òigh, mu'n cuairt duit,*
>> The graces, maiden, have assembled around you
> *Gu meudaichinn d'uaill 's gach puing;*
>> To add to your dignity at every point;

(MacCoinnich, I, 1834, p. 63)

while his *'Oran an t-Samhraidh'*, and notably his song in praise of Gairloch, *'Moladh a' Bhàird air a Thir Fèin'*, abound in pleonastic expressions:

> *Gur h-i Gearrloch an tir bhàdheil,*
>> Gairloch is a friendly land,
> *'S an tir phàirteach, bhiadhar,*
>> Freely sharing and abundant,
> *Tir a' phailteis, tir gun ghainne,*
>> Land of plenty without stinting,
> *Tir is glainne fialachd,*

Land of the finest hospitality,
An tir bhaineach, uachdrach, mheallach,
Land of milk, cream and honey,
Chaomhach, channach, thiorail;
Mild, pretty and comfortable;
Tir an arain, tir an tacar
Land of bread and plenteous venison
Sithne, 's pailteas iasgaich.
And rich fishing.

(Mackenzie, J, 1877, p. 286)

Although William Ross was a native of Skye, it is a striking fact that hardly ever in his works that are extant do we find any reference to the land of his birth. He was born in the year 1762 at Sithean, near the village of Broadford, where his ancestry could be traced back for several generations. His father seems to have been a man of more than average intelligence, and his calling, that of packman (*'m'athair ri màlaid riamh'* – 'my father was always carrying a pack', as the poet says of him), would undoubtedly have sharpened powers already acute, and afford him a vast and varied experience of life. There can be no doubt, however, that whatever qualities of mind the bard derived from the paternal stock, he inherited the poetic genius through his mother, who was a daughter of the famous piper and poet, John Mackay, *'Am Pìobaire Dall'*.

While he was still a lad the family removed to Morayshire and, at the grammar-school of Forres, the future poet soon gave early promise of his latent powers. He excelled especially as a student of the classics, while his frequent itineraries in the company of his father throughout the Highlands and the Isles widened his outlook and perfected his knowledge of Gaelic, of whose cultivation he was always an ardent devotee.

Once again the family residence was changed, this time to Gairloch, the land of his mother's people, where he was appointed parish schoolmaster. Ross possessed those physical and mental attributes that go to the making of the ideal teacher. His tall and commanding figure, his striking features and his beautiful auburn hair, were qualities that endeared him to the young mind, while his engaging personality, his gift of rich humour and his ripe scholarship, were bound to impress his older pupils.

He was a general favourite. Few could tell a tale or recount a topical incident better than he and in the singing of a song he had no equal. In addition, he was an accomplished violinist, so that his company was much sought after, especially on market days and at marriages. He was fastidious about his own appearance nor was he unmoved by that of others. It is related of him that once, as he met a local bard who was on the way to attend a sister's wedding, this obsession got the better of him, so that he could not refrain from commenting on the figure cut by the latter, whose shabby coat accorded ill with his haughty bearing. Ross thus accosted him:

'S ann tha phròis air bàrd an Rubha,
The Bard of Point is full of pride,
On tha phiuthar dol a phòsadh;
Since his sister is going to be married;
Ach 's neonach leam mun d' fhàg e'n tigh,
But it is a wonder to me, before he left the house,
Nach d' rinn e malairt còta.
That he did not change his coat.

The retort of the poet from *Rubha* affords a direct reproof to all meddlers:

Tha 'n còta taitinn rium fhin –
The coat satisfies me –

Tha e min, is tha e blàth;
 It is soft and warm;
'S mur b'e meud do dhonoilean,
 And, but for the extent of your lack of breeding,
Dh' fhaodadh tusa leigeil da.
 You would leave it alone.

    (MacCoinnich, E, 1967, p. 307)

It is said of Ross that he frequented the tavern rather freely, an allegation to which he adverts in his poem in praise of whisky.

Thogadh ort nach b' fheairrde mis' thu,
 It is reported to you that I had not been the better for you,
Gun ghoid thu mo chuid gun fhios dhomh;
 That you secretly stole my means;

    (Mackenzie, J, 1877, p. 289)

There may have been some justification for the patronage he bestowed on the inn, he being early a victim to chronic asthma. This trouble eventually developed into phthisis and he was advised to leave the moist seaboard of Gairloch for the uplands of central Perthshire.

Dh' fheuch an fhearr a gheibh mi slàint',
 To try to improve my health,
A' tigh'nn gu àird nan Garbh-chrìoch.
 By coming to the Rough Bounds.

    (Mackenzie, J, 1877, p. 287)

It was then he composed 'Moladh a' Bhàird air a Thir Féin'. He did not remain long there, for he was never happy, nor did he benefit much in health by the change of scene and air.

It was shortly after his return to Gairloch that he met the lady whose influence was to cloud the remainder of his short life. This was Marion Ross, a native of Stornoway, to whom he composed those soul-subduing lyrics that have no equal in our language. 'Feasgar Luain' was his tribute to her on their first meeting; 'Cuachag nan Craobh' expresses the cruel torment of unrequited love; while that sad swan-song, 'Oran Eile', is pervaded throughout by a note of resignation, feebly raised by the broken heart, for which this world and its affairs are resolved to nothingness:

Cha dhùisgear leam ealaidh air àill,
 I cannot start an ode at will,
Cha chuirear leam dàn air dòigh;
 I cannot compose a poem;
Cha togar leam fonn air clàr,
 I cannot raise a tune on the harp,
Cha chluinnear leam gàir nan òg;
 Or listen to the laughter of youth,
Cha dhirich mi bealach nan àrd
 I cannot climb the mountain pass
Le suigeart mar bha mi'n tòs,
 With vigour as was my wont,
Ach triallam a chadal gu bràth,
 But I go, forever to sleep,
Do thalla nam bàrd nach beo.
 In the hall of the bards that are gone.

    (MacCoinnich, I, 1834, p. 174)

and this wonderful genius departed for the *"halls of the bards that have gone"* in 1791, at the early age of twenty-eight years. He lies buried in the old graveyard of Gairloch, where an unpretentious stone erected in 1850, with an inscription in English and Gaelic, marks his grave.

In memory of William Ross
Who died aged 28 years
1791

This stone, discovered in 1955, while a grave was being dug, is distant from the commemoration stone erected in the cemetery in 1850.

CHAPTER XV

Family History, 1800–1900

The MacDonalds

On the death of Alexander, the first Lord MacDonald, in 1795, his eldest son, also named Alexander, succeeded. The young laird had been educated at Eton and at St. Andrews and, like his father, he was disinclined to spend much of his time in his native island. Indeed, he resided for the most part in England and abroad, but when he did revisit his home he was always active with schemes to improve the lot of his people. As one writer says of him;

He lived on terms of cordial intimacy with his clansmen and tenantry, whose interests it was his chief pleasure to promote; while the greater proportion of his income was expended on the improvement and the decoration of his estate.

It was he who, in 1815, built the present castle at Armadale. His intention, originally, was to have it constructed of the marble of Strath, a project that was not carried out. The mansion was designed by a certain Gillespie Graham and, although it was externally so very uninspiring, its internal architecture was both elegant and grand. Its magnificent staircase, made of the marble of Strath, its oak panellings, its noble stained window, were features that made some amends for an eminently commonplace exterior.

At the behest of the laird, young plantations of trees were established in Sleat and elsewhere in Skye, while the development of the fishing industry was his ever-present concern. At Kyleakin he built a 'general stores', the first shop in Skye, in order that their simple needs might be the more accessible to his people. All were welcomed to his castle at Armadale, with its ever-open door and its kindly cheer. Even during its owner's prolonged sojournings abroad, the hospitality of that mansion was never stinted, for his factor had instructions to attend to the convenience of any who might care to enter. He was so highly respected by his people that, when he toured his estates, his principal tenants vied with one another in their endeavours to do him honour.

Owing to his absences from home, he was ignorant of the extent to which emigration was draining the manhood of his clan, while it has been said that he knew nothing of the ruthless evictions that were perpetrated during his chiefship.

In the portrait that is extant of him, there is the pleasing expression of a cultured man, an eye radiating kindliness and good sense, although at the same time betokening a disposition suggestive of reserve, if not bordering on shyness.

Sir Alexander, the tenth baronet, and second Lord MacDonald, died unmarried, in June, 1824, when he was succeeded by his brother. In 1824, *Ailean Dall* (Allan MacDougall) composed a panegyric on Glengarry, when he was stricken with fever in London, in which he refers to the death of Lord MacDonald -

> *Seo a bhliàdhna gun eibhneas*
>> This is the year without joy
>
> *Fhuair Clann Dhòmhnuill an leireadh ma thrath*
>> Clan Donald already have suffered a severe blow
>
> *Sgeul duilich ri èisdeachd*
>> Sad tale to tell
>
> *Chaill iad ceannard nach creubhadh am mal*
>> They lost a chief who would not extort the rent
>
> *Bàs a Mhorair Shlèibhtich.*
>> The death of the Lord of Sleat.

(Dughalach, A, 1829, p. 81)

Godfrey, Nineteenth Chief and Third Lord

Godfrey Wentworth was born in Edinburgh in the year 1775. Educated at Harrow, he proceeded thence to Oxford, leaving the latter institution to enter upon a military career in 1794, when he was barely twenty years of age. He was an athletic and handsome man, being well over six feet in height, and when, five years afterwards, he returned to England from active service in Holland, an event happened that was to be of momentous consequence to the House of Sleat. The youthful soldier fell in love with a young English lady, Louisa Maria *'Edsir'*, the offspring of a morganatic alliance between the Duke of Gloucester,

brother of George III, and the beautiful Lady Almeria Carpenter, daughter of the first Earl of Tyrconnell.

Owing to the barrier set by the young lady's guardians to the marriage, an elopement was resolved upon and carried out. The ardent lovers agreed to live together as husband and wife and, as Godfrey was still a native of Scotland, for nothing had supervened whereby he should be denationalised, such a contract as he then formed constituted valid wedlock according to the law of his land. When, in addition, he returned to England in 1803, with the rank of colonel, and was duly married at Norwich by an ordained clergyman, the legitimation of his child, Alexander, born before that ceremony, was thus unquestionably established (MacDonald, DJ, 1978, p. 435); for, as Lord Skerrington avers in his decree, in the case brought by Sir Alexander MacDonald of Thorpe Hall against Lord MacDonald in the year 1910:

> *Upon the evidence, I am satisfied that Godfrey MacDonald's domicile of origin was Scottish and there is no reason to suppose that, prior to the year 1803, he had acquired a domicile in England. … It follows, therefore, that the pursuer's grandfather, Alexander, was legitimated by the marriage of his parents in 1803 and that decree must be pronounced to that effect.*

(ibid., p. 437).

As is well known, however, it happened that, on Godfrey's death in 1832, the succession devolved on the second son, the presumption being that the first was illegitimate. The latter succeeded to the English estates of Thorpe and Gunthwaite, while Godfrey, his younger brother, entered into possession of the Scottish estates and became chief of his clan. It is fitting here to observe that, although succession to estates is determined by law, the dignity of chief rests solely on the choice of the members of the clan.

Godfrey, Twentieth Chief and Fourth Lord

This young chief, living somewhat extravagantly, soon found himself deeply involved in debt. In order to meet the demands of creditors, he was forced, in 1847, to sell portions of the family patrimony, including the whole of North Uist, and Kilmuir in Skye. He was married to a Yorkshire lady, and they had two sons, who became successively chiefs, namely, Somerled, who died unmarried in 1875, at the early age of 25 years, and Ronald Archibald, who succeeded as the twenty-second chief of *Clan Uisdein*, and the thirtieth in descent from Somerled, '*Rex Insularum*'.

At this stage, it may be of interest to quote a statement from the '*Book of Clan Ranald*', by Neil MacMhuirich, of the long line of *sennachies* and bards in the family of Clan Ranald (there seem to have been eighteen of them from their progenitor *Muireach Albanach*). "I have", he declares, "*no male descendants to set down of Donald, Lord of the Isles, except Sir Donald* (this was his own contemporary, '*Do'ull a' Chogaidh*'), *son of Donald, son of Sir James, son of Donald Gorm Og, son of Gillespic, son of Donald Gorm Sassanach, son of Donald Gorm, who was killed at Eilean Donain, who was son of Donald Gruamach, son of Donald Gallach, son of Hugh*", the first of Sleat (MacBain, A & Kennedy, J, 1894, p. 215).

> *'Nuair dh' éireas Clann Dòmhnuill*
>> When Clan Donald will arise
> *Na leomhainn tha garg,*
>> These ferocious lions
> *Na beò-bheithir, mhòr, leathann,*
>> Like dragons large and full bodied
> *Chonnspuinneach, gharbh;*
>> Heroic and rough
> *Luchd sheasamh na còrach,*

>> Men who would uphold justice
> *Do'n òrdugh lamh-dhearg;*
>> Whose badge the Red Hand
> *Mo dhòigh-sa gu'm ghòrach*
>> In my view it would be foolish
> *Dhaibh, tòiseachadh oirbh.*
>> Of them to set about you.

(Mackenzie, J, 1877, p. 72)

The MacLeods

John Norman, Twenty-fourth Chief

As has already been stated, General MacLeod, the twenty-third chief, died in 1801, and was succeeded by his son, John Norman, who was the offspring of his second marriage. On his homecoming from Edinburgh, in 1809, as a young man, a song of welcome was composed by the clan bard, Donald MacLeod, the first stanza being:

> *Tha m' inntinn air lasadh*
>> My spirits are kindled
> *Aig uiread mo chlaisneachd*
>> By what I have heard
> *Mu sgeul tha air tachairt*
>> Of the news that have reached us
> *MacLeòid air tighinn dhachaidh*
>> Of the homecoming of MacLeod
> *Le choirichean neartmhor*
>> With his confirmed charters
> *Gu tur nan clach snaighte*
>> To the tower of the hewn stones

Far am b' fhuirneasach
> Where there was entertainment

Sgaipteach do chairdean.
> Lavishly given to your friends.

(MacLeòid, D, 1811, p. 9)

For some years the young chief had been engaged in a costly law-suit with MacLeod of Gesto over the question of boundaries, the latter winning his case. When the lease of the farm of Gesto expired in 1825, the chief had his revenge by evicting his tenant, incurring, by his action, the displeasure of many of the leading men of the clan.

The dispossessed clansman was Neil MacLeod, the last of the name in Gesto. He is said to have been somewhat eccentric in his manner but he was a keen student of the lore of Skye and an outstanding authority on the art of *pìobaireachd*. The Rev. Alexander MacGregor says of him: *"He knew almost every pìobaireach in existence, their names, composers, origin, and the causes for composing them"*. MacGregor saw in his possession a large MS collection of this branch of music, containing about 200 pieces, some from their appearance distinctly ancient, though others, deciphered on different paper, were obviously more modern. Of them he published about a score, the compilation being known as *'The Gesto Collection'* (Mackenzie, A, 1889, p. 193).

The 'Gesto' hospital at Edinbane is named after a son of this last MacLeod of Gesto, who, after having amassed a considerable fortune in India, as an indigo planter, returned to his native island, and bought the lands of Greshornish and Orbost. He gave munificently of his wealth, setting apart an enormous sum of money for the endowment of the hospital, in which much good work has since been done for the suffering poor of Skye. On the death of this benefactor, the estates passed to his grand-nephew, who assumed the name of Robertson-MacLeod (*ibid.*, p. 198).

In the early part of the century, the parliamentary representative for the county of Inverness was Charles Grant of Glenelg, who won the election of 1826 by a vast majority over Godfrey, third Lord MacDonald. On the passing of the First Reform Act in 1832, the Chief of MacLeod opposed the 'sitting' member, by whom he was, however, defeated by a few votes.

This chief was married to an English lady named Anne Stephenson. They had a family of six daughters and two sons, of whom Norman, the elder, succeeded to the chiefship on the death of his father in 1835. His lament by Lady D'Oyly is in the *Oranaiche* (Sinclair, A, 1879, p. 294).

Norman, Twenty-fifth Chief

This chief was only twenty years of age on his accession. He was a linguist of considerable ability, having spent some time both in Germany and in France, in order to make himself proficient in the languages of these countries. In addition, he had studied law, became a member of one of the Inns of Court, but he had never practised to any great extent.

During those times of trial and grave anxiety that followed the failure of the potato crop in 1845, the chief was seldom from home but was constantly engaged in devising means for the alleviation of distress. The noted generosity of his house was never better exemplified than on this occasion. It is now no secret that he had spent so much of the family inheritance in supplying the immediate wants of his people that he was faced with ruin. It was in consonance with the altruism of his nature, and the practical bent of his mind, that he did not consider it beneath his dignity to become even a wage-earner, if nothing better would offer, in order to recoup the fallen fortunes of the estate. He, therefore, accepted an appointment as a clerk in the Home Office, where he acquitted himself with such ability that for several years he held the post of Principal Secretary in the

Department of Science and Art. He continued in office until his 69th year, when he retired as a pensioner.

He was a man of splendid physique, always active and alert, and endowed with a mind of transparent disinterestedness, prompted solely by a desire to do good – a man worthy of the name of chief, by the most rigorous connotation of the term.

He was twice married, first to the Hon. Louise St. John, and, on her death, to a Hungarian lady, Baroness Hanna. By the first marriage he had a family of four sons, three of whom were Roderick Charles, a Canon of the Church of England, an able student of Highland history, who was for many years resident in Morpeth; Sir Reginald, who after a long period of government service, culminating in the office of Permanent Under-Secretary for Scotland; and Norman Magnus, who was born in 1839 and became chief in the year 1895 (*ibid.*, pp. 185–6).

Norman Magnus, Twenty-sixth Chief

As a young man he chose a military career, being also for several years in the diplomatic service in South Africa. He was responsible for the introduction of Coolie labour into Eastern South Africa, while, in the turmoil of 1878 and 1879, with the Basutos and Zulus, he played a prominent part.

As a chief, he had always been active with schemes for the amelioration of the lot of his people, and especially busy with the formation of small-holdings and the erection of good houses for his tenants, who became peasant-proprietors after the repayment, on easy terms, of the initial outlay. A man of patriarchal appearance, this venerable chief, who attained the age of ninety years and died in 1929 was in very truth the father of his people.

Na Leòdaich am pòr glan,
    The MacLeods are a clean crop
Cha b' òlach 'ur siol:
    Nothing rank in their seed
Dream rìoghail gun fhòtus,
    A Royal stock without blemish
Nan gòrsaid, 's nan sgiath.
    Of the cuirasses and shields
Gur neartmhor, ro eòlach,
    Stalwart and intelligent
'Ur 'n òigfhir, 's 'ur liath;
    Are your youths and your old
Gur h-e cruadal 'ur dual'chas
    Your heritage was hardihood
A dh' fhuasgail sibh riamh.
    Which kept you ever free.

(Mackenzie, J, 1877, p. 73)

CHAPTER XVI

The Lesser Clans and Septs of Skye

The MacKinnons

This clan occupied Strath from very early times. The Rev. John MacKinnon, who wrote the *'New Statistical Account'* for his parish in 1841, says that the district was *"known to have been populated by the MacKinnons since 1354"*; and there is a mention of Dun Ringell on the shores of Loch Slapin in an Act of Council of 1360, where it is referred to as Castle Findanus – a name which suggests that it was even then in the possession of the MacKinnons. They moved the family seat to Castle Moil, or Dunakyn ('Fort of Hakon') as it was called, probably in the latter half of the 15th century.

> *An Strath Fhionnghain gheal*
>> The white Strath of MacKinnon
>
> *'S an grinne beus gun small*
>> Of the most attractive quality without blemish
>
> *An strath is cruaidhe clach*
>> The Strath of the hardest rock
>
> *'S an sgaitiche cu 'us bean;*
>> And the most incisive dogs and women;
>
>> (Mackay, JG, 1922, p. 337)

and:

> *A choinnle Chill mo Ruighe*
>> Light of Kilmaree
>
> *A Mhic ionmhuinn Fhionghuine*
>> Beloved son of Fingion
>
> *An talc tus catha du chuir*
>> Strength at the onset of battle
>
> *A mharcuigh Strath Shuairdail.*
>> O knight of Strath Suardal.
>
>> (Watson, WJ, 1922, p. 212)

Dean Munro, who made a tour of his diocese in 1549, makes mention both of Dunringill and of Dun Akin as castles in Skye, but he does not say whether or not they were then occupied. It has already been shown that, when the attempt was made in 1513 to raise Sir Donald of Lochalsh to the dignity of Lord of the Isles, the venue of the rebels was Dun Akin (MacDonald, A & A, 1896, p. 319).

In an account written in 1577 it is stated that

Strathvardeil pertains to MacKynvin, given to him by MacConneil (MacDonald) for to judge and decide all questions and debates that happens to fall between parties for playing of draughts and dice. It will raise eight score men. He has a castle called Dewnakin.

(Skene, WF, 1890, p. 432).

In consequence of the relationship they bore in the past to the Lords of the Isles, the MacKinnons had always placed themselves under the banner of the MacDonalds of Skye. During the Commonwealth they fought against Cromwell and were present with the other clans at the Battle of Worcester. In the first Jacobite Rebellion they took the field under the Chief of Sleat, a contingent of one hundred and fifty of the clan fighting at Sheriffmuir. For the part they took in that rising, the estate was forfeited, but it was purchased for the family by Sir John Grant in 1723. The chief of the time, *Iain Dubh*, was pardoned in 1727 and the estates were restored to him. Ever loyal to the Jacobite cause, they showed no hesitancy in ranging themselves on the side of Prince Charlie, when the Highlanders were once again called to arms in 1745. In that rebellion the MacKinnons were commanded by the chief in person, and by two members of his house, namely, Captain Lachlan of Corry, and Captain John of Elgol, the latter of whom is so well known to fame for the part he played, with his chief, in aiding the Prince's escape from Skye. The chief and his captain were both captured and suffered imprisonment for their activity in that adventure. On the passing of the Indemnity Act, they were released with other Jacobite prisoners, after having been twelve months in a prison-ship near Tilbury Fort. When the news of his pardon was being conveyed to him, the chief was reminded by the then Attorney-General, of the debt of gratitude he owed his king for allowing him his freedom to return home. The answer of the old warrior chief was in keeping with his fearless and independent spirit: *"Had I the king in my power, as I am in his"*, he declared, *"I would return him the*

compliment by sending him back to his own country" (Lamont, D, 1913, p. 78). His manliness made a deep impression on his persecutors for "they saw he was involved in the rebellion from the spirit of chivalry". In *'The Lyon in Mourning'* it is stated of him by Bishop Forbes that *"he used to say he hoped God would not take him off the earth, but on the field of battle, fighting for the House of Stuart"* (Forbes, R, 1975, Vol. III, p. 152).

This chief married, as his third wife, a daughter of *Mac Ghille Chaluim Camachasach* (MacLeod of Raasay of 'The '45'), whose son became guardian to his nephews of Strath, Charles and Lachlan, on the death of their father in 1756. Young *Mac Ghille Chaluim* did all in his power to preserve the estate in possession of the family of MacKinnon but, in 1765, it was privately sold by MacKinnon of Mishnish to the MacDonalds of Sleat. It has remained the property of the latter House, with the exception of the district of Strathaird, which has since frequently changed ownership and was possessed by a Mr. MacAlister in 1786.

Several members of the family of MacKinnon have distinguished themselves in the service of the church of their native island. Reference has already been made to the Rev. Neil MacKinnon, the first Protestant minister of Skye. He was the nephew of Sir L. MacKinnon, fourteenth chief of Strath. In the year 1653 he was translated to Sleat, when he was succeeded by the Rev Farquhar MacLennan, who was followed in the Ministry of Strath by Donald, third son of the above Rev Neil MacKinnon and his wife Johnat, daughter of MacLeod of Drynoch (Lamont, D, 1913, pp. 90–1).

In 1632 the Rev. John MacKinnon was presented by John, Bishop of the Isles, to the chapel of Eynort of Minginish, and also to that of St. Assind of Bracadale (Innes, C, 1854, p. 357).

The famous hereditary succession of ministers of this family began in Strath with Donald, the grandson of the poet, *Lachlan Mac Thearlaich Oig*. The Rev. Donald was born in 1731, and, after a period of service in the Outer Isles, was translated to

Strath in 1771. It was he who constructed the famous genealogical tree of his clan. He was succeeded by his son, John, the compiler of the *'New Statistical Account'* for his parish, and the father of many eminent sons. One of them, the Rev. Dr. Donald MacKinnon, completed the ministerial succession in Strath, another was Surgeon-General Sir William MacKinnon (Lamont, D, 1913, pp. 95–6).

The crest of this clan consists of a boar's head, erased argent, holding in its mouth the shank-bone of a deer proper. In addition to this design, they show in their arms the castle triple-towered of the MacLeods, a lymphod with sails furled, and a hand holding the crosslet, emblematic of their relationship with the MacDonalds. The supporters of the arms are a lion dexter; sinister, a leopard; both proper. Above the escutcheon appears the Latin motto, *'Audentes fortuna Juvat'* ('Fortune favours the brave'), and below occurs in Gaelic, *'Cuimhnich Bàs Alpein'*. The badge of the MacKinnons is the Pine.

The Nicolsons

The origin of this sept is very obscure, and those stray references we meet with in the early records concerning it are of little significance. Hugh MacDonald, the Sleat sennachie, who wrote a history of the MacDonalds in the reign of Charles II, says that Somerled, in his expedition to the northern isles of the Hebrides, *"killed MacLier in Strath, and Olay the Red killed MacNicol in North Uist, likewise"* (Skene, WF, 1847, p. 284). This authority also makes mention of *'MacNicol of Portray'* as one of the sixteen members of Council of the Lord of the Isles and, as that dignity was ended in 1493, the Nicolsons must have been, even at that early time, of some consequence in Skye.

> *Clann 'ic Neacail a' bhrochain*
> Nicolsons of the gruel

'S an droch aran eorna
> And the bad barley bread

Nam potagan mine
> Of the oaten bannocks

'S nan criomagan feola
> And the fragments of meat

Brochan Chloinn Neacail
> Nicolson's gruel

Tog air sop i
> Lift it on a straw

Lite Chloinn Neacail
> Nicolson's porridge

Tog nad uchd i.
> Lift it in your lap.

(MacKay, JG, 1922, p. 337)

The Rev. A. Campbell, who had been successively schoolmaster and parish minister at Portree, towards the end of the eighteenth century, says that the Nicolsons had occupied Scorrybreck since the time of the Danes; while the Rev. J. Morrison of Bragar, who, under the name of *'Indweller'*, wrote an account of his native island in 1680, mentions the Nicolsons as one of the three oldest clans of Lewis and he states that the heiress of that family, a lady named Margaret, had been forcibly espoused by a MacLeod after he had massacred all the males of her kindred. The tradition persists in Lewis that the Nicolsons were in possession of the island before the MacLeods and that for three centuries they had occupied the stronghold of Castle Sween (Mackenzie, WC, 1903, p. 60–1).

Skene says that the Nicolsons are *"descendants of MacKyrcol"*, who lived in Coigeach and Assynt from about 1200 to 1450; and it has been suggested that the variant, *'Mac Reacail'*, may be referable to this eponym. This form is, however, only a case of consonantal change for ease in pronunciation; note 'Gregall' in the genealogy. In 'Collectanea de Rebus Albanicis', Skene (1847, p. 54) quotes a MS wherein is given a genealogical list of chiefs, going back from the year 1450, as follows: John, Ewen, John, Nicail, Aigh (Hugh), Neaibl, Nicail, Gregall, Gillemuir, *"son of Seailb, son of Torquil, son of Totin, son of Thorstein, son of Deacuil, son of Erbhle, son of Harold, son of Murdoch, son of Fogal, son of Paul, son of Allan, son of Carfin, son of Teague, son of Olave, son of Torc of Dublin, son of Harold, son of Osman, son of Ard"*. If we assign twenty years to each, this would place the last-named in the early part of the tenth century.

The first authentic reference to this family in Skye occurs in the reign of James IV, when, in 1507, we find that royal protection was extended to *"Mulconil MacNicol and others of Trouternes"* (Reg. Sec. Sigil. 20 August 1507). . The person against whom this guarantee had been craved, and granted, was the fratricide and usurper, Gillespic *Dubh*, a son of the first chief of Sleat, who, after having gained the royal favour, became bailie of Trotternish in 1511. Again, when in the year 1580, a summons 'was raised' at the instance of John, Bishop of the Isles, against many leading men in Skye, who had failed to pay the teinds due to the church, the name of '*McConneill McNicoll of Trouternes*' is cited (Reg. Sec. Sigil. 25 July 1581). In the following year the king conferred the confiscated property of several island chiefs on the Bishop of the Isles; and among the dispossessed were *"Macconeill MakNicoll, officar of Trouternes, and Nicoll his brother"*, both of whom were declared rebels, and were *"denounced at the horn"* for their remissness in the payment of church dues (Donaldson, G, 1982, p. 69).

After that John, who is mentioned by Gregory as chief in 1500, the succession of chiefs probably was Alexander, Donald, Malcolm, Donald, Malcolm, John, Malcolm, Donald, and Norman (Nicholson, JG, 1988, p. 29). The last marked the end of the line of the chiefs of Scorrybreck and he emigrated to Tasmania in the early years of the nineteenth century. Of the foregoing, there were some who were ministers as well as chiefs, the most notable being the Rev. Donald, who was an Episcopalian minister in Trotternish from 1663 until 1696. On account of his uncompromising attitude to the re-establishment of Presbyterianism in Scotland, he relinquished his charge in the latter year. He died in 1697, leaving an enormous progeny of more than a score of children. One of these, Alexander, was the last clergyman in Skye of the Episcopalian church that was instituted during the reign of Charles II (*ibid.*, p. 16).

Malcolm, the great-grandson of the Rev. Donald Nicolson, a man of striking personality, was greatly revered in Skye because of his unswerving loyalty to the customs of the past and his eagerness to foster the traditions of his race. The unbounding liberality of this chief was remembered for several generations. He died in 1813 aged 87.

Donald, the father of the last chief, was married to Margaret, sister of Sir John MacDonald of Scalpay, Adjutant-General of the Forces. Two of their sons were officers in the Army, the older, Lieutenant Malcolm, being a man of powerful physique and commanding presence. His promising career was cut short by a fever in India, where also died his brother, Lieutenant George Nicolson. Colonel Macinnes, in his *'The Brave Sons of Skye'*, makes mention of a Captain Samuel Nicolson of Tote (Mac-Innes, J, 1899, p. 165).

The armorial bearings of this family consist of a chevron with 3 hawks' heads. The crest is a hawk's head, overall bearing the motto *'Sgorrabreac'*. The badge is the Trailing Azalea, a plant that grows abundantly on the hills of Skye.

The MacAskills

The MacAskills are one of the oldest families in Skye. They are traditionally said to be of Irish extraction, the account being that an ancestor, who had been embroiled in dissensions in Ireland over the succession to a throne, was forced to leave that country and seek the protection of MacLeod of Harris, who gave him lands in Skye. The root, *'Asketill'*, however, points to a Norse origin for this clan, the word meaning 'sacrificial vessel of the gods'.

From very early times this sept occupied the district of *Rubh' an Dùnain*, where the ruins of the family residence may still be seen. Before the MacDonalds took possession of *Dun Sgathaich*, it is said to have been held by the MacAskills as wardens of that fort under the Norse kings of Man. In after days, when reiving prevailed, they filled the office of *comes litoris,* or coast-watcher, to the MacLeods and one of them always did duty as commodore on board the principal galley of the chief of that clan.

Mention has already been made of the exploit of a member of this family, one, William MacAskill, who played such a prominent role in the discomfiture of the forces of the Lord of the Isles at the Battle of Sligachan, early in the sixteenth century. Tradition credits the clan with men of phenomenal physique and extraordinary strength (MacLeod, RC, 1927, pp. 57–8)

Many members of the family served the country, both in the Army and the Navy, and several are known to fame. Two brothers were officers in the American War of Independence – one, Captain John, who was tacksman of *Rubha,* and a younger brother, William, who afterwards rose to the rank of major-general and acted for a time as Governor of Mauritius. He died in 1815. Another clansman who had a distinguished military career was Major-General Sir John MacAskill. He entered the service of the East India Company and took part in the fighting in India in the early years of the nineteenth century. After the massacre of General Elphinstone and his army by hostile Afghan tribes in 1841 and when Sir Robert Sale was dangerously beleaguered in Jalalabad, General MacAskill, as second in command to General Pollock, led the relieving army and rendered distinguished service in that brilliant piece of campaigning. He was serving under Sir Hugh Gough when the Sikhs broke out in rebellion in 1845 and in a minor engagement he was mortally wounded as he was leading his men to the charge. Three of his sons attained commissioned rank, serving chiefly in India (MacInnes, J, 1899, p. 160).

The Beatons

References have been made to members of this famous family on several occasions in connection with their services both to Medicine and to the Church. We meet with the name in Skye as early as the middle of the fourteenth century, when mention is made of a certain John Bethune, who married Margaret, daughter of the second chief of the MacLeods. They early figure as hereditary physicians to the MacDonalds, and the first of that illustrious line is said to have been one of the name of Peter, who, for his services, was given a tract of land, free of all burdens, on condition that he trained one of his sons, preferably the oldest, if he showed any aptitude, to continue the practice of the art for the benefit of the chief and his people. Of his family, the person chosen to carry on the professional succession was the second son, a man named Angus, and he was one of the most noted of his race. He wrote a treatise on the practice of medicine.

The empiric skill of the family was transmitted in unbroken succession from father to son until we come to one who was perhaps the most distinguished of the line. That was Neil, the great-grandson of Angus, who lived during the latter part of the sixteenth and the early portion of the seventeenth century. Said to have been illiterate, he yet was possessed of a wonderful knowledge of herbs, and especially of their medical properties, which he was able to extract in a manner known to himself alone. His skill was so great, not only as a physician, but as surgeon as well, that, according to Martin, his marvellous cures were *"attributed to a compact with the devil"* (Nicolson, A, 1958, pp. 104–6).

In the eighteenth century, when men who were duly qualified practitioners began to appear, these empiricists naturally came to lose their prestige. Then the genius of the race began to express itself in other spheres of usefulness and the Church claimed many of them. Of these, the Rev. John Bethune was minister of Bracadale, where he died in 1708 and has been described as *"an able divine and a learned physician"*. His son, the Rev. Kenneth Bethune, a scholar of note, was minister of Kilmuir, where he died in 1739, while the Rev. William Bethune, who served the parish of Duirinish, and wrote the *'Old Statistical Account'* of that district in 1791, was one of those ministers who so impressed Dr. Johnson, both by their learning and their lofty morality, that he says he could not converse with them *"without wishing, as his respect, that they had not been Presbyterians"* (Johnson, S, 1984, p. 108). The Beatons, some of whom adoped the form *Bethune,* claim to be a sept, both of the MacDonalds and the MacLeods.

The MacQueens

The MacQueens are said by tradition to have been descendants of a member of the human dowry conferred on the daughter of the Irish chief, O'Cathan, who was married to Angus, *'Lord of Trotternish'*, a son of the Lord of the Isles. The MacQueens were said to be of the same stock as the MacDonalds, being descended from *Conn of the Hundred Battles.* The gift consisted of twenty men drawn from each of three tribes and, according to the Rev. Alexander MacGregor, who was parish minister of Kilmuir about the middle of the nineteenth century, the MacQueens were the descendants of one band and they occupied Garrafad for three hundred years. A branch of the family held the lands of Rigg and Totterome for a time. Their rent was a number of salmon to be given to the MacDonalds of Sleat.

Frequent references are made to members of this clan in the history of Skye. Several of them had served the Church, and a remarkable record stands to their name in that son succeeded father as minister in the parish of Snizort for four generations. They were Archibald, who became Episcopalian minister there in 1642; Donald, his son and successor, who, despite his non-jurancy, is said to have been in *"possession of that church"* in 1710; the Rev. Archibald, erudite, pious and zealous in doing good, and finally the Rev. William, who served the disjunct parish of Snizort at the same time that his famous brother, Donald, was the parish minister at Kilmuir. Mention has also been made of the Rev. Angus MacQueen and the Rev. Edmund MacQueen, who were ministers in the parish of Sleat.

Many of them are known to fame as soldiers. There were two who took part in the Jacobite Rebellion of 1745 – one, Malcolm, a loyalist, who fell on Culloden, and another, Archibald, a Hanoverian, was an officer under Major Hugh MacDonald of Armadale, who commanded the contingent of MacDonald Militia. Major Donald John MacQueen, a grandson of the Rev. Dr. Donald MacQueen of Kilmuir, a man of striking appearance, rendered distinguished service during the Peninsular War, and was present in almost all the sanguinary engagements of that titanic conflict. He died in 1836. He had two sons – John Archibald, a lieutenant, who fought in the first Afghan War, and in the Sikh Wars, and the other, Captain George MacQueen, who distinguished himself in the Indian Mutiny (MacInnes, J, 1899, p. 72).

The Martins

Like the MacQueens, the Martins are said to have been descendants of the men brought to Trotternish by *Nighean Chathain,* though another tradition has it that their progenitor was a noted sea-riever named *Aonghus na Gaoithe* (Angus of the Wind), who settled at Marishader.

One of the most notable members of the sept was Martin Martin, who, in 1693, wrote an important treatise on the Western Isles – a work which is our best authority for the social conditions in Skye at that time. He had been educated for the medical profession but it would appear that he had never practised. He graduated MA Edinburgh in 1681, and in 1710 entered Leyden where he qualified as an MD. For several years he acted as tutor in the family of MacLeod at Dunvegan. He died, unmarried, in London.

A member of the family, who occupied the lands of Bealach and Duntulm, is still remembered as a man of huge build and prodigious strength. This was Martin of Bealach who lived during the latter half of the eighteenth century. In a lament of high poetic merit composed on his death by Neil MacNab of Kilvaxter, his praises are sung as follows:

Bha thu foghainteach làidir
 You were handsome and strong
Bha thu spioradail, tàbhachdach, ciùin;
 Lively, firm and calm
Dreach an t-samhraidh mar shnuadh ort
 Like the aspect of summer your expression
Cha robh naimhdeas no fuachd 'nad do ghnuis
 Neither enmity nor aloofness in your countenance
Fiamh a' ghair' air do mhalaidh
 The image of laughter on your brow
Pailt bhlàths ann an sealladh do shùl
 Much warmth in the glance of your eyes
'S mor a chaoidh thug do bhàs
 Your death brought great sorrow
Do 'n mhuinntir a dh' fhàg thu 's an Dùn.
 On those in the Dun.

(Budge, D, 1976, p. 584)

The Reverend Donald Martin, who succeeded the Rev. Dr. Donald MacQueen as parish minister of Kilmuir in 1785, was of the family of Marishader.

The armorial bearings of this sept are composed of three wolves' heads with the crest, which is a tiger rampant holding an arrow point downwards, the supporters consisting of two tigers. The motto is *'Constant and Faithful'*.

The Clan MacInnes

Hugh MacDonald, the historian of Sleat, says that this clan once occupied the lands of Morvern, and he recounts the important role they played under Somerled against the Danes.

The first of the family to settle in Skye is traditionally said to have been a certain *Niall a' Bhogha* ('Neil of the Bow'), so called on account of his prowess as an archer. On one occasion, the sennachie says, his cattle were being raided by a party of MacLeods, near Corry in Strath. Neil attacked the reivers single-handed, killing twelve of them and recovering his stolen stock. His skill was transmitted to his descendants, who were noted archers. This may be the reason why they formed such an important unit in the ranks of Clan Mackinnon, to whose chief they acted as bodyguard in times of war (Lamont, D, 1913, p. 80).

CHAPTER XVII

Social Conditions, 1800–1900

The Church

In dealing with the general conditions of the people during the latter portion of the previous century, reference was made to the buoyancy of spirits that prevailed in the face of great trials. They had songs for every labour, and they took care to sing them. They were passionately fond of the dance; and the fiddle, if not the bagpipe, was kept in every house, and most could handle these instruments with skill. The ancient tale was listened to with the closest attention, while the works of the bards were held in the highest degree of reverence.

As the century advanced towards its close, however, this native joyfulness of heart began gradually to subside. The cruel reality of emigration had cast its shadow over the whole island, as near and dear ones were severed, in many cases for ever, from those left behind. The separation was always a poignant one and the sight of the emigrant ship, with its sorrowing human freight, sailing away to unknown shores, made an impression on those who remained that time could not erase, with the result that there was induced a gravity of outlook on life that the people had never before experienced. Music and the tale now failed to bring consolation to the heavy heart and many came to feel that

their sorrows could be assuaged only *in the ways of religion*. Coincident with the new frame of mind, an evangelising spirit was abroad. In the year 1805, one of its agents came to Skye, in the person of a certain John Farquharson – a man who, though practically illiterate, conveyed his message with an enthusiasm that surmounted all bounds. Many travelled long distances to hear this perfervid evangelist proclaim the gospel in a new light and his labours were rewarded by numerous converts. Among the most noted of these was blind Donald Munro, who had lost his eyesight as a result of smallpox when he was about fourteen years of age. He was born at Achtaleathan, near Portree, about 1773 and died in 1830. This wonderful man, who has been called the *'Father of Evangelical Religion in Skye'*, had been, in his early days, the doyen of fiddlers in the district of Trotternish. That instrument, which had erstwhile been the pride of his heart, became, in his changed state, the means of his mortification; while the genius that had been so ably displayed in the musician began, under the new influence, to manifest itself as powerfully in the missioner whose burning zeal created a real revival wherever he preached. By the force of his personality and the power of his eloquence, he exerted a tremendous sway over the minds of the people, and when, as on one occasion, he asked his hearers to show their renunciation of all forms of 'worldly pleasures' by bringing their musical instruments to the head of Loch Snizort, on a day appointed, for a public conflagration, the response was so general that a veritable 'mountain' of fiddles and bagpipes was there accumulated and consigned to the flames (Nicolson, AW (undated), pp. 3–11).

The orthodox church looked with scorn on this new movement that, as yet, touched the lay population only and was confined almost wholly to Trotternish. Soon, however, it was to permeate Duirinish and Bracadale, chiefly through the instrumentality of the Rev. John Shaw, who ministered successively in these parishes. Mr. Shaw had been appointed assistant to the Rev. Mr. William Bethune of Duirinish in the year 1811. Two years later, on the death of Dr. Roderick MacLeod, he was translated to Bracadale. He has been described *"as an excellent and faithful minister"*; and, by all accounts, he worthily deserved that praise. He died in the 39th year of his age, and the 12th of his ministry, and was succeeded by the Rev. Mr. Roderick, the youngest son of the Rev. Mr. Malcolm of Snizort (Gillies, D (undated), p. 11).

A galaxy of able lay preachers now arose in the northern and western parts of Skye – men who, with the burning fervour of proselytes, endeavoured to *"hasten the Kingdom of Glory"*. Among them were Donald Munro, already mentioned; Alexander MacLeod, tacksman of Ungnacille; Donald MacQueen, and several others and their ranks were greatly strengthened by the fact that the Rev. Mr. Roderick now came under the influence of the new faith.

We have already seen that, on the death of Mr. Shaw, he had been translated from Lyndale, where he had served as a missionary, to the parish of Bracadale in the year 1823. Possessed of a striking personality and a rare turn of eloquence, the young minister ably maintained and furthered the pioneer work of his predecessor. When, in 1838, he returned to his native parish, he carried into his new sphere of labour the zeal and the energy that had produced such remarkable results in his last charge.

In Bracadale the cause of evangelism suffered no arrestment when it lost the services of Mr. Roderick for his successor, the Rev. John Glass, was a man richly indued with the new faith. The influence of these two ministers was powerfully felt even in the neighbouring parishes, with the result that many developed such strictness of outlook that they deemed it not improper to refrain from baptising their children and from partaking of the Sacrament, if they disapproved of the officiating clergyman, or even if they thought that an unconverted person was present at the 'Lord's Table'. Indeed, this attitude of mind had become so settled in Skye that the Rev. A. Clark, minister of Duirinish, writing in 1841, says *"it has to some extent come to be regarded as a proof of piety to avoid partaking of the sacrament"*; and he declares that communion services had been in abeyance in his own parish for eleven years, until about 1840, *"when thirty-five persons partook of the sacrament"*.

Those who came under the power of the new faith based their principles of conduct on the tenets of the Puritans. All forms of secular recreation were unsparingly condemned by the preachers, and their renunciation was heartily observed by the people. *"I have raised the standard against shinty and tobacco both"*, writes Mr. Roderick, *"and with some measure of success"* (Gillies, D (undated), p. 99).

Such, then, was the state of affairs in Skye when the Disruption took place in 1843. The people of the North and West of the island were ripe for secession, and showed it in no uncertain way. Writing in 1841, the Rev. Coll MacDonald, parish minister of Portree, speaks of the loyalty of his people to the Established Church: *"So inviolable is their attachment to it"*, says he, *"that lately some of them, hearing of disputes which at that moment unfortunately disturbed and agitated our venerable church, and dreading that these arose from the hostility of Roman Catholicism* and other sectarians, were heard solemnly to declare, in presence of the writer of these pages, that sooner than the church of their fathers should suffer violence or change, and far less annihilation, they would suffer their heads to be cut off" (Second Statistical Account of Portree); and he observes elsewhere "*There are no sectarians of any description in this parish*". How far he misunderstood the temper of the people, subsequent events prove, for, when the schism took place, the great majority of his congregation on the mainland of Skye threw in their lot with the Free Church and practically the whole population of Raasay and Rona seceded.

The same tale could be told of the other parishes in the north and west of Skye but only a few families left the establishment in Sleat, and still less in Strath, the latter parish being long looked upon by the adherents of the Free Church as "*the home of infidelity*".

Of the ministers of Skye, all remained faithful to the old church with two exceptions, namely, the Rev. Roderick MacLeod of Snizort and the Rev. John Glass of Bracadale. These two dedicated themselves, body and soul, to the cause of the new church and, though for many years they laboured under grave difficulties, their work was greatly lightened by that whole-hearted zeal, the faithful adherence and the unfailing generosity which one always finds associated with any new movement. For many years all their meetings were held in the open air. The congregation of the Free Church of Snizort was refused a site for a church for many years. The people met for worship in the open and, as Mr. Roderick's successor, the Rev. Joseph Lamont, observes,

my predecessor often preached with the hailstones dancing on his forehead, his hearers wiping away the snow before they would sit down; and, when the shower was passed, they could not be distinguished from the ground, except by their faces.

Alexander MacLeod of Ungnacille, later missionary in Portree, describing his itineraries in the *Highland Missionary Society's Journal*, tells that, ministering to people on the east side of Raasay, he could not find a house large enough to accommodate the congregation and had recourse to a cave, at the seashore, where they were sheltered from a severe storm.

This state of affairs continued until the munificent Major Fraser entered into possession of a portion of the north of Skye. He readily granted a site for a church, which was built at Uig, contributed generously to its building fund, declining to exact any rent for it during his life-time. But see the lines on him by the poetess, *Màiri Mhòr nan Oran* (Big Mary of the Songs, or Mary Macpherson):

> *Ged a lion thu suas do shaibhlean*
>> Although you filled up your barns
> *Le foirneadh nan daoine coibhneil*
>> By encroaching on the kindly people
> *Gheibh thu fhathast duais na thoill thu*
>> You will get the reward you deserve
> *'S cha dean saibhreas a dh' fheum dhuit.*
>> And wealth will not do you any good.
>>> (Mac-Bheathain, A, 1891, p. 214)

The prejudice against the new sect was as marked in the other parishes of Skye as it was in Snizort. The petitions of the people of Portree for a site on which to build a church were scornfully rejected and the pleas of the adherents in Kilmuir went unheeded until the year 1860 (Gillies, D, (undated), p. 84). Indeed, if all accounts be true, such was the bitterness shown to the Free Church, and we have the testimony of the Rev. Mr. Reid of Portree for it, that several people had been evicted from their holdings for no other reason than that they were members of the new church.

A few particulars concerning the ministers who served in the several parishes of Skye at this time now fall to be recorded. We have seen that the Rev. Alexander Campbell was the incumbent at Portree at the beginning of the nineteenth century. He was a graduate in Arts of the University of Aberdeen and, on the completion of his course there, he was appointed schoolmaster and catechist at Portree by the Commission of the Royal Bounty, in the year 1791. In the last year of the century he became minister of the parish, as successor to the Rev. John Nicolson. At the early age of forty-one years he was killed by falling from the top of a stair in his house, and the death of their minister under such tragic circumstances, and in the prime of life, made a deep impression on his parishioners. It was said of him then that *"his erudition was varied and extensive, and he was noted for his liberality and benevolence"*. He took a deep interest in the lore of the past, and was a gleaner of note of the poetry that still floated about on the breath of tradition, some of which was published in *Reliquae Celticae* (MacBain, A & Kennedy, J, 1892, Vol. I) and *Leabhar na Feinne* (Campbell JF, 1872, Vol. I). He himself was a poet of no mean order. Nor did he neglect the primary duties of his calling, but laboured indefatigably for the spiritual benefit of his flock. In 1791 he was commissioned to compile the *Statistical Account for the Parish of Portree*, and, as he was a native of the island, he was well qualified for the work.

This man of sterling qualities was succeeded, in 1811, by the Rev. Coll MacDonald. *'Mgr Cólla'* was a man of forceful character and great industry. In 1825 he succeeded in building a church for the parish, the manse having been constructed in 1811 and, through his influence and zeal for education, he was responsible for the establishment of two schools, one in his own parish and the other in that of Snizort. He has been described as a man of *"high moral worth"* and the account goes on to say that *"he was always ready to forward the best interests of the poor and to give sound direction and advice in matters both sacred and secular"*. He wrote the *'New Statistical Account'* for his parish, a production that stamps him at once as a 'man of affairs'. In the bitterness of the strife that centred around the Disruption his name was much maligned, while from the great numbers that defected from his charge, it would appear that his ministry failed to appeal to those who were carried away by the new evangelical movement in this part of Skye. He died in 1854 at the age of eighty-one years, and was succeeded by the Rev. H. MacArthur, who had been appointed his assistant during the previous year. Mr. MacArthur served the congregation until 1867, when he was followed by the Rev. John Darroch, M.A., who, in 1894, was succeeded by the Rev. A. Black.

The first minister of the Free Church of Portree was the Rev. Duncan MacEachran. He was admitted to this church in 1849 but remained only for two years, when he chose to go to Cromarty. After him the Rev. James Reid was settled on the congregation in 1853 and, for the long period of forty years, he faithfully served the church. This mild-mannered and cultured gentleman was greatly beloved by the people of the parish, though the last years of his life were clouded by the secession of a large number of his congregation in 1893. The Rev. Mr. Reid died in 1896, and was followed by the Rev. Norman MacLeod, who had been appointed colleague and successor two years previously.

The first minister of the Free Church in Raasay was the Rev. William MacDougall, who was inducted there in 1851. It was during the following years that several townships on this island were cleared and the ruthless work so weighed on the mind of the minister that he resigned this charge in 1855. His successor was the Rev. Mr. Kippen. The *Teachdaire Gaidhealach* of Australia produced in Hobart, Tasmania, in 1857, mentions the call given by the Free Church in Raasay to Mr Kippen. He remained there until 1868, and in the following year came the young and able Mr. Galbraith, who was called to Ferintosh in 1890.

In the adjacent parish of Snizort the Rev. Malcolm MacLeod ministered until his death, in 1833, when the Rev. Simon MacLachlan was presented to the charge. Five years afterwards, on Mr. MacLachlan's translation to Cawdor, the pastorate devolved on his predecessor's famous son, the Rev. Mr. Roderick MacLeod, who returned to his native parish from Bracadale. Mr. Roderick, born in 1795 in Glen Haultin, graduated M.A. of Aberdeen at the age of twenty years. In 1818 he was appointed missionary at Lyndale, whence, in 1823, he was transferred to Bracadale, on his being presented to that church by MacLeod of MacLeod. During the period of his incumbency in Lyndale, the athletic young minister was a general favourite among those in the higher circles in Skye and he used to remark, concerning his nomination to Bracadale, that it was more for his proficiency as a marksman than for his fitness for his calling as minister of the gospel, that he was offered this preferment. In Bracadale he built a church in 1831. We have already referred to his work there, and his continuance of it in Snizort. He was deprived of his charge in 1843, a misfortune that served only to stimulate him to higher endeavour. A man of fearless disposition and herculean strength, he was endowed with marvellous powers of endurance that were often tested to the full. For several years he ministered to his own people in Snizort as well as to those who followed the Free Church in the parish of Portree and his services were in constant demand in other parts of the island. It has been said of him that *"after passing nights without rest, while journeying by sea and land, he would preach with the greatest vigour"*. His last illness was brought about by exposure in an open boat during a wet and stormy night, as he was returning from South Uist, where he had been preaching for several days (Gillies, D, (undated), pp. 113–4). He was Moderator of the Assembly of the Free Church in the year 1863, and died in 1868. Mr. Roderick was succeeded by the Rev. Joseph Lamont, a man of great amiability and an earnest worker, but lacking the personality of his famous predecessor. He was followed by the Rev. Mr. MacDougall, who had been translated thither from Lochs in Lewis; after him came, the Rev. Donald MacArthur.

The Established Church, having been rendered vacant by the expulsion of Mr. Roderick in 1843, was filled in the following year by the Rev. Angus Martin.

About the year 1837 the Baptists had established themselves in this parish, attaining such an ascendancy as to curb the Revivalist movement there for a space. The efforts of this sect were, however, effectively counteracted when the Rev. Roderick MacLeod became the minister of the parish in 1838.

On the translation of the Rev. Donald Martin to the Chapel of Ease in Inverness in 1808, the Rev. Donald Ross, a graduate of Aberdeen, was appointed minister of Kilmuir in the following year. In 1810 a new church was built above the shore of Score Bay, the whole cost being borne by the liberal-minded Alexander, second Lord MacDonald. In 1822 Mr. Ross left Kilmuir for Rogart, and was succeeded by the Rev. Robert MacGregor, whose successor was his scholarly son, Alexander. It was the last who compiled the highly instructive account of this parish for the *'New Statistical Account'* in 1841. The Rev. Alexander MacGregor had been minister in Inverness prior to his coming to Kilmuir in 1844, and continued to serve the parish until 1851. Mary Macpherson composed a beautiful lament on him (*vide, Celtic Magazine*, July 1833, p. 436, and Mac-Bheathain, A, 1891, p. 186).

In 1853 he was succeeded by the Rev. John MacIvor, who had been translated thither from Sleat, where he had officiated for close on ten years. After Mr. MacIvor came the short-lived ministry of Mr. Mackenzie, followed by the long-continued incumbency of the Rev. James Grant. Mr. Grant is reputed to have been a large-minded man, keenly interested in public affairs, while his abilities as an administrator often proved of great help to the local bodies to which he gave his willing service. After him came the scholarly Mr. MacPhail, whose immediate successors were the Rev. Mr. MacLean and the Rev. Mr. Stewart.

It was during the ministry of the Rev. Robert MacGregor that this large parish was divided, a *quoad sacra* charge having been constituted at Stenschol by authority of the Assembly in 1833. A minister had been appointed to serve this district in 1829. He was the Rev. John Nicolson, a graduate at the University of Aberdeen, who had previously officiated as missionary in Minginish, where he had been ordained by the Commission of the Royal Bounty in 1816. The first minister of the Free Church of Kilmuir was the Rev. Christopher Munro, who, in 1864, was translated to Strathtay. His successor, the Rev. J.S. MacPhail, who had previously served in Sleat, went to Kilmuir in 1873, continuing there until the year 1888, when the Rev. D.A. MacDonald, was appointed to the charge.

In Duirinish, the scholarly William Bethune was succeeded, in 1811, by the saintly John Shaw, who was translated to Bracadale in 1813. After the church had been vacant for a year, it was filled by the Rev. James Suter, a graduate in Arts of Aberdeen, who, in addition to his ministerial duties, was tacksman of Feorlig, as well as chamberlain to MacLeod of MacLeod. Under the date of 13 May 1818 is a letter from him, to MacLeod of MacLeod, on estate business (MacLeod, RC, 1939, p. 18). It was during the ministry of Mr Suter that a new church was built in Dunvegan in 1832. Mr. Suter died in 1839, and his assistant, the Rev. John Glass, was appointed his successor. This minister, as we have seen, came under the influence of the new movement in the church, and when in 1838, he was translated to Bracadale, he continued the work that the Rev. Roderick MacLeod had fostered there. His successor in Duirinish was the Rev. Archibald Clark, the compiler of the *New Statistical Account* for the parish. In 1842 Mr. Clark was succeeded by the Rev. Angus Martin, whose short ministry of two years terminated when he was translated to the parish of Snizort, on the deposition of Mr.

Roderick. The next minister of Duirinish was the Rev. Duncan MacCallum, who continued to officiate there until 1888. After him came the Rev. Mr. MacLean, the compiler of the valuable *Typographia Scoto Gadelica* (MacLean, D, 1915) and who was followed by the Rev. Mr. Mackenzie, the last minister of the Establishment in Duirinish.

In the Free Church of this parish the ministers were the eloquent and evangelical Mr. MacColl, on whose translation to the district of Fort Augustus, there came the Rev. Mr. MacRae – '*MacRath a' Loin Mhoir*, large in body and sanguine in endeavour, a man who enjoyed a wide reputation as a healer, especially amongst the adherents of his own sect.

In the same year that the *quoad sacra* charge was formed at Stenschol, another was established in Duirinish, its first minister being the Rev. Roderick Reid, M.A. When, however, the congregation was reduced, owing to defections, in 1843, he was translated to Lewis. Mr. Reid has been described as a "*man of moderate principles, and temperate passions.*" In 1884, the Rev. Donald MacCallum was elected to the charge. He was an ardent democrat and, during his ministry he played a prominent part in the crofters' agitation. In 1887 he left Skye for the island of Tiree.

In Bracadale, the Rev. John Shaw succeeded the Rev. Dr. Roderick MacLeod in 1813, and on his death, in 1823, the Rev. Roderick MacLeod was translated thither from Lyndale. In 1839 the Rev. John Glass became minister of this parish, and on his dismissal in 1843 because of his adherence to the Free Church, the Rev. Neil Mackinnon was appointed parish minister. In 1856 there came the Rev. John Tolmie, who, eight years later, was succeeded by the Rev. Roderick Morrison.

The second minister of the Free Church in Bracadale was the Rev. John Finlayson, brother-in-law of Rev Roderick MacLeod. He was translated from Ness in Lewis to Bracadale in December

1843, but was killed in February 1844 as a result of a fall from a gig (Ewing, WM, 1914, Vol. 2, p. 231).

The Episcopalian chapel at Caroy was restored in 1838, and its minister was the Rev. William Greig, whose congregation then consisted of four families.

In the parish of Strath there was the illustrious succession of MacKinnons. At the beginning of the century the Rev. Donald MacKinnon was minister of this parish, being in 1826 succeeded by his son, John, who had served in the parish of Sleat since 1812. The Rev. John MacKinnon compiled the *Statistical Account* for his parish in 1841. In 1840 the congregation ceased to meet for worship in the old church of Kilchrist, or Kilchro, *"owing to its state of disrepair"*, and a new church was then erected in Broadford. In 1856 the Rev. John MacKinnon was succeeded by his son, the Rev. Dr. Donald MacKinnon, a man of eminent ability, a fearless protagonist of the evicted crofters of Skye, and a real friend to those in distress. *An Gaidheal* of February 1874 reported under the title, *A Pluralist in Skye:*

> *There is in the Island of Skye a minister, in one of the parish churches, who occupies the pulpit which his father, grandfather and great-grandfather have filled in succession and who is training his son to be his successor. Chairman of the School Board, road contractor for the district, noted breeder of setters, a knowing judge of cattle, occupant of four large sheep farms in addition to his glebe, verging on three score years, preaches two sermons, one in Gaelic, the other in English every Sunday.*
>
> (Lamont, D, 1913, pp. 95–6).

On the translation of the Rev. John MacKinnon from Sleat in 1826, the Rev. Alexander MacIvor, M.A., who had served for some years as schoolmaster in Glenelg, where his father was minister, became the new incumbent. When Mr MacIvor went to Dornoch in 1843, his brother, the Rev. John MacIvor, became minister of the parish. Mr. John was a man of gigantic physique, large in heart as well as in body, and he is still remembered for his lovable nature and his great liberality. On his translation to the parish of Kilmuir in 1853, there came the following succession: The Rev. John Forbes, who ministered there for ten years; the Rev. Donald MacDonald; and, seven years afterwards, the Rev. Archibald MacNeil. In 1882 the Rev. Alexander Cameron was inducted here, being succeeded in 1914 by the Rev. Mr. Ross.

It would appear that the old church of Kilmore, built in 1681, was still used for worship in 1841. The parish manse was erected in 1815, the same year as the castle of Armadale, the plan of which, by Gillespie Graham, was used in the designing of the manse.

The first minister of the Free Church in the parish of Sleat was the Rev. J.S. MacPhail, and he continued to officiate there for the long period of twenty years, after which he was transferred to Kilmuir. His most notable successor was the Rev. Finlay Graham, who was a zealous advocate of the cause of the crofters during the early eighties of last century.

About the year 1890, the Free Church began to exhibit signs of schism, when the proposal for union with the United Presbyterian Church was being mooted. On the passing of the Declaratory Act in 1892, the indications of cleavage took definite form, with the result that a new church was set up. It was called the Free Presbyterian Church of Scotland and its leaders were the Rev. Donald MacFarlane of Raasay and the Rev. Donald MacDonald of Shieldaig. In certain parts of Skye, notably in the parishes of Portree and Duirinish, this new sect had a large following.

The Morals of the People

As a result of the revivals that took place in many parts of Skye in the early years of the nineteenth century, two facts emerge. In the first place, the preachers of the new evangelism waged war persistently against such popular recreations as secular music, the ancient tales and the traditional barderie, with the result that much of the native culture, developed during the course of ages, has been irretrievably lost.

In the second place, there supervened a decided change in the conduct of the people, so far as their attitude to temperance was concerned. Thus the Rev. A. Clark of Duirinish, writing in 1841, says, in effect, that at marriages and funerals the riotous revelries that prevailed in previous years were then unknown; and he continues: *"The people are generally remarkably sober. Their hospitality continues as unbounded as ever; but in their exercise of it, the rules of temperance and decorum are very rarely violated, and every excess is condemned and discouraged"*; and the Rev. Coll MacDonald of Portree declares that such vices as profane swearing and drunkenness *"are less prevalent than they were twenty years ago"*.

Still, a large amount of strong drink was then consumed in Skye. In Bracadale alone there were, according to the Rev. Roderick MacLeod, five licensed ale houses and, he adds: *"Whisky is retailed in various other places, to the manifest injury of the temporal interests of the people, and the progressive and sure destruction of their morals"*. Mr. Roderick was, of course, one of the stoutest advocates of temperance the Church then possessed, and it was characteristic of the man to denounce, in no unmistakable terms, any extension of the traffic in excisable liquors. The construction of a distillery in Carbost, Minginish, in 1830, deeply offended the principles of this ardent reformer. In referring to it on one occasion, he characterises it as *"one of the greatest curses that, in the ordinary course of providence, could befall this or any other place."*

On the whole, the standard of morality that prevailed among the people was a high one. They were peaceable and law-abiding; so much so, indeed, that it is very rare to find an instance of recorded crime.

Stanhope, who made a tour of Skye in 1805, adverts to the jail that had 'recently' been built at Portree, and his observation on it is, *"it is principally in terrorem, as it is always empty"*. The Rev. A. MacIvor, writing in 1841, states that the only criminal offence known to have been committed in the parish of Sleat since the year 1827 was one of theft, *"and the culprit was an imbecile"*; while the Rev. John MacKinnon, writing at the same time of Strath, has nothing worse to record of the conduct of his parishioners than to deplore the importation by gangrel-bodies of ragmen, tinkers, and egg-wives, of such vices as *"tea-drinking, tobacco-chewing and smoking"*! Of the parish of Portree, the Rev. Coll MacDonald says: *"The people are powerfully under the influence of moral principles, so much so that heinous crimes are seldom or ever seen or heard among them"*.

In the parish of Snizort, on the other hand, Mr. Donald Fraser, the compiler of the *'Second Statistical Account'*, remarks on the degeneracy of morals among the people, their proneness to quarrel, their litigious propensities and their disposition to thieving. This is truly a staggering statement when collated with the contemporary accounts of the other parishes and one that can be accepted only with a large amount of reservation. Indeed, the only facts that can at all be adduced in support of this sweeping asseveration is a statement by the minister of the parish of Portree to the effect that, in 1840 (a year when a phenomenal wave of crime overtook the island), as many as sixteen persons had been sentenced to imprisonment at Portree, *"four of them for house-breaking"*. He adds that, owing to the insecurity of their confines, the prisoners often escaped, and that they were made desperate by the inhumanity of their treatment. No attempt was made to heat the cells, no bedding was provided for them, and the means of subsistence were so scanty that they were often starving.

The Housing of the People

The housing of the people showed no improvement on the conditions prevailing during the previous century. In the vast majority of cases, the cattle were under the same roof as the people themselves. The dwellings were still the same long, low-roofed structures and rarely was there any attempt made to divide them into chambers. Where partitions did exist, these were chiefly of drystone; some were of wattled-work, woven of straw or reeds, while, owing to the great dearth of timber, there were very few of wood. They seldom reached higher than the top of the walls of the house; above that was black emptiness, permeated by the peat reek that fumigated and deodorised the noisome atmosphere.

Near the fire, which was in the middle of the floor, was a cast-iron pot of enormous capacity, containing dyeing decoctions, whose pungent odours drew attention to its presence in every household with any pretensions to skill and well-regulated industry.

There was, of course, no incentive to change these conditions. Indeed, should the tenant aim at improving the amenities of his house or his holding, there was often imposed an increase of rent as a result of his labours. Besides, people were prohibited in most parishes from gleaning thatch for their dwellings, as the cutting of rushes, and especially the pulling of heather, were held to interfere with the preservation of game. Thus a crofter from Sconser, who had been cited to appear before the Royal Commission in 1882, declared that the houses in his district were the worst in Skye, because the people were not allowed to take thatch from the hills. *"A neighbour of mine"*, he added, *"went out to cut heather for ropes, and the huntsmen came upon him and they threatened to shoot him if they found him there again. They were afraid we would disturb the muirfowl"*. A witness from Milovaig in Glendale, who came before the same court, deponed that, owing to the prohibition in vogue in his district against the pulling of heather, the condition of their dwelling-houses was *"most deplorable"*. And the same sad state of affairs is epitomised in the *'Report of the Commission'*, wherein it is declared that *"the habitations of the people are of a character that would imply physical and moral degradation in the eyes of those who do not know how much decency, courtesy, virtue, and even mental refinement, survive amid the sordid surroundings of a Highland hovel"*.

In the latter portion of the nineteenth century, wooden partitions were erected in some houses, and separate doors were made for the cattle and the human inmates. At the same time, a few sought to effect internal improvements by improvising a sort of wooden chimney that was suspended against the end wall of the kitchen, but this contrivance proved, in most cases, to be a very ineffectual ventilator. Many outhouses also were constructed, and soon a few of the so-called 'white houses' began to make their appearance in the more progressive areas. But it was not until the following century was on its way that their number came to exceed that of the old 'black houses'.

General Conditions of the People; Their Diet, Clothing, etc.

During this century the people came, more and more, to depend on the potato as their principal article of food. The enormous increase in its cultivation is shown by the fact that, whereas in one parish of Skye the yield was 5,000 barrels in 1801, it had risen to 32,000 barrels in 1841. We have seen that great privations resulted from a failure of this crop, even towards the end of the previous century, when people were less dependent on it than they were at this time. The inclement weather that prevailed in 1807, and again in 1817, greatly impaired the crop, and there was much suffering in Skye, but worse times were to follow. In the summer of 1835 the weather had been so wet that a blight

supervened which ruined the potato fields. During that winter, and the spring of the following year, many were in a state bordering on starvation, and, for several years afterwards their plight had not much improved. It has been said that, in 1837, *"half the people of Skye were destitute"*. The Rev. Roderick MacLeod, who wrote the *'Second Statistical Account'* for Bracadale in 1841, in speaking of the food of the people, reports: *"They are not considered ill-provided who can feed on potatoes and salt, and during the last season even that would have been a luxury to many of them"*. The dependence of the people on the potato crop is adverted to by those other ministers in Skye who were responsible for the compilation of the *'New Statistical Account'* for their respective parishes at this time. The Rev. A. MacIvor of Sleat says: *"The food of the people consists chiefly of potatoes and fish, sometimes with salt and sometimes without"*. Alluding to the conditions that obtained in the parish of Duirinish, the Rev. A. Clark declares: *"Butcher meat is almost unknown among them, and very little meal is used"*; while it would appear that in the district of Portree the people did not fare any better. The minister of that parish, the Rev. Coll MacDonald, states that *"no people on earth live on more simple and scanty diet than those in this parish. The greater number of them subsist on potatoes of the worst kind, sometimes with, but oftener without, fish"*. A medical man who spent a couple of years in Raasay about 1850, remarks: *"The prevailing disease is poverty, and the remedy is food"*.

The distresses of these years were not so general, nor so acute as they became after 1845. That year, and during the three succeeding summers, the blight played havoc with the crops, so that in many cases the people were not able to raise enough potatoes to provide seed for planting in the following spring. Destitution was so widespread that the government appealed for funds for the alleviation of distress, and employment was given in the construction of new roads and the repairing of those already existing.

In 1848 a Committee of Relief was inaugurated for the West Highlands, and a Captain Eliott was appointed Inspector-General for the whole area. Writing in August of that year, he reports that *"the potato failure in Skye is virulent, decided, and on the increase. The cereal crops are perhaps an average, and from the wet weather they are still growing, and they afford no prospect of harvest under five or six weeks to come"*.

The local agent of the Committee was Captain Fishbourne, a man entirely devoid of sympathy with the people. He constantly inveighs against them for what he considers their lack of self-dependence, and their proneness to look for help from others without doing anything in return. In substantiation of his statement, he cites the case of thirty-five men who, as he alleges, left the employment of MacLeod, although they were earning 10s a week, *"merely on the speculation that they would obtain Committee meal"*. The people, however, complained that while they worked hard, and for long hours, the wages were low, and Captain Fishbourne himself mentions the case of a man who, with his wife and family, had worked at netmaking from Monday morning till Saturday night for the aggregate wage of 4s 8d.

The work provided consisted of road-making, the construction of piers, the building of march dykes, draining land, spinning, knitting, and netting. Of these employments, road-making absorbed 1441 persons.

Philanthropic agencies, also, were busy, but none was so unsparing of his means and his energy in that respect as Norman, twenty-fifth Chief of MacLeod. That generosity, which had graced the House of Dunvegan down the years, was never practised with greater liberality and genuine disinterestedness than on this occasion. It is said that the estate was spending from £175 to £225 a week and, when the chief was warned of the imminence of financial disaster, he would answer that *"ruin must be faced rather than let the people die"* (MacLeod, RC, 1927, p. 180).

Godfrey, Lord MacDonald, too, was tireless in his efforts to relieve the distress and it is on record that, in 1849, he was supplying numerous families with meal free of charge. Still, there was no alleviation of the suffering and many were constrained, as on previous occasions of want, to haunt the foreshores for shellfish, that with dulse – 'kail' was often their sole means of subsistence for weeks on end. So great was the state of destitution that, in 1850, the Rev. Roderick MacLeod, minister of the Free Church at Snizort, wrote to the Secretary of State for Home Affairs: *"Death from starvation must be the inevitable result if we are denied extraneous aid, as we have no available local resources of any kind".*

The state of poverty that prevailed during the first portion of this century is shown also by the lack of the other amenities of life. Great difficulty was experienced in providing clothing, many going bare-footed even in winter. Some were constrained to make use of meal bags as outer garments, and more often as underclothing, for children. The Rev. Coll MacDonald reports of his own parish in 1841: *The people have little of night or day clothing. The children nearly approach absolute nakedness';* and the Rev. Roderick MacLeod ascertained that, in the parish of Bracadale, *'one hundred and forty families had no change in night or day clothes".*

The Clearances and Emigration

We have seen that the trade-boom in the sale of the black cattle had been maintained without intermittence until the beginning of the nineteenth century, and that one of the immediate results of it was a steady appreciation in the price of such land as could conveniently be used for the purposes of pasturage. Incidentally,

it created a keen demand for more land on the part of those who could afford to pay extra rent so that several of the smaller farmers, and large numbers of crofters, were callously squeezed out. The system of multiple farming, too, was in vogue – a principle characterised by the Rev. Roderick MacLeod of Bracadale as *"a decided disadvantage to the whole population".*

Reference has also been made to a new industry, namely, kelp-making, that was then introduced, and was to provide a means of subsistence for a time for those who were dispossessed. Such people built lowly homes along the shores and were able to live in moderate comfort so long as the price of kelp was maintained at the higher level. When, however, in 1825, the tax on barilla was repealed and a start was made in utilising for commercial purposes the enormous deposits of sulphate of potash at Strassfurt in Germany, a rapid decrease in the demand for Hebridean kelp ensued, so that in the short space of a little more than a year its price fell from £30 to £2 10s a ton. So long as the industry of kelp-making was lucrative, fishing, and even farming, were to a large extent neglected: when it was no longer profitable to pursue it, the spectre of starvation haunted all who had no other means of support. The exodus to the Colonies was once more resumed, and many a home-sick heart was divided from the Misty Isle *"by a waste of seas".*

About the same time that the trade in kelp was on the decline, an event happened that was destined to play a greater part in the depopulation of our island than any that had preceded it. That was the accidental discovery that the Cheviot breed of sheep could withstand the rigours of a Highland winter. A feverish demand for sheep farms, in consequence, ensued and factors were busy devising plans for getting rid of the crofters who occupied the more fertile townships. Whole communities were soon cleared out of certain districts, and places that once rang with the merry voices of children were now converted into deserts, where nothing could be heard but the bleat of the polled sheep of the borders, the bark of the collie and the language of the stranger, for several wealthy farmers from the Scottish mainland entered into possession of tacks in Skye.

In his *'Oran nan Ciobairean'* the poet, *Ailean Dall*, depicts the situation in a graphic manner.

Thàinig oirnn do Albainn crois,
　A cross has come to us in Scotland,
Tha daoine bochda nochdte ris,
　And poor people are exposed to it.,
Gun bhiadh, gun aodach, gun chluain,
　Without food, clothing or ease,
Tha 'n àirde tuath an déidh a sgrios.
　The North land has been devastated.
Chan fhaicear ach caoirich is uain,
　One sees only sheep and lambs,
Goill mu'n cuairt dhaibh air gach slios,
　Lowlanders around them on each moor,
Tha gach fearann air dol fàs,
　All cultivated land is going wild,
Na Gaidheil is an ceann fo fhliodh.
　The Gaels with their heads under dirt.
Cha chluinnear geum ann am buaile,
　One does not hear lowing in the fold,
Chaidh 'n crodh guail'-fhionn a suim,
　The white shouldered cattle are out of fashion,
Cha n eisdear luinneag, no duanag,
　One cannot hear a song or ditty,
Bleoghan mairt aig gruagach dhuinn
　From brown haired maids milking cows.
On chaidh ar cuallach an tainead
　Since our cattle stock was thinned
'S tric tha pathadh 'gar claoidh;
　Often we are tormented by thirst;

'N aite nan càirdean a bh' againn,
　In place of the friends we had,
Linnseach ghlas am bun gach tuim.
　There is a grey sluggard at the base of every knoll.
(MacKenzie, J, 1877, p. 302)

The work of depopulating the straths of Skye went on apace. The grassy slopes on the west side of the island considered being eminently suitable for the rearing of Cheviots, clearances on a wholesale scale were then effected. From Duirinish, Bracadale, and Minginish people were evicted. The population of Bracadale in 1841 was 1824. By 1881 it had dropped to 929. The whole of the land in this fertile area was divided among six tenant farmers, namely, Talisker, Glenbrittle, Drynoch, Ebost with Ullinish, Ose, and Totarder. Glenbrittle, which was occupied by crofters in fairly comfortable circumstances, was now converted into a sheep-run. The flats and the slopes of Eynort and of Tuasdale, two of the most picturesque spots in Skye, bear the records of the clearances in unmistakable characters even to this day. A large community was driven off the former and the manse was converted into a shepherd's cottage; from the latter about a dozen families were cleared away. Sixteen families were expelled from the adjoining lands of Krakinish and as many as thirty were forced to evacuate Fernilea. All these took place in Minginish but a similar tale could be told of Bracadale, from one district of which, namely, Feorlig, seventeen families were removed in 1840.

And Trotternish did not escape. The populous district of Scorrybreck was cleared from end to end. The fertile south end of Raasay suffered a similar fate and numerous townships there were wholly given over to the rearing of sheep. Indeed, few districts escaped the effects of the change. The work of depopulation was carried into Strath, where, among other districts, two populous townships, Borreraig and Suisnish, were ruthlessly cleared by the notorious Ballingall, Lord MacDonald's factor. This was in 1852 and, as some of the crofters offered resistance, they were forcibly evicted and their dwellings razed to the ground in order to prevent their return. It was a time of snow. One man, who did return to his home in Suisnish, was found dead the following morning at the door of his ruined house, having perished in the night from exposure and cold. It has been said that as many as 2000 were dispossessed of land and home on the estate of MacLeod and that the number for the whole island amounted to 3500 persons.

The evicted were in some cases provided with alternative accommodation, but invariably on those parts of the estate where the soil was inferior or exhausted. Hundreds were intruded on the crofting areas, where extreme overcrowding, with all its attendant evils, soon prevailed. A few instances will suffice to show the extent to which this congestion had been allowed to go. Two of the townships of Braes, namely, Penichorran and Achnahanaid, were divided among five and four tenants, respectively, about the year 1823. By 1883 the number of crofters had been increased to twenty-six in the former, and in the latter to seventeen, exclusive of several squatters.

Multitudes more could find no site for a home in the land of their birth, and the only course open to them lay in emigration to the Colonies. In a report published in the *Highland Missionary Society's Journal*, Alexander MacLeod, Tacksman of Ungnacille, later Missionary in Portree, says that in July 1833, a ship, the *Adrian*, was at anchor in Portree, having aboard a great number of emigrants, to whom he preached. In 1837 a contingent of 459 was shipped off to Australia and, during the years 1840 and 1841 as many as 600 souls sailed to that continent and to America from the parish of Portree alone. Indeed, emigration was considered to be the only expedient for relieving the difficulties of the situation, and many philanthropically-minded people formed associations for the purpose of raising funds in order to help those who might be induced to go abroad. By many the action of these agencies was thought to be a most commendable one, most of the ministers of Skye giving it their blessing. The Rev. Coll MacDonald of Portree was enthusiastic in his praise. *"It cannot fail"*, he wrote in 1841,

> *to afford the highest satisfaction to every well-regulated mind to see the efforts now made by noble men, proprietors, and others connected with the Highlands of Scotland, for transferring the poor and labouring classes of the community to the British colonies … The highest praise is due to Lord MacDonald for his liberality in this beneficent work and patriotic enterprise, he having expended large sums of money, both this year and last, in conveying the poor people on his property to America.*

In 1851 a society, under the presidency of Sheriff Fraser of Portree, succeeded in securing £7200, by means of which it was able to provide for the passage of 200 emigrants from Skye; while in 1854, 129 persons sailed from Raasay in one day, when, it is said, the wailing of these unfortunate people could plainly be heard on the opposite shore at Braes as they were being dragged on board the emigrant ship in Clachan Bay. In 1857, the *Teachdaire Gaidhealach* of Australia notes *"At the beginning of this year, many a pitiable family left Skye for America and Australia."*

Mention has already been made of the removal of the crofters from Borreraig and from Suisnish in Strath, and it is interesting to record the account given of the incident by Sir Archibald Geikie, the famous geologist, as it represents the impressions of one who was an eye-witness of the event, and is noted for the accuracy of his observations and the impartiality of his statements.

Geikie was always a welcome guest at the manse of the MacKinnons in Kilbride and concerning one of his many visits there he writes:

One of the most vivid recollections I retain of Kilbride is that of the eviction, or the clearance of the crofters of Suisnish. The corner of Strath between the two sea-inlets of Lochs Slapin and Eishort had been for ages occupied by a community that cultivated the lower ground, where their huts formed a kind of scattered village. The land belonged to the wide domain of Lord Macdonald, whose affairs were in such a state that he had to place himself in the hands of trustees. These men had little local knowledge of the estate; and though they doubtless administered it to the best of their ability, their main object was to make as much money as possible out of the rents, so as, on the one hand, to satisfy the creditors, and, on the other, to hasten the time when the proprietor might be able to resume possession. The interests of the crofters formed a very secondary consideration. With these aims, the trustees determined to clear out the whole population of Suisnish and convert the ground into one large sheep farm, to be placed in the hands of a responsible grazier, if possible from the south country.

I had heard some rumours of these intentions, but did not realise they were in process of being carried into effect until one afternoon, as I was returning from my ramble, a strange wailing sound reached my ears at intervals on the breeze from the west. On gaining the top of a hill on the south side of the valley, I could see a long and motley procession wending along the road that led from Suisnish. It halted at the point in the road opposite Kilbride, and there the lamentation became long and loud.

As I drew nearer, I could see that the minister, with his wife and daughters, had come out to meet the people and bid them all farewell. It was a miscellaneous gathering of at least three generations of crofters. There were old men and women, too feeble to walk, who were placed in carts, the younger members of the community on foot were carrying their bundles of clothes and household effects, while the children, with looks of alarm, walked alongside.

There was a pause in the notes of woe as the last words were exchanged with the family of Kilbride. Every one was in tears; each wished to clasp the hands that had so often befriended them; and it seemed as if they could not tear themselves away. When they set off once more, a cry of grief went up to heaven; the long plaintive wail, like a funeral coronach, was resumed; and, after the last of the emigrants had disappeared behind the hill, the sound seemed to re-echo through the whole wide valley of Strath in one prolonged note of desolation. The people were on their way to be shipped to Canada. I have often wandered since then over the solitary ground of Suisnish. Not a soul is to be seen there now; but the greener patches of field, and the crumbling walls, mark where an active and happy community once lived.

Incidents such as this drew from our island bard, Neil MacLeod, many of his most affecting poems and what a close parallel to the account we have quoted is given in his *'Cumha Eilean a' Cheò'!*

Ach tha 'n comunn air sgaoileadh,
> But the community has scattered

'S iad air faondradh 's gach àit'
> Being driven everywhere

'S cha tachair sinn comhlà,
> And we will not congregate

Air Di Dòmhnaich mar bhà.
> On Sunday as was our wont

Aitean còmhnuidh ar n-òige,
> The dwelling houses of our youth

Air an còmhdach fo'n làr;
> Are covered under the earth

Far 'n do shaothraich ar sinnsir,
> Where our ancestors laboured

Iomadh linn agus àl.

　　For many a generation and age.

(MacLeòid, N, 1924, p. 125)

The lot of the emigrants was always a hard one and for several years they were condemned to terrible privations in the land of their adoption. Writing in '*The Celtic Monthly*' in 1879, Alexander Mackenzie, who had done so much on behalf of the dispossessed crofter of the Highlands, says:

Fathers, mothers and children bound themselves away as virtual slaves in some settlements for a mere subsistence. Some lived in huts with only bushes as roof and had to walk some eighty miles through deep snow, and through trackless forests, in order to obtain a few bushels of potatoes, or a little flour, in exchange for their labour, dragging the commodities back on their backs. Some boiled buds of birch as food for their children; and in one case a small supply of seed potatoes, brought a long distance and planted, was taken up and the splits eaten.

But the wicked work of eviction went relentlessly on. The veriest pretext was often considered sufficient justification for turning a whole community adrift. When Lord MacDonald's factor, Ballingall, wished to extend the deer forest of Sconser, in 1853, two families of crofters and seven of cottars were cleared off Aricharnach, eight from Moll and sixteen crofters, in addition to several squatters, were removed from *Ceann nan Creagan* and *Torra Micheag* and we have seen that, several years previously, the people of Coillemhor were deprived of their hill grazing, and no one was allowed to possess sheep. The crofts of the people of Sconser were not protected from the deer, so that the crops were destroyed year after year and yet, such was the fear of eviction that no one dared to raise his voice in protest. A general policy was also pursued of still further curtailing the common pastures of crofting townships for the benefit of the adjoining sheep farmer. The grazing of Ben Lee had thus been filched from the crofters of Braes, and let to a tenant in 1865; and this practice had been continued so long, although no abatement in rent was vouchsafed those dispossessed that a spirit of revolt was beginning slowly to simmer in the minds of the people of Skye.

The year 1875 marked the commencement of a period of prosperity in the fishing industry off the West Coast of Ireland. Multitudes of our islesmen hired themselves as crews in the fishing-boats of Campbeltown and Carradale and good wages were earned. As a result of the comparative comfort they thus enjoyed, young men spent the winters at home, where the local fishing was prosecuted with moderate success. Early marriages were the rule. New settlements were clamantly needed but, instead of meeting this demand, people were still being extruded on all sides. The experience they had gained away from home was, however, beginning to have its effect on the minds of the young men of the island; so that they were now no longer disposed to suffer tamely every injustice that might be heaped upon them by those in authority. They began to question the justice of rack-renting and the insidious practice of preying on the common pastures of the townships. Resentment at the grievances under which they laboured was gradually growing in intensity. It had found expression in Staffin; in Glendale it had assumed alarming proportions. There the crofters had left their stock on Waterstein in defiance of an interdict and three of the leaders were arrested, tried and committed to prison for a period of two months.

In the district of Braes a crisis was approaching. The grazing of Ben Lee was due to run out of lease in 1882 and the crofters of the three southern townships were negotiating for its restoration to themselves. Time and again they declared their willingness to pay, in the aggregate, a higher rent than that paid by the 'sitting' tenant; but their plea went unheeded.

When redress was denied them, they took matters into their own hands. They allowed their sheep to stray over the whole range of the mountain, and some went so far as to refuse to pay rent until their claims should be recognised.

Certain men amongst the agitating crofters were marked out for punishment. In order to have them evicted from their holdings, the Sheriff's officer in Portree, with two assistants, went to the Braes to serve notices of ejectment. The officer in charge was Angus Martin, who was also clerk to Alexander MacDonald, factor to Lord MacDonald, his assistants Ewen Robertson and Norman Beaton, Sullishader, who was a ground officer. The officials were met on the way to Braes by the women and children, who forced them to burn the documents on the public highway, in addition to heaping other indignities upon them.

This glaring act of deforcement raised the ire of the chief legal authority for Inverness-shire, the notorious Sheriff Ivory, and he determined to crush this spirit of lawlessness by the use of stern measures.

He asked the Chief Constable of Glasgow to send fifty policemen to Skye in order to meet an emergency and the requisition was so peremptory that, it is said, the men were despatched without the sanction, or even the cognisance, of the magistrates of the city.

The Braes folk knew well that their action in interfering with the Sheriff's Officer would be viewed with severity by those in authority and they were informed of the intention to have summons served on them again, and this time with the assistance of a strong body of policemen. Watchers took turns on prominent positions and a rude system of telegraphing was agreed upon, whereby intelligence could be brought to the people immediately the police and the officers of the law had left their headquarters in Portree. Owing to the fact that the period had expired during which summons for eviction could legally be served, the vigilance of the sentries had abated, with the result that the inhabitants of Upper Braes were taken by surprise when, at 6 o'clock on the morning of the 17th April, 1882, a force of forty-seven Glasgow constables and ten local policemen, with two sheriffs and their officers, reached the northern boundary of Gedintailor before they were observed.

At the opposite march of that township the invading force was met by a hurriedly summoned body of the people of Balmeanach and Penichorran, about one hundred strong, many of them dishevelled and in a state of deshabille, for news of the invasion had come to most of them whilst they were still in bed. Disappointment was written large on every countenance as all were aggrieved that the policemen had been permitted to penetrate so far into their territory without opposition, and in the heavy rain that was falling, the kindly old folk, as they stood there trembling on their staffs, presented a pitiable sight. It must here be added that most of the able-bodied men of the district had already left home for the Irish fishing and that if they had been present that day a situation fraught with alarming consequences would have developed.

As it was, matters soon assumed an ugly aspect, for no sooner had certain men been arrested and a start made by the police to return, than, at the instigation of the women, a general attack was launched against the expeditionary force. Sticks and flails were wielded with telling effect and volleys of stones were hurled with unerring aim. The road goes through a narrow gorge at a place called *Allt nan Gobhlag*, and there the police were assailed on both flanks with relentless vigour. The order was now given by Captain Donald, of the Glasgow detachment, to charge the attackers, who, however, did not yield an inch. The party in charge of the prisoners, together with the law officers, had meantime passed through the narrow defile and, seeing this, the rearguard of the force rushed through 'at the double'. But the worst was yet to come. About 300 yards to the north, the road is cut along the face of a steep declivity, which rises almost sheer from the sea to a height of about 400 feet. The place is called *'An Cumhang'*, the crofters' *'Torres Vedras'*, where they confidently believed they could stop the progress of any force that might be sent against them and where, for days previously, they had been busy gathering boulders, which they heaped in readiness for the fray on the brow of the hill.

A race for this strategic point now started in deadly earnest and a small body of the natives having secured it first, they began to make good use of their post of vantage. An avalanche of boulders was sent hurtling down the precipitous slope, so that several of the policemen were grievously injured. For a few brief moments the police were brought to a standstill. Move, however, they must for, to halt in such a position would be tantamount to suicide, now that the numbers on the hill were rapidly increasing. A desperate rush was therefore made by the policemen, and they succeeded in forcing a way through.

Having now gained the more open ground, the constables, who had hitherto used their batons only, began to retaliate with stones also and the crofters, incensed to fury for having lost their position, closed with the police in grim hand-to-hand strife. Many heads were bruised and the marvel is that all escaped with their lives. The women fought like Amazons and several of them were severely mauled, one old woman being in a critical condition for several days after the fight. As the road now lay through open country, the crofters withdrew from the conflict. (MacLean, N, 1945, pp. 95–122).

Nuair thainig e cheud uair
  When he came the first time
Le leth-chiad aingeal ga riaghladh
  With fifty 'angels' under his command

Chuir e coignear an iarrain
  He put five men in irons
Ann an criochan Beinn Lith.
  On the bounds of Ben Lee.

(Mac-Bheathain, A, 1891, p. 111.
Mary Macpherson is referring to Sheriff Ivory)

The prisoners Alexander Finlayson, Malcolm Finlayson, Peter MacDonald, Donald Nicolson and James Nicolson, were lodged in the prison at Portree, pending their removal for trial to Inverness. There they were convicted and sentenced to pay fines. These fines were soon subscribed by sympathisers and the men returned home the day following their trial. By some they were looked upon as heroes, by others as martyrs, who were being persecuted under a ruthless system. The whole island was seething with discontent. Warships were sent to the lochs of Skye; troops were despatched ashore and marched through the disaffected areas in order to overawe the people. Wiser counsellors, however, advised an impartial inquiry into the condition of the crofters, and a Royal Commission was set up by the government of Mr. Gladstone in 1883. It was composed of six members, four of whom were landlords, namely the chairman, Lord Napier, Mackenzie of Gairloch, Cameron of Lochiel, and Fraser Macintosh, and only two who had no direct interest in the land, Professor MacKinnon and Sheriff Nicolson. This Commission gave of its time unstintingly. Its first session was in Braes. By the end of a year it had issued its report, after having accumulated an enormous mass of evidence. Soon the public came to know of the scandalous extent to which rack-renting had been carried on, and the unrighteous methods that had been practised to deprive a defenceless and unsophisticated peasantry of the land which had been occupied by their families for many generations. *"Notwithstanding the studied caution of the language"*, says Mr. MacFarlane, a Member of Parliament of that time, *"the report discloses a state of misery, of wrong doing, and of patient long-suffering without a parallel in the history of our country".*

The immediate consequence of the work of the Commission was the passing of the Crofters' Holdings Act in 1886, when, among other privileges, the provisions of fair rent and security of tenure were vouchsafed the smallholder. Commissioners were appointed to fix an equitable rental, and it was then that the glaring height to which the rapacity of landed proprietors and their factors had arisen was brought to light. Thus, the Commissioners assessed one croft in Braes at a rental of £3 10s, whereas its tenant had been paying £11 10s for several years previously. In the townships of Balmeanach and Gedintailor the average reduction of rent amounted to 50 per cent, whilst the arrears accounted against crofters in the same district were written off to the extent of 70 per cent.

The benefits that flowed from the Crofters' Holdings Act can best be appreciated when we consider the conditions under which the crofter laboured before it received legislative enactment. Owing to the keen demand that existed for land, no compunction was shown by factors to any who might, for the time being, find it difficult to pay his rent. He was peremptorily ejected from his home and his holding was conferred on the highest bidder. It was easy to obtain offerers, for, despite the drain of emigration, the population was increasing, and those who had already been dispossessed were eager to resume occupancy of a plot of ground at any price. The ingoing tenant was obliged to hold himself responsible for the payment of any arrears that might have been incurred by his predecessor, with the result that many a poor, though industrious family was destined to suffer extreme want for many years, in order to meet the heavy obligations that were imposed upon them. But so strong was the love of the homeland in the hearts of these people that they would submit to any conditions rather than jeopardise the continuance of their tenure.

It is difficult for us to understand the mentality of a people that would permit the exercise of such tyranny with impunity and, in our thoughtless moments, we are prone to accuse them of slavish subservience to lairds and their factors. But the traditional reverence for the chief still persisted among them, and their implicit faith in the principle of *"what is, is right"*, led them to endure their cruel lot uncomplainingly and impute it wholly to the will of an All-wise Providence.

Màiri Mhòr in her poem Fios gu Clach Ard Uige says of the clergy:

> *Tha luchd teagasg cho beag churaim*
>> The preachers have so little care
> *Faicinn caradh mo luchd dùtcha*
>> Seeing the ill treatment of my Isle's folk,
> *'S iad cho balbh air anns a chubaid*
>> And so silent about it in the pulpit
> *'S ged bu bruidean bha gan èisdeachd.*
>> As if brute beasts were listening to them.
>>> (Mac-Bheathain, A, 1891, p. 215)

Hence it happened that regulations imposed on them by tacksmen or factors received their unquestioning obedience. When necessity compelled them to take heather, rushes, or seaware, from the lands of neighbouring farmers, they met the claims of the latter for compensation by rendering personal service. When their common grazing was curtailed for the benefit of the adjacent farmer, they submitted without demur. When deer destroyed their crops, they raised no protest, lest they should incur the ill will of the factor. A witness from Sconser, before the Royal Commission of 1883, declared, *"We dare not kill the deer which come to our crofts for fear of eviction"*; while another from Torrin deponed that, in his township, they suffered much loss from the incursions of deer and he adds, *"I was paying five shillings of dog tax to enable me to keep deer off my ground. The shooting-tenant's gamekeeper came to the back of my house and shot my dog fifty yards off. The dog was lying beside my wife and daughter, who were lifting potatoes at the time. I complained to the fiscal, who however, averred I had no right to keep a dog".* Instances of tyrannous actions of this nature could be multiplied indefinitely but enough has been written to show what cruel wrongs were inflicted on a defenceless and law-abiding people.

The land agitation, and its concomitant incidents, powerfully affected the imagination of the people, and many gave vent to their feelings in song. Chief among the bards who were moved by the stirring events of those times were Neil MacLeod, Mary MacPherson (*Màiri ni'n Iain Bhàin*), Donald MacCallum, and Neil MacPherson (*Niall Ceannaiche*). In his *'Oran nan Croit-earain Sgiathanach'*, the first of these raises a sympathetic note:

An sluagh bha cho càirdeil,
    The people who were so friendly,
Cho suairc', is cho bàidheil,
    So civil and so warm,
Rinn uachdarain stràiceil
    Haughty landlords
Am fàsgadh ro theann,
    Squeezed them too tightly,
Tha saors' air am fàgail,
    They are bereft of their freedom,
Tha 'n raointean 'nam fàsaich',
    And their fields are a wilderness,
'S tha caoraich an àite
    And the sheep have the place
Nan àrmunn 's a' ghleann.
    Of the heroes in the glen.

(MacLeòid, N, 1924, p. 131)

Congestion – Cottars

By the year 1811, the runrig system of tenure had come to an end in Skye. Thereafter the land was divided into crofts, and, owing to the circumscribed areas under cultivation and especially the small amount of souming each lot was allowed to carry, these portions were often insufficient to support a family even in a favourable year. The margin of comfort could never be large under the circumstances, and the condition of the occupiers was worsened by the extraneous demands made upon them. On account of the great increase in the population, many squatters settled on the new holdings, so that it often happened, according to the Rev. Coll MacDonald of Portree, that as many as three families occupied one plot of ground.

The evil of congestion was so accentuated during the time of the clearances, that by 1840 a grievous state of affairs prevailed all over Skye. Thus the Rev. A. MacGregor says of Kilmuir that, while there were only 190 divisions of land, there were as many as 421 families in the parish, and the Rev. A. MacIvor declares that as many as 225 families then paid no rent in his own parish of Sleat. These cottars built a house on the holding of a relative, or at the margin of the high-water mark by the shore, and were given a small portion of land, that could ill be spared by the recognised occupier, so that they might raise a crop of potatoes. In the *'Report of the Board for the Relief of Highland Destitution'*, issued in 1850, there is abundant evidence of overcrowding in the parishes of Skye. Thus one district, of the extent of 3676 acres, was allocated among 334 families of crofters, while it maintained a parasitic population of 1200 souls. In another, an extent of 205 acres over all was occupied by nine tenants. They cultivated 42 acres, which, in a good year, produced 61 bolls of oats. Their stock comprised 24 cows, 16 sheep, and 6 horses, and they paid £84 in rent; and here were ten families of cottars. A third extended to 161 acres, of which only 22 were under cultivation, and it was divided among four tenants, each of whom could raise about 8 bolls of oats. They had each 2 cows, 5 sheep and a horse, and on their land lived 11 families of squatters, who were parasitic on the rent-paying tenants.

Agriculture

On the larger farms the cumbersome old wooden plough had been discarded in the early years of the nineteenth century, but it continued to be used by certain of the smaller tenants, a number of whom shared one among them. In most cases it was manufactured locally, and it cost about £2 15s. It ceased to be used after 1820.

The crooked spade was still the implement responsible for the tillage of what was by far the greater portion of the arable land, for, owing to the weight of the old-fashioned plough, which required four horses to pull it, a 'pan' was formed in the soil, and this interfered with the free movement of moisture to and from the surface.

On account of the fact that no attention was paid to suitable methods of drainage, the ridge system of cultivation, *'Feannagan Taomaidh'*, described in previous pages, was still the vogue. This was the invariable practice in the rearing of potatoes, which were then the principal crop of the island. The increase in its cultivation was enormous, for, as already shown, whereas the quantity raised at the beginning of the century in one parish of Skye was 5,000 barrels, as many as 32,000 were grown in 1841.

Among the larger tenant-farmers, a regular system of rotation of crops had been introduced, and, in addition to potatoes and oats, crops of hay, barley, and a small quantity of turnips, were grown, although, according to the Rev. A. Clark, turnips and clover *"were utterly unknown"* in Duirinish in 1841. All the writers of the time declare that, owing to the unfavourable weather conditions, the hay crop was always greatly impoverished before it could be secured.

The allotments of the crofters were so small that the principle of rotation could not be exercised, so that intensive cultivation of one or two crops was the rule. After some years the soil was thus rendered useless for cultivation, its poverty being accentuated by the lavish use made of seaware for manuring purposes. When the soil was put 'out of heart', their only remedy was to leave it fallow sometimes for four and five years and yielding nothing but weeds.

It has already been shown that no incentive was given to the smaller tenants to improve the condition of their holdings. Indeed, if they did make any effort, with a view to their amelioration, they were faced with the possibility of an increase in their rent. This unwise and unjust practice was in vogue all over the island. Writing in 1841, the Rev. A. Clark, minister of Duirinish, says, in effect, that the crofters were deterred from making any improvements for the reason that they were tenants at will, *"and they will not bestow their labour on land which may become another's before the end of the year"*. Even as late as 1883, we find witnesses before the Royal Commission deploring the fact that, from their own experience and that of their neighbours, they were precluded from effecting improvements on their crofts. Thus one witness declared: *"I tried to improve my croft by working it; but my reward was that my rent was raised 5s in the £. I did no more for it. I worked like a horse, going four miles for mud for the soil"*.

> *Mur be eagal an da mhail*
> If it were not for the fear of doubling of the rent
> *Bheireadh Tiridh da bhar.*
> Tiree would yield a double crop.
>
> (Oral tradition)

A deterrent not confined to Tiree.

In an experiment designed to counteract these disabilities,

Glendale was bought by the Board of Agriculture (now the Scottish Office Department of Agriculture and Fisheries) and, only reluctantly, did the crofters agree to become peasant proprietors (MacLeod, RC, 1939, pp. 123–4).

Trade and Industries

The trade in the sale of the native black cattle still lingered on, for, even as late as 1840, we find that the annual exportation from the parish of Bracadale alone amounted to 450 head. During the Napoleonic Wars an exorbitant price was secured for this breed, and a brisk trade was then effected. By the middle of the century the sale of sheep had become an important business, though hitherto confined chiefly to Bracadale, from which as many as 4500 were sold yearly. The average prices realised for animals then were as follows: £7 for a horse, £6 10s for a cow, £1 for a cheviot sheep, and 16s 6d for a blackfaced sheep with lamb.

As already stated, the trade in kelp-making, once so vigorous, began steadily to decline, the several stages in its decay being marked by the importation of barilla from Spain after 1817, the abolition of the salt duty in 1825 and especially the discovery of the great potash deposits of Germany. The work was, however, prosecuted until the middle of the nineteenth century and in 1841 about 80 tons of kelp were produced in the parish of Duirinish; though the sale, according to the Rev. A. Clark, did *"little more than repay the cost of making it"*.

Long periods of depression overtook the fishing industry during this century, as had happened often before that time and has since. It was prosecuted with a fair amount of success at the beginning of the century, but from that time it suffered a gradual falling-off, so that by the year 1830 the herring appeared to have abandoned the lochs of Skye altogether. Writing in 1841, one of our ministers observes, *"Indeed, there is reason to fear that the herring fishing will disappear from our coast"*; while another, the Rev. John MacKinnon of Strath, in seeking a cause for the decline of the industry at that time, suggests that *"it is due to the destruction of the spawn on the East Coast of Scotland"*. The slackness in this industry continued until about 1879, when an improvement set in that was maintained for several years.

Nor was the decline in the fishing trade due to lack of enterprise or initiative on the part of the people, for all were keenly susceptible to the importance of the industry. With a view to its development on the western seaboard of Scotland, the Scottish Fishery Society established a station at Stein of Waternish, among other places, in 1787. There a pier was constructed, houses and 'stores' were built; but the venture proved a failure, and the Society was forced to sell their property there at a loss of £1241. Alexander, second Lord MacDonald, with characteristic altruism, spent large sums of money in the first years of the nineteenth century, building fishing-boats and in hiring expert fishermen from the East Coast of Scotland, in order to train the people of Skye in the best methods for prosecuting the industry, but his efforts were unavailing.

This public-spirited chief probed every avenue that might lead to the prosperity of his people. At the very beginning of the century he established a store at Kyleakin, the first *'shop'* in Skye. It was owned by himself and it was the means of supplying the simple wants of the inhabitants. *"To the hopeful it hinted at the future extension of commerce on a large scale"*, writes Stanhope in 1805, but these sanguine forecasts were never realised, though many small shopkeepers were soon to establish businesses all over Skye, so that, about the year 1840, according to the Rev. A. Clark, *"as many as forty people retailed merchandise"* in the parish of Duirinish alone.

Although all his endeavours had so far been attended with failure, Lord MacDonald tried other schemes to improve the lot of his people. Hopes being entertained at that time that the

Tertiary coal of Skye might prove a profitable undertaking, he induced trained miners to come from the South by the offer of high wages, and a start was made at Braes, and at Camusbàn in Portree Loch. Owing, however, to the thinness of the seam, its discontinuity and the great difficulty of mining the coal, the work was finally abandoned after repeated trials had been vainly made to strike profitable seams.

Lord MacDonald was also interested in the marble of Strath. He had, indeed, often spoken of using that stone in the building of his castle at Armadale, but that project, too, never materialised, though much of the Strath marble was used in the construction of the great staircase of the castle, while large quantities of it went to the paving of the lobby of Hamilton Palace, and numerous consignments were sold to the Board of Ordnance for the making of millstones. It was, however, abandoned by the last named as the presence of crystals of tourmaline in the marble made it impossible to cut to the required dimensions.

A lime kiln, erected at Broadford, was the scene of a successful business for many years and the lime produced there was of very high quality. The price charged to the tenants on the estates of MacDonald was 6d per boll for building and 4d when the material was to be used merely for the purposes of manure.

The draining of St. Columba's Loch, near his residence at Mogstadt, had also engaged the attention of this good chief. The work had been begun as early as 1715, but it was left in abeyance owing to the troubles that flowed from the Jacobite rebellions. It was resumed in 1763, only to suffer suspension once more before it could be brought to completion. In 1819 Lord MacDonald employed a large squad of men to re-open the drains. The main trench is about ¾ mile long, 35 feet deep in parts, 114 feet in width at the top, and 9 feet at the bottom. After working at it constantly for five years and spending about £10,000 on it, the undertaking was at last completed in the year 1824. Owing, however, to the difficulty of keeping the branch

ditches free of aquatic plants, drainage is impeded, and the soured soil produces a fertile growth of sedges, to the detriment of the production of hay.

In the early portion of the nineteenth century there were two, and even three, meal-mills in every parish. The millstones were produced from the granophyre of the island of Raasay, a rock peculiarly suitable for such a purpose and there was a considerable trade in their manufacture. These millstones were supplied, not only to Skye, but to the adjacent mainland as well, sums varying from £9 to £12 a pair being charged by the masons for the finished article.

The practice of tanning leather by means of the bark of the birch, and the roots of *tormentilla vulgaris*, was continued until the middle of the nineteenth century and most of the people fashioned their own shoes, or brogues, at that time. Many also made their own clothes, but before the middle of the century itinerant tailors came to be engaged in the work, for which they received a mere pittance.

Until about 1840, all sacks for holding grain were made locally from sedges, or from straw, and the collars used as harness for horses were manufactured from the same materials.

The manufacture of fishing nets was carried on in most homes, and during the period of the 'potato famine' it received much encouragement from philanthropic agencies in Skye. Although there was a large amount of production then, the wages paid were very low. The women were adepts at this work, many still practising the art when the second portion of the nineteenth century was well advanced.

About the year 1840, the wages paid for hired labour in Skye were as follows: Farm workers, employed for the year, received from £5 to £10 in the case of men, while women, who served either indoors or in the fields, were paid at a rate varying from £3 to £4 a year, with board and lodgings.

Labourers, hired for casual work, earned 1s a day in summer

and 9d in winter; while artisans, such as masons and joiners, were paid from 2s 6d to 3s for a day's work of at least twelve hours' duration.

Means of Communication

The eighteenth century was drawing to its close before any thought was given to the construction of roads in Skye. In the year 1799 it had been decided by Parliament to lay a road between Kylerhea in Strath and Lochbay in Waternish, but it was long after that year before the track was completed. According to the testimony of one, Stanhope, who toured Skye in 1805, there was no trace of a road anywhere on the island except the old tracks. In 1801 MacLeod of MacLeod contracted the road between Stein and Sligachan, employing a man, Tulloch, as sub-contractor. The crofters gave their labour free. It is said that the construction of the high bridge, near Drynoch, cost £2,000 (MacLeod, RC, 1939, Vol. II, p. 115).

In the year 1804, a memorial was addressed to the Commissioners of Roads by the Chief of Sleat, Lord Alexander, urging them to proceed with the construction of the road already surveyed from Kylerhea to Stein, with branches, one of which, it was suggested, should proceed northwards from Sligachan, by Portree, to Aird of Trotternish, and another from Broadford towards the south, by Kinloch, to Ardvasar. Lord Alexander pointed out that, in order to foster trade in the rearing and sale of black cattle, then the principal industry on the island, it was essential that good arterial ways should be made. It was decided to proceed with their construction immediately.

In 1806 interested parties, such as Colonel MacDonald of Lyndale and James MacLeod of Raasay, petitioned the Commissioners to grant facilities for the laying of a road from the west of Skye at Dunvegan to join the proposed northern road at Snizort, for that way came the cattle from the Long Island to the market at Portree. Though this was the last of the main roads to be surveyed, it was the first to be completed. The contract for it was secured by Colonel MacDonald himself, and the work was finished, and very favourably reported on, by the year 1811.

> *'S mi gun coisicheadh le sunnd*
> I would traverse with cheer
> *An rathad ùr troimh thìr MhicLeòid.*
> The new road through MacLeod's country", sings the
> nostalgic sailor in foreign parts.
>
> (Oral tradition)

Meanwhile, progress was slow in the construction of the other roads of Skye, and certain of the contractors were faced with financial ruin. The most difficult section of all proved to be that between Kylerhea and Sconser. In 1812 the Broadford-Ardvasar Road was finished. In the following year the section from Kylerhea to Sconser had been completed, but it was in a very unsatisfactory condition, owing to the state of the bridges and the surfacing.

The year 1816 saw the completion of that portion of the north road from Sligachan to Portree, its continuation to Uig being effected in 1819.

Of the road that was first proposed for Skye, that from Kylerhea to Stein, certain sections, such as that from *Tigh a' Phuirt* in Sconser to Sligachan, and a large portion in Bracadale, had not yet been contracted for, and it was not until 1825 that the latter was completed.

By the year 1840, stretches of good roadway had been constructed in several parishes. The Rev. Roderick MacLeod of Snizort, who wrote the *Second Statistical Account of Bracadale* in 1841, stresses the decided benefit to his own district of the formation of a *'parliamentary road'*. An interesting commentary is made in the same year by the Rev. A. Clark of Duirinish on the

conservatism of the people and their prejudices against innovations in any shape or form. He states that

> *for some years after the construction of roads, the common people would not, on any account, travel on them, alleging that stones and gravel bruised their feet. They preferred to follow the old paths, uneven and boggy as these were.*

For some years, even after the middle of the century, there were several places in Skye, inhabited by considerable communities, which were not served with roads. In the *Report of the Crofters' Commission of 1884*, mention is made of the isolation of the townships of Mugarry and Glenmore, which, with a population of over 200 souls, were *"without even a tolerable track, though they were situated some four miles from any constructed roadway"*.

The first steamship service to Skye was inaugurated by Messrs. Hutchison about 1830. Previous to that time, communication with Glasgow and the south was effected by means of sailing vessels ("Packets" as they were called) which, owing to the calls made at numerous intermediate ports, took ten to fifteen days to complete the voyage. By 1840 a steamboat plied weekly between Glasgow and Skye. But the sailings ceased during the months of winter. A pier and a store were built in Dunvegan in 1869 (MacLeod, RC, 1939, p. 110).

Owing to the inadequacy of the transport services then, much inconvenience and loss were sustained by the people of Skye. Even as late as the 'early eighties' of last century, fishermen in Glendale were constrained to use turbot as bait for cod and ling, as the last two alone could be preserved for sale by drying.

Population

It has already been shown that the population of Skye had been increasing steadily towards the end of the eighteenth century, and it now falls to be recorded that the increase was well maintained during the first part of the nineteenth century. In the year 1801, when a census was undertaken for the first time in Britain, the population of Skye was discovered to be 16,000. The growth advanced year by year until, by 1841, when it had attained its peak, it had reached 23,000, thus representing an advance of 44 per cent during a period of forty years. Captain Fishbourne, who, we have seen, was stationed in Skye as Inspector by the Committee for the relief of destitution in 1848, says the population of Raasay then was 975, and of Rona 116.

The growth in population during these years is a remarkable phenomenon, when we bear in mind the repeated drains made by emigration. The increase is attributable to two causes – first, to the practice of vaccination, which arrested the ravages of smallpox, and, secondly, to the division of land into holdings in the first and second decades of the nineteenth century, and the subsequent sub-division of these crofts by the original occupiers among their relatives.

As a result of the potato famine of 1845, the clearances, the consequent emigration, and the constant trek to the south in search of employment, a steady decrease in the population set in after 1841. In 1861 it had dwindled to 19,000; twenty years later it was 17,700, and by the beginning of the present century it had declined to 13,800 – a decrease of 40 per cent in the space of sixty years.

The practice of recording vital statistics had been introduced in 1800, but the first entry in the parochial registers of Skye was not made until 1803, in the district of Minginish, which, for several years, kept a record distinct from that of its parish (Bracadale). The first entry in the register of the parish of Portree is in September, 1806; for Strath it was made in 1820, and in 1823 both for Snizort and for Kilmuir. It is noticeable that for several years entries are made in a very desultory manner, an irregularity which was continued until the middle of the century. Thus in the register for the parish of Portree, there is only one item, a birth, for the year 1806. The following year is a blank. Two births are recorded for the year 1808, and they took place in April; one occurs for December, 1809 and another for August, 1810. Several notifications of birth appear for the year 1811, and the numbers are well maintained until March, 1813, after which, with the exception of two entries in 1814, there is nothing until June, 1815. So far as marriages were concerned, the period 1806 to 1811 is entirely a blank, nor is there any record of one from January, 1812, until September, 1816. The great proportion of marriages, when recorded, fall between January and March of each year.

The Span of Life

Instances of individual longevity are no more remarkable during the nineteenth century than they were in the previous one; and, as the practice of the registration of births had not become a regular institution during the early part of this century, the ages ascribed to certain members of the community must be recorded with caution. The Rev. A. MacGregor, who wrote the Statistical Account of Kilmuir in 1841, makes mention of the death of a John Nicolson in Staffin, a man noted for his knowledge of the traditional tales and poetry of the Gael, who was reported to have lived to the age of 105 years. At the same time, the Rev. John Mackinnon considers it worthy of notice that one of his parishioners, *"who never wore but the kilt,"* had accomplished a walk of twenty-four miles in one day, although he was in his 84th year.

Diseases

The dread scourge of smallpox that had so often before taken a heavy toll of life in Skye had been effectively stayed by the introduction of vaccine, but its incidence was still a matter to be feared and numerous deaths resulted from it. Fevers also were common and their visitations cut off many people. Typhoid had been virulent in Raasay about the year 1850, and it recurred frequently in Sconser until the close of the century.

There are few recorded cases of consumption during the early part of the nineteenth century. The Rev. A. Clark, writing of Duirinish in 1841, states that *"fatal diseases, especially consumption,"* were unknown in that parish, and in 1860 a certain Dr. Morgan, who had been resident in the island of Raasay, says he *"did not come on one case of phthisis"* during his sojourn there. That the island of Skye was not, however, wholly free of this disease is evidenced by the fact that the parish minister of Portree, the Rev. Coll MacDonald, avers that such a plant as coltsfoot was considered to be beneficial in the curing of bronchial affections – *"and consumption."*

Most of the people who write of that time avert to the prevalence of *"severe rheumatic complaints,"* which they ascribe to the humid nature of the climate. *"As might naturally be expected,"* writes the Rev. Coll MacDonald, *"the variable and humid state of the atmosphere, in all seasons of the year, is found highly injurious to the human constitution and produces among the inhabitants many diseases, rheumatics, asthma, fever and consumption."*

Weather

In discussing the climatic conditions that prevailed in Skye until the end of the eighteenth century, we have seen that, contrary to traditional notions, the state of the weather in our island had

not suffered any appreciable change down the years. We also saw that many of those who were responsible for the compilation of the *Statistical Account in 1793* often refer to the sensible deterioration in our climate, and it is significant of our tendency to praise the past that those clergymen, who wrote accounts of their respective parishes fifty years later, repeat the same popular illusion. *"The seasons have undergone a decided change"*, states the Rev. Coll MacDonald in 1841, but, as has already been shown, all the evidence that is available goes to disprove that assertion. Indeed, when we come to consider all the records, the conclusion is forced upon us that the climate of Skye has been remarkable only for one feature. That has been its constancy in its inconstancy!

Wet seasons have happened in the past as often as they occur to-day. Certain years are specially singled out for the severity of the weather that prevailed. Such were 1807 and 1817, when, owing to the storms and rains, crops were grievously damaged. Again, 1833, 1835, and the two succeeding years stand out as periods of widespread destitution, owing to inclement weather conditions. In 1844 and 1845, right on till 1850, the summers had been excessively wet, a condition that led, in those years, to the development of that blight which ruined the potato crop in our island, as in other places on the western seaboard of the kingdom. *"It is very rare, indeed"*, declares one of our ministers in 1841, *"that there is in this parish a favourable seed-time; and in harvest, heavy rains and strong gales of wind prevail, by which the corn crops are either lodged or shaken; thus, all the hopes of the husbandman are in a great measure frustrated"*. Another of our parish ministers observes that *"the chief obstacle to the improvement of agriculture is the raininess of the climate, which renders it difficult to secure a crop, though it should be reared"*.

So severe was the climate about the middle of last century that the Rev. Coll MacDonald states: *"There is no natural wood growing here* (parish of Portree), *with the exception of a small quantity in the island of Raasay, and even this was almost annihilated in 1836 and 1837, those years of memorable destitution, when, from the wetness of the seasons, the people were unable to secure their peats"*. In their extremity they were forced to consume their turf huts as fuel. Lots were cast as occasion demanded, in order to ascertain whose house was next to be destroyed and the responsibility for the maintenance of the family thus deprived of a home was determined by the same principle. *'The Inverness Courier'* of March, 1837, comments on the state of destitution brought about by inclement weather which then prevailed in Skye, as follows:

Crowding round the miserable fire, thus scantily supplied, and with only at long intervals a handful of meal and potatoes, we know not that the history of the British people ever presented such pictures of severe, unmitigated want".

It was reported in *An Gaidheal* for April 1864 that,

"So far the winter fishing, both for herring and ling, has turned out a failure all over the Highlands, principally in consequence of the rough boisterous weather experienced over the West coast during the past three months.

Paupers

The nineteenth century was well advanced before any attempt was made for the relief of destitution by communal effort. Those who, by bodily infirmity or feeble-mindedness, were unable to maintain themselves, were thus almost wholly dependent on the charity of neighbours, except for the meagre contributions the churches were able to make for their support. From this last source they received a dole varying from 2s to 15s a year – a miserable pittance that was ridiculously inadequate for their needs, but their people saw to it that they seldom suffered from want. Writing in 1841, the Rev. A. MacIvor of Sleat says *"Rent-payers consider it a duty to put aside a certain portion of their potatoes and corn for the poor, whose wants have hitherto been thus supplied"*. They begged from house to house and none was ever turned away, although some of them, especially the insane, were often a source of trouble and danger to their hosts. The condition of those who, by age or infirmity, were unable to fend for themselves, must have been miserable in the extreme.

The able-bodied idiots, who roved at large over the island, contributed much to the entertainment of the young by their idiosyncrasies. Some of the most notable of these were: *Gilleasbuig Aotrom*, light in spirit as well as in head and famed for his practical jokes and the cleverness of his repartee; *Alasdair MacGuirmein*, noted for his gargantuan appetite; and *Lachlain na Ciste*, a morose churl with the strength of a gorilla, who lugged a wooden box about in his peregrinations and was the unfailing butt of all who delighted in boyish pranks.

Pastimes and Habits

That gaiety of temperament, which characterised the people of Skye in the past, still persisted vigorously during the early years of the nineteenth century. Their fondness for singing, in spite of their privations, was the wonder and the delight of every stranger who happened to sojourn in their midst. We have elsewhere referred to the pleasing effect it produced on Dr. Johnson, when he landed on the island of Raasay, to hear the song of the harvesters. Stanhope recounts a similar experience that fell to him in Skye. *"I do not know of anything more pleasing"*, says he, *"or anything that brings one more in touch with plain unsophisticated nature, than the sounds of these untutored female voices singing in unison with their hands"*; and the same writer states that *"the rowers sang"* as he was being ferried over to Scalpay.

He also records the pleasure it gave him to hear the bagpipe played in Raasay House by a Mackay of the famous line, *"who, after MacCrimmon, was considered to be the best piper in the Hebrides"*. This was in 1805; but a change was soon to come.

That transformation was wrought by the revivals. We have seen that the playing of musical instruments, the singing of secular songs and the telling of the ancient tales, were all put under a ban, and that those who had the faculty for these arts mortified the talent, either voluntarily or under the coercive influence of public opinion. In Trotternish, Bracadale and Duirinish, the new outlook was most developed, for there the work of the evangelist had been more intensive than elsewhere on the island. In these localities the ceilidh was no longer an institution. The people became less sociable and the native lightness of heart was damped under a cloud of gloom. *"It is rare to hear a song sung now"*, says the Rev. A. Clark of Duirinish in 1841, *"still rarer to hear the pipe or the violin"*. Thus it happened that much of the precious heritage of our race was irretrievably lost.

All gatherings, except those held for religious purposes, were viewed with disfavour, with the result that none but the wayward now joined in the dance. At the waulkings, the women no longer sang their rhythmic labour-song, as they heartily tossed the web from hand to hand, and innocent assemblies for athletic contests, and even such games as shinty, were practically discontinued. The Rev. A. MacGregor of Kilmuir tells us that, by 1841, the piper's lament was no longer heard at funerals, although, *"a few years ago, as many as two pipers were always present"*.

Marriage functions also had lost much of their pristine hilarity, so that for several years before and after the Disruption only five or six persons attended the celebration and, according to one of our parish ministers of that time, the marriage feast consisted of *"potatoes and herring, with a glass of whisky"*.

Superstitious Practices

Superstitious beliefs lingered on among the people generally, even as late as the middle of the nineteenth century. The writers of the *Second Statistical Account of 1841* make frequent mention of the survival of irrational beliefs as was indicated by the scrupulous care people exercised in order that they might not violate certain time-honoured practices.

Especial credence was given to the power of the moon to shape the course of events, so that most were careful to observe its particular phase before they undertook certain works. They still imagined that, in its crescent stage, it communicated *"a growing quality to substances"*; and then they carried out such operations as sowing the seed, the slaughtering of animals, the shearing of sheep, and the clipping of human hair. They would not begin to plough, to reap, to cut timber or peat, until the moon was in its wane, for then alone would the natural juices depart and drying be expedited. It should be added that a sneaking regard for these observances may even still be noticed in certain parts of Skye.

The belief in witchcraft, in second sight, and in fairies, was entertained by many after the middle of the nineteenth century, and the existence of 'the evil eye' exercised a strong influence over the mind of the credulous, even as recently as the beginning of the present century. The possession of that power, like its cognate talent, second sight, was held to be, in some cases at least, an involuntary faculty that might be developed in one at any time. To guard against its intrusion, according to the compiler of the *Statistical Account for Snizort in 1841*, there was pronounced every morning, while the person was engaged in the operation of washing the face, the following incantation:

Gu'm beannaicheadh Dia mo shùil,
　　Would that God would bless my eye
'S beannaichidh mo shùil na chi

And my eye will bless all it sees
Beannaichidh mise mo nabuidh
　　I will bless my neighbour
'S beannaichidh mo nabuidh mi.
　　And my neighbour will bless me.

Numerous instances of superstitious practices have come under the writer's observation, even at the end of the century under review, and mention may be made of three. One was the case of an old man who peregrinated a township, carrying in a vessel a sample of a cow's milk that was alleged by him to have been robbed of its essence by the 'evil eye'. He went thus from house to house, in the hope that the possessor of the spell, by the act of looking on the milk, would thereby restore its lost virtues.

Another example was the application of a serpent's head to a local swelling on a cow that was supposed to have been stung by an adder; and the last was the rite performed on a heifer, sickening, as was thought, under the influence of the evil eye, by sprinkling the animal with water in which a silver coin had been dipped and a live cinder quenched. When this remedy failed to effect a cure, a band of cloth was tied round the middle of the animal and an incantation was uttered somewhat as follows:

Ge b'e co leag ort an t-sùil
　　Who so cast his eye on you
Gum mùch i air fein
　　May it press on himself
Gum mùch i air a thùr
　　May it press on his home
Gum mùch i air a spréidh.
　　May it press on his cattle.

(Carmichael, A, 1928, Vol. II, p. 68)

Fauna

We have seen that in the previous century the number of sheep on the island was less than the stock of cattle, but in the nineteenth century, owing to the demand for wool and the formation of large sheep farms, the number of sheep increased by leaps and bounds. The small native breed now came to be replaced by that secured from the crossing of the *'Caoraich Bheaga'* (little sheep), as the former were called, with the larger variety from the South. This happened about the beginning of the century, and the resultant variety, though far superior to the original breed in size, was much inferior both as regards the quality of the wool and the savour of its mutton.

Some of the smaller tenants continued to rear the indigenous sheep even until the middle of the century, for the Rev. A. Clark states that there were several of them in Duirinish in 1841. Long before that time the larger farmers were beginning to dispense with the larger breed of blackfaced sheep and to introduce the Cheviot.

The noted black cattle were still being reared in considerable numbers during the earlier part of this century, for they were held in high estimation by dealers from the South. So likely, indeed, were they to continue the dominant breed that, when agreements were composed for a long period of time contracts came to be proverbially referred to as lasting so long *"as white milk can be got from black cattle"*. *"Cho fada agus a thig bainne geal o bhoin dhuibh."* (Traditional).

Cattle and horses constituted the wealth of the people of Skye until about 1810, when they were superseded by sheep. During the earlier portion of the century a large number of horses was kept, and they were so hardy as to be able to maintain themselves in the open all winter. Consequently, their number was much in excess of what was necessary.

Some of the larger farmers kept a few hogs, but these animals never rooted themselves in popular favour in Skye. The number of goats was being gradually reduced, though a few persisted in the feral state even as late as the first decade of the twentieth century.

The Rev. A. MacIvor of Sleat states that no moles, polecats, or hares existed in Skye when he wrote the *Statistical Account* in 1841, and he adds that the hare had been twice introduced, but *"it had disappeared"*.

Military

Mention has already been made of the great demand for men that took place during the course of the American War of Independence. An even greater need for soldiers arose when the excesses of the French Revolution, and their consequences, threatened the stability of the whole of Europe. Hundreds of our men were then taken into the Army, many of them being forced to join through the efforts of the 'Press Gang'.

In order to meet the possible contingency of a French invasion, a regiment of volunteers was raised in Skye in the year 1798. It was established purely for the defence of the island, and it consisted of ten detachments, officered by the local gentry, many of whom were retired soldiers. On the conclusion of the Peace of Amiens, in 1802, this volunteer force was disbanded. It was shortly afterwards to be resuscitated, when our relations with France came once again to be strained and, in 1803 it was decided to raise two regiments in Skye for Home Defence. One of these was commanded by James MacLeod, the last chief but one, of Raasay, and by Alexander MacDonald of Lyndale, both holding the rank of lieutenant-colonel. The great victories that were won through the skill of Lord Nelson rendered the continuance of this force unnecessary, and it was demobilised in 1814. The flow of men to the Army, and in a lesser degree to the Navy, was, however, steadily maintained from the closing years of the eighteenth until about the middle of the nineteenth century. According to a statement made by the Rev. Dr. Norman MacLeod, the island of Skye made a contribution to the fighting forces of the Crown during a period of forty years, from 1797, of *"21 lieutenant-generals and major-generals, 45 colonels, 600 commissioned officers, 10,000 common soldiers, and 120 pipers"*. The Rev. Roderick MacLeod, Free Church minister of Snizort, once quoted this assertion at a meeting of the Assembly in Edinburgh as he was inveighing against those responsible for the depopulation of Skye to provide more room for sheep, and he added the clause: *"Besides no insignificant number of officers and men to the British Navy"*. It is said that this information was supplied by one who was himself a distinguished son of Skye, namely, Sir John MacDonald, the son of Norman MacDonald of Scalpay; and as he was Adjutant-General of the Forces, he was in a position to acquire accurate knowledge.

In one of her poems, the bardess, *Màiri ni'n Iain Bhàin*, refers to the same facts:

> *Bha corr agus deich mile*
> > More than ten thousand
> *Bho'n rìgh a ghabh an t-òr*
> > Who took the King's gold
> *Gu onair 's dion na rìoghachd*
> > For the honour and defence of the Kingdom
> *A Eilean grinn a' Cheò.*
> > From the beautiful Isle of Skye.
>
> (Mac-Bheathain, A, 1891, p. 4)

That an island so circumscribed in area, and of so scanty a population, should have furnished such a large number of men to the Army and the Navy, seems truly phenomenal, but from the observations of others who were conversant with the facts, one is justified in concluding that the statement may not be unduly exaggerated. Thus, Alexander Smith, the author, who was the son-in-law of a famous military officer of Skye, Lieutenant Charles MacDonald of Ord, says:

Of the miniatures of portraits kept in every family in Skye, more than half are soldiers, and several have attained to no mean rank.

Another authority, General Stewart of Garth, observes:

There are so many old soldiers settled in Skye receiving pensions for wounds, and length of service, that the circulation of so much money is no small advantage to their native isle. … Whilst so many soldiers returned home to enjoy their country's reward, I have access to know that an equal number settled in other parts of the kingdom after their discharge;

and Colonel Alexander MacDonald of Treaslane, writing in 1848, declares that the conditions prevailing in Portree on the day the pensioners were being paid were paralleled only by those that obtained on a market day in the village.

Several of the distinguished soldiers have already been referred to, notably, Sir John MacDonald, son of Norman MacDonald, tacksman of Scalpay, who had attained the rank of Adjutant-General of the Forces. He was a man of striking appearance, whose square face and widely-set eyes bespoke the man of forceful disposition and steady deliberation. He had rendered renowned service in the wars of the Peninsula and of Egypt. He died in 1850 at the age of 80 years.

He had a brother who was no less distinguished than himself. This was General Alexander MacDonald, whose name will ever remain fresh on the pages of history as the hero of one of the most daring exploits in the annals of war. When his contingent was surrounded by dense masses of the French on the fateful field of Fuentes Donoro, and escape seemed impossible, he succeeded in bursting through the serried lines of the enemy – an adventure that has deservedly been named 'The Brilliant Feat of Arms'. He died in 1856, in the 70th year of his age. Two other members of the MacDonalds of Bernisdale and of Scalpay, nephews of the foregoing, are also known to fame. One was Major-General Norman MacDonald, brave and debonair, who fought on many a field, and culminated a career of distinction in the Crimea. He died at an advanced age in 1892. The other was Brigadier-General the Right Hon. J.H.A. MacDonald, who, though only a volunteer officer, yet possessed such brilliant military talents that he gained for himself the title of 'The Heaven-born Soldier'.

From among a notable galaxy of the family of MacLeod, a few names are singled out. There was Lieutenant-General Sir John MacLeod (*Seoc Unish*), a son of 'The Old Trojan', Donald MacLeod of Bernera, and his third wife, Margaret MacLeod of Greshornish. He was a man of most commanding presence. A full-brother, Sir Charles, also rose to the rank of lieutenant-general. He won distinction in India, especially in the Mahratta War of 1817, and is said to have been *"exceedingly handsome"*. Another son, Alexander, of the Mansfield West India Man, having purchased Harris in 1779, erected, at Rodel, a memorial to his father. Part of the inscription reads: *"In his 75th year, he married his third wife, by whom he had nine children. Died aged 90 in 1783."*

Of the MacLeods of Gesto many had raised themselves to rank and to fame, but chiefly in the service of the Netherlands. The most outstanding of them was Major-General Norman MacLeod, whose son, Lieutenant-General Norman MacLeod, had a brilliant career in the Dutch Brigade; while a grandson rose to the rank of vice-admiral in the naval service of that country.

The MacLeods of Borline are represented in the military annals of the early part of the nineteenth century by Major-General Norman MacLeod, who saw service in Cape Colony, in Spain, and in India during the Mahratta War. He was a man of impressive appearance, tall and muscular, with features that bore a striking resemblance to those of the Duke of Wellington. He was drowned in the Irish Sea in 1831. Another of this famous family was Major-General William C. MacLeod, who spent the greater part of his life in India. He died in 1880. His son was the distinguished Indian officer, Major-General Donald MacLeod, C.B., D.S.O.

Of another branch of the clan, the MacLeods of Orbost, the most notable men were two brothers, Donald and Alexander. They served chiefly in India, and both attained the rank of major-general.

Another who served in India was Captain Alexander MacLeod, of Vatten, on whose death a touching elegy was composed by *Dòmhnall nan Oran* (Donald MacLeod) (See MacLeòid, D, 1811, p. 107).

Another farm in Duirinish, Varkasaig, produced a distinguished son in General Sir Donald MacLeod of the Indian Army. He died in 1843, and his only daughter, Mary, was married to John MacLeod, the last chief of Raasay.

Of the Raasay MacLeods, the most eminent was General Sir John MacLeod, who, from his outstanding skill as a gunnery officer, was made Director-General of Ordnance on the express recommendation of the Duke of Wellington. He occupied this post, specially created for him, until his death in 1833.

The MacAskills of *Rubh' an Dunain* and their offshoot of Bracadale occupy a position of high distinction in the military history of Skye. As references have already been made to some members of that famous family, we need only make a passing mention of certain of them here. The best known were Major-General William MacAskill, who became Governor of Mauritius. He died in 1815. There was also Major-General Sir John MacAskill of Bracadale, who was mortally wounded in India in the year 1845.

Of the family of MacKinnon the most famous soldiers of the nineteenth century were Major-General Henry MacKinnon, youngest son of William, thirty-second chief. He fought in Egypt, and afterwards in Spain, where he was killed while leading his men through a breach in the walls at the storming of Ciudad Rodrigo. In writing of his death, Southey says: *"Perhaps the country has never sustained so great a loss since the death of Sir Philip Sydney"*. His nephew, Major-General Daniel MacKinnon, was another of our islesmen who had led a brilliant career in India. Then there was Major-General Sir William MacKinnon, a brother of the Rev. Dr. Donald MacKinnon, who was the last of the famous succession of ministers in the parish of Strath. His proved efficiency and his conscientious attention to duty won for him the golden opinion of his Parliamentary chiefs. He entered the army in 1853, and was in both the Crimean campaign and on the personal staff of Lord Clyde during the Indian Mutiny. He fought against the Maoris from 1863 to 1866 and was at the fall of Kumasi as Principal Medical Officer. He retired in 1896 from the post of Director General of the Army Medical Services and died in 1897. By his will, £2,000 was left to Edinburgh University to fund the Mackinnon Bursary. (MacInnes, J, 1899, pp. 208–10).

It was no doubt the prowess of men such as these that our sweet-voiced bard, Neil MacLeod, so beautifully extols in one of his songs:

> ... *na laoich a bha gaisgeil*
>> The valorous heroes
> *A cheannsaicheadh feachdan 's a' chòmhraig,*
>> Who would conquer hosts in the strife,
> *Gu buadharra, cruadalach, smachdail*
>> Victorious, hardy and commanding
> *Nach lùbadh fo chasan luchd fòirneirt;*
>> Who would not cower beneath the feet of oppressors;
> *Fo shuaicheantas luaineach am bratach*
>> Under their waving emblems and banners

> *'S na pioban le'n caismeachd ri ceol daibh,*
>> Pipes with their tuneful marches,
> *Cuir fuinn air na suinn bha gun ghaiseadh,*
>> Raising the ardour of the faultless gallants,
> *Nach tionndadh le taise 's an tòrachd.*
>> Who would not turn faint-hearted in the pursuit.
>> (MacLeòid, N, 1924, p. 167)

Education

In a previous section we have seen that schools had been erected in all the parishes of Skye during the eighteenth century and, in addition to the parochial schools, others had been built in several districts. Thus we find that before the middle of the nineteenth century there were as many as five in Bracadale, while in the adjoining parish of Duirinish the number at the same time was no fewer than ten. In the parish of Portree there was, however, but one school in 1841, and in large districts like Braes, whose school-population was then about 120, and the townships of Glenmore and Mugarry, with an aggregate of 50 children between the ages of 6 and 15 years, no provision whatsoever was made for secular education. In these places the 'subscription schools' were kept on occasion, but, as they were so poorly paid, few teachers with any qualification could be got to serve in them. By the middle of the century a branch parochial school had been established in Raasay, where the 'Three Rs' were taught. About that time, also, it happened that a public-spirited colonial, named MacDiarmid, who was born in Borve, bequeathed a sum of £1000 for the endowment of a school in his native township and another in the district of Braes. In the former place, some £200 of the capital had been spent in the building of a schoolhouse and its appurtenances, but the balance of the fund still allowed a yearly salary of £35 for the schoolmaster. This school was well attended, and it continued for some years to be in a flourishing condition.

There was a parish school in Snizort, while a school was set up in Uig, about 1845, on 'the Assembly Scheme'. Kilmuir was then served by the parochial school, in which the average number of pupils was 70 in summer and 130 in winter, but, according to a writer of the time, the attendance was very irregular, on account of the inability of the parents to provide their children with suitable clothes and to supply books. In this parish there had been established, long before the middle of the century, another school, in which the medium of instruction was exclusively Gaelic, and, indeed, most of the schools on the island, apart from the parish school, were of this type. In 1811 the Gaelic School Society began to found schools in the Highlands, and it was as a result of the efforts of that patriotic organisation that some were built in Skye. But those who had the cause of the Gaelic language at heart had reason even then to deplore the indifference shown by the people to the welfare of their native tongue. Several of the ministers who wrote an account of their parishes in 1841 advert to the growing tendency on the part of those who were constrained to go South in quest of employment to return with a smattering of English, which they intermixed with Gaelic by way of airing their knowledge of the foreign tongue.

Following a circular addressed to Highland Parishes, at the instigation of the *Gaelic Society of Inverness* in May 1876, as to whether they thought it was advisable to give instruction in Gaelic, it is noteworthy that, as published in *An Gaidheal*, Vol. II, p. 155, both Sleat and Strath were against such teaching. The parishes indicating approval show that the number of children was as follows:

Carbost (Bracadale)	70	Stein	90	Clachan	22
Struan	60	Halin	90	Bernisdale	125
Soay	26	Kilvaxter	125	Kensaleyre	60
Glenbrittle	20	Kilmaluag	70	Uig	140
Borodale	50	Portree	180	Glenhinisdale	33
Borreraig	50	Torran	60	Staffin	100
Dunvegan	60	Glens	30	Valtos	90
Vatten Bridge	170	Rona	20		

Even in those districts where schools existed, there does not seem to have been any great desire on the part of the people to take advantage of the opportunities provided for the education of their children. One of the ministers, who wrote in 1841, inveighs against the prevailing unconcern for learning and even goes so far as to suggest the desirability of introducing *"the compulsory regulations of Prussia"*, in order to overcome it. His assertion is borne out by the observation of another minister, who, writing at the same time of the parish of Bracadale, with its five schools, asserts that there were about 400 children between the ages of 6 and 15 years, and no less than 800 adults, who were wholly illiterate. As the adult population of Bracadale at that time was 1769, we see that over two-thirds of the people belonged to that category. That a gradual advance was, however, being made is shown by the declaration of the Rev. A. Clark of Duirinish in 1841, that, whereas two-thirds of the adult population of his parish could neither read nor write, only one-half of the children between 6 and 15 years were in a state of absolute illiteracy.

The salaries of the parochial schoolmasters of Skye in 1841 ranged from £23 a year, which was paid in Duirinish, to £30 in Kilmuir. Those teachers who served in schools other than that of the parish were paid from £8 to £25 per annum – sums which were sometimes supplemented by fees, but these were in most cases merely nominal. It is significant to find that the stipends of the parish ministers at the same time varied from £150 in Bracadale to £271 in Strath.

As was to be expected, those parochial schoolmasters who had cast in their lot with the Free Church were dismissed from their charges in 1843, and schools had to be built by the new denomination for the children of their adherents.

The Poetry of the Nineteenth Century

We have seen that, during the previous century, only one bard of note could be claimed for Skye and that even he had produced his best work furth the island. In the succeeding century, however, several poets make their appearance, though it must at once be stated that in none of them do we find the fire and the depth of feeling that characterise the works of William Ross.

Taking the chief poets of the nineteenth century in their chronological order, the first we meet with is Murdo MacLeod, son of *Alasdair Og Thriaslain*, who occupied a farm on the western shores of Loch Snizort. Of his works only one piece has been preserved, and it takes the form of a dialogue between the young bard and his kindly mother, who exhorts him, in the most winning way, to forsake his libidinous manner of life. She assails him with many a homely thrust, while the poem sparkles with such rare wit, and exhibits such a range of experience and such consummate mastery of the intricate art of Gaelic versification, that the reader is forced to conclude that this piece is but one of many that the author had composed, but which have been lost, like the works of many others of our island bards. The following verse, among other features, shows his skill in metrical technique:

Ministear no Pàpa
Minister or Pope

A dh' fhàilnaich 's a' ghniomh sin,
Who failed in that work,
Olc no math a rinn iad
Whether they did well or ill
Chan fhaighnichear dhiots' e.
Will not be inquired from you.
'S bh' fhearr dhut a bhi céilidh
You would fare better spending time
Ri ceusadh do mhiannan
To suppress your desires
'S ma rinn iadsan eucoir
And if they have committed impropriety
'S iad féin a bheir diol ann.
It is they who will pay for it.

(MacKenzie, J, 1877, p. 399)

Murdo MacLeod emigrated to Carolina about the year 1810, and we hear no more of him.

Donald Macleod (Dòmhnull nan Oran)

A poet of whose works much more is extant is Donald MacLeod, 'Do'ull nan Oran'. This noted bard was a native of Glendale, where he was born at Pollosgainn, in 1787. His father, from whom he inherited his genius, was a farmer in a small way and was, besides, a man of such intelligence and incisiveness of expression as marked him off from the common run of his fellows.

Donald was an only child, and seems to have received an education as good as could be obtained locally at that time. He early showed signs of the genius that was latent in him for, while still a boy of fifteen years, he produced his first poem, '*Oran Aitreamh Ruairi*', descriptive of a dwelling-house that had been erected by a relative:

'S ann an Steinn a thog thu 'n aitreamh
    It was in Stein you built your mansion
Anns am faighte ghloinne lionta
    Where the flowing glass was to be got
Ruma glas is fion na Frainge
    Grey rum and wine of France
Uisgebeatha 's branndaidh riomhach
    Whisky and costly brandy
Gheibhinn ann gach seorsa bidh
    I would get there all manner of food
Chan urrain mi dhoibh 'ga chunntas
    That I cannot enumerate for you
Cruithneachd is briosgaidean Innseach
    Wheat and Indian biscuits
Muc 'ga sgriobadh 's muilt 'g an ruagadh.
    Pigs scraped and wethers dispersed.

              (MacLeòid, D, 1811, p. 173)

As incidents in his early life moved him, he continued to compose on a variety of subjects. When he was about the age of twenty years, the 'Press Gang' was active in Glendale, as elsewhere in Skye, and, in order to shield his son from their attentions, his father secured for him an appointment as collector of road taxes on the estate of his chief. That office suited a man of his talents in an admirable way for, under the varied experience it afforded of men and things, his mind rapidly developed. He was deeply interested in the general lore of the Highlands, his mastery of the vocabulary and the idiom of the Gaelic language being so marked that he soon came to be recognised as one of the best story-tellers of his day in Skye. The originality of his wit, the point of his ready repartee, were known to all while the flick of his satire, stinging, but seldom vindictive, was never administered at the expense of personal dignity.

In 1811, when he was twenty-four years of age, he published an anthology of verse, miscellaneous and original, running to about 270 pages. It contained seventeen poems of his own compositions, some humorous, some martial, and a few amatory pieces, all of which possess considerable merit.

His best known humorous piece is *'Oran Mhurchaidh Bhig'*, a dialogue between a local elder's horse, whose dignity had been sorely affronted, and a hapless herd-lad who presumed to ride it home in the saddle. The poem is full of droll banter and amusing exchanges of wit. The metrical scheme follows that of *'Cabar féidh'*, otherwise it owes nothing to that great masterpiece. The first part of each verse is the effusion of the discomfited halflin, the remainder the withering retort of the insulted steed:

Thuirt esan is e 'g éirigh,
    He said as he arose;
Mo léirchreach, mar phrannadh mi,
    This bruising is my discomfort
Cha dean mi tuilleadh feuma
    I am rendered useless
'S a bheist bheir thu ceannach air,
    And you will pay for it, you brute
Ged tha thu leis an éildeir,
    Tho' you belong to the Elder
Chan éirig air m' anam thu;
    You are no ransom for my soul
'S ma 's e mo ghalair bàis e,
    And if this is the cause of my death
Gu'm pàigh thu ri m' allaire.
    You will pay for the funeral.

              (MacLeòid, D, 1811, p. 43)

The spirited animal rallies the upstart thus with scorn:

A Mhurachaidh bhig nam biodh tu glic,

If you were wise, Little Murdo

Cha b'ann ri sud a dh' fhanadh tu.

You would not have waited for that

Ach dhol dachaidh, gun aon each,

Going home without a horse

O'n chleachd thu bhi'd fhear cairiste.

Since your lot is that of a hired servant

Bha m' eòlas ort da bhliadhna,

I have known you for two years

'S tri miosan a bharrachd air,

And three months beyond that

'S chan fhaca mi each diollaid

And I never saw a saddled horse

Dol riamh gu do dorus leat.

Taking you to your door.

(MacLeòid, D, 1811, p. 43)

In the same sarcastic strain is his *'Rann Molaidh a' Bhàta'*; while its sequel, *'Rann Firinn'*, is a diverting description of a crazy hulk long past its best:

Bha i sgallach breac mar dheile

She was blotched and spotted

Air dhroch lochdradh:

Like a board badly planed

Bha sruth dearg bho cheann gach tàirne

There was a red streak from the head of each nail

Mar a' chorcair.

Like scarlet.

Mar bha meirg air a cnamh,

As the rust had corroded her

'S a làr 'ga grodadh,

And the floor boards were rotten

Bha nid nan corruichin cosag

The nests of the slater were

'Na buird mhosgain.

In her dry rotted timbers.

(MacLeòid, D, 1811, p. 156)

His satire on the elders of Lonmore, produced later in life, is no less amusing; but it is somewhat marred by the introduction of personalities. Although, by all accounts, the conduct of our bard was always exemplary, it would appear that the local elders, in a censorious mood, had been told of some peccadillo or other, and that their strictures had aroused his ire, for he assails the back-biting busybodies of the church with venom in his words:

Ma gheibh thu drama bho dhuin' uasal,

If you get a dram from a gentleman,

Tha thu 'n uair sin air do mhàbadh,

You are traduced,

Ma chuir thu car thar do ghualainn,

If you turned your head on your shoulder,

Sealtainn bhuat le feithe-ghàire,

To look with a becoming smile,

Bheir Iain MacAlasdair suas thu –

John, son of Alexander, will report you

Leugh thu ' 'N Cuairtear' air an t-Sàbaid,

If you read the Cuairtear on Sabbath,

Fuiling a nise do bhinn

Suffer now your condemnation

Bho Chalum Seang 's bho Eoghainn Tàilear.

From 'Slim' Malcolm and Ewen the tailor.

(MacLeod, JN, 1922, p. 128)

His love affairs were no whit more fortunate that those of many a brother bard. When he was about twenty years of age he came under the spell of a neighbouring farmer's lovely daughter, a Miss Stewart of Borrodale. She heartily reciprocated his feelings; but her relatives did much to ruffle the course of true love, until her untimely death obviated the necessity for further interference. One of the lyrics he composed to her shows touches of beautiful imagery. It is called *'Luinneag Ghaoil'*, of which the following is the first stanza:

Dh' fhàg mi slàn mo sgàthan beòshlaint,
    I left hale for my sustaining image,
Snathnean m' àraich, 's geard mo dhòchais;
    The cord of my nurture, the guard of my hope,
Càil mo bhlàthais, is fàin' mo stòldachd,
    The cause of my warmth and the ring of my calmness,
Bàigh na h-òigh le deòin nach tréig mi.
    The love of the maid I shall not willingly relinquish.
                (MacLeòid, D, 1811, p. 222)

A similar verdict is due his *'Oran Reisimeid 'ic Shimidh'*, which he wrote at the age of twenty-three. This is a poem of a very high order, marked by untrammelled freedom of movement, pleasing conceptions, and well-knit vigorous verse:

Chan eil cùnntas air fasain
    There is no account of the plenishments
Fo'n chrùn th' aig Righ Shasuinn,
    Under the crown of the King of England,
Nach eil ionnsaicht am pearsa
    That have not been learned in person
Na th' aca de àireamh
    By all they have in their muster.
Is mùirneach ri 'm faicinn iad,
    Grand is the sight of them,
Is cliùiteach ri 'n claistinn iad,

Renowned the report of them,
Is lùghmhor an casan,
    Fleet are their feet,
'S is bras an cath-làmh iad.
    And impetuous in hand to hand combat.
Is àllainn an crioslachadh,
    Magnificent their plenishings,
Sgabardach, biodeagach
    With scabbard and bayonet
Stàilinneach, pistealach,
    Of steel and pistols,
Slioslannach, deàrrsach,
    With glittering side arms,
Sgàrlaideach, leasaichte,
    Clothed in scarlet,
An càradh fo itean,
    With feather bonnets.,
Thug stàtaichean meas daibh,
    Esteemed by noble men,
Nach fiosraich mo chànain.
    Beyond my powers of description.
                (MacLeòid, D, 1811, p. 62)

His lament, composed in 1808, to Donald MacDonald, who died in Greshornish, is suffused with genuine feeling, and possesses high poetic merit. Witness the fine rhythmic flow of the following verse:

Nam b'ann le fòirneart luchd dò-bheirt
    If it had been by violence of evil doers
Thigeadh leònadh ann ad charaibh
    That wounds have come your way
Dheannte feòlach d' chòmhnadh
    Carnage would happen in assisting you

Le spionnadh dhòrn 'e le cruaidh lannan

    By strength of fists and blades of steel

Le neart Chlann Dòmhnuill 's nan Leòdach

    By strength of Macdonalds and MacLeods

'S gach urra mór leis bu toigh thu

    And of each important person who favoured you.

Bu chomunn gòrach a steòrnadh

    It would be a foolish person who would plan

Do chur air fògradh dha d' aindheoin.

    To banish you against your will.

                    (MacLeòid, D, 1811, p. 31)

An elegy he wrote about the same time, on the death of Captain Alexander MacLeod of Vatten, who had served with distinction in India, is marked by great wealth of imagery and very deep sympathy (MacLeòid, D, 1811, p. 107).

When he was about twenty-four years of age, he relinquished his post as collector of road-taxes for that of fisherman to the castle. Soon, however, the fever of emigration affected him, like many another in Skye, and he set off for America. He did not remain long in exile, for he returned to his native dale in 1833, when he set up in business as a general merchant.

At the age of sixty he married a girl of nineteen years, and they had a family of four sons and six daughters. Two of the former were bards – Neil, the polished gentleman, the exquisite lyricist, and John, the wayward sailor-lad, whose patriotic lays and rollicking wit entertained his associates in many a foreign port.

The harassing cares of a large family were not conducive to the exercise of the Muse, so that, with the exception of two poems, he produced nothing of note in later life. His 'Oran an Uillt Mhóir' and 'Oran do Thungaig' show a mind beautifully attuned to Nature's soothing influences, and in them he depicts the scenes of his native vale with that quiet charm and loving grace that one so often meets with in the works of his famous son.

Donald MacLeod died in 1873, at the ripe old age of eighty-six years, and he was buried in the ancient churchyard of Kilcomgan, in Glendale.

It is a sad commentary on our lack of interest in the poets of our race that the works of a bard of such pronounced genius as Donald MacLeod should have been suffered so long to remain in broken and scattered fragments, with none to consider them worthy of being gathered together and presented to the world as a connected whole. Rev Donald Maclean in *Typographica Scoto Gadelica* (1915) says that the family had in manuscript, many of his poems, never printed, and that a prospectus had been produced, soliciting subscriptions for an enlarged edition. *"An sealladh nach fhaicear"* ('A sight that will not be seen') (MacLean, D, 1915, p. 265).

Mary MacPherson (Màiri ni'n Iain Bhàin)

In the year that *Do'ull nan Oran* died, namely, 1873, the voice of another genius was raised in song. It was that of the bardess, Mary MacPherson, the daughter of a crofter in Skeabost named John MacDonald, or, as he was locally called, *Iain Bàn MacAonghais Oig*. Her mother was Flora Macinnes from Uig. Mary, who was the second youngest of a large family, was born at Skeabost in March, 1821. Having been brought up like other young women in her station of life, she early became proficient in those rural pursuits and domestic arts that were then the duty and the pride of every maiden to master.

In her twenty-seventh year she was married to a shoemaker in Inverness, one Isaac MacPherson, and they had a family of four children. Her husband died in 1871, and in the following year an event happened that was destined to become the turning point in her life. She was accused of a certain misdemeanour, found guilty (unjustly, as most declared at the time), and sentenced to a term of imprisonment. The sense of injustice, coupled with the infamy inflicted on her good name, so rankled in her spirit that it seemed to have inducted the gift of poetry – a faculty that had hitherto given no manifestation of its presence. The alleged misdemeanour happened in Inverness and was the taking of clothes that belonged to her mistress.

'S e n' dh fhuiling mi de thaire
    It was the degree of harassment I suffered
Spogan easbuigean is baillidh
    At the hands of bishops and baillies
Chur a faothar air mo nadur
    That put the edge on my nature
Is ola chraidh g'a deanamh geur dhomh.
    And the oil of pain sharpened it.

Bha mi fada bho mo chairdean
    I was far from my kinsfolk
'Nuair a thuit mi anns an araich
    When I fell in the conflict
'S ged nach cualas riamh mo bhardachd
    And though my poetry had never been heard
Chuir an tamailte ri cheil i.
    The shame put it together.
                    (Mac-Bheathain, A, 1891, p. 216)

In Tha mi sgith de luchd na Beurla (I am tired of the English speaking folk) *she protests her innocence.*
Bu mhath dhomsa mar a thachair
    It was as well for me as it happened
Nach robh chogais ga mo thacadh,
    That my conscience did not choke me,
Sud a ni' a chum an taic rium
    For that is what gave me support
'Nuair a thachair dhomh bhi' 'm eiginn.
    When I happened to be in dire straits."
                    (Mac-Bheathain, A, 1891, p. 225)

Soon after this incident she removed to Glasgow and, although she had then attained the advanced age of fifty years, she decided to enter the nursing profession. With a view to qualifying for that calling, she became a probationer at the Royal Infirmary, where, after serving a few years, she obtained a certificate.

During this period, and for some time after it, she joined in the social life of Highlanders in the cities of the South with characteristic fervour, being a welcome guest at the 'gatherings' of her isles-folk in particular, and of Highlanders generally, in Glasgow and Greenock. In celebration of these functions she often composed, and sang, songs that evoked a large amount of enthusiasm at the time, but now that the scenes have changed, and the personalities represented have passed away, one is forced to admit that the great majority of these effusions have no permanent value. Indeed, but few of her productions are worthy of preservation. She was incapable of sustained effort, her imagery was too fleeting and superficial, and we tire of her pleonastic and rambling treatment of her subject. In *'Nuair Bha Mi Og'*, which is one of her best efforts, she rouses us momentarily with a pleasing sentiment here and there, only to accord us a shock elsewhere by her commonplace observations. In another of her most popular pieces, *'Soraidh le Eilean a' Cheò'*, she depicts beautiful vignettes of scenes in her native isle, but displays them in such rapid succession, and in such a haphazard manner, that the mind wearies in following her, so that the whole production too often resolves itself into a glorified tourists' guide.

In the year 1882 she retired to her native district, where a house, 'Woodside Cottage', was placed at her disposal, rent free, by the generous proprietor, Lachlan MacDonald of Skeabost. At that time the land troubles were agitating the island, and she championed the people's cause in speech and song. Many of her poems were then composed, though few of them possess much poetic value.

Among her works appear a large number of elegies; but in these, as in her political songs, she betrays the shallowness of her genius, borrowing largely from the works of other bards. Her most meritorious production in this branch of poetry is her *'Tuireadh air Cluainidh'*, or lament for MacPherson of Cluny. Her *Marbhrann* ('lament') for Mrs MacDonald, Viewfield, is also worthy of mention, (Mac-Bheathain, A, 1891, p. 65), while, in *The Celtic Monthly*, July 1883, there is a very praiseworthy lament by her for Rev Alexander MacGregor. It is noteworthy that in her works the love lyric occupies a very subordinate position, a trait to be accounted for by the fact that she was well advanced in years before she began to express herself in song.

Through the munificence of her patron, MacDonald of Skeabost, her poetry was published in the year 1891. It was taken down from her dictation (for she could not write) by John White, Inverness, and an introduction was compiled for the volume by the erudite scholar, Alexander MacBain.

Always fond of company, she degenerated in her old age into a mere gadabout, and during her wanderings she died suddenly in Portree in 1898, at the age of eighty years. She was buried in Inverness, where, in the chapel burial-ground, a monument was erected to her memory by one who had often been the subject of her songs – Charles Fraser Macintosh, M.P. for Inverness.

Sheriff Nicolson

Alexander Nicolson was the son of Malcolm Nicolson, who was proprietor of the small estate of Husabost, in the parish of Duirinish. Here the future sheriff was born in the year 1827. He was educated privately, and at an early age proceeded to Edinburgh University, where he gained high honours both in literature and in philosophy. During the illness of Sir William Hamilton he was appointed deputy to that renowned philosopher and he afterwards became assistant to Professor MacDougall. Sir Archibald Geikie, who was one of his students in 1856, makes mention of the impression made on him by the *"big-boned Celt with a look of strength and kindliness in his large and strongly-marked features"*.

> *Tha laoch dhuibh ann a Husabost*
>> There is a hero in Husabost
> *Is duinleach, tha mi cinnteach*
>> And a warrior, I am sure
> *Nach dealaich ris a bhreacan*
>> Who will not abandon the tartan
> *Fhad s' bhitheas Neacalach 's san Riogheachd."*
>> As long as there is a Nicolson in the Kingdom.
>
> (Mac-Bheathain, A, 1891, p. 81)

At this time he intended to qualify for the ministry. With that end in view, he attended classes in the Faculty of Divinity, only to discover that he could not conscientiously pursue his studies, for, in his own words, *"the officer's uniform in that excellent body is painfully tight"*.

Thereupon he turned his attention to journalism, writing voluminously for several periodicals in an easy, graceful style.

On his father's death he decided to enter the legal profession, and was 'called to the bar' in 1860. Owing, however, to that erraticism which has so often proved the undoing of some of the most brilliant members of his race, the great expectations entertained of him failed to materialize and, as Geikie says, *"this most gifted and genial man became the most unsuccessful of the advocates who paced the floor of Parliament House"*.

In 1865 he was one of the commissioners appointed by the government to inquire into the state of education in the Highlands, and he gave of his abilities and his energies with zeal to that endeavour. Indeed, it was work of this nature, necessitating his attention only for a time, that best suited his genius, which was meant to sparkle, but not to emit a continuous fire.

In Edinburgh he was a member of several exclusive clubs, notably the 'X' and the 'Red Lion', at which his company was much sought, because of his affability, his brilliance, and his rare wit. When Sir William Thomson, afterwards the great Lord Kelvin, in his presidential address to the British Association in 1871, propounded the theory that life came to the earth through the broken fragments of meteorites, Nicolson delighted the members that evening at the Red Lion dinner by singing his clever skit on the 'British Ass', one verse of which is quoted:

> *To Grecian sages charming*
> *Rang the music of the spheres:*
> *But voices more alarming*
> *Salute our longer ears.*
> *By science bold, we now are told*
> *How life did come to pass.*
> *From world to world the seeds were hurled,*
> *Whence sprang the British Ass.*

Long-delayed preferment at length came the way of the briefless barrister, when, in 1872, he was appointed Sheriff of Kircudbrightshire, but he was not happy there, for he missed the congenial life of the capital.

> *'S tha Siorram MacNeacail am breacan cho grin*
>   And Sheriff Nicolson in so elegant a tartan

Gaisgeach rioghail nam buadh
   Kingly hero of talents
Sheinneadh duanag gu binn
   Who would sing a sweet song
Chridhe fearail an t saighdear
   Manly soldier's heart
'S mar maighdean e ciuin
   And gentle as a maiden
Suil mar lainnir nan leug
   An eye like the shine of the jewels
Bhios air eideadh mo ruin
   That are in the adornments of my love
Sealgair damh chroicaich 's an ard chreachan ghlas
   Hunter of the antlered stag in the high corrie
Bheireadh bradan gu bruaich
   Fisher of salmon
As an fhuar linne chas
   From the swift cold river.
Bi ceartas is trocair triall co' ruit
   Justice and mercy will go with you
'S ant saoghal
   Throughout your life
'S claon bhreithe gu brath
   And never a foolish judgement
Cha toir armunn mo ghaoil.
   Will my love give.

(Composed by Mary MacKellar)

When his friend and admirer, Professor Blackie, succeeded in founding the Chair of Celtic in Edinburgh, it was confidently expected that Nicolson would become its first occupant. But, to the regret of many, he declined the proffered post.

In 1881 he published his unique compilation of Gaelic proverbs, a work that, for fulness of material and evidence of

scholarship, will remain a monument to his name so long as the language of the Gael is spoken. In *An Gaidheal* of 1873, he has a letter to the Editor, from Kircudbright, asking for proverbs and intimating he is to prepare a new edition of MacIntosh's *Gaelic Proverbs*. (MacIntosh, D, 1785, 1st Edition) When the land troubles in the Highlands had at last commanded the attention of the government, Sheriff Nicolson was nominated as one of the Commissioners, and we can trace his work in several portions of the epoch-making report produced by that august body.

In 1885 he was transferred from the Stewartry to Greenock, but there also he evinced no enthusiasm for his work, and, to the disappointment of all, relinquished his profession and retired to Edinburgh in 1889. His retirement, however, failed to bring him happiness. He suffered from periodic fits of depression, and his end came suddenly on the 20th of January, 1893. Sir James Crichton-Browne, in referring to his death, says of him: *"He was a big man with a big heart, which was ever in the Highlands, or more particularly in the Hebrides, the glories of which he celebrated in a few exquisite lyrics"*. His best efforts were in praise of his native isle, all of them being characterised by a healthy patriotism and a beautiful sentiment blended with a noble reverence. Thus, in his pæan on the Isle of Skye, he writes:

Many a poor, black cottage is there
Grimy with peat smoke;
Sending forth in the quiet evening air
Purest of incense.
Reared in these dwellings have brave ones been
Dear ones are still there.
Forth from their darkness I've seen
Coming pure linen;
And like the linen the souls were clean
Of them that wore it.

(Sharp, EA, 1896, pp. 270–1)

His martial song, *'Agus Ho Mhórag'*, extolling the prowess of Highland soldiers on the field of battle, shows his great power of fitting words to a difficult metrical scheme:

Many were their deeds of arms
'Gainst the swarms of Hyder Ali.
Leagured close in Mangalore
Tippo and his hordes they baffled.

The same wonderful command of language is shown in his masterly translation of that greatest of sea-epics, *'Birlinn Chlann Raoghnuill'*, by *Alasdair Mac Mhaighstir Alasdair:*

Drive the mountain-monsters onward,
Ho ro hùg a bhi;
Pounding grey-backed swirling eddies,
Ho ro hùg a bhi;
Send the surge in sparkles skywards,
Ho ro hùg a bhi;
Hoary-headed seas upswelling,
Ho ro hùg a bhi.

His works are scattered throughout various publications. In *An Gaidheal*, July 1872, is a translation by Nicolson of a poem of Professor Ayton's called *Ruathar Mhic a Phearsain* (MacPherson's Rant). The fascinating articles on the Cuillin he so much loved, appear in *'Good Words'*. Two of his poems, together with a brief memoir, are given in Edward's *'Modern Scottish Poets'*, and the Rev. W.C. Smith, D.D., published several of his works and a sketch of his life in the year 1893.

Neil Macleod

Neil MacLeod was born at Pollosgain, in the district of Glendale, in the year 1843. He was the son of Donald MacLeod (*Do'ull nan Oran*), and the strong poetic strain in the father made itself early manifest as a dominant trait in the son.

He was brought up like other boys in his station in life, but with this difference: he had a father whose mind was richly stored with the legendary and historical lore of the Highlands, and who could relate it in a manner that few could equal. The influence of such an upbringing on a youth whose faculties were naturally receptive and keen can scarcely be over-estimated. Often he adverts to these happy days in the morning of his life, when:

> *Ann an dùbhlachd gharbh a' geamhraidh*
> > In the rough gloomy winter
> *Cha b'e am bu ghainn' ar spòrs;*
> > No whit less was our diversion,
> *Greis air sùgradh, greis air dannsa,*
> > Time for sporting, time for dancing,
> *Greis air canntarachd is ceòl;*
> > Time for music by mouth and instruments;
> *Biodh gach seanair aosmhor, liath,*
> > Hoary old grandfathers,
> *'G innseadh sgialachdan gun ghò,*
> > Relating faultless tales,
> *Mu gach gaisgeach fearail, greannmhor,*
> > About the many, handsome heroes,
> *Bh 'anns a ghleann nuair bha iad òg.*
> > Who were in the Glen when they were young.
>
> (MacLeòid, N, 1924, p. 2)

In his twenty-second year he left his native glen for Edinburgh, where he was to spend the remainder of his days. He was employed there by the firm of R. & R. MacLeod, tea merchants, the principal partner in which was his cousin. His work as agent for this company brought him into contact with all manner of people, among whom his unfailing courtesy and healthy humour made him a general favourite. We need not wonder, then, that his services were often in demand wherever Highlanders were wont to foregather in the cities of the south.

In 1889 he married Katherine Stewart, the daughter of a schoolmaster in Kensaleyre. They had a family of two daughters, and a son who won distinction in the medical profession, and secured the degree of M.D. from the University of Edinburgh.

When the Bard retired from business in 1911, he was presented with an illuminated address. A notable assemblage met to do him honour, and Professor Mackinnon paid a high tribute to his talents as a writer. He was not, however, to enjoy his retirement long, for his health had now become impaired and he died in September, 1913.

Neil MacLeod has had the unique experience, for a Gaelic bard, of seeing his works pass through four editions in the course of his lifetime. The first collection of his songs was published in 1883, under the title of 'Clàrsach na Doire', and such was its popularity that a second edition was called for ten years later. Other impressions were soon to follow. A third appeared in 1902, a fourth in 1909, while a fifth was produced in 1924.

Among his works the love-lyric holds a predominant place, no fewer than twenty of his poems falling in this category. In a very notable way he sustained this type of song on a plane as high as was customary among Gaelic bards of the past. While he does not fail to dwell on the physical charms of her who inspired his song, he is attracted the more by her mental qualities and spiritual traits. True love rarely exulted with more rapturous ecstasy over a tocherless maiden than it does in 'Coille Chaoil':

Chan 'eil fearann, chan 'eil fonn
    Neither farm nor croft
Aig mo rìghinn òig;
    Has my young maiden
Ach tha cridhe glan 'n a com
    But a pure heart
Aig mo rìghinn òig.
    Has my maiden.
Ged a bhiodh ar bothan lom,
    Though our hovel should be bare,
Is ar sporan gun bhith trom,
    And our purse light,
Bhithinn sona ris an tom,
    I would be happy in the lea of a mound,
Le mo rìghinn òig.
    With my young maiden.

            (MacLeòid, N, 1924, p. 68)

In that noblest of his works, *'Màiri Bhaile Chrò'*, the poet's art has touched a level seldom attained by the master minds of any clime or age. Throughout this great lyric the poet is so engrossed in rapt adoration of his subject that the self is almost wholly effaced.

Ged bheireadh baintighearna dhomh 'lamh
    Though I might wed a lady fair
Le saibhlean lan a dh' òr
    With coffers filled with gold
Gu lionmhor buaireas agus cradh
    That riches bring but cross and care
Tha 'n caradh ris an t seòrs'
    'S a tale that's oft been told
Gu'm b` annsa bhi air cosg nan tràth
    I'd rather list the cuckoo's voice

Le sith is gràdh 'n a choir
    As through the glen I go
An gleann nan cuach, 's ruith nam ba
    About the kine, along with thee
Le Màiri Bhaile Chrò.
    Fair Maid of Ballchro.
    (MacLeòid, N, 1924, p. 17– Translation by D. MacKay, Ledaig)

And he had plumbed those cruel depths into which the love-lorn are sometimes drawn, to be swirled hither and thither until the helm is finally wrenched out of the hand of reason. In that sad song, *'Bi Seumas Leam a' Nochd'*, he kindles our sympathy for the island Ophelia even more powerfully than does Shakespeare himself.

Just as through his amatory poems sounds a clear clean note, so in his satires and humorous pieces there is a complete freedom from that personal bitterness and those crudities of expression, tainted with obscenity, that too often mar the works of some of our other bards. Neil MacLeod was by nature incapable of administering a wound to his fellows; he soared superior to those petty feelings that seek to besmirch and annoy. But his sparkling wit glints through every stanza, delighting us with its playful banter and sheer harmlessness. One wonders whether the philosophic resignation of the old maid, who is prepared to throw herself on any man that may offer, has ever been more cleverly defined than in his *'Oran na Seana Mhaighdinn'*:

Ma gheibh mise fear gu brach
    If I am ever to get a man
Plaigh air nach tigeadh e
    Plague on him for his dilatoriness
Ged nach can mi sin ri cach
    Though I shall not mention it to others
B'fhearr leam gun tigeadh e

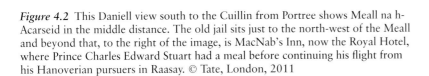

Figure 4.1 According to Daniell (1769–1837), an English landscape and marine painter, and engraver, this is Castle Broichan. Actually the castle's name is Brochel. During July and August 1815 Daniell journeyed around the islands of Eigg, Rum, Skye and Raasay, together with the Hebridean Islands of Harris and Lewis. His trip continued up the west coast of Scotland, around the north coast, out to the Orkney Islands and down the east coast as far south as Dundee. He arrived in Dundee in October 1815. This mammoth journey resulted in 139 aquatint prints being finally published, the last completed in 1821. © Tate, London, 2011.

Figure 4.2 This Daniell view south to the Cuillin from Portree shows Meall na h-Acarseid in the middle distance. The old jail sits just to the north-west of the Meall and beyond that, to the right of the image, is MacNab's Inn, now the Royal Hotel, where Prince Charles Edward Stuart had a meal before continuing his flight from his Hanoverian pursuers in Raasay. © Tate, London, 2011

Figure 4.3 Today Liveras is conjoined to the village of Broadford. This view from the sea takes in Corry Lodge which was built around 1790 as their residence of the MacKinnons of Corry. In the background is Beinn na Caillich.

Figure 4.4 Loch Coruisk, a fresh-water loch lying just to the south-east of the Cuillin. Not only was it captured thus by Daniell but was also painted by J.M.W. Turner, Sidney Richard Percy and Alexander Francis Lydon.

Figure 4.5 Portree on the Isle of Skye. © Tate, London, 2011.

I wish he would come
'N a mo laighe seo leam fhin
    Here I lie all alone
'S tha e coltach ris gu'm bi
    And it is likely long to be
Ma tha leannan dhomh 's an tir
    If there is a lover in the land for me
Sgriob air nach tigeadh e
    Bad luck on him for delaying
Ged a bhiodh a sporan gann
    Although his purse would be light
Dhannsainn na 'n tigeadh e.
    I would dance at his coming
Ged a bhiodh a leth shuil dall
    Although he be blind of an eye
M' annsachd nan tigeadh e.
    I would love him if he came.
Biodh e dubh, no biodh e donn
    Be he black or be he brown
Biodh e direach biodh e cam
    If he is straight or be he bent
Ma tha casan air is ceann
    If he has legs and a head
Dhannsainn nan tigeadh e.
    I would dance at his coming.

            (MacLeòid, N, 1924, p. 64)

In *'Turus Dhòmhnuill do Ghlaschu',* comedy is skilfully blended with tragedy in a graphic description of the situation that develops when an unsophisticated islander falls into the clutches of the city harpy and her associates.

Throughout his works there glows a love of home that borders close on piety, reaching its highest pitch in his *'Cumha Eilean a' Cheò',* where he declares:

Thigeadh bochdainn no beairteas,
    Come poverty or riches,
Thigeadh acaid no leòn,
    Come grief or wound,
Chaoidh cha sgar iad mo chuimhne
    Never will they sever my memory
Bho na glinn sin ri m' bheò;
    From those glens while I live;
Ged a shiubhlainn gach rioghachd
    Though I were to traverse
Is gach tir fo na neòil,
    Every kingdom under the sun,
Bidh mo chridhe gu deireadh
    My heart will be forever
Ann an Eilean a' cheò.
    In the Island of the Mist.

            (MacLeòid, N, 1924, p. 125)

Like the other bards of our people, he was readily susceptible to Nature's influences, but what strikes us as strange is that, while he enthuses over the beauties of *'doire, cuartag, agus glac',* grove, path and hollow, his native hills had for him so slight an appeal. Thus his references to the Cuillin convey to the reader but little of the glamour and the grandeur of these majestic mountains, while his poem on Quiraing is utterly lacking in anything that inspires.

He shows a marked tendency to point the moral, a large proportion of his poems being didactic in character. But while he may teach in some of them, none can say that he ever poses as the prude whose chief end is to preach to his fellows. Through them all there breathes the spirit of an earnest and clean-minded man. His *'Taigh a' Mhisgeir'* is a faithful exposure of the evils of intemperance. To him has been revealed, in a manner vouchsafed to few, the secret of the problem of life and, if it be granted that they possess most who lay least store on the material things of this world, then Neil MacLeod was truly rich in all that makes life worthwhile. When 'the world is too much with us', it would be a good corrective were we to repeat that wish of his, *'Ri Taobh na Tràigh'*, so simple in expression, so sublime in sentiment!

> *Tha cuid an tòir air stòr 's air maoin,*
>> Some seek material wealth,
>
> *'Gan ruith bho'm breith gu'm bàs.*
>> Chasing after it from birth to death.
>
> *Chan fhaigh iad fois, cha bhi iad saor*
>> They never rest and are never free
>
> *Ma chi iad sin aig càch:*
>> If they see anything possessed by others:
>
> *Thoir dhòmhsa sith, is gràdh, is gaol,*
>> Give me peace, charity and love,
>
> *Ri taobh nan sruthan tlàth,*
>> Beside the gentle streams,
>
> *Mo bhothan beag fo sgàil nan craobh,*
>> My little cottage under the trees,
>
> *'S mo lios ri taobh na tràigh.*
>> And my garden beside the sea.
>
>> (MacLeòid, N, 1924, p. 135)

The same purity of outlook that guided his life pervades the whole of his works. His diction is always choice – he never wrote a word at which the most finical could take umbrage, and the polish of his verse is superior to that of any of our bards. He was a master of the art of versification, showing marvellous powers in adorning his lines with those subtle touches – alliterative effects, topic linkages, and rhythmic stresses, that lend such a charm to the best of our Gaelic poetry:

> *Tha 'n oigh ann seo bu bhinne guth,*
>> The maid is here of sweetest voice,
>
> *Bu ghile làmh, 's bu ghrinne cruth,*
>> Of whitest hand and neatest form,
>
> *'S an com a bha mar eal' an t-sruth,*
>> And the body that was like the swan of the stream,
>
> *Gun dreach, 's gun bhlàth;*
>> Without beauty or bloom;
>
> *'S a cuailean dualach, clannach, dubh*
>> And her hair ringletted, curled and black
>
> *Gun chìr air chàmh.*
>> Withered without a comb.
>
>> (MacLeòid, N, 1924, p. 170)

Nor was his prose writing ability a whit inferior to that of his bardic compositions. Such writing of his is scattered throughout several publications, such as the *Transactions of the Gaelic Society of Inverness* and the *Transactions of the Gaelic Society of Glasgow*, and some choice specimens appear at the end of his *Clarsach an Doire*.

More recently there have appeared publications by other Skyemen, *viz* Angus Robertson: *Cnoc an Fhradhairc*, an eclogue, *Orain na Ceilidh* and a novel, *An t-Ogha Mór*; Neil Ross's *Armageddon* and Sorley Maclean's *Dain do Eimhir*, as well as numerous pieces in various magazines. In addition to these there is a large mass of material, some in manuscript, which is in a high order of quality, though, perhaps, of local interest and appeal, by Neil MacPherson (*Niall Ceannaiche*), *and* Duncan, his son; while Charles Matheson (*Tearlach a' Phosta*), with his incisive wit and lively humour and catchy tunes, has long been a favourite in his local district and among those who know his works.

CHAPTER XVIII

The History of Raasay

On the dissolution of the Lordship of the Isles, in 1493, Raasay and Rona, with the adjoining islands, together with the peninsula of Waternish, and the island of Isay, in Skye, became part of the territory of *Siol Thorcuil*, as the MacLeods of Lewis were called.

About the year 1510, the ninth chief of that clan, Malcolm by name, ceded to his second son a portion of his far-flung dominions, consisting of the islands of Raasay and Rona, with certain portions of the adjacent mainland, namely Coigeach and Gairloch. The name of the new chieftain was Calum Garbh, and the line of which he was the first is accordingly known in history as *"Clan 'ic 'ille Chaluim Ratharsair"*.

As was natural enough, this branch continued for some years to form an integral part of the parent stem. A reference is made to them as a separate entity when, in 1518, Sir Donald MacDonald of Lochalsh made an incursion into Morvern to avenge himself on the MacIans of Ardnamurchan, who had so consistently opposed his pretensions to the Lordship of the Isles. It is mentioned that among those who accompanied him as his allies were the MacLeods of Raasay. That they still owned MacLeod of Lewis as their superior is shown in a statement by Hugh MacDonald, the sennachie of Sleat, who, in referring to

this episode, says: *"Raisay had a consultation with his chief, the laird of Lewis"* (MacDonald, A & A, 1896, p. 325).

In the encounter that ensued between the forces of Sir Donald and the MacIans at *Creag an Airgid*, it is stated that MacIan fled, but was closely pursued, and finally captured. The account closes with the remark that he was *"killed by the laird of Raisay"*. Even as late as 1549, the Chief of Lewis was still suzerain to the MacLeods of Raasay, for in that year Dean Munro observes: *"This same Mac Gille Chaluim should obey M'Cloyd of the Lewis"* (Munro, RW, 1961, p. 70).

At that time, and for fully two hundred years thereafter, the islands of Raasay and Rona were components of the extensive parish of Snizort in Skye. Indeed, one of the earliest notices we meet with concerning these islands, apart from a reference made to Raasay as a point in the route of King Haco, when he came with his mighty Armada in 1263, is the statement that, in 1501, James IV, the Scottish king, presented to a certain Sir Nicholas Berchame *"the vicarage of Kilmolowok in Rasay, one of the annexes of Snesford"* (Innes, C, 1854, p. 346). (It may be noted that the title, 'Sir', was given to such as possessed the degree 'Bachelor of Arts'.) In the ancient churchyard of Clachan the ruins of this chapel may still be seen, now almost embedded in the swelling turf, the result of countless burials. Like many another in the Highlands, this church was dedicated to St. Moluac, and a semi-circle of eight crosses was set at intervals to demarcate its precincts and form a sanctuary. Some of these crosses were still standing when Dr. Johnson visited the island in 1773, though the church was then *"unroofed and ruinous"*.

The successor of Sir N. Berchame would appear to have been a certain Sir Norman MacPherson, whose decease in the year 1626 rendered the vicarage of *'Sneisfort'* vacant once more. The incumbency then devolved on one whose name was destined to become a familiar one in the history of the Western Isles. That was Sir Donald Monro, Dean of the Isles, who in 1549 made a tour of his diocese, and left on record a most interesting, if somewhat unreliable, account of it. He describes Raasay as wooded with birch, and with large stretches of fertile land, well cultivated, while its seas abounded with fish. He also states that there were many deer on the island then, although in Dr. Johnson's time there were none. The Dean states further:

> There are in it twa castles, to witt, the Castle of Kilmorocht and the Castle of Brolokit, with twa faire orchards at the saids castells, with ane paroche kirke, callit Killmolowocke; … The land 'perteins to McGyllychallum of Raarsay be the sword, and to the bishope of the iles be heritage.
>
> (Munro, RW, 1961, p. 70).

Kilmorocht was the seat of the MacLeods after Brochel (*'Brolokit'*) was abandoned. Martin refers to it as a *'Tower'* (Martin, M, 1716, p. 164). See also *MacFarlane's Geographical Collections* (Mitchell, A, 1906–8).

In the account given of Rona the Dean says that it was well wooded, and assiduously farmed for it produced abundance of corn. He states that it was inhabited by a lawless people, *"scant of any religion"*; while the harbour, in the middle of the island, *"is guyed for fostering of thieves, ruggairs, and reivars, till await upone the peilling and spulzeing of poure pepill"*. Anent this it is significant that one of the coves in 'The Harbour' of Rona is still known as *'Port nan Robairean'*, or the Harbour of Thieves. Of Rona, as of Raasay, it is stated: *"This ile perteins to McGyllychallum of Raarsay be force, and to the bishope of the iles be heritage"* (Munro, RW, 1961, pp. 70–1).

In those days title deeds had not become a vogue in the Highlands, so that possession, especially *'by force'* was four parts of the law. *"What care I"*, said a MacDonald of Keppoch, *"for titles given on sheepskin; I claim my rights and titles by the edge of this sword"*. We have abundant evidence of it that the MacLeods of Raasay had on all occasions refused to acknowledge the Bishop of the Isles as their lord, for in *'Acta Dominorum Concilii et Sessiones'* we find that, on 14th March 1532, an action was brought at the instance of *"ane Reverend fader in God, Farquhar, Bischop of the Ilis and Commendatour of Colmekyll"*, against *"Mac Gille Chaluim, callit of Raasay"*, for his remissness in paying dues to the see of Iona; and, again, according to a statement quoted in reference to the sources of the rental of the Bishopric of the Isles in 1561, Raasay is entered as a part of the property of the bishop (Skene, WF, 1847).

These incidents, with the exception of the last, took place during the chiefship of the first of the *Mac Ghille Chaluims*, Malcolm *Garbh*, or 'The Brawny', as he was called. Very few facts have been gleaned concerning this chief, the time of his death even being uncertain. It is probable that he lived until 1556, for in that year a charter for his lands was given under the government seal to *'Malcolm Gillichalum Garbh'*. In *'The Baronage of Scotland'*, by Sir Robert Douglas of Glenbervie, it is said that he 'died in the reign of Queen Mary'.

Malcolm left two sons who were known to history, namely, Alexander, the heir, and 'John of the Axe', *Iain na Tuaighe*. It would appear that the second Chief of Raasay did not long survive his father, and that the guardianship of the young heir devolved on his uncle, *Iain na Tuaighe*. In the *Miscellany of the Scottish History Society*, (Campbell, H, 1926) on the history of Craignish, there is the following account of *Mac Ghille Chaluim* of Raasay's second son

> *happened on the shores of Craignish with a birlin, where he met a woman who had been the concubine of Campbell of Craignish and she married MacLeod. She was the great grandmother of Iain Garbh MacLeoid and is buried in Raasay where her grave may be seen to this day.*

> (Campbell, H, 1926, p. 232).

Now it happened that this 'John of the Axe' had been carrying on clandestine relations with the wife of his uncle, Roderick MacLeod, tenth Baron of Lewis. About the year 1539, the undutiful wife eloped with her youthful lover, and lived with him in Raasay, where, after her divorce by her first husband, she was probably married to *Iain na Tuaighe*. The fact that she was a MacKenzie of Kintail would not commend her to the clansmen of Raasay, who, at that time, were at war with her people over the lands of Gairloch. And when one of her daughters was betrothed to Alasdair Roy, the head of the MacKenzies of Gairloch, a real offence was given to the men of Raasay, with the result that the island was seething with indignation because a woman of their name had entered into the bonds of wedlock with one whose clan had been their most bitter foe for over half a century.

About that time the wife of 'John of the Axe' died, and he married shortly afterwards a kinswoman of his own, the daughter of Allan MacLeod, chief of the Gairloch branch of the family. She had a brother named Roderick, a man who was noted in that barbarous age for dark schemings and acts of cruelty that gained for him the agnomen of *'Nimheach'*, or 'Venomous'.

When a son was born of the second marriage, the ambitious Roderick conceived a scheme whereby he sought to remove all who had a prior claim to his nephew on the chiefship of *Clann 'ic ille Chaluim*. Being a man who, by his resource and cunning, had gained the respectful awe of all who knew him, it was an easy matter for him to wheedle his own kinsfolk to listen to his proposals.

To carry out his treacherous object, he sent an urgent message to Raasay, inviting the regent, with his sons and those of the late chief, to meet him post-haste on the island of Isay in Dunvegan Loch. He informed them that he would reveal matters of supreme importance of the clan, and that he wished all those related to the chief to meet and decide in secret conclave how best they might meet the contingency that had supervened. All obeyed the summons with one exception, the youngest son of Alexander, the last chief, who was then fostered from home under the care of a devoted warrior named Malcolm MacNeil (*Calum Mac Nèill*).

On arrival of his relatives in Isay, the crafty *'Nimheach'* received them with feigned cordiality, and they were sumptuously entertained. After he had regaled his guests with viands and wine, he announced that he was going to hold a consultation with the regent and all his relatives individually at first and that, after he had ascertained their respective views on the situation, all were to return to the banqueting-chamber, where they would discuss collectively their course of action. The unsuspecting regent followed his scheming kinsman into a room at the far end of the house, but no sooner had he entered than he was murdered by two hired assassins, who were stationed one on each side of the doorway. Having thus disposed of his principal victim, the heir to the chiefship was next summoned and he met a similar fate. All the other guests were likewise dealt with as they entered the chamber of death.

The man of treachery was, however, foiled in his designs. Well might he exclaim, with Macbeth:

There the grown serpent lies, the worm that's fled,
Hath nature in him that will venom breed,

for no sooner had *Mac Nèill* heard of the massacre than he conveyed his foster-son to the charge of Campbell of Cawdor.

Meanwhile, 'Roderick the Venomous' made for the island of Raasay, where he placed himself in the hands of a few influential clansmen. He declared to these that he had discovered the existence of a secret understanding between their regent and the MacKenzies, a contract utterly prejudicial to the interests of their clan; that immediately he became aware of it he decided, from purely patriotic motives, to act without delay and had accordingly rid them of men who were so base as to become traitors to their own race. The story was readily believed by the MacLeods, who, as already stated, had been incensed because of the matrimonial relations that had been entered into with their inveterate foes. Roderick was hailed as the saviour of the clan. He was appointed guardian to his nephew, the young son of the murdered regent, and was installed in Brochel Castle, where he lived with all the pomp of chief.

But Malcolm MacNeil, the faithful foster-father of the rightful heir, was not idle. He took his protégé back to Raasay, maintained him there, it is said, in a cave, and, by degrees, began to reveal him to such as, he had convinced himself, had discovered the true aims and the traitorous designs of *Ruairidh Nimheach*. He finally succeeded in winning to his side a band of resolute men, among whom was the warden of Brochel Castle. An attack was made on that stronghold by night; entrance was easily effected, but the usurper had escaped by lowering himself from the battlements on the landward side and he made for Gairloch, only to be expelled shortly afterwards, it is said, by the MacKenzies.

It is difficult to ascertain what his end was, but we find that, in August, 1569, when Donald Gormson, the Chief of Sleat, and MacKenzie of Kintail, had been induced by the Privy Council to submit their disputes to arbitration at Perth, the former was there enjoined '*to cause Rory MacAlan, alias Nevynnach, and all utheris, the said Donaldis kins … desist fra all trubbling or invasion of the said Lord of Garlauchis landis, rowmis, possessiones, etc., in all tyme cumin, and Donald will neither support, aide, not give said Rory any maner of maintenance, but expel him and pursue him to the uttermost.*' In the following year this mischief-maker was again in trouble, when he was denounced by the Privy Council for molesting men engaged in the fishing industry in Loch Broom. He was then referred to as 'MacLeod of the lands of Lochgair' (MacKenzie, A, 1889, p. 347).

There is difficulty in assigning an exact date to the Massacre of Isay, but that diligent student of Highland history, Donald Gregory, places it in the year 1568, and, when we consider the date of the strictures passed on its perpetrator by the Privy Council, a fact to which allusion has already been made, that time is highly probable (Gregory, D, 1881, pp. 211–12). The *Letterfearn MS* is our only written authority for the event, although there is a mass of oral tradition bearing on the incident, stray echoes of which may still be heard in Raasay, and possibly in Waternish as well. That celebrated warrior and poet of Clan Donald, *Do'ull Mac Iain 'ic Sheumais*, the first of the MacDonalds of Kingsborough, thus refers to it in a fragment of an '*iorram*', or rowing-song:

An tulgadh seo gu Eilean Iosaidh,
    This rocking to the Isle of Isay,
Far an d' rinn MacLeòid an dinear,
    Where MacLeod made the dinner,
Far an d' rinn MacAilein diobairt;
    Where the Son of Allan perpetuated an extirpation,
Dhoirt e fuil, 's gun chaisg e ìotadh.

He shed blood and slaked his thirst.

(MacDonald, A & A, 1911, p. 32)

As a result of the disputes that tore the island of Lewis asunder, owing to the rival claims of the three Torquils, sons of Roderick, the last chief, the king granted a charter in 1572 to the oldest of the claimants, Torquil *Connanach*, and in this deed it is expressly stated that, failing heirs to the assignee, the estates were to devolve on the oldest representative of the MacLeods of Raasay. It was probably in the previous year that young Malcolm, the foster-son of Malcolm MacNeil, and son of Alexander, the last chief, assumed the leadership of his clan. There is extant an account of the island written in 1577, that falls therefore during the period of his suzerainty.

> "Raasay", it runs, "*perteins to the Bishop of the Isles, but it is occupied and possessed by a gentleman of MacLoyd Lewis kin, called Gilliechallum Raarsa. He has ane castil called Prokill. It (Raasay) is eight markland, and will raise eight hundred men. It pays yearly to the Bishop of the Isles sixteen marks, and to the captain thereof sundry tributes better than five hundred marks. There are no woods, but high crags. It is commodious for corn and all kinds of bestial, especially horses.*

(Skene, WF, 1890, p. 433).

Like many other chief of that age, Malcolm, third of Raasay, seems to have been remiss in the payment of his dues to the Church, for, in the year 1580, when an action was brought by the Bishop of the Isles against those who had failed to meet their ecclesiastical obligations, mention is made of Malcolm *Mac Ghille Chaluim* of Raasay, with Norman MacLeod 'of Harris', and Donald *Gorm* of Sleat. "*They had intromitted with mailes, fermes, teinds, and dewties perteining and belonging to the Bishop of the Isles, each of them for their own part of crops, in the years of God 1572, 1573, and divers uther years*".

The young Chief of Raasay appears to have been a man of many parts. He was a bard, but all that is now extant of his works is represented by a fragment that has been preserved in the *Fernaig MS*. It consists of five verses of an elegy recounting the transience of worldly things:

> *Shaoghail is diomhain do mhuirn,*
>> Oh world, short lived is the enjoyment of you,
> *'S mairg a dhubhar le droch chuirm',*
>> Pity to be depressed over a poor feast,
> *An triuir bu phailt ri mo rè*
>> The three most bountiful of my time
> *Ni air mhaireann duibh ach an ath sgeul.*
>> Nothing is left but the tale.

⚜ ✹ ⚜

> *Nis bho chaidh an triuir sin seachad*
>> And since those three have passed on
> *'S gun bhith ann neach gu taobhadh*
>> And no one with whom to associate
> *Ach iad mar ghiomaich am faiche,*
>> Since they are all as lobsters in their burrows,
> *'S ro-bheag mo thoirt ort, a shaoghail.*
>> Small is my reliance on you, world.

(Watson, WJ, 1932, pp. 236–7)

Like other members of his line, he was noted for his princely generosity, and we find that he is styled *'an t-slat fhial'* ('the generous staff') by *Alasdair MacMhurchaidh*, a famous bard of Kintail, who flourished about the middle of the seventeenth century. This chief was a skilful diplomat, and a mighty warrior

as well. In 1588 he took a prominent part in a memorable incursion made into Caithness by a force composed of Macintoshes, Mackays, Munros, and the MacLeods of Assynt. All these clans were the allies of the Earl of Sutherland, who had received a 'commission of fire and sword' against the Earl of Caithness for the murder by the latter of George Gordon, who, by way of insult, had cut the tails off the Earl's horses. On the approach of this formidable array, the men of Caithness fled to the north, ruthlessly pursued by the invaders. Much booty was taken, the event being accordingly called '*Latha na Creiche Mòire*', or the 'Day of the Big Foray'. "*A great prey of catell and goods was taken away*", writes Robert Gordon in his '*History of Sutherland*', "*the lyk whereof was not sein in that countrey for many yeirs; all which spoil was divyded among the army according to the rites and customs then used in such cases*", and he appends the reflection, "*Thus do we alwise see the poor and common sorte of people to suffer for great men's follies*". And suffer the people did, for the town of Wick was besieged and sacked, while, in the rage for devastation, it was proposed by some that the church be given to the flames. Wiser counsels, fortunately, prevailed to prevent that act of sacrilege. Some of the more ardent raiders, however, burst into the sacred building, mention being made of *Mac Ghille Chaluim* of Raasay and his son, John. According to Robert Gordon, the latter found a case of lead containing the ashes of the heart of one of the Earls of Caithness, "*the ashes of which heart was throwne with the wind by John Mack Gil Chalm Rasey*". This is probably the person referred to in *The Wardlaw Manuscript* (Mackay, W, 1905, p. 230), for the year 1597 in "*a dreadful slaughter at Lagy Vraid (Logy, Conon) betwixt John MacKillichallim, a Mackleud, and a brother of the Laird of Raasay and another gentleman, John Bain, brother of Bain of Tulloch. This John Mackillichallim was a vile, flagitious, profligat fellow and a ravaging robber, picked quarrells with all men everywhere, frequented marcats etc.*".

Few in that age were more accomplished raiders than the men of Raasay. They were skilful seamen, the geographical advantages they enjoyed in their situation, between Skye and the mainland, making it an easy matter for them to carry on their depredations. Hence they were always in the foray, often with their chief at their head, and, despite many threats and denunciations by those in authority and frequent sentences of 'putting to the horn', they could not be suppressed. In 1592 it is stated that *Mac Ghille Chaluim* of Raasay had been "*released from the horn for any cause bygone*"; but this act of clemency could not win his restless clansmen over from the thrilling sport of rieving. Indeed, in the following year they had carried out a most successful raid on the lands of Alexander Bane of Tulloch, when, in the month of September, "*Mac Gille Chaluim Rasa, John his son, Alexander Ley, Andrew Ley, Angus Pyper, Hucheon Mac In Glas, Alexander MacIain 'ic Rory, John Mac William Dow* (surnames as we know them now were then seldom in use), *with their accomplices, broken men and sorners, stole 240 cows, 500 sheep, 200 goats, and 20 horses; and they had often committed such acts*" (MacKenzie, A, 1889, p. 353). In 1594 they were summoned to appear before the Privy Council in order to answer this charge of 'rief', but, as usual, they did not comply. The ceremony of putting them 'to the horn' inevitably followed, *Mac Ghille Chaluim* and his accomplices being declared rebels.

But the sentence of outlawry was soon to be revoked. A full pardon was extended to the clan, while on 10th July, 1596, a complacent sovereign conferred on their chief a charter, wherein he is described as "*Mac Ghilli Chaluim, son and heir of Alister vic Gillichalum of the lands of Raasay, Ire,*" etc., all which districts are declared to have once been the rightful property of the Bishop of the Isles, but "*now belonging to the king by Act of Annexation*" (ibid., p. 357).

At this time the internal commotions in the island of Lewis had become so acute that the territory was forfeited to the

Crown, and, in view of the waning fortunes of the reigning house, *Mac Ghille Chaluim* of Raasay began to see his chances of self-aggrandisement. He tried to cultivate the friendship of powerful neighbours who might be useful in helping forward his claims. Accordingly, he entered into a bond of manrent with Donald *Gorm Mór* of Sleat, thus initiating a contract that was to remain inviolate for over two centuries. A ceremony associated with this undertaking was the bequeathing of his sword by the dying chief of either clan to the survivor of the other, Dr. Johnson stating that this outward sign of friendship had been observed when, on the death of Sir James MacDonald in Rome, in 1766, his sword was given to MacLeod of Raasay.

In consequence of a transaction with MacKenzie of Kintail, the cause and details of which are unknown, the lands of Raasay were resigned to that chief, who restored them again to the original possessors. This was done on the understanding that the MacLeods were to own allegiance to Lord Kintail and were to provide a *birlinn* of twelve oars for the use of their superior. The charter was compiled at the Castle of *Eilean Donain;* and it is noteworthy that the assignation was made to *"the umquhile Malcolm MacGillichalum of Raasay"*, indicating that that chief was then dead.

This happened in 1610, a year that is memorable in the history of the family of Raasay. The feuds between them and the MacKenzies of Gairloch, for possession of the latter district, had been waged intermittently throughout the century. At the battle of *Loch an Fhéidh* in Glen Torridon, the MacKenzies inflicted so disastrous a defeat on the mainland branch of the MacLeods that the latter were forced to evacuate their estates there; and they never succeeded in regaining them. Of the principal men of the sept, one, John MacAllan MacRory, probably a grandson of 'Rory the Venomous', was taken prisoner, while another, John Holmach MacRory, supposed to be the uncle of the foregoing,

fled the country and made for the island of Raasay (MacGregor, A, 1907, p. 142).

In August the following year, Murdo MacKenzie, the oldest son and heir of MacKenzie of Gairloch, with Alexander Bane of Tulloch, set sail for Skye at the head of a goodly band of warriors. According to some, their intention was to seize John Holmach, while others suggest that MacKenzie's aim was to secure the hand of the only daughter of Donald *Dubh* MacRuairi, who was the direct heir to the estates of Gairloch, now that John MacAllan was a prisoner and John Holmach an exile. By this union the MacKenzies hoped to gain the legal right to the district which they then held by the sword.

Whatever the motive for the expedition, and the latter is the more probable one, MacKenzie's galley was forced by stress of weather to put into Clachan Bay, where it dropped anchor opposite the site of the present mansion-house.

On hearing of the presence of the strange ship, it is said that the young laird of Raasay, 'MacGillichaluim Og', with twelve men, went aboard, but when MacKenzie and Alexander Bane saw who were visiting them they hid themselves below deck. By some means or another, Raasay had ascertained who were aboard, and, having bought a quantity of wine, returned home. There he held a consultation with a devoted member of the clan, one, 'MacGillichalum Mór MacDho'ull 'ic Neill', a man of shrewd intelligence and gigantic strength, as to the course of action they should pursue against the young laird of Gairloch and his confederates.

MacNeil advised him to commission his brother Murdo to gather as many men as possible without delay, while MacNeil himself and a picked band of men would accompany their chief to the Gairloch galley on pretence of buying more wine; that they should then have recourse to stratagem, seize MacKenzie and, having made him their prisoner, hold him in durance until they had succeeded in inducing his clan to have him exchanged for John MacAllan MacRory.

Mac Ghille Chaluim Og was only too willing to embark on this project. Returning to the galley with his men in two boats, more wine was bought and, now that MacKenzie and Bane had revealed themselves, MacLeod insisted that the whole quantity be quaffed there and then in company with the men from Gairloch. The proposal met with the hearty approval of all, while the MacLeods showed such unstinted generosity in disposing of the liquor that most of their guests were soon intoxicated; and all retired to their bunks with the exception of four who had abstained from partaking of the wine, as they were apprehensive from the beginning of sinister motives on the part of their hosts.

Seeing that MacKenzie had now been deserted by most of his men, MacLeod laid hold of him, declaring that he was a prisoner. The former, who was a powerful man, released himself, asserting he would scorn to yield to any MacLeod, and with one blow he felled the Laird of Raasay. The followers of the latter, roused to fury because of the discomfiture of their chief, immediately drew their dirks. As MacKenzie was stepping backwards in order to obtain more room to wield his sword, his heel struck the gunwale of the ship and he fell into the sea. Being a strong swimmer, he made for the peninsula of Aird, on the Skye side of the sound; but he was not allowed to go far, for the MacLeods on shore, noticing the commotion on board the Gairloch galley, put to sea, pursued the fugitive, and battered him to death with their oars.

Meanwhile the fight was proceeding in grim earnest on board the ship and, as each of the men from Gairloch, who had previously retired inebriated below the deck, tried to return to the scene of contest, he was killed by the MacLeods as soon as his head appeared in the hatchway. But the four men of the MacKenzies who had refrained from drinking were giving such a manly account of themselves, that Raasay, MacNeil and their twelve followers were also among the slain.

Now the men from the mainland had succeeded in disposing of their enemies on board not a moment too soon, for their ship was beset on all sides by bands of resolute men of the Raasay clan. So gallantly, however, did the defenders acquit themselves, aided as they were by the comparative height of their galley, that a heavy toll was taken of the MacLeods. As more boats were rushing from shore, filled with fresh enemies, the MacKenzies, concluding that their position was becoming desperate, cut their cable, and, hoisting sail before a favourable breeze, soon outstripped their pursuers and reached Gairloch in safety (MacGregor, A, 1907, p. 143).

In referring to this incident, Sir Robert Gordon, author of '*A History of Sutherland*', written in 1630 says

In August, 1611, there happened an accident in the ile of Rosay, wher Gilcalme, laird of that iland, and Murthow Mackenzie (the laird of Garlogh his sone), wer slain with divers others.

The brief career of *Gille Chaluim Og*, the fourth chief of Raasay, was thus cut short in the fight in Clachan Bay; and the succession devolved on a boy named Alexander, whose name is mentioned in a deed of gift by the King in 1617, to Andrew, Bishop of the Isles, of all sums owing to his majesty by the chiefs of Skye and '*Alexander MacGillichalum of Raasay*'. In that year King James I, after the Act of Annexation of all the ecclesiastical properties of the realm, "*gave and set free, to the umquhile Malcolm MacGilliechalum father of the said Alexander, heritably the whole lands of Raasay, extending to eight merklands of old extent, and also the lands of Ire, Tottua, Carrabost, Ware, Sallader, Vinsinort* (these are, of course, in Snizort), *extending to three merklands, and all and sundry the fortalices, on condition of payment to the Bishop of the Isles of twenty-four marks of* old duty and £1 13s 4d of new augmentation"; and he is further obliged to make provision for the king, or his representative, when either happened to come to his territory (MacKenzie, A, 1889, pp. 358–60).

Again, in the year 1628, his name appears appended to a document drawn up and signed at Duntulm by the chiefs of Skye, Sir Donald MacDonald, John MacLeod and Sir Lachlan Mackinnon, together with Seaforth, when they bind themselves to do all in their power to preserve the deer and the roe on their estates, and to punish all who might be guilty of poaching (Skene, WF, 1847, pp. 190–3).

This chief lived till about 1643. He was married to a daughter of John MacLeod, second of Drynoch, and they had two sons, Alexander, his heir, and John, whose descendants carried on the succession on the death of Alexander, brother of the seventh chief, *Iain Garbh*.

Alexander the sixth chief of Raasay, was married to Sibella, daughter of Mackenzie, the first of his line in Applecross. By her he is said to have had one son, *Iain Garbh*, his heir, and two daughters, Janet and Julia, though *Màiri ni'n Alasdair Ruaidh* states, in her lament on the death of *Iain Garbh*, that there was another son:

B'e sgeul cràiteach do'n mhnaoi a dh' fhàg thu,
    A painful report it was to the wife you left,
'S do t'aon bhràthair a shuidh 'na t-àite;
    And to the one brother who succeeded you;
Diluain Càisge chaidh tonn bàit' ort,
    On Easter Monday a whelming wave overtook you,
Craobh a b` àird' de'n abhal thu.
    Who was the tallest tree in the orchard.

              (Watson, WJ, 1932, p. 30)

The older of the daughters, Janet, was married to Duncan MacRae of Inverinate (*Donnacha nam Pios*), the compiler of the *Fernaig M.S.* She composed a lament on the death of her husband by drowning. The song was traced by Captain Matheson of Dornie (MacKinnon, D, 1885, pp. 311–39). The younger daughter died unmarried.

N'an iomradh sibh, 'illean sheinnean
    If you row lads, I shall sing you a song
dhuibh oran Air mo lamh cha be binneas bu bheus di
    My hand on it, sweetness is not a feature of it
Tighinn a nuas Caolas Scalpaidh, 's ann
    Coming through the Kyle of Scalpay,
a chuala mi naigheachd
    I heard the news
B'e mo dhiubhail mar thachair 's be 'm beud e
    My devastation is what has happened and sad it is
Gu robh Dunnachadh Mo Cridhe ga ghiulein air lighe
    That Duncan of My Heart is carried by the flood
Fear mor meanmnach tighearnail beusach.
    The great, spirited, lordly, talented.

Iain Garbh succeeded his father on 20th August, 1648. He was married to Janet, daughter of the celebrated Sir Rory *Mór* of Dunvegan, and he was considered to be the strongest as well as the most handsome man of his age. *Màiri ni'n Alasdair Ruaidh* sings his praises in her lament:

Bu tu 'm fear curanta mor,
    You were brave and great,
Bu mhath cumadh, is treòir,
    Of good shape, form and prowess,
'O d' uilinn gu d' dhòrn,
    From elbow to fist,

'*O d' mhullach gu d' bhròig.*
   From crown to foot,
Mhic Mhuire mo leòn,
   Son of Mary, my paining is,
Thu bhith 'n innis nan ròn,
   That you are in the abode of the seals,
'*S nach fhaighear thu.*
   And cannot be recovered.

                (Watson, JC, 1934, p. 26)

This popular chief met his death by drowning as he was on his way home from Lewis, where he had been attending a christening in the family of Seaforth. Off the north-east coast of Skye his galley was overtaken by a gale so wild that the ship foundered, and all aboard were lost. The sennachie, with his characteristic disposition to hyperbole, still refers to the severity of that storm when "*the waves rose high as the Cuillin, and the boulders of Mol Stamhain were hurled far above the shore cliffs and deposited on dry land*".

His death was universally mourned, and, as has already been stated, *Màiri ni'n Alasdair Ruaidh* composed a touching lament. It is entitled '*Marbhrann do Iain Garbh Mac 'Ille Chaluim Ratharsaidh*', and is written in the best strain of that wonderful poetess. Her equally famous contemporary, *Pàdruig Mór Mac-Crimmon*, gave expression to his grief in that epic *piobaireachd*, '*Iain Garbh Mac 'Ille Chaluim*', that is rightly considered by the masters of our classic music to be at once the loftiest and the most soul-subduing melody of its kind.

The Wardlaw Manuscript, the journal of the Rev Fraser, in giving events of the year 1671, refers to the unusual severity of the weather:

Spring dry, cold and tempestuous, summer and autumn wet, a cruel year. This April the Earle of Seaforth, dwelling in the Lewes,

a dreadful accident happened … His lady, being brought to bed there, the Earle sent for John Garv M'Cloud of Rasay to witness the christening and after the treat and solemnity of the feast Rarsay takes leave to goe home and after a rant of drinking upon the shore, went aboard his birling and sailed with a strong North gale of wind and whether by giving too much sail and no ballast or the unskillieness of the seamen or that they could not manage strong Dutch canvas saile, the boat whelmed, and all the men drowned in view of the coast. The Laird and sixteen of his kinsmen, the prime, perished non of them found, a greyhound or two cast ashore dead and pieces of the birling. One Alexander Mackleod in Lewes, the night before had voice warning him thrice not to go with Rarsay for all would drown in there return, yet he went, being infatuat and drowned with the rest. This account I had from Alexander his brother the summer after. Drunkenness did the mischief.

                (Mackay, W, 1905, pp. 498–9).

In Raasay there is a tradition to the effect that one of the sisters of *Iain Garbh* composed a new lament to his memory every recurring Friday for a whole year but only four of them have been preserved. One is *Mi am shuidh' air an Fhaolinn*, a lengthy elegy through which runs a note of poignant sorrow and is characterised, at the same time, by a wealth of imagery, which stamps the composition as the work of a great genius. The first and last verses are given:

Mi am shuidh' air a Fhaolinn
   I am sitting by the shore
'*S mi gun fhaoilte 's gun fhuran*
   Without cheer or welcome
Ri cha tog mi fonn aotrom
   I cannot sing a light song
Bho Dhihaoine mo Dhunaidh
   Since Friday of my misfortune

Nochd is iosal do chluasag
    Low is your pillow this night
Air leacan fuara na tuinne
    On the cold slabs of the sea
'S ann an clachan gun traghadh
    In a graveyard with no ebbing
Tha mo ghràdh sa air uiridh.
    Is my love couched.

(MacLean, S, 1977, p. 385)

It has been stated that this renowned chief was drowned at the early age of twenty-one years, but in consideration of the following facts we are forced to question that assertion. We know that he was served heir to his father in 1648, and there is extant a bond signed on the 10th March 1661, by 'John MacLeod of Raasay', in conjunction with Sir James MacDonald of Sleat, Colonel Roderick MacLeod of Talisker, and Lachlan Mackinnon of Strath, in which they undertake to repay a sum of 4000 merks to Sir Robert Farquhar of Meanie, who had lent that amount to MacLeod of Assynt. Again, in 1688, it is recorded that his sisters, Janet and Julia, were served *"heirs of line, conquest, and provision"* to their father, *"Alexander MacLeod, alias MacAlaster vic Gillichalum … in the lands of Raasay, including the towns, lands, islands, and liegrassings of Kilmiluach, Ausach, Balliechurn, Balliemeanach, Invervig, Glam, Moisnes, Crochill, with the pertinents of Sciepadell, Hallag, Leaghk, Kamiorich, Liebost, Slagadine, Slachro, Fearne, Stair, Ire, Shuashnesmore, Shuashnesbeg, Inneraross, Boradell, Glen, Kylehan, and the two islands commonly called Rona and Fladda, together with Ire, Tott, Carobost, Glengrast, Ugisarder, Knockshint, Penniemore, Penniecappan, in the barony of Trotternish, and in the other towns, lands, islands and others of Fortuna Rasaye, in the parish of Snizort"*. (Even as late as 1790 the annual rental of the lands of Raasay in Snizort amounted to £140.) In the same records ('The Retours') there occurs a puzzling statement to the effect that in the year 1630 lands, which appear to be identical with several of those quoted above, had been granted to *"Alexander M'Leane MacFerquhard MacEachan, in the lands of Rasey, viz., Clachan, Oistage, Innervig, Clam, Maenes, Browkill, Awoynes, Phladda, Ronnha, Skrebidell, Halleg, Larg, Lebost, Naseiring, Lagan, Achositore, Ire, Swysnes, Inneraros, Borrodaill, Ramisdall, extending to eight merklands, and in the lands of Ire, Tuych, Carrabost, and Wygsadder in Trotternish to the extent of three merklands"* (Innes, C, 1854, pp. 247–8).

Iain Garbh was succeeded by his brother, Alexander, who died about a year afterwards and he was succeeded by his cousin, also Alexander, grandson of John, brother of Alexander 6th of Raasay. According to Sir Robert Douglas, in *'The Baronage of Scotland'*, this chief obtained from his cousins, Janet and Julia, who are described as *'heirs of line'*, a resignation of all the family estates in his own favour; and he was duly infeft in these lands by charter, dated August, 1692. When Janet, the sister of *Iain Garbh*, married Duncan MacRae, her claim to the succession was annulled.

Alexander was married to Catherine, the daughter of the famous warrior, Sir Norman of Bernera. Little is known of this chief. He is probably the one referred to by Martin Martin in his *'Description of the Western Isles'* as follows:

Mackleod is a cadet of the family of that name. His seat is in the village, Clachan. The inhabitants have as great veneration for him as any subjects can have for their king.

(Martin, M, 1716, p. 164).

A member of this family is referred to as having played a distinguished part in the War of the Spanish Succession. He was

Colonel Aeneas MacLeod, a trusted officer under the Duke of Marlborough.

The succeeding Chief of Raasay was Malcolm, the tenth of his line. He was married to Mary, daughter of Alexander MacKenzie of Applecross, by whom he had three sons: John, his successor, Dr. Murdoch of Eyre, and Norman, who was an officer in the pay of the States General, and is mentioned as having been living in retirement at Eyre with Dr. Murdoch, where Dr. Johnson and Boswell visited him in 1773. There was also a daughter, who was married, as second wife, to John Dubh Mackinnon, chief of Strath.

In addition to these children Malcolm had eight others, the progeny of a second marriage with a clansman's daughter, Janet MacLeod, or, as she is locally referred to, *'Bantighearna Dhubh Osgaig'* ('The Black Lady of Oskaig'). The most notable of her children was the Rev. Malcolm MacLeod (*Maighsteir Calum*), who was minister of Snizort until his death in 1832, and was the father of the famous 'Mr. Roderick' and Isabella, wife of the Rev. John Finlayson, Free Church Minister of Bracadale.

The chief lived during the stirring times of 'The '45' and, being an ardent loyalist, he was early eager to join the rebellion. His desires were not, however, to be realised so soon as he would have wished, owing to the vacillating attitude of the other chiefs of Skye to the cause of Prince Charlie. His conference with Sir Alexander MacDonald at Sconser has already been alluded to, and, when he discovered that that chief was no longer disposed to throw in his lot with the Jacobites he decided to act alone.

After having, as a precautionary measure, conveyed the estates to his oldest son, whom he persuaded to remain at home, he mustered one hundred men of his clan, and, with his second son, Dr. Murdoch of Eyre, and his cousin, Captain Malcolm MacLeod of Brae, made for the south in November 1745. Having joined the men of Clanranald, they met the Prince at Stirling on his retreat to the north. They were present at Falkirk, where the fading

fortunes of the Jacobites enjoyed a temporary revival and, with the rest of the Highland army, they suffered defeat on Culloden. Thence they returned home, all except fourteen of them, who had fallen in the rebellion. Dr. Murdoch of Eyre was wounded on Culloden, a bullet entering one shoulder and lodging in the other.

Shortly after the return of the MacLeods to Raasay, the search for the chief became so keen that he was constrained to leave his own country and seek safety in the wilds of Knoydart. As soon, however, as he heard that the Prince had landed on his island, he returned, in the hope that he might be able to help his royal fugitive. His galley met that of Mackinnon of Strath as the latter was conveying Prince Charlie from Elgol to Morar, but *"they evaded each other, as they were both apprehensive of danger"* (Boswell, J, 1955, p. 140).

Now, when the intelligence was brought to the forces of the government that a contingent from Raasay had set out to join the Prince, measures were immediately taken to harass their lands. Thus it happened that a certain Captain Hay, who commanded a government tender, landed on the island of Rona a party which indulged in an indiscriminate slaughter of all the cattle there. Thence they proceeded to the north end of Raasay, where *"they plundered two or three small townships"*.

About the middle of May, 1746, the ruthless Captain Ferguson invaded the island, despatching a party on shore under the command of a Lieut. Dalrymple. The work of devastation was then resumed with unbridled vindictiveness. The chief's residence at Clachan was burned to the ground, after the windows and the most precious part of the plenishing had been taken possession of by the soldiery. When an entry had been effected, prior to the burning of the house, it was seen that the plate and some of the furniture had been removed, and, according to *'The Lyon in Mourning'*, a former servant, a young lad, who was captured by the destroyers, was forced to betray where the household goods were hidden, *"in a cave about a quarter of a mile from the house"*. All the other houses on the island, with the exception of those in townships that had escaped the observation of the Hanoverian troops, were similarly consigned to the flames (Forbes, R, 1975, Vol. 2, pp. 78–81).

On his return from Knoydart, the chief, with his two sons, John and Dr. Murdoch, his cousin, Captain Malcolm of Brae, and five clansmen, went in hiding to the island of Rona. Thence Captain Malcolm set off for Kingsborough, in order to acquaint the MacDonalds with the news of the escape of the Prince from Skye, but, finding *"all the tracks beset with soldiers"*, he deemed it prudent not to proceed. On his return to Raasay, he found that the island was once again overrun by the Militia, who were feverishly searching for the chief, as news of his return had got abroad.

This visitation had been organised in a very thorough manner. A Captain Scott was in command and a landing was effected first in Rona, where the chief was known to be in hiding. In their endeavour to obtain news of him, the party tried to coerce the people to turn informers. With that end in view, it is said, they lashed two men in Rona so that one died, and the other had not recovered from the punishment when the account of the atrocity was given to Bishop Forbes, two years later.

Foiled in their search in Rona, the soldiers then invaded Raasay. There they exacted a terrible revenge on the people. According to an estimate given to Bishop Forbes of the damage that was wrought, it is stated that upwards of two hundred and eighty cows and seven hundred sheep were killed, in addition to several horses that were *"shot for pleasure"*. Over three hundred houses were burned down, the growing crops were destroyed, and thirty-two boats, great and small, were set on fire. On the intercession of Sir Alexander MacDonald, one boat was left for young Raasay, another having been concealed in a cove by Captain Malcolm of Brae, but both were afterwards taken to Lochindal by command of the Earl of Loudon.

According to a contemporary computation, there were one hundred and twenty families in Raasay at that time, and their suffering must have been appalling, deprived as they were of all their stock, and their crops ruined. And the lands of the Raasay MacLeods in Skye did not escape. So terrible, indeed, was the devastation wrought there, that families were forced to evacuate their homes, fleeing to the neighbouring districts and leaving waste their own lands *"as they are to this day"* (1748).

On his return from Skye, after his activities in connection with the escape of the Prince, Captain Malcolm of Brae was one day observed by some soldiers, who, mistaking him for the chief, had him forthwith closely watched. For a night or two he lived in the open, occasionally changing his place of concealment, until one morning he was discovered by a band of the Militia. Being swift of foot, he succeeded in breaking clear, and made for *"the top of the island"*. On the way he encountered a party of between fifty and sixty men, under Captain Scott. His speed, and his knowledge of the terrain, however, saved him; while a man, Donald Nicolson, who accompanied him, was taken, and rigorously interrogated as to his knowledge of the Prince's wanderings and the place of concealment of his chief. The loyal fellow, refusing to give any information, was tortured so savagely by the soldiers that *"he was left for dead"*.

That night Malcolm made for a cave in the left bank of Inver Burn, known locally as 'Uamha Caitriona Duibhe'. There, with only *"a few crumbs of bread and cheese"* in his pockets, he spent three days and nights. Desperate with hunger, he left his hiding-place to seek food and shelter in the house of a relative, Murdo MacLeod, who lived in Brae. Early the following morning, while he was still sleeping, the soldiers were seen approaching by the lady of the house. She immediately raised the alarm and Malcolm had just succeeded in making his escape when the house was surrounded. He made for his retreat, and although closely pursued, and once or twice fired upon, he managed to reach it in safety. Near the cave he met a boy, whom he coerced to follow him, lest the lad, falling into the hands of the enemy, should betray his place of concealment. Three more nights and days dragged wearily on in the cave, until he was finally forced to let the famishing youth go free. The net had meanwhile been tightened around the districts of Inver and Brae, so that it was impossible for anyone to be abroad without being seen by the soldiers. On leaving the cave, the boy promised he would return with food, but he had barely gone half a mile when he was captured and compelled to tell all he knew.

That evening, as Malcolm was cautiously looking about him, in the failing light, he noticed on a rock above his cave a small band of soldiers, who covered him with their muskets. There was now no course open to him but to surrender, and he was taken before MacLeod of Talisker, whose soldiers had effected his capture. Without ado, he was whisked off to Portree, where he was kept in close confinement in a guardhouse for two days, with Donald MacLeod of Galtrigill as his fellow-prisoner.

From Portree they were sent to Applecross Bay, where General Campbell was known to be on board the '*Furnace*'. So long as the General remained with the ship, the prisoners were treated with humanity, but once he left they were exposed to the tyrannies of Captain Ferguson, "*one of the most barbarous men ever set loose on the Highlands*". For weeks the '*Furnace*' cruised about the Hebrides, a floating prison-house, the sufferings of the captives being cruel in the extreme. Early in the evening they were forced below decks and, as no beds were provided, they were obliged to lie on coils of rope and on the stones used as ballast. Their rations were inadequate – they had to subsist on half the amount given to the mariners, while the food was always stale, and often decomposed. During the whole time they were on board they were given no change of garments, and Malcolm "*had not one shirt to change another*" (Forbes, R, 1975, Vol. 3, pp. 123–8).

It was thought by his captors that he was the chief, and he did what he could to confirm them in their delusion, for he knew that so long as that belief was held the island of Raasay would be free from further molestation. Hence it was that, when preparations for his court-martial were being made in London, the evidence against him was found to be perplexingly conflictory. Many a ruse was tried in order to procure information against him. People would visit him, professing to be his friends. One of these paid informers, a man of the name of Urquhart, he found most difficult to dispose of, owing to his pertinacity. This person posed as a Jacobite, talking much about the exploits he had had in Edinburgh and at Inverness in the company of the men from Raasay, but Malcolm "*kept him off with long weapons and discreet returns*".

The most reliable clue the officials of the government possessed for the identification of the Chief of Raasay was that he was bow-legged and 'hen'-toed, whereas Malcolm's legs were discovered, on examination, "*to be straight and stout*" (*ibid.*, Vol. 1, pp. 145–6). The credulous may find in this physical deformity of *Mac Ghille Chaluim*, together with his frequent breaches of the Moral Law, as expressed in the seventh commandment, the fulfillment of that famous prophecy, attributed to '*Coinneach Odhar*', the '*Brahan Seer*':

'*Nuair a thig MacDhò'uill Dhuibh, bàn,*
    When a fair haired chief of the Camerons, appears
MacShimidh ceann-ruadh,
    A redhaired Fraser chief,
Siosalach claon, ruadh,
    A Chisholm weak minded,
MacCoinnich mór, bodhar, agus
    The Great MacKenzie, deaf and

MacGillechaluim camachasach,
   MacLeod of Raasay bow legged,
Iar ogha Iain Bhig a Rig,
   The great-grandson of Little John of Rigg
Is e sin MacGillechalum
   That MacLeod of Raasay
Is miosa thàinig, no thig.
   Is the worst that has been or will be.

(Oral Tradition)

Despite the fact that no incriminating evidence could be obtained against him, Malcolm was kept in detention until the passing of the Amnesty Act, on the 4th of July 1747. Through the activities of Jacobite enthusiasts, a subscription was raised for him in London and a means of conveyance thus procured for him and for Flora MacDonald, who was set free on the same day. It was considered by the friends of the latter that Captain Malcolm would make an excellent escort for Flora, and they travelled north under the sobriquets of 'Mr. and Miss Robert-son', in order to evade the attentions of the curious. Thus it was that Malcolm was wont afterwards to observe: *"I was taken to London to be hanged; but I was sent back in a post-chaise with Flora MacDonald".*

There was great enthusiasm among his clansmen on his safe return. Shortly afterwards he received a letter from Bishop Forbes, from which one may infer the large amount of havoc that had been wrought in Raasay by the soldiers of the king. In his note the Bishop says:

I congratulate you on your safe return to you own place – I wish I could say to your own fireside. But I hope that that and all other losses will be made up to you with interest in due time.

Captain Malcolm occupied that district of Raasay which is situated to the north of Balmeanach, and to the east of Holo-man. He is accordingly designated 'Malcolm MacLeod of Brae'. When Dr. Johnson and Boswell were touring in the Highlands, Captain Malcolm, as the representative of his chief, went to Corry, in Strath, in order to escort the famous literati to the island of Raasay. They were ferried thither in *"a good, strong, open boat, made in Norway"*, Malcolm, as helmsman, singing the while for the benefit of the oarsmen, and to the delectation of his guests, the well-known Jacobite song, *'Tha Tighinn Fodham Eirigh'*, the whole company, with the Rev. Dr. Donald MacQueen, taking up the refrain.

Malcolm was then sixty-two years of age, and he is described by Boswell as follows:

He was hale and well-proportioned, with a manly countenance, tanned by the weather, yet having a ruddiness in his cheeks, over a great part of which his rough beard extended. His eye was quick and lively, yet his look was not fierce; but he appeared at once firm and good humoured. He wore a pair of brogues, tartan hose which came upon near to his knees and left them bare, a purple camblet kilt, a black waistcoat, a short green cloth coat bound with gold cord, a yellowish bushy wig, a large blue bonnet with a gold-thread button. I never saw a figure that gave a more perfect representation of a Highland gentleman. I wished much to have a picture of him just as he was. I found him frank and polite in the true sense of the word.

(Boswell, J, 1975, p. 113).

In addition to his many other qualities of body and mind, Captain Malcolm was an excellent exponent of pipe-music and a noted composer as well. The best known of his works is *'Fàilte Phrionnsa'* ('Welcome to the Prince'), composed by him shortly after his release from prison.

He was the son of John III of Rigg. He was born in 1711, and died without progeny. The territorial designation *'of Rigg'* passed to his brother, Norman, who is known in the history of Skye as the father of two eminent men – Captain Norman of Camustianavaig, and Captain John of Ollach, both of whom had distinguished careers as officers in the British Army during the American War of Independence.

We have seen that, prior to his participation in the rebellion of 1745, the Chief of Raasay conveyed his estates to his son, in order to guard against their alienation from the family in case of defeat. The heir was an ardent Jacobite, and, as previously shown, played an active part in the escape of Prince Charlie. When he was advised by Captain Malcolm to avoid the Prince, as the latter was being taken to Raasay, he characteristically replied that he was proud to get the opportunity of giving what small service he could to the Jacobite cause, and that he would render it even although it should cost him his head.

This man was afterwards John, the eleventh of Raasay. He was married to Jane, daughter of MacQueen of Totterome, and they had a large family of three sons and ten daughters. It was during his chiefship that Dr. Johnson paid his visit to the island in 1773. The impression made on the famous litterateur by the manner of his reception in Raasay is worth re-quoting,

> *Such a seat of hospitality amid the winds and the waters fills the imagination with a delightful contrariety of images. Without is the rough ocean and the rocky land, the beating billows, and the howling storm; within is plenty and elegance, beauty and gaiety, the song and the dance. In Rasay, if I could have found a Ulysses, I had fancied a Phaeacia.*
>
> (Johnson, S, 1984, p. 80).

Boswell too, gives an illuminating account of Raasay at that time. He observes that the island was comfortably self-supporting, for there was, *"abundance of black cattle, sheep, and goats"*. Many horses also were reared, and they were employed in the customary operations of agriculture. They were, however, seldom used as beasts of burden, for there were, of course, no roads on the island then and, as most of the houses were built close to the shore, the carriage of goods was done chiefly by sea. Fishing was plentiful, crops flourished. *"Rasay"*, he says, *"is a place where one may live in plenty, even in luxury"*. There was a great variety of game, and plenty of it – grouse, pigeons, and 'blackcock in extraordinary abundance'; but there were no deer, hares, or rabbits.

Like Dr. Johnson, Boswell pays a high tribute to the laird. *"Rasay"*, he says, *"has the true spirit of a chief. He is, without exaggeration, a father to his people; and so far is he from distressing his clan that, in the present rage for emigration, not a man has left his estate"*.

MacLeod 'registered arms' in 1779. These consist principally of a burning mountain; the crest, which is 'the sun in its splendour'; supporters, two savages with flames on heads and hands each standing on a burning mound, and the motto *'Luceo non Uro'* (I shine, but do not burn). The badge is the red whortleberry (*Lus nan Crainnseag*), which is found in abundance in Raasay. His letters to Dr. Johnson, and to Boswell, mark him as a man of cultivated taste and of sober judgement; while his wife must have been a woman of considerable ability and great common sense to have prepared her many daughters for the high positions that were later to be occupied by some of them in society.

We need not wonder, then, at Johnson's observation on the amenities of life, and especially on the domestic felicities, in the household of Raasay: *"More gentleness of manners, or a more pleasing appearance of domestic society, is not found in the most polished countries"*.

Of their daughters, the celebrated Miss Flora was one of the most handsome women, and perhaps the greatest beauty of her age in the Highlands. She was married to the Earl of Loudoun but she died soon after the birth of a daughter, also called Flora, who became the wife of the Marquis of Hastings, a Governor-General of India. Another daughter, Margaret, was married to Martin Martin of Bealach, a man of pleasing address, and still remembered in Skye for his phenomenal strength.

The second daughter, Isabella, became the wife of a Major Ross of the Royal Artillery. On his first visit to Edinburgh, Burns became *"acquainted with Miss Isabella MacLeod of Rasa, to whom I composed 'Raving winds around her blowing'"*. In Currie's edition of Burns, Isabella is mentioned (Barke, J, 1974, pp. 279 & 438). One of their daughters, Elizabeth, was married, as his second wife, to the famous artist, Sir Charles D'Oyly, whom she met in India while living there with her cousin, the Marchioness of Hastings. On her return from India, Lady D'Oyly brought with her an elegant set of pipes, which she presented to the celebrated piper of the family, Angus Mackay, the son of John MacKay, MacLeod of Raasay's piper, who won the Highland Society of London's medal in 1792. John MacKay left Raasay in 1824, on the death of James the 12th Chief, and became the piper at Drummond Castle. He returned to Skye and died at Kyleakin. Angus, his son, in 1838 compiled and published a collection of *Pìobaireachd* and about 183 tunes in manuscript, recorded from his father's *Canntaireachd* (Campbell, A, 1948, p. 9). Angus MacKay composed *'Lady D'Oyly's Salute'*.

Lady D'Oyly was a poetess of considerable power and lofty taste. Of her compositions the best known is the breezy, yet easy-flowing love-song, *'Thàinig an Gille Dubh'* (The Raasay Love Lilt). The aptness of its imagery, its faultless rhyme, and the harmony of its assonance, are a delight to the mind and to the ear alike. Two quatrains are quoted:

Gur guirme do shùil
Bluer your eyes

Na'n dearcag fo'n driùchd,
Than the blaeberry in dew,
'S gur finealt do ghnùis
Finer your features
Na ùr-ròs mheanganan.
Than fresh roses on branches.

⁂

Ged bhitheadh a' ghaoth
Though the wind
Ri sgoltadh nan craobh,
Would rend the trees,
Gun cumadh mo ghaol
My love would keep
A taobh 's na marannan.
Her (ship's) side to the wind.

(MacKenzie, J, 1877, pp. 379–80)

Another of her songs is *'Oran do'n Eilthireach'*, in which the exile yearns for –

O Ghàidhealtachd ghaolach,
Oh beloved Highlands,
Nan cladach, 's na faoileann,
Of the shores and beaches,
Nan innis, 's nan aonach uain'.
The Islands and the green slopes.

(Mac na Ceardaich, G, 1879, p. 282)

In addition to *'Cumha Mhic Leòid'* and *'Oran do Phrionnsa Tearlach'*, she composed another love-lyric, *'Mo rùn air mo Leannan'*, in which she sings:

Is math thig air mo ghràdhsa
　　Well becomes my love
Cota grinn air dhath sgàrlaid
　　A coat of scarlet
'S ann aig tha 'n cul faineach
　　His is the curly hair
Is bòidhche.
　　Most beautiful.
Suil mheanmnach, chiuin mheallach,
　　A lively eye, calm and bewitching,
Nach feargach a sealladh,
　　Never angry of look,
'S bu dearbh thu ri d' ghealladh
　　And true to his promise,
An còmhnuidh.
　　Always.

　　　　　　(Mac na Ceardaich, G, 1879 p. 330)

For pictorial effect, another of her amatory compositions, *'Oran Gaoil',* can compare with anything in our language:

"Tha sùil mo rùin-sa gu meallach cùine,
　　The eye of my love is bewitching and calm,
'S mar dhearcag dhù-ghorm fo dhriùchd a' fàs;
　　Like a dark blue berry growing under dew;
Mar ghrian ag éirigh moch maduinn chéitein
　　Like the sun rising early on a May morning
Tha sealladh m' eudail gu h-éibhinn tlàth.
　　His aspect is joyous and mild.
Do dheud cho dìreach fo bhilibh min-dhearg,
　　Your regular teeth and smooth red lips,
Am beul na fìrinn fo 'm mìllse fàilt;
　　Truthful mouth of the sweetest welcome;
Chan iarrainn sùgradh ach pog bho chùr'-bheul,
　　I seek no other pleasure than a kiss from your sweet lips,
Co riamh thug sùil ort, 's a dhùilt dhut gràdh?
　　Whoever that saw you would deny you, Love?

　　　　　　(Mac na Ceardaich, G, 1879, p. 336)

Lady D'Oyly died on the 1st of July, 1875.

Of the sons of John, the eleventh chief, the second, John, died young; the third, Malcolm, was a captain in the Indian Army, and the oldest was James, the heir, and successor.

Sometime after the accession of this, the twelfth Chief of Raasay, the menace of Napoleon was felt even in Skye, there being much talk of a French invasion. In the attempt to meet such a contingency, two battalions of volunteers were formed in 1803, and there was eager enthusiasm to join them. They were commanded respectively by James MacLeod of Raasay and Alexander MacDonald of Lyndale; but, as already stated, the necessity for continuance being obviated by the victories of Nelson, they were disbanded in 1814.

This chief initiated schemes with a view to improving the amenities of the island, making large additions to the mansion-house – a work which proved so costly that the estate was sunk deeply in debt. He died in 1824, when he was succeeded by his son, John, who was married to a daughter of that famous soldier of Skye, General Sir Donald MacLeod, the son of MacLeod of Bharkasaig. They had an only daughter, who died young.

As all efforts to relieve the weight of debt on the estate proved unavailing, the creditors were reluctantly constrained to sell it. In 1846 the historic family of *Clann 'ic Ghille Chaluim* severed their connection with their lands in Raasay and in Rona, and John, the thirteenth chief, emigrated to Australia. Lady D' Oyly in her *Oran do Ratharsair* (Song to Raasay) says:

Iain Oig Mhic 'ille Chaluim
　　Young John MacLeod of Raasay

Mun d' rugadh thu bha e air aithris

    Before you were born it was said

Gu falbhadh uatsa do thuath 'us d'fhearann

    That your people and your land would leave you

Do chliu 's do bhuaidh

    Your reputation and your influence

Is do lamh bhi' falamh

    And your hand be empty

Reic thu d' oighreachd 'us do dhuthaich

    You sold your estate and your domicile

Bha aig do theaghlach

    That was in your family

'O am nan Stiubhart

    Since the time of the Stewarts

Ach is ioma cridhe tha briste, bruite

    But many were the heavy and sore hearts

'Nuair chur thu cul riu.

    When you turned your back on them.

                       (MacLeod, N, 1899, p. 178)

The new proprietor was a Mr. Rainy from Edinburgh, and the period of his tenure will long be remembered on the island. It was then that many districts were ruthlessly cleared of their inhabitants to make room for sheep. Ninety-four families, resident in twelve townships, namely, Suishnish, Eyre, Upper Fearns, Lower Fearns, Upper Hallaig and Lower Hallaig, North and South Screapadale, Castle, Manish, and *Doire Dhomhain*, were dispossessed of their lands between the years 1852 and 1854, while on the 6th of May of the latter year as many as 129 were shipped to Australia; and, as the Rev. Mr. Galbraith observed in his testimony before the Crofters' Commission in 1883, *"by far the greater number of these were sent away against their will"*.

Mr. Rainy was succeeded by his son, who was prepared to do all in his power for the comfort of the people, but his promising career was cut short by death in 1872. From the *Northern Ensign*, quoted in *An Gaidheal*, August 1872, it states that Raasay is

for sale, rental is £1,500 of which a native of Sutherland pays £1,000 for sheep farm, ... and gardens famous for fruit, especially gooseberries, a hot house which cost £1,500 is in the garden but in disrepair. Close beside the garden entrance is a stone slab which was dug out from an old Celtic ruin and bears Celtic hieroglyphics, which have defied efforts to make out what they are. The improvements made by the late proprietor's father cost about £15,000. Lord Middleton said to be an offerer. The executors of the late Mr Rainy will not give the island to any harsh landlord for fear of turning out the people.

The following month (September), An Gaidheal reported that "The estate of Raasay and Rona was exposed for sale in Dowell's rooms, Edinburgh, on Friday at upset price of £50,000 and after keen competition was secured by George Grant MacKay of Rosehall and Oban." Mr. G.G. Mackay's sole aim was to make pecuniary gain by the purchase. This gentleman disposed of the island about three years later to Mr. Armitage, a humane man, who sold it eighteen months afterwards, "at a fancy price", to Mr. Wood. The new proprietor was an enthusiastic sportsman, wholly bent on converting the island into a game preserve. The deer were carefully protected, some 2000 pheasants were annually reared, while the stock of rabbits had increased to such an enormous extent that, according to the Rev. Mr. Galbraith, as many as 14,000 were killed yearly by the company of eight gamekeepers then employed on the island. The home-farm was well developed, and about 1880 it carried a stock of 3,000 sheep while for the accommodation of the farm workers a small township was formed at Oskaig. Good slated houses were then erected, each occupier paying the exorbitant rent of £10, in addition to an assessment of £3 for an acre of ground attached to his dwelling.

The Woods remained in possession of Raasay and Rona until the year 1912, when the islands were bought by Messrs. Baird & Co., the ironmasters of Coatbridge. In 1922, while still retaining the valuable mineral rights, that company sold their property to the Board of Agriculture for Scotland.

The interesting ruin known as Brochel Castle, perched on a lofty mound on the east of Raasay, occupies what is perhaps a stronger position than that of any other castle-fort in the Western Isles. The unique eminence on which it was reared is an outlier of Torridonian conglomerate mainly composed of littoral deposits. Rising sheer above the rocks of the shore, it presents an unscalable front on all sides from the land, while its only doorway, which is on the seaward side, is so difficult of approach as to have rendered it impregnable in its day.

Like all our ancient castles, it is built on no conceivable ground-plan, but follows the configuration of its site, occupying every corner of it. It seems to have been three storeys in height, and a striking feature of its walls is the smallness of the stones of which they are constructed, corner-stones and lintels alone being of a large size.

The fort is said by tradition to have belonged to the Mac-Sweens, possessors of the Lewis before the MacLeods whose chief, Malcolm, ninth of his line, ceded Raasay and other portions of his dominions to his second son, also named Malcolm, in the year 1510. When Sir Donald Monro, Dean of the Isles, toured his diocese in 1549 he made mention of this castle under the name of *'Prolokit'*, where *"was a fair orchard"*. It was a convenient seat for the MacLeods so long as they held Coigeach and Gairloch as well as Raasay and Rona. When, however, they were expelled from their possessions on the mainland after their defeat at *Loch an Fhéidh* in Glen Torridon in 1610, the family residence was changed from Brochel, with its exposed anchorage, to Clachan, on the western seaboard of the island.

Alexander Campbell, schoolmaster, and subsequently parish minister of Portree at the beginning of the eighteenth century, states that the last chief of the MacLeods to occupy Brochel Castle was the famous warrior, *Iain Garbh*, who was drowned off Staffin in 1671. The same writer declares that it was a place of considerable size, being capable of 'accommodating 800 persons'. He adds that in the courtyard was a spring of water, fed probably by an artificial channel, traces of which may still be seen running from the hill on the west. The last of the roof collapsed about 1780, the oak joists being still visible when the account already quoted was published in 1795.

APPENDICES CONTENTS

APPENDIX 1

ALEXANDER NICOLSON – A BIOGRAPHICAL NOTE

In the 19th century Clearances the Nicolsons were evicted from Scorrybreac and joined the displaced people crowded into the Braes of Trotternish, near Portree. Writing in 1884, Groome [1] described the area as 'cold, unkindly and barren', with a 'pitiful' proportion of arable land. He stated:

'The little that is under cultivation is in the hands of crofters, who have a hard struggle for life, and have generally to eke out their scanty means of subsistence by taking part as 'hired-men' in the east coast herring fishing. The townships between Loch Sligachan and Tianavaig Bay are known as The Braes, and the inhabitants of them have, during the last three years (1881–84), earned a somewhat unenviable notoriety for their lawless proceedings in connection with alleged land grievances.'

The 'lawless proceedings' was a reference to the crofters' protests over rents and land rights which led to rent strikes and the 1882 Battle of Braes (see pp. 262–3). In 1884, the government set up the Napier Commission to travel the Highlands and investigate the crofters' grievances. The Commissioners began their work by visiting Braes and the first witness to give evidence to them was Angus Stewart of Peinnchorrain.

In 1881 Iseabail MacLeod, a niece of Angus Stewart, married Somhairle Mor Nicolson in Portree and they set up home together in Achnahanaid. The 1891 Census found them, their son Alexander, his elder sister and a younger sister and brother living in a house described as '1 room with 1 or more window'. By the time of the 1901 Census, they had moved to a house with '2 rooms with 1 or more windows', the elder daughter had left home and Iseabail had given birth to another daughter and five more sons.

Alexander's daughter, Ishabel Beal, describes his early years:

My father was born in 1884, in Achnahanaid, Braes. He was the second child and first son in a family of ten. His father, Somhairle Mor, was a crofter fisherman, and thus often away from home. His mother Iseabail was the daughter of Donald MacLeod and Catherine Stewart. These grandparents lived nearby at Balmeanach and my father, as he grew, was often with them. He always said that "the brains came from the Stewarts". I am sure that his grandmother's stories instigated his love of the history of Skye.

The people of Braes may have been poor but they were fortunate in one respect: in 1831 Mr Donald MacDiarmid of South Carolina established a fund of £2050 to erect and endow schools at Borve (in Snizort) and Braes [2]. In 1884 the Braes school had an average attendance of 32 [3]. It was located at the southern end of Ollach and drew its pupils mainly from Balmeanach, Gedintailor and Peinnchorrain [4]. (Alexander's mother Iseabail was brought up in Balmeanach and her mother was brought up in Peinnchorrain, so they may have been educated at the school.)

In 1892 the MacDiarmid Endowed School was replaced by a new Braes Public School, which was located at the north end of Ollach, only a mile or so from Achnahanaid, opening the possibility of education for the young Nicolson children. The new school had two teachers, two pupil teachers and a roll of 170 children. It is possible that it may have inherited some books from the Endowed School but other resources were limited: inspectors reported that the infant classes had only 15 slates for 59 pupils and for the first two winters there was no fuel for heating, so the children had to bring peats with them to heat the school [5].

According to Alexander's daughter Ishabel, these were not the only problems: "the pupils knew no English and the teacher knew no Gaelic" and, to make matters worse, if the teacher was drunk (which was often) he would send the children home. "However in spite of very inadequate schooling, he pursued his own education avidly and, remarkably, became a pupil teacher, a difficult position I should think where there were so many siblings and cousins. At one point, a young teacher came to the school for 6 months. This teacher pointed to him resources which would guide him to begin the path to university entrance. (As an example of the problems of self-education, he was prepared for translation from Latin to English but not *vice versa*. He also began to learn French until a visitor scoffed at his pronunciation. One day on Ben Lee, as he watched over the sheep, he realised the truth of Pythagoras' Theorem.)"

The school records refer to 'A Nicholson' (sic) as one of two recipients of 'Merit Certificates' in 1898–99 and state that he served as a Pupil Teacher from 1901 until 1905. When Portree Public School was recognised as a Higher Grade Public School, A Nicolson was one of the first 12 candidates from Skye, Glenelg and North Uist who travelled there to sit the national school-leaving certificate.

In 1906 Nicolson took the Glasgow University entrance examination [6] and travelled to Glasgow to study for a Master of Arts. However his financial support appears to have run out before he could complete his studies. In the summer of 1907 he spent a month as a teacher in Lochmaddy, North Uist, and from 1909 onwards he taught full-time in primary schools in the Glasgow area to support himself, continuing his University studies on a part-time basis. He finally graduated in 1913. His daughter Ishabel says, "His Master of Arts degree was widely-based and hard-won. As medallist in geology he was offered a job in South Africa but the beginning of the First World War prevented that. His maths qualified him for his teaching career but his love of Gaelic and the history of his island prevailed".

University and the schools of Glasgow also brought him into contact with the world of radical politics. Among others, he got to know James Maxton, a teacher who had graduated from Glasgow University in 1909 and later became leader of the Independent Labour Party. According to his nephew Sorley MacLean, 'The most intellectual of my relations was a sceptic and a Socialist (my uncle in Jordanhill, Alex Nicolson). Apart from his dangerous opinions he appeared a better man than all my religious acquaintance'. MacLean was particularly impressed by hints that his uncle had come into contact with the great Scottish revolutionary socialist, John MacLean [7]. This political involvement led Nicolson to become a conscientious objector in the First World War and from 1916 to 1919 he was imprisoned in 'Princeton Work Centre' (Dartmoor Prison). He later said that when locked in a narrow cell with a high small window he sometimes despaired but seeing the planet Venus through that small window kept him sane.

After the war was over, he returned to teaching in Glasgow, where he met his wife, Janet Davidson. In the years that followed, they raised a family and he continued his studies and writing.

Alexander Nicolson was an invited guest at one of the most celebrated inter-war events at Glasgow University, in which he had been an interim lecturer in Celtic, a role perhaps overshadowed by his better-known achievements as lecturer in Gaelic at Jordanhill College. On 20th June 1933, Albert Einstein gave the first Gibson Lecture in Mathematics, under the heading of "About the origins of the General Theory of Relativity". The lecture was delivered to an audience of 1,500 people in the Bute Hall. The following day, the University Principal, Professor Robert Sangster Rait, who himself had spent part of his childhood on Skye and had attended school in Portree, held a luncheon in Einstein's honour in the Principal's residence. Nicolson was among the invited guests there also, and attended along with his friend Professor Magnus Maclean of Glendale, who had worked closely with Lord Kelvin at the University for many years and whose work in that role had been known to Einstein. It is related that Rait, Maclean and Nicolson were drawn into earnest discussion by Einstein on the place of the Gaelic peoples in Scotland and it fell to Professor Maclean to respond to Einstein's questions about Bonnie Prince Charlie and Flora Macdonald. On hearing what would, no doubt, be an erudite and learned exposition from the Glendale scientist, Einstein thought deeply and said to Maclean, who was by now seventy-five years of age, "Not only are you highly knowledgeable but you are also a highly active Gael"! The exchange, and the approval for Maclean's spontaneous scholarship, in the presence of Rait, former Historiographer Royal for Scotland, the world's first professor of Scottish History and knighted that same year, gave Alexander Nicolson the opportunity to challenge Maclean to prepare a paper on Flora Macdonald for the Gaelic Society of Glasgow of which he was an office-bearer. The result was that Professor Maclean delivered his final formal Lecture to the Society, of which he had himself been one of the founders, just four months later, on 31st October 1933, and Nicolson, always quick to spot a literary allusion, used his position as one of the editors of the Gaelic Society of Glasgow's fourth volume of papers, to publish Maclean's learned article on Flora Macdonald and, echoing Einstein's words, to name the volume, 'The Active Gael'.

He built a notable reputation for his 'lantern slide' lectures on Skye and on Gaelic culture and language. Following his lecture on 'The Coolins' to the High School Ceilidh, one newspaper report observed that 'To followers of shinty Mr Nicolson is well-known as the goalkeeper for the famous Glasgow Skye combination. In his lecture Mr Nicolson revealed himself as something which is, perhaps, more rare than a first-class shinty goalkeeper, namely a scientist who is also a poet'. The reporter described the mountain views in the slide show as a 'revelation', commenting on 'the lecturer's prowess as a climber' and regretting only that more was not said about 'the occasion when, mist bound, he and some companions spent a moonlit night on the spur of Bruaich-na-Frith – "not daring to sleep"'.

His daughter Ishabel remembers:

My predominant memories of him are writing at the living room table, with a spread of books and papers around him. When he acquired a camera, he recorded historically important sites in Skye and the life of its people. From these he compiled lantern lectures which he delivered to Highland and other societies. He promoted Gaelic by teaching in evening classes. He lectured in Gaelic to Highland students at Jordanhill and Notre Dame Colleges. During the Second World War he took the place of Angus Matheson as Celtic lecturer at Glasgow University. Thereafter he became the first teacher of Gaelic in two Glasgow schools until his retirement.

He loved the mountains. Sometimes, if the weather was good enough, he would spend 3 days and nights on the tops. This love of the lonely places and his knowledge of botany, geology and history he passed on to his children. He was a polymath as well as a Gaelic scholar.

Alasdair Beal, with assistance from Ishabel Beal,
Richard Beal and Cailean Maclean

1. F.H. Groome, Ordnance Gazetteer of Scotland (1882–4); © 2004 Gazetteer for Scotland.
2. *Ibid.*
3. MacDiarmid Endowed School Log Book.
4. *Ibid.*
5. Braes Public School Log Book.
6. *Ibid.*
7. Somhairle MacGill-Eain, *Dain do Eimhir*, ed. C. Whyte, Birlinn, Edinburgh, 2007, 'Autobiographical Sketch', p. 268.

Photograph taken by Alexander Nicolson in Achnahanaid, Braes about 1920, showing his brothers Calum and James working in the field with their father, Somhairle Mor. The two little boys in the background are his nephews Calum and Sorley MacLean; the former later became a noted folklorist and the latter a celebrated poet. © Alasdair Beal.

Alexander Nicolson in Raasay. © Alasdair Beal

APPENDIX 2

PREHISTORY OF SKYE

'Edifices, either standing or ruined, are the chief records of an illiterate nation'.

Dr. Johnson, *A Journey to the Western Isles of Scotland*

As the content and arrangement of his opening chapter makes plain, Nicolson did not consider it his purpose to attempt an historical narrative based upon the meagre handful of archaeological material available in his day. Even now, over 60 years after he wrote, we are little further towards that goal of writing a text which might reasonably claim to chronicle over five thousand years of human settlement on Skye before our first recorded historical event, – the missionary activity of St Columba in the later 6th century. Nicolson was quite clear in his own mind as to the distinction between his main purpose, that of writing a history of people and events, and that material he must necessarily treat as a preliminary to it. For him 'history' was a narrative of human events drawn from the rich mass of written and oral transmissions; yet for the seemingly endless ream of earlier life only archaeology (for him, that which had to be inferred from the welter of physical remains) was available as a source of information.

Yet whereas Nicolson well knew the limitations of the archaeological data, he was no less acutely aware of its value in revealing the long and complex history of settlement activity in Skye, and in showing how this activity extended back into times as equally remote as had been demonstrated for anywhere else in Scotland. Even here though, whereas many might feel it sufficient to tidily tuck away into their opening paragraphs, material in which they have little interest but do not wish to be criticised for disregarding, he was determined to discharge this duty to the best of his abilities, and accordingly set himself the challenging task of acquainting himself with the archaeological literature. It is clear that, while he is not entirely as at ease with the nature and context of his material, his rigorous academic probity would not allow him to discharge an obligation so peremptorily; his approach is more than just a passing nod of respect to that youngest of tools in the toolkit of historical enquiry, – the emergent discipline of archaeology.

It is salutary to recall that at the time Nicolson was writing very little had been done in the West to relieve him of the necessity to look at the results of work elsewhere in Scotland (notably to the Orkneys). Apart from general texts and specialist articles there was really little then available specifically on Skye. He confirms what we know from the historical chapters which follow his archaeological account, that he had an impressively thorough familiarity with a remarkably wide range of sources. He omits no record of 'archaeological' observations in these early accounts, such as Martin Martin's account of the souterrains at Camustianavaig (*Martin, M, 1716*), or Pennant's observations and remarks concerning 'Bronze Age' vessels (*Pennant, T, 1774*). In other respects the work of near-contemporary scholars in adjacent areas encouraged a confidence in his theme; and certainly here the work of Beveridge in North Uist had demonstrated the potential of such material, and revealed comforting nearby analogies to some of the structural forms encountered here (*Beveridge, E, 1911*). At the same time, excavating on the mainland at Glenelg and just opposite Skye, Alexander Curle had recovered something of the structural history and material culture of those living around the brochs of Dun Telve and Dun Troddan (*Curle, AO, 1916 and 1921*) which helped form in Nicolson's mind a picture of life around similar structures in Skye.

There can be little doubt however, that the most influential, and indeed timely, source to come to his notice was the *Ninth Report of the Royal Commission on Ancient and Historical Monuments and Constructions of Scotland*. Appearing just two years before the publication of Nicolson's own work this '*Report ...*' was an inventory of archaeological monuments and buildings of historical interest garnered in a sweep of the Outer Hebrides, Skye and the Small Isles by the Commission's inspectors and surveyors (*RCAHMCS,1928*). For its day the work was a prodigious undertaking of field recording blended with sensibly considered historical analysis; to this day their rigorously applied meticulous standards continue, through successive volumes, to enlarge our understanding of Scotland's history to an unequalled degree.

Nicolson was well aware that excavation had taken place on Skye – indeed he refers specifically to the work of the Countess Vincent Baillet de Latour at Dun Beag (*Callendar, JG, 1921*). Surprisingly however, he omits to mention by name her other excavations; that at Dun Totaig, in Duirinish (*RCAHMCS, 1928, pp. 161–2. No 519*), and at Dun Fiadhart, Duirinish (*MacLeod, FT, 1915*), although both of these must surely have been familiar to him. Yet he does add archaeological items which appear nowhere else, and which have clearly been gathered through purposeful enquiry (such as the 'flake factory' at the Braes), while his account of the 'bloomery' on Raasay shows him to be not averse to a little archaeological investigation at first hand.

From the sources he has plainly consulted, the question must have arisen in his mind as to the best model for presenting his material, and here several paths lay open to him. Certainly a narrative of sorts could be written taking the nationally received storyline and adapting it to local circumstances, simply by dropping in the names of those local examples which seem to exemplify its truth. It is the familiar, '*The Neolithic people were the first farmers, and from the pottery found under No 47 Willow Drive we know one of them lived here*' theme that monotonously reverberates around the information panels of the nation's smaller museums to this day. That he chose not to imitate this widespread model is interesting, as is in particular his largely eschewing all reference to periodisation.

The division of prehistory on the basis of technological achievement so assiduously established by our Scandinavian colleagues in the mid-19th century, and which had given us our Stone, Bronze and Iron Ages is, with one, almost accidental exception, totally disregarded by Nicolson. Rather he chooses to gather his material into category headings, 'Stone-circles', 'Duns and Brochs' etc., then pointing out examples of these and lightly highlighting aspects of them. Yet, these categories are, without exception, structural in theme. They deal with structures of various sorts rather than more abstract themes, such as prehistoric '*Agriculture*' '*Fishing*' and '*Modes of Dress*' for example, as appears later in the work. Moreover, the opening sentence itself makes plain his model; it is just what might 'impress' the 'wayfarer' who wanders the Skye landscape. He had noted its successful employment by the writers of the *RCAHMCS 9th Report*, and was not slow to see the relevance of this approach for his own work.

In the half a century intervening since he wrote, archaeology has certainly made great advances. Nationally the picture is, in many respects, a radically different one from that of the 1930s. Within Scotland in particular it is only necessary to refer the general reader to such seminal works as Graham and Anna Ritchie's, *Scotland; Archaeology and Early History* (1985) or *Symbols of Power at the Time of Stonehenge* (Clarke, DV, Cowie, TG & Foxon, A, 1985) and the bibliographies therein, to note the pace and extent of the change. Sadly though, it cannot be claimed that the advance in knowledge has been evenly distributed geographically; however, it seems that the imbalance which in previous decades has seen little resourcing of archaeological strategies in the Hebrides is now being addressed through the current programmes of work undertaken in the Western Isles, both by outside agencies, and (particularly heartening), the determination of local community-based groups to understand and develop their own archaeological heritage.

In Skye until quite recently the movement has been more 'measured'. Certainly from time to time casual discoveries, such as flint arrowheads, axeheads, and the occasional hoard of bronze weapons, have been made, which add further to the quantity and breadth of material Nicolson has already noted. Of these casual discoveries mention must be made in particular of the survival of some wooden objects discovered in different parts of the island. Only under exceptional conditions will organic material survive for any length of time in the ground, usually only in extremely dry or, as the peat offers here on Skye, extremely waterlogged circumstances. In 1931 a wooden barrel was found at Kilmaluag, Trotternish (*Ritchie, J, 1941*). It was made from birch and contained 'bog-butter', a fatty material that on analysis appears closely akin to butter. It has been C14 dated to between AD 246–346, and matches the discovery of several alder barrels with similar contents found at Kyleakin sometime before 1886 (*Anderson, J, 1885*). An elaborately carved wooden bowl of alder found at Talisker in 1979 has recently been radiocarbon dated to between AD 85–245 (*Barber, J, 1982*). A second alder bowl discovered near Glen Bracadale has been dated to between AD 20–205 (*Crone, BA, forthcoming*). Apart from these small portable objects, very little archaeological excavation has taken place since the 1930s, to bring Nicolson's record of prehistoric discoveries up to date. Brief reference might be made of those which add to the fabric of his archaeological narrative.

Within three years of the appearance of *History of Skye*, W Lindsay Scott had found flint material and beaker pottery indicating domestic occupation within a cave at *Creag a' Chapuill, Rubh' an Dùnain* (Scott, WL, 1934). In the 1970s beaker pottery, together with barbed and tanged flint arrowheads, were found in what may have been a burial context at Elishader in Trotternish (*unpublished information in National Museums of Scotland*). Inevitably however, most effort has again been devoted to the 'Iron Age', the millennium straddling the BC/AD divide. Particularly useful as an overview of the situation has been Anne MacSween's survey, *The Brochs, Duns and Enclosures of Skye (1985)*. From the great welter of archaeological forms that litter the Skye landscape it is sad to see the moth-like fascination by outside agencies with the 'dramatically monumental' continuing to dominate our archaeology, the brochs and duns. So it is that excavation has taken place at Dun Ardtreck (*1964–5 – Mackie, EW, 1967 and forthcoming*), Dun Flodigarry (*1979–1982 – Martlew, R 1985*), and Dun Colbost (*1990 – MacSween, A; Personal information*). At the same time Manchester University has excavated two circular homesteads at Achnacloich, in Sleat (1988–1991 – Burney, C; Personal information).

In 1988, *Dualchas* (Skye and Lochalsh District Council Museums Service) was formed, having a Heritage landscape remit. In addition to expanding the Sites and Monuments record of archaeological discoveries through a planned programme of archaeological field survey and recording, the Service is active in the fields of excavation and monument restoration. As part of an integrated general strategy, in 1988 *Dualchas* excavated a rectangular homestead with souterrain at Tungadale, Glen Bracadale (*Miket, R & Wildgoose, M; forthcoming*) and a souterrain on Raasay the year following; subsequent excavation work includes examination of shielings at Torrin, Strath as part of a wider shieling study programme (1990–92 – Wildgoose, M & Miket, R; forthcoming), and a circular stone homestead at *Coille a' Ghasgain,* Ord (1993 – Wildgoose, M, Burney, C & Miket, R; forthcoming).

The main purpose of this note is to provide a context for Nicolson's discussion of the prehistory of Skye and a supplement on what further work has taken place since he laid down his pen. Nevertheless it would be a singular failing not to remark how the use of archaeology as a tool has been extended into areas which indeed might well have surprised Nicolson. As an example, the architectural history and evolution of shielings worried neither Nicolson nor the writers of the 9th Inventory, yet since their day Malcolm MacSween has shown it to be an invaluable and major element in the distinctive agricultural regime, an understanding of which can benefit greatly from just this kind of approach (MacSween, M, 1959; MacSween, M & Gailey, A, 1961). Similarly, much has been written from the economic history point of view of the kelp industry in Skye, without any clarity as to its archaeological manifestation; the examination of a kelp-burning site might indeed add much to what we think we know from other sources. In the island's archaeological narrative, the magnificently monumental might well contain moments of high drama but the thread which unites the whole work runs rather through the commonplace and less imposing structures.

There is clearly great potential in the years ahead to expand upon those few building blocks then available to Alexander Nicolson. The unattainable ideal of course is of a Skye recounting a coherent story derived virtually solely from its own archaeological material; a sturdy framework of sites and finds which indeed intermeshes with a national picture, but equally can demonstrate what might be unique and individual in its personality. To achieve this in both a healthy and successful manner will require local initiatives to establish and maintain an integrated programme of work in place of the many caprices which have characterised much previous activity; in effect, channeling the impulses of external agencies into a partnership of exploration. Taking these initiatives will in turn require an adequate information base, and access to the appropriate training whereby these tools might be deployed in a manner which will allow the area to explore its own heritage for the future well-being of all whom it touches.

APPENDIX 3

GENEALOGY OF CLAN DONALD OF SKYE

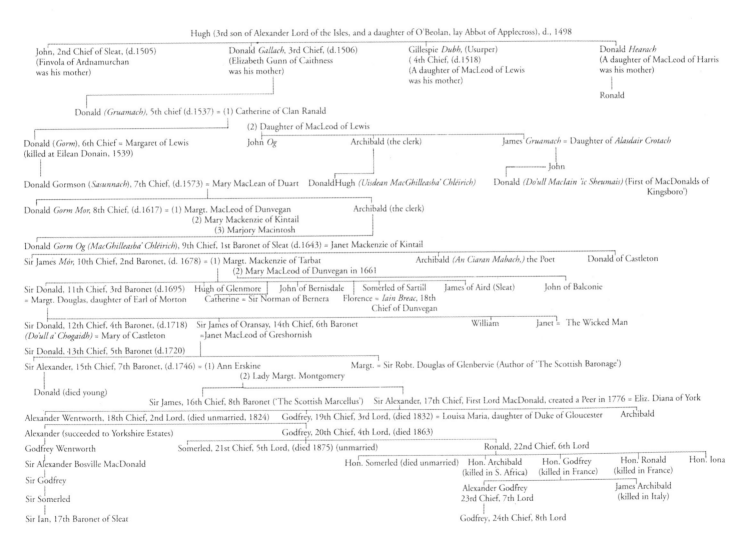

Hugh (3rd son of Alexander Lord of the Isles, and a daughter of O'Beolan, lay Abbot of Applecross), d., 1498

John, 2nd Chief of Sleat, (d.1505) (Finvola of Ardnamurchan was his mother)

Donald *Gallach*, 3rd Chief, (d.1506) (Elizabeth Gunn of Caithness was his mother)

Gillespie *Dubh*, (Usurper) (4th Chief, (d.1518) (A daughter of MacLeod of Lewis was his mother)

Donald *Hearach* (A daughter of MacLeod of Harris was his mother)

Ronald

Donald *(Gruamach)*, 5th chief (d.1537) = (1) Catherine of Clan Ranald

(2) Daughter of MacLeod of Lewis

Donald *(Gorm)*, 6th Chief = Margaret of Lewis (killed at Eilean Donain, 1539)

John *Og*

Archibald (the clerk)

James *Gruamach* = Daughter of *Alasdair Crotach*

John

Donald Gormson (*Sasunnach*), 7th Chief, (d.1573) = Mary MacLean of Duart

DonaldHugh (*Uisdean MacGhilleasba' Chléirich*)

Donald (*Do'ull Maclain 'ic Sheumais*) (First of MacDonalds of Kingsboro')

Donald *Gorm Mor*, 8th Chief, (d.1617) = (1) Margt. MacLeod of Dunvegan (2) Mary Mackenzie of Kintail (3) Marjory Macintosh

Archibald (the clerk)

Donald *Gorm Og (MacGhilleasba' Chléirich)*, 9th Chief, 1st Baronet of Sleat (d.1643) = Janet Mackenzie of Kintail

Sir James *Mór*, 10th Chief, 2nd Baronet, (d. 1678) = (1) Margt. Mackenzie of Tarbat (2) Mary MacLeod of Dunvegan in 1661

Archibald *(An Ciaran Mabach,)* the Poet

Donald of Castleton

Sir Donald, 11th Chief, 3rd Baronet (d.1695) = Margt. Douglas, daughter of Earl of Morton

Hugh of Glenmore Catherine = Sir Norman of Bernera

John of Bernisdale

Somerled of Sartiil Florence = *Iain Breac*, 18th Chief of Dunvegan

James of Aird (Sleat)

John of Balconie

Sir Donald, 12th Chief, 4th Baronet, (d.1718) (*Do'ull a' Chogaidh*) = Mary of Castleton

Sir James of Oransay, 14th Chief, 6th Baronet =Janet MacLeod of Greshornish

William

Janet = The Wicked Man

Sir Donald, 13th Chief, 5th Baronet (d.1720)

Sir Alexander, 15th Chief, 7th Baronet, (d.1746) = (1) Ann Erskine (2) Lady Margt. Montgomery

Margt. = Sir Robt. Douglas of Glenbervie (Author of 'The Scottish Baronage')

Donald (died young)

Sir James, 16th Chief, 8th Baronet ('The Scottish Marcellus')

Sir Alexander, 17th Chief, First Lord MacDonald, created a Peer in 1776 = Eliz. Diana of York

Alexander Wentworth, 18th Chief, 2nd Lord, (died unmarried, 1824)

Godfrey, 19th Chief, 3rd Lord, (died 1832) = Louisa Maria, daughter of Duke of Gloucester

Archibald

Alexander (succeeded to Yorkshire Estates)

Godfrey, 20th Chief, 4th Lord, (died 1863)

Godfrey Wentworth

Somerled, 21st Chief, 5th Lord, (died 1875) (unmarried)

Ronald, 22nd Chief, 6th Lord

Sir Alexander Bosville MacDonald

Hon. Somerled (died unmarried)

Hon. Archibald (killed in S. Africa)

Hon. Godfrey (killed in France)

Hon. Ronald (killed in France)

Hon. Iona

Sir Godfrey

Alexander Godfrey 23rd Chief, 7th Lord

James Archibald (killed in Italy)

Sir Somerled

Godfrey, 24th Chief, 8th Lord

Sir Ian, 17th Baronet of Sleat

GENEALOGY OF THE MACLEODS OF DUNVEGAN

Leod, son of Olave the black = Daughter of MacHarald (Armunn)

Norman, 2nd Chief, (d. c.1320) = ? Fingula MacCrotan, daughter of an Irish chief

Malcolm, 3rd Chief, (d. c.1360) = Daughter of Earl of Mar

John, 4th Chief, (d. c.1392)   Norman (Harris)   Murdo of Gesto   Fingula = Mackenzie, 6th of Kintail

Malcolm (died young)   William (*Cléireach*), 5th Chief, (d. c.1402) = Daughter of MacLaine Lochbuy   Daughter = Lachlan of Duart

John (*Borb*), 6th Chief, (d.1442) = Margaret, grand-daughter of the Earl of Douglas   Norman whence (1) *Clann ic Uilleim* (2) *Clann Alasdair Ruaidh*   George

William (*Dubh*), 7th Chief, (d.1480) = a Maclaine of Lochbuy   Norman whence (1) MacLeods of Drynoch (2) MacLeods of Balmeanach (3) MacLeods of Meadle (4) *Sliochd Iain 'ic Leòid*   Margaret = Roderick, 3rd of Lewis   Daughter = Lachlan, 7th of Duart

Alasdair *Crotach*, (d.1547) 8th Chief, = Daughter of Lachlan MacLean of Duart   John (*Iain a' Chùil Bhàin* or *Iain Og*), 10th Chief

William (*Uilleam na h-Uamha*), 9th Chief, (d. 1551) = Agnes Fraser, daughter of 4th Lord Lovat   Mary ("Heiress of the Isles")   Donald, (murdered at Lyndale)   Norman, 12th Chief, (d.1585) = (1) Julia, MacLean of Duart (2) Daughter of Earl of Argyle   Daughter = James *Gruamach* of Castle Camus   Nine other daughters   Norman   John (*Iain Dubh*, or *Og*), 11th Chief, (d.1560) (*de jure*)   Norman, 11th Chief (*de facto*)

William, 13th Chief (d.1520) = Janet Macintosh of Dunachton, John, 14th Chief (d. young c.1596)   Sir Rory *Mór*, (d.1626) 15th Chief = Isabella of Glengarry   Alexander of Minginish whence MacLeods of Ose and MacLeods of Ferinica   Margaret = Donald *Gorm Mor*   Daughter = Torquil Dubh of Lewis

John (*Iain Mór*,) 16th Chief (d.1649) = Sibella of Kintail   Sir Roderick of Talisker   Sir Norman of Bernera = dau. of Sir James MacDonald   William of Hamera whence MacLeods of Waterstein   Donald whence MacLeods of Grishornish   Janet = *Iain Garbh* of Raasay   Five other daughters

Roderick ('The Witty') 17th Chief (d.1664) = Margaret dau. of Sir John Mackenzie of Kintail   John (*Iain Breac*), 18th Chief, (d.1693) = Florence, dau. of Sir James MacDonald   Mary = Sir James *Mór* of Sleat as 2nd wife   Sibella = Thomas Fraser of Lovat   Three other daughters

Norman (died young)   Dau' = Stewart of Appin

Roderick, 19th Chief (d.1699) = Lady Isabel Mackenzie, Anne = Donald MacLeod of Bernera ('The Old Trojan')   William   Norman, 20th Chief, (d.1706) = Anne Frazer of Lovat   Isabel = Stewart of Appin   Janet = Sir James Campbell of Auchinbrech

John, 21st Chief   Norman ('The Wicked Man'), 22nd Chief, (d.1772) = (1) Janet, dau. of Sir Donald of Sleat (2) Ann Martin

John d.1766   3 daughters   (Natural Children)

Norman ('The General',) 23rd Chief (d.1801) = (1) Mary MacKenzie of Suddie (2) Sarah Stackhouse   Maj. Alex MacLeod of Lochbay   Capt. MacLeod of Cyprus

Norman (killed on board Queen Charlotte)   Mary = Col. N. Ramsay   John Norman, 24th Chief (d.1835) = Ann Stephenson   Three daughters

Norman, 25th Chief (d. 1895) = (1) Hon. Louisa St. John

Norman Magnus, 26th Chief   Torquil Olave   Sir Reginald, 27th Chief   Dame Flora, 28th Chief = Hubert Walter   Joan = Robert Wolridge Gordon   John, 29th Chief   Roderick Charles

GENEALOGY OF THE MACLEODS OF RAASAY

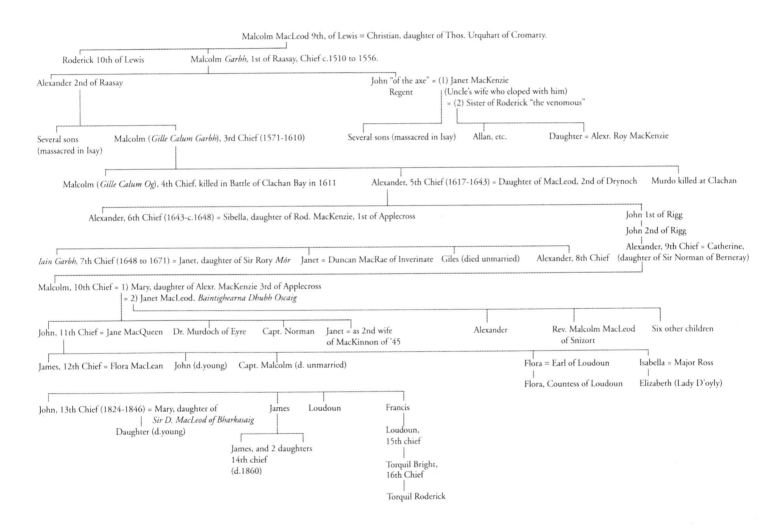

Malcolm MacLeod 9th, of Lewis = Christian, daughter of Thos. Urquhart of Cromarty.

Roderick 10th of Lewis

Malcolm *Garbh*, 1st of Raasay, Chief c.1510 to 1556.

Alexander 2nd of Raasay

John "of the axe" = (1) Janet MacKenzie
Regent (Uncle's wife who eloped with him)
= (2) Sister of Roderick "the venomous"

Several sons (massacred in Isay)

Malcolm (*Gille Calum Garbh*), 3rd Chief (1571-1610)

Several sons (massacred in Isay)　Allan, etc.　Daughter = Alexr. Roy MacKenzie

Malcolm (*Gille Calum Og*), 4th Chief, killed in Battle of Clachan Bay in 1611　Alexander, 5th Chief (1617-1643) = Daughter of MacLeod, 2nd of Drynoch　Murdo killed at Clachan

Alexander, 6th Chief (1643-c.1648) = Sibella, daughter of Rod. MacKenzie, 1st of Applecross

John 1st of Rigg
John 2nd of Rigg
Alexander, 9th Chief = Catherine,
(daughter of Sir Norman of Berneray)

Iain Garbh, 7th Chief (1648 to 1671) = Janet, daughter of Sir Rory *Mór*　Janet = Duncan MacRae of Inverinate　Giles (died unmarried)　Alexander, 8th Chief

Malcolm, 10th Chief = 1) Mary, daughter of Alexr. MacKenzie 3rd of Applecross
= 2) Janet MacLeod, *Baintighearna Dhubh Oscaig*

John, 11th Chief = Jane MacQueen　Dr. Murdoch of Eyre　Capt. Norman　Janet = as 2nd wife of MacKinnon of '45　Alexander　Rev. Malcolm MacLeod of Snizort　Six other children

James, 12th Chief = Flora MacLean　John (d.young)　Capt. Malcolm (d. unmarried)

Flora = Earl of Loudoun
Flora, Countess of Loudoun

Isabella = Major Ross
Elizabeth (Lady D'oyly)

John, 13th Chief (1824-1846) = Mary, daughter of
Sir D. MacLeod of Bharkasaig
Daughter (d.young)

James　Loudoun　Francis

James, and 2 daughters
14th chief
(d.1860)

Loudoun,
15th chief

Torquil Bright,
16th Chief

Torquil Roderick

APPENDIX 4

ENUMERATION OF THE MACLEOD CHIEFS

In the past, various authors have used different criteria in assessing the numeration of the MacLeod chiefs. What follows attempts to reconcile, and to a limited extent, account for the discrepancies arising.

The MacLeods – The History of a Clan (Grant, IF, 1959) followed by *The MacLeods – The Genealogy of a Clan* (MacKinnon, D and Morrison, A, Section 1, 1968).

1   Leod
2   *Tormad*
3   Malcolm
4   *Iain*
5   William
6   *Iain Borb*
7   *William Dubh*
8   *Alasdair*
9   William
10 Mary
11 Donald
12 *Tormad*
13 William
14 John
15 *Rory Mor*
16 *Iain Mor*
17 *Rory Mir*
18 *Iain Breac*
19 *Rory Og*
20 Norman
21 John
22 Norman (Red Man)
23 Norman
24 John Norman
25 Norman
26 Norman Magnus
27 Sir Reginald
28 Dame Flora

The MacLeods of Dunvegan (MacLeod, RC, 1927), following Mackenzie, A, 1889)

1   Leod
2   *Tormad*
3   Malcolm

4 *Iain*
5 William
6 *Iain*
7 William
8 Alexander
9 William
10 Donal
11 *Tormad*
12 William
13 *Rory Mor*
14 *Iain Mor*
15 *Rory Mir*
16 Iain Breac

18 *Iain Breac*
19 Roderick
20 Norman
21 John
22 Norman (Wicked Man)
23 Norman
24 John Norman
25 Norman
26 Norman Magnus
27 Sir Reginald
28 Dame Flora

History of a Skye, followed by *The Book of Dunvegan* (MacLeod, RC, 1938), with one exception, *vide infra*

1 Leod
2 Norman
3 Malcolm
4 John
5 William
6 *Iain Borb*
7 *William Dubh*
8 *Alasdair*
9 William
10 *Iain a Chùil Bhàin*
11 *Iain Dubh* or Norman, grandson of 10
12 Norman
13 William
14 John
15 *Rory Mor*
16 *Iain Mor*
17 *Rory Mir*

After the death of Dame Flora, her grandson, John Woolridge Gordon, succeeded her as John MacLeod of MacLeod, 29th Chief. With the death of John Macleod of Macleod in 2007, he was succeeded by his son Hugh Macleod.

Until the death of William the 9th Chief, numbers are in agreement. Mary is entered as 10th Chief by Dr Grant but it would appear that she had never been accepted by the Clan. Canon MacLeod (MacLeod, RC, 1927, p. 94) has Donald as 10th Chief and *History of Skye* places *Iain a Chùil Bhàin* as No 10. Dr Grant refers to the latter as 'usurper' on no evidence offered by her. She quotes *"another MS history"* (Grant, IF, 1959, p. 121, fn), which merely confirms the account given in *The Bannatyne Manuscript* on which both Canon MacLeod and the *History of Skye* are based, saying *"next heir was Iain Oge, grandson of Tormad, brother of Iain, the 6th Chief."* (See also MacLeod, RC, 1938, p. 5). Thus, the whereabouts or even survival of Donald and Norman, brothers of the late Chief, being unknown, made *Iain a Chùil Bhàin*'s succession acceptable to the Clan. Indeed, when Donald, brother of William, 9th Chief, reappeared, Canon MacLeod states that the Clan rejected him and continued *Iain a Chùil Bhàin* as Chief, during his life (MacLeod, RC, 1927, p. 95).

On *Iain*'s death, however, Donald's claim was upheld but he was murdered almost immediately, before he could be installed as Chief, by *Iain Dubh*, *Iain a Chùil Bhàin*'s son. The Clan then elected as chief Norman, son of *Iain a Chùil Bhàin*'s deceased eldest son, Norman (*ibid.*). This child chief, who should correctly be counted as 11th in line, was also murdered by his uncle, *Iain Dubh*, who occupied Dunvegan Castle and acted as a usurping chief for a period of two years.

He was driven out in favour of the missing Norman, brother of William, the 9th Chief, who succeeded as 12th Chief, although Canon MacLeod (*ibid.*, p. 98) refers to him as 11th. As he also omits mention of John, the grandson of Norman, he numbers *Rory Mor*, John's uncle and successor, as 13th (*ibid*, p. 119) instead of 15th as generally accepted.

Although Canon RC MacLeod (*ibid.*) numbers Donald 11th, and *Tormad* (Norman) 12th, a genealogy almost exactly as in *History of Skye* appears in his posthumous *Book of Dunvegan* (MacLeod, RC, 1939, p. xxxvi), the exception being that he names the grandson of *Iain a Chùil Bhàin*, whom he calls *Norman*, as 12th Chief following *Iain Dubh*. Norman, brother of William 9th becomes the 13th Chief, but the numbers are realigned by the omission of John the infant, named as 21st Chief by Dr Grant and *History of Skye*.

APPENDIX 5

A NOTE ON ST COLUMBA'S ISLAND, SKEABOST

Writing in 1930, Nicolson had only the evidence of the Rev Malcolm Macleod in the Old Statistical Account which merely states that the ancient church on the Island in Snizort River was probably once the metropolitan church of Skye. Research carried out later this century, particularly among Vatican papers, now shows the extent of that understatement. The late Professor Cowan of Glasgow University says,

The Diocese of Sodor [the Sudereys are the South or Western Islands of Scotland, so called by the Norse to distinguish them from the Nordereys, the Orkneys and Shetlands] *or the Isles appears on record shortly before 1079 when Rolwer died as Bishop and was buried in the Isle of Man ... although evidence exists that earlier Celtic bishops had been at work in Man and the Western Isles in preceding centuries. The 12th Century bishops bear a variety of titles including Skye, Man, Sudereys and Sodor, and appear to have recognised the authority of York until 1153, when they were placed under Trondheim ... The rights of Trondheim were reduced to a nominal level after 1349, when a Papal Grace excused the bishop from a personal visit to Trondheim to profess obedience. ... Such a far flung diocese must have been difficult to administer and it is possible that, from the 12th century, administrative burdens were being divided between Man, which was the title borne by the early archdeacons, and Sodor, although no archdeacons bearing that title appear until 1220. In the 13th century, archdeacons bearing the titles of Man and Sodor, respectively appear in 1219 and 1235x44, but as their periods of office do not coincide, the evidence of such division is inconclusive. On the other hand, even before the Great Schism, which resulted in the emergence of two lines of bishops based on Man and the Isles respectively, a separatist trend is observable in the Scottish part of the diocese. A group of Canons in Snizort in Skye along with the clergy of Skye elected a bishop, 1326x1331, and it is possible that this community possessed a separate existence from the 11th century, when an earlier Bishop of Skye is recorded.*

(Cowan, IB, 1978, pp. 15–16).

The history of the diocese of the Isles at Snizort is described as shadowy until 1499, when the Campbells, taking immediate advantage of the forfeiture of the Lordship of the Isles succeeded in having John Campbell, then Bishop of the Isles transferred to Iona, The 'earlier Bishop' referred to by Cowan is identified as Hamond filius Iole/Wimond who obtained consecration as Bishop of Skye from Archbishop Thomas of York in 1079 (Watt, DER, 1969, p. 197).

Archdeacon Monro writing in 1549 says of Iona that

the abbey was the cathedral kirk of the Bishoppes of the Iles sin the time thai was banist out of the ile of Man be the Inglismen.

(Munro, RW, 1961, p. 62).

Dr MacQuarrie says, however,

It must be doubted whether this had been so since the explusion of the Scots from Man in c 1331 ... It cannot be a coincidence that it is around the same time ... that the clergy of Skye elected a bishop to rule the diocese from the church at Snizort. But it is not until the outbreak of the 'Great Schism' in 1378 when Scotland and England were divided in the support of different Popes, that there is a continuous succession of Scottish bishops of the Isles at Snizort and English bishops of the Isles in the Isle of Man.

The position of Snizort as Cathedral of the Bishops of the Isles in the 14th and 15th centuries has been established beyond reasonable doubt, but it is curious that its history is so obscure that it was unknown to Archdeacon Monro in the 1540s and was not rediscovered until this present century. The ruins of a mediaeval church on an island in the Snizort River at Skeabost Bridge indicate the site of this obscure and little known Scottish Cathedral of the Isles. The siting of their cathedral in such a remote place may have been felt as an inconvenience by the Bishops of the Isles. In 1433 Bishop Angus (MacDonald, son of Donald of Harlaw, Lord of the Isles) petitioned the Pope for permission to move his cathedral from Snizort to a more suitable site within the Diocese and in 1498, the Earl of Argyle petitioned that the abbey of Iona be erected into 'the bishoppis sete of the Iles, quhil his principall kirk in the Ile of Man be recoverit fra Inglismen'..... in the following year the Abbacy of Iona was granted to the Bishop of the Isles 'in commendam', ie the bishop was allowed to occupy the abbey and enjoy the revenues without performing the abbot's duties or taking the Benedictine habit.

(MacQuarrie, A, 1987, pp. 369–70).

It is clear that the history of Snizort had been deliberately suppressed. Archdeacon Monro had been vicar of Snizort (Innes, C, 1854, p. 255) and he must have known from older parishoners of the earlier exalted role of the Snizort Church.

APPENDIX 6

A NOTE ON THE BATTLE OF WATERNISH (*BLÀR MILLEADH GÀRAIDH*)

Donald MacKillop, a native of Berneray, but who has faithfully studied the lore of Waternish, has composed what is probably the finest song written in the Gaelic bardic tradition which has appeared this century – *Coille an Fhàsaich* – which is a place in Waternish. He feels (personal communication) that the title *Milleadh Gàraidh* is the product of folk etymology and that the place is actually called *Millegearraidh* as is a place in Berneray which is topographically similar.

He argues logically that the people of Waternish would not have ruined a perfectly good and useful wall by tipping it over their slain enemies, when they could have so conveniently been thrown into the sea, a method of disposal not unknown in island history. In an article on *Social Life in Skye*, the author does not dispute the spoiled dyke theory, but the editors (Professor Watson and Alexander N Nicolson) add a footnote *"Properly written 'Millegearraidh', a Norse word meaning 'middle field'."* (Mackay, JG, 1924, p. 130).

APPENDIX 7

DONALD MACDONALD OF GLENHINNISDALE

Donald MacDonald, who published the earliest collection of *pìobaireachd* written in staff notation (MacDonald, D, *c.* 1820) got his tuition from the last of the MacArthur pipers who served the MacDonalds of Sleat in that capacity. In an article in the Celtic Magazine in 1887, Rev Alexander MacGregor described a meeting with Donald MacDonald and his father in 1837 in Donald's house and workshop in the Lawn Market in Edinburgh.

He had been established there as pipemaker and piper to the Highland Society of London by the patronage of Sir John Sinclair, whose wife was a daughter of Lord MacDonald. Donald played a fine *pìobaireachd, The Gathering of the Clans*. He was a small man, extremely corpulent and 82 years of age but he played well under the critical eye of his father John, who, naturally, was then over a hundred years old.

John Macdonald was a very colourful character and, although it was not known whether he, himself, had played, he knew a vast amount about *pìobaireachd* and had known many important historical individuals during his long life.

As a herd boy, in his teens, he had encountered MacDonald of Kingsburgh, when he was conducting Prince Charles Edward to spend the night in his home. John had shown the party the well which is still identified as *Tobar a' Phrionnsa* near the Glenhinnisdale River. Nearly thirty years later, he had seen the famous Dr Samuel Johnson at Kingsburgh. He had wondered who the man was in the strange broad brimmed hat, *"a lusty, stout man, somewhat like my son, Donald there, but probably stouter"* and had enquired of Dr Donald Macqueen, who accompanied Johnson. The minister said in Gaelic that it was the great Englishman who made the English language, to which John replied, *"ma ta, a' Mhinisteir, bha glè bheag aige ri dhèanamh"* ("Well, indeed, Minister, he had precious little to do.")

APPENDIX 8

THE ROUT OF MOY

The impact of *Cha till MacCruimein* on oral and piping tradition may well be explained by the tragic series of events leading to the death of Donald *Ban*.

Tradition has it that he was made prisoner at the skirmish at Inverurie, where MacLeod's inexperienced companies had been recklessly exposed by Lord Loudoun to be out numbered and out manoeuvred by a force of Jacobites from Aberdeen (Forbes, R, 1975, pp. 344–45). The Jacobite pipers refused to play a note while their distinguished colleague was a prisoner and Donald *Ban* was released only to be killed at the Rout of Moy.

The Muster Roll of the independent companies, raised by MacLeod of MacLeod to help in the suppression of the Rebellion of 1745, is dated June 1746, when Malcolm MacCrimmon is named as the piper to Macleod's own company (MacLeod, RH, 1985, p. 378) and it is not known to which company Donald *Ban* had been attached, although it is certain that he was beside Lord Loudoun at the Rout of Moy. The legend of the part played by the blacksmith of Moy, who was sent out by the wife of Macintosh of Macintosh to patrol the roads and who, with four men, routed Loudoun's forces, is one of the best known incidents in the story of the Rebellion. It was communicated to Bishop Forbes by two of Prince Charles' non combatant domestic servants (Forbes, R, 1975, Vol. II, pp. 136 and 247). Other records, however, appear to justify the term 'legend'.

Captain Malcolm Macleod, himself a piper and knowing Donald *Ban* well, was present at Moy that night as a member of the Prince's guard. He would have made it his business to find out exactly what had happened. In discussing the event with Forbes, he did not deny the story about the blacksmith but could not confirm that he had been instrumental in causing the death of Donald *Ban* (Forbes, R, 1975, Vol. I, p. 149). The campaign was over and Malcolm's erstwhile enemies had again become his friends and he would not have wished to embarrass them if he knew the truth was otherwise but he did add, almost as an after-thought, *"It is thought that Lord Loudoun's men who fired wounded some of their own companions."*

Lord Loudoun's report of the incident to the Duke of Cumberland (Maclean, A, 1989, p. 24) shows that the blacksmith, if he was involved, could not possibly have fired the shot that killed Donald *Ban*. He describes how he sent a detachment of thirty men and an officer by a different route to prevent warning of his approach reaching Moy Hall. The detachment *"saw or thought they saw four men"* and opened fire on them. This threw the main body, by now a mile away, into such confusion that five companies ran away and the remainder, whom he was able to muster, were *"ten deep and all presented, and some dropping Shots, one of which killed a piper at my feet"*.

The manuscript account of Aeneas Macintosh, who knew Macintosh's lady, on whose virtual doorstep all this happened, throws a clear light on Loudoun's rather bumbling report. The detachment, he said, had mistaken peat stacks for an enemy and opened fire. The main body returned the fire in panic and killed a piper, who was among them (Macintosh, AM, 1903, p. 337).

APPENDIX 9

CHARLES EDWARD STUART'S ROUTE FROM PORTREE TO STRATHAIRD

In dealing with that epic overnight walk, Nicolson offers his own theory about the route taken and, in this, he is possibly mistaken. It will be remembered that Captain Malcolm MacLeod, the Prince's guide, says of his plans for the journey *"for I dare not lead you the direct road, but take you byways, and go here and there cross country to keep as far as possible from the parties scattered up and down."* (Forbes, R, 1975, Vol. 1, p. 134).

Local tradition in Strath, as communicated by John Mac-innes, Dunan, agrees with the generally accepted story that it was through Strath Mor that the Prince entered Strathaird. This tradition is the more significant in that it derives from a one time native of Luib whose ancestor, John MacArthur, appears on the Muster Roll of the Prince's army. (Livingstone, A, Aikman, CWH and Stuart Hart, B, 1984, p. 170). It also accommodates Nicolson's point about the traditional site of *Tobar a' Phrionnsa* (The Prince's Well) at the foot of Marsco, which the travellers reached after by-passing Sligachan. It details the next stage of the journey as through the glen between Marsco and *Beinn Dearg Mheadhonach*, the place where daybreak found them (about 3.00 am) and certainly evocative of the Prince's remark, *"I am sure the Devil cannot find us now."* From there the route followed up hill to the pass, named on the OS map as *Mam a' Phobuil* (the Pass of the People) but known locally as *Mam a' Phrionnsa* (the Prince's Pass). It was downhill then through *Coire nam Bruadaran* (the Corrie of Dreams) to the head of Lochainort and along the slopes of Glasbheinn Mhor, above Aricharnach, into Strath Mor, by the path still identified on the OS map, avoiding all the populated areas.

APPENDIX 10

REVIEWS OF THE FIRST EDITION OF THE HISTORY OF SKYE

Inevitably, a work as seminal as the *History of Skye* attracted the attention of the press, and following its publication there were a number of reviews. A dozen of these reviews have been traced.[1] Seven were favourable without exception; four, while being favourable, and indeed enthusiastic, uniformly indicated areas in which improvements could have been made. These might be summarised as:

1   The absence of a table of contents (*The Times Literary Supplement*, adding, '*in a work otherwise remarkably complete*');
2   The lack of source references;
3   The omission of translations for the Gaelic poetry and prose.

An attempt has been made in the present work to remedy these general criticisms. Indeed there is evidence that the author had done so in the lost second edition. However, the author's knowledge of the oral and written literature of the Highlands was so vast, that the source of some of his material has remained elusive.

One review, however, was so remarkable in the breadth, depth and hostility of its criticism that it justifies separate treatment here. This is a matter of sadness as it came from the pen of another giant on the subject of Skye's history, The Rev Dr. Donald MacKinnon of Portree. Dr. MacKinnon was an excellent historian, with a profound knowledge of the genealogy of countless Skye families. He was indeed singularly well equipped to write a history of Skye, and might well have considered doing so. So persistent was the author of this hostile review in pursuit of his quarry that, not content with publishing it in the *Northern Chronicle* on 16 July 1930, Dr. MacKinnon republished it, with some amendments, in pamphlet form, in April 1931. On the second occasion, he fulsomely expanded on the criticism made by other reviewers, as already detailed above. And yet, though his comments may be considered justifiable in places, we detect something else besides. It is not the present purpose to act as an apologist for Alexander Nicolson; the fact that a second edition, purposely intended to adhere faithfully to his intent, demanded extensive revision and amendment, clearly indicates the imperfections of its first form. However, observation from a distance of over half a century reveals more to this rather scathing review than one of mere academic dispute.

Many of Dr. MacKinnon's criticisms were plainly of so trivial

a nature as to warrant little discussion. Some indicated minor Gaelic spelling aberrations which, where appropriate, have been corrected in the present edition. However, where such spelling versions might be understood to conform with the Skye pronunciation of earlier writers, they have been left unaltered. In judging a work so complex and wide-ranging as the *History of Skye*, a few printers' errors and the occasional slip of the author's pen might well be expected to escape the proof reader. It might, for example, seem harsh of the reviewer to remark that a proof reader failed to pick up on a line omitted by the printer which gave a completely different cast to the meaning of a sentence, and then elsewhere to pick up on this unintentionally distorted meaning as a product of the author's misinterpretation of information.

In the field of family history, Nicolson was criticised for considering Norman, son of Leod, to be the first MacLeod of Dunvegan, on the *then* reasonable basis that two brothers, Norman and Torquil (sons of Leod) were the progenitors of the MacLeods of Dunvegan and of Lewis respectively. Recent work (Matheson, W, 1981, p. 324) indicates, however, that the relationship may have been otherwise, and that Leod might correctly be named as the first of the MacLeod Chiefs of Dunvegan. Dr. MacKinnon also found Nicolson wanting in his sequence of the MacLeod Chiefs, as he did not adopt Canon RC MacLeod's

(then current) version. As is apparent in *Appendix 3* of the present work, Canon MacLeod was far from consistent in his placing of the Chiefs, and subsequently came to adopt a sequence almost identical to that of Nicolson. Similarly, in the history of another family, the reviewer devoted much space in demonstrating the illegitimacy of Hugh MacDonald, the first Chief of Sleat, as if it were a matter of grave contention, which it certainly was not.

In the field of ecclesiastical history, Dr. MacKinnon was indeed an expert, and well equipped to offer comment. As with his remarks dealing with the military history in Skye, any criticism from one so profoundly knowledgeable demanded deeper consideration. It is therefore a matter of some regret to those currently attempting to remedy the deficiencies and omissions from the consideration of the book's reviewers, that Dr MacKinnon failed to substantiate, through reasoning and references, some of the errors he alleged in Nicolson's sources; all the more so in that such a charge of omission is one levelled at Nicolson.

In the six decades which have elapsed since the work first appeared, these two Titans in their field have been gathered to their fathers. Each dedicated his life to understanding the history and traditions of the Gael, leaving a substantial and lasting scholarly legacy, without which we would all be immeasurably the poorer.

1   Below is a list of newspapers which carried reviews at the time of publication (1930):

The Scotsman (2 reviews)   The Stornoway Gazette
The Glasgow Herald   The Oban Times
The Times Literary Supplement   The People's Journal
The Edinburgh Evening News   The Weekly Herald
The Dundee Advertiser   The Northern Chronicle

APPENDIX 11

GENERAL WORKS RELATING TO SKYE AND PUBLISHED SINCE 1930

The number of publications appearing since 1930, which either wholly or in part refer directly to Skye, is legion and indeed no attempt is made here to encompass them all. Rather the list given below is a selective one which allows the general reader to extend beyond Nicolson's framework of references.

Basin, E. 1977, *The Old Songs of Skye; Frances Tolmie and her Circle.*

Bell, B.R. and Harris, J.W., 1986, *An Excursion Guide to the Geology of the Isle of Skye.*

Charnley, R. and Miket, R., 1992, *Skye: A Postcard Tour.*

Cooper, D., 1970, *Skye.*

Craig, D., 1990, *On the Crofters' Trail: In search of the Clearance Highlanders.*

Douglas, H., 1993, *Flora Macdonald, The Most Loyal Rebel.*

Draper, L. & P., 1990, *The Raasay Ironstone Mine.*

Gifford, A., 1992, *Highlands and Islands,* in 'The Buildings of Scotland' series.

Hunter, J., 1976, *The Making of the Crofting Community.*

MacDonald, A. R., 1938, *The Truth about Flora MacDonald.*

Macdonald, D.J., 1978, *Clan Donald.*

Macdonald, I., 1980, *A Family in Skye, 1908–191.6*

MacKenzie, W., 1934, *Old Skye Tales.*

MacKinnon, D. and Morrison, A., 1976, *The MacLeods – The Genealogy of a Clan,* Section 1, The MacLeod Chiefs of Harris and Dunvegan (3rd Edition).

Ibid, Section 2, *The MacLeods of Talisker, Berneray, Orbost, Luskintyre, Hamer, Greshornish, Ulilinish* and *Dalvey.*

Ibid, Section 3, *The MacLeod Cadet Families, descended from William XIII Chief, Norman XII Chief, Iain Borb VI Chief, William Cleireach V Chief, and Malcolm III Chief.*

MacLean, A. and Gibson, J.S., 1992, *Summer Hunting a Prince.*

Maclean, S., 1943, *Dain do Eimhir agus Dain eile.*

Maclean, S., 1970, *Four Points of a Saltire* (MacLean, Hay, Neil and MacGregor).

Maclean, S., 1977, *Spring Tide and Neap Tide* (Reothairt is Contraigh).

Maclean, S., 1985, *Ris a' Bhruthaich.*

Maclean, S., 1986, *Obscure and Anonymous Gaelic Poetry in the Seventeenth Century in the Highlands.* Inverness Field Club, pp. 89–104.

Maclean, S., 1987, *Poems 1932–1982.*

Maclean, S., 1989, *O Choille gu Bearradh* (*From Wood to Ridge*).

Maclean, S., 1990, *O Choille gu Bearradh* (*From Wood to Ridge*) (2nd Ed).

Maclean, S., 1991, *O Choille gu Bearradh* (*From Wood to Ridge*) (3rd Ed).

MacNeacail, A., 1970, *Briseadh na Cloiche.*

MacNeacail, A., 1976, *Poetry Quintet.*

MacNeacail, A., 1980, *Imaginary Wounds.*

MacNeacail, A., 1983, *Sireadh Bradain Sicir* (*Seeking Wise Salmon*) (Drawings by Simon Fraser).

MacNeacail, A., 1984, An Cathadh Mor; *The Great Snowbattle* (Drawings by Simon Fraser).

MacNeacail, A., 1990, *Rock and Water.*

MacNeacail, C., 1975, *Bardachd Chaluim Ruaidh.*

MacPhie, A., 1981, *Cunnartan Cuain.*

MacSween, A., 1985, *The Brochs, Duns and Enclosures of Skye,* in *Northern Archaeology,* Vols V and VI, 1984–5.

Miket, R. and Roberts, D.L., 1990, *The Mediaeval Castles of Skye and Lochalsh.*

Morrison, A., 1986, *The Chiefs of the Clan MacLeod.*

NicGumaraid, C. and M., 1974, *A' Choille Chiar.*

NicMhathain, S., 1931, *Dain Spioradail.*

Nicolson, J., 1989, *I Remember: Memoirs of Raasay.*

Reed, L., (undated) *The Soay of our Forefathers.*

Sharpe, R., 1978, *Raasay, A Study in Island History* (Documents and Sources).

Sharpe, R., 1982, *Raasay, A Study in Island History.*

Sillar, F.C. and Meyler, R., 1973, *Skye.*

Watt, E., 1972, *A' Bhratach Dhealrach.*

Watt, E., 1987, *Gun Fhois*

APPENDIX 12

PLACE NAMES AND MAP REFERENCES

Achtaleathan, Achtalean NG 468 461
Altavaig or Eilean Flodigarry NG 479 717
Annishader NG 432 511
Ardnish NG 672 239
Ardvasar 632 034
Aricharnach NG 555 276
Armadale NG 638 038
Ashaig NG 692 239
Baile Ghobhain, Balgown NG 386 690
Balmeanach, Braes NG 529 345
Balmeanach, Duirinish NG 322 434
Balmeanach, Raasay NG 560 409
Beal, Beil, Am Bile NG 503 445
Bealach Udal NG 755 206
Bealach, Trotternish NG 414 732
Ben Tianavaig NG 511 408
Bernisdale NG 402 503
Berreraig, Bearreraig NG 516 530
Bharkasaig, Bharcasaig NG 256 425
Blaven, Blabheinn NG 531 217
Bòrd Cruinn NG 368 794
Boreraig (Strath) NG 618 164

Bornaskitaig, Bornesketaig NG 376 716
Borreraig (Duirinish) NG 190 535
Borrodale NG 161 488
Borve NG 448 483
Brochel NG 585 463
Camusban NG 494 424
Camusfhionary, Camasunary NG 517 187
Camustianavaig NG 508 390
Carbost (Minginish) NG 380 317
Caroy NG 309 433
Castle Camus or Knock Castle NG 670 086
Clachan, Raasay NG 546 364
Claigean, Claigan NG 237 537
Coire na Creiche NG 439 257
Colbost NG 209 493
Corrichatachain, Corrie-chat-achan NG 622 226
Corrie, Corry NG 641 241
Crossal NG 455 320
Cuidreach NG 379 595
Druim nan Cleoc(hd) NG 538 292
Drumuie NG 456 464
Drynoch NG 406 317

Dun Ringell, Dun Ringill NG 561 171

Dun Sgathaich, Dun Scaich NG 595 119

Duntulm NG 414 742

Ebost, Eabost NG 317 392

Edinbane NG 345 509

Elgol NG 519 138

Eynort NG 379 266

Eyre NG 414 529

Eyre Point, Raasay NG 580 340

Fearns NG 588 355

Feorlig NG 299 436

Fernilea NG 365 339

Fiskavaig NG 327 340

Fladda Chuain, Fladaigh Chuain NG 361 812

Flodigarry NG 464 717

Galtrigill NG 181 544

Garrafad, Garafad NG 493 676

Gedintailor NG 521 352

Gesto NG 356 367

Glam NG 558 427

Glen Vargill, Glen Varragill NG 479 360

Glenbrittle NG 412 215

Glenhinnisdale, Glen Hinnisdal NG 406 577

Glenmor, Glenmore NG 435 402

Greshornish NG 341 540

Hallaig NG 591 383

Hallin NG 249 588

Hamera, Hamara NG 170 495

Harlosh NG 287 417

Harta Corrie NG 478 231

Healabhal NG 221 444

Holoman NG 554 398

Hungladder NG 391 711

Idigil, Idrigill (Duirinish) NG 251 364

Idigil, Idrigill (Uig) NG 376 636

Isay NG 219 566

Isle Ornsay, Isle Oransay NG 703 123

Kilbride NG 589 205

Kilchrist NG 616 201

Kildonan NG 354 540

Kilmaree, Kilmarie NG 549 173

Kilmartin (Staffin) NG 488 668

Kilmore, Cill Mhor NG 654 070

Kilmuir (nr Dunvegan) NG 259 472

Kilmuir (Trotternish) NG 382 704

Kilvaxter NG 385 696

Kingsborough, Kingsburgh NG 395 551

Kinlochainort NG 538 277

Krakinish, Kraiknish NG 371 235

Kylerhea NG 784 203

Liveras NG 643 242

Loch Duagrich NG 401 398

Loch Eishort NG 618 147

Loch Leathan NG 504 517

Loch Siant, Loch Sheanta NG 471 698

Lochbay NG 266 545

Lon Fearn, Lonfearn NG 520 620

Luib NG 563 278

Lyndale NG 368 547

MacLeod's Maidens

Manish NG 554 458

Marishader NG 492 639

Marsco NG 508 250

Meadle, Meadale NG 389 348

Mogstadt, Monkstadt NG 377 675

Mugarry, Mugeary NG 445 388

Ollach NG 513 367

Orbost NG 257 431

Ord NG 616 135

Osdale NG 240 443

Ose NG 312 409

Oskaig NG 550 381

Ostaig NG 647 059

Pabay NG 675 268

Peingown NG 401 715

Penichorran, Peinachorrain NG 525 331

Pooltiel NG 158 503

Rigg NG 519 565

Roag NG 272 439

Roisgil, Roskill NG 279 450

Rona NG 620 566

Rubh' an Dunain NG 387 162

Rubha Hunish NG 408 767

Sartil, Sartle NG 463 679

Scalpay NG 612 293 NG 458 678

Sconser NG 522 322

Score NG 401 725

Scorrybreck NG 496 449

Screapadale, Screapadal NG 580 444

Sgeir Mhor NG 493 433

Shulista NG 425 746

Sithean NG 629 224

Skerinish NG 410 523 GB

Skinidin NG 224 477

Skudaborg, Skudiburgh NG 372 648

Sligachan NG 489 297

Stein NG 263 566

Stenschol, Stenscholl NG 478 680

Strathaird NG 552 179

Suardal (Duirinish) NG 239 509

Suardal (Strath) NG 624 210

Suisnish NG 592 159

Suisnish, Raasay NG 553 343

Sullishader, NG 478 433

Talisker NG 324 299

Tarskavaig NG 589 097

Tormore NG 617 015

Torra Michaig, Tormichaig NG 536 316

Torrin NG 579 209

Totarder, Totardor NG 371 398

Totterome, Tottrome NG 507 541

Troday, Troddday NG 444 786

Trumpan NG 225 611

Tuasdale, Tusdale NG 357 250

Ullinish NG 325 377

Unish NG 237 657

Vatten NG 285 438

Waterstein NG 145 471

ALEXANDER NICOLSON – SELECT BIBLIOGRAPHY

History of Skye, First Edition, MacLaren, Glasgow, 1930. (Second edition of which was published by Maclean Press, Skye in 1994).

Mairi, Nighean Alasdair Ruaidh, delivered on 22 December, 1931, in '*The Active Gael, being Papers Read before the Gaelic Society of Glasgow*', Volume IV, Glasgow, 1934, pp. 114–140.

Modern Gaelic: A Basic Grammar, Archibald Sinclair, Glasgow, 1936.

Gaelic Riddles and Enigmas, Archibald Sinclair, Glasgow, 1938.

Am Breacadh; a Basic Gaelic Reader, Glasgow, A. Sinclair, 1939.

Comhairleach Sgiathanach, Seirbhis a' Chrùin, An Comunn Gaidhealach 1943, pp. 103–111.

Oideas na Cloinne, Archibald Sinclair, Glasgow, 1948.

Cumha Ni'n Dhomhnaill Riabhaich, Ossian, Glasgow University Ossianic Society, 1951, pp. 22–23.

Mairi Nighean Alasdair Ruaidh, Gairm, Aireamh 8, Glasgow, *An Samhradh*, 1954, pp. 316–317.

An Ite Sheunta, Gairm, June 1955, No 12, p. 305.

The MacBeths – Hereditary Physicians of the Highlands, in *The Transactions of the Gaelic Society of Glasgow*, Volume V, 1958, pp. 94–112.

Guidebook to Isle of Skye and Adjacent Islands, Archibald Sinclair, Glasgow. Various editions from 1931, including versions in which the publication was called *Handbook to the Isle of Skye*.

Manuscript of lectures on Gaelic Literature delivered by Alexander Nicolson at Jordanhill College, National Library of Scotland, Sorley Maclean Papers, Reference number MS.29732.

The Geology of Skye, in Glasgow Skye Association, *Souvenir Book of the Jubilee Gathering, St Andrew's Halls, Glasgow, 2nd December, 1921*, Celtic Press, Glasgow, 1921, pp. 31-47

BIBLIOGRAPHY

Adams, F., 1970, *The Clans, Septs and Regiments of the Scottish Highlands*, Revised by Innes, T.

Aikman, C.W.H., 1984 (see Livingstone, A.).

Anderson, J., 1885, *Notice of a Bronze Cauldron found with several small kegs of butter in a moss near Kyleakin, in Skye: with notes of other cauldrons of Bronze found in Scotland*, in *Proc Soc Antiq of Scotland*, Vol. XIX, 1884–5, pp. 309–15.

Barber, J., 1982, *A Wooden Bowl from Talisker Moor*, in *Proc Soc Antiq of Scotland*, Vol. CXII, 1982, pp. 578–9.

Barke, J. (Ed.), 1974, *Poems and Songs of Robert Burns*.

Beveridge, E., 1911, *North Uist*.

Blaikie, W.B., 1916, *Origins of the '45*.

Boswell, J., 1955, *Tour of the Hebrides*, Collins Edn.

Brichan, J.B. (Ed.), 1855, *Origines Parochales Scotticae (The Antiquities Ecclesiastical and Territorial of the Parishes of Scotland)*, Vol. II, part 2. (See Innes, C. (Ed.), 1854 for Vol. II, part 1).

Brown, P.H. (Ed.) 1911, Register of the Privy Council, 1673–6, 3rd Ser, Vol. 4.

Budge, D., 1976, *Baird An Eilean Sgiathanach: Clann-an-Aba, Throdairnis*, in *Trans Gaelic Soc of Inverness*, Vol. XLVIII, 1972–74, pp. 584–601.

Callander, J.G., 1921, *Report on the Excavation of Dun Beag, A Broch near Struan, Skye*, in *Proc Soc Antiq of Scotland*, Vol. LV, 1920–21, pp. 110–131.

Cameron, A., 1871 (See MacBain, A, and Kennedy, J).

Campbell, A., 1720 (See Campbell, H, 1926).

Campbell, A., 1948, *Kilberry Book of Ceol Mor*.

Campbell, H. (Ed.), 1926, *The Manuscript History of Craignish by Alexander Campbell, c. 1720*, in *Miscellany of the Scottish Hist Soc*, Vol. IV, 3rd series, pp. 187–292.

Campbell, J.F., 1872, *Leabhar na Feinne: Heroic Gaelic Ballads collected in Scotland chiefly from 1512 to 1871*, Vol. I

Campbell, J.L., 1984, *Highland Songs of the Forty-Five*.

Carmichael, A., 1928, *Ortha nan Gaidheal (Carmina Gadelica): Hymns and Incantations*, Vols I & II (Ed E Carmichael Watson)

Chambers, R., 1934, *History of the Rebellion of 1745–1746*.

Clarke, D.V., Cowie, T.G. and Foxon, A., 1985, *Symbols of Power at the Time of Stonehenge*.

Conellan, O. (Ed.), 1860, in *Trans Ossianic Soc (Dublin) for year 1857*, Vol. V

Cowan, I.B., 1978, *The Mediaeval Church in Argyll and the Isles*, in *Trans of Royal Scottish Church History Soc*, Vol. XX, pp. 15–29.

Craig, K.C., 1949, *Orain Luaidh Mairi Nighean Alasdair*, air an cruinneachadh le K.C. Craig.

Crone, B.A., *A Wooden Bowl from Loch a' Ghlinne Bhig, Bracadale, Skye*, forthcoming in *Proc Soc Antiq of Scotland*.

Curle, A.O., 1916, *An Account of the Ruins of the Broch of Dun Telve, Near Glenelg*. Excavated by HM Office of Works in 1914 in *Proc Soc Antiq of Scotland*, Vol. L, 1915-1916-21, pp. 241–254.

Curle, A.O., 1921, *The Broch of Dun Troddan, Glean Beag, Glenelg, Inverness-shire*, in *Proc Soc Antiq of Scotland*, Vol. LV, 1920–1921, pp. 83–94.

Dasent, W. (Ed.), 1894, *The Orkneyinga Saga and King Hacon's Saga*.

Donaldson, G. (Ed.), 1982, *Register of the Privy Seal of Scotland (1581–1584)*, Vol. 8.

Dughalach, A., 1829, *Orain, Marbhrannan agus Duanagan le Ailean Dughalach, filidh Mhic-ic-Alasdair*.

Edwards, D.H., 1881, *Modern Scottish Poets*.

Ewing, W.M. (Ed.), 1914, *Annals of the Free Church of Scotland 1843–1900*, Vols 1 and 2.

Forbes, D., 1698, *Family of Innes*.

Forbes, D., 1815, *Culloden Papers*.

Forbes, R., 1975, *The Lyon in Mourning*. 3 Volumes, Ed. Paton, H. (Reprint by Scottish Academic Press).

Gillies, D. (undated), *The Life of the Very Rev Roderick Macleod of Snizort, Skye*.

Gillies, E. (Ed.), 1786, *Sean Dain agus Orain Ghaidhealach (The Gillies Collection)*.

Goss, D., 1774, *Chronicon Maniae*, Vol. 2 (See also Munch, PA).

Grant, A., 1803, *Poems on Various Subjects*.

Grant, I.F., 1959, *The MacLeods – The History of a Clan*.

Gregory, D., 1881, *History of the Western Highlands and Isles of Scotland*.

Guthrie, E.J., 1885, *Old Scottish Customs (Local and General)*.

Henderson, G., 1911, *Survival of Belief among the Celts*.

Hennesey, W. (Ed.), 1887, *Annals of Ulster; Chronicles of Irish Affairs*, Vol. I.

Hennesey, W. (Ed.), 1893, *Annals of Ulster; Chronicles of Irish Affairs*, Vol. II.

Hennesey, W. (Ed.), 1895, *Annals of Ulster; Chronicles of Irish Affairs*, Vol. III.

Hennesey, W. (Ed.), 1901, *Annals of Ulster; Chronicles of Irish Affairs*, Vol. IV.

Hume-Brown, P. (Ed.), 1911, *Register of the Privy Council (1673–1676)*, 3rd Series, Vol. 4.(Ed.)

Huyshe, W., 1922, *Adamnan's Life of St Columba*.

Innes, C. (Ed.), 1850, *Origines Parochales Scotticae (The Antiquities Ecclesiastical and Territorial of the Parishes of Scotland)*, Vol. I.

Innes, C. (Ed.), 1854, *Origines Parochales Scotticae (The Antiquities Ecclesiastical and Territorial of the Parishes of Scotland)*, Vol. II, part 1 (See Brichan, JB (Ed.), 1855, for Vol. II, part 2).

Johnson, S., 1984, *A Journey to the Western Isles of Scotland* (Penguin Classics).

Knox, J., 1975, *A Tour through the Highlands of Scotland and the Hebride Isles in 1786*.

Laing, S. (Ed.), 1844, *Heimskringla Saga; Chronicle of the Kings of Norway* Vol. III (1914 Everyman Edition).

Lamont, D., 1913, *Strath, in Isle of Skye*.

Livingstone, A., Aikman, C.W.H. and Stuart Hart, B. (Eds), 1984, *Muster Roll of Prince Charles Edward Stuart's Army, 1745–46*.

MacBain, A. and Kennedy, J. (Eds),1892, *Reliquae Celticae, Texts, Papers*, Vol. I (Collected by Cameron LLD, A).

MacBain, A. and Kennedy, J. (Eds) 1894, *Reliquae Celticae, Texts, Papers*, Vol. II.

Mac-Bheathain, A. (Ed.), 1891, *Dain agus Orain Ghaidhlig le Mairi Nic-a-Phearsoin (Poems and Songs by Mary MacPherson)*.

MacCoinnich, E., 1967, *Da Bhard a Gearrloch anns an ochdamh linn deug*, in *Trans Gaelic Soc of Inverness*, Vol. XLIV, pp. 297–309.

MacCoinnich, I. (Ed.), 1834, *Orain Ghaelach le Uilleam Ros*.

MacDhòmhnuill, R., 1776, *Comh-chruinneachadh de Orain Ghaidhealach le Raonull MacDhomhnuill as an Eilean Eigg (The Eigg Collection), athleasaichte le Padruig Turner, 1809*.

MacDonald, A. and A., 1896, *The Clan Donald*, Vol. I.

MacDonald, A. and A., 1900, *The Clan Donald*, Vol. II.

MacDonald, A. and A., 1904, *The Clan Donald*, Vol. III.

MacDonald, A. and A., 1911, *MacDonald Collection of Gaelic Poetry*.

Macdonald, D., c. 1820, *A Collection of the ancient martial music of Caledonia called Piobaireachd, as performed on the Great Highland Bagpipe*.

MacDonald, D.J., 1978, *Clan Donald*.

MacDonald, H., 1847, *Fragments of a Manuscript History of the MacDonalds written in the Reign of Charles II*, in *Collectanea de Rebus Albanicis*. Iona Club, pp. 283–324.

MacDonald, P., 1784, *A Collection of Highland Vocal Airs by Patrick MacDonald*, Minister of Kilmore.

Macfarlane, W., 1900, *Macfarlane's Genealogical Collections, A General Collection Concerning Families in Scotland, made by Walter Macfarlane 1750–1755*. 2 vols, Scottish History Society, first series, No 33, Edited Clark, J.T.

MacGregor, A., 1907, *History of the Feuds and Conflicts among the Clans*.

MacInnes, J., 1899, *The Brave Sons of Skye*.

Macintosh, A.M., 1903, *Macintosh and Clan Chattan*.

MacIntosh, D., 1785, *A Collection of Gaelic Proverbs and Familiar Phrases accompanied with an English translation*.

Mackay, A., 1838, *A Collection of Ancient Piobaireachd or Highland Pipe Music*.

MacKay, J.G., 1922, *Social Life in Skye from Legend and Story*, in *Trans Gaelic Soc of Inverness*, Vol. XXIX, Part 1 (pp 260–90) and Part 2 (pp 335–54).

MacKay, J.G., 1924, *Social Life in Skye from Legend and Story*, in *Trans Gaelic Soc of Inverness*, Vol. XXX, Part 3 (pp 1–26) and Part 4 (pp 128–74).

McKay, M.M., 1980, *The Rev Dr John Walker's Report on the Hebrides of 1764 and 1771*.

MacKay, W. (Ed.), 1896, *Records of the Presbyteries of Inverness and Dingwall*.

(1643–1688) *Scottish Historical Society*, 1st Series, No 24.

Mackay, W. (Ed.), 1905, *Polichronicum seu Policratica or A True Genealogy of the Frasers* by Rev James Fraser, Minister of Wardlaw, now Kirkhill, in *Scottish History Society*, 1st Series.

MacKenzie, A., 1889, *History of the MacLeods, and Genealogies of the Principal Families*.

Mackenzie, A.M. (Ed.), 1964, *Orain Iain Luim: Songs of John MacDonald, Bard of Keppoch*, Scottish Gaelic Texts Society

MacKenzie, J., 1877, *Sar-obair nam Bard Gaelach or The Beauties of Gaelic Poetry* (4th edition), with an Historical introduction by James Logan.

Mackenzie, W.C., 1903, *The History of the Outer Hebrides*.

Mackie, E.W., 1967, *Dun Ardtreck*, in *Current Archaeology 2*, pp. 27–30.

Mackie, E.W., forthcoming, *A Corpus of Brochs*, in *Brit Archaeol Reports*.

Mackie, J.D., 1972, *A History of Scotland* (Pelican Series).

MacKinnon, D., 1885, *The Fernaig Manuscript* in *Trans Gaelic Soc of Inverness*, Vol. XI, 1884–85, pp. 311–39.

MacKinnon, D. and Morrison, A., 1968, *The MacLeods – The Genealogy of a Clan* – Section 1 (MacLeod Chiefs of Harris & Dunvegan).

Maclean, A., 1989, *The Summer Hunting of Seventeen forty-six*, in *Trans Gaelic Soc of Inverness*, Vol. LV, 1986–88, pp. 21–46.

MacLean, D., 1915, *Typographia Scoto Gadelica, or Books printed in The Gaelic of Scotland from the year 1567 to 1914*.

Maclean, N., 1945, *The Former Days*.

Maclean, S., 1943, *Dain do Eimhir*.

Maclean, S., 1977, *Some Raasay Traditions*, in *Trans Gaelic Soc of Inverness*, Vol. XLIX, 1974–76, pp. 377–97.

Maclean-Sinclair, A. (Ed.), 1898, *Na Baird Leathanach: The MacLean Bards*, Vol. I.

Maclean-Sinclair, A. (Ed.), 1900, *Na Baird Leathanach: The MacLean Bards*, Vol. II.

MacLeod, A, (Ed.), 1978, *The Songs of Duncan Ban Macintyre*, Scottish Gaelic Texts Society.

MacLeod, F.T., 1915, *Notes on Dun an Iadhard, a Broch near Dunvegan*, excavated by Countess Vincent Baillet de Latour, Uiginish Lodge, Skye, in *Proc Soc Antiq of Scotland*, Vol. XLIX, 1914–15, pp. 57–70.

MacLeod, J.N., 1922, *Domhnall nan Oran, am Bard Sgitheanach*, in *Trans Gaelic Soc of Inverness*, Vol. XXIX (1914 -19), pp. 119–33.

MacLeod, N., 1899, *Caraid nan Gaidheal (The Friend of the Gael)*.

MacLeod, N., 1899, *Beagan Dhuilleag bho Sheann Bhardachd Eilean a' Cheo*, in *Trans Gaelic Soc of Inverness*, Vol. XXI (1896–7), pp. 171–86.

MacLeod, R.C., 1927, *The MacLeods of Dunvegan (from the time of Leod to the end of the 17th century)*.

MacLeod, R.C., 1938, *The Book of Dunvegan*, Vol. I, 1340–1700.

MacLeod, R.C., 1939, *The Book of Dunvegan*, Vol. II, 1700–1920.

MacLeod, R.H., 1985, *The Independent Companies of the 1745 Rebellion*, in *Trans Gaelic Soc of Inverness*, Vol. LIII, 1982–84, pp. 310–93.

MacLeòid, D., 1811, *Orain Nuadh Ghaeleach*: Maille Ri Beagain do Cho-Chruinneachadh Urramach na'n Aireamh (author known as *Dòmhnall nan Oran*).

MacLeòid, N., 1924, *Clarsach an Doire: Dain, Orain is Sgeulachdan* (5th Edition).

MacMhathain, U., 1939, *Orain Iain MhicFhearchair: A bha' n a bhard aig Sir Seumas MacDhomhnaill*.

MacMhuirich, D. (Ed.), 1868, *An Duanaire – Co-thional ur de dh orain, de dhuanagan, etc*.

Mac na Ceardaich, G., 1879, *An t-Orannaiche (The Gaelic Songster) Co-thional taghte de dh'Orain, etc*.

MacQuarrie, A., 1987, *Kings, Lords and Abbots – Power and Patronage in the Mediaeval Monastery of Iona*, in *Trans Gaelic Soc of Inverness* Vol. LIV, 1984–86, pp. 355–375

MacSween, A., 1985, *The Brochs, Duns and Enclosures in Skye*, in *Northern Archaeol*, Vols 5 & 6, 1984–5

MacSween, M., 1959, *Transhumance in North Skye*, in *Scot Geog Magazine*, Sept 1959, pp. 75–88

MacSween, M. and Gailey, A., 1961, *Some Shielings in North Skye*, in *Bull Board of Celtic Stud*, Vol. 5, pp. 77–84

Maidment, J. (Ed.), 1845, *An account of Lewis and some of the other Western Isles from the Collections of Macfarlane of that ilk*, in *The Spottiswoode Miscellany*, Vol. II, pp. 333–58.

Martin, M., 1693, *A Description of the Western Islands of Scotland* (1st edition).

Martin, M., 1716, *A Description of the Western Islands of Scotland* (2nd edition), (Reprint, Thin, 1970).

Martlew, R., 1985, *The Excavation of Dun Flodigarry, Staffin, Isle of Skye* in *Glasgow Arch J*, Vol. 12, pp. 30–48.

Matheson, A., 1953, *Gleanings form the Dornie Manuscripts*, in *Trans Gaelic Soc of Inverness*, Vol. XLI, 1951–2, pp. 310–81.

Matheson, A. (Ed.), 1952, *Ortha nan Gaidheal (Carmina Gadelica): Hymns and Incantations*, Vol. V.

Matheson, A. (Ed.), 1971, *Ortha nan Gaidheal (Carmina Gadelica): Hymns and Incantations*, Vol. VI.

Matheson, W. (Ed.), 1970, *The Blind Harper (An Clarsair Dall): The Songs of Roderick Morison and his Music*, Scottish Gaelic Texts Society.

Matheson, W., 1981, *The MacLeods of Lewis*, in *Trans Gaelic Soc of Inverness*, Vol. LI, 1978–80, pp. 320–37.

Miket, R. and Roberts, D.L., 1990, *The Mediaeval Castles of Skye and Lochalsh*.

Mitchell, A., 1900, (See Macfarlane, W.).

Mitchell, A. (Ed.), 1906, *Geographical Collections relating to Scotland, made by Walter Macfarlane*, Vol. I, Scottish History Society, 1st Series.

Mitchell, A. (Ed.), 1907, *Geographical Collections relating to Scotland, made by Walter Macfarlane*, Vol. II, Scottish History Society, 1st Series, Vol. LII.

Mitchell, A. (Ed.), 1908, *Geographical Collections relating to Scotland, made by Walter Macfarlane*, Vol. III, (with Clark, J.T.) (Eds), Scottish History Society, 1st Series, Vol. LIII.

Morrison, A., 1968 (See Mackinnon, D.).

Morrison, H., 1899, *Songs and Poems in the Gaelic Language by Rob Donn*.

Munch, P.A. (Ed.), 1774, *Chronicon Manniae*. Revised by Goss, Rt. Rev. D.

Munro, J. and R.W. (Eds), 1986, *Acts of the Lords of the Isles (1336–1393)*, Scottish History Society

Munro, R.W. (Ed.), 1961, *Monro's Western Isles of Scotland*.

Nicholson, J.G., 1988, *The Clan Nicolson*, 2nd edition with new preface by Iain MacNeacail of MacNeacail and Scorrybreac, *Chief of the Highland Clan MacNeacail*.

Nicolson, A., 1958, *The MacBeaths – Hereditary Physicians of the Highlands*, in *Trans Gaelic Soc of Glasgow*, Vol. V, pp. 94–112.

Nicolson, A.W., (undated) *The Life of Donald Munro*, the Blind Fiddler who became Skye's most famous evangelist.

O'Baoill, C. (Ed.), 1972, *Bardachd Shilis na Ceapaich, c. 1660–c. 1729; Poems and Songs by Sileas MacDonald, c. 1660–c. 1729*, Scottish Gaelic Texts Society.

O' Rahilly, T.F., 1942, *A Hiberno-Scottish Family O' Muirgheasain*. Morrison, in Scottish Gaelic Studies, Vol. V, pp. 101–5

Pennant, T., 1774, *A Tour in Scotland and Voyage to the Hebrides*.

Ritchie, G. and A., 1985, *Scotland: Archaeology and Early History* (paperback edition).

Ritchie, J., 1941, *A Keg of 'Bog-butter' from Skye and its Contents*, in *Proc Soc Antiq of Scotland*, Vol. LXXV, 1940–41, pp. 5–22.

Robertson, A., 1919, *An t-Ogha Mor* (2nd edn. 1980).

Robertson, A., 1938, *Orain na Ceilidh*.

Robertson, A., 1940, *Cnoc an Fhradhairc*.

Ross, N., 1950, *Armageddon*.

Sacchaverell, W., 1859, *Accounts of the Isle of Man, its Inhabitants, Language, etc.*

Scott, W.L., 1934, *Excavation of Rudh' an Dunain Cave, Skye*, in *Proc Soc Antiq of Scotland*, Vol. LXVIII, 1933–4, pp. 200–223.

Sharp, E.A. (Ed.), 1896, *Lyra Celtica: An Anthology of Representative Celtic Poetry*.

Sinclair, A., 1879 (See Mac na Ceardaich, G.).

Skene, W.F., 1847, *Collectanea de Rebus Albanicis: General Papers relating to the Highlands of Scotland*. Iona Club.

Skene, W.F., 1886, *Celtic Scotland; History of Ancient Alban*, 2nd Edition, Vol. I.

Skene, W.F., 1887, *Celtic Scotland; History of Ancient Alban*, Vol. II.

Skene, W.F., 1890, *Celtic Scotland; History of Ancient Alban*, Vol. III.

Skene, W.F., 1902, *The Highlanders of Scotland, their Origins, History and Antiquities*, 2 parts.

Spottiswoode Society, The, *1845* (See Maidment, J., 1845).

Stevenson, J.H. (Ed.), 1984, *Register of the Great Seal, 1560–1568*.

Stewart, A., 1812, *Elements of Gaelic Grammar in Four Parts*.

Stewart, D., 1885, *Sketches of the Institutions and Customs of the Highlanders of Scotland*.

Stuart Hart, B., 1984 (See Livingstone, A.).

Turner, P. (Ed.), 1809, *Comh-chruinneachadh de Orain Ghaidhealach le Raonull MacDhomhnuill as an Eilean Eigg (The Eigg Collection) athleasaichte le Padruig Turner*.

Walker, J., 1812, *An Economical History of the Hebrides and Highlands of Scotland*, 2 vols.

Walker, J., 1980 (See McKay, M.M., 1980).

Warrand, D. (Ed.), 1923, *More Culloden Papers*, Vol. I.

Warrand, D. (Ed.), 1925, *More Culloden Papers*, Vol. II.

Warrand, D. (Ed.), 1927, *More Culloden Papers*, Vol. III.

Warrand, D. (Ed.), 1929, *More Culloden Papers*, Vol. IV.

Warrand, D. (Ed.), 1930, *More Culloden Papers*, Vol. V.

Watson, J.C. (Ed.), 1934, *Gaelic Songs of Mary MacLeod*, Scottish Gaelic Texts Society.

Watson, J.C. (Ed.), 1940, *Ortha nan Gaidheal (Carmina Gadelica): Hymns and Incantations*, Vol. III.

Watson, J.C. (Ed.), 1941, *Ortha nan Gaidheal (Carmina Gadelica): Hymns and Incantations*, Vol. IV.

Watson, W.J., 1922, *Classic Gaelic Poetry of Panegyric in Scotland*, in *Trans Gaelic Soc of Inverness*, Vol. XXIX, 1914–19, (poem on p. 212; article on pp. 194–235).

Watson, W.J. (Ed.), 1929, *Rosg Gaidhlig – Specimens of Gaelic Prose* (2nd edition).

Watson, W.J., 1932, *Bardachd Ghaidhlig: Specimens of Gaelic Poetry, 1550–1900* (2nd edition).

Watt, D.E.R., 1969, *Fastii Ecclesiae Scoticanea in medii aevi ad 1638*, Scottish Record Society New Series, Vol. I.

NOTES

1 The Bannatyne Manuscript (MS History of the MacLeods, in the Dunvegan Muniments) is believed to be the work of Sir William MacLeod Bannatyne, well known as an archaeologist, and son of Roderick, a great-grandson of Sir Norman MacLeod of Bernera. However, it was possibly re-written by Bannatyne William MacLeod of the Glendale family. Although the latter lived most of his life in India, he may have inherited a draft from his cousin, Sir William MacLeod Bannatyne. This Manuscript should not be confused with another manuscript of the same name. The Bannatyne Manuscript by George Bannatyne, was published in four volumes (1928–1934), Ed. Ritchie, WT (Scottish Text Society).

2 The Letterfearn Manuscript. Gregory D (1881, pp. 210–12, fn) refers to a Manuscript which he identifies as *the Letterfearn Manuscript*. This is unknown to the National Library of Scotland but, from Gregory's text, might equate with a manuscript history of the MacKenzies, known to have been in the possession of L MacKinnon of Letterfearn. It is known that Lachlan MacKinnon of Corrie also held Letterfearn (Cameron A, 1871, pp. 133, 135). The importance of this Manuscript to the present work is that it contains the sole reference to the Massacre of the MacLeod of Raasay heirs on the Island of Isay by *"Ruairi MacAllan Macleod, surnamed Nimhneach, ie venomous ..."*

INDEX

THE
PADDY
H🍀PKIRK
STORY

What the reviewers said:

Irresistibly engaging and packed with infectious enthusiasm.
Classic & Sports Car

A well-illustrated and complete story, nicely written and liberally laced with Hopkirk quotes.
The Automobile

Disarmingly honest.
Motorsport News

Full of amusing detail about the jolly Irishman who over five decades gained outstanding successes in every kind of event.
Motor Sport

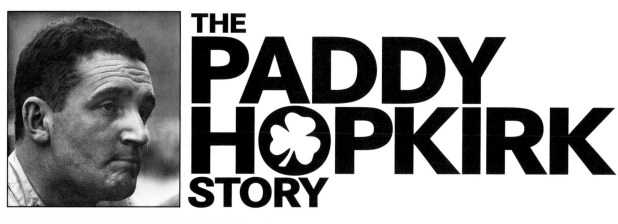

THE PADDY HOPKIRK STORY

A DASH OF THE IRISH

Paddy Hopkirk

June 2012

Haynes

Bill Price WITH **Paddy Hopkirk**

First published in July 2005
Reprinted 2006

A catalogue record for this book is available
from the British Library

ISBN 1 84425 110 1

Library of Congress catalog card no. 2005925519

Published by Haynes Publishing,
Sparkford, Yeovil, Somerset, BA22 7JJ, UK

Tel: 01963 442030 Fax: 01963 440001
Int. tel: +44 1963 442030 Int. fax: +44 1963 440001
E-mail: sales@haynes.co.uk
Website: www.haynes.co.uk

Haynes North America Inc., 861 Lawrence Drive,
Newbury Park, California 91320, USA

Edited and expanded by Jon Pressnell
Designed by Richard Parsons
Printed and bound in Great Britain
by J. H. Haynes & Co. Ltd, Sparkford

Contents

Acknowledgements

Paddy on the 1969 Circuit of Ireland; author Bill Price is beside him, in the rally jacket, pondering on a misfire afflicting the special ultra-lightweight Mini. (Esler Crawford)

When researching the rally and race career of a driver with such a long history it was necessary to obtain the help of many people. I am most grateful for the assistance I have had from Paddy's family and from the following, who in some cases have also loaned or supplied photographs:

Kathy Ager, Peter Allen, Autopics, Jonathan Balck, Raymond Baxter, Hugh Bishop, BMIHT, John Brigden, Peter Browning, Maurice Bryan, Bernard Cahier, Willy Cave, Garry Chapman, Rootes photographer H R Clayton, Jeremy Coulter, Beatty Crawford, Esler Crawford, Ron Crellin, Brian Culcheth, Dan Daley, Andy Dawson, Paul Easter, John Edmund, John Evans, Norman Ewing, Robin Eyre-Maunsell, Nick Faure, Brian Foley, Tony Fowkes, Foto Jelinek, Ernie Garbutt, Lewis Garrad, Richard Grant, Den Green, Ian Hall, Charles Harbord, Chris Harvey, Justin Harrington, Terry Harryman, Andrew Hedges, Eric Hopkirk, Jenny Hopkirk, Kate Hopkirk, Patrick Hopkirk, William Hopkirk, Mike Hughes, Arthur Jolley, Peter Jopp, Sydney Jordan, Robs Lamplough, LAT Photographic, Sandy Lawson, Joyce Liddon, Tim Loakes, Bobby Longmuir, Stephen Layton, Tony Mason, Ernest McMillen, Wynne Mitchell, Larry Mooney, Bob Montgomery, Brian Moylan, Eithne Murray, Chris Nash, The National Motor Museum, Peter O'Gorman, Photo Erpe, Alec Poole, Frederic Reydellet, Paul Richardson, Peter Riley, Graham Robson, Maurice Rowe, The Royal Irish Automobile Club, Michael Taylor, Simon Thomas, Emma Scott, Fiona Scott, Guy Smith, Michael Turner, Stuart Turner, The Ulster Automobile Club, Patrick Vanson, Brian Waddell, Bob Whittington, Gerald Wiffen, Mike Wood, Philip Young, Robert Young, Alan Zafer.

I am also grateful to the book's editor, Jon Pressnell, for the extensive additional interview material he supplied.

I hope I have not missed too many names; if I have, you will know, and I trust you will accept my thanks and apologies.

Bill Price

Foreword

Paddy Hopkirk is one of those evergreen people who has sustained a reputation, a style, an approachability, a charm and a recognition which seems to have gone on forever and which also looks like it will never end.

I have been lucky enough to have known Paddy since the early '60s when I first met him at Jim Clark's farm in the borders of Scotland to celebrate a birthday. Paddy was a big name then, and now, 40 years later, the name of Paddy Hopkirk still has amazing power, even with younger enthusiasts.

He was, of course, a wonderful rally driver, giantly successful in his prowess behind the wheel, particularly that of Minis, something that is stamped in the annals of motorsport's history. But he did race successfully also – instantly recognisable in a Mini, particularly in my mind coming through Woodcote Corner at Silverstone, his head cocked to one side with his Herbert Johnson crash-helmet at a jaunty angle.

Paddy's success in business over the years has also allowed him to continue to grow and progress beyond the driving-gloves-and-crash-helmet period of his life, but more than anything else that Irish charm has endeared him to so many people over the years that, no matter where he goes around the world, he has friends, and if you are lucky enough to spend time with him, you will be mesmerised by the many memories and tales that he so vividly recounts.

He still keeps up a hectic and busy business life, has a very wide range of friends in every walk of life and with Jenny, his wife, currently being High Sheriff of Buckinghamshire, this provides him with a new dimension in which to exercise his mind and pride.

Paddy was a tough competitor and unlike an awful lot of other people who have won a lot, carried his charm, which was always disarming, with great style.

Paddy Hopkirk is a friend whom I am very happy to boast about. I am sure the readers of this book will enjoy enormously the tales told by such an interesting and successful man.

Sir Jackie Stewart OBE

Photo courtesy of Eoin Young.

Chapter 1

In the beginning

The early years

Patrick Peter Barron Hopkirk was born at St Clair, 29 Windsor Avenue, Belfast, on 14 April 1933. His mother Kathleen had married Captain Francis Cecil Hopkirk, an engineer in the British Army who had spent some time building the railways in India. Paddy had two sisters, Eithne and Elsie, and two brothers, Frank and Eric. His mother in all had eight children, but three died after birth, leaving Paddy the youngest of the five surviving children.

"Like many 'last born', Paddy was probably a little spoilt as a baby," recalls his brother Eric. "In 1943 he became ill with a serious kidney infection and was in bed for what seemed months. Father brought in a specialist who did not seem to be able to sort the problem out, so he found another doctor and eventually Paddy recovered. I remember how thin he looked, after being poorly for so long".

During the War the family had moved to Cairnbin, at Whitehouse, on the north side of Belfast. Francis Hopkirk had a wonderful garden with six greenhouses and grew considerable quantities of tomatoes, cucumbers and grapes. "I took grapes round to the local clergyman as there always seemed to be so many," says Paddy. "I also remember being taken down into the cellar during an air raid, and sheltering under our billiard table. Dad later built a thick concrete shelter down there – he was a very practical man".

Paddy's brothers and sisters (left to right) Paddy, Eithne, Elsie, Eric and Frank – back of St Clair, March snow 1936. (Paddy Hopkirk)

Ulster and Southern Ireland: a world of difference

The Ireland of Paddy's youth and young adulthood was a very different place from the Ireland of today – and this was reflected in the motoring scene of the time.

"Northern Ireland was very much more like England, while the South was much more of a farming community. The cars weren't well kept – if you dinged your car you didn't worry about it. The Northerners were more like Scots – you always polished your car at the weekend. Down in the South they were more interested in getting from one horse-race to the next, or from one pub to the next. Northerners were always dapper and well-dressed – we were known in the Republic as 'The Black Northerners'.

"We used to think we were superior to the Southerners. If you saw a nice shiny car in Dublin, with spotlights and a couple of car club badges on it, it nearly always had a Northern plate. When it came to the Circuit of Ireland, this was organised by the Ulster Automobile Club. Again it was the Northern Irish coming in.

"There were quite a few well-off enthusiasts in Dublin in the Royal Irish Automobile Club, such as Cecil Vard and Jack Tuohey, who were great friends of mine.

"When I was selling Toyotas in Northern Ireland, 84 per cent of our employees were non-Catholic. Maybe this was because there were more non-Catholics working in the retail motor industry overall."

Paddy was soon on four wheels. "There was a steep hill in Whitehouse Park next door and I had a 'guider' – a trolley with four pram wheels and rope steering – and got push-started down this hill, which was quite exciting".

The family bought a house in Portrush on the northern coast, to get away from the danger of bombing. Eithne and Elsie both went to Armagh Convent. When Eithne wanted to get a job, her father would not let her – he persuaded her to study domestic economy, and she became a very good cook and used to cook for the whole family at home. This was certainly appreciated by Francis Hopkirk, recalls Paddy. "We all ate very well – my Dad liked his food and a drop of good wine". Elsie, meanwhile, did an art and dress-designing course at Belfast Technical College, married an Irishman and went to live in Northern Rhodesia for several years.

Paddy grew up in comfortable conditions, but in reality the family was not part of the moneyed classes. "We looked prosperous, and everybody thought we were well-off. Dad was very keen on driving, on cars, and all mechanical things, and he had a couple of Rolls-Royces during the war – not both at the same time – so we would have appeared prosperous. We lived in a very nice house and we lived very well, but in fact when Dad died

there was very little there. I would say 'God Bless Him', because he spent his money on bringing his family up, and not on himself. He spent money on our education, and we were very well educated – we went to public schools in Ireland, and to university."

Paddy's mother and father, Kathleen and Francis Cecil Hopkirk. (Paddy Hopkirk)

The young Paddy reclining aboard his father's motor cruiser, the Cairnbin; *boats of one sort or another were an integral part of Paddy's youth in Northern Ireland, and a passion he returned to in later life. (Paddy Hopkirk)*

Paddy started his education at the preparatory school at the Fortwilliam Park convent and then at St Malachy's College in Belfast. In 1945 he followed his brothers to Clongowes Wood College, at Naas in County Kildare, where he was a boarder until 1949.

"This was pretty much Ireland's Eton," says Paddy of this somewhat stern Jesuit institution. The staff there were quite strict and if you stepped out of line you would be punished by the priests, who would slap you with this leather implement. If you were caught smoking you were given 'twice nine' – 18 strokes with a 'pandy bat' on your backside, which wasn't very pleasant!" His time there, he says, did not leave him with any strong religious beliefs. "I'm not very pro-Jesuit at all. I married a non-Catholic, and I regret to say I didn't watch the Pope's funeral. I'm not anything really. I think I'm a good Christian, and I see myself as more a Catholic than a non-Catholic – one good thing about the Catholic religion, and something it shares with the Jewish religion, is that I think it teaches strong family unity. The family unit is breaking down in our society, and I think that's what's going wrong. We were taught you should stay married to one person, and keep it in your trousers."

Frank, meanwhile – "much cleverer than me," according to Paddy – progressed to Queen's University and studied law, becoming a young barrister, while Eric went to Trinity College Dublin to study engineering, becoming a civil engineer.

"I played cricket, rugby and tennis at school and also did some sprinting, but wasn't that good at any of them with the exception of tennis and running," remembers Paddy of these days. "I transferred to Garvey's College in Belfast, where I passed the London Matriculation which was my passport into Trinity College Dublin."

Paddy was good with his hands, remembers brother Eric, who recalls some amazing Meccano constructions Paddy created. But soon there was another hobby – and one that brought to the fore another of Paddy's natural aptitudes. "There was an aero-modellers club and I took up building aeroplanes, some of them control-line models – we had a special room for laying out the plans and glueing all this balsa wood together. I became head of this club and I used to buy the kits from a model supplier in Cirencester. I used to get a discount and sold them on to members, making a small profit – I suppose I was already a bit of a wheeler-dealer, and this must have been the first sign of my business instincts".

A first taste of power – in an old bath-chair

As a schoolboy Paddy had his first taste of powered transport – a motorised bath-chair called a Harding bequeathed to him by the clergyman to whom he had delivered grapes during the war. This eccentric device was powered by a 250cc JAP engine, with a little drip-feed oil tank above it, a motorcycle three-speed gearbox, tiller steering, and braking only on the rear wheels. It was, remembers Paddy, something of a challenge to drive. "It was rather unstable, but with the rear-wheel brakes I soon got into the habit of turning it by slapping on the handbrake. It only had the chain drive to one rear wheel so when you let the clutch out quickly it took off to the left! I think it was what made me a good driver. It's like skiing – if you start when you're young, you're usually better."

This was all with the approval of the boys' father, says Eric Hopkirk. "There was a house opposite ours which housed German PoWs in Nissen huts in the grounds and which had a long drive. Father obtained permission for us to drive the Harding round the grounds, which was where Paddy started to learn car control". All the brothers played together with the car, remembers Paddy. "Frank drove the Harding on the public highway first, because I didn't have a licence. I remember once setting off with Frank for Portrush, about 60 miles away, and breaking down with overheating before we got halfway!"

Amazingly, Paddy found and purchased this very Harding, some years ago, and it is now awaiting restoration. "I'd been on the John Dunn radio show, and John had asked me how I'd started driving, and I'd told him about the Harding. The next day somebody rang up the BBC and said they had a Harding. They were in Dulwich, in London, and the Harding had apparently been thrown out by somebody in Belfast. I went to Dulwich, and this guy had his little council house. He had motorcycles in the bedroom, in the dining room, in the front room – he was mad about restoring motorcycles. And he had this Harding, in bits, in boxes. I looked in the boxes, and there was the numberplate – 'IJ 9670'. It was my old bath-chair. I bought it, and unfortunately it's still lying in crates in my barn waiting to be restored."

Motorcycle days

Useful trainer though the Harding was, there were soon other attractions: when he was 15, Paddy graduated to motorised transport of his own, acquiring a bicycle equipped with a clip-on engine behind the saddle, with friction drive to the rear tyre. "Drive was via a roller – when you operated the clutch it went down onto the tyre. It was awful, but it allowed me onto the road."

After the war, Paddy's father had turned to civil engineering and had became Managing Director of Tennant's Tar Distillers in Belfast, a company specialising in the supply of bitumen and tar to contractors and county councils in Northern Ireland. By now, the family had moved to a big house in Somerton Road back in Belfast, with a tennis court and a long drive where Paddy could practise his driving, and in 1949, at the age of sixteen, he decided to take up motorcycling.

His parents were worried about his safety and Paddy remembers how his father persuaded him that a motorcycle combination would be more appropriate. "I couldn't wait to get a motorcycle but my Dad didn't want me to have one, and bought a big secondhand Triumph 650 'twin' from a place in Holywood. It was fitted with a heavy sidecar, which Dad insisted on – rightly so. Motorcycles are dangerous things, and that was especially so in the Belfast of that time, with its cobbles and tramlines. Crossing the tramlines on a bicycle or a motorbike on those cobbled streets was something special!

"The Triumph had a gate change on the side of the petrol tank. My brother took me down

Paddy (centre), with friends from the Clongowes school aero-modellers club, of which he was the head; he bought the balsa kits at a discount, and sold them on at a modest profit. (Paddy Hopkirk)

Paddy's first four-wheeled motoring was at the helm of this 1922 Harding invalid carriage, which had a 250cc JAP engine driving one rear wheel by chain. (Paddy Hopkirk)

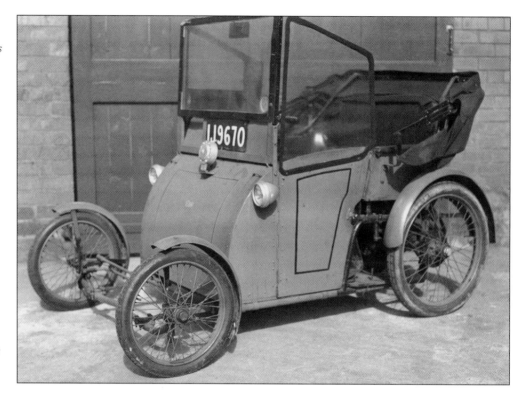

Paddy with the Harding; the JAP engine and chain drive are clearly visible. (Paddy Hopkirk)

to collect it and I paid over the money and then drove it back to Belfast. When we got home he told me I drove it much too fast because he had seen me getting it sideways on the cobblestones…"

Paddy used the Triumph as daily transport to go to Garvey College on the other side of Belfast. "The motorcyle-and-sidecar was a great machine. You could steer it with your body, with the accelerator, or with the brakes. A 'combination' is a great piece of kit. It teaches you a lot about handling – especially not to let the sidecar come up on a left-hand bend! It was good fun…"

By now Paddy was developing an interest in motor sport and was often seen around Belfast co-driving in an MG TC and then a TD with his friend Bobby McMillan. "His family was in the steel erection business, and he had more money than I did. The TD was quite modern, with its independent front suspension, but the TC was something else. If you changed direction when going backwards, the front came round. The kingpins were very angled, so the car would centralise when you were driving. But when you went the other way the opposite happened – it tried to steer one way or the other. It was a very hard car to do driving tests in – although in its day I'm sure it was regarded as a great bit of engineering."

In passing the London 'matric' exam, Paddy qualified for a place at university and in 1951 he decided to take up Engineering at Trinity College Dublin. "Trinity was a Protestant university, and normally special permission would have to be granted for a Catholic to take a place there. As I didn't ask for permission, this was probably the first time that I was ex-communicated!"

Initially there was no place to read Engineering, so the first year saw Paddy reading Agriculture, lodging in digs at 88 Lower Baggott Street run by two old spinsters, one of whom seemed to be drunk most of the time and used to hide gin bottles under her chair. The 650 Triumph was now replaced by a new Triumph Thunderbird 650cc 'twin' with sprung rear hub. Paddy found the new bike a big improvement, even if the sprung hub was hardly a great advance, in terms of rear suspension. "The bike had a good headlamp and was great for driving at night. Father, very wisely, insisted that a sidecar – a Watsonian – be fitted to this machine as well".

Paddy kept the Triumph in Belfast and didn't take it to Dublin. During the 1951 university vacation, he embarked on a tour of Europe with the Triumph combination, accompanied by his law-student friend John Gullery, who was at Queens University. "I remember going over on the ferry to Stranraer complete with our tent and camping gear and a pressure cooker. These cookers were all the rage and we found it great for camping, as you could put all the food in it and in no time it was cooked. About halfway between Stranraer and Carlisle, at Castle Douglas, we stopped for the night. After a good camp meal we went into town, found the local dance hall and ended up well oiled.

"What we hadn't realised was that we had set up camp near a lake, and in the middle of the night I remember waking up and hearing this noise in the tent. I shone my torch and was petrified to see a large water rat consuming the remains of our food. I leapt into the air screaming, taking the tent, tent poles and guy ropes with me. We didn't get much sleep that night! I wrote a diary, calling it *Nine Countries on Three Wheels*, as a photographic record of this six-week adventure.

"Our trip took us to Dover, down through France to Biarritz, Spain and Portugal, back to France along the south coast, and then into Italy – visiting the leaning tower at Pisa and then going on to Rome. We went as far south as Naples and then headed north into Austria, visiting Innsbruck and Klagenfurt, over the Grossglockner Pass, to Lichtenstein and Switzerland, through France via Reims to

Paddy with his second side-car combination, the Triumph Thunderbird 650cc 'twin', with its sprung-hub rear, and its Watsonian 'chair'. (Paddy Hopkirk)

home, covering a total of 7000 miles. We didn't camp all the time and often used youth hostels for overnight accommodation. After crossing the Channel, on the way home somewhere in Kent, we had two punctures and with the help of a friendly AA man, who also gave us a bed for the night, we got it fixed. In those long-gone days the whole trip was quite an adventure for two 18-year-old students on a motorcycle combination!"

Paddy's first real car, an Austin Seven Chummy, registration number CMM 463, outside the family house in Belfast. (Paddy Hopkirk)

On to four wheels: Paddy and his Austin Seven

The move from motorcycle to four wheels came with the purchase of an Austin Seven Chummy from a Belfast barrister friend of Paddy's brother Frank. "Ah! The 'Saucepan Seven' – it had the registration number CMM 463, and the girls used to look at the number plate and call it the Cement Mixing Machine," remembers Paddy. "I took it to bits and repainted it. I learnt about re-cellulosing and engineering, and I took it completely to bits. When I'd finished, it was immaculate. Austin Sevens had quarter-elliptic springs at the back and when you went round a corner one spring became longer than the other, and you got rear-wheel steering. I had huge tyres on the back, too, and I think that made its handling even worse.

"I recall an engine blow-up when a connecting rod went through the crankcase, known as putting a leg out of bed. A guy said he'd repair it, and we were in fact able to patch the hole. He was an aluminium welder somewhere in Belfast – I think he worked at the shipyard. The engine may have had a skimmed head, if I recall correctly – and it probably had a straight-through exhaust, to make you think you were going faster than you really were...

"I suppose I had the Austin because I could

Paddy (second right) at a black-tie party in Belfast, with then girlfriend Dierdre Clark (third right) who was also at Trinity; sister Elsie Hopkirk is on the far left, with her future husband, and Bobby McMillan, whose MGs Paddy shared, is in the centre. (Paddy Hopkirk)

afford it. I have good memories of it, because it used to take me to Dublin – a hundred miles away. I used to do it in two-and-a-bit hours. I knew the road like the back of my hand, and it was a fairly good road. I think I even kissed a couple of girls in it – or tried to. It was like my own little house. When you're a kid and you have a tree-house, you get into it and it's your little home. That's how the Austin was for me. At that time of my life it was a coveted car. I remember seeing my girlfriend off, getting into the car on a wet night, in the rain and with the wiper going, lights on, and it bringing me home. It was a great comrade. You know that independent feeling you get when you're a kid, and you have your own power, your own independence..."

After he had rebuilt the little Austin Paddy entered some local rallies, this marking the start of his career as a rally driver. Maurice Bryan was also at Trinity and he recalls his first meeting with Paddy on the 1952 Droicheadnua Bridge Night Trial. "I was assisting with the recovery of an MG Y-type which had gone into a bog when Paddy came along in his Austin Seven with its maroon mudguards. I soon realised that he was a rather jolly person with a definite sense of humour."

The first rally Paddy competed in as driver was an Ulster Automobile Club Trial on a Saturday afternoon which consisted of 'plot-and-bash' map references and then driving tests on the public roads. These events were the backbone of Irish motorsport, says Paddy. "You'd meet at a pub, which was the starting point. They'd hand you a set of map references, and you'd rush to your car and plot the references onto the map, and then you'd got to drive to these points. It was good fun for the navigators! Then you'd get to a crossroads in the middle of the Wicklow mountains, say, and they'd just close the road. There were no police or anything, and they'd put down chalk lines and pylons, and you had to drive up and round and reverse and you were timed to the second. The winners were those who had a combination of being 'clean' on the road and had the fastest times on the driving tests."

Driving tests became Paddy's forte – that fooling around in the Harding had borne fruit. "Driving tests are a wonderful way of testing someone's driving ability and their brain-to-hand coordination without having to spend much money," he says today. "I think if you can do driving tests well you can handle a car well. I'm not saying you'll be a Formula 1 winner, but it's a good way of finding out if someone has the ability to drive.

"Northern Ireland was built on it – we were so good at it. We won the Ken Wharton Trophy every year, against England, Wales and Scotland. We were light years ahead on

Paddy's first win was with this Volkswagen Beetle, on the 1953 Cairncastle Hill Climb. (Paddy Hopkirk)

In a newer Volkswagen Beetle on a 1954 university rally just on the outskirts of Dublin, in snowy conditions. (Paddy Hopkirk)

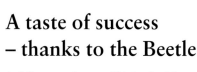

handbraking, going backwards, and throwing the front end, because we all just did it so much. One year for the Ken Wharton I was captain of the Northern Ireland team, and we came to Droitwich in the Midlands, and we were eight seconds behind on the last test. It was on TV, Raymond Baxter was commentating, and the whole of Northern Ireland was watching. There was a box you had to go backwards into, and do a three-point turn and come out again. I was in an Austin-Healey Sprite. I went in flat-out. I remember I closed my eyes, flicked the front end – and did a '180'. I kept my foot down and came out again – nine seconds off everybody else's time. We won the Trophy, and I went back to Belfast with the rest of the team to a heroes' welcome."

Paddy was able to transfer to Engineering – which was a four-year course – for his second year, but soon after, in 1952, he dropped out of university. "I wasn't very academic, and by then I'd joined the Ulster Automobile Club and I wanted to spend more time rallying," he says. "Father was wonderful and didn't try to stop me leaving Trinity, although he must have been disappointed when he realised that I was more interested in cars".

A taste of success – thanks to the Beetle

A fellow student at Trinity had been Michael O'Flaherty, who was also reading Agriculture. He was the son of Stephen O'Flaherty, who owned and ran the Dublin VW importer, Motor

The driving test tricks that make for a winner

Taken in 1955, during the Sligo Trial, this photo shows Paddy is in an oval-window Beetle, tackling a reversing test. "That's how we used to hang out of the windows on driving tests," he says. "How did we do that? If I tried today I'd crick my neck. But we were really good. We could judge the tests so well. What we'd do was put a bit of tape in our sightline on the front mudguard. If that bit of tape crossed the line you knew that was the centre of the wheel crossing the line, so you'd save a second or two there..."

Distributors, which had a CKD assembly plant at Ballsbridge – renamed 'Testicle Viaduct' by Paddy's crowd. In 1952, to finance his rallying, Paddy got a job as a car salesman with their retail outlet Ballsbridge Motors, which was owned by Motor Distributors. He was soon rallying with a Beetle, as he recalls.

"The VW was a very good car in those days, especially in driving tests, as it had the engine over the rear wheels. It was a very strong car, and I won a lot of events in it. The suspension was marvellous. With its independent rear and the rear engine it handled like a dream over the rough roads. The other cars had suspension with a solid rear axle, and over rough roads they weren't as good. In the South of Ireland the roads were very rough – the asphalt roads at the time were more in the North. We had things like the 'Cork 20' Trial, which was 20 hours of really dirty roads all over Co Cork and Co Kerry, all through the night – the roads were called 'boreens', and were the little white roads on the map, 'boreen' being the Irish word for 'little road'.

"I worked with Pat Moylett, who was a lovely man, selling mainly VWs and Mercedes. I think I was a good salesman, and it was a good job – it kept me talking cars, and I met some nice people in Dublin. The job gave me the advantage of getting my car serviced and so on at the right price, and I was co-driver for Michael O'Flaherty on various events. Stephen was very good to me and loaned me a Beetle on occasions. I eventually bought a secondhand 1131cc Beetle locally, the one with the split rear window, and I used this in trials and auto-tests. I won my first prize in the Beetle, in the Cairncastle hill climb, and was offered my first free car from

Volkswagen for the 1953 Circuit of Ireland – from Isaac Agnew, who was the Belfast VW importer."

This was the first of many Circuits in which Paddy competed, the entry fee in 1953 being three guineas for members of the UAC. The following year Paddy – by then working for Paddy Beggin at Dublin's B & K Motors – had one of his first successes on a major event when on the 1954 Circuit of Ireland he led the event on the first day in his Beetle, going on to finish second in class. At the garage test at Bangor, Paddy made fastest time against potentially much more powerful cars.

Success in the event was important in putting Paddy in the public eye. "Competition driving and rallying in Ireland was a bit like football is today in England. It was a bit like in Finland, where if you were a good rally driver you got noticed and got a lot of publicity in the papers. And the Circuit of Ireland was the big one – a very tough rally with long distances and night driving. It was a well-run event, with wonderful roads and wonderful tests. It was held over Easter, and all the press came to Killarney for the weekend, just as the international press all congregated in Monte Carlo for the Monte. Every journalist in Ireland was in Killarney, looking for a story, so it automatically generated good publicity. It was Ireland's equivalent to the Monte Carlo or the RAC Rally, and the roads were quite unique. On the Sunday we'd go to beautiful places such as the Tim Healy Pass, so it was good for photographers as well as journalists – and there was always a hell of a good party in Killarney afterwards! "

As a regular competitor, Paddy soon became involved in motor club activities and in 1954,

The top Beetle men at a rally in the west of Ireland. Left to right are Heber McMahon, Paddy, and T P O'Connell. (LAT)

In the Wicklow Mountains on the 1955 MG Car Club Trial, with a nice clean Volkswagen Beetle; the co-driver is John Garvey, who was also at Trinity. (Paddy Hopkirk)

at the AGM of the Dublin University Motor Cycle & Light Car Club, Paddy was elected honorary treasurer. "It was a very casual club run by active undergraduates, and with Paddy's sense of humour the finances sometimes looked a bit haphazard!," remembers Arthur Jolley.

Brothers Frank and Eric were very keen yachtsmen in the family 17-ton ocean-racing yacht *Glance*, and were regular competitors in races such as the Fastnet, where one year they were dismasted. Paddy was an occasional crew member and was on board during two or three races, including the Cowes to Benodet race and the 1954 Cowes to La Coruna race, in which the Hopkirks won their class. Paddy had a strong stomach and did not suffer much

from sea sickness. "When you are ill at sea, they say there are two stages of sea sickness. In the first you're worried in case you are going to die, and in the second you're worried in case you are not! Once while we were becalmed in absolutely flat seas in the middle of the Bay of Biscay we spotted some French tuna-fishing boats and when one came into range we shouted 'Avez-vous un poisson s'il vous plaît?' and they shouted 'Oui, oui'. We held up a bottle of gin. We threw a line across and they attached a bucket to it and we hauled it in with this huge tuna fish in it and we sent back a bottle of gin! They shouted 'fantastique!' – and we had tuna to eat for days". Eric Hopkirk remembers the incident well. "When we got ashore we thought we'd been ripped off, but then we found out that a whole tuna was worth much more than a bottle of gin."

One step up: Paddy and his TR2

During his time at Trinity, Paddy had been friendly with Matt McQuaid, whose brother was the Archbishop of Dublin and Primate of All Ireland. Matt ran the Standard-Triumph assembly plant in Dublin, and in 1955 Paddy was offered a Triumph TR2 at the right price. "The roads weren't that good in the '50s but I used to drive home to Belfast at the weekends in the Triumph flat-out – it was great, and it was certainly a good bird-puller! Matt kept mentioning my name to Ken Richardson, team manager of the Triumph rally team, and this may have helped get my name known in Coventry."

Paddy contested a number of events in the green TR2, including road races at Phoenix Park, Kirkistown and Leinster, and the Craigantlet Hill Climb as well as trials and rallies, and met with some success. "The TR2 was outstanding in its day – it was strong and simple, and it was quick and lovely to drive. I surprised myself at how well I did in it at Phoenix Park, and it was also a good car for driving tests. It was less good, though, on rallies that had very rough roads – the solid rear axle didn't do it any favours."

The 1955 Phoenix Park race meeting was his first outing in the Triumph. It was at this event that Paddy showed that he could be just as much a force to be reckoned with in Irish racing as he was in rallies and trials. His new acquisition went well, but after winning Heat

Two the car unfortunately suffered a broken throttle linkage in the final.

In the Leinster Trophy race there were no fewer than eight TR2s running, but Paddy won the TR2 battle despite mounting the pavement at one stage, finishing fourth overall. "The Belfast Triumph distributor was driving a TR2. He was just in front of me and he went off the road and turned the car over, being quite badly injured. It was a downhill bit and I have always felt a bit guilty. I was perhaps pushing him a bit because my car was not as fast on the level parts of the course."

To participate in motor sport at this level didn't require anything to speak of in the way of modifications to the Triumph, says Paddy. "I don't think I did a thing to the engine – I just got in the car and drove it. That's what has changed these days – competition cars are so different from those you can buy. In our day it was just a question of blowing the tyres up a bit and going and racing it. Certainly my cars were probably less prepared than a lot of other people's – I didn't have the money and I didn't have the time. But I've always believed that the result rests with the driver – especially downhill. It's going downhill that tests people, whether it's Schumacher or anyone else. If you can drive downhill quickly on a loose road, it doesn't matter what car you've got. A well-driven 2CV can go as quickly downhill on the loose as a Porsche. It's all about balance – a bit like skiing."

In the 1955 Craigantlet Hill Climb, Paddy was competing against insurance broker Ernest McMillen, also in a TR2, but his friend Ernest – "quite a driver" – got the better of him this time, winning the class. For that year's 1000-mile Circuit of Ireland Paddy reverted to a Volkswagen, on loan from Belfast dealer Agnews. With stockbroker John Garvey co-driving, Paddy won his class and was eighth overall.

His car was looked after by an excellent VW specialist called Larry Mooney, who worked for Stephen O'Flaherty and prepared most of his Beetles for rallies. Larry was an early witness of Paddy's uncanny car skills: "I will never forget seeing Paddy on a driving test at Baldonnel after he had moved on to a Ford Anglia. On the test Paddy braked heavily, and with the nose of the car down and the rear wheels in the air somehow the rear of the car was swung over the pylons, allowing the car to reverse immediately into the next box or 'garage'. It was quite amazing!"

In September 1955 Paddy was back to the TR2 for the 900-mile Irish Rally with John Garvey. There were 44 starters and this time Paddy finished first overall. With another win in the TR2 in October of that year, on the Circuit of Clare, Paddy once again showed how competitive he was in the Triumph.

At the end of 1955, with his determination and skill at autotests, and accompanied by his friend John Garvey, a competent rally co-driver, Paddy won the Hewison Trophy, awarded by the Royal Irish Automobile Club for the most consistent trials driving in the 26 counties. As reported in his old college magazine, *The Clongownian*, Paddy had a

Mixed field: Paddy at the famous Phoenix Park circuit in 1955 in his newly-acquired Triumph TR2. (Paddy Hopkirk)

Competing in the 1955 Baird Memorial Trophy race, Kirkistown, again in the Triumph TR2. (W McCandless)

crossing a clearly constituted border. "In those days I was frequently crossing the border between the North and South. What we tend to forget now is that the North and South of Ireland were two different countries, with their own border controls and customs houses. There was always the added nuisance of being stopped and having passports checked, just like going through any other European border of the time."

At this time another change of employment came about through his father, who was still MD of Tennant's Tar Distillers in Belfast. Paddy was given the opportunity of taking a job as a draughtsman at the company branch in Dublin, called Irish Tar Distillers, where brother Eric was also working. "Father probably thought I would come in and eventually run the business. But I don't think I had my heart set on that. It was just a way of using my engineering skills, and it gave me the opportunity to spend more time rallying." It was in February 1956 that Paddy started his new job in the drawing office: "I remember doing some engineering drawing, with Eric teaching me, and we did some drawings for a pipeline down in the Dublin docks, for Esso Petroleum. This particular pipe had to be lagged to keep the bitumen warm as it was designed to take the bitumen in from the ships.

"Percy Wallace was my boss and he was a good man, often turning a blind eye when I took off extra time to go rallying. I was rallying-mad by now but was earning enough

remarkable year. This was the first time that Paddy had entered this competition and he was driving his own Volkswagen against the most experienced drivers in the country. At the end of 1955, as no club colours had been presented for some years, the DUMC & LCC decided to present colours to Paddy Hopkirk, John Garvey, Sam Logan, Mike Heather and David Felton.

Among the events being organised in the south were trials organised by the Irish Motor Racing Club, the IMRC. As Paddy was only too well aware, competing in events in Northern and Southern Ireland meant

A real road-race: Paddy in the Wicklow mountains during the 1955 Leinster Trophy race, in his Triumph TR2. He finished fourth overall. (Paddy Hopkirk)

Paddy with his great friend John Garvey at the 1955 MG Car Club prize-giving dinner at Dublin Airport, where they picked up a number of trophies. (Pictorial, Dublin)

The family yacht Glance pictured at Cowes. The boat gave Paddy his first taste of ocean racing, and participated in events such as the Fastnet. (Beken Cowes)

money to keep my rallying going, doing events virtually every weekend. Eric had gone straight from Trinity into his job with Irish Tar Distillers and we shared a flat at 6 Lower Fitzwilliam Street with two others. Our accommodation changed somewhat when the four of us rented this nice big house in Blackrock, Co Dublin." The atmosphere in the new house was enlivened by boisterous parties, as Eric Hopkirk remembers. "These parties were usually rather large, especially by the time we had invited yachting, rallying, Belfast and Dublin friends, and often they went on all night." It was at one of these that Paddy, as he confesses, put on a show for his guests.

"I had bought a Ford special built by T P O'Connell in Sligo. It was like a Dellow – it was a great little thing for playing around in, as it was very light and so it went like hell. I did a few driving tests in it, and it was fantastic, as you could see all four wheels. One evening we had a party at Blackrock and we all got pretty inebriated. I remember driving the special up and down the street doing handbrake turns and so on to impress the visitors, but out of their sight I managed to turn it on its side. I pushed it back onto its wheels and was very pleased that no one saw me over-doing it that badly. But that was the sort of thing you could do in those days – on a main road in Dublin, in the middle of the night! Can you imagine doing that now?"

Youthful capers or not, Paddy was building a reputation in Irish motor-sport events. It was to be only a matter of time before he moved on to bigger things.

Chapter 2

Start of the big time

1955–1958

The purchase of his Triumph TR2 brought Paddy's name to the notice of Ken Richardson, who had overseen much of the development of the TR and who between 1954 and 1962 was Standard-Triumph's competitions manager. In 1955, at the tender of age of 22, Paddy received a call from Richardson. "Matt McQuaid had always been telling him about this young Irish driver who was doing well in a TR2 and I think he just said 'Yeah, yeah'. But then Johnny Claes died. He was a Belgian bandleader, I think, and he'd been entered in the Monte Carlo Rally in a Standard Vanguard. Ken had tried all the other drivers he knew but they were all tied up, so he called me.

"I jumped up and down and told the Irish newspapers that I'd got a works drive on the Monte. I was all over the Irish press. And then Ken phoned up the next day and told me that the Monte Carlo authorities wouldn't accept a change of driver. I said 'Oh God, it's all over the press and everything. He said 'Look, I'll give you a drive on another event'..."

Works debut: the 1956 RAC and Tulip rallies

"I sent Ken Richardson a solicitor's letter every other day, reminding him of what he'd said," recalls Paddy. "He told me later that he hadn't wanted to give me a drive at all, but in the end he gave me a drive in the RAC Rally – I think maybe I embarrassed him into it!

Paddy driving his Standard Ten up Prescott Hill Climb during the 1956 RAC Rally, his first works drive. (Charles Dunn)

Paddy and the 'monkey-on-a-stick'

Paddy's Volkswagen days might have been drawing to a close, but there was one throwback to the Beetle that was to resurface later: the famous VW jack.

"At BMC I was responsible for them using the monkey-up-a-stick VW jack," says Paddy. "I was the instigator of that.

We used to use wind-up jacks, but I persuaded them to get VW jacks and modify them for the Mini. They were very clever. You pushed the thing under the car, pushed the lever downwards, and the outer collar gripped on the tube, with no teeth or anything. It was so quick..."

Anyway, John Garvey and I came over and did the RAC in a Standard Ten – which was a bloody good car. In those days the RAC had driving tests on the promenade at Blackpool, around pylons and so on. The first few tests I cleaned up, achieving three zeroes for fastest in class, because I could use the handbrake and everything. So Ken Richardson was in a bar somewhere in Blackpool when he heard on the radio that some unknown young Irish driver was leading the rally. He nearly fell off his bar stool – and I never looked back. From that day on, I think I was always Ken's blue-eyed boy!"

This first foray into international rallying might have proved Paddy's potential, but it wasn't, in the end, a success for the Hopkirk-Garvey équipe, the Standard Ten merely being classified as a finisher. "I remember we made a 'horlicks' of it in Yorkshire and then we holed the sump, ripping the drainplug out," says Paddy. "The RAC Rally hadn't gone into the forest in the '50s and we hadn't considered a sumpguard necessary".

A better result – appreciably so – was achieved on 1956 Tulip Rally, with the Hopkirk/Garvey duo, this time in an unmodified Standard Eight, coming third overall and being part of the team that won the manufacturers' prize. The organisers were so surprised that these diminutive cars had done so well that they ordered the engines to be stripped and measured to ensure no cheating had taken place. This revealed nothing untoward: the secret, says Paddy, was that the cars were well-prepared and had good back-up.

Life in the fast lane with Ken Richardson

Paddy was now accepted as part of the Standard-Triumph team. "I didn't get a fee

when I joined. I was only too pleased to get a works drive, but they of course paid day money to cover our expenses – so long as we didn't live it up too much!"

The team, fielding mainly the small Standard Eights and Tens and the Triumph TRs, was effectively managed by the undoubtedly able but certainly colourful Richardson. "He was a good guy," says Paddy. "He knew about engineering, and was a top-rate mechanic – he could listen to an SU carburettor, for example, and tell if it was going up and down as it should do. He was a very hard worker – a workaholic. He lived on his nerves. He didn't want food, sleep, or anything like that. He didn't look healthy – he was very thin and wiry. He smoked a lot and he drank. I wouldn't say he over-drank, but he liked his nicotine and his alcohol. He liked life, and didn't take himself too seriously. That was

Rough stuff on the 1956 Circuit of Ireland – a typical boreen driving test. (Paddy Hopkirk)

Paddy and John Garvey at the finish of the 1956 Tulip Rally in their Standard Eight (car no. 201); they finished third overall and were members of the winning team. (B Ietswaart)

what was so nice – I can't stand people who take themselves too seriously!"

At the time, however, Paddy had certain reservations about Richardson – reservations that he now regrets. "Here he was, a married man, and he was chasing the ladies. I thought this was terrible! What an idiot I was! In fact he was a very good family man, and his wife stood by him. I completely misjudged him, and so I suppose I didn't have the respect for him that I should have had.

"If I met him now I'd have that respect. I think I used to judge people a bit too much on that. I was pretty narrow-minded. I was brought up a Jesuit boy, and they brought you up that you could rob someone, or shoot someone, but kissing someone was completely out of the question. They used to make us keep our underpants on in the shower in case we'd get excited. Sex was a terrible thing, and all the more so outside marriage."

To the hills: interlude in Ireland

Paddy's international rally programme allowed time for other events and he still had his own TR2. Down in Tipperary, the 1956 Dungarvan Hill Climb was to see the battle between the TR2s of Paddy and Mike Heather renewed in no uncertain manner, with Paddy coming out on top with a time six seconds faster. There was also an epic battle between Paddy and Joe Flynn, in a blown MG TC, resulting in a shared FTD of 1 minute 48.2 seconds.

Paddy at Cranfield Airfield in 1956 where despite this incursion into the straw bales – from which he recovered – he finished third in the Scratch race. (Paddy Hopkirk)

Ready for departure for the '56 Alpine. The Bristol Freighter awaits Paddy and Willy Cave, plus Ken Richardson (second right) and Kit Heathcote. (LAT)

Paddy in his works Triumph TR3 on the infamous Gavia Pass, on the way to winning a coveted Coupe des Alpes on the 1956 Alpine Rally. The picture clearly shows the challenging nature of the road surface in 1956. (Paddy Hopkirk)

On the Enniskerry Hill Climb, Paddy was again in the TR2, coming third in the Open Handicap class and fifth in the Open Scratch class with a time of 46.76 seconds. FTD was made by a 1098cc Cooper, with a time of 43.63 seconds.

A bridge too far: the 1956 'Midnight Sun'

In May 1956 it was off to foreign parts with the works team for Sweden's Midnight Sun Rally – or, to give it its full title, the *Svenska Rallyt till Midnattssolen*. Three TR3s – for Ken Richardson and Kit Heathcote, Annie Bousquet and Jo Ashfield, and Paddy with BBC man Willy Cave – were included in an entry of 200 cars. Cave takes up the story:

"I'd been navigating for Johnny Wallwork in national and club events in the North of England, and then he got a drive in a works Standard Ten on the 1956 RAC Rally. This was the first time I had met Ken Richardson, and he seemed to like my work. Two or three weeks later he phoned up and asked whether I

The scene looks more like a Monte Carlo Rally as the works Triumph TR3 comes down through the snow during the 1956 Alpine. (Paddy Hopkirk)

and drag on the front and rear to catapult the car through each newly revealed twist. In 16 kilometres it was over – and we were just six seconds late. From then on I wasn't frightened! Paddy didn't shout at me in the car, but he did shout at the pretty teenage Swedish girls, sliding open the side window and saying 'Wait for me – I'll be back!'.

"We were given little photocopy strips of map showing each special stage, but they were about 100,000:1 scale, and no good at all for reading the road. I'd therefore bought an up-to-date map which showed a useful new bit of road to get us across the river over a splendid bridge, so I took it. I guided not just Paddy but the entire Triumph team down the new road. I was relieved to see the great pillars of the bridge standing up above the birch forest. Yes, the bridge was finished – but it wasn't yet open to traffic. The old ferry was still working but had just left for its journey to the other side. Mr Richardson was not pleased with me!

"We did the Solleftea 1200-metre hill climb and were chastened to find our time equalled by a huge Ford Fairlane. On the middle of the second day we were back in the middle of Sweden and had to do three laps of the Karslkoga circuit in races of five cars at a time. Leaving the circuit, I checked the roadbook stamps and so on but didn't realise until the next control that we had been given someone else's roadbook. Panic! And then the axle started to whine, as it had lost oil from a loose casing…

"The final test was on the seafront at Saltjobaden, and was actually a tie-decider. The results were announced next morning and we had not done very well; the regulations had favoured the smaller cars".

would like to navigate in one of his cars on the Tulip Rally. I'd already signed up to do the Tulip in a private entry so couldn't go. He rang back a bit later and said 'Pity about the Tulip, but come on the Midnight Sun. I've got this new whizzkid who's been winning driving tests all over Ireland. He's never been abroad, never been on the continent, and I think you're just the man with the experience to look after him and bring him home safely'.

"We flew to Stockholm to pick up our car. The Standard-Triumph distributors in Stockholm extended the most wonderful hospitality to us during our stay. The best part of two days was spent on the 600km 'assembly run' to Ostersund, with competing cars starting from six starting points. We added stoneguards to the lights and bought caps with enormous peaks because the sun spends eight of the 24 hours near the horizon.

"When we were waiting at one of these 'scrambly' stage starts, and feeling rather nervous, Paddy said to me 'It might help you to know that I have never had a crash on a rally'. I've been frightened before and I will be frightened again, but this occasion will certainly rank as a most special experience. Paddy was superb, fighting with the steering wheel, a man possessed as he stabbed at the brake and accelerator, balancing the thrust

Tyres and 'Gatso': the 1956 Alpine

Paddy was in a TR3 for the 1956 Alpine Rally, which that year innovated by taking in Yugoslavia. Willy Cave was again Paddy's co-driver, and vividly remembers the event.

"Ken Richardson held a team meeting in his hotel room, going through the route in some detail, discussing times, traffic and road conditions and so on. Tyres were subject to some concern as the cars had to finish on the same tyres that they started with, according to the regulations. We learned the value of

– at least I don't think he did. Things did change a bit when we started to be able to go faster than him.

"Anyway, on the final night we did the 'Hell Fire Loop', which was very narrow, and we thought we'd lose time here. Gatso said 'I'll tell you what we'll do here. I'll book out, drive 100 yards up the road, and you'll book out a minute behind me and I'll lead you round'. He was therefore sacrificing one of his precious minutes, but he got in with about a minute and a half to spare and we were two and a half minutes early! It was like following the grand master – he was a lovely driver.

"I always remember Marcel Becquart coming up to us. He was a perfect French gentleman, and he spoke English with a thick French accent. He said 'On theese section I 'ave been told to go like *sheet off a shovel*. I know what *sheet* mean, but please what ees *shovel*?'

"We won a coveted Coupe des Alpes, not to mention the prize money of 250,000 francs, which we shared. If the timed climb and circuit of the Dolomites hadn't been virtually cancelled, and the rain hadn't come down during the last two days, the tyres wouldn't have made it."

Paddy and Maurice 'Gatso' Gatsonides (right) watch team manager Ken Richardson receiving the team prize on the 1956 Alpine Rally from a young admirer. (Paddy Hopkirk)

Paddy, again with John Garvey, managed third in class in the Triumph TR3, on the 1957 Tulip Rally. (E Jelinek)

rotating the wheels, including the spare, to even out the wear to avoid losing our coupe. It was enormously exciting, but there was this fear of going into Yugoslavia. If we broke down, there was no support and we didn't know if we would ever get out again. We had visions of funny money and terrible petrol, and we expected to get heaps of punctures. In fact we had four or five, and seemed to be forever fitting new tubes. We finished on bald tyres and during the last 24 hours I said to Paddy 'If I hear you squealing the tyres once more, I'll thump you!'. On the Vivione, the exhaust came adrift in a gully in a woodyard and we had this awful noise all the way over the pass. It was terrible and we thought 'That's it', but just before the finish the exhaust went quiet again. Don't ask me how – it was unbelievable! It was very hot, and at one point Paddy said 'Willy, will you tell me which country we are in, because I think I ought to buy a drink at the next control ?'..."

Maurice Gatsonides was the team leader, and was partnered on this Alpine by Frenchman Marcel Becquart. "Gatsonides was very serious about his motor sport," says Paddy. "He was the first man ever to mention the word 'reconnaissance' to me. He practised the whole route and made lots of notes. He was a sharer. He didn't keep secrets to himself

Irish mix: Anglia and Beetle

Towards the end of 1956 Paddy bought a Ford Anglia in Dublin. "Why did I buy an Anglia? I suppose it was because it was after my VW days and I needed something cheap to compete in – but also because it was good for driving tests. It had a three-speed gearbox, so first and reverse gears were opposite each other, so for parking in a 'garage' and going out again you didn't have to stir around in a plate of porridge to find the right gear. After a few events I had the engine modified by Louis Carter, a wonderful tuner and motorcycle racer in Dublin. He put an SU carburettor quite high up on the engine with quite a bit of ram effect from the manifold, and it went like hell."

Despite this new car, in which he won a few driving tests, Paddy was back in a VW Beetle for the Cork 20-hour Navigation Rally, winning the Conway Cup for the best times in the driving tests and being a member of the winning Volkswagen team with Cecil Vard and Sam Logan.

Paddy and John Garvey on the famous Midnight Sun Rally in Sweden in a Standard Eight – badged as a 'Vanguard Junior'. The car was underpowered and Paddy, who had not quite mastered the technique of driving on loose narrow roads, finished well down the field. (Paddy Hopkirk)

1957: a year of disruption and sadness

The year 1957 was not good for motor sport, with the Suez crisis and the closing of the Suez Canal. Petrol rationing was introduced in the UK and numerous rallies and races were cancelled, including the RAC and Alpine rallies.

However, the Tulip Rally was held and Paddy was teamed up with his friend John Garvey in a works Triumph TR3, registration TRW 737. They achieved a reasonable result, with a third in class and 20th position overall. With different tyres, Paddy might well have done better. He does not have fond memories of the Dunlop Duraband tyres used. "They were amazing. They had a steel band in them, or something, and the roadholding was superb. But when they lost grip it was like the tyre had gone flat, and you span. We all spun at Zandvoort – me, John Waddington, and Tommy Gold, who later went off on the Freiburg Hill Climb and ended up on the top of a tree – and we were all blamed for it. But we blamed the tyres. We all had big problems. It would suddenly be like someone had let the back axle go. It would suddenly go. They were very good in one way, and not so good in another. It took us a long time to be able to judge their behaviour, and know where the limit was – it made the driving very difficult. I don't know whether the upside outweighed the downside – it's a question I couldn't answer. But I reckon they were dangerous."

In Ireland, many rallies and trials continued, and Paddy used his Ford Anglia with some success in hill climbs, trials, rallies and races. The Midnight Sun was also run, and the Standard-Triumph team entered Standard Eights badged as Vanguard Juniors, with a chrome grille, to match the Swedish market specification. Paddy was accompanied by John Garvey and they managed to finish 22nd overall.

Meanwhile, the Hopkirk family had moved from Somerton Road to Newtownbreda and this is where they suffered a great personal loss. In October 1957 Paddy's father, who had been suffering from heart problems, died. "Heart disease, they called it," says Paddy. "I've got some old 16mm film of him, and you can see him going downhill – becoming more and more ill-looking." The death of Francis Hopkirk resulted in Paddy's brother Frank taking over the running of the Tennants Tar Distillers business while Paddy moved back to Belfast and lived in a small house there which he shared with his other brother, Eric.

Paddy with Jack Scott in their Triumph TR3A on the 1958 Monte Carlo Rally, here in the Massif Centrale after they had extracted themselves from an off-road excursion – note the damage to the front of the car. (Paddy Hopkirk)

1958: Paddy's first Monte – and a new co-driver

On the international scene, a strong Triumph team equipped with TR3As was entered in the 1958 Monte: Maurice Gatsonides with Marcel Becquart, John Waddington with Mike Wood, Paddy Hopkirk with Jack Scott, and Annie Soisbault with Tish Ozanne. The cars were fitted with a perspex screen inside the windscreen, a long backrest on the passenger seat, front and rear windscreen defrosters, a Halda, an Eolopress inflator/extinguisher, two-speed wipers, and a radiator blind. The cars were driven in convoy from Coventry to Lydd and crossed over to Le Touquet on a British United Airways Bristol Freighter.

Mike Wood was meeting Paddy for the first time. "Nobody seemed to know him, as he had done most of his rallying in Ireland. I remember he had a good sense of humour and was always first to the bar! He did manage to stir things up sometimes, in a typical Irish manner. On an RAC Rally when we were at a golf club which was the breakfast halt somewhere up north, Paddy asked for cream to put in his coffee. The waitress said 'Oh no, we don't have that at this time of day'. Paddy's response was 'Jesus Christ, don't you

know that the war is now over up north!'…"

Paddy now had a new co-driver, Jack Scott, as he recalls. "On the 'Cork 20', a 20-hour-long difficult night event, for two years running I won it on the driving tests and Jack Scott won the navigation bit with someone else. I was in the bar one night, talking with Jack, and I said 'Look, this is ridiculous. You're winning the navigation and I'm winning the driving – why don't we get together?'. That was it – Jack became my

Paddy's training in Irish driving tests helped him into fifth overall in the manoeuvrability test at Monaco. This competition was not, alas, included in the overall results of the rally. (Erpe)

Paddy showing off his driving test skills on the way to winning the 1958 Circuit of Ireland. (Belfast Newsletter)

co-driver. Jack was in the jam business – R&W Scott of Edinburgh was the company – and he ran the firm's Dublin factory.

"He was a terrific guy, with a great sense of humour. He was also a wonderful pianist and we had some memorable sing-songs including popular tunes such as *These Foolish Things* adapted to his own words. He created some interesting variations to the lyrics of well-known songs, and these closed down a few bars over the years…"

On the Monte Paddy and Jack Scott started from Paris. Conditions were not good, recalls Paddy. "I remember going up this col with the snow getting deeper and deeper. I was behind Mike Couper's Austin Westminster which had wipers on the headlamps. He was able to see

much better than us until he stuffed it off and there it was in the ditch with the cables from the headlamp wipers tangled around the front of the car. We remarked that his headlamp wipers wouldn't be much use now. We had no studs and the car was sliding all over the place. It was so cold in the Massif Centrale and although we had the radiator blind right up, the engine temperature didn't get up to normal – which of course affected the heater."

Mike Wood, co-driving John Waddington, didn't have it any easier. "The snow was terrible. We had to keep stopping to clear snow from the signposts because we couldn't see the junctions and we had no recce notes. Then Ron Faulkner in a Jaguar spun in front of us and went over the edge, and we swerved to avoid him and pushed the front wing onto the tyre. After making sure they were OK, we managed to get the wing clear and continued."

At Dole, only five cars made it – including Paddy, despite his having gone off the road into a field. With a superhuman effort he managed to regain the road, only to go OTL (outside time limit) a little later. The appalling weather conditions resulted in the Paris and Munich starters coming off worst, with only one car from each city getting through to Monte Carlo. Maurice Gatsonides finished sixth out of 58 finishers but John Waddington and Paddy salvaged a little pride for the

The winning team on the 1958 Circuit of Ireland – left to right are Ernest McMillen, John Haslett, Paddy, Jack Scott, Desmond Titterington, and Brian McCaldin, photographed with Paddy's winning car and the trophies. (Paddy Hopkirk)

Paddy, a member of the winning Standard Pennant team, swings around a pylon at Hastings during the 1958 RAC Rally. (Gifford Boyd)

Coventry team by coming third and fifth respectively in the manoeuvrability test that was run after the rally had finished.

On a lower register, Paddy was chosen to lead the Northern Ireland team in the Ken Wharton Memorial Trophy autotest in 1958 for teams from England, Wales, Scotland and Northern Ireland. Raymond Baxter had come up with the idea for the format of this event, the idea being that it was suited for Saturday afternoon television; organisation was by by the Hagley & District Light Car Club and the event was televised by the BBC, who were to cover the event for a further ten years. Paddy was team captain for the Northern Ireland team for four years, and his team was victorious in 1959, 1960 and 1962.

Flying the Pennant: the 1958 RAC Rally

The Monte had not been a very good start to the year, and the RAC Rally wasn't much better, arctic conditions again playing a decisive part in the results. The rally was to be known this year as 'The Rally of the Tests', with 20 hill climbs and high-speed and manoeuvrability tests along the 1800-mile route. There were starts from Blackpool, Hastings and Le Touquet – although nobody opted for the French start – and the routes converged on the Prescott Hill Climb. Deep snow afflicted at least half of the route, and conditions were so severe that in the

The 'Pathfinder' who couldn't find his way

"Air Vice-Marshal Donald Bennett was a hero during the Second World War. His men used to fly ahead of our bombers and drop red flares over the targets to help them deliver their bombs in the right place. He was known as 'Pathfinder' Bennett and drove Fairthorpe cars made by his company in Denham, Buckinghamshire.

On one tricky bit of rally navigation he unexpectedly turned right up a small road and, of course, everybody followed 'Pathfinder', including us. Shortly he was coming back in the opposite direction at a rate of knots, as his navigator had obviously made a mistake. It was good bar talk afterwards. I now often play tennis with his son Torix and we still laugh about the incident."

1958 Alpine Rally: Paddy and Jack Scott ready for the 'off' in Marseilles, in their Triumph TR3A. (Paddy Hopkirk)

convince him we were genuine, and told him we would arrange for new parts to be sent up from the factory straight away. The staff were wonderful, and fitted an axle from a second-hand Standard Ten in the showroom in one hour and four minutes!"

As a result, Paddy and Jack arrived rather breathless at Test 10 at Charterhall. On Test 11 at Otterburn, which was a 100-yard dash, Paddy was fastest in class, and he was also fastest on Test 12 at Otterburn, which was a simple pylon forward and reverse layout. Their troubles were not yet over, as when they were on the A20 approaching Hastings the Standard suffered a broken windscreen – the final drama of an eventful RAC Rally. Nevertheless, their efforts resulted in the Team Prize.

At the finish, Ian Hall, who was with the Rootes team, recalls how Paddy was keen to start the post-event celebrations. "At the finish about half-a-dozen of us, including Paddy, all carrying our bags, were walking to the hotel together and we stopped in front of the commissionaire. Paddy put down his bags, looked up to this formidable figure and said 'Do you sell Guinness?'. 'Yes, sir' came the answer, to which Paddy replied 'Well, you can start pulling the pints now then!'"

Otterburn area cars became stuck on the special tests. Paddy was in a Standard Pennant – a tarted-up version of the Standard Ten – and near Kelso his rear axle started to become noisy.

"We stopped at this garage which was a Standard-Triumph dealer – Tweedsmuir Motors of Kelso – and spoke to this old chap with a flat hat. We explained we were with the works team and had an axle problem. He said 'Oh aye, you've got to be careful these days, you get some right-rum-buggers coming up from the south, sum cum in 'ere tother day and drove off without paying.' I said 'Yes, you've got be careful of these people coming up from London'. He replied 'No, these rum-buggers were from Wigan.' I managed to

Back on their home territory, Paddy and Jack Scott competed on the Circuit of Ireland in a Triumph TR3A. Triumph entered a team of three cars. The rally started on Good Friday in foul weather and at the end of the first stage Desmond Titterington in his TR

The flailing tyre on the Stelvio Pass which signalled retirement for the TR3A and Paddy's departure from the Triumph team. (Paddy Hopkirk)

was leading, with 161.6 points against Paddy's 161.8 points. The Tim Healy Pass test was run downhill and at the end of the second stage Paddy was first and Titterington second. On the Corkscrew Hill Climb, Paddy was fastest with a time of 69.2 seconds followed by Titterington at 69.4 seconds. The pair had quite a battle, but in the end Paddy won the event overall, with Triumphs filling the top seven places in the overall classification.

This season was notable also for the success that Paddy achieved with an Austin A35 fitted with a Speedwell conversion. The car was Paddy's own, and it was tuned by Billy Rainey in Belfast. During 1958 Paddy won his class no fewer than ten times in hill climbs, sprints and race meetings.

Feeling deflated: an unfortunate Alpine

All this contrasted with Paddy's continued participation in top-flight international rallies. Next up was the Alpine Rally, an event which attracted considerable British interest, there being no fewer than 40 British competitors in 1958 out of a total entry of 62 cars.

Paddy and Jack Scott were first away from the start in Marseilles in their green TR3A with stoneguards on the headlamps. This was the first time that the works TR3As ran with 2.2-litre engines. On the Stelvio pass teammate Annie Soisbault hit a wall right in front of the Shell film cameras, but Paddy, as he recalls, was also in trouble.

"The car was 20 seconds faster up the

Stelvio with the 2.2-litre engine but on the way up the pass, with its 48 hairpins, we had a puncture in the left-hand rear Dunlop Duraband tyre. I was on for a second consecutive Coupe des Alpes which would put you in the frame for a Gold, and so I decided to keep going to remain penalty-free. We made it to the top but the engine overheated with the strain and we were forced to retire. It was probably a case of bad judgement on my behalf, resulting in Ken Richardson saying 'You are a pratt, what did you do that for?'. In effect I got the sack, because that was my last Triumph drive. I spoke to Ken's son recently, and apparently it was in everybody's mind that we'd fallen out. But we hadn't, really. I was very fond of Ken, and he was quite right to sack me."

Three rivals, probably not telling each other the whole truth. Left to right are Les Leston, Peter Jopp and Paddy. (LAT)

Chapter 3

The Rootes years

1959–1962

Paddy didn't have a drive for the 1959 Monte Carlo until asked by Les Leston to replace journalist Gordon Wilkins in his Riley One-Point-Five. Leston, one of motor sport's more colourful characters, had a shop in Holborn selling go-faster gear, and in his early life, before becoming a racing driver, he had been a drummer in the famous Ambrose Orchestra as well as being a mean tap-dancer. Paddy jumped at the chance to partner Leston. "I really wanted to be on the rally, to have the chance of meeting people. I knew Les, as I was selling gloves, clothes and overalls and all that sort of stuff for him in Northern Ireland."

With Leston on the Monte

The Riley started from Glasgow, and after arriving at Dover crossed the Channel to Boulogne with the other competitors in the famous old car ferry the *Lord Warden*. On the mountain circuit, between La Grave and Peille, on some unexpected ice, Leston skidded through a parapet wall, landing on the roof of a Citroën ID19 which had already gone off the road in the same place. The Citroën made quite a good landing platform, and with the help of some gendarmes and a jack Les and Paddy regained the road and

Paddy in his first role as a co-driver, having been kindly offered a lift by Les Leston in his Riley One-Point-Five for the 1959 Monte Carlo Rally. (Paddy Hopkirk)

continued. In the main event they were not very well placed, being 82nd overall and second in class, but Les did the manoeuvrability test at Monaco and was 13th fastest.

Les Leston's volatile temperament nearly caused an incident on the return journey, as Paddy recalls. "We'd been to the prize-giving and that night, after the rally, Les decided that he wanted to go straight home in the Riley. Driving with great panache, Les crossed a white line and was stopped by a motorcycle policeman. The policeman of course came to my window, thinking it was a left-hand-drive car. Les leaned across and was very abusive and said 'What the f*ck do you want?' He was asked for his licence, to which he said 'ta gueule' – French for 'shut up!' – with the result that the policeman started to draw his revolver, shouting 'Papiers! Papiers!'. I was a bit alarmed, quickly crossed myself, and sank down into my seat, saying 'For Christ's sake, Les'. Eventually, after some formalities, we drove off, much to my relief."

Les Leston in his Riley One-Point-Five, with Paddy co-driving, on the way to Monte Carlo. (LAT)

On the 1959 Safari – in a Hillman Husky!

After the Monte, Paddy happened to be in the Metropole Hotel. He was in the right place at the right time, as he recounts. "Propping up the bar with a gin-and-tonic was Basil Cardew, Motoring Editor of the *Daily Express*, with Norman Garrad, the Rootes team manager, who was 'god' in those days. Mike Hawthorn had been scheduled to drive a works Hillman Husky in the forthcoming Safari rally, but sadly had just been killed on the Hogs Back near Guildford. Norman said to Basil 'Who am I going to get to drive his car in the Safari?'. Basil said 'There's a young Irish driver I know who is very good and has just been sacked by Triumph'. I happened to be walking through the foyer and Norman called me over to the bar. He said 'Would you like to drive for us on the Coronation Safari?' Imagine my excitement – an offer to drive for the Rootes Group team! I've forgotten how many times I said 'Yes, Sir'.

"Norman was someone you always looked up to, who ruled by example – rather a supremo. I thought he was particularly good at weighing up and picking drivers with potential. I didn't get paid a fee, but the day-money expenses were more generous than

with Triumph and we could sometimes make a bit of money out of it."

Norman Garrad was certainly a character, as well as being, according to Raymond Baxter, the first really professional team manager in international rallying. "He was quite different from Ken Richardson", confirms Paddy. "He was very professional, certainly, but he delegated more. It was an army style of management rather than doing it yourself. And just as he was immaculate himself, so were the cars – he was an attention-to-detail man. Everyone thought that the Rootes team was simply the best team to be with, in those days."

Rootes driver Ian Hall is among those with fond memories of Garrad. "He wasn't one to dash about at a service point and clean a windscreen, for example. At home, though, he fought the management behind the scenes, to get the best deal for the team." Graham Robson has a slightly different perspective from his days with the team. "I felt that there was no real team spirit. There were no team orders. Although Peter Harper was in effect team captain, I think Norman Garrad believed that he got more out of his drivers by allowing personal rivalry to prevail."

Delighted by his works drive, Paddy was unconcerned by such issues as he prepared to do battle on the Safari in the diminutive

*Paddy, fag in hand, on his first works drive with the Rootes Group: team manager Norman Garrad is in the centre and co-driver Ron Dalton stands in front of the duo's Hillman Husky, during the 1959 Coronation Safari in Kenya.
(Paddy Hopkirk)*

Hillman estate car. "It was a horrible thing – there was no sound-deadening in it, and on rough roads the noise was appalling." Although teamed with local driver Ron Dalton in the Husky, Paddy did his recce with Peter Jopp. Paddy recalls having trouble with their recce car, and being given a lift by fellow Ulsterman Ronnie Adams in his Humber. Paddy was very impressed at the speed Adams was maintaining on the loose surfaces. "It was the first time that I had met Ronnie and he made me realise how I couldn't really drive properly on loose roads. Ronnie was a wonderful driver, and was great fun, too, with an eye for the ladies!"

Paddy had to retire their car after holing the sump and running a big end. Peter Harper was less fortunate: he crashed heavily and broke his arm. Peter Jopp picked him up to take him to the next control and he was screaming in pain, to such an extent that Jopp, with a single punch, knocked him out to keep him quiet. This act of kindness resulted in his being presented with the Samaritans award at the finish.

For Paddy the Safari was a great experience. "I liked the Safari because it was unlike anything in Europe and was such a fantastic challenge – partly because I didn't know anything about driving on the loose. What with the dust, the mud, the huge holes and wash-aways, the river crossings and the wild animals, it had everything. You had to have a lot of luck and local knowledge."

*The Husky at speed before retiring with a holed sump.
(Paddy Hopkirk)*

1959 continued: ups and downs with the Rapier

Rootes were one of the teams to have decided on a busy European rally programme and Paddy's next event – partnered by Jack Scott – was to be the 1959 Alpine Rally, this time in a Sunbeam Rapier. The Alpine had always been a tough event and that year was no exception, with four stages totalling 2397 miles, 58 starters – and only 27 finishers. The first stage, Marseilles to Cortina, was 770 miles, the second stage, Cortina to Merano, was 415 miles, the third stage, Merano to St Gervais-les-Bains, was 407 miles, and the final stage, St Gervais to Cannes, was 805 miles.

"The cars were beautifully prepared, and with the Rapier the Rootes competition department made the best of a small family saloon," says Paddy. "I'd say the cars we drove were quite a bit removed from the ones you could buy from your local showroom – much more so, probably, than had been the case over at Standard-Triumph." Paddy remembers in particular how the Rapier had been adapted to have overdrive on all gears – as opposed to only on third and top, as on the production Rapiers. "This virtually gave us an eight-speed gearbox – it was wonderful. You'd stick the car in first gear, let the clutch in, and as it was coming up to 4000–5000rpm you'd flick the switch on the gearlever and you'd get overdrive first gear, then you'd change out of that into second and then again into overdrive – and in came the power like a supercharger. But we were always told not to use overdrive in first and second too much, because the overdrives couldn't take the torque.

"We were also told by the mechanics not to go above 6500rpm. Peter Harper was with Peter Procter and they were taking about ten seconds off me on hill climbs such as the Col d'Izouard and Col d'Allos. In the bar one night during the event I was talking with Peter, Procter and he asked me what revs we were using and I said 6500rpm, as instructed. He said 'Try 8000rpm!'. I said 'Really?', but next day I used up to 8000rpm and was taking three seconds a stage off Peter Harper – which didn't amuse him. I got on alright with Peter, but he didn't like the idea that somebody in the team was challenging him – especially a hungry young driver such as myself. Still, that's the sort of rivalry you get in any team, and Norman Garrad probably realised that, and just let it happen."

Paddy and Jack finished an excellent third overall and first in class, winning a Coupe des Alpes and the *Autocar* Trophy for the best British car, with team-mates Jopp and Leston and Ivor Bueb with Tish Ozanne completing a clean sweep in their class.

The toughest rally in Europe was the Liège–Rome–Liège, but Paddy, in a Sunbeam Rapier with Irish co-driver Cecil Vard, had no luck and retired from the rally. Peter Jopp recalls a prank involving Paddy. "I was with Les Leston in another Sunbeam and Les was doing radio broadcasts for the BBC. Paddy, as the up-and-coming star, loved doing interviews, and we kidded Paddy into doing an interview in our hotel room, with a shower head as a microphone. I had the 'microphone'

Paddy maintains a tight line on the 1959 Dungarvan Hill Climb, driving his MkI Austin-Healey Sprite. (Brian Foley)

Cecil Vard, a well-known furrier who was normally a first driver, accompanied Paddy in his Sunbeam Rapier on the 1959 Liège–Rome–Liège rally. (Robyns)

in my hand and soon after Paddy started his story, I switched on the water! How many Irish swear words do you know?…"

Although now a Rootes works driver, Paddy had a relatively quiet year on the home front, and so was able to fill in with a number of events in the Austin-Healey Sprite he had bought. At the AGM of the Dublin University MC & LCC held in West Chapel in November, Arthur Jolley was appointed president, and David Felton as Captain, and Paddy was nominated as one of ten committee members.

It was around this time that Raymond Baxter first met Paddy. "I first came across Paddy when he was a member of the Northern Ireland team competing in the Ken Wharton Memorial Trophy, which was a competition I invented for BBC Television and which was held at a manor house in Droitwich. Ginger Cowgill was head of BBC Television Sport and he used me to fill in 'bits' so I came up with this driving or autotest competition for the best autotest drivers in the country. I thought Paddy was an exceptionally jovial happy-go-lucky and charming Irishman, and he was astonishingly quick at driving tests. He drove his own Austin-Healey Sprite at this first running of the event. It went down on television fairly well, I guess.

"When Paddy joined the Rootes team he was very much a team man, and very competitive. Having said that, when I was with Peter Harper if ever Paddy came up behind us on a special section, there was no way that Peter would give way to his teammate. This happened on one occasion when Kling in the works Mercedes came

up behind us and Peter wouldn't let him through and Kling complained to the organisers. I liked Paddy very much and I admired him as a sportsman and an excellent driver. We could always be sure of a good *craic* when Paddy was around!"

To finish his first year with Rootes, Paddy was entered in the RAC Rally in a Sunbeam Rapier, with Jack Scott as his co-driver. The first test was on the seafront at Blackpool

This is what happened on the first attempt when Paddy was asked to demonstrate a front-end throw in front of a large crowd after the 1960 Gran Canaria Rally. (Paddy Hopkirk)

immediately after the start, and Paddy was fastest car in his class. On the Rest-and-be-Thankful Hill Climb, run in pouring rain, he was again fastest in his class. At the Aintree test, comprising three laps of the club circuit, the rain was pouring just as hard, and again Paddy did a quick time. The weather at the Prescott Hill Climb was fine, but this time Paddy was beaten in his class by Peter Harper.

Near the end of rally they lost 15 minutes, because someone had turned the 'Control' approach sign round. This was later revealed to be Les Leston, who had decided to have a little joke, and who recalls Paddy going up this road the wrong way and coming tearing back down again. The Sunbeam suffered a broken axle at Druids Corner after one lap of the Brands Hatch test, and was forced to retire.

1960: treading water in a lacklustre year

The first event for 1960 was the traditional Monte Carlo rally, with Paddy and Jack Scott this time starting from Oslo with team-mates Jopp and Leston, both duos in Rapiers. The cars were equipped with the new Duraband studded tyres for the first time. There was three inches of snow at the start and the competitors met violent snowstorms and sheet ice on the autobahn in Germany on the way to Monte. On the Col de Lachaux, which had 6ft snow banks, Paddy went off into a snowdrift, despite the car being fitted with snow chains. "We had some sponsorship from Lucozade," recalls Paddy, "and a picture appeared in *Autosport* of me offering a bottle of the stuff to Les and Peter, as they slithered past in their Rapier".

Co-driver Viscount 'Kim' Mandeville enjoys a cigarette before the 1960 East African Safari – the Rapier retired with a broken differential while in the lead. (Paddy Hopkirk)

East Africa now beckoned again. The eighth Safari, now called the East African Safari, saw Paddy in a Rapier with local driver Viscount 'Kim' Mandeville. "He was an ex-Army officer who was based in Kenya and had done a lot of local events, and was a very good co-driver. He was the son of the Duke of Manchester and had a beautiful wife. He was a serious boozer and used to keep a bottle of brandy under the seat of the car. During the recce a little black boy ran across the road and I had to swerve to avoid him. 'Kim' said 'What did you do that for?' – hopefully not typical of the local ex-pats! During the rally, whenever we came into a petrol station with a queue, 'Kim' would say 'Use the handle'. I would say 'Viscount Mandeville's car is back there' and all the locals would bow and scrape and get out of the way and we were immediately at the front of the queue! These colonial types…"

On the Mzenga section near Dar-es-Salaam the Sunbeam nearly hit a leopard, but after 30 hours Paddy was leading. However, the car became bogged in mud – losing 100 minutes – and then retired with a broken differential.

With Paddy away on the Safari and unable to compete in the Circuit of Ireland, he loaned his Austin-Healey Sprite to Cecil Vard and Jack Scott. Vard often borrowed cars from Lincoln and Nolan, the BMC importers, and in return Paddy was loaned his Mini for the Midland Circuit Trial organised by the Irish Centre of the MG Car Club and starting in Dublin. He finished first in the up-to-1000cc saloon class.

Paddy was still very much associated with Les Leston and he was one of the guests of honour along with Stirling Moss and Norman Garrad at the opening of a new London show-room for Les Leston in High Holborn.

The Gran Canaria Rally didn't feature on many manufacturers' rally programmes but Paddy was entered in a Sunbeam Rapier with Lewis Garrad – son of Norman – doing the co-driving. "The reason we went to the Canaries Rally was simple," says Garrad. "We

The Hopkirk/Scott Sunbeam Rapier approaches the summit of the Gavia Pass during the 1960 Alpine Rally. (Paddy Hopkirk)

Jack Scott watches a leisurely top-up before the 1960 Alpine Rally in which the Rapier he and Paddy shared was to finish sixth overall. (Paddy Hopkirk)

Paddy and Jack Scott watch their Sunbeam Rapier being unloaded at Stockholm for the start of 1961 Monte Carlo Rally. Note that the car has no sumpguard and is fitted with Dunlop Duraband studded tyres. The pair finished second in class. (Paddy Hopkirk)

the Rapier being the lone British entry. There were 46 cars, and the wearing of crash helmets was compulsory during the whole event. Paddy has mixed recollections of the rally. "There were a lot of regularity tests and a few driving tests and they hadn't seen driving tests done with front-end throws and the like. It was a very difficult rally, a stupid rally. We did well on the driving tests but cocked up some of the regularities. I was asked to do this demonstration of handbrake turns and front-end throws in the square on the Sunday morning after the rally. I managed to turn the car over doing a front-end throw, but the car was righted and the organisers said 'Thank you very much'. I said 'No, I will demonstrate it again' – and with some oil now on the road it went very well and the crowd, estimated at 12,000, went mad. I felt like a champion bull-fighter in a bull-ring."

Lewis Garrad recalls winning a huge trophy which caused all sorts of problems with the British Customs on return – but he got through with the comment "It's all part of our export drive, you know!".

The Tulip Rally was another 'Did Not Finish' when the Sunbeam Rapier suffered a broken halfshaft near Castellane in France, resulting in the wheel coming off. Despite having a new halfshaft delivered by motorcycle from the dealer in Nice, Paddy stopped to help another team member and was outside the time limit at the control on the Col de Leques.

had a very capable dealer on the island named Juan Dominguez who sold a large number of Rootes cars and vans. During a visit to the Export Division in UK he asked for support in his territory. The Competitions Department was asked to provide two cars, a Rapier for Paddy and an Alpine for Juan. Yours truly volunteered to go as co-driver with Paddy…"

The cars were shipped to the island, with

Paddy and Rapier round the harbour corner during the final test on the Monaco Grand Prix circuit at the end of the 1961 Monte Carlo Rally. (Rootes)

For that year's Alpine Rally Paddy was again in a Sunbeam Rapier, and with Jack Scott as co-driver finished sixth in the Touring Category and second in class. Despite his works drives with Rootes, Paddy managed to fit in some events in Ireland with his Austin-Healey Sprite. In the Castlemaine Hill Climb in August, he entered the Sprite and shared it with his girlfriend, Betty Cordner, managing second place in Class B, for open cars up to 1250cc, with Betty finishing third in the same class. Paddy now had a bungalow at Cultra, between Holywood and Bangor, bought from a pair of famous Northern Irish stage comedians, Jimmy Young and Jack Hudson, and he renamed it 'Stelvio'.

The year 1960 saw Paddy's first trip to USA, when he was entered in the short 'enduro' race at Riverside, a supporting race at the US Grand Prix meeting which unfortunately clashed with the RAC Rally. Two Sunbeam Rapiers were shipped over in the liner *Queen Mary*, the second car for Peter Harper. The Rootes drivers found they were up against Jaguar 3.8s driven by Briggs Cunningham and Walt Hangsen. These went off into the distance, but the two Rapiers held third and fourth positions in the race until Paddy retired when his car lost a wheel.

"The Rootes PR man in the States was a wonderful guy – or so it appeared – by the name of Henry Henkel," remembers Paddy. "He took us down from the Mission Inn, where we were staying, to a beach resort

called Salton Sea where he and his beautiful wife were living. 'S&S' was famous for low flying and testing, because it was 300ft below sea level.

"About a year later Henry Henkel came to London and was visiting Lord Rootes in Park Lane on his way to Switzerland. He had a very large suitcase with him which was, as it turned out, full of cash, and he was on his way to place the money in a Swiss bank account. It came out later that it was the biggest swindle in the motor trade and involved Price Waterhouse, the US auditors for Rootes. He had been selling cars to the dealers under HP agreements, but the cars were fictitious. Despite this, Henkel had the cheek to call on and stay with his boss, Lord Rootes – with the money with him in the suitcase!"

Visiting the Riverside circuit, California in 1960 for the saloon car race. Left to right are John Panks, head of Rootes North America, Norman Garrad, Paddy, Henry Henkel (behind Paddy), and Peter Harper. (Paddy Hopkirk)

Arrested development: the 'better' brakes that weren't

One of the shortcomings of the early Rapiers was brake fade, in the days before the cars were fitted with disc front brakes. "We actually had the brake fluid boiling," Paddy recalls. "Going down the Alps you were always stamping on the brakes to check they were still there – you had to pre-pump them.

"I remember one year when we were practising for the Alpine we saw this Rapier outside the restaurant, stuffed full of gadgets and instruments. I went into the restaurant and said 'You must be from the Rootes Group – I didn't know you'd be coming out'. The guys said 'We're not here for the rally – we're from the Engineering Department. We're out

here brake-testing'. I said 'Oh really? We've had a lot of trouble with brake-fade, with the drum brakes'. One of the engineers said 'Oh you won't fade them now, because we've modified them'. I asked who'd been doing the driving, up and down the Alps. 'We have', he said. 'Have you really tried the brakes hard?', I asked. 'Of course we have', came the reply. 'We're engineers...'

"So we got into the car and tried it – and we faded the brakes. I think they were upset with us because we'd blown all their statistics and they had to go back to the drawing board. It's the old story – the test guys don't always drive the cars to the limit."

Paddy mixing it in his Sunbeam Alpine during the '61 Le Mans. (Paddy Hopkirk)

Rich mix for 1961: Rapiers, Alpines and Elvas

Rootes didn't have written contracts with their drivers, but Paddy was retained by the team for their 1961 competition programme. This kicked off with the Monte Carlo Rally, with Paddy and Jack Scott starting from Stockholm in a Sunbeam Rapier shod with a choice of long-stud and short-stud Dunlop Duraband tyres. Leaving Charbonnières, Paddy's wipers stopped working, but they clocked out of the control and had them fixed by Lucas mechanics, losing four minutes which was soon made up on the road section.

Paddy and Peter Jopp seemingly having just spotted a bird while in the pits at Le Mans with their Sunbeam Alpine before the 1961 race. (Paddy Hopkirk)

Peter Harper and Paddy were fast on the Monaco GP circuit test, moving ahead of the class-leading Volvo of Andersson, but team mate Mike Parkes crashed his Rapier on the GP circuit when his left-hand front wheel pulled over the studs. The Rapiers suffered rather from wheel failures, Paddy recalls. "I think the PCD – the Pitch Circle Diameter – was too small, so the studs were too close to the centre, and the wheels used to pull off. I lost a wheel that way once or twice, I seem to remember."

The AC de Monaco handicap system favoured heavy cars with small engines and it was not surprising that the French press predicted a Panhard win. Predictions proved accurate, with *The Motor* magazine running the headline 'Panhard Win Rally of the Handicaps', after the French saloons with their 850cc engines scooped the first three places in the general classification. Paddy and Jack finished second in class behind Harper/Proctor, and 13th overall. Analysis after the event suggested that on scratch overall the results would have read first René Trautman in his Citroën, second Erik Carlsson in his Saab estate, and third Gunnar Andersson in his Volvo.

After the Monte it was off to North America again, this time for a visit to Sebring, Florida, for the 12-Hour Race, in a Sunbeam Alpine entered by Rootes USA. At this stage the Sunbeam name was not very well known in the States, as Paddy remembers. "We all stayed at a motel nearby, which was full of Americans.

Paddy and Jack Scott discuss their plans with team-mate Mary Handley-Page (from the aircraft manufacturing family), before the 1961 Alpine Rally in which they finished an excellent third overall. (Rootes)

'You guys race-car drivers?', they asked us. We said 'Yes', and they asked us what we were driving. I said 'Sunbeams' and they laughed. 'That's not a car', they said. 'That's a make of washing-machine!' They'd never heard of Sunbeam cars."

There was a minor mutiny before the race, resulting in Peter Jopp acting as 'union convener', as he recalls. "The drivers had a union meeting about money. We were being paid £10 a day but the motel we were staying at was £12 a day which left us nothing for food. We all agreed, and I was detailed to go to Norman Garrad to ask for more day money. Norman nearly exploded when I presented the drivers' proposition to him but he did see reason and arranged with a friend, the local bank manager, to get us some more cash."

In the race the Sunbeam crew became involved in an entertaining class battle with the Abingdon MGAs. However, the engine in Paddy's car overheated and a long delay in the pits for a change of head gasket, plus heavy tyre wear, all contributed to the MGs emerging as the class winners, with Paddy and Peter Jopp managing fourth in class.

Paddy had won the Circuit of Ireland in 1958 and was pleased to have a works Rapier for his local event in 1961. There were 134 entries, with starting points in Belfast, Omagh or Dublin on Good Friday. The rally started with two difficult navigation sections, 'cleaned' by only two crews including Bill Bengry (VW), with Paddy ending up with

14 penalties. In the driving tests, the best performance in the class gained zero penalties, and despite considerable pressure from Adrian Boyd in his fast Daimler SP250, Paddy came out winner with a lead of only 6.2 points from Robert Woodside in an Austin-Healey Sprite.

With Paddy's already proven ability on tarmac, it was not surprising that he was entered in a two-car team of 1.6-litre Sunbeam Alpines for the Le Mans 24-Hour Race. Although preferring rallying to racing, Paddy admits to a soft spot for Le Mans. "I liked the spectacle – and of course, like the Monte Carlo, it got a lot of publicity. It was more interesting than just going round and

High spirits meant that two fully-clothed adults ended up in the pool after the 1961 Alpine Rally – Paddy and Tiny Lewis (left). (Paddy Hopkirk)

Paddy wrestling with his ill-handling Formula Junior Elva at Kirkistown in 1961: he finished third overall in the Formule Libre race. (Ulster Photographic)

Paddy in his Sunbeam Alpine uses a little more of the road than was intended, on a front-end throw during a driving test on the 1961 Rhodes Cup trial. (Brian Foley)

round in circles, too, because there were differing weather conditions in the course of the 24 hours – and we rally drivers were more in our element. In the morning, when you're at your lowest ebb, we were good, because as rally drivers we were used to it. And if there was a bit of fog or wet, it was right up our street, whereas the racing drivers didn't like it at all. They'd say 'My God, my windscreen has steamed up. What do I do now?'. For us it was just normal..."

Peter Harper and Peter Procter shared a Harrington-bodied Alpine for the 1961 event but the car for Paddy and Peter Jopp had

normal hardtop coachwork. "The cars weren't highly tuned, but the engines were well put-together and very strong," says Paddy. "I think they were a lot better than we thought they were – quite a lot of technology went into making them better than the production engines." After 11 hours, while lying 24th overall, problems with the overdrive brought the car into the pits where, in the excitement, the gearbox oil was topped up. However, under the race regulations it was not permitted to replenish any oil within 25 laps, and the pit official disqualified the car. After the race the problem was found to be electrical, which was a little ironic. The Peter Harper car achieved a splendid result by winning the Index of Thermal Efficiency, and celebrations were in order, as Paddy recalls.

"We had some fire crackers, which Peter Jopp had purchased, the type with string hanging out of each end. After the race, 'drink was taken', as the saying goes, and we went round to the bedrooms where some of the crews were 'at it'. We attached some of these bangers between the door and frame with drawing pins. When the 'visitors' went back to their own beds at four o'clock in the morning, there were a number of loud explosions which I think woke up half the hotel and must have embarrassed the culprits!"

Another excellent result was achieved on the 1961 Alpine Rally, with Paddy and Jack finishing third overall out of only 25 finishers. The Rapiers also won the Gatsonides Cup for the fastest times on the special tests. During the post-rally festivities, Paddy was

thrown into the hotel swimming pool, closely followed by Oliver Speight of Dunlop, 'Tiny' Lewis, and Tommy Gold, the latter wearing a dinner jacket borrowed from David Seigle-Morris, who was less than pleased.

At this time changes were about to take place in the BMC Competitions Department at Abingdon, an organisation which was to play a significant part – to say the least – in Paddy's career. During an Alpine Rally, Ian Appleyard had sounded out Marcus Chambers as to whether he would be interested in joining his expanding retail motor group in Yorkshire. Chambers thought about it for some time and when Appleyard repeated the offer in 1961, he decided that perhaps he would like to spend more time at home. So, with a considerable increase in salary, he decided to accept the offer of becoming the Service Manager of Appleyards of Bradford. This posed a problem for John Thornley and the BMC Competitions Committee. Following a recommendation from Chambers, Stuart Turner was invited to Abingdon for an interview. Turner, who had been writing the 'Verglas' column on rallying in *Motoring News*, says the interview was quite brief. On 24 July he received a letter from John Thornley, inviting him to join the company as BMC Competitions Manager, as soon after September 1st as possible, at a salary of £1250 per annum. This would allow a month's overlap before Chambers finally left Abingdon for pastures new.

Meanwhile Paddy, with his interest in circuit racing, arranged to meet Frank

Nichols, who made Elva cars. They met at Brands Hatch where Paddy had a test-drive in one of his Formula Junior cars, which had suddenly come to prominence. Paddy made a misjudgement in thinking that the car was quite exciting and he and his friend Charles Eyre-Maunsell – the Rootes distributor in Northern Ireland – bought a car each, Paddy's with a BMC A-Series engine and Eyre-Maunsell's with a Holbay-tuned Ford unit. "The Elva was a pig," says Paddy. "It was terrible. It steered badly, and I couldn't keep it on the road. It was frankly dangerous. There was no design in it – it was just a bitza that

Paddy with an ex-Abingdon MG Midget, behind his Alfred Street premises in Belfast. (Brian Foley)

Competing in another ex-Abingdon MG Midget, in the Brentford Market driving test, during a London meeting. (Esler Crawford)

Once again minus his co-driver, Paddy in his Rapier tackles the final test on the Monaco GP circuit during the 1962 Monte Carlo Rally. (Rootes)

should never have been sold. Charles hated his, too, and changed it for a Lotus 18. That was a much better car – I couldn't keep my hands off it!"

Paddy competed in a number of hill climbs and races with his car, but remained unhappy with its handling. "I put the Elva off the road in 1962 at Dunboyne in the Formula Junior meeting and Charles Eyre-Maunsell kindly loaned me his Lotus. Ken Tyrrell had the full works team of Coopers over with John Love and Peter Procter and I led his cars into the first bend – which rather surprised the works drivers, and me too! I remember their wheels almost being in my cockpit and thinking that they were very rude, these English drivers! I finally finished third behind the two Tyrrell cars. I was really thrilled by it. Ken Tyrrell came up to me afterwards and said 'You don't hang about', or something like that. I later turned down an offer from Ken Tyrrell to

Paddy winning the 1962 saloon handicap race at Phoenix Park in his Hillman Minx 'HOP 750', fitted with the engine from a Le Mans Sunbeam Alpine. (Brian Foley)

drive Formula Juniors for him, but it was the start of my racing for him and John Cooper in Mini-Coopers."

In the Dunboyne race meeting, featuring the Holmpatrick Trophy, Paddy crashed Charles Eyre-Maunsell's Elva in practice: coming out of the Sheaf of Wheat railway bridge, he missed a gear and dumped the car in a deep gully. In the Trophy race he drove his Sunbeam Alpine but the water-pump pulley hit the radiator when he went over a yump on the circuit, damaging the radiator and causing retirement; the engine mountings were standard Rootes items, and were too soft to restrain the engine properly. In the later Kirkistown race meeting, once again in the Sunbeam Alpine, he was luckier, winning the race for MGA and Sunbeam cars.

So, with the end of another busy year approaching, it was time for the RAC Rally, with Norman Garrad entering a team of Rapiers. Team-mates Tiny Lewis and David Stone were lucky not to suffer serious injury after Paddy crashed through a five-bar gate on a gated road high in the Yorkshire moors, smashing his lights. When Peter Harper arrived in another of the Rapiers, he saw the car in front slow and then drive over the remains of the gate. Peter kept going but Tiny Lewis was next on the scene and failed to see the top spar still swinging backwards and forwards loosely. The spar came through the windscreen at an angle and out through the passenger window. When Tiny glanced across he thought his co-driver's head had been knocked off but in fact he had ducked

Top: Paddy's Sunbeam Rapier tops the summit of the Col d'Izoard on the way to third place in the 1959 Alpine Rally. (Studio Erpe)

Above: Paddy and Jack Scott by Cannes harbour display their coveted Coupe des Alpes (their second) after the '59 Alpine. (Paddy Hopkirk)

Right: A smart Paddy Hopkirk posing in Belfast with one of his first Standard Ten Tip Top sales vans. (Paddy Hopkirk)

Above: The 1071cc Mini-Cooper S in which Paddy won the 1964 Monte Carlo Rally is kept in original condition. (BMIHT)

Left: Attention to detail in preparation is what wins rallies – Gerald Wiffen, a total professional, built many of Paddy's winning cars including the '64 Monte winner. (BP)

Opposite: The winning car near La Turbie, all lamps ablaze. (LAT)

Above left: This Michael Turner painting depicts Paddy during the 1964 Monte Carlo. (Michael Turner)

Above: The National Anthem is played for the winners of the 1964 Monte Carlo Rally. (LAT)

Left: Paddy in his Austin-Healey 3000 streaks along the Cooper Straight during the 1965 Guards 1000 race at Brands Hatch. (Jan and Alaster Smith)

Opposite top: Paddy ditch-hooking during the 1966 RAC Rally. (BMIHT)

Opposite bottom: Paddy is towed from the finish of the 1967 Rally of the Flowers in San Remo by Tony Fall, after freewheeling over the line with a broken driveshaft coupling. (Mike Wood)

Above: Paddy and Ron Crellin collect their trophies from King Constantine of Greece after winning the 1967 Acropolis Rally. (BP)

Below: Raising the dust on the 1967 Acropolis Rally. (Mike Wood)

Above: Paddy and Ron Crellin with journalist Gordon Wilkins and their winning car, after the 1967 Alpine Rally. (Mike Wood)

Below: Paddy at speed on a 'selective' during the '67 Alpine. (Mike Wood)

Above: On a special section during the 1967 Alpine Rally. (BMIHT)

Below: Paddy giving instructions to a local rally driver during the Austrian rally drivers' course in 1967. (BP)

sideways out of the way! Fourth overall and a member of the winning team was a good result for Paddy, but there were some tensions in the Rootes team, as Ian Hall recalls. "Paddy got very irate with Peter Harper on this event because Peter thought they had a gentleman's agreement that he should not be beaten by Paddy. When Paddy took one minute off Peter he didn't think it was playing the game."

Paddy was again a natural choice to be included in the Northern Ireland team for the Ken Wharton Memorial driving tests, this time driving an MG Midget. The Irish boys, including Dr Thompson Glass and Robert Woodside, came second to the Midlands team.

So 1961 came to an end after a fairly quiet season for the Rootes works team, but with a number of excellent results for Paddy and Jack Scott. Norman Garrad confirmed another year with the team, and once again it was to the snow and ice of the French Alps and Monte Carlo to start the New Year.

1962: Monte success – and back to Le Mans

Paddy and Jack started from Paris with new equipment on the Rapiers including a 20-gallon fuel tank, an adjustable snow deflector on the bonnet, and spot lamps under the bumper. The scrutineers made competitors disconnect swivelling roof lamps before the start. Interestingly, the reporter for *The Autocar* noted that at least half the cars were fitted with seat belts but only one crew appeared to have them fastened. How things have changed!

The cars started from Paris in slightly damp weather, with the temperature around 50 degrees fahrenheit. With the mild weather most of the cars discarded their studs and Norman Garrad sent his studded Dunlop Durabands on to Chambéry. The first snow and ice appeared on the Col de Granier but most starters found the rally to be mainly snow-free. Paddy had few problems and finished an excellent third overall. Graham Hill, who was included in the works team, was penalised at the finish when one of the official seals was found to be broken. Not only did Paddy and Jack win the prize for the best-placed Paris starter, but they were part of the winning manufacturers team and won the RAC Challenge Trophy for the best-placed British crew. It was a good effort all round.

Having won the Circuit of Ireland in 1958 and 1961, there was the chance of a hat trick on the 1962 event. Paddy was entered in a Rapier with his regular co-driver Jack Scott and they achieved their aim by coming in first overall yet again, with Paddy's friend Cecil Vard second overall in a Mini. There was a slight hiccup at the end when a protest was submitted on behalf of Volkswagen, claiming that the Rapier should not have had overdrive operating on all forward gears. This was thrown out when the scrutineers found that this mod was quite legal.

Paddy certainly didn't spare the horses, as fellow Trinity man Maurice Bryan, co-driving Peter Jenkins in a Borgward, recalls: "I remember coming in towards Belfast doing about 70mph because of delays caused by holiday traffic and being overtaken by Paddy at some colossal speed. It was quite frightening!"

Rootes prepared three Sunbeam Alpines for

The Lotus 18 Formula Junior borrowed from Charles Eyre-Maunsell being driven in a real road race through the streets of Dunboyne – complete with lamp posts, telegraph poles, kerbs and street furniture – in 1962; Paddy finished third overall. (Esler Crawford)

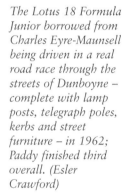

Tension at the start of the 1962 Knockagh Hill Climb, as Paddy prepares to grapple with the terrible handling of his BMC-engined Formula Junior Elva. (B E Swain)

the 1962 Le Mans 24-Hour Race, with Paddy and Peter Jopp driving 9203 RW and Peter Harper and Peter Procter driving 9202 RW, and one spare car in reserve. One interesting modification carried out by Thomas Harrington Ltd was the reprofiling of the boot and rear wings so that they were level. Paddy's car began to suffer from low oil pressure, and when a big end starting to complain the car was brought into the pits.

"Under the regulations you weren't allowed to change the oil, so the mechanics dropped the sump, changed the bearings and used my future wife Judith's tights to sieve the oil to get rid of the metal particles and so on," remembers Peter Jopp. "The damage had been more severe than expected, and the car retired at about 10.00hrs on the Sunday, after 187 laps, leaving Paddy with a long walk back to the pits."

After the race Paddy was able to acquire a spare Le Mans engine from the Rootes competitions department and this was fitted to the Hillman Minx which he had over in Ireland. The car was entered in the Phoenix Park race meeting where Paddy finished first in the ten-lap saloon car handicap race at an average speed of 75.95mph. "The car didn't

handle that brilliantly, but it went like hell," recalls Paddy of this unlikely Rootes hot-rod, which he remembers racing just this once.

The Rootes team made a big effort for the 1962 Acropolis Rally, fielding a team of Rapiers. But it was all to no avail, as Ian Hall recounts. "For the Acropolis it took about a month – or so it seemed – to get there. You had to get down to Lyons on the train, drive to Marseilles, and then go on a Greek ship to Piraeus. The three Rapiers all ran their big-end bearings within a space of only a few miles of each other shortly after the start, due to an oil-feed problem, and we had to make our laborious way back on another crazy boat. During this journey, Paddy revealed that he had had a drive around Glyphada in the Pat Moss works Healey and was amazed at the power of the car. He was itching to drive a Healey, and this dominated his conversation for the next week as we returned home".

Paddy confirms this story. "I was absolutely knocked out by the performance of the Healey. It was easy to win rallies with that sort of power." The apple of temptation had been plucked, and it was soon to be the beginning of the BMC adventure for Paddy, and the even greater fame that was to follow.

Chapter 4

The move to BMC

1962–1963

Following the disaster on the 1962 Acropolis, Norman Garrad insisted that all the Rapiers should be returned to England for examination, which left Paddy without a car for the Alpine Rally. Stuart Turner had been at Abingdon for less than a year when in June he received a letter from Paddy asking for a works drive, saying 'I want to drive cars which are capable of winning rallies outright – even if I'm not!'

Stuart Turner obviously thought that here was the chance to get Paddy into the Alpine, but when asked by Paddy if he could be released to drive an Austin-Healey 3000, Norman Garrad replied 'Certainly not!'.

Turner had known Paddy from his pre-Rootes days. "I was teamed up with Paddy when we won the team prize with Standard Pennants on the RAC and got to know him

well on Alpines and Tulips. I never co-drove with him, though – two awkward and opinionated sods in the same car would have been too much!"

Eventually Paddy was taken on by Turner as part of the BMC team. Paddy was now working with the most talented team manager in the business. "I admired Stuart enormously," he says. "He was very clever in the way he organised servicing, he was terribly keen on recceing, and he was very supportive of anything the drivers wanted. And he listened – he was a very good listener. He invented ice notes – he just had a very innovative mind. If everybody said 'Go left', he'd go right, to see if that was possible. He was very challenging like that. He was a real team leader – the mechanics all respected him terribly. They'd work all night for him, just because they loved it.

Paddy's first works drive in an Austin-Healey 3000 was on the 1962 Liège–Sofia–Liège Rally; he is seen here crossing the Italian/Yugoslavian border before retiring prematurely with broken rear suspension. (BP)

Timo Makinen: a virtuoso at the wheel

"Timo was terribly quick – terribly! I just admired his talent – and enjoyed his company. He was good fun – he didn't take himself too seriously. Rauno was more serious – he was very dedicated. Timo was more talent than dedication. He could drive anything. I remember we all went out to some party after a talk we'd given up in Bradford or somewhere. Timo drove the service barge back, with us and the mechanics, and Stuart. There was really bad snow, and boy did he handle that car well, without spikes or anything. He had an extraordinary feel for a car. I have the highest respect for him."

"The other thing was that he had the support of the BMC hierarchy. Alec Issigonis, George Harriman and the others thought very highly of him. Stuart certainly had the ear of Alec Issigonis. He could get anything done at BMC through Issigonis. He just by-passed all the board meetings and approval and all that nonsense. He was straight down to the production line and getting the part changed so it could be properly homologated. For example I remember that the gearbox mounting, at the back, was a weakness on the Mini when we started to put a lot of power through it, because the torque of the engine wanted to twist it in the opposite way to the direction in which the wheels were turning, and you got the gearlever extension jumping up and down. So Terry Mitchell at MG redesigned it to put a ball inside a cap, with rubber then moulded around it, so that even if the rubber failed the mounting didn't fail – because if it did then the whole engine flapped about.

"With Stuart, with the mechanics, and with Abingdon, we were probably the best-organised team in rallying. We hadn't necessarily got the best cars, but we'd got the best-prepared cars. Good drivers, good cars, very good mechanics, and a very good team manager – it was a winning combination."

Big Healey debut: the 1962 Liège

Paddy's first event for Abingdon was the 1962 Liège–Sofia–Liège Rally, in an Austin-Healey 3000 with Jack Scott co-driving. It was an eventful rally for the Abingdon team. Stuart Turner decided that to save time when refuelling, the team should have its own supplies at critical controls. The author was sent with fellow-mechanic Johnny Lay and a Dunlop flexible fuel tank to Titograd, Yugoslavia. The tank was filled up with some difficulty at the local petrol station well before the rally was due and the service point set up near the control. There was little time for servicing, and with the Pat Moss Morris 1100 in trouble with broken rear suspension and the John Gott MGA arriving with a split fuel tank it was rather chaotic for a time. Paddy arrived with three minutes in hand, refuelled and was away.

The roads through to Dubrovnik were very rough and Paddy suffered rear suspension problems on this section, retiring with broken suspension at Dubrovnik. He wasn't sorry. "We arrived in Dubrovnik covered in dust, very stressed, and with the rear spring sticking up through the driver's seat into my backside.

Pressing on, over the rough gravel roads of Yugoslavia – which weren't closed to normal traffic – even coming in the opposite direction. (Paddy Hopkirk)

I was never so relieved in all my life when the mechanics said they couldn't repair it. I was really sore!" Damaged car or not, some felt that Paddy had a way to go in mastering the demanding Big Healey. "I wasn't that impressed with Paddy's driving on the Liège," says Tony Ambrose. "His times weren't that good – he couldn't hold a candle to Rauno Aaltonen." Paddy feels this is unfair, although he admits that there was a certain learning curve with the Healey.

"Of course I got better – especially on the loose. I was learning all the time on the loose. The Scandinavians were always superb on the loose, with their left-foot braking. They could go into a bend too fast, and get it round. I wasn't good enough at left-foot braking to do that. In general the car handled quite well, but it's true that downhill on the loose it was lethal.

"The thing with the Healey, though, was that the power was so outstanding that you didn't need necessarily to go that fast around bends, as in between the bends it was so quick. I think the power and the performance made up for all the discomfort. It was a hairy monster, really, but it was good for me, in terms of results. I was glad, all the same, when the Mini saved me from it – front-wheel drive was great! For my style of driving, which was cautious, front-wheel drive was much more forgiving. The Scandinavians were much wilder – they were much more aggressive and much faster than I was at that stage. I found that with the Mini I could be a bit wilder. I drove it much more to its limit, extracting more of its potential than had been the case with rear-wheel-drive cars."

In Northern Ireland, another change of car took place when Paddy purchased an MGA Twin Cam from his old friend Robert Woodside. Paddy raced the car at Dunboyne circuit but without much success. It was not unknown for Abingdon to occasionally loan out cars to the works drivers for UK rallies, sometimes using the exercise to test components. One of these events in 1962 was the London Rally, when Paddy was given one of the new Morris 1100 saloons; unfortunately the car retired with a slipping clutch. The 1100 had of course only been launched in August that year.

Racing was still on the Hopkirk agenda, and for the International Six-Hour Touring Car Race at Brands Hatch in October Paddy was invited to share a Riley One-Point-Five with Alan Hutcheson. Alan had been successfully campaigning the Riley, prepared by Barwell Engineering with support from Abingdon, but this time the car retired when the right-hand front wheel fell off at South Bank corner.

Peter Riley, who later became involved in Paddy's business ventures, was only briefly a team-mate because he went to drive for Ford just after Paddy joined BMC. "I thought he was a good safe driver but in the Ford team I think he was regarded as an ordinary talented works driver. His subsequent results, I think, proved he was more than an 'ordinary' talent."

Paddy understands what Riley means: he says he might not have been out-and-out fast, but he was someone who conserved his mechanicals and got to the finish when other faster drivers might have been forced out as a result of having over-abused the machinery.

Sharing a Riley One-Point-Five with Alan Hutcheson in the 1962 Brands Hatch Six-Hour race; later a wheel sheared off. (BMIHT)

"I wasn't that quick – I didn't want to die, and I didn't like having accidents. But I finished a lot of events because I was good with gearboxes. I changed gear a little bit slower than other people. And of course the Finns, with their left-foot braking, put a lot more strain on the cars. They went faster – Timo was terribly quick – because of course you can go faster with left-foot braking because it's more forgiving. It's a bit like traction control – you keep the power on, and the brakes on, and therefore the wheels don't stop turning. Also you don't get punctures as easily, because if you go into a loose surface with a wheel locked there's a risk the tyres will get cut. But if the wheel is turning, you won't get cuts in the tyres.

"Not helping the mechanicals, I think that Timo was changing gear without using the clutch – if he was left-foot braking he had to – and he was very quick. But I was finishing events – and you've got to finish an event to win. The Alpine, for example, was very hard on driveshafts, transmission and everything, and I remember one year the gearbox was starting to misbehave, but I nurtured it through. I don't like to boast, but I was good on gearboxes..."

The 1962 RAC in a Healey – and Paddy's first Monte in a Mini

For his first appearance in a home International for BMC, Stuart entered Paddy and Jack Scott in the 1962 RAC Rally in an Austin-Healey 3000. "I liked the RAC Rally so long as it was not an icy, snowy event," says Paddy, who was lined up with a formidable BMC entry of eight cars – including three more Big Healeys, driven by Pat Moss, Don Morley and Peter Riley. After hitting a rock and bursting a front tyre and damaging the front suspension in the Bin Forest, Paddy drove two miles on the rim to the end of the stage to arrive at the finish in Bournemouth second in the general classification behind winner Erik Carlsson in his Saab. This was an excellent result, matching that of Pat Moss the previous year and confirming Paddy's talent in a more powerful car than he had used in the past.

After the RAC, Paddy returned to Northern Ireland to take part in the Go-As-You-Please Rally in his Sprite. Other competitors

Paddy's first Monte Carlo rally for BMC: here he and Jack Scott are seen leaving Paris at the start of the 1963 event, in their 997cc Mini-Cooper. (Paddy Hopkirk)

included regulars Ernie Robb in a Sprite, UAC honorary secretary Gordon Neill in a Herald-Climax, and Ronnie McCartney in a Mini-Cooper. The rally started on the Clandeboye to Newtownards road and consisted of eight driving tests in local quarries in the Newtownards area, finishing in Donaghadee. Many of the competitors made errors on these tests and although Paddy did not excel, his aggregate times resulted in another local victory for him.

For his introduction to the Mini, Paddy was to have a go at the 1963 Monte. Carrying out practice for the Monte was essential, but Paddy did not like recces, which he found boring.

"We'd make our notes and then we'd go out at three o'clock in the morning to practice them, in the hope that nothing was coming the other way. We'd try the sections flat-out – at the maximum. I remember practising all December with the Monte notes, going out and trying the notes, changing them, reversing back down and saying 'No, that bend – I think we can take it flat' and then changing the notes from 'very fast' to 'flat'. It was important work. Good notes, well read, are worth times 10–15 per cent faster, and you're much safer – especially with ice-notes, which made you safer still. Stuart was very generous about recceing, given that we were on day-money, but it was an essential part of winning. Recces

During a test session at Finmere airfield for the 1963 Sebring MGBs. Left to right are Stuart Turner, his wife Margaret Turner, Don and Erle Morley – and Paddy, trying to be funny. (BMIHT)

were also important in that they enabled you to get to know your co-driver better, because you spent so much time together."

The 997cc Group 1 Mini-Cooper was prepared by Brian Moylan, and Paddy was a little surprised to be called down to Abingdon by Stuart Turner to practise fitting snow chains. Although Paddy's car was identified by the registration '407 ARX', the actual car was '17 CRX', the number being changed to help the preparation schedule. Paddy and co-driver Jack Scott started from Paris alongside teammates Pauline Mayman and Val Domleo in another Mini-Cooper, and Christabel Carlisle and Timo Makinen in an Austin-Healey.

That year all Athens and Lisbon starters were eliminated by snowy conditions but conditions in France were not much better.

Ice-notes: another Abingdon innovation

One of the many Turner ways of getting one ahead of the opposition was in his use of ice notes to accompany the pace notes that had already been prepared – and practised – in advance. Paddy recalls how they operated:

"We used a crew of experienced co-drivers to go ahead and go over the stages and mark our notes with where the ice was – so not only did we know whether the bend was left or right and how fast it was, but we also knew whether there was any lethal ice around. The guys would mark our notes in red for where the ice was, and then give us back the notes. It was bloody well organised – Stuart made sure the ice-note crews had copies of each rally car's notes to mark-up.

"The ice-crews who were making the ice notes also helped us make the decision about what tyres and spikes to use. The Finns – and in particular Timo – were very good at helping Stuart with tyre selection. The Finnish tyre-spikers were very knowledgeable, and I think Timo's input was very helpful.

"The thing is that spikes on asphalt are no good, and the longer the spikes the worse they are on asphalt. But the deeper the snow the longer the spikes you need. So when you have an event that starts low down, goes over the top of a mountain, and then down the other side, you get varying degrees of snow and ice as you go higher, and then on the north side, going down, you get a hell of a lot more. So the judgement you have to make is what length of spike you use for the amount of ice you are likely to encounter – and that is a difficult decision to make. "

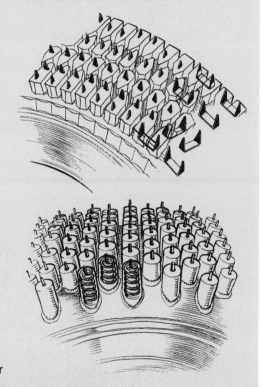

Above: Finnish spiked remoulds on a Dunlop SP carcass. Top is the 'chisel' by Rengas-Ala and bottom the spring-steel spiral or 'porcupine' by Kelhu. (Autocar)

The Mini-versus-Citroën rivalry continues on the GP circuit during the '63 Monte. (LAT)

The Donald Healey Motor Company team representing BMC at Sebring in 1963, ready for the 12-hour race – Paddy, in very short shorts, is with Denise McCluggage and Stuart Turner, with Christabel Carlisle on his immediate right. (Paddy Hopkirk)

Paddy, Bob Olthoff and Christabel Carlisle taking a short holiday break in Nassau on their way home from the 1963 Sebring race. (Paddy Hopkirk)

"I remember the very cold weather down in the south of France and having a lot of trouble with the windscreen freezing up," says Raymond Baxter, having his first drive with the team, starting from Stockholm in an MG 1100 with Ernest McMillen. "Ernest said 'There is only one thing for it' and produced a half bottle of brandy which he had been keeping for medicinal purposes, and splashed some on the windscreen!"

Bo Ljungfeldt in his Ford Falcon was fastest on all six special tests but lost time on the road with various problems. The only serious problem that affected Paddy was when Jack Scott's trousers started to disintegrate, requiring frequent repairs with safety pins, but this did not prevent them coming in sixth overall – not bad for someone who originally said he wanted to drive an Austin-Healey 3000! Once again showing off his skill as an auto-test driver, Paddy made fastest time in the manoeuvrability test after the rally.

Soon after the Monte, at the AGM of the Dublin University Motorcycle & Light Car Club Paddy was elected an honorary life member of the club in recognition of his worldwide rally successes. A further diversion came when the London Motor Club organised an 'Autobog' at Brands Hatch for the BBC *Grandstand* programme, specially for Monte runners and with commentary by Raymond Baxter. The circuit, made up of the grandstand road and main car park, soon became a morass of mud after a quick thaw dispersed new snow fall. In the final, Paddy had a desperate battle with Pat Moss in an Anglia, the two racing alongside each other with Paddy at times holding the driver's door open to see where he was going. This battle between Paddy and Pat was a feature of the event, with Paddy eventually finishing second overall behind Makinen in an Austin-Healey 3000 – Timo showing off his skill at the wheel of the powerful Healey with its special Finnish spiked tyres.

Paddy, in a Mini entered by the Cooper Car Co, leads Alan Hutcheson (Riley One-Point-Five) and a Jaguar during the May 1963 International Trophy Meeting at Silverstone; he finished second in class. (Harold Barker)

Racing the Mini

One of the first race meetings at which Paddy appeared in a works 997cc Mini-Cooper was at Snetterton in the Lombank Trophy Meeting. Paddy was not placed in the race.

Ginger Devlin had been running racing Minis for Cooper, the cars being in British Racing Green and with engines prepared by Morris Engines Branch under the guidance of BMC's respected engine man Eddie Maher. Devlin had been given the job of preparing a special twin-carb Mini with in effect a Formula Junior engine, and a remote-control gearchange, for John Cooper to take to Longbridge. This was before a 'tweaked' version of the Mini had been planned by BMC. Showing this car to the management at Longbridge so impressed them that it resulted in the birth of the Mini-Cooper, launched in September 1961 in 55bhp, 997cc form.

"Paddy's business was going well," recalls Devlin, "and I remember him bringing into our workshop his new Paddy Hopkirk accelerator-pedal extension; there were about eight of them on a card. We always welded an extension on the race cars for heel-and-toe gearchanging, but this one just bolted on in five minutes."

Abingdon decided to enter two of the new MGBs at Sebring and with the Donald Healey Motor Co also entering cars, Stuart Turner asked Geoff Healey if Paddy could drive one of his Austin-Healey 3000s with Donald Morley co-driving. They covered 187 laps, finishing fourth in class.

By now Paddy was a convert to the Mini. "I was at Oulton Park driving the 997cc Mini-Cooper for the Cooper Car Co – I think because I had made an impression on Ken Tyrrell and John Cooper driving the Formula Junior Lotus in Ireland against the Cooper cars, when I'd beaten the works cars into the first corner at Dunboyne. In fact Ken did actually offer me a works drive in his single-seaters. Anyway, Stuart turned up in a new 1071cc Mini-Cooper S. I had the chance to drive the car outside the circuit and I thought it was fantastic. It was a different kettle of fish from the Cooper. It wasn't just the engine – it had bigger brakes and other differences."

It was no hardship, then, for Paddy to be allocated a Mini-Cooper for the 1963 Tulip Rally, with Henry Liddon as co-driver; the duo came in second overall. Jack Scott had indicated to Stuart Turner that he would be giving up regular co-driving owing to the pressure of running his jam-manufacturing business, hence the new man in the passenger seat. "I got on so well with Jack," says Paddy. "He spoke the same language, and we gained some excellent results together and he became a very good friend of mine. I didn't want him to go".

Le Mans starts: a question of technique

"I was good at Le Mans starts," says Paddy. "I used to practise a lot. I used to leave the car in gear – as you got in you hit the clutch and the starter at the same time. You couldn't hear anything, because of the noise from the other cars, so you had to look at the rev-counter to see if the engine had fired. You let it go up to 6000rpm and then you let the clutch out with a bang. They were good fun, Le Mans starts! Stirling Moss was very good at them. I remember asking him whether he left it in gear or not – he agreed that if you didn't leave it in gear, when you depressed the clutch it could be hard to get the car into gear quickly. Also you didn't need the handbrake on if you had the car in gear."

First Le Mans for the MGB

There was still in effect a BMC ban on official entries in long-distance European races, in the aftermath of the 1955 Le Mans disaster, so an entry in the Le Mans 24-Hours with an MGB was made in the name of Paddy's co-driver, Alan Hutcheson. Paddy recalls that his team-mate's performance might have suffered from his antics the night before the race. "I was in the room next door to Alan and he had this gorgeous blonde girlfriend. Some of the noises during the night from next door were rather distracting – we were holding tumblers to listen through the wall! In the morning I didn't think he was that fit, and I said 'I think I'd better do the first bit and start the race'. He said 'Oh no, no, I'm the first driver, I'll do the start'. Of course, almost immediately he went off into the sand at Mulsanne Corner. Alan could appear to be a bit arrogant sometimes, and I think some Ferrari had come up behind him and at the end of the Mulsanne straight was out-braking him, and I think he said 'I'll show that bastard' – and promptly put himself in the sand. He was a quick driver and very kind to me."

The car was stuck in the sand for one hour 25 minutes, while Alan dug frantically with his hands and anything he could lay his hands on including his crash helmet, as Paddy remembers only too well. "An exhausted Alan managed to free the sand-filled car and get it back to the pits just in time for me to take over before the car was *hors de course*. I took over to keep us in the race, and there was sand coming out of everywhere!"

During the race the mechanics carried out one tyre change and one precautionary pad

Paddy's second attempt at the Liège–Sofia–Liège Rally in an Austin-Healey 3000 was more successful, he and new co-driver Henry Liddon finishing sixth overall. Here they are seen anxiously entering Yugoslavia. (BP)

change, and the MG went on to finish 13th overall. The car was actually classified 12th overall, however, as the gas-turbine Rover-BRM which finished 8th was not officially categorised, on account of its means of propulsion. In what was one of the slower cars, Paddy drove a steady and skilful race, as Richard Harwood, an apprentice with Smiths Industries spectating at the Esses, testifies: "I was so impressed by the way in which Paddy drove that car," recalls Harwood. "Lap after lap he held the same line, just on the limit through those corners, just missing the wreckage of a Lola which had lost it just after the Dunlop bridge and was parked in a dangerous position."

Paddy reckons that as a rally driver his cornering technique looked different from that of the racing boys. "If it's a slow car you have to go quickly through the corners to make up for the slowness on the straights. We rally drivers probably looked quicker than we were, though, because we were a bit sideways..."

Alpine and Liège: Paddy returns to the Big Healey

Immediately after Le Mans, Paddy left the circuit and drove down to Marseilles in an Austin Westminster for the start of the Alpine Rally. Back behind the wheel of a Big Healey, Paddy was fastest on St Baume, the first stage, but then went off the road. His old team-mates from Rootes, Peter Harper and Ian Hall, were in a Sunbeam Rapier fitted with a limited-slip differential for the first time. Peter threw the car into a hairpin in his usual way and promptly rolled the car. Ian Hall takes up the story...

"After sorting this out, which took some time, we continued up the col and half way down on the road section there was Paddy's car pointing at Marseilles. He was sitting there with about 4000rpm on the clock, dropping the clutch trying to get back onto the road. Every time it jumped forward, it seemed to move further over the edge. We attached two tow ropes to the Healey and tried to pull him out. But the Rapier didn't have enough grip on the tarmac and the back end just skidded across the road as soon as Peter put the power on. Sitting beside the road with Jack Scott, Ian realised that Paddy did not know that they were out of the rally and thought they had stopped to lend a hand. Paddy kept saying alternately 'Thanks for helping' and 'You bastards, you can't go and leave me now'.

"I said to Jack 'What are we going to do?' Jack's reply was to the effect that 'You can leave the bloody thing there – I'm not going another mile with Paddy in his current state of mind!'..."

In compensation for his bad luck on the Alpine, and the disappointment of his first Healey drive in the Liège–Rome–Liège, Paddy was more fortunate on the 1963 Liège, getting the Big Healey home in this rough marathon in sixth place overall.

Tour de France triumph

It was back to a Mini-Cooper for the Tour de France. This was a long, very tough endurance event, but Stuart Turner reckoned that if good reliability were maintained a result could be obtained with the 1071cc Mini-Cooper S. Paddy's car, '33 EJB' – which was to become even more famous – was prepared by Johnny Organ and was included in a line-up of three more Mini-Coopers and an MGB. During the 90-minute race at Spa the car ran on a good helping of Radweld as the radiator was leaking. At Rouen, Paddy was ninth overall in the race and on the Aubisque Hill Climb he was second-fastest overall. One of the most spectacular sights was during the 1½-hour race

Paddy and Henry in their Austin-Healey 3000 leaving Yugoslavia during the 1963 Liège. The Healey is a sidescreen-equipped MkII rather than the winding-window MkIIA introduced during 1962. (Paddy Hopkirk)

at Le Mans when three Minis came round lap after lap in tight line-astern formation. "I learnt so much about slipstreaming here, with the three of us almost touching bumpers," says Paddy. "Effectively you had 300bhp driving one 'shape', the front car breaking the wind and the rear car taking the drag. This gave us about 10–15mph extra speed on the straights, but the two trailing cars at the back had to keep weaving out of line to avoid overheating. Going round Le Mans in a Mini wasn't much fun, but this made it a bit more exciting!"

At the Pau Circuit the Hopkirk/Mini combination was sensational in the rain, the little Mini swapping places with the 7-litre Ford Galaxie of Henri Greder. "The Galaxie blew us out on the straights because it had hundreds of horsepower more, but on the twisty bits at the back of the circuit I would come out in front again," recalls Paddy. "It was a real David-and-Goliath thing, and we got the sympathy of the French, thanks to the event being covered on French TV for the first time, for 20 minutes a day."

The Cooper S held together and finished third overall and first in the Index of Performance, a tremendous result of which Paddy says the BMC top brass were at first unaware. "We were at the Motor Show in London immediately after the Tour, on the BMC stand. I remember Sir George Harriman coming up and saying 'Hello! Are you still working for us?' – all that sort of stuff. I said I'd just done the Tour de France, and he said 'What's that?'. Then the doors opened and all the French BMC dealers descended on the stand, and instead of ordering ten Mini-Coopers they were ordering a hundred each – that sort of thing. The Mini-Cooper had made its mark in France, and I think BMC woke up at last to the fact that rallying sells motor cars."

Whether or not sales of Minis in France really jumped tenfold – the main Paris distributor is said to have requested a still-impressive three times his normal quota – the team certainly deserved the post-rally party held at La Fiesta near Nice Airport. It was a lavish affair featuring food and drink from many nations served by staff in national costumes, with champagne being dispensed from a petrol pump. Unfortunately there was a go-kart track in the complex and one can no doubt visualise the scene as many well-oiled drivers and mechanics tried to prove their skills. Rally driver Geoff Mabbs managed to shear off the stub axle on one kart and BMC mechanic Brian Moylan overturned his, collecting nasty grazes on his chin and leg not to mention dire results to the trousers of his best suit.

Back in Britain, Stuart Turner arranged test sessions at Silverstone in October and November, to evaluate driver performance. The second of these, in November, sticks in Paddy's mind. "This was the second time that I really met Jackie Stewart. He was brought along by Ken Tyrrell, who was one of the observers, as he had shown some promise in the Tyrrell Formula 3 car".

There was a line-up of nine rally/race drivers including Roger Mac, Timo Makinen, Warwick Banks, John Fitzpatrick, Clive Baker, Rauno Aaltonen and Harry Kallstrom. The drivers all had to do three laps each in each of the nine cars available. Paddy was fastest or second fastest in eight of the cars, but did not have a go in the Formula 3 car which was reserved for drivers with F3 experience. Jackie Stewart was impressive, with the fastest time in the F3 car but also the fastest time in the race Austin-Healey 3000, the MGB, and a Mini fitted with Hydrolastic suspension. Geoff Healey and Stuart Turner were judges. "Naturally I didn't mind these test days," says Paddy. "But I didn't always feel comfortable about them. It kept you on your toes as you knew that Stuart was always looking for new talent".

Year end: the 1963 RAC Rally

The year 1963 closed for Paddy with the RAC Rally, in which he was entered in Mini-Cooper S registration 8 EMO; his co-driver was Henry Liddon, and the car was prepared by Gerald Wiffen. "We had a wonderful team of mechanics," says Paddy. "They were all good, but Gerald was particularly meticulous and was a very nice guy whom I got on with really well. He was a totally professional hands-on engineer".

It was a very wet and muddy RAC and the Minis were fitted with new dural sumpguards. The strengthening strips welded on the outside of these wore through, however, and the guards had to be reinforced during the overnight halt at Blackpool. A further innovation was that quartz-iodine bulbs were now available, although only in single-filament

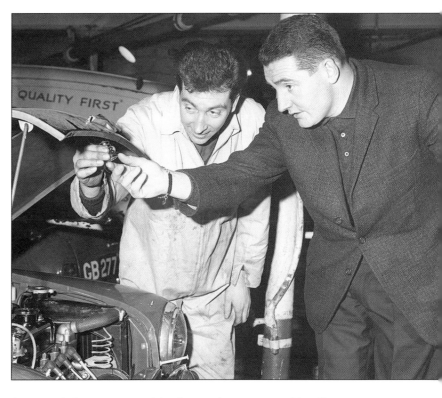

form, and these were used in the spotlamps for the first time. Paddy was the best-placed BMC driver, finishing fourth, just in front of Timo Makinen in a Healey.

The Monte Carlo regulations were out by now and it was time to think about recces. With preparations in full swing at Abingdon, now it was 'all systems go' for the mechanics and the crews, as they readied themselves for the Monte in January.

Gerald Wiffen, Paddy's regular mechanic, who built the car, showing Paddy round his Mini-Cooper S before the 1963 RAC Rally. (BMIHT)

Paddy splashes through the mud on a forest stage during the '63 RAC, in which he eventually finished fourth overall. (Paddy Hopkirk)

Chapter 5

The big one

Winning the Monte in 1964

So now Paddy had been with the BMC team for 18 months, having competed in nine events – four in a Mini, four in an Austin-Healey 3000 and an MGB at Le Mans. Competitions Manager Stuart Turner was looking for an outright win with the 1071 'S', so the emphasis would be on Minis for the 1964 Monte. Indeed, the Mini-Cooper S was now the rally car to have and there were no fewer than 38 Mini-Coopers on the entry list, more than any other model.

Well aware of the danger of starting all his cars from one place, Turner split the crews between Oslo, Paris and Minsk. "That was something that cost quite a lot of money, but he was correct to spend the money," says Paddy. "If we'd all started from the same place, we could have ended up with a total wipe-out and lost all three cars. I would think Stuart was quite innovative in starting us all over the place. It made things more complicated for the mechanics, and it was probably an expensive thing to do, but it was a good way of hedging his bets, and also getting wider publicity for the Mini."

Behind the Iron Curtain

It is hard to imagine now the adventure of travelling behind the Iron Curtain, especially to the Soviet Union: visas for the crews, carnets for the cars, the currency restrictions and the constant feeling of being watched by gentlemen in dark coats and fur shapkas…the difficulty of communicating with the outside world…and of course the rather restricted diet, even in the best hotels. All those intrepid travellers who did venture behind the 'Curtain' were certainly very relieved when they crossed back into Western Europe.

Douggie Watts, the chief mechanic, decided

Look, no snow: kicking up the dust on a dry special stage. (BMIHT)

that as '33 EJB' had competed in the all-tarmac Tour de France, it could also do the Monte. For preparation the car was allocated to Gerald Wiffen, who had been with the Competitions Department from the start. As can be seen from the brief car specification at the end of the book, a number of interesting modifications were incorporated, including one Halda Tripmaster, fitted with a magnifying glass obtained from a jewellers in Abingdon. There were also headlamp washers, and Triplex's newly-developed heated windscreens. The recce crews had the opportunity of trying the new screens in Alpine conditions, and Paddy was one of the drivers who told Stuart Turner that the gold-film heating membrane in the laminations reduced visibility at night and was very tiring, particularly in foggy conditions.

"In the dark they reduced your light – it was like driving in sunglasses," says Paddy. "During the rally I had mine removed – the advantages didn't outweigh the disadvantages. But later Triplex developed heated screens with wires in them. The trouble with these was that when you shortened your focal length in fog it was like being in prison – the little fine wires came into your vision. You started to notice the screen and the wires."

In addition, Lucas was trying out new brighter headlamp bulbs which used iodine gas in the glass envelope, following on from the iodine spotlamps used on the previous year's RAC Rally. It was decided to fit these bulbs to the Monte cars, which necessitated dipping to small 576 Lucas foglamps, mounted outboard in a position directly below the headlamps, as the iodine bulbs had only a single filament. The team maintained its long-term association with Dunlop, this

Paddy at speed on the Col de Turini, in rather more typical conditions. (LAT)

being in the capable hands of their Rally Manager, Oliver Speight. A selection of SP and Weathermaster tyres was available, with different configurations of studs, together with racing tyres.

This year the handicap system for the rally was an attempt by the Automobile Club de Monaco to even out the performance of the cars. The 'factor of comparison' was determined by the cubic capacity of the car expressed in litres, and this should have given the unmodified Group I cars an advantage. However, if dry conditions persisted, the smaller-engined cars were going to find difficulty keeping in front of the powerful V8s on handicap.

Ford of America had entered a team of Falcons in 1963 which had astounded the rally world by winning all of the timed special tests. For 1964 Ford entered eight Falcons, powered by 4.2-litre V8 engines developing around 300bhp, and with a formidable crew line-up including Graham Hill, Anne Hall, Bo Ljungfeldt, Peter Harper, John Sprinzel and Peter Jopp.

Joining Paddy and Henry Liddon from Minsk would be team-mates Raymond Baxter and Ernest McMillen, also in a Mini-Cooper. Paddy had done a lot of practising. "I've never worked so hard in my life. During the recce, one place we stayed was Gap and we seemed to be forever returning to the town after yet another run over the local stages."

The team was very fortunate to have a real 'Mr Fixit' working for it, in the form of Dan Daley of MAT Transport. He made arrangements for the rally cars to be shipped to Gdansk on a Polish Lines vessel from London Docks, accompanied by mechanics Gerald Wiffen and Bob Whittington – the latter recalling that the staple diet on the boat seemed to be red cabbage.

On arrival at Gdansk the cars were unloaded by crane, and in freezing temperatures the convoy set off for Warsaw on very snowy and icy roads. Paddy and Henry, travelling with Raymond Baxter and Ernest McMillen, flew to Warsaw to meet the mechanics, who had managed to get the rally cars into a heated garage as protection from the sub-zero temperatures. The crews then drove in convoy to Minsk, leaving the mechanics to wait for the rally to come through Warsaw two or three days later.

Raymond Baxter, who had been a team-mate of Paddy's when driving for Rootes in Sunbeam Rapiers, had joined the BMC team and was in a Cooper S. "It was good to be back with Paddy. He was always good for a laugh, a bit of a boyo in the best possible sense. I thought Henry Liddon was a remarkable chap – quiet, studious and very amusing, The Intourist hotel in Minsk was awful and we were quite sure that the rooms were bugged, so we made sure we said the right things! As Ernest has reason to remember, we all went to

Paddy and Henry Liddon discuss the 1964 Monte Carlo Rally route with Stuart Turner (centre) in his office at Abingdon. (Bernard Cahier)

'Dexies' kept Paddy running...

How did Paddy keep awake on long-distance through-the-night rallies? In common with other rally drivers – and with RAF pilots and others during the Second World War – he took amphetamine or 'speed', in the form of Dexedrine tablets, known colloquially as 'brown-and-clears' or 'Dexies'.

"We used spandules of Dexedrine – 'No-Doze' as they called them in the States. They were capsules full of little different-coloured things. Some would dissolve immediately and others would dissolve in say half an hour. So they would work over a period – and they certainly kept you awake. They were a 'wakey-wakey' drug, available on prescription – I think kids used to take them before exams. I don't think it was against the regulations – I suppose drugs then weren't the problem they are today. I don't think we boasted about it – but I'm sure the other teams were doing the same.

"The Dexedrines made you very happy. I remember people saying 'Well, don't they affect your judgement?'. I said 'Nothing affects your judgement more than falling asleep at the wheel!'. I'd rather be slightly impaired but eyes open. The one thing they did was they put you right off food, so you didn't eat anything – and if you did eat something then they didn't have the same effect. They were better on an empty stomach. But when you came to the finish, at a control, about half a beer and you were totally whistled. Probably the cheapest way to get drunk quickly I can imagine would be to take Dexedrine first!"

the circus where there were some lovely roller-skating girls. Being behind the Iron Curtain felt all very sinister…"

Paddy had come prepared. "Knowing that such luxuries were in short supply in the Soviet Union, I had taken a supply of ladies' nylon stockings which I persuaded the hotel chef to swap for a huge tin of Beluga caviar. My intention was to sell it to the Hôtel de Paris in Monaco, but needless to say we ended up scoffing the lot, washed down with copious amounts of vodka and champagne, at our victory party."

The quartet certainly weren't bored in Minsk, says Ernest McMillen. "As we were booking into this enormous Russian hotel, there were two very attractive girls at the other end of the counter. Paddy said quietly 'Look at those girls!'. The girls heard his comments and said 'Hello boys, we're from Southend' – they were in Minsk with the circus group.

"There were endless receptions for us, and the circus group were also staying in our hotel. Every evening when they returned from their performance a party seemed to take place and we got to know them all quite well. On our last night we were given tickets and invited to attend the circus as guests of honour.

"During the performance the spotlight fell on me and the ringmaster called me into the ring. I became part of the roller-skating act, flying around the platform in front of the crowd. Then they sat me on the edge of the skating platform knowing I would fall off, which of course I did. But this was all part of the act, and as I fell the girls were waiting to catch me."

Paddy, meanwhile, recalls an afternoon tea-dance at the hotel. "When the band took a break to have their vodkas, some members of the Dutch team started to play modern western jazz on the instruments left behind, and we started to do the twist. The locals couldn't believe what these western 'barbarians' were doing, because their normal dances seemed to be the waltz and foxtrot!"

The temperature in Minsk was about 20 degrees below freezing and the crews found some difficulty starting the Minis which had been parked outside all night. The local Russians were not impressed with the Minis, with their east-west engines and front-wheel drive, and on seeing them being towed around the town to start the engines were reported to comment that at least their Volgas and Moskviches were fitted with electric starter motors…

"Before the start in the square in Minsk, the military set up this huge searchlight operated by a noisy and smelly diesel generator," remembers Paddy. "This dumb squaddie controlling the light trained it into the sky not realising that his three-million-candlepower-

Meals at the wheel

"It wasn't like nowadays, when you have a First Class chef getting the diets right," says Paddy of on-rally nourishment. "We used to have Heinz self-heating soup, and I remember Shippham's Chicken Supreme in tins. I think one of the reasons we had that was that the makers used to give it to us free-of-charge. You'd arrive at a control and the mechanics would be doing something, and they'd say 'Are you hungry?' and they'd give you a tin of the stuff.

"Otherwise we ate quite a lot of sweets and chocolate, and we used to drink a lot of Lucozade. And of course at every control the town mayor would hand you a bag of goodies from the town area – dried figs, biscuits, whatever it was. The car was always being stuffed with food. Every control point was honoured and excited to see the Monte Carlo Rally go through."

plus beam was focussed on the local overhead electric cables. The insulation melted, there was a dead short, and the whole of Minsk was plunged into darkness."

The first car started from Minsk at 34 minutes after midnight on Saturday 18 January, the route taking the cars through Poland, Germany and Holland to the start of the common route at Reims. Denis Lowe, the chief Morris Motors photographer from Cowley, flew to Minsk with colleague Ken Smiles to cover the start, and they flew back to London with their film, which was shown on BBC TV that night.

Paddy above all recalls the freezing conditions. "It was terribly cold and on the Russian part of the route there was a fur-hatted soldier at every junction. God they must have been cold. They had huge fur-lined boots and were covered in fur and looked like tea cosies with a gun poking out, this in turn being used as a pointer if you wrong-slotted. There was quite a lot of snow in Eastern Europe and the cold was relentless.

"When we crossed from the Soviet Union into Poland I shall never forget people dropping notes into the car pleading 'Take us with you – get us out of this place'. It was heartbreaking. I remember a very nice Polish doctor who came up to me at one of the control points. He spoke good English, and seemed really desperate to escape his own country."

The author was teamed with Den Green and Johnny Lay in one of the service 'barge' Austin Westminsters and particularly remembers servicing at Frankfurt in the middle of a freezing night. The area near the control was a sheet of ice and unfortunately the water container had been left on the roof-rack. The MGB driven by the Morley brothers arrived with a leaking radiator and of course needed some water. As the container was frozen, it was decided to warm it up with a welding torch. To help out, Ernie McMillen offered to hold the welding nozzle but was a bit too keen and soon melted a hole in the can. The day was saved when the Saab mechanics lent some water.

The Mini-Cooper S scrabbles for grip on light snow. (Paddy Hopkirk)

Paddy at speed on the Col de Turini during the '64 Monte. The car is in Morris form, which was generally – but not invariably – the case with the works rally Minis. (Maurice Rowe)

Nearly there – Paddy three-wheeling on the final laps on the Monaco Grand Prix circuit. (BMIHT)

Getting serious: into France

At Reims, Paddy confirmed that he would like to have his gold-laminated heated windscreen changed for a standard laminated one, and this was duly done. Now the rally really started, with the common route incorporating ten sections including five special stages. The road conditions were patchy, with some ice and snow, and fog and heavy hoar frost adding to the unpredictability.

Paddy and Henry arrived at the small floodlit area surrounding the start of the first *épreuve à moyenne spéciale chronometrée*, or special stage, at St Disdier, wearing special spectacles with dark red lenses. "It was commonsense, really," says Paddy. "If you're in a lot of bright light your pupils get smaller to stop the light getting in your eyes. It takes a while afterwards for your eyes to adjust when you then go into darkness. So we used to come into places such as Chambéry, where the special stages were starting over the mountains,

A final pose with all the trophies on the bonnet before leaving the Palace in Monte Carlo. (Paddy Hopkirk)

and there was lots of light, what with the mechanics, the photographers and everything else, and then we'd go straight off to a special stage. So we wore these dark glasses so that when we went into that special stage our eyes were wide open – which was absolutely right and worked very well. But they all thought we were a bunch of posers...

"It was again something Stuart Turner did. He went to some professor at Cambridge where we discussed all sorts of things, such as our pace notes. We used phrases such as 'fast left', 'fast right', 'medium left', 'medium right', and so on. I remember this guy looked at the language we were using. What we were worried about was the co-driver being misunderstood, or making a mistake, and us missing a bend. I remember he gave an example, from the world of aviation. When they wanted full power they used to say 'take-off power' – meaning full power as used at take-off. One day somebody was coming in to land and was under-shooting the runway. The pilot said 'take-off power' to the co-pilot, but the co-pilot took the power off instead of putting it on. So our language was looked at, but actually it was thought it was very good the way we had it, and we left it alone.

"This was typical of Stuart. He was always thinking outside the envelope. He put heart monitors on us as well. I remember on a recce Stuart would say 'Meet Joe Bloggs. He's from somewhere-or-the-other, and he wants to

wire you up for heart monitoring'. Or it would be someone looking at the food we were eating, or something. Stuart was at the start of what happens today in rallying and racing – the man who drives the machine is very important."

On the first special stage of 23kms from St. Disdier, which included the 4370ft Col de Fenestre, Paddy achieved a time of 16 minutes 13 seconds, beaten only by the powerful Ford Falcon of Bo Ljungfeldt with a time of 15 minutes 54 seconds. When taking the 'factor of comparison' into consideration, the penalties on this stage were Paddy 325.46, Bo Ljungfeldt 332.85 – which gives an indication of how much faster the Fords needed to go to beat the Mini. On the second special stage (29 miles from La Madelaine to Gap) Paddy's time was 34 minutes 11 seconds with the Falcon at 33 minutes 53 seconds. On the third stage, Paddy and Ljungfeldt were equal, with Henry Liddon reported at the time as complaining "If we take ten seconds between two corners, the blooming Falcons take five. One of them overtook us on the second section when we were really on the limit".

On the fourth stage, the Falcon was 28 seconds faster than the Mini and this was to be the pattern, with the Falcon beating Paddy by 17 seconds on the Col de Turini. On arrival in Monte, Paddy held the lead from the Saabs of Erik and Pat Carlsson respectively. Whether this would still have been the case had Paddy not indulged in a bit of quick thinking earlier in the rally is another matter. Whilst in France he had mistakenly gone the wrong way up a one-way street – and promptly been stopped by the local gendarme. Had the officer stamped his road book as a result of this infringement Paddy would almost certainly have been penalised. He thus played a variation on the old 'Englishman Abroad' number, explaining in execrable French that he had already retired from the rally, and was hurrying home to the funeral of his mother. After hearing a tearful Paddy tell him *ma mère est morte* he let the Mini go, the road book unstamped.

After a rest day, all that remained was the three-lap test on the Grand Prix circuit. The highest-placed 120 cars ran in ten heats of 12 cars, so it was on with the racing tyres. The 'factor of comparison' was not used on this test, but nevertheless the Saabs had to take ten seconds a lap off Paddy for him to lose his overall lead. Ljungfeldt made up enough time to move in front of the two Carlssons, who in turn were split by Timo Makinen's Mini, but Paddy drove quickly and safely to keep ahead.

At first, though, he didn't know that he'd won. "In those days you didn't have the electronic calculating devices you have today, and you didn't know the results until the start times and the finish times for the stages were taken into Monte Carlo and subtracted from each other so you got the gross times. Stuart stopped us when we were coming down the Turini and asked me how we'd done. I said that I didn't know but that we hadn't gone off the road and had done our best. We didn't know. I remember the French journalist Bernard Cahier ringing me at four o'clock in the morning to say 'I think you've won.'..."

Victory!

So Abingdon had not only won outright, but had secured the Team Prize with Timo Makinen and Rauno Aaltonen, and won the GT category with the Morley brothers in their MGB. Had Paddy thought that a Mini could win the Monte? "No. No way. Maybe Stuart did, I don't know. The Fords had the performance, but the thing is that that year there was a lot of snow, and the roads were very narrow as a result of how they'd snow-ploughed them clear. So the Mini was particularly good. But we'd practised well, and we had our notes. It was a combination of things – like everything."

The win was also a surprise for BMC, says

Paddy with Mini designer Alec Issigonis (left) and famed racing driver Juan Manuel Fangio, on a balcony at the Hôtel de Paris in Monte Carlo, celebrating with the caviar from Minsk. (Bernard Cahier)

Paddy relaxes in the Hôtel de Paris swimming pool after his Monte victory. (Bernard Cahier)

What a line-up! This group was captured in the Hôtel de Paris after the 1964 Monte Carlo Rally. Back row left to right are Donald Morley, Tony Ambrose, Patrick Vanson, Erle Morley, Alec Issigonis and Henry Liddon; front row left to right are Mme Joan Cahier, Jo Bonnier, Graham Hill, Juan Manuel Fangio, Paddy Hopkirk and Stuart Turner. (BP)

The BBC's Raymond Baxter interviews the winning crew at Southend Airport after they have arrived on the Carvair aircraft from Nice. (BP)

Paddy. "I don't think the BMC boys back home hardly even knew the rally was on. Suddenly they got a phone-call from BMC PR man Tony Dawson saying 'Do you realise that you've won the most famous rally in the world, and the world's entire press is here?'. I had *Life* magazine from the States interviewing me, and you know it really was a shock – I was suddenly in the public eye. This was when people went to Skegness or Clacton for their holidays, and Monte Carlo was a very glamorous place. I had a telegram from the Prime Minister, Sir Alec Douglas-Home, and I was later given the keys to the City of Belfast..."

For the team it was not all celebration, however, as Stuart Turner broke the sad news to the crews that Doug Hamblin, the deputy workshop foreman, had been killed in a road accident near Henley-on-Thames on the way to Dover and a service point. Understandably this put a big dampener on proceedings.

At the Hôtel de Paris an afternoon tea-party was organised with a photo-shoot, and among the guests were Graham Hill, Juan Manuel Fangio, Jo Bonnier and Mini designer Alec Issigonis. "I thought it was a great honour to be in the presence of Fangio and be photographed with three of the greatest GP

Left: The revolving platform at the London Palladium, with Bruce Forsyth in the foreground. (BMIHT)

Below Left: Entering the back entrance to the stage at the London Palladium. When asked by Bruce Forsyth what was the most difficult part of the event, Paddy answered "getting the Mini through the stage door". (BP)

Below: Bruce Forsyth congratulates Paddy, on the stage of Sunday Night at the London Palladium. *(BMIHT)*

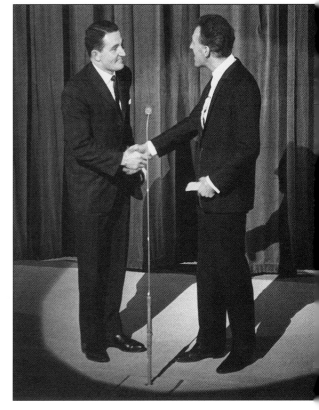

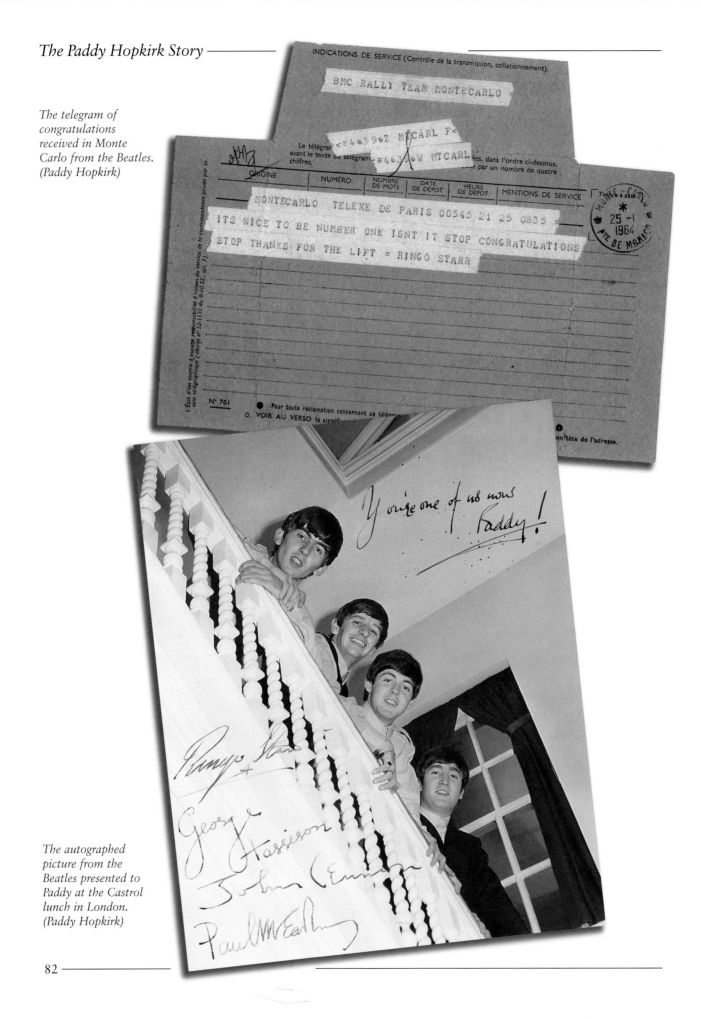

The telegram of congratulations received in Monte Carlo from the Beatles. (Paddy Hopkirk)

BMC RALLY TEAM MONTECARLO

MONTECARLO TELEXE DE PARIS 00545 21 25 0835 =
ITS NICE TO BE NUMBER ONE ISNT IT STOP CONGRATULATIONS
STOP THANKS FOR THE LIFT = RINGO STARR

You're one of us now Paddy!

Ringo Starr
George Harrison
John Lennon
Paul McCartney

The autographed picture from the Beatles presented to Paddy at the Castrol lunch in London. (Paddy Hopkirk)

Watch out Jimi Hendrix! At the Castrol celebration lunch given by the oil company's senior executives Paddy is presented with a guitar, the autographed Beatles photo – and a Beatles wig. (Paddy Hopkirk)

Another Racing Car Show photo-call. Is John Cooper trying to sign Paddy up for his race team? (Den Green)

drivers of the time," says Paddy, who then went on to a rather lavish party organised at Le Pirate, with Alec Issigonis and his great friend the suspension designer Alex Moulton both in attendance. "Issigonis was charming. It was all 'Oh Paddy! How wonderful!' and 'Oh dahling – I'll have another Dry Martini'. He had a funny laugh – he wasn't like a car engineer at all. He was more like someone from the theatre. He almost seemed peripheral to what was going on.

"We arrived in good form and had never seen flaming torches like these at the entrance to a restaurant before, let alone a fire-eater belching flames. It was fantastic. Although it certainly was a good party, our thoughts were with Doug Hamblin's family back home."

There was a bit of a problem at the end of the party when Tony Dawson realised that he did not have the means to settle the balance of the bill. After some discussion with *le patron*, it was agreed that the balance could be settled direct with the Publicity Department at Cowley.

Tony Dawson organised a British United Air Ferries Carvair to fly the winning team home

from Nice to Southend Airport. The Carvair was new to BUAF, and on the way out the pilot buzzed the airport at Lydd so that the ground staff could get a look at their new aircraft in flight. The flight from Nice was fairly subdued, and at Southend a sizeable reception committee was on hand including John Thornley and the mayors of Abingdon and Southend.

The car and crew then appeared on ITV in *Sunday Night at The Palladium* with Bruce Forsyth. There was a brief interview with Paddy and when Bruce asked him what was the hardest part of the journey, Paddy answered "Getting the car through the stage door into here!" In all it was a priceless piece of publicity.

Paddy received many telegrams, and one

which he treasures most was from Ringo Starr. "The Beatles were in Paris at the time of the Monte, but Ringo Starr had been delayed in London. BMC Publicity arranged for him to be collected at Orly Airport, and mechanic Brian Moylan with Stuart Turner met his flight in Pauline Mayman's rally Mini. After being filmed leaving in the Mini, Ringo soon transferred to a chauffeur driven Rolls to be whisked into Paris. When Ringo saw that a Mini had won the Monte Carlo he sent that telegram. I never met him myself, and never met the Beatles, but Castrol got them to sign a photograph for me, and they sent me that electric guitar – hence the 'You're one of us now Paddy!' on the photo."

Naturally enough, there was a hectic round of public appearances for the winning crew

Paddy with Graham Hill at a reception for London's 1964 Lord Mayor's Show. (Paddy Hopkirk)

and a request was made to appear on the *BBC News* in Belfast. Dan Daley helped make this happen. "I got in touch with Shorts of Belfast, the aircraft manufacturer, and suggested they might like to send one of their aircraft over to get Paddy to the BBC *Six o'clock News* on time. Surprise, surprise, they agreed, and the aircraft flew into RAF Abingdon, a stone's throw from the factory."

Paddy remembers his arrival in Belfast. "We arrived at Nutts Corner airfield, where a BBC car was waiting. I drove the car and when I got to Sandy Row in Belfast I turned right at a no-right-turn and was immediately stopped by a policeman. He said 'Who do you think you are, Paddy Hopkirk?'. That's absolutely true! The BBC man said 'Of course it is – we're trying to get to the studio in time'. He let us go and I rushed into the studio just as the *Six o'clock News* was starting".

Outside the business premises in Alfred Street, brother Eric had a 'Welcome Home' banner erected in the street to celebrate the win and there was a family dinner party in Belfast held at Chimney Corner restaurant where a very proud mother invited a total of 18 of the family, including Eithne, Elsie, Eric and Frank, and friends, such as Desmond Titterington and Stuart Turner, to celebrate the victory. The owner, Tony McCusker, got hold of a model vintage car and decked it out with comp number 37 for the occasion. The menu read just like a Monte celebration dinner:

Hors d'Oeuvres Ruski de la Minsk
Potage Hopkirk
Tournedos Monte Carlo
Sauté Champignons Monaco
Sweet Corn BMC
Croquettes Palladium
Soufflé Henri Liddon

The morning after...

There was not much prize money in international rallying but the crews were paid bonuses by team suppliers such as Dunlop, Lucas, Champion and so on. Paddy and Henry were also both given new Mini-Coopers by George Harriman after the Monte win and Stuart Turner was awarded a bonus of £500. "We both sold the cars to a dealer without taking delivery of them, which probably didn't please Stuart very much but at the

time was the only practical thing to do," confesses Paddy.

There is one last – and bizarre – footnote to the story of the '64 Monte. A week or two after the event a BMC replica of '33 EJB' was stolen from a parking place in London's West End. The thief was brought to justice and when asked in court to give his reasons for 'borrowing' the car, he said he was merely wanting to have a go in the car to see how a Monte-winning Mini handled...

"Suits you, Sir". Paddy modelling a Gannex raincoat, as immortalised by Labour PM Harold Wilson, in the company of Reg Harris, the racing cyclist and Gannex man. (Larkin Bros)

Chapter 6

Very Mini

1964–1966

The publicity following the 1964 Monte win had not abated when the crews attended their next event, at Prescott. Once again, the BBC decided to run a 'Mini Monte' for a selection of Monte runners in works cars, to be shown on their TV *Grandstand* programme. The event consisted of timed runs up Prescott Hill, but Paddy had bad luck when the rotor arm came adrift on an early run. This put him out of the results, so he finished 12th overall. Owing to publicity commitments, '33 EJB' was not available, so Paddy drove the car used in the Monte by Rauno Aaltonen.

Every effort was made to capitalise on the Monte win, with Paddy and Henry Liddon touring many BMC factories and Fort Dunlop, home to the suppliers of the winning tyres. There were many requests for interviews, and in the course of one John Sprinzel paid generous tribute to Paddy's skills. "There are two Paddy Hopkirks, one on show to the public and the other to fellow competitors – the fun-loving practical joker," said Sprinzel. "He is full of party spirit, and apparently free of the tedious responsibilities of a works driver. Those who heard his spirited rendering of *The Foggy Foggy Dew* in Warsaw during the recent Monte Carlo Rally must be puzzled at the sort of driver the capitalists are employing these days. Paddy's greatest dislike is practising, but there are few drivers who pay such attention to detail, or who are so thorough in the monotonous task of pre-rally practising; he repeatedly disclaims the dedication that all top-line drivers must possess."

Paddy testing Mini suspension on the Downs near Letcombe Regis. (BMIHT)

The Healey climbing the Turracher Höhe during the 1964 Austrian Alpine Rally. (Artur Fenzlau)

Back to the Healey: Sebring and the Austrian Alpine

American crews were called upon to drive the Abingdon-prepared MGBs in the Sebring 12-hour race but Geoff Healey asked Paddy to drive an Austin-Healey 3000 for the Donald Healey Motor Co, with Grant Clark co-driving. The car suffered tyre problems early on in the event but this was resolved in uncompromising fashion when Clark rolled the car out of the race.

There was a bit of a gap in the works drivers' schedule before the next rally. With regular co-driver Henry Liddon, Paddy was entered in an Austin-Healey 3000 in the Austrian Alpine. This was the new BJ8 MkIII model launched in February 1964, and modified in May with a revised rear suspension using twin radius arms in place of the previous Panhard rod, in order to increase the Healey's legendarily poor ground clearance. Despite being pushed on some of the tighter stages by the Polish driver Zobieslaw Zasada in a tiny Steyr-Puch, Paddy achieved yet another win for the Big Healey.

"With all its power, the Healey was particularly suitable on the steep, hilly Austrian roads," says Paddy, who recalls a close shave on the rally. "I remember Henry being told *ein bus kommt* by a German, at the start of a stage. I said 'What does that mean?' and Henry said he didn't know. Imagine my surprise when we met this enormous bus coming the other way, nearly causing a serious head-on. I now know what that piece of German means!"

Paddy and Henry Liddon in their winning Austin-Healey 3000 crossing the Austria/Yugoslavia border during the 1964 Austrian Alpine Rally. (Artur Fenzlau)

Paddy in the 1964 Targa Florio, driving the special-bodied Donald Healey Motor Co Sprite which he shared with Tommy Wisdom. (Bernard Cahier)

A special Sprite for the Targa

An outing for the Cooper Car Co Mini team at the Silverstone International Trophy race, alongside team-mate John Fitzpatrick, was followed by a run in Sicily on the Targa Florio. This was a disappointment, as the special lightweight open Austin-Healey Sprite which

Three-wheel drifting the works Mini-Cooper S to another class win, during the 1964 International Trophy Meeting at Silverstone. (Paddy Hopkirk)

Paddy was sharing with journalist and veteran competitor Tommy Wisdom retired with a broken halfshaft. The Austin back axle wasn't known for its strength, so this was no reflection on the car's preparation, but Paddy recalls that the cars run by the Healey works in Warwick were not as smart as those from Abingdon.

"They were always a bit tattier, and seemed to have been built on more of a shoestring. But beggars can't be choosers, and I was contracted to BMC and when I was asked to drive for Healey it was a question of *force majeur*. I liked Geoff Healey a lot though, and I remember that at Le Mans he and his wife Margot were a bit like a Mum and Dad – she did the soup and cooked everything. Donald Healey was so charming, too. He was a man who not just loved cars but loved life – he liked his nightlife and beautiful girls. All the women loved him – he was always smiling. He didn't look like a motor engineer at all."

Paddy was no luckier on his next international event, a second DNF ('Did Not Finish') following when his Acropolis Rally came to an end after the battery cable shorted out on his Mini-Cooper S.

Return to Le Mans for the MGB

Meanwhile, the 1963 Le Mans result had been encouraging, so next it was back to France for the 24-hour race, with the 'droop-snoot' MGB,

registration BMO 541B. Sporting race number 37, the same competition number as on the Monte-winning Mini, the MG had Andrew Hedges as co-driver. Apart from Paddy falling off a Moulton bicycle in the paddock before the start, slightly damaging his good looks, the race was more or less trouble-free.

Abingdon mechanics Den Green and Nobby Hall were on pits duty, and Green recalls an incident during one of the pit-stops. "After a driver change, with Paddy handing over to Andrew, Nobby and I were invited up to the Castrol suite for something to eat. Next thing we were called back because Andrew had come in unexpectedly. Andrew said 'I think we'll have to have a touch of brakes, chaps!'. When we jacked the car up the pads were down to the backplates, and the piston had started to push through the metal of the pad. We had a hell of a job changing them, as everything was red hot." Another minor problem was that during one refuelling stop the fuel filler cap was broken by the *plombeur*, but a replacement was borrowed from Marcus Chambers, who was running a Sunbeam Tiger from the Rootes pit.

The MGB won the *Motor* Trophy, finishing 19th overall and second in class to a Porsche 904 GT, the car having covered 287 laps, or 2392 miles, at an average speed of 99.9mph. "That wasn't bad going," says Paddy today. "But I don't think Le Mans is a great skills challenge. I wouldn't rate it as my proudest achievement. But because of the publicity and the fact that it was racing rather than rallying, and I was known more as a rally driver, then I suppose I took pride in it from that point of view."

Top Left: The MGB, winner of the Motor Trophy, *on the scrutineering ramp before the 1964 Le Mans 24-hour race. (BMIHT)*

Above: Den Green and Nobby Hall with Paddy and Andrew Hedges, in the pits before the '64 Le Mans. (BMIHT)

Left: Paddy coming through the 'esses' during the race. (BMIHT)

Left: Andrew and Paddy soak up the atmosphere after finishing the 24-hour race. (BP)

Henry Liddon gives
the victory sign to the
photographer during
the 1964 Alpine Rally.
(Paddy Hopkirk)

'For what we are
about to receive' –
a photo shoot for
Shippham's Chicken
Supreme, with
Pauline Mayman, at
Abingdon. (BP)

Bad luck in the Alpine...

It was back to a Mini-Cooper S for the Alpine Rally, the car alas retiring with suspension problems. Things had started to go wrong before then, however. The author was in a service car with Brian Moylan and Robin Vokins, and one of the service points was at Sigale. When Paddy arrived he wanted the rear brake shoes changed. There were also some modified rear hubs to fit, these having been brought out from England by Doug Watts.

This was a routine job but – as sometimes happens – the change did not go smoothly. With time running out, Liddon saying they had to go, and Paddy shouting 'Quick boys, think of the coupe', the reluctant rear drum was hastily banged on with a mallet. Liddon said 'Just put the wheel nuts on finger-tight, and I'll tighten them the other side of the control'. Unfortunately, with the delay he clocked in late – which meant that they had lost their coupe. However, the car was forced to retire later with those suspension problems. "I probably blamed the mechanics at the time, rather unfairly, as even the simplest jobs can sometimes go wrong," says Paddy today.

and in the 'Guards' –
not to mention the Liège...
and the Tour de France

Driving a Mini-Cooper for the works Cooper team in the Guards Trophy race at Brands Hatch was rather a short-lived exercise, as despite a successful practice session Paddy was forced into the pits when the fanbelt failed on the warm-up lap, and so he was a non-starter.

The Spa–Sofia–Liège Rally was always a challenge and the 1964 event brought about another retirement for Paddy, driving an Austin-Healey 3000. First an oil leak just after Kranjska Gora lost them 30 minutes, and then finally near Paracin, just south of Belgrade, retirement beckoned after the gearbox decided to provide the crew with only second gear. Looking at the service schedule, it is amazing to see that the service crew in Yugoslavia carried only one spare wheel/tyre in their car. We must have had faith in the Dunlop tyres. This was to be the last year that the event was run in this format, and fittingly it was won by Rauno Aaltonen and Tony Ambrose, also in an Abingdon-entered Austin-Healey 3000.

The good result of the previous year was not

Top left: Paddy's Austin-Healey 3000 negotiating the rough Yugoslavian gravel during the 1964 Liège, before gearbox problems intervened. (BP)

Above: Ready for the 'off' – the start of the 1964 Tour de France Automobile. (BP)

Left: Close formation at Clermont-Ferrand during the 1964 Tour, with Paddy (no.19) just at the head of the trio of Minis. (Paddy Hopkirk)

Paddy in conversation with the Duke of Edinburgh, at the Motor Show. (Sutton Photographic)

Minis during testing and the damaged car remaining on my drive for a few days waiting collection by Abingdon. While it was there, a police car stopped and the driver came to the door and asked where the accident had happened. I told him it had happened messing about on private land, as I didn't think I should drop Paddy in it."

While the new fluid-and-rubber Moulton-designed Hydrolastic suspension improved the Mini's ride for normal road use – albeit at the cost of a certain amount of fore-and-aft 'shunt' – it was less satisfactory for the rally cars, says Paddy. "It used to pump up – the wheelbase was too short, and you'd go over a few bumps and the front would go down-down-down as all the fluid displaced to the back. It was good on the 1800, with its long wheelbase, but on the Mini it was awful. They sorted it a bit by putting a one-way valve in the system."

Stuart Turner was always talent-spotting and in October a BMC driver test-day was held at Silverstone. Using two Austin-Healey 3000s, a Sprite, an MG Midget, an MGB, and 1275cc and 970cc Cooper S Minis, the best times achieved by each driver were recorded – with Paddy showing his speed by achieving fastest times in four of the cars.

A second BMC Silverstone test day was held on 4 November with a slightly different list of drivers, and including Jackie Stewart, brought along by Ken Tyrrell, who obviously rated this up-and-coming driver. Again, though, Ken Tyrrell would only let those drivers with current F3 experience drive the Formula 3 car. Overall, Jackie Stewart was outstanding, with Paddy once again being quickest of the rest. At least being in the single-seater made some sense to Paddy, unlike the tests in the other cars: "I can never understand why people take road cars on a race track to test them. Racing cars should be tested on real race tracks and

to be repeated on the Tour de France, which was listed on the FIA calendar as a race for the first time, instead of a rally. Paddy and all the Abingdon cars retired, with the exception of Pauline Mayman, who won her class.

Goodbye rubber, hello Hydrolastic

Hydrolastic suspension was launched for the Mini in September 1964 and Longbridge sent down one of their Engineering cars for evaluation. Tony Ambrose found a good loop in a section of forest at the back of Hartley Wintney, and although Abingdon didn't have permission for using this land it got away with testing cars there several times, as Tony Ambrose recalls.

"I well remember Paddy rolling one of the

Colonialism in the service of rallying?

"We were as good as everybody else – if not better – when it came to servicing," says Paddy. "The service planning was very good. Not only that, but the English co-drivers were excellent – people such as Henry Liddon were great planners and worked everything out. They were very well-travelled – and I

think it was also a bit of a colonial thing. In those days the British were better travellers. For some of the other teams foreign countries were very foreign. But with the British it was 'We've been here before. We've been to Brunei...' Travelling to India, say, was no problem for the British."

road cars should be tested on real roads, especially loose surfaces – that sorts the men out from the boys."

Paddy generally looked after his rally cars, but on the RAC this year he put his Mini-Cooper off the road into a tree on the eight-mile Blackcraig stage, causing his retirement. Ron Crellin has a few memories about the event. "I remember doing some stage notes for it. We were in a Morris Oxford, posing as photographers and with all the right passes. I was lying across the back seat with a pad with all these carbon papers to turn out about seven copies. We would arrive at a stage start, tell the marshals we were going to find a suitable spot for pictures and would be waved through. Jack Scott would read out the notes while I wrote them down. At the end of each page another seven copies had to be assembled. At the end we would go round the corner and I would have the horrendous job of sorting out these seven sets of notes. Our runner would then rush off with the notes for the crews.

"It was decided to do the same thing on the Scottish Rally, this time with Andrew Hedges driving and Jack Scott reading out the notes, with Mike Wood as one of our runners. At one of our meeting points for the note collection, we were seen by Ian Hall of Rootes passing over these sheets. Stuart said 'Drop it!' That was it…"

At this stage Paddy became a journalist – at least in name – when for 1965 *Autosport* magazine introduced a regular item called 'From The Rally Seat', with Paddy as the regular contributor. "I would get this phone call from Wilson McComb, the BMC Competitions Press Officer who would ask what I had been up to and he would come up with the text. I got a small fee for my name above the articles."

Paddy getting out of shape in one of Geoff Healey's Austin-Healey 3000 race cars during a Stuart Turner driver test-session at Silverstone. (Paddy Hopkirk)

All smiles from Paddy as he collects an Austin Mini-Cooper S test car he has just purchased to take back home to Northern Ireland. (BMIHT)

A rare dry stage on the 1965 Monte – in which, owing to severe snow, Paddy was one of only 35 cars to arrive in Monte Carlo. (BP)

Another Monte win – but not for Paddy

There was no change in the driver line-up for 1965, as Paddy had already committed to a two-year agreement at an annual fee of £4000. There was to be a big effort for the 1965 Monte Carlo Rally after Paddy's win in 1964. The influence of the Finns, Timo Makinen and Rauno Aaltonen, ensured that the latest in studded tyres were obtained, with considerable co-operation from Dunlop. In addition to the Dunlop Weathermasters with pop-in studs, Kelhu 'spirals' and Rengas-Ala 'chisels' were sourced from Finland. Sorting out the distribution of the different types of tyre was a demonstration of Stuart Turner's organisational abilities, says Paddy. "He made sure that we had the minimum number of tyres with the maximum choice – the maximum number of permutations. Logistically it was very clever. It was a bit like one of those challenges you get in the army – you're trying to get across a river and the boat only carries so many people, and you have to work out how do you do it down to the last person.

"This sort of thing was typical of Stuart. He'd ring you up in the middle of the night and say 'We'll leave two long spikes at *that*

control, pick some more up *there* that we'll give to the other car...and we'll have three sets for *that* car'. The mathematical permutations of having been given 200 tyres, with differing spike lengths, having six cars running, and trying to work out which wheels should be in which place at the right time was a Chinese puzzle, and Stuart was bloody good at it."

For the first time Lucas alternators replaced the dynamo and – as before – quartz-iodine bulbs were fitted to some of the lamps. Four of the BMC team cars, including Paddy's, used Hydrolastic suspension, and a new design of Triplex heated windscreen was also fitted, omitting the gold tint from the previous year; as mentioned earlier, this was still unsatisfactory, as far as Paddy was concerned.

An early casualty even before the start was the Raymond Baxter 970cc Mini-Cooper S, which threw a con-rod on the way from the docks, about 125 miles from Minsk. Dan Daley of MAT tried valiantly to air-freight out a new engine, but with all the Iron Curtain bureaucracy this proved impossible.

Paddy and Henry Liddon started from Stockholm in a Group 2 car prepared by Gerald Wiffen, with mechanic Peter Bartram in attendance, and had a reasonable run to St Claude. The report of the section from St Claude to Monte Carlo in one motoring magazine admirably summed up this gruelling section. 'The 500 odd miles were among the most devastating in the rally's history', the magazine wrote. 'The average speed of 35mph is all right if you can see where you are going. It was like driving into a frothing milk shake. Over 170 cars were swallowed out of the rally here where 8 inches of snow fell in two hours.'

After Chambéry only Timo and Paddy had clean sheets, but then Paddy hit a rock just on the edge of a hairpin. "It was stupid – really stupid. I wasn't even going fast at the time. You can't afford to do things like that – you have to concentrate 110 per cent."

As a result of this incident, Paddy lost 30 minutes having the tie-rod bracket welded, and was lying 18th in Monte Carlo before tackling the mountain circuit. The bracket was welded again on leaving the parc fermé for the circuit. Rally officials did not want Paddy to start the Monaco–Monaco section, because of the suspension damage, but Brian Moylan and a French BMC mechanic welded the tie-rod in 14 minutes to get them going. More welding was carried out at Sospel, with another 23 minutes lost, but just before Puget-Théniers the suspension collapsed and Paddy was out. After getting the car mobile, Paddy picked up John Fitzpatrick and Raymond Joss, who had crashed over the edge of the Gorge de Cians just after Beuil in their Austin 1800. Despite retiring on the mountain circuit, Paddy was placed 26th overall in general classification, and first in the Group II class. After a fantastic drive, Timo Makinen and Paul Easter were the winners and again there was a terrific party at Le Pirate.

Also in January, Paddy appeared in the *Irish Independent* Sports Star of the Year programme on Eire TV. In a separate award, Paddy was also chosen as one of the Caltex 'Sports Stars of 1964' and was presented with his award at the 'Sports Stars Banquet' at the Gresham Hotel, Dublin, in February.

Two famous Scots: Jim Clark and Jackie Stewart

Paddy had by now become a world traveller, never in one place for very long. Despite this, during 1965 he moved to England. "I bought a little two-bedroom mews house in Belgravia from Lady Gore, with a double garage underneath. From an investment point of view, it was

the best thing I ever did. It had one of those remote ultrasonic garage-door openers, but the trouble was that when a taxi with squeaky brakes went by in nearby Chapel Street, the door used to open..."

It was about this time that Jim Clark became a lodger. "Jim and I got on very well, and he wanted a place in London. I had a spare room, so Jim rented it from me. He was hardly ever there, because like me he was living out of a suitcase, but I had the honour of having him in my house.

"He was the most lovely, charming, well-mannered man. He wasn't just good at Formula 1 – he was good at everything. He was a wonderful motorcyclist, and his rally-driving was terrific. He could really put a rally car sideways in the dirt – he knew all about rally-driving. On one Scottish Rally he was in a Cortina. My God he put up some good times! But above all I remember him as a lovely guy, and a very modest guy – he hated the press, and he hated publicity. He just wanted to get on with the job. He was very shy, really. But the girls! The women used to rush after him!"

Paddy was at a party in Scotland when an amusing incident took place. "One year Jim invited me to his birthday party in Scotland. There were very few girls, but shortly after I remarked on this Jim said that there was a

A happy team after the 1965 Monte – left to right in the back row are Paul Easter, Henry Liddon and Tony Ambrose, while in the front row are Rauno Aaltonen, Timo Makinen and Paddy. (BP)

Paddy hugging the cliff face on his way to winning the 1965 Circuit of Ireland. (BP)

Paddy hugging the cliff face on his way to winning the 1965 Circuit of Ireland. (BP)

nurses' home down the road. I remember phoning up and saying 'There is a bit of party on here at Jim's – you know, Jim Clark – and would any of the girls like to come?' There was a lot of squealing on the phone so I said I would go down and pick them up in his van. I was already in good form and when I got there I said 'Are there any girls available for the party?'. The reaction was…well let's say that I had to beat them off with a shovel!

"There were some lovely girls and the evening was progressing well until suddenly I felt someone tugging my sleeve. I turned round, looked down, and it was Jackie Stewart. He said 'How do ye drive round that turn at Oulton Park? Do ye take it flat or something?'. I was talking to a girl and I turned round to Jackie and said 'Why don't you leave me alone? Can't you see I'm busy?'. Jackie was only drinking milk at the time. He was very serious – all he wanted to do was motor racing.

"Weeks later BMC were tyre-testing at Silverstone with a Big Healey and Jackie Stewart turned up with the Ken Tyrrell team. Ken said 'Can Jackie have a go in the car?' A bit snootily I said 'Go away, we are professional rally drivers tyre-testing'. But he persisted and said 'Can't you let him have a go?'. I said 'That little guy is probably useless. I met him up at Jim Clark's party, and he was just a pest!' Anyway we let him have a go and he was only about two seconds a lap quicker than any of us. I said to Timo and Rauno 'We'd better get rid of him quick, or we'll be out of a job!'…"

Victory in Ireland – and a wet Sebring

Retirement in Sweden – all four works Minis gave up the ghost, with broken diffs caused by lubrication problems in the freezing conditions – was followed by success in the Circuit of Ireland. Paddy was paired with Terry Harryman as co-driver in the Mini, and the duo came in first ahead of four Ford Cortina GTs.

This was Harryman's first drive with Paddy since he had been with him in his special Hillman Minx back in 1963. "I must have done something right, because I was rather surprised when Stuart Turner phoned me to see if I could do the Circuit, especially as I had already been approached by Graham Robson, then the Triumph team manager. While we were on a recce of the stages, we couldn't get into the Rostrevor Forest, and I remember walking the whole length of that stage making notes!

"Paddy decided that he had to demonstrate how to do a 360 degree spin. The first one ended with us up a bank but the repeat was OK. Not satisfied with that, he gave a demonstration of left-foot braking. Paddy didn't think he'd mastered it, and during the rally I didn't notice him trying it out very often."

The victory had not been all plain sailing, as after Stage Four one of the driveshaft couplings failed. To speed up the change the

mechanics turned the car on its side and did the job in 12½ minutes. After the rally the BMC team were challenged by Ulster TV to demonstrate a coupling change in front of the cameras, but this time the job took 14 minutes.

Immediately after Ireland it was off to Sebring, this time in a Donald Healey Motor Co Sprite coupé shared with Timo Makinen. With about five hours of the race to go, the heavens opened, causing serious flooding of the track, the water being so deep that wheels and tyres were floating about in the pit area. During this cloudburst Timo Makinen was driving and, using his rally-driver skills, he passed one of the leading Chaparrals in front of the pits and made up two laps on the race leaders before it dried out. "Timo told us when he got back to the pits that he had to open the driver's door on left-hand corners to let the water out," recalls Paddy. "With the rain, all the racing cars were stuffed. But for us it was just like a bit of a wet special stage!" The duo's efforts were rewarded by a second-in-class placing.

From one of the many requests for assistance from BMC dealers on the continent, one which Stuart Turner did accept was to enter a car in the International Luxembourg Slalom. The invitation was sent by Charles Saviola, boss of the local Morris dealership, and the author drove a Mini over to Luxembourg. Practice day was held in dry conditions, with no problems with the Mini. Next day there was a parade of drivers carrying their national flags, including Timo Makinen who had arrived from the Tulip Rally having just won his class. Timo did some demonstration runs in the wet with his Tulip Rally Mini-Cooper S before the slalom started.

The weather improved for the timed runs, with Paddy being quite spectacular, beating virtually all the powerful race machinery to win his class. Unfortunately, the event was marred by an accident at the start/finish line when a Porsche 904 ran into a group of spectators, causing at least two leg fractures.

Targa '65 – the Midget shows its mettle

In the world of MGs, much interest had been generated by the three MG Midget coupés which had been built at Abingdon. Dick Jacobs had persuaded John Thornley to build these cars, two of which had been campaigned successfully by him and were usually referred to as the Dick Jacobs Midgets. The two cars were returned to the custody of the Competitions Department in 1965 and an official BMC entry was made for one in the Targa Florio, for Paddy and Andrew Hedges. During Friday practice, Stuart Turner sent the car off on a full tank so he could check the fuel consumption and tyre wear, and he calculated

During practice for the 1965 Targa Florio, Paddy Hopkirk marks a kilometre stone as 'flat-out bend ahead'. Paddy and Andrew Hedges finished second in class in one of the Dick Jacobs MG Midget coupés. (Andrew Hedges)

Paddy drifts through Paddock Hill Bend at Brands Hatch during the 1965 Guards 1000-mile race, in which he finished fourth overall; his co-driver was Roger Mac. (LAT)

that the Midget could do 5.6 laps on a full tank of 81 litres (18 gallons) and that the tyres should complete the race distance. Practice times for Paddy and Andrew were 47.11 minutes and 48.29 minutes respectively.

Paddy started the race and lapped consistently, with times in the region of 44.30 to 44.50 minutes, coming into the pits at the end of the third lap for rear tyres and two pints of oil. After five laps the car was in the pits again for the driver change, refuelling, new rear tyres, four pints of oil and for the dampers to

be adjusted to the maximum. It was quite a good result but not fast enough to beat the Abarths, which duly won their class. The MG finished second in class, and 11th overall.

"I have to say that was a hell of a performance," says Andrew Hedges. "We were very near to winning the class, which is probably one of the finest performances that an MG Midget has managed in a motor race, but the little Abarth beat us. I remember going right round the course with Paddy, walking every corner, painting our little marks up on kilometre posts and so on. It paid dividends. We used a Fiat hire car and I think we had to take it back at least once for some new tyres."

Castrol made a film of the event called *Mountain Legend* and one of the camera crews was on a corner where Paddy spun the Midget. Paddy did a spectacular reverse spin turn to resume the correct direction on the circuit but the film crew had no sound recording of the spin. When editing was taking place the film crew came to Abingdon to dub in the sound. The author had to perform a number of reverse spin turns in the MG car park up near the boiler house with the same MG Midget, for the sound recordist…

The 1965 'Guards' in a Big Healey

The idea of the Guards 1000 Race at Brands Hatch in May was to give amateur drivers some experience in long-distance racing. This was too good an opportunity to miss and two cars were entered by Don Moore with both the Austin-Healey 3000 and MGB prepared at Abingdon, but with Moore building the MGB engine. As the report in *Motoring News* commented, 'the Don Moore entries had "works" written all over them including the mechanics'. Paddy was teamed with racing driver Roger Mac in the Healey. After a rolling start behind Roy Pierpoint in a Ford Mustang, the first half of the 1000-mile race got under way. Refuelling was by five-gallon churns and when the car came into the pits for fuel after 1 hour 20 minutes it was leading, although it relinquished the lead during the driver change. With Paddy at the wheel, a rear tyre threw its tread, costing three minutes in the pits, then Roger Mac had a coming-together with a Sprite, causing some body damage and another pit stop. Despite having some broken spokes and a fractured brake pipe, the BMC duo were lying eighth overall at the end of the first day. It was permitted to take the cars away overnight and the two Abingdon cars were whisked away to a BMC dealer locally for a thorough going-over by the Abingdon mechanics. The second part of the race was less eventful for Paddy and Roger, and they worked their way up the field to come in fourth overall and second in class by the time the second session of 189 laps had been completed.

Le Mans 1965 – return of the 'B'

The Le Mans 24-hour race was becoming a habit for the Hopkirk/Hedges duo and for the third year running an Abingdon-prepared MGB was entered. "The car would do about 126mph down the Mulsanne straight but when the Cobra driven by Sears/Thompson slowed with mechanical problems, we managed about 132mph with a tow from the Cobra's slipstream," recalls Paddy. "We were held up by a number of unscheduled pit stops. One of them was when I spotted a pit signal showing 'PIPE'. I came in and asked why I had been called in for a PeePee ...

"All that was wrong was that the mechanics

had spotted that the exhaust pipe was loose. Later the Dunlop R7 tyres started rubbing on the bodywork, and while Andrew was driving he had a blow out, causing him to complete half a lap on the flat. Towards the end we had been pressing on and gaining 21 seconds a lap over the Rover-BRM driven by Graham Hill and Jackie Stewart, hoping to overtake them and gain tenth place overall and the *Motor* Trophy. However, a calliper seal suddenly let go and we had no brakes, so we had to slow and put up with eleventh." This would be the last Le Mans for the BMC team, and the result was a good effort in what was very much a production car.

Left: It must be all over – Paddy and Andrew Hedges share a joke at the '65 Le Mans. (BP)

Below: Paddy and wife-to-be Jenny with chief mechanic Tommy Wellman, in the pits before the 1965 Le Mans 24-hour race. (BP)

Above: Chasing a Ford GT40 down a tree-lined straight. (BP)

Right: The long-nose MGB at speed on the way to its second-in-class. (BP)

Europe calling – off to Germany

The entry in the 1965 Nordrhein/Westfalen Rally was mainly to support the BMC importers in Germany and their publicity campaign. Paddy was fastest in all the tests except at the Nürburgring, where Andrew Hedges was fastest in an MGB, but the marking system prevented a good result.

After the rally, Paddy reported on it for the *Autosport* 'From The Rally Seat' column. 'Navigation was by 2-inch-to-the-mile black-and-white maps, with only time controls marked. There were lots of by-roads just like the Welsh countryside – I saw more German farmyards than I ever knew existed', he wrote. 'If Stuart Turner had known about the marking system, he would never have sent works cars. On one test the driver and co-driver had to run to the car in a Le Mans type [of] start. The Circuit of Ireland was a better event 10 years ago!'. Indeed, Paddy was sufficiently uncomplimentary about the event, saying he'd never compete in it again, that the organisers responded in kind and said they wouldn't accept an entry from him anyway...

On the Alpine Rally, Paddy and Henry were awarded a Coupe des Alpes and also collected the Coupe d'Argent for winning three non-consecutive coupes. "We used

Dunlop R7 racing tyres but if the event were run again, I'd use Dunlop SP3s because of all the loose gravel," says Paddy today. "When we had fuel pump trouble on the first night, Henry got under the car at a petrol station to change over the fuel pumps. The attendant wasn't paying attention and allowed petrol to overflow all over Henry, soaking his shirt. To prevent petrol burns, and because of the lack of time, Henry took off his shirt and was topless during the next section. This caused a number of ribald comments from other competitors, who suggested he might be posing for the Mr World competition – this was way before the Chippendales were heard of !"

At the annual Competitions Committee meeting at Longbridge where Stuart Turner presented his plans for the following year, Paddy was named as one of the team drivers for 1966, with a two-year agreement and a fee of £5000 a year. Interestingly, Rauno Aaltonen's fee was proposed at £6000 plus £50 a start. Expensive, this Flying Finn!

Top: Paddy at a press conference with Swedish rally driver Evy von Korff-Rosquist before the 1965 Nordrhein/Westfalen Rally. (Inge Wigger)

Above: Henry Liddon looks relaxed on the 1965 Alpine; he and Paddy finished fourth overall. (BP)

Left: Paddy rounds the Nürburgring Karussell on the 1965 Nordrhein/Westfalen Rally. Despite winning all but one of the special stages, he was only placed sixth overall. (Paddy Hopkirk)

Above: Celebrating the millionth Mini at Longbridge in 1965. Alec Issigonis (left) talks to Timo Makinen, while Paddy stands beside smiling BMC boss Sir George Harriman. (LAT)

Right: Paddy exits the rooftop sauna at a Helsinki hotel following his sixth position overall in the 1965 1000 Lakes rally – one of the best results achieved by a non-Scandinavian driver. (Paddy Hopkirk)

Right: Game for anything: this happy bunch of hunters comprises (from the left) Ken Gregory, former manager of Stirling Moss, Graham Hill, graphic designer Jim Kelso, actor Donald Houston, Paddy, and – holding the labrador – Les Leston. (LAT)

Flying the flag for BMC in 1965: Stateside and Scandinavia...

Another item discussed was a request by BMC Hambro, in the US, for an appearance at Bridgehampton – "a rather narrow and twisty circuit set in sandhills rather like Zandvoort", recalls Paddy. This was agreed on condition that BMC North America would foot the bill for cars and drivers. So an MGB was sent to the Bridgehampton 500 for Paddy to drive – with the Flying Finns both in MG Midgets.

Graham Whitehead was the boss of BMC North America and employed the Roland company to promote MG and Austin-Healey products. "After the race there was a big party out in the country with champagne flowing and all these guests, and it took us some time to realise that most of them were employees of the Roland company," says Paddy. "It seemed that the company were making use of the race weekend to hold a big company get-together and it was probably the first time that I became suspicious of PR companies and their motives!

"Graham was responsible for getting me onto one of those TV game shows – *To Tell The Truth*, which was a sort of simplified version of the UK show *What's My Line?*. There were four people on the stage and the panel had to guess who was the real rally driver and at the end I had to get up and reveal that I was the real Paddy Hopkirk. Of course the average American didn't recognise me anyway, so it wasn't that difficult!"

Back in England, Paddy and Henry competed in the London Gulf rally in a Mini, but retired from the event in Dovey forest with a leaking water pump. The rally was marred by the death of Volvo driver Tom Trana's co-driver in a road accident.

Historically, non-Scandinavian drivers hadn't fared well on the 1000 Lakes Rally in Finland, but this year Paddy was accompanied by Kauko Ruutsalo, service manager of Oy Voimavaunu, the Morris importer in Helsinki. They only completed a one-week recce, during which Paddy took out a journalist for a yumping exercise, achieving a distance of 22 metres which he regards today as more than respectable. This showmanship didn't stop one local newspaper thinking Paddy was a forlorn hope, and running a

Paddy charges through a forest stage on his way to a second-in-class on the 1965 RAC Rally. (BP)

headline before the rally stating 'Paddy's tragedy is being in the same team as Timo and Rauno'.

In the rally Paddy had an 'off', hitting a hut, denting the petrol filler and knocking out the rear window. "We had to make a temporary cardboard rear window to keep out the fumes. Still, we managed sixth overall, which wasn't too bad I suppose for a non-Scandinavian."

...and Australia and New Zealand

Support of BMC markets overseas was always important, and trips to Australia became a regular feature in the busy programme. The Armstrong 500 at Bathurst was one of the most important events on the calendar and Paddy and Timo Makinen were despatched to compete in this long-distance saloon car race.

Paddy enjoyed himself. "The Minis were locally-prepared Australian-built cars, to very strict regulations and close to showroom spec – you couldn't even fit a Paddy Hopkirk throttle pedal! Accommodation was at the National Fitness Camp at Bathurst – in a sort of Nissen hut on stilts. This turned out to be a fantastic trip. Wherever we went we had to demonstrate spin turns, handbrake turns and so on, and the Aussies loved it."

The Minis were hard on tyres, which gave the race to the Cortinas. The Fords finished first and second overall but Paddy and Timo were third in class behind the class-winning Mini of Brian Foley and Peter Manton. After Australia, Paddy and Timo went on to New Zealand and were guests at the Wills Six-Hour Race at Pukekohe. The proceedings were enlivened before the race by a demonstration by the two BMC drivers, in Minis, doing spin and handbrake turns, which had the crowd crying "More, more!".

Works drivers were often in demand, and for the London-to-Brighton Run Paddy was invited to take part in a 1901 Renault, owned by Philip Fotheringham-Parker and co-driven by Jack Kemsley, organiser of the RAC Rally. It was extremely cold and damp but there was a bottle of brandy under the seat and Paddy recalls that there was not much left by the time the team eventually arrived in Brighton – "but at least we didn't freeze to death!".

The 1965 RAC Rally will probably be remembered best for the battle in the snow between Timo Makinen in his Big Healey and Rauno Aaltonen in a Mini. Paddy,

Timo Makinen (left), Paddy and author Bill Price at a service halt on the 1965 RAC Rally. (BP)

The 1965 Craigantlet Hill Climb saw Paddy competing in his own Mini-Cooper S. (Paddy Hopkirk)

Meeting another royal: Paddy chats to the Earl of Snowdon, a well-known Mini enthusiast, during a Racing Car Show. (Paddy Hopkirk)

meanwhile, was in a Mini. "I remember near Newcastleton the front tie-rod nut came off, despite the fact that the Nylok type had been replaced by castellated and split-pinned nuts. We didn't have a nut but were able to borrow one from a spectator. On the Loch Achray stage the oil cooler split and we were fortunate that the Ford service crew near the end of the stage was prepared to give us some oil. This RAC was unusually snowy and icy and I learnt to left-foot brake effectively on this event. I still couldn't do it like a Finn, but I'd use it when faced with sheet ice, downhill, with no studs!"

'We woz robbed': the controversial '66 Monte

What can one say about the 1966 Monte Carlo Rally, when the leading BMC, Ford and Rootes cars were all disqualified over an alleged infringement of the regulations relating to the headlamp bulbs? 1966 saw the introduction of new Appendix J regulations. To clarify some of the amendments, Stuart Turner and Henry Taylor of Ford went to the FIA, and came away reasonably satisfied.

The Monte regulations favoured cars complying with the new Group I 'showroom' category and Turner made the decision to enter three cars in this category. Meanwhile Paddy was off on the recce. "After the RAC Rally we flew from Lydd to Geneva on the British United Air Ferries flight with our RAC car fitted with a Group I engine. We had a number of punctures during the recce and we had one rather startling incident. While stopped, talking to Jorma Lusenius who was on his recce, there was a bang, rather like a shotgun going off, immediately behind us. One of our Mini front tyres had exploded – the wire bead had broken, the tyre had come off the rim and the tube was right outside the tyre. It was a good thing it didn't happen when we were ear-holing down the Col de Porte a few minutes earlier!"

Come the rally proper, Makinen and Aaltonen were lying first and second, with two Fords third and fourth, in front of Paddy in fifth spot, when the rally arrived in Monte Carlo. Late on Tuesday evening, with the crews

Above: Paddy in full flight during the 1967 Gallaher 500 race at Bathurst, Australia, his Mini appropriately be-decked with shamrocks. (Autopics)

Right: Paddy entertains the spectators on the 1968 Monte Carlo Rally. (BMIHT)

Top left: At speed in the 1968 Sebring 12-Hour Race, Florida, in the MGC GTS which Paddy shared with Andrew Hedges; the duo won their class. (BP)

Left: Paddy and Andrew Hedges fielded an MGB GT – not an MGC – in the 1968 Targa Florio. They finished twelfth overall, and second in the GT category. (LAT)

Above: Paddy, Jenny, journalist and TV presenter Mike O'Carroll and Joan Nash before the start of the 1969 Circuit of Ireland. (Mike Wood)

Right: Paddy supervises the refilling of a jerrybag during the 1968 London-to-Sydney Marathon. (BMIHT)

Above: Despite this photo of Paddy and Tony Nash, it wasn't all smiles on the 1969 Austrian Alpine Rally with the MkI Triumph 2.5 PI. (Mike Wood)

Right: Paddy holding the football World Cup before the London-to-Mexico World Cup Rally. Left to right are footballer Geoff Hurst, Paddy, England manager Alf Ramsey, Lord Stokes, and Brian Culcheth. (BMIHT)

Opposite: Paddy ducks while Tony Nash drives their hired VW Beetle across a typical bridge in Brazil during a recce of the 1970 World Cup Rally route. (Brian Culcheth)

Left: Tony Nash, Neville Johnston and Paddy wait for the start of the 1970 London-to-Mexico World Cup Rally at Wembley Stadium. (BMIHT)

Below: Paddy's Triumph bears the scars, after falling off the road in Colombia during the 1970 World Cup Rally. (Brian Culcheth)

Opposite right: Paddy and Tony Nash unwind after the World Cup Rally with some local Mexican girls. (Alan Zafer)

Opposite bottom left: The Hopkirk family enjoy some skiing at Courchevel in 1980. (Paddy Hopkirk)

Opposite bottom right: The Explosive Ordnance Disposal team at work with their robot outside Paddy Hopkirk's shop in Belfast. (Paddy Hopkirk)

Above: Paddy completes a driving test during his winning drive on the 1982 Lombard RAC 'Golden Fifty' Rally. (Paddy Hopkirk)

Left: Paddy and Brian Culcheth display their trophies after winning the 'Golden Fifty' Rally. (Brian Culcheth)

now tucked up in bed, a notice went up on the official noticeboard stating that the traffic authorities were concerned about the dipping system of some cars, and there would be an inspection in the morning in the parc fermé. The competitors would be split up into three groups reporting at 11.00, 12.00 and 13.00 hrs. In the morning the crews assembled at their allotted hour and one crew member was asked to go to his or her car and switch on and dip the headlamps while what looked like a hat-box lid was held in front of the headlamp. No action was taken but after the mountain circuit had started, another bulletin was posted specifically mentioning certain cars. The Minis were said to have headlamps which dipped by using a rheostat to dim the quartz-iodine bulb, which was indeed the case, and probably wasn't strictly in conformity with the rules. They could also dip by switching to the foglamps, but this was not signalled to the rally authorities.

Out on the mountain circuit Paddy had a problem with a loose sumpguard and over-heating, but the mechanics kept the car going. "We were using spiked tyres called 'chisels' but they wore out quickly because the snow had been broken up by earlier competitors. I put knobbly pop-ins on the front but this gave the car fantastic oversteer. Rob Slotemaker, who followed us at one stage, said he had never seen a Mini going so sideways!" Eventually Paddy spun off into a rock, but luckily without much damage. The three Minis put up a fantastic performance over the circuit, to arrive at the finish in the first three positions overall.

The author will always remember when the BMC contingent arrived in Monte Carlo from Lisbon, and he went to the Bec Rouge restaurant behind the Hôtel du Helder in Monte with the mechanics and drivers. The head waiter was aware that we were the BMC team and during conversation made it clear that a British car would not win this year. The way he put it suggested that – one way or another – the Minis would not win, almost as if it had been planned by a higher authority.

But that was just the beginning of an amazing few hours. The leading cars were driven to Garage Riviera for final scrutineering, where the most detailed stripping ever seen at a motor-sport event took place, even counting the teeth in the gearbox – as Raymond Baxter remembers only too well. "There was the most incredible effort by the 'shruggers' to find a technical irregularity with the winning cars," he recalls, using the nickname for the scrutineers that his old friend the Allard driver Goff Imhof supposedly first coined. "Whenever you ask any of the officials a question they just shrug their shoulders," Imhof apparently once remarked…

No technical discrepancy could be found, except in the front track on Paddy's car. The car had suffered accident damage and it was only after it was pointed out that the track should be measured at a pre-determined ride height, shown on the homologation form, that the scrutineers accepted the dimensions. At 19.00hrs the results were posted and, to everyone's dismay, the Minis, Fords and Rosemary Smith's Imp were not listed.

Above left: Paddy arrives in Monte Carlo with his car – badged this time as an Austin – clearly showing the scars incurred on the mountain circuit. (BMIHT)

Above: Paddy and Henry Liddon on the mountain circuit during the 1966 Monte Carlo Rally. (BMIHT)

"They were out to nobble us"

Although he says he didn't feel the threatening atmosphere some felt before and during the ill-fated 1966 Monte Carlo, Paddy does say that he had heard that the French were out to get the British. His stronger recollections are of the post-event attempts to find illegalities in the winning Minis. "I remember being called in by the man in the black suit and his saying 'We're going to disqualify you because you've modified the cars – you've changed the track'. I said 'What the hell are you talking about?'. He said 'No, no. You've changed the track. You're disqualified'. Then Rauno said to me 'My car's still in the parc fermé'. So I said 'We've still got one car in the parc fermé. Do you want to go and check that?'. They checked it – and the track was correct. They came back again. 'No, no. This-and-that is wrong'. Then they took the wheels off and weighed them, and they counted the number of teeth in the gears. They tried everything. And then eventually they got round to the lights. They were out to nobble us – there's no doubt about it."

Stuart Turner submitted a protest which was rejected, resulting in the protest being sent to an FIA tribunal for a final hearing. The atmosphere in Monaco was unbelievable but, despite the result, Longbridge decided to fly the team cars home by Carvair aircraft to London Airport and the 'winning' car appeared at the London Palladium, this time with compère Jimmy Tarbuck asking the questions. "It was like war was going to break out," Paddy recalls. "It was very nationalistic. They played *Rule Britannia* and everybody stood up. If there'd have been a Frenchman within sight he'd have been shot!

"We thought the disqualification was a put-up job by the French. The lights didn't help us win the rally. They tried everything else. If only they'd been straight about it. Technically of course they were right, in that we couldn't protest it. But it didn't help us win the rally. It's a bit like saying that because you'd put a green roof on your car instead of a red roof you were disqualified. It didn't actu-

ally make the cars go any better – or make us see any better. It was a total technicality. They couldn't find anything else. It was very unfair. It was biased – and the organisers had been noted for that before. It was big money, of course – car manufacturers fighting for market. It was becoming serious stuff. But it actually gave the Mini more publicity than if we had just won it straight. It really gave the press something to write about!

"I did a live interview in the Monte Carlo studio on a direct link with Ludovic Kennedy, the BBC current affairs presenter, in the BBC studio in London. I was terrified what he might ask me, because I'm no politician. I knew that I was in front of an intelligent man, and I didn't want him to ask me too many intelligent questions, in case I couldn't answer them. But I think I did alright. I remember saying that the whole thing was a disgrace, and that got quite a lot of publicity outside the sporting fraternity – the disqualification became an international incident."

Right: All disqualified! Paddy, Rauno Aaltonen, Timo Makinen, Rosemary Smith (Rootes) and Roger Clark (Ford) return to England after the '66 Monte. (BP)

Far right: Is this the French division of the Paddy Hopkirk fan club? Flag-waving on the 1966 Monte... (BMIHT)

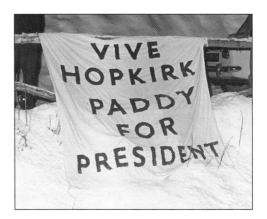

Enter a special lady – and the end of a professional 'marriage'

This was a memorable period for Paddy in more ways than one, as he recounts. "It was about now that I met Jenny. I went for a drink at the London Eaton Mews house of power-boat racing champion Tim Powell, with a pretty model girl called Joan Harkness from Belfast, and Andrew Hedges – who was accompanied by a blonde called Jenny. I quite fancied Jenny and some weeks later I came back from a rally and was keen to meet her again. I phoned Andrew from abroad and asked him if he could find me a nice partner to take to the MG Car Club dinner. He said 'Do you remember that blonde who was with me at Tim Powell's? She lives in Chelsea with two friends, so make sure you get the right one – her name is Jenny Manser'. Jenny worked for a big advertising agency, Geers Gross, and was free, so off I went with my prize catch to the MG Car Club dinner-dance at the Rembrandt Hotel, Knightsbridge. The guest speaker was Michael Christie, who was a hero of mine because I remember him coming over to Northern Ireland to do the Craigantlet Hill Climb. He had a smart team of mechanics in matching overalls looking after his car – the outfit looked very professional and made an impression on me. I sat on his table at the dinner and it was a memorable evening – Michael Christie was really nice, and I chatted up Jenny! I called Jenny the next day and we met for lunch, and I was hooked."

Paddy and Henry Liddon had now been together as a team since the 1963 Tulip Rally and they both now thought that it would be an idea to make a break, and have a change of crew mate. "Henry was the epitome of the English gentleman, and I liked him a lot, but he used to drive me mad," confesses Paddy. "He was the sort of guy who if you were peeing down his leg would say 'That's nice and warm'. I think his silences drove me nuts. I wished sometimes he'd say more, but he was so polite. The trouble is that with a co-driver you get to know them so well that it's almost like being married. And I think Henry and I needed a separation. It wasn't that we'd come to dislike each other – I think it was just that our cultures were too far apart.

"I think I used to annoy him. I'd won the Monte, and in that sort of situation you can

become quite pleased with yourself. I'm sure I fell into that trap. You think you're a great rally driver. So what? Great rally drivers can be a pain in the backside. I'd rather be a good surgeon and go and save some lives, or go and do something useful in life. I steered my kids away from rallying for that reason. I think it's a selfish sport. Anyway, with Henry I just decided that we had grown apart, and I felt it was time for a change before we fell out. I think we just saw too much of each other."

Ron Crellin had worked with Stuart Turner previously, doing ice-notes on the Monte with Donald Morley and Julien Vernaeve, and had competed in a works car with Tony Fall on a number of rallies. Turner asked him if he would consider sitting beside Paddy and he jumped at the chance.

His baptism of fire was the next event on the BMC calendar, the Italian Rally of the Flowers. Ron was pleased to find he didn't have to make any special adjustment for his new driver. "Paddy had his own pace notes

Paddy with new co-driver Ron Crellin before the start of the 1966 Italian Rally of the Flowers. (BP)

Paddy and Jenny relaxing at Glyphada Beach after the 1966 Acropolis Rally. (BP)

Working it hard on a typical Rally of the Flowers road. (BP)

Paddy, Graham Whitehead (MG's US boss), Andrew Hedges and Stuart Turner at the 1966 Sebring race meeting. (Den Green)

which I fell straight into without having to modify the way we used them."

The rally was very rough and the Mini suffered a serious water leak, constantly boiling and requiring regular topping-up. The radiator and fan were eventually changed at a BMC service point, but with a very tight time schedule the mechanics had to finish the job on the other side of the control. The delay of 30 minutes resulted in four minutes of road penalty at the next control. Not only that, but the 'gulp' valve on the inlet manifold was letting oil into the engine, causing a misfire, and the jack broke. Ron was not impressed with sixth in class on his first event with Paddy...

Testing at Silverstone was followed by a visit to Florida for the Sebring four-hour and twelve-hour events. Paddy was co-driving with Peter Manton in a Mini-Cooper S in the 'sedan' race but was forced to retire – and things didn't improve in the longer event. Paddy and Andrew Hedges put in a respectable qualifying time of 3 minutes 42.4 seconds in their MGB, giving them a good grid position, but on the second lap of the race a rocker arm fractured and the car lost 17 minutes in the pits while it was replaced. The car circulated consistently for $10\frac{1}{2}$ hours (157 laps) until a broken con-rod caused instant retirement.

There was a great party after the race and true to character Paddy was first in the swimming pool. Timo Makinen, meanwhile, was arrested by the local sheriff, who caught him racing round the block with a Mini Moke, doing handbrake turns...

Now came the chance to do the European Touring Car Championship Four-hour Race at Monza, this time for Don Moore, the famed engine tuner, in a 970cc Cooper S. Don Moore wouldn't run the car on wide rims and racing tyres, recalls Paddy, but insisted on running $3\frac{1}{2}$in wheels with Dunlop D7 tyres – in effect C41 covers constructed in racing rubber. "The engine was a beaut, but in practice we could only manage ninth fastest in class because the Fiat Abarths were very fast. I hadn't raced on a banked circuit before but the advice from Don was 'Take your hands off the wheel and let the car find its own position on the banking' – good advice. In top gear the engine would pull about 8200rpm with a 3.9 diff, or about 115mph. The car was beautifully prepared and we finished fifth in class."

Upside-down in Ireland

When you look at Paddy's rally record, he seldom retired through crashing. One exception was the 1966 Circuit of Ireland, when Paddy was in a Mini with Terry Harryman. "At about 04.30hrs on the Lough Eske stage in Donegal, we were doing about 75–80mph and took off over a brow. The car came down on its nose in the middle of the road, bounced to the left, demolished a tree, missed a wall and spun down the road on its roof. I remember seeing wall-road-wall-road-wall in the head-lights as we went round and round. All I could see were sparks, then the driver's door came off and I scraped my shoulder and elbow on the road. After about 100 yards the car flipped onto its wheels. The passenger door was jammed, and the roof was down to the bonnet – I remember thinking that a roll bar would be an essential piece of equipment in the future!

"I had turned off the ignition before the car stopped, and I scrambled out and ran down the road with a torch to warn the next car. In the confusion I ran in the wrong direction. The next competitor slowed to have a look at the accident and was hit up the back by Charles Eyre-Maunsell."

Terry Harryman thinks the Hydrolastic suspension contributed to the accident, and Paddy is inclined to agree. "It pumped up. It was that old pumping-up action again. We went up, and when we came down again there was no front suspension, as all the fluid had displaced to the rear. So the car landed on its bloody front bumper and we went over."

The incident remains a vivid memory for Harryman. "We took off twice and the second landing threw the car over. When we disentangled ourselves from the wreck, we were disorientated and, as Paddy says, we ran in the wrong direction to warn the next car. The next car was Vic Elford in his Lotus Cortina and it was his lights which illuminated our driver's door firmly wedged in the branches of a tree."

Success in the 1966 Austrian Alpine – and a disputed Acropolis win

The next 'headline' event was the 37th Austrian Alpine (*Internationale Österreichische Alpenfahrt*, to give it its full name), and Paddy won this for the second time, despite fairly

Above: Paddy on the start ramp of the 1966 Circuit of Ireland, with Terry Harryman. (BP)

Left: Paddy presses on between the snow banks to win the 1966 Austrian Alpine Rally. (Foto Jelinek)

strong opposition from team-mate Tony Fall and some semi-works Porsche 911s. Based at Velden, the rally had a strange regulation limiting the number of road wheels that could be used, and no official outside service was allowed. The Abingdon boys therefore did their usual thing, setting up unofficial service points out of sight of the route and – hopefully – any officials. Typical of how the unexpected can mess things up, one of the Austin Westminster service 'barges' hit a deer and was severely damaged.

Tony Fall eventually retired after hitting a pile of logs and damaging the steering, leaving Paddy to score another victory for BMC. "The final test was a five-lap race at Klagenfurt airport, with Ron watching out for low-flying aircraft! We ran over a snake which looked about 4ft long, but we didn't know if it was dead or alive. Ron said it was 14ft long – but then he always was prone to exaggeration..." Of the 57 starters, 37 cars finished. There was no post-rally scrutineering, but a rather

Above: No doubt where this is, as Paddy and Ron Crellin start under the Acropolis in Athens; the duo were placed third overall, after the disputed servicing incident. (BP)

Above right: The going was very rough for the little Minis with their limited ground clearance: full-length dural sumpguards were used, plus skidplates under the battery and silencer, while the brake callipers had protective guards over the hydraulic hoses. (BP)

long-drawn-out prizegiving, with gold and silver coins included among the trophies given to the winners.

The team went to a restaurant for a meal, in the hotel's VW Microbus. The driver wanted to impress Paddy and everyone was glad to arrive in one piece. After a good meal, Paddy ordered Irish coffee and the waiter made such as mess of it that Paddy was furious and asked for a new set of ingredients. He then proceeded to demonstrate how to prepare an Irish coffee without mixing up all the ingredients – the proper Irish way!

Paddy and Ron had gone straight from the Austrian Alpine to Greece to recce the Acropolis. The friendship between Paddy and Jenny was now getting serious and Jenny came out to Greece to join the BMC party. Jenny made quite a mark in Athens, says

Paddy. "She was wearing a trouser suit with a lace panel up the side of her leg, and this resulted in her picture appearing in one of the leading Athens papers the next day, the paper proclaiming that a new style from London had now arrived in Greece."

During the rally a rock went through the sumpguard, damaging the gearbox and causing an oil leak. Fortunately Paddy and Ron came across an MGB beside the road and it turned out to be someone from the BMC Doucas garage. He had some oil on board, which saved the day.

At one service point, recalls Ron, the mechanics were obliged to park within the control area because space was very tight, and they did this with the apparent blessing of the officials. "When we arrived, Brian Moylan indicated that there had been some moans

Right: With no ramps available, Paddy's car undergoes a driveshaft coupling change during the 1966 Acropolis Rally; Hardy-Spicer inner joints were now used instead of Moulton rubber joints. (BP)

More on that Acropolis penalty...

Peter Browning, in his book The *Illustrated History of the Works Minis*, gives a more detailed explanation of the Acropolis wrangle over the alleged servicing of Paddy's Mini within a control area. 'The reason for Stuart's insistence in protesting was that the action of the Stewards was not in accordance with the international rally regulations, that the control area in question was not satisfactorily defined owing to considerable traffic congestion, and the control warning sign was obscured by parked vehicles', Browning writes. 'Most significant, it was agreed by the control marshals at the time that no penalty was called for and the official road book was marked accordingly. Finally, quite a number of other competitors found themselves in the same position at this control, but Paddy was the only driver singled out for penalisation.'

about their service slot, but Paddy said 'Oh, to hell with that – just get on with the job!'. We won the event but were penalised 420 marks for booking in early at the control and 120 marks for working on the car in the control area. This placed us fifth overall."

Paddy remembers the incident well. "What happened was that they had a regulation – as in every rally, I think – that you were not allowed to service your car within 100 metres of the control. The 'Control' sign was very close to the service point, and when we put the quick-lift jack on the front of the car the car went up in the air and forwards so that it was about 1cm in front of the sign – and Ford took a photograph of it.

"I'd won the rally, and suddenly a notice went up saying there'd been a protest. I remember Stuart Turner and myself going into the rally HQ in Athens just as the Ford Competition Manager, Henry Taylor, walked out. He said 'Congratulations, Paddy'. And then ten minutes later a notice went up saying that I'd been penalised for servicing within the area of the control. Ford had done a deal – and when Henry Taylor said 'Congratulations' he knew I'd been penalised. That night Stuart and I went back into Glyphada, to Henry Taylor's bungalow, and I hauled him out of bed by the lapels of his pyjamas and said 'You rotten sod, don't you ever do that to me again'..."

Afterwards it was established that Paddy had not in fact booked in early, so that penalty was dropped, which moved him up to third place. Stuart Turner protested the other penalty, but a long meeting of the stewards failed to find in Paddy's favour. The protest went to the FIA and it was not until 12 October in Paris that the final results were ratified, with Paddy and Ron declared third overall.

German interlude – 1966

Next it was over to Nürburgring for the European Touring Car Championship Six-hour Race with John Rhodes. Famed for his spectacular tyre-smoking antics, Rhodes is remembered by Paddy as the quickest Mini racer of them all, but on this occasion he slightly over-cooked things in practice. "He took the car out for the last practice lap on the narrow rims and put the car off the road, through a Bosch advertising sign and down a 15ft bank. Luckily the car was not badly damaged. This was the race where the limited-slip diffs had been set up until they were virtually locked and the car, running on very big tyres, was very difficult to drive. I remember going out in the car for the first time and scaring myself rigid. 'The whole thing is one big slide', John had said – and it was, too! The LSD nearly tore the arms out of us, but boy was the thing quick!"

To support the BMC market throughout Europe, Stuart Turner included the German Rally in the schedule. This time Paddy had Chris Nash co-driving. "In Frankfurt I received a phone call from Stuart Turner to tell me that our entry was in doubt because of the rude comments I had made in *Autosport* about the previous year's rally. I wrote to Baron von Diergart and apologised to the club for hurting their feelings, and assuring them that the criticism was well meant, and our entry was accepted. Chris had been regular co-driver to Chris Knowles-Fitton and this was his first continental event. He adopted a very professional approach to the job and was soon getting the hang of the pace notes. The first night the weather was bad with dense fog. At Nürburgring we had a ten-lap test, but the

Paddy in his element on a typical special stage on the 1966 RAC Rally. (Ron Crellin)

car had been consuming a lot of oil and on the seventh lap serious oil surge caused the bearings to run."

This was the first works drive for Nash. "It felt absolutely fantastic. I did a short recce with Paddy and tried hard to get to grips with his pace notes, spending hours writing them up before the rally. We were doing reasonably well in the rally, but were not leading, when we retired with piston trouble. The mechanics were a super bunch and really looked after their new 'novice' co-driver. After we retired and were having dinner at a local hotel – and when the adrenalin effect had diminished – I ended up asleep face-down on the tablecloth. Paddy offered me a job running his shop in Belfast, but I declined as I had other commitments. Later that year I remember doing a club rally in Wales competing against Paddy, with my co-driver Bob Bean. At the end of the event we were tying with Paddy on penalties but the win went to Paddy on the basis that he had gone furthest with a clean sheet."

That year's Alpine Rally began with scrutineering in blistering heat in Marseilles – as Paddy remembers all too well. "Ron was sitting in the car. Next thing I knew was that he was lying on the ground, having passed out and fallen out of the car. The doctor said it was caused by too much sun, and Ron spent Saturday and the rest of Sunday recuperating and was OK for the start. During the rally an oil leak developed, caused by something coming through the gearbox casing from inside. We bodged it with Gun Gum exhaust repair putty, but at the Swiss border we lost all the oil and that was that."

Paddy occasionally borrowed cars from Abingdon to do non-international events. "I borrowed a Mini-Cooper S from Abingdon for the Shenstone Rally, but as Ron Crellin was Clerk of the Course, Richard Harper came as my co-driver. The car had no trip meter but Ron said 'That's no problem, Richard does it all off the maps' – and he did! He was a wonderful map-reader. At the finish, we had lost four minutes, along with Malcolm Gibbs and Bob Bean. The decider was a special test on white roads, which we won. One of the winner's prizes was a Paddy Hopkirk rally jacket!"

Down-Under again

It was always enjoyable to go to Australia, despite the distance, and this year Paddy had an entry in the 1966 Gallaher 500, on the wonderful Mount Panorama circuit at Bathurst, with Brian Foley. Cars in the Gallaher 500 were classified within price brackets, with the Mini-Cooper S cars entered by BMC Australia in Class C, for cars costing £1021 to £1350.

Alas, the Mini was forced to retire with engine failure on lap 28. After this Paddy participated in the Southern Cross Rally, in South Eastern Australia, starting and finishing in Sydney, with Garry Chapman as co-driver. Chapman had been asked to pair Paddy by Evan Green, who was BMC Australia's Public Relations Officer. "He asked if I would navigate for an overseas driver, probably because I was South Australian champion from 1960 to 1963. I had also been co-driver to Erik Carlsson in 1965. Paddy was a very cheerful person and a true professional."

The Southern Cross Rally car was locally prepared and there hadn't been time to obtain some of the special parts requested from Abingdon. On the rally, the suspension collapsed, a brake leak occurred – caused by a loose union – and the regulator box developed a fault. Despite this, Paddy and Garry managed third in class.

This was quite a rough rally, says Paddy, so he wasn't so unenthusiastic about the Mini's Hydrolastic suspension. "The rubber-cone suspension was never very good on rough roads – the car became very jumpy. Hydrolastic was definitely better on rough terrain – it was much smoother. It was just the 'pumping up' that we had to get under control".

Hard work with Hill
– the '66 RAC Rally

The home International was always the RAC, this year sponsored by newspaper *The Sun*, which meant there were orange roundels on the doors of the cars. Unlike today's modern rallies there were 63 stages on this event, incredible though this may seem.

Graham Hill was signed up to drive an Abingdon Mini on this event, and received tuition at Bagshot from Paddy in the presence of the BBC TV *Wheelbase* film crew. "Graham found it difficult at Bagshot," says Paddy. "He just couldn't get the hang of front-wheel drive on the loose, and we ended up off the road several times. I was amazed at how difficult he found it, but I suppose with racing and rallying it's like the difference between say ice-skating and skiing. Graham was after all one of the most competent racing drivers I ever knew. He was a lovely character, never took himself too seriously, and had a fantastic sense of humour – he was a very funny man, and a wonderful story-teller. It's a pity more of the modern racing drivers haven't got those qualities.

"When we were on the rally, South of Aviemore the fanbelt came off and we drove ten miles without one. A new belt failed to cure the overheating which had resulted, until Timo suggested changing the thermostat, which solved the problem. The car had good torque, as we were using the relatively mild 510 camshaft. We only had one minor excursion on the rally and then in Yorkshire we went up an escape road where three other cars had already gone. We backed up, put it in first gear and a driveshaft broke, putting us out."

Driving tuition from Paddy before the 1966 RAC Rally, at Bagshot test track – left to right are Graham Hill, journalist Maxwell Boyd (lighting a cigarette) and Paddy. Note the trademark helmets of Graham Hill (left) and Paddy. (Den Green)

'Family' photo outside the Competitions Department at Abingdon just before the 1966 RAC Rally. Left to right are Paul Easter, Simo Lampinen, Mike Wood, Stuart Turner, Rauno Aaltonen, Tony Fall, Paddy Hopkirk, Timo Makinen, Henry Liddon, Ron Crellin. (BMIHT)

Peter Browning takes over

Not many personnel at Abingdon were aware that Stuart Turner was contemplating a move. However, just before Christmas Peter Browning received an unexpected phone call. "The phone rang and John Thornley's secretary called me up to his office. John said 'Do you know that Stuart is leaving?'. I said 'No'. He said 'I would like you to take on the job'. I said 'You must be joking – no way'. John said 'Sit down and we'll talk about it'. I said that I didn't know anything about rallies, except what I'd picked up when I went round with Wilson McComb, then the Competitions press officer. John said 'Yes, but you've done quite a bit of timekeeping with the team. You'll soon pick it up'. Stuart had never said anything to me about the job but it seemed that John Thornley had made his mind up."

So another era was coming to an end. Paddy could sense that things were changing, but at least he had no qualms about the new man at the top. "The Mini was getting less competitive, and other people were learning, and getting better. Obviously stepping into Stuart's shoes must have been very difficult, but Peter was very well respected, and he was very good at adminstration."

Chapter 7

Paddy's best year
1967–1968

Soon after the RAC Rally, Paddy and Jenny became engaged, and photographs of the couple appeared in motoring magazines and a few national newspapers. The usual busy Abingdon programme for the year to come thus looked as if it might be punctuated by the sound of wedding bells...

For the 1967 Monte, Turner had Peter Browning looking over his shoulder in preparation for his taking over as team manager. "I remember sitting in on a briefing session one Saturday morning, all about the tyre choice complications, which was all beyond me. Stuart was making notes on little square pads and when he'd finished he asked me to go over the yard to the *Safety Fast* office to make some photocopies. The copying machine was very tired and the precious notes started to smoulder. I ended up making up the notes from the charred remains and my memory. It was rather a steep learning curve!"

Revenge is sweet: the '67 Monte

Following the lighting problems in 1966, there was a determination to have another go at the Monte and Paddy and Ron Crellin started from Athens in a car prepared by Gerald Wiffen; the main reason for the Athens start was to help relations with Doucas Brothers, the local BMC agent, after the problems on the Acropolis the previous year.

There were no recriminations from Longbridge after the 1966 Monte headlamp problems. The attitude was 'Let's show them!'. For the 1967 event a tyre-limit category was introduced, with those cars opting for only eight tyres per section having a distinct advantage, and being identified by yellow backing to the competition numbers.

Tests were carried out on dry tarmac, with

Characteristic Mini understeer uphill on a very slippery surface during the 1967 Monte. (Paddy Hopkirk)

Dunlop using different types of stud near Monte Carlo to check stud retention, bearing in mind it was quite possible with changing weather that the cars might have to cover a considerable mileage on dry roads. Cars entered in the limited-tyre category had to carry four spare wheels/tyres, so Terry Mitchell at MG designed a special quick-release wheel clamp which would hold two of the wheels securely on the rear seat pan. After all the controversy in 1966, Turner asked Paddy to take his recce car to M. Sobra of the AC de Monaco to show and obtain permission for this modification. The clamp arrangement was approved by the organisers but they declined to put this in writing.

After an early start from Athens, Paddy and Ron found the road was blocked by heavy snow and trucks as they approached Larissa, and they had to take a diversion via Volos. From the border with Greece and Yugoslavia to Skopje the road was hard-packed snow, with one pass blocked by snow drifts, as Paddy recalls.

"We dug for 20 minutes and then backed the car and charged the drift, luckily only just coming out the other side so we could continue. The trouble with a drift is that if you get into one and you don't get through it, the car sinks down under the pressure of its own weight, and it's like being moulded into an ice cube – you'll never get it out.

"On the road to Belgrade and through to Sarajevo the weather was bad, with snow and ice, but when the road became blocked again, out of nowhere about a hundred people appeared and managed to push the offending vehicles out of the way. There was snow all the way up the Adriatic coast until we crossed into Italy, and with freezing fog and ice to contend with this time we were grateful for the electrically-heated windscreen."

Bad weather or not, the duo didn't miss a trick when it came to wrong-footing the competition, as Ron Crellin recalls. "During the recce we had discovered a possible short cut on the Col de Granier test. On the rally, Tony Ambrose, who was doing ice-notes with his wife, was instructed to park his car across the road with the bonnet up to block the short cut. Interestingly, no-one tried to use it ..."

On the 800-mile Monaco–Chambéry–Monaco section all the BMC works drivers opted for four plain Dunlop SP tyres and four half-studded (200-stud) SP44 Weathermasters which were 'branded' with the car's rally number by an official. At the Chamaloc

service point, Paddy changed tyres front to rear and at the end of this section Vic Elford (Porsche) was leading Paddy by 37 seconds, with Makinen four seconds behind and Aaltonen a further 17 seconds back. Paddy's engine had suffered some overheating, despite changing the thermostat and adding Radweld, and at Levens the engine was boiling. Then, to cap it all, the temperature gauge broke.

"We were asked why we had dropped from second overall to sixth after the mountain circuit", says Paddy. "It was purely due to tyre choice. I had selected four plain and four studded and the studs had worn out just when we needed them. It snowed heavily and we spun at least twice due to lack of grip." Ron Crellin confirms this. "The car was all over the place, because the tyres were bald and had no grip – we were constantly up the banks and parapets!"

With Paddy and Ron finishing sixth overall and Rauno Aaltonen and Henry Liddon declared the winners, it was a popular result for the Abingdon team – and sweet revenge after 1966's debacle.

Soon after the Monte it was back to business for Paddy, with the opening on 5 February of his accessory shop in Dublin, at 5 Lincoln Place, just behind Trinity College. Jim Clark and Rootes Group rally-driver – and Irishwoman – Rosemary Smith were guests of honour.

Rally co-driver Gregor Grant, founder/editor of Autosport *magazine, shares a joke with Paddy and Ron Crellin at the end of the '67 Monte. (Studio Erpe)*

Pushing it: 1967's Italian Rally of the Flowers

Next on the agenda was Italy's Rally of the Flowers, an event that became the subject of some controversy, as Ron Crellin relates.

"On the last stage while leading and just before the finish in San Remo, we caught up and passed a lorry. About halfway through the stage, going uphill, there was bang and a driveshaft coupling disintegrated. Both Paddy and myself had the same idea. The lorry soon arrived, and despite the language barrier we persuaded the driver to give us a bit of a nudge to get us over the hill. We built up speed and after one or two more nudges crossed the flying finish. The lorry drove past and we booked in at the control. We were at the top of a mountain with just one more control halfway down, before the final control in the square.

"We were now with Douggie Watts and Peter Browning with their service 'barge', and although the coupling was reconnected, it would not drive the car all the way to the finish. We had lost about 2½ minutes on the stage but if we could reach the final control on time, the penalty would not be too severe. We

set off, with Douggie taking over where the lorry left off. It was not easy, as there were so many hairpins, but the 'barge' would give us a nudge and Paddy would hurl the car as fast as possible through the hairpins to keep up the momentum. If a photographer was visible on a bend, Douggie would hold back so as not to give the game away. We freewheeled into the time control halfway down without further penalty, but had to push the car from the control.

"As soon as we were out of sight of the controllers, Douggie took over the pushing again, the Mini's boot now looking rather crumpled. We reached the promenade at the foot of the hill where the road was almost flat, with the last control just after a tunnel in the town. The pushing vehicle got up to about 80mph to be able to back off and make it look like we had made the finish under our own steam. We emerged like a cork from a champagne bottle and freewheeled, blipping the throttle, to the control table. Once we had booked in, Paddy engaged gear and let out the clutch; the car lurched forward and stopped. We of course looked suitably surprised to have a mechanical failure just after the finish. What luck!

"Tony Fall gave us a tow to the hotel. Meanwhile, at the finish John Davenport,

Paddy spots something more interesting than rally cars, before going on to second place on the 1967 Rally of the Flowers. Left to right are Ron Crellin, Paddy, mechanic Dudley Pike, and Tony Fall. (BP)

writing for *Autosport*, reckoned the car had been pushed and tried his hardest to find out. In his rally report he said '...with the results now final and no one having said anything official, the mystery is complete.'.

"To finish the story, in his 'From The Rally Seat' column, also in *Autosport*, Paddy said 'Thank you John Davenport for blowing the gaff on our final 23kms from Baiardo to the finish.' He wasn't happy about John's indiscretion..."

Today Paddy still recalls the incident with amusement. "We were very lucky. It was a case of quick thinking – of seizing the opportunity. It meant that we also got the prize-money for finishing second. Better second place than nothing!"

Paddy's popularity was emphasised when the BMC Competitions press officer, Wilson McComb, doing a survey, asked some young motoring enthusiasts to name two famous rally drivers. The answer was: Hopkirk 54 per cent, Makinen 46 per cent and Carlsson/Aaltonen 15 per cent. So, after his 1964 Monte win, and his subsequent successes, Paddy was still very much at the top of the popularity poll.

The life of a works rally driver was a busy one, and appearances at motor club functions were all part of the scene. In March, a rally panel consisting of Paddy, Stuart Turner, Tony Fall, Mike Wood and Tony Ambrose entertained a crowd of 400 Lancashire Automobile Club members to a talk and film (on rally testing) at the Dunkenhalgh Hotel, Clayton-le-Moors. The evening was scheduled to last for two hours but eventually ran from 7.30pm until 11.00pm. As Stuart Turner had already announced that he was leaving BMC, this was the last meeting of a BMC panel to include him.

With four wins already on the Circuit of Ireland, it was an obvious choice for the local hero to be entered in this event, in a Cooper S, and again with Terry Harryman co-driving. "We ran out of petrol running into the Killarney control, after being incorrectly directed by the Garda," recalls Paddy. "But we made it to a petrol station where I told the attendant to 'Put five bob's worth in'. We booked in with two minutes to spare."

At the Killarney halt, Paddy was leading and he maintained his lead to win the rally from Adrian Boyd in a Mini-Cooper S and Charlie Gunn in a Lotus Cortina. This was Paddy's fifth win on the Circuit. Terry Harryman pays tribute to his uncanny skills. "Paddy was the first world-class driver I had competed with

A pensive Paddy waits for the author to check the brake adjustment before he continues on his way to win the 1967 Circuit of Ireland with Terry Harryman. (BP)

and I had been rather in awe of his standing the first time I went with him for BMC in 1965. His car control was superb, helped I am sure by his experience in driving tests and hill climbs. This resulted in his being a very 'clean' driver coupled with great determination."

Within an hour of the finish of the Circuit, Paddy was at the airport with Alec Poole to catch a plane for Sebring. The event was an important shop window for MG cars. With support from BMC Hambro, entries were made in the three-hour saloon car race with a Mini (for the first time), and in the 12-hour race with an MGB GT. John Rhodes was co-driver in the Mini and the pair achieved a class win despite problems with the refuelling rig. The MGB GT was the first Abingdon entry for this model, but because it had not yet been homolgated in Group III, it had been entered in the Prototype category. Nevertheless, a class victory was achieved, with regular long-distance co-driver Andrew Hedges, just in front of the team MGB driven by Makinen and Rhodes.

Revenge Part II: victory on the Acropolis

After a successful Monte, the team felt it was time for revenge again, this time in Greece. In a Mini-Cooper S prepared by Robin Vokins, Paddy and Ron Crellin headed home the Lancia of Andersson and the Lotus Cortina of Söderstrom to win the Acropolis Rally – helped by his usual nifty performance in the event's driving tests. Paddy's engine lost oil pressure during the final Tatoi circuit race, so he stopped before the line and crossed only when the flag fell, to ensure the win. "The year 1967 was a year when I won events I could really feel proud of having won, and it was particularly sweet to win the Acropolis after I'd been robbed of my victory the year before," says Paddy. "This was all the more so as the Mini wasn't the best car for it – a bigger car with more ground clearance and a longer wheelbase would have been better for the terrain."

One of the new lightweight MGC bodies was being prepared for the Targa Florio, fitted with a 2-litre MGB engine. Paddy and Timo Makinen drove this, with Alec Poole and Andrew Hedges entered in another MGB. The Hedges/Poole car crashed with Hedges driving, but despite poor handling and trouble with the brakes Paddy and Timo finished ninth

Paddy asks mechanic Gerald Wiffen about his diet while chief mechanic Tommy Wellman looks on, before the 1967 Sebring 3-hour race. (Gerald Wiffen)

It wasn't all hard work: off St Petersburg, Florida, after the 1967 Sebring race, and Paddy lands his lunch. (Paddy Hopkirk)

Despite the unique hardness of the rough special stages on the 1967 Acropolis, Paddy went on to win. (BP)

Paddy testing the four-cylinder MGB GTS on the Thruxton circuit, in preparation for the 1967 Targa Florio. Essentially an MGC, the GTS ran with a 150bhp 2004cc B-series engine, as the six-cylinder 'C' had not yet been announced. (BP)

overall, and third in class behind two Porsches. Good result or not, Paddy loved the Targa. "What a wonderful event! The thing I'm most proud of is of having driven in the Targa Florio. It was something else. It was unique. You were racing around the mountains, and it was just like one long special stage, only without a co-driver to read your notes – it was a good race for rally drivers, in fact. I think the Targa course is one of my best memories of driving a fast car on a road circuit, with all its variations of corners, gradients, towns and villages."

A happy Paddy and Ron Crellin before the 1967 Acropolis Rally. (BMIHT)

Right: Jenny and Paddy signing the register after their marriage in 1967 – 38 years on, the couple are still happily married. (BMIHT)

Best man Andrew Hedges in full flow at the wedding reception at the Hyde Park Hotel, London. (BMIHT)

Wedding Bells

Paddy was having to devote some time to preparations for his wedding to Jenny, which would take place in Chelsea, on Friday 30 June. "I was a Catholic and Jenny was Church of England but I suppose I wasn't a very good Catholic. I had to find a church and I went to Brompton Oratory but they said 'No, you live in Belgravia so you must go to Cadogan Street'. Here I met Father Archer. I said 'I want to get married' and he said 'OK. What's the name of your fiancée?'. I told him it was Jenny Manser. I said 'Have you any other questions?' and he said 'No'. But I said 'I'm a Catholic and Jenny is C of E'. He said 'That's fine'. I almost fell over at this relaxed attitude compared with Northern Ireland. Father Archer said 'The only thing is that I will have to give her some instruction, which is part of our tradition'. I asked if Jenny could have her minister at the service, and he said 'Of course you can – you can have a rabbi if you like'.

"So Jenny went for her instruction and at the last session he said 'There is one last thing I should mention. Do you realise in the Catholic Church there is no form of birth control, mechanical or otherwise? That's the way we work. Do you understand?'. Jenny said 'Of course I understand, but what if I take the pill secretly and don't tell Paddy? How do we stand? Father Archer looked up and said 'I think you're laughing!'. Jenny had to sign a piece of paper saying she would bring any children up in the Catholic faith, but I don't think they require that any more."

So on Friday 30 June 1967, Paddy and Jenny were married at 3.30pm in St Mary's Church, Cadogan Street, Chelsea. Andrew Hedges was best man and there was a large gathering of family and friends to celebrate, including many of the BMC team. During Paddy's speech at the reception in the Hyde Park hotel, Alec Poole, who had brought in a 28lb weight with chain and clamp, attached it to Paddy's ankle, secured it with a padlock, and then threw the key out of the window into the gardens of Hyde Park.

"Luckily the padlock hadn't clicked closed properly, as otherwise I'd have needed a welding torch to cut it off," recalls Paddy. After the reception at the Hyde Park Hotel, the couple left for their honeymoon in Portugal, arriving at Faro to collect an MGB GT which the BMC importer had laid on for their use.

"With friends like mine, you want to keep your eyes on your feet when making your own wedding speech": Paddy padlocked – or almost – at his wedding. (BMIHT)

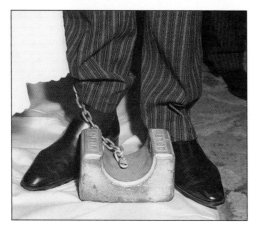

Ron Crellin about to climb aboard the winning Mini at a crowded control during the 1967 Alpine Rally. (BMIHT)

A typical Alpes-Maritimes special stage during the rally. (BMIHT)

Back to business: the '67 Alpine

The Alpine Rally was still one of the great road races of the era and from the entry list it seemed there would be fierce opposition from continental teams. Paddy had loved the Alpine since his Triumph days. This year he had pace notes for all the tight stuff – just as well, as Ron Crellin remembers one tight section after another. "I seemed to be forever turning over pages of pace notes. It tended to get a bit out of hand as the sections came so thick and fast."

The car was a lightweight Mini, with aluminium bonnet, boot lid and doors, and perspex side windows and rear screen. Running without bumpers, it weighed nearly 1cwt less than a Group II car, and was entered in the Group VI prototype category. Paddy felt that the performance was down until it was discovered that the regulation Group VI brake cable had not been slackened off and was holding the rear brakes on. "It was a good car – it was lovely to drive and went bloody well. It was fantastic downhill."

Brian Culcheth was driving an Austin 1800 on the Alpine, and this was the first time that he had a close team relationship with Paddy. "He was a great team man, always willing to help and share information with us. In my

Paddy lifting a wheel on his way to victory. The Mini was a lightweight Group VI car with an auxiliary front radiator. (BMIHT)

opinion, this was one of Paddy's greatest drives – against serious opposition. At the last overnight halt, when Paddy was lying sixth overall, he said to me 'We can win this rally'. I was very impressed that Paddy seemed to have the confidence to believe that he could win. I was disappointed that the film that the BMC photographic team from Cowley took was never produced."

Out of the 79 starters only 15 finished – and Paddy scored the victory that he'd predicted, having moved up from the seventh place he was holding at the end of the first stage, and having profited from the retirement of the rapid Alpine-Renaults. 'Paddy plays it cool' read the *Autosport* headline announcing his victory in front of two very quick Alfa Romeo GTAs.

Nautical interlude

Paddy had always enjoyed boats, having been a good rower as a child and having often gone sailing with his brothers. "Being brought up in Portrush, in Nothern Ireland, I could do anything in a dinghy," he says. During the summer of 1967 he had a taste of another competitive nautical sport when he was invited by Tim Powell to crew an offshore powerboat with Norman Barclay – the boat, called *UFO*, being owned by Powell. They were entered in the

Cowes-to-Torquay race and Paddy recalls a near-disaster when they were practising.

"We had been out for a practice run and as we came alongside the pontoon in the harbour a pressman on the side shouted out 'You're sinking'. There were two flaps in the stern which opened at speed to drain the bilges. They hadn't closed, and as we trickled in we hadn't noticed that water was coming into the boat. Tim opened the engine hatches and shouted to Norman 'Quick, get it out to sea'. Water was now high up and swirling around the engines and carburettors, causing them to cut out.

"Tim sprayed the ignition with this new wonder liquid, Rocket WD-40. Suddenly the boat took off, almost throwing Tim off the stern, the water quickly drained out, and we made it back to shore! WD-40 had saved the day."

But within ten minutes of the start of the race Paddy was injured. "Some oil had leaked onto the floor where I was standing and at the same time the hand grip I was holding started to pull away from the bulkhead. The terrific pounding caused my foot to slip and I broke my toe. Despite the pain and the rough conditions, we managed third overall."

This was not Paddy's only powerboat race, as he was also a crew member in *Vivacity*, a boat owned by Sir Max Aitken and piloted by

Tommy Sopwith, this time in the Miami-to-Nassau race. It was powered by turbo-diesel engines and was very fast, but blew the transmission after about half-distance.

Paddy continued to sail, too, and was to become involved with ocean racing after his retirement from rallying, competing in the Admiral's Cup and a couple of Fastnet races. "I'll tell you something. If you want to find out what men are made of, bad weather on a boat is the best test of all. You have a four-hour-on, four-hour-off watch when you're racing, and you're tired and wet. Within ten hours you discover who's worth it. I think co-driving is very similar – you spend a lot of time with a guy, you sleep in the same room. You get to know people well. I hadn't got the personality to suffer fools lightly, and to be polite to people I didn't like, so I was quite choosy. If there were any duffers, I don't remember them, and when I look back at friends such as Alec Poole or Tony Nash, I don't think we had one cross word, not even on something as long as the London-to-Sydney Marathon."

The globetrotting continues...

Paddy was journeying across the world again in late 1967, destination Australia, for the Southern Cross Rally, in which he drove an Abingdon-prepared Mini-Cooper S, again with local co-driver Garry Chapman. The car was using Koni dampers on the front for the first time, in conjunction with the Hydrolastic suspension, but the Mini retired with a broken gearbox. "I thought the suspension on this car was terrific and spoke to Alec Issigonis about it at the London Motor Show," says Paddy.

This beefed-up suspension was fitted for the Tour de Corse, a rally that should have suited the Minis. In fact, though, the 1967 event was not a success for the BMC cars, and became known at Abingdon as the 'Rally of the Fan Belts'.

Paddy was driving 'GRX 5D' with Ron Crellin, using knock-on Minilite wheels for the first time on a rally. "We had wheels come loose twice, and on one occasion couldn't get a wheel off because it was jammed," says

A French journalist rushes in for a quick quote during the 1967 Tour de Corse. (DPPI)

Paddy. "The things obviously required some further development. We had terrible trouble with them – I don't think we ever got them right."

More seriously, the car suffered from overheating from the start and despite filling bags of water at Bains de Guitara, Paddy was forced to retire with overheating and a slipping fan belt at Pont d'Altiani, with the Aaltonen/Liddon car retiring at the same place with a similar problem. "On the first stage the lights dimmed and the temperature went up. Despite having the belt adjusted it happened again, until we went out with no lights and overheating. The belts were checked after the rally and found to be faulty, although there had been murmurings about sabotage while we were in Corsica."

Whenever possible, as has been mentioned, the Competitions Department supported BMC national companies in Europe and it was the enthusiasm of Dr Henry Krackowizer, the publicity boss of BMC Austria which was instrumental in arranging an Austrian rally-drivers course in conjunction with the Ö.A.M.T.C (Österreichische Automobil Motorrad-und Touring Club). The author took a Mini-Cooper S out to Vienna with mechanic Dudley Pike, and met the Austrian drivers and their cars at an army training area outside the city.

Paddy and Rauno Aaltonen were earmarked as the instructors for the weekend. "We set up a school in the old army building on the training area, so we could explain driving techniques using a blackboard," recalls Paddy. "There was one Austrian driver with a Citroën DS who was a pain in the backside. He was particularly cocky and reckoned he could beat everyone else. On the demo run he managed to turn his car over, much to everyone's delight. Rauno, with his German, taught those whose English was not too good and I took the other batch. We had to invent a stage by selecting a section of road with various types of corner."

After instruction, the Austrians were taken out in the Mini by their instructor, followed by the instructors – rather bravely – sitting beside the Austrians in their own cars. Despite a number of accidents, proceedings ended with a timed competition to judge how they had all fared. It was a successful flag-waving weekend, despite the carnage.

No one could have predicted the fate that was to befall the RAC Rally, the last event of 1967. The newspaper *The Sun* again sponsored the rally, but, as we all now know, at the eleventh hour the Ministry of Agriculture ordered its cancellation due to the widespread outbreak of Foot-and-Mouth disease. Paddy and Ron Crellin had been entered in a Group VI Mini-Cooper S, fitted with a Weber carburettor. Cancellation resulted in a fairly lengthy party at the Excelsior Hotel, Heathrow, the start venue, but with TV now short of footage, a number of the works cars were asked to take part in a televised stage next day. Paddy – and Timo Makinen with his injection Mini – accordingly took part in the 'RAC Rally Camberley Stage' for TV – with less than auspicious results. The stage was very rough and on his first run Paddy suffered a puncture, and so didn't do the second run, deciding to save the car further damage.

It was the time of year for manufacturers to consider their future driver line-up and there were suggestions that Paddy might be tempted away from BMC to a continental team. A news item in *Motor* magazine stated: "After six years with BMC, there was now a fairly steady tramp of foreign boots across the cobbles towards a certain Belgravia Mews house, with gentlemen from foreign car factories waving bags of lire or marks in front of the contract-signing hand." Paddy was not tempted, and was reported as saying "It took me six years to learn how to speak English so I think it is too late to start learning another language now. Maybe I will stay with BMC."

The Competitions Department Christmas dinner was always a lively affair and this year, for Paddy's benefit, some of the mechanics wrote the script for a sketch to the music of the carol 'God Rest You Merry Gentlemen'. It went like this:

God rest you merry rally-men
The thought makes us dismay
For Paddy Hopkirk Ltd
Was founded on this day
With steering wheels and junk like that
For which he makes you pay
Oh, Oh tidings of jackets and gloves
jackets and gloves
Oh, Oh tidings of jackets and gloves

It is reasonable to say that, measured in terms of outright rally victories, this was Paddy's best year. "When you're at the top and winning, the graph usually goes down after that," says Paddy. "I don't know that I thought that much about it. I was never a long-term strategist type of thinker – I was probably living more day-to-day..."

Monte '68: the year of the 'split Webers'

The Monte regs were usually out in October with the team carrying out an initial recce of the route before Christmas and then another immediately after Christmas. The latter wasn't a very profitable exercise, according to Mike Wood. "We went over to France again to continue our recce near Gap. Unfortunately several feet of heavy snow covered the area, preventing us getting on to the stages. After waiting for a day or two for things to improve, we decided to drive out of Gap. Down the road we were met by Paddy and Ron coming the other way in their recce car, with Ron engrossed in the Michelin Red Guide, looking for the next restaurant to sample. There wasn't much else to do and I think that week taught me how to really eat French food!"

This was the author's hat-trick of Lisbon starts. The group had a good run down with Paddy's car on a trailer and once again everyone was very well looked after by the Morris importers, Almeida, and in particular Henrique Bastos, their service manager. Soon after the start, Paddy's car had a small problem in Spain when the pipe to the overflow tank came off, spraying Ron with anti-freeze. Paddy and Ron also complained of freezing

fog in the Massif Centrale, and were again glad of the heated windscreen.

In 1966 the headlamps had been a problem, and now there seemed to be a problem concerning the carburettors fitted to the Minis, this being described in *Motor* magazine as 'The Great BMC Carburettor Scare'. On arrival in Monte Carlo, Peter Browning was called to a meeting of the Sporting Commission to be told that the scrutineers had doubts about the eligibility of the carburettors. Appendix J stated that carburettors were free so long as they could be fitted to the inlet manifold without an intermediary device. Abingdon had fitted modified Weber carburettors, which became known as 'split Webers'.

Once again differences in the rally regulations between the French and English text were highlighted, ending with Browning being given the opportunity of changing the carburettors back to SUs. He refused, and asked for time to consider the withdrawal of the cars from the rally – he wasn't prepared to put the teams through the wringer on what was left of the rally if they were going to be disqualified at the finish. The Sporting and Technical Commissions discussed the matter further, but without making a final decision. After a phone call to Longbridge and the fact that now the organisers had accepted that the

Using the ditch for some more grip on the Col de Turini, during the 1968 Monte. (BMIHT)

The 'split' Weber carburettor

The carburettors at the heart of Peter Browning's concerns were Weber twin-choke units ingeniously modified by Abingdon. The original idea came from Finland, where Timo Makinen had spotted it, and it was put into practice by the Comps Department's engine wizard, Cliff Humphries.

In essence two standard Webers were cut in half, retaining the float chamber, and the two left-hand halves used each as a single-choke carburettor. To fit these re-fashioned carbs to the standard manifold, SU-type flanges were welded to the Weber bodies. This tweak gave the Downton-head 1275cc engine an output of about 92bhp at 6500rpm, on a compression ratio of 12.6 to 1 – an increase of 6bhp or so.

Regulations for Group II, in which the cars were running, clearly said that the standard carburettors could be replaced by others of a different size, provided that the number used remained the same and that they could be mounted on the standard inlet manifold without any intermediary device and with the use of the original attachment points. However, in the original French the regulations included an additional phrase, stipulating that the carburettors should be 'without modification or deformation'.

Peter Browning had sent details of the split-Weber installation to the FIA and to the organisers, ahead of the event, to avoid a repetition of the 1966 headlamp fiasco, and nothing had been said. But when the cars had arrived in Monte Carlo, after the Concentration Runs, the Sporting Commission informed him that there were doubts about the eligibility of the carburettors.

Browning argued that the carburettors were not modified, and that although they followed Weber design principles and used Weber parts they were in fact entirely new prototype carbs designed and made in England; furthermore an additional stub, which was the subject of some contention, was not an intermediary device, as it was welded to the carbs and formed an integral part of the carb body.

Although no definitive ruling emerged from the meeting with the Sporting Commission, leaving the BMC team open to a protest by another competitor, the carbs were not 'protested' after the rally; however, all the Minis had their carburettor installations minutely dismantled in the post-event scutineering, in a fruitless effort to find discrepancies with the regulations or the homologated specification of the cars. As Peter Browning relates in his book on the works Minis, the gentleman zealously overseeing operations was the same individual who in 1966 had officiated over the scrutineering that had led to the disqualification of the entire BMC team...

carburettors had been fitted in good faith, it was decided not to withdraw the entry. This created a problem because most of the service team had dispersed and were out on the town. However, everyone was rounded up, leaving Browning to sort out the final service details.

With the dry conditions, it looked like racing tyres for all the tests on the leg from Monte Carlo to Vals-les-Bains and back. However, the late decision to continue in the rally had repercussions at the service point at Pont des Miolans, when the Dunlop van driven by Gordon Pettinger arrived too late – resulting in Timo, Rauno and Paddy going off on 3000-mile-old studs instead of the racing tyres they wanted. However, Tony Fall, who was a late number, had a selection of tyres, while at Bedoin the ice-note crew of Julien Vernaeve and Bob Freeborough reported a 95 per cent dry road on the Col de Perty, so the Minis all selected racing tyres. Leaders after the Parcours Commun were Alpine-Renault, Porsche, Porsche, then Rauno's Mini, followed by a Lancia, and then Paddy and Tony Fall in their Minis.

One of the Lancias and one of the Alpine-Renaults crashed on the mountain circuit, leaving the two Porsches to come home first and second overall ahead of the convoy of Minis – Aaltonen, Fall and Hopkirk, in that

Paddy and Andrew Hedges scored another class win at Sebring in 1968 with the MGC – now sporting its correct six-cylinder engine, in alloy-head iron-block form. Bored out from 2912cc to 2968cc, it developed 200bhp at 6000rpm, on triple Webers. (BMIHT)

order. The dry conditions had prevented a fifth Mini victory in the most famous rally of all. Oh for some more snow!

Team managers and competitors alike were rather interested in leaflets which were distributed at the end of the Monte describing a new long-distance rally to be called the *Daily Express* London-to-Sydney Marathon: it was to cover 10,000 miles, with there being £10,000 prize money. The cynics said it would never happen.

After the Monte, Ron Crellin – now 37 years old – announced that Paddy would have to find another co-driver as he was retiring from professional rallying, mainly because he had problems getting the time off work. Even on this Monte he had been obliged to use up some of his annual leave. The two-year partnership had been one of the most successful during the period but now Ron, a surveyor with a well-known building society, was putting aside his maps.

In February Paddy was featured in a film which was part of a Ministry of Transport campaign to encourage drivers to wear seatbelts. There was quite a lot of publicity, resulting in Paddy being photographed assisting the Minister of Transport, Barbara Castle, with the full-harness seatbelt buckles in a Mini.

Paddy drove one of the MGC GTS cars in the Sebring 12-Hour Race, with old mate Andrew Hedges, finishing tenth overall and first in class, thereby achieving the best position ever for a BMC car in this race. There was less good news on the Circuit of Ireland, where Paddy, partnered by Irish friend Terry Harryman, retired with a broken differential.

Above: A typical boreen through Ballaghbeama Gap, during the 1968 Circuit of Ireland. Paddy's Mini retired with differential failure. (Esler Crawford)

Left: Early days for the jerribag, as Paddy and Terry Harryman are refuelled at Rathcoole during the event. (Esler Crawford)

One of the flat, dusty forest stages in Canada during the 1968 Shell 4000 Rally – note the cover over the auxiliary radiator. (BMIHT)

Wind of change: the formation of British Leyland

It was in May of this year that another milestone in the history of the British motor industry occurred with the merger of the Leyland Motor Corporation and British Motor Holdings to form the British Leyland Motor Corporation, headed by Lord Stokes. Stokes was in favour of value-for-money events such as entering cars in TV rallycross, where the cars could be exposed relatively inexpensively to an audience measured in millions. At Abingdon, the Comps Department was renamed the British Leyland Competitions Department. With a reduction in the rally programme and uncertainty concerning the

department's future, Peter Browning was obliged to tell most of the drivers that their contracts would not be renewed for 1969. This was with the exception of Paddy, who was on a two-year contract, and Brian Culcheth.

Although BMC had competed at Sebring since the late '50s, the team had not entered any rallies in North America. This was to change with a two-car entry in the International Shell 4000, in support of BMC Canada. Paddy was in a 1275cc Mini-Cooper S with local co-driver Mike Kerry, the rally starting from Calgary and crossing Canada to finish in Halifax, a distance of 4000 miles.

The event was memorable in various ways for Paddy. "I knew a fellow called Carlo von Maffi, a racehorse trainer and breeder, and when we arrived in Calgary he sent a chauffeur with a large Mercedes to collect us from the airport. We went to his house for dinner, complete with butler in white gloves, which was all very splendid. He was a big hunter, too, and there were stuffed polar bears all about the house.

"I remember we went to have a look at one of the stages which was normally closed in winter, up a hill near Banff, and had to cut the chain keeping the barrier down. When we were way up this road we saw what we thought were a couple of blokes. As we got nearer we realised that they were huge bears, and they started walking towards the car. When they saw us they turned and ran off – it was amazing.

"On a special stage during the rally, near Toronto, we came over a brow and there was a large truck blocking the road. In front of the truck was the Porsche 911 of Zasada and he was having a confrontation with the driver, who eventually produced a gun. We said 'We're on the Shell 4000 Rally' but the truck driver said 'I don't care a sh*t what you're on, my children walk to school down this road and I ain't having any of you guys blasting down here!' The stage had to be cancelled..."

On the second day the Mini suffered from overheating and the team decided to fit an additional radiator to the front of the car. Unfortunately, the attention of the organiser, James Gunn, was drawn to the potential ineligibility of this modification, and he sent a note to Peter Millard of BMC Canada, saying that the car could continue while further enquiries were made. Two days later, after a stewards' meeting, a letter to Millard stated that the car was not eligible, so Paddy was out.

Tying up '68:
Targa and the TAP

Jenny went down to Sicily with Paddy for the Targa Florio, where he was driving an MGB GT with Andrew Hedges. "It was a very hard circuit to remember – I think it was 25 miles long. Because you didn't have a co-driver with you, I remember going out with Andrew, to mark the kilometre stones with signs. I remember marking 'FL' on a stone, for 'Flat Left', and then Lancia going out that night and changing the sign – not to nobble us, but because they wanted their own signs, and there wasn't enough room for both sets of signs. We should have done a deal that we all used the same notes – that would have made it a lot easier!"

Paddy and Andrew Hedges certainly had a good run that year, finishing second in class – and then had the occasion to relax in style, as Paddy recalls. "As well as our cars, Anthony Bamford had entered an MGB, painted in yellow JCB colours and driven by Tony Fall and Peter Brown. After the race Anthony said to us 'Would you like to come over to my father's yacht?'. This was moored in Palermo harbour. We were staying at Cefalu, east of Palermo, so Rauno, Timo, Andrew and myself, with Jenny, drove our race cars, still with race numbers, and blasted into the harbour area to find all these huge boats moored there.

"We couldn't find the Bamford boat, and as the evening was drawing in we were about to leave when we heard a voice shouting down to us 'Are you friends of young Anthony?'. We looked up and there was Joe Bamford on the deck of this huge ship. It seemed to take ages just to climb the ladder to get on board, it was so big, and there we were on this beautiful yacht. This was my introduction to JCB – to think that Joe Bamford had started out in life as a bicycle mechanic, and now he had all this!"

With the retirement of Ron Crellin, Tony Nash was now invited to co-drive with Paddy, their first event being the second TAP Rally in Portugal. The rally followed the pattern of the Monte Carlo, with several starting points, although Lisbon and Oporto starters only covered 800kms before the common route commenced at Madrid. The first test was ten laps of the Jarama racing circuit, with 20 cars at a time going round. The second test was five laps of a banked track round a football

stadium, with only the driver aboard; Paddy was fourth fastest, behind a Porsche 911, a local Mini-Cooper S and a Renault 8 Gordini. The second leg was incredibly difficult because of the small-scale maps, and of the 155 starters only 42 reached Oporto at the end of the section. The lead became a battle between Paddy and old team-mate Tony Fall in a Lancia Fulvia, but this was settled by a closed level-crossing gate on a four-minute section on the final leg, resulting in Paddy and Tony coming in second.

This had not been such a good year as 1967 and – as Peter Browning commented later – 1968 seemed to be a season of second places for Paddy.

A corny publicity shot with Tony Fall (centre) and Paddy in stetsons, before the 1968 Shell 4000 Rally in Canada. (BMIHT)

Paddy showing Barbara Castle, the Labour government's Minister of Transport, how full-harness rally seat belts work, during a campaign to persuade people to use safety belts. (BMIHT)

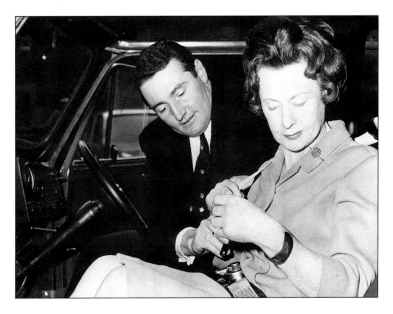

Chapter 8

The long drive
1968–1969

The London-to-Sydney Marathon was thought up over a lunch attended by press baron Sir Max Aitken, chairman of Beaverbrook Newspapers, Jocelyn Stevens of Beaverbrook Newspapers and Tommy Sopwith, racing driver and owner of Equipe Endeavour. A committee including racing driver Jack Sears, Tony Ambrose, Dean Delamont of the RAC and Jack Kemsley, the RAC Rally organiser, eventually decided on an overland route to Bombay, shipment of the competitors to Fremantle on the P&O liner *Chusan*, and a daunting route across Australia to finish in Sydney, a total of 10,000 miles later.

Paddy's 1800 under preparation at Abingdon for the 1968 London-to-Sydney Marathon. (BMIHT)

The 'Land Crab': slow but tough

The BMC 1800 was chosen as the Abingdon team entry, it being judged the most suitable on account of its strength and its ability to cover rough roads at high speed thanks to its Hydrolastic suspension. Although the 'Land Crab', as the 1800 was affectionately nick-named, was never going to have the agility of the Mini, it was not without its virtues, as Paddy gladly recognises.

"It was a slightly unknown quantity, but we knew it would be very well prepared, and on unknown rough terrain it made sense. It was only ever going to be a long-distance car – it was never going to be a short-distance competition winner. But it was strong as hell, and with its Hydrolastic suspension and wheel-at-each-corner design it had fantastic roadholding.

"I remember doing a special stage up and down a mountain the other side of Kabul. The thing was sluggish going up – it drove me up the wall. To make up time, coming down I drove like a man possessed. I drove that car down that rough road – and I'd never driven on one quite that bad – and the thing was amazing. On rough roads it was the nearest thing to a Citroën. The roadholding! You could chuck it anywhere – it was a very safe car. We did an excellent time for the stage, considering how slow the car was going up the

hill, and ended up running fourth or fifth by the time we arrived at Bombay."

There was much discussion on whether to go two-up or three-up, with the decision finally taken to run three-man crews – another reason why the 1800 was chosen. Going three-up meant a weight penalty, in that a third person and their possessions was being carried, amounting to at least an extra 1½cwt, and in hindsight Paddy is still not sure if he made the right decision. "It might have been a mistake. But the marathon was a very long endurance test, and I like my sleep. We also wanted a really good mechanic on board – and Alec Poole was a very good mechanic. So I decided to run three-up – as did Andrew Cowan, who won the event. But the Citroën that nearly won was two-up. We didn't actually *have* to have a three-man crew. That said, it was bloody good fun with the three of us – I really enjoyed myself and thought at the time that I'd done the right thing."

It was Paddy, with regular co-driver Tony Nash, who had picked Alec Poole, son of the proprietor of BMC's Dublin importer/assembler, Booth Poole, as his third crewman – despite Clive Baker, who had carried out quite a lot of the testing at Bagshot, having been pencilled in for the position. "I took Alec because he was a bloody nice reliable guy, a good mechanic – and a very good driver, who had won the European Championship. I had known him some years because I knew his father. As for Tony, he had done quite a few

Above Left: Tony Nash, who as well as being co-driver on the Marathon was Paddy's partner in a Mini on five rallies, including Paddy's BMC swansong, the 1970 Scottish Rally. (BP)

Above: Alec Poole, the MG apprentice who was the third member of the Marathon team in the 1800. (BP)

Right: Paddy and Tony Nash try out their headsets during the pre-rally shakedown for the Marathon at Thruxton circuit. (BMIHT)

events with me, and was a lovely guy. He was in the car business in Bristol, and was quite wild."

The mechanical specification of the cars was free and the organisers marked the engine and body of each car to ensure that these components were not changed during the event. One important comfort was the fitting of wool seat covers to ensure the crews were kept cool on the hotter sections of the route and warm during the earlier and colder European sections.

London to Bombay – via Afghanistan

The start of the Marathon was from Crystal Palace, where massive crowds surrounded the cars; even Lord Stokes was present. Paddy was looking forward to what was to come. "I liked the idea of the marathon, because it was a long-distance event. Racing was essentially driving round in circles. European rallies normally stayed within their own countries, whereas this was a real adventure – this was going somewhere, like climbing Mount Everest. Actually trying to go somewhere, into new territory – that made sense. That was exciting."

The rally to Bombay was more or less without incident for Paddy and his crew. But that's not to say that this part of the rally wasn't memorable – especially when the cars reached Afghanistan. "The King of Afghanistan closed

Above: Some of the team at Thruxton during the shakedown. Left to right are Tony Nash, Henry Liddon, Tony Fall, Paddy Hopkirk, 'Gelignite' Jack Murray, Peter Browning, Rauno Aaltonen, George Shepheard, Alec Poole and Mike Wood. (BMIHT)

Right: The British Leyland team at the start of the Marathon at Crystal Palace, with Paddy standing to the left of Lord Stokes (centre). (BMIHT)

the roads – we had nothing on them. But when you stopped to check your tyres or something, people suddenly came out of holes in the ground. We had a puncture in Afghanistan in the middle of nowhere. There was a small hut about 100 yards away with three chaps inside drinking tea. We accepted a drink of this nice hot tea. I don't know what was in it because I was as high as a kite for about a day!"

The arrival in India was memorable. "Millions came out to see the rally," remembers Paddy. "It was like driving through a sea of people – all immaculately dressed in their best white robes. You had to swerve the car to get them to pull back, and sometimes you couldn't get out of the car to service it – while of course people would also pinch bits off the cars. In Bombay a well-spoken Indian journalist opened the door of the car and said to me 'I was educated at Oxford. Just follow me'. He took us to a press room, where a meal was laid on. I asked him what would happen if I ran over one of the people lining the route. He looked left and then right and said in that inscrutible Indian way 'He gets injured'. The police were beating them back with sticks..."

In the docks at Bombay the cars all received a thorough going-over by the mechanics. Although the 1800 engine spec was designed to cope with the varying quality of fuels en route, it was interesting to see that the Hillman Hunter of Andrew Cowan had a high-compression cylinder head fitted at Bombay. At this stage Paddy was in fourth

place with 22 penalties. "We were getting on really well in the car, with never a cross word. I drove all the stages and Alec shared the rest of the driving, particularly on the long road sections."

Alec Poole's fond recollections of the Marathon start with the journey out. "The trip on the *Chusan* was fantastic, with wonderful food and great parties. It got to a stage where the captain had the swimming pool emptied each night and covered with a net to stop inebriated rally drivers falling into the water half-naked."

The *Chusan* had been specially diverted to Bombay to collect the rally cars – at some expense, but with P&O having been persuaded that plenty of good publicity would result. Alas this was somewhat torpedoed by a jaded Paddy Hopkirk, when the ship arrived in Fremantle. "When I got off the boat BBC TV stuck a microphone under my nose and asked what I thought of things so far. I said I thought the sea journey was the best advertisement for air travel ever. Apparently P&O were very upset, as my remarks went out on prime-time TV..."

Peter Browning, meanwhile, recalls one of his less bright ideas. "I remember doing a recce in Australia in a light aircraft, with a sandstorm blowing, the pilot trying to keep as low as possible, and with the windscreen being peppered with sand. I can't believe that I was so stupid that I thought I could do a recce from the air and get down any detail which would be useful."

Bottom Left: A confident thumbs-up from Tony Nash (left), Paddy and Alec Poole, before setting off. (BMIHT)

Below: Paddy at speed on the Marathon – although in reality speed was not one of the attributes of the rugged 'Land Crab'. (BP)

Into Australia – the going gets tough

On the section from Marvel Lock to Lake King, Paddy had two punctures and damaged the steering rack. "We were on this tight sandy section, with sections of the road made up with slabs of concrete, when we hit the edge of one of these slabs which was standing proud," recounts Alec Poole. "The steering-rack housing was fractured about six inches from the end, so we did still have steering – but it was rattling all over the place, with the front wheels pointing in strange directions. At the next service point a new steering rack was fitted by the mechanics.

"I also remember the Snowy Mountains on the last night. We finished the stage and we were at a service point drinking coffee and eating sandwiches. None of the other competitors seemed to be stopping for long and Paddy said to Tony 'What have we got next?'. Tony said 'Don't worry, mate, we've got four hours down the main road to the next control'. We set off down this road and it was bend after bend after bend. It didn't seem to matter, as we assumed we would quickly be onto a straighter bit with dual-carriageway or whatever. After about an hour, Paddy said 'Surely we should be getting on to a better road soon?'. Tony said 'I've been starting to get a bit worried about the time myself'. We realised then that we ought to press on a bit. So Paddy started really motoring but the time had already been lost and we lost several minutes. You could say that in effect lost us the rally, because we were beaten by six minutes by Andrew Cowan in his Hillman Hunter at the finish, but he may have had some setbacks too. We realised afterwards, talking to our Aussie crew, that when the recce had been carried out the section was still closed by snow, so accurate notes hadn't been made."

Drama: the Citroën accident

On the last day, Lucien Bianchi in his Citroën was leading with about 110 miles to the finish at Warwick Farm. Jean-Claude Ogier, the co-driver, was driving when the car was involved in a head-on collision with a local Mini driven by an apprentice electrician. As the DS was a left-hand-drive car being driven on the left-hand side of the road, this resulted in the passenger's side taking the full impact, and Lucien Bianchi (who was asleep) received serious injuries. Next car along was the 1800, as Paddy recalls. "It was awful. Lucien was conscious but there was a lot of blood streaming down his face. Alec jumped out to try to get Lucien out of the car. Jean-Claude had already got out, but was staggering around in shock. Alec reached into the car to try to reach Lucien's legs and felt a loose shoe and for a moment thought Lucien had lost a foot. The cars were locked together and the next thing was that the Mini caught fire. Alec went to the boot of the 1800 and pulled out one of those small Simoniz aerosol fire extinguishers. He opened the bonnet and, being met by flames, quickly shut it again and squirted the extinguisher through the grille, managing to put out the flames. Lucien was lucky that this small extinguisher did the trick."

At least the team was well equipped for such emergencies, says Alec Poole. "We were carrying bolt-cutters in the car, because of the possibility of locked gates in the outback. But even with these I couldn't cut through the crushed door section to free Lucien."

Leaving Alec and Tony attending the injured, Paddy turned round and sped off up the road for a mile, to where he had seen some photographers standing by a ford. Paddy said 'We need help. There's been a smash. Is there a doctor anywhere?'.

The men returned to the accident scene and one of them phoned for an ambulance using a taxi two-way radio. They managed eventually to cut Bianchi free and an ambulance arrived and took him and the Mini occupants to hospital. Bianchi suffered a broken leg and severe hand and face injuries while the people in the Mini were lucky to receive only lacerations. Once the situation was under control, Paddy carried on, and just made the next control in time. "Later a rumour circulated that BMC had hired a kamikaze crew to go out and crash into the leading Citroën as

Right: Australian mechanics change the damaged steering rack, while Alec Poole checks the oil on the 1800. (BMIHT)

Below: Ah! That's better! The team enjoys a beer after finishing second overall. (BP)

revenge for the previous problems on the 1966 Monte Carlo Rally," recalls Paddy. This of course was absolute nonsense. Nor is it the case, says Paddy, that the 1800 would have won had it not stopped to help Bianchi and Ogier.

He remains very critical of the NSW police, whom he described at the time as 'twits'. "I remember driving through one small settlement in the middle of the night, flat-out, and we were stopped by a police officer. He said 'You might think that this is one small quiet sleepy part of Australia which doesn't matter, but that's the way it is going to stay!'. They were like a bunch of SS men; there were seven police cars following us from Nowra, but where were they when Lucien crashed? Don't talk to me about the Australian police!"

Left: Paddy receives a special award from Donald Crosby of the Cork Examiner – note the picture of the London-to-Sydney 1800 engraved on the salver. (Cork Examiner)

Bottom left: Innes Ireland (second from left) shares a joke with Alec Poole, Tony Nash and Paddy, on their return from Australia. (BMIHT)

An honourable second

Was the apparently unlikely victory of the Hunter a surprise, or had Paddy seen it as serious competition? "Oh yes, it was serious competition. It was very well prepared, and Andrew Cowan was no idiot. It was a very good team. But the rally was only won on the last half day. It could have been Bianchi, it could have been us. We knew we were up for winning it – with a bit of luck, if someone had to drop out, as we weren't in the fastest car. But the mistake we made near the end, on the section we hadn't recce'd, cost us time. The trouble was that with the 1800 you couldn't make up much time if you got behind, because you couldn't just put your foot down. You had

to keep moving the whole time, as it was quite a sluggish car. Had we run two-up instead of three-up there is no doubt that the weight-saving would have increased our performance uphill, and over those long stages this could have made quite a difference, but it wouldn't have been such a happy journey with only two people."

No one ever remembers who comes second in a rally and the prize money of £3000 was not really much consolation. However, Paddy did appreciate the telegram he received from Terence O'Neill, Prime Minister of Northern Ireland, and which read 'Many congratulations on a gallant effort and splendid placing. Delighted to see an Ulsterman once more up with the winners'.

Above: A welcome-home kiss from Jenny at London Airport, after Paddy's return from the Marathon. (BMIHT)

1969 – The shrinking Comps Department – and Paddy goes rallycrossing

Jenny was still working for major advertising agency Geers Gross, and on Paddy's return from the marathon the couple went to a drinks party at the Chelsea house of Bob Gross, as Paddy recalls. "At this party I met this big Australian guy, Wylton Dickson, who told me he was the promoter for the football World Cup. He said 'What do you do?' and I said 'I've just been to your country on a rally'. He said 'What's a rally?'. I explained, and later in the evening he came over to me and said 'Why don't we have a World Cup Rally?'. I thought to myself that he should go and have another drink. Here is this guy who doesn't know what a rally is and he's suggesting something like that...

"But after the party I checked up on Wylton and found out he was no fool and was a real entrepreneurial promoter. I was later phoned by him, and he asked me if I thought a rally to Mexico was a good idea. I liked the idea and put him in touch with Dean Delamont of the RAC. So with sponsorship from the *Daily Mirror*, that's how the World Cup Rally got off the ground."

The Competition Department now moved into the New Year with sadness that the team had in effect been split up, with only Paddy and Brian Culcheth being retained, but looking forward all the same to a relatively busy programme.

There had been no problem getting approval to compete in the TV rallycross series and to give the BMC 1300 some exposure it was decided to include a 1300 in BL's entries at Lydden Hill for this BBC event. The car was fitted with an injection engine and it was felt it could make a good showing. Paddy drove the car in the rather muddy televised contest and achieved good results, coming sixth overall against some well-tried Mini rallycross cars. Interestingly, for later rallycross events the 1300 had the suspension changed from Hydrolastic to a Mini-style rubber-cone system. Whatever

Paddy churns up the snow at a televised Lydden Hill rallycross meeting early in 1969. (BMIHT)

Kate Hopkirk

Born in October 1969, Kate's first two schools were in London and she then went on to St Mary's Convent in Ascot where she became Head Girl. Kate left school to take a two-year HND course in advertising and marketing at Bristol Polytechnic. After successfully completing this course Kate decided to do some travelling and spent nine months visiting various parts of the world including four months working in Sydney, Australia. While in Australia, Kate decided on nursing as a career and returned to London where she did her general nursing training, a three-year course, at St Thomas's. Until she married she continued at the hospital, later working as a practice nurse attached to a number of GP practices. In 1997 she married Hugh, an investment manager with a merchant bank. Kate and Hugh's first daughter, Molly, was born in 2001, followed by daughter Jessica in 2003.

"As far as Dad's rally career is concerned, my memories are mainly of going to the odd rally finish," says Kate. "He's always rather underplayed his rally-driving and it wasn't until we went to an amazing museum in Northern Ireland full of Minis that I realised what a celebrity Dad was. The second time was when we went to the party that BMW put on at the factory in 2004, with all the Mini clubs.

"Growing up with Dad, I remember we had these amazing Sunday lunches which went on forever, with jokes, games and card playing well into the evening. He has always been such fun – a really cheeky fellow. I can see why people remember him so well."

the suspension, however, Paddy was no great enthusiast for rallycross. "I hated it. It was such a chancey business because it all depended on how much mud you did or didn't get on your windscreen. I don't think it was a very skilful sport – it was a bit like banger racing."

Another house move became a necessity when Paddy and Jenny announced that they were expecting an increase to the family. They bought a four-bedroom house in Kensington and later moved again, still in Kensington, to a bigger house with seven bedrooms and five bathrooms, which was to be the family home until the Hopkirks left London to live in the country in 1983.

Circuit of Ireland '69: a question of wheels

With five wins on the Circuit of Ireland, Paddy was keen to compete in his home event again. In February 1969 he went to Thruxton to carry out some testing with a selection of tyres and a limited-slip differential. He did about 30 laps and it was decided that he would take 12in Dunlop Weathermasters for the forest stages and a selection of 10in and 12in race tyres for tarmac, retaining the limited-slip differential.

In an attempt to build a really lightweight car, mechanic Roy Brown was instructed to carry out the maximum of lightening to all possible components, and the body was constructed with aluminium boot, bonnet and doors, without the characteristic Mini seams. Unfortunately the engine, fitted with a single Weber carburettor, failed during the running-in period, with a faulty cam follower, reducing preparation time.

The mixing of the two wheel diameters on the Circuit of Ireland car emphasised one of the fundamental challenges in using the Mini as a rally car, namely the use of small 10in wheels. "The small wheels were a problem – they reduced ground clearance, and you couldn't get the power through to the road," says Paddy. "There were more powerful engines coming through, but that was no good if you couldn't get the power down. And the ground clearance was a big problem. We were riding on the sumpguards – which were very strong, as a result – and this was breaking the cars up. It was shaking them to pieces. Bigger wheels improved the ground clearance and stopped us wrecking the car over rough terrain, and they probably gave us better traction. But on 12in wheels for the Circuit of Ireland the car handled like a pig. I found it very difficult to drive, as it had poor directional stability – I could hardly keep it on the road. After seven stages, the 12in wheels were replaced by 10in ones, and this did improve the handling. Even later Rover-era Minis never handled that well on 12in wheels – although I'm not technical enough to say, I think it was a question of steering geometry."

Apart from low oil pressure on the Killarney loop, the most worrying failure was the fracture of two of the new adjustable front tie-rods. The mechanics managed to obtain standard tie-rods from a private service crew and the car ran on these to the end, Paddy and Tony finishing second behind the Ford Escort Twin-Cam of Roger Clark and Jim Porter, with Adrian Boyd third in another Mini-Cooper.

A night stage for Paddy on the 1969 Circuit of Ireland; he eventually finished second overall. (Esler Crawford)

Sebring – and a brush with Customs

The annual trip to Sebring was to be the last event for the MGC GTS models, after only two such sorties. It was decided to sell the cars in the States as there was no budget available to continue development, which was sad. In the race Paddy, with regular co-driver Andrew Hedges, came in a respectable 15th overall and ninth in the Prototype class, after completing 195 laps. Nearly forty years after the event, Paddy confesses to having relatively hazy memories about the MGC. "It was a big, strong car, and I remember it as being very torquey. In fact, when you put your foot down the whole car twisted – great fun! But I don't remember getting terribly excited about driving it. These sort of cars weren't great for the job, but they were made good by very good preparation. Attention to detail, on things such as the wiring, that was where BMC was so meticulous. The Lancias – for example – were real high-performance cars, but it doesn't matter how quick a car is if the seat frame breaks or the lights go out. Our cars weren't so high-performance, but they were strong and reliable. There was a lot of commonsense put into the cars. It wasn't high-tech engineering development. If you could find a better bracket off a bicycle that would do the job, then you'd use it – and usually what the mechanics did find was good."

Paddy and Tony Nash leave the start of the 1969 Circuit of Ireland in the lightweight Mini-Cooper S. Note the magnesium sumpguard and the lack of external body seams. (Esler Crawford)

Talk of the 1969 Sebring brings to mind for Paddy a story concerning his miniature Minox camera. "I already had a secondhand Minox but on the way to the US I stopped at Shannon Airport, where I saw a new one at a knock-down price in the duty-free shop and duly bought it. Travelling back from the States with Bob Olthoff, he admired my new Minox and because they were still expensive he bought my old one. I said 'To avoid duty at London Airport, I'll bring my old camera through Customs and you can bring my new one through because you're South African'. We had the respective receipts and so all was well. Some time later, coming back from Nice, the Customs man at Heathrow said 'Have you got a camera? If so, can I see the receipt?'. I got the receipt out of my wallet. He said 'The serial number isn't the same as the one on the camera'. I thought quickly and said 'I know what's happened. A friend of mine had an identical camera and his had a cracked lens so I lent him mine until he got it fixed. He must have picked up the wrong camera by mistake when he gave mine back'. The Customs man was now very annoyed, searched all my baggage, and seized the camera. Outside the airport I phoned Bob, told him what had happened and asked if he'd back up my story. A few days later Bob went into the airport with his camera and the receipt, they believed him, and he got my camera back.

"Some months later I was in my flat in Belfast and there was this guy outside in a greasy raincoat, sitting in a Hillman Minx. He knocked on the door and said 'I'm from Customs and Excise and I have a warrant to search the house'. During the search he found the Minox and a projector, and one or two other things on which I hadn't paid duty. He then asked to go down to my office and proceeded to go through everything, looking for paperwork with 'Olthoff' on it, but of course found nothing.

"He left, and next thing I knew I'd received a summons to appear at Uxbridge Magistrates Court where, despite having a very good barrister, I was fined £3000 – or three times the value of the goods. As I came out of the Court this Irishman came up and said 'Hello Paddy, do you have time for a pint?'.

"We had a chat and he said 'I'm the chief investigator for the Customs and I read about what happened at London Airport, so I knew there was something funny. I found out from Minox where the camera was supplied, went to Shannon and found the receipt with your signature, so I knew I had you by the balls! We want publicity to stop other people smuggling and you are well known so you were done!'

"The story made the front page of the *Daily Express*, with the headline 'Irish rally driver caught smuggling'. Interestingly, when I won the Monte it was 'British driver wins the Monte Carlo Rally'..."

Paddy in his MGC GTS, seen in front of some bigger machinery, achieved one of the best results ever recorded by an MG in the 1969 Sebring 12-Hour Race. (BP)

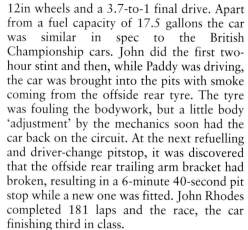

One of the first outings for the Triumph 2.5 PI was on the 1969 Austrian Alpine Rally, as part of the development programme. (BMIHT)

Paddy maintains a tight line on one of the hill climbs with his injection Mini, during the 1969 Tour de France Automobile – note the knock-on wheels. (Paddy Hopkirk)

A return to Triumph

The new BL management wanted to use Triumph models to promote the sporting image of the company, and Abingdon were having good help from Ray Henderson at Triumph with development of the Triumph 2.5 PI. However, an exploratory entry in the Austrian Alpine found a weakness in the clutch, and the car was sent home on the train.

In June, the European Six-Hour Touring Car Race was held at Brands Hatch. This was one of the events included in the Mini race programme, and Paddy was teamed up with John Rhodes in an injection car fitted with 12in wheels and a 3.7-to-1 final drive. Apart from a fuel capacity of 17.5 gallons the car was similar in spec to the British Championship cars. John did the first two-hour stint and then, while Paddy was driving, the car was brought into the pits with smoke coming from the offside rear tyre. The tyre was fouling the bodywork, but a little body 'adjustment' by the mechanics soon had the car back on the circuit. At the next refuelling and driver-change pitstop, it was discovered that the offside rear trailing arm bracket had broken, resulting in a 6-minute 40-second pit stop while a new one was fitted. John Rhodes completed 181 laps and the race, the car finishing third in class.

Three cars were entered in the revived Tour de France Automobile, run in September, with two 1275cc Coopers for Paddy and John Handley, with Brian Culcheth in a Group I car. During their recce Paddy and Tony had a frightening experience, as Paddy recalls. "It was one of my scariest moments in a rally car. I was coming down the Chamrousse near Grenoble with Tony Nash in the passenger seat and our suitcases in the back, and we came to a hairpin which had some gravel. The back end came round and I gave the steering full lock. The car was still fitted with racing tyres, and I hadn't used full lock before with these tyres fitted. The tyres locked up in the wheelarch, sending the car straight over the edge. We ended up jammed between the rock face and a tree, upside down. I could hear the fuel pump running and smelt petrol.

"Tony and I placed our feet against the windscreen and managed to push the glass out, coming out of the car with nothing to hold onto. We had to hang onto the car until a local threw us a rope so we could get back to the road. John Handley and Paul Easter then came along and we sorted things out, with Paul taking a picture for evidence!"

The Tour de France was a gruelling 5000km event, its 3000-odd miles comprising ten circuit races and eleven hill climbs. Paddy lost time at Albi with a loose heater hose and then, before the Nogaro race, a broken valve spring was diagnosed. With no time to remove the cylinder head, some clever work through a plug hole enabled the mechanics to change the spring without time loss. Despite problems with a lower suspension arm and then a puncture during the race, Paddy and Tony won their class.

For Paddy and Jenny it was time to celebrate with the birth of their first child, Kate,

on 26 October 1969. "We weren't yet into the era where fathers closely followed the births of their children and were present at the delivery," says Paddy. "I was in a pub next to St Mary's Hospital Paddington when I heard the news – a wonderful moment."

The entering of three Triumph 2.5PIs in the RAC Rally was in effect a development and test exercise for the forthcoming *Daily Mirror* London-to-Mexico World Cup Rally. Paddy wasn't hugely impressed by the big six-cylinder Triumphs. "They were very nice comfortable cars on the road, but they reminded me a bit of the Rapiers, in that we were using the best we had – which was a very nice saloon car, but something that was light years behind as a competitions car. I think I committed a dreadful *faux pas* with Lord Stokes. Somebody from TV asked me how I thought things were going, and I said that the most difficult thing would be winning the rally in this car. I think that PR-wise I didn't do myself any favours..."

This was the first time that Abingdon had entered a team of non-BMC cars in an international rally, with Andrew Cowan and Brian Culcheth making up the RAC team with Paddy. "He was great fun to have as a team-mate, and a lovely guy," says Cowan. "He was extremely competitive, aggressive and cunning, and I am not sure if he really shared information with his team-mates."

The event was to experience more than its usual share of snow and ice, which did not favour the rear-wheel-drive Triumphs, which had to be fitted with chains on several stages. At Pantperthog Paddy's car lost all gears

except top, so a gearbox change became a necessity. Overcrowding caused chaos at the Machynlleth Control and with the car up on the ramp in the local BL Dealer and time running out, Peter Browning resorted to running Tony Nash up to the Control, where Tony was able to book out minus car in the mêlée! However, the clutch was now not working and although the mechanics tried to fix the release mechanism, Paddy completed the rally clutchless, all the same finishing second in class.

Now the big challenge was the London-to-Mexico World Cup Rally, and the next few months were to be occupied with preparations for this marathon.

Above left: Paddy on the third Clocaenog Special Stage of the 1969 RAC Rally. (E G Hodgkins)

Above right: A tea break on the 1969 RAC Rally. Left to right are Johnstone Syer, Paddy, Gunnar Palm, Brian Culcheth and Tony Nash. (BMIHT)

Below: Paddy's first Jaguar E-type coupé at Browns Lane. (LAT)

Chapter 9

World Cup year 1970

With sponsorship from the *Daily Mirror*, all the talk now was about the London-to-Mexico World Cup Rally.

Originally it had been intended to run a team of the then-secret new Range Rovers, but production delays prevented the test programme getting under way in time. Peter Browning therefore had to go for an alternative. With the emphasis placed by Donald Stokes on the Triumphs as BL's sporting models, and with the experience of the MkI version on the 1969 RAC Rally, it was decided to enter four MkII Triumph 2.5PIs. "It was marketing trying to dictate what the Competitions Department used, rather than the other way round," says Paddy. "In the Stuart Turner days we used the car that had the best chance of winning, and I don't think we ever even discussed it with the marketing people.

"But the Triumphs were very good for this sort of event. They were solid, and they handled very well. With the fuel injection the cars also had the advantage of being fitted with a metering unit controlled by a big lever on the dashboard, so we could adjust the mixture to compensate for the high altitude in the Andes. There was so little oxygen at that height that we had very little power – we were down to about half in some places."

Practising for the 1970 World Cup Rally in typical South American 'outback' terrain. (BP)

A little whisky goes down well...

A recce of the route in South America was essential, and with BL having a number of local agents, a standard Triumph 2000 was brought down from Leyland Peru by Ulrico Ossio for the first recce. Ulrico was to be the third crew member in the Andrew Cowan Triumph. He met Tony Nash in Santiago but before long it became obvious that the unmodified car was not strong enough, while the 2000 also suffered a fair number of punctures. Brian Culcheth returned home on Christmas Eve, requesting properly prepared cars for the next recce. In January, Paddy, Andrew Cowan and Brian Culcheth left for Rio de Janiero to start a second recce – carried out in three VW Beetle hire cars. For the third recce, however, two of the Triumph 2.5PIs used on the RAC Rally were shipped to South America.

"The cars were shipped to Buenos Aires and we couldn't get them out of Customs," remembers Paddy, who was to share a car with Tony Nash and his old friend and business partner Neville Johnston. "While waiting for the release of the cars, which meant hanging about in a central Buenos Aires hotel for about a week, we went to every cinema there was, to see whatever films were shown in English with Spanish subtitles. It was good for us, and passed the time. Understanding English, we could laugh at the jokes – which often didn't seem to translate – and this caused the locals to turn round and look at us, which was a laugh in itself.

"But we were getting bored and I remembered that during the 1964 Monte I had met Fangio. So I said 'Let me phone him and see if he can help with getting the cars out of customs'. Fangio didn't speak English but I got through to his secretary who did, and she said 'Oh yes, Mr Fangio remembers you. He'll see what he can do'.

"The next thing we knew was that two large guys had turned up at our hotel. They asked 'Have you got some money?'. We said we had, so off we all went to the local supermarket and bought a case of Scotch. Then it was off to the docks with these two guys, and they went

One of the road hazards found during a recce of the World Cup Rally route in South America. (BP)

into the customs house with the whisky. Ten minutes later the cars appeared at the back! Fangio was like a local god in that part of the world, and his magic had worked..."

There was quite a lot of flooding and on one section, with Paddy driving, one of the recce cars gulped up some flood water into the air intake, resulting in a bent con-rod. This resulted in a modification to the rally cars to prevent the possibility of this happening on the event.

Paddy treated the recce very seriously, says Brian Culcheth. "He was very professional, and would discuss each section with his team-mates and there was much talk about whether to run two-man or three-man crews. The pace notes were simplified to include mainly the rough and dangerous sections, as full notes were found to be too detailed for the crews to be able to concentrate on for 500 miles."

Paddy experimented with the effect of altitude by running with and without oxygen on the 15,650ft Agua Negras pass, and on the team's return to England a visit to the Institute of Aviation Medicine at Farnborough was arranged.

"We went to Farnborough and spent a day in the de-compression chamber with a Red Arrows crew. That was very interesting. They reduce your oxygen level and you make stupid decisions. After writing nursery rhymes on a pad we were subjected to a simulated 24,000ft altitude. This wasn't too uncomfortable, and while we were at this altitude we were asked by the instructor to write out the same rhyme again, with very interesting results. It was like a spider walking across a sheet of paper after walking in ink. As a result we were convinced that we should have oxygen available in the Andes. In the event, the lack of oxygen affected some people much worse than others, and I coped fairly well. Perhaps I've just got a small brain..."

Preparations for the rally did indeed seem endless, with the crews requiring innoculations for yellow fever, typhoid, cholera and smallpox. Betting was taking place, too, with Ladbrokes quoting Paddy as favourite at 10-to-1, Rauno Aaltonen and Roger Clark at 11-to-1, and footballer Jimmy Greaves at 12-to-1.

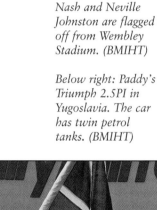

Below: Off at last – Paddy with Tony Nash and Neville Johnston are flagged off from Wembley Stadium. (BMIHT)

Below right: Paddy's Triumph 2.5PI in Yugoslavia. The car has twin petrol tanks. (BMIHT)

Across Europe...

The start was from Wembley Stadium in the presence of Lord Stokes and England football team captain Bobby Moore, and was further enlivened by 'Gelignite' Jack Murray letting off thunderflashes on the start ramp. With the route passing through Munich, Vienna, Budapest, Belgrade and Sofia, the first problems were experienced in Yugoslavia. Closure of a bridge caused a road blockage and the Triumph crews were not happy. Mike Wood and mechanic Martin Reade had checked this out when they did their recce, but understood it would be repaired in time.

The results of the European leg were determined by this 'prime', with Paddy and Brian Culcheth lying sixth equal at the Monza control. The 'prime' in Portugal, from Ville San Pietro to Camporossa, was 65 miles long and Paddy waited for daylight to complete this stage. Brian said it was incredibly easy. At the major BL service point in Lisbon the results showed Brian Culcheth lying sixth, Paddy eighth, and Andrew Cowan eleventh overall.

Paddy on 'Gelignite' Jack

"Jack Murray was a legendary character from the days of the Round Australia Rally. He obtained his nick-name Gelignite from his trick for overtaking fellow competitors in the dusty outback. He used to throw out sticks of the explosive to distract the car in front with the bang, making them think they had a blow-out so they slowed down and he could pass. Very young looking for his age, he was a strict teetotaller and very fit too. I always remember his unique name for alcohol – he used to say it was like drinking 'battery acid'. He was a member of the 'bare footers club' for people who water-ski at high speed without skis. We saw him do this on the Hawkesbury River at his weekend shack, up the river inland from Sydney."

Far left: Prince Michael of Kent, Gavin Thompson and Paddy at Wembley for the start of the rally. (LAT)

Left: Paddy and Tony Nash with their respective wives, Jenny and Joan, at the start of the rally in Wembley Stadium. (BP)

Paddy skates over the loose gravel on the San Remo 'prime' during the European leg of the rally. (BMIHT)

...and into South America

There was now a lull while the rally cars were shipped to Rio de Janiero on the Royal Mail Lines ship *Derwent*, a 12-day journey. The restart of the rally was in Rio de Janiero. The BL team stayed at Rio's Hotel Gloria, with their stay enlivened by Rosemary Smith, driving a Maxi in the rally, who donned a white bikini by the hotel swimming pool, causing as much publicity as the rally cars.

The competitors were now faced with the prospect of a marathon drive to Mexico. On the dirt roads and narrow wooden bridges through to Uruguay the Triumphs lost time on the impossible stage from Tacuarembo to Salto. From Montevideo, the capital of Uruguay, it was on to Buenos Aires, and to a chaotic service point at the Shell station in Salidillo.

"I remember lying in the back of the Triumph on a road section trying to sleep and looking up at the stars," says Paddy. "In Australia on the Southern Cross rally, Evan Green had told me about the stars and how the Southern Cross points towards the South Pole. As I looked at the stars I suddenly realised that we might be going in the wrong direction. I said to Neville, who was navigating, 'I think we're going in the wrong direction'. He said we weren't, and there was a bit of an argument. I said again 'I'm sure we're going in the wrong direction'. So Tony stopped the car, we had a look at the map, and we realised we were actually wrong. Luckily it was a long section so we soon made up the time lost."

These 'primes' were a disappointment for the Triumphs, as they expected to gain some time over the faster Fords, but the target times proved to be too easy. At Santiago there was a rest day, followed by a re-route through the Limite road tunnel as the result of a landslide. Consequently the drivers missed out one of the highest parts of the route. All the same, the stage from Rodeo to La Vina was 510 miles, with the road climbing to over 15,000ft, as Brian Culcheth recalls only too well: "It was the toughest section of the rally. It was rather like driving from Edinburgh to Dover, mainly in fog, on unmade roads strewn with rocks and animals, as fast as you could."

It was on this section that the Andrew Cowan car was involved in a serious accident. Having waited for a time, so as to start the 'prime' to take advantage of daylight, they caught up the 'Beauty Box' 1800 driven by the ladies crew. Blinded by the dust the 1800 was throwing up, Cowan missed a corner, and the car went off the road and dropped about 30ft, landing upside-down. All three crew members were injured but the local emergency services did a good job, and eventually they were all safely in hospital, their rally over. Brian Culcheth had to be carried from his car at the finish of the stage, and Paddy was also exhausted. "We didn't really know if the co-driver could read the notes and still concentrate for a full 13 hours continuously, but Tony did it. In the blinding heat it was a fantastic effort."

Paddy was in trouble on the section finishing at La Paz. With approximately 80km to go, a broken quillshaft (the intermediate shaft in the differential torque tube) brought his car to an abrupt halt. Willy Cave and Peter Jopp, in an Austin 1800, came along and found Paddy without any drive to the rear wheels. He had been in touch with the service crew at La Paz but was certain of losing time even if the spare parts arrived quickly.

"We towed the Triumph for about 60km, stopping several times to conceal the tow rope whenever a helicopter buzzed around," remembers Peter Jopp. "We were constantly watching in the mirror, worried that we would be seen by another competitor giving an illegal tow. Afterwards, Paddy very kindly sent us a very nice bottle of brandy as a thank you."

There was a major service point at La Paz, and mechanic Den Green was sent off by Peter Browning with a local driver in a jeep, carrying a new quillshaft. "We hadn't gone far when we came across Bill Bengry in a Rolls-Royce, filming the rally. We stopped and he asked us where we were going. When he realised we were going off to help Paddy, he said 'Jump in, this Rolls is a bloody sight quicker than that thing!'. When we got to Paddy, Neville Johnston had the car all in bits ready to fit the new shaft." Neville Johnston had been Paddy's racing mechanic in his Formula Junior days and was a dab hand at building gearboxes, and Paddy made it into La Paz with ten minutes to spare.

"The 560-mile 'prime' from Cuzco to Huancayo, including the Ticlia Pass, was gruelling, with the altitude averaging 13,000ft and an average speed set at 50mph," remembers Paddy. "I was glad to have the oxygen bottles on board at this altitude, and with the adjustable metering unit the engine ran without the over-fuelling problems which some cars experienced."

The BL mechanics had a service point in the BL factory in Lima, where Paddy had new halfshafts fitted. The first four cars to arrive at Lima were on time, including the two leading Fords and Brian Culcheth and Paddy, with everyone else losing time. There were now only 30 cars still in the rally.

Paddy was on the way from the last 'prime' before Cali in Colombia, trying to make up time on a downhill section, when he lost concentration for a moment and slid off the road on a muddy corner, losing about an hour. "It was a stupid accident. The radiator and oil cooler were damaged, but Neville did a wonderful job and managed to get us going, and at Cali, after the restart, the mechanics did some more panel bashing, to keep us going.

"I remember the road down into Buenaventura was an awful twisty little road with lots of lorries, and very dangerous. This was where we were to get on the Italian Lines ship *Verdi* for the sea trip to Cristobal. The hotel in Buenaventura was disgusting, with one rusty fridge, covered in ants and maggots, and a local barman with flies all over his nose. We were even scared to drink the bottled Coca Cola. I went out round the back and saw the swimming pool, which had about a foot of filthy water in it and a dead dog lying in the bottom. I went back into the bar and said to the crowd 'There's a swimming pool out the back! Anyone coming for a swim?'. With a cry of expectancy there was a rush for the door. When they saw this rotting corpse at the bottom I very nearly joined it! In contrast, when we got on board the *Verdi* it was like Claridges – it was super-luxurious and we had a great party that night en route to Panama."

Paddy and his crew unload their car on the quayside in Lisbon, before shipment to South America. (BMIHT)

Last leg: end of the adventure

It was a two-day trip to Cristobal through the Panama canal. The 16th stage was from Canoas to Cartago (220 miles) through the coffee plantations, and Paddy put up a strong performance. "This was the 'prime' we had practised between finishing the European section and restarting from Rio, and it paid off, with us winning the stage with a time six minutes faster than Hannu Mikkola in the leading Ford Escort. When we got back to England I was entertained to lunch at the Costa Rican Embassy and they presented me with a certificate recording my win on their 'prime' and the fastest time ever across Costa Rica. Our performance on the Panama-to-Mexico section also won us the Mexico Coffee Institute Award, with prize money of £500."

Cars arrived as much as 11 hours early at Oaxaca, leaving time for some sleep before tackling the 140-mile 'prime' from Oaxaca to Tuxtapec. Culcheth started first, with Paddy second, and although Rauno Aaltonen overtook both Triumphs he only gained three minutes – not enough to affect the results. After a gentle run to Fortin, the surviving 23 cars were escorted to the Aztec Stadium, a distance of 200 miles, by police on Harley-Davidson motorcycles.

Paddy, Tony and Neville had survived their various problems to come home in fourth place, winning prize money of £1500. "It was a great experience – a great adventure," says Paddy. "I'd have liked to have done better, but it would have been hard to beat the Escorts.

Paddy on a rough gravel road in South America on his way to fourth place overall. Note the two roof spotlamps now fitted. (BMIHT)

They were out to win, and the Escorts were real rally-winning cars, as well as having good drivers." Final overall positions were first Hannu Mikkola, Ford Escort, second Brian Culcheth, Triumph 2.5 PI, and third Rauno Aaltonen, Ford Escort.

The BL team was well looked after in Mexico City, with a party at the residence of the British military attaché and a splendid dinner and prizegiving laid on by the organisers. The team was welcomed home with a reception and lunch at the Lancaster Hotel, attended by Lord Stokes. After the rally Johnny Evans, who had built Paddy's Triumph, received a cut-glass sherry decanter and six glasses from Paddy, with a note saying this was in appreciation of the excellent build quality of the World Cup car – a very nice gesture.

Scottish swansong

Plans had been made before the World Cup to enter two cars in the Scottish Rally. So after the anti-climax of returning from this marathon event, entries were confirmed for Paddy and Tony Nash in a Mini 1275GT (XJB 308H) and Brian Culcheth in the Triumph 2.5PI World Cup test car – now fitted with triple Webers. Andrew Cowan had been down to drive the Triumph, but was still recuperating from his World Cup accident.

The rally became an epic struggle between Paddy in the Mini and Brian in the Triumph. "We were driving the former World Cup 1275GT with a new engine after the original had failed in Italy during the rally, and with the central long-range fuel tank removed," remembers Paddy. "We used 12in wheels, but it just wouldn't handle over the rough so we reverted to 10in wheels, with a slight reduction in ground clearance."

This was to be Paddy's last event for BL – and it was a messy end to his professional career. At the end of the rally, a protest was lodged with the organisers on behalf of Harry Kallstrom (Lancia), alleging that the leading Triumph had taken a short-cut on the Culbin stage. This was eventually sorted out in favour of Brian Culcheth/Johnstone Syer, with Brian finishing first and and Paddy second in the general classification.

That 1275GT Mini thus had a treble historical significance: it was Paddy's last BMC/BL works car, it was the last works Mini to appear in a UK rally, and it was one of Abingdon's very last rally Minis. Although no

sentimentalist when it comes to old cars, Paddy tried to buy the car after the rally. "I said I didn't want to sell it. I wanted to keep it, in a museum, as one of the last works Minis built. But it was knocked out to some dealer..."

The end: October 1970 – Abingdon closes, Paddy retires

With Lord Stokes now very much controlling the purse strings in his new empire, things were not looking good for Abingdon, with the rug having already been pulled from under the MG Car Club and Austin-Healey Club offices. Peter Browning had been trying to get the board to approve his programme for the next year without success, and in July he tendered his resignation in protest, offering to stay on until his successor had been appointed. He attended a meeting at Longbridge, expecting to discuss his replacement with George Turnbull, but it was a terrible blow to the staff at Abingdon when he returned late in the afternoon to announce that the Competitions Department would close on 31 October.

Something unique and very special had been destroyed, as Paddy acknowledges. "Big companies have to change to survive, and Abingdon was a bit of a law unto itself. Although it was part of BMC it was away from everything else. There was a culture that was away from 'Red Robbo' and the unions. In the Competitions Department they were all little entrepreneurs, almost, if you know what I mean. When a company gets bigger as the result of a merger, you always wonder about the people at the top, especially the accountants. I don't think we thought a lot of Lord Stokes, but maybe he knew something that we didn't.

"John Thornley, who ran MG, was a good man, and great fun, and Norman Higgins, the Financial Director at Abingdon, was the most down-to-earth accountant I've ever met. I think he bent the rules something rotten, adjusting the budgets to make sure the Competitions Department got what it wanted. I don't think Stuart ever wanted to do something that he wasn't allowed to do because he didn't have the money.

"Driver-wise, Stuart and his team got what they wanted. Whether it was good for the British Motor Corporation I don't know, but it got results. When you look at Stokes closing

Patrick Hopkirk

Patrick was born in March 1971 and went to school in London until he was nine years old and then to Worth Abbey, a boys' boarding school near Crawley run by Benedictine monks. Patrick represented the school at rugby, football, cricket and tennis. He also took part in the Duke of Edinburgh Awards scheme, winning the Bronze, Silver and Gold medals. With the Knights of Malta he went many times to Lourdes as a volunteer helper.

"I used to get a bit embarrassed with Dad and his cars. He was always changing cars and when he came to school I didn't know what he would turn up in next, so I used to get a bit of a ribbing from my classmates," he recalls."As children we went on skiing holidays in France and Italy and in the summer we'd go down on holiday to Devon or Cornwall as a family. In fact we went on family holidays until in our 20s, and when we got fed up with English summer weather we went to Spain for the sunshine."

After A Levels, Patrick chose to go to Trinity College Dublin for four years, to read Theology and Classical Civilisation, but he subsequently changed course to read Geography and Sociology. While a student he obtained some work experience in his father's factory and when he finished at Trinity he got a job with Quaker, and worked for them for a year selling soft drinks all around NW London.

In 1995 Patrick joined Paddy's business for two years and then went off to do a Post Graduate Certificate of Education in Geography at the University of London. After experience in various British schools he obtained a teaching job at St Georges in Buenos Aires, Argentina. During his time in South America he took the opportunity to see some more of South America and visited Chile, Bolivia and parts of Brazil.

The collapse of the Argentine economy in 2001 saw Patrick back in the UK, and he has rejoined Paddy, and his partner Paul, in their sales and marketing business. He is still very active, playing football, cricket – and tennis for the Queen's Club 2nd VI. He has recently been appointed a school governor in London.

Patrick sees his Dad as a very modest person, but someone with a natural skill at PR. "He never really talks about his rally-driving with the family because I think he is very conscious of being an old rally-driver and perhaps boring people by talking about it..."

the department down, I think it was costing £300,000 a year or something. A lot of people would have given their right arm to have that at such a low budget. It wasn't money that was winning rallies – it was bloody good organisation and bloody good people."

As soon as it was announced that Paddy was leaving the team, he received an offer from Cesare Fiorio, the Lancia team manager, to drive for them in Fulvia HF coupés. He had already had experience of the little fwd V4 Lancias, and been most impressed, but all the same he was not swayed by the offer. "I remember driving Ove Andersson's Lancia while practising one year for the Monte – we had a drink together, and just swapped cars. I thought it was fantastic! I remember thinking how difficult our job was. But in the end I decided I didn't want to drive for the Italians and eat spaghetti all the time."

"Anyway, we were blessed with our lovely new daughter Kate, and I think I had really decided to retire from the rally game. It's not really a married man's sport – and in any case I'd started a new UK business in 1969, and that was something that demanded my attention. I used the end of the Competitions Department as an excuse to retire, really."

So with the sadness of the closure of the Competitions Department, a final dinner was held at the Bear Hotel in Wantage, with the printed menu being less than flattering about Lord Stokes.

Things were going to change now for Paddy, in his first year away from rallying. However on the family front there was more excitement, when Paddy and Jenny were blessed with an addition to their family in the shape of Patrick, born at St Mary's, Paddington, on 5 March 1971.

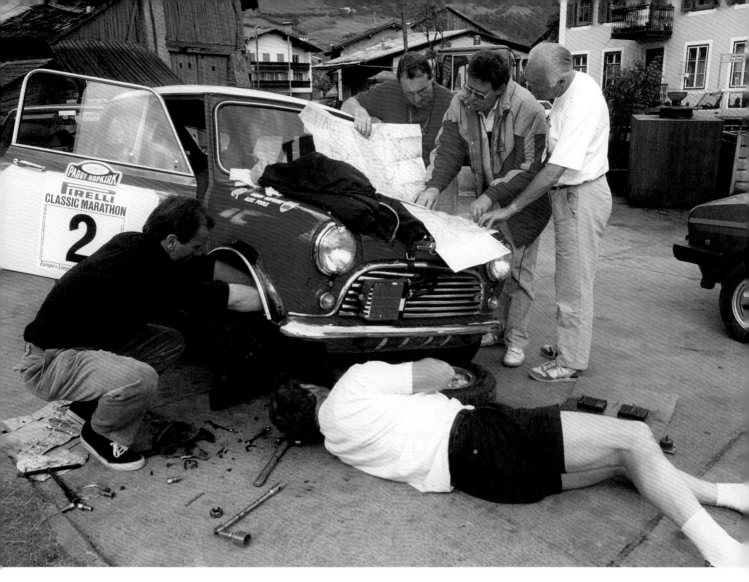

Above: Simon Wheeler and Alec Poole (underneath) change a driveshaft while Paddy consults the maps with Bob Freeborough and Philip Cooper of the Pirelli 'management' crew, during the 1989 Pirelli Classic Marathon. (Chris Harvey)

Right: The happy winners in the Dolomites. Alec and Paddy with '6 EMO' just after crossing the finishing line of the last special stage on the 1990 Pirelli Classic Marathon. (Esler Crawford)

Left: The ex-works car which Paddy and Alec Poole drove in the 1989 Pirelli Classic Marathon being shown off to the Mill Automotive Group staff. (Paddy Hopkirk)

Opposite: Issued on 26 April 2001 by Eire's post office, to commemorate the centenary of the Royal Irish Automobile Club, this stamp depicts Paddy on the 1964 Monte. (LAT)

Below: Ron Crellin and Paddy with the 1994 Monte Mini, in the company of John Cooper (second right) and Stuart Turner. (Paddy Hopkirk)

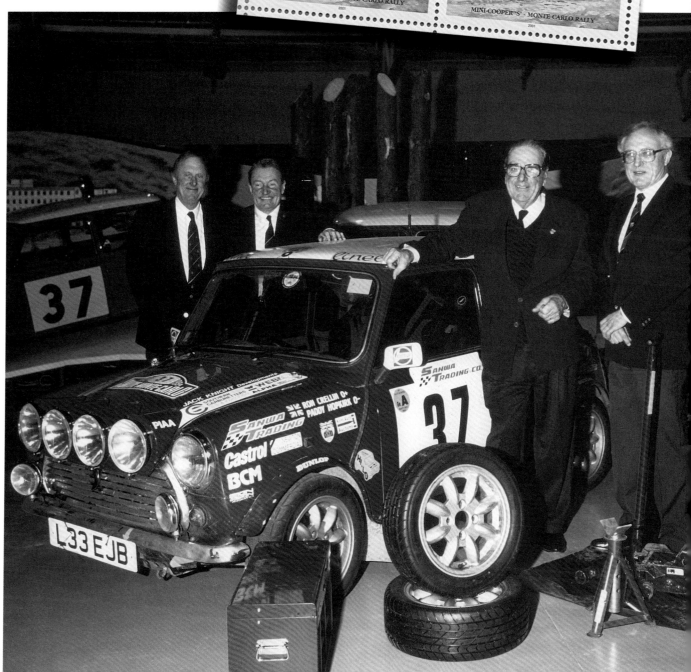

Opposite top: Family group taken in 1989. Left to right are Jenny, daughter Kate, sons William and Patrick, and Paddy. (Paddy Hopkirk)

Opposite bottom: The Acropolis Rally 50th anniversary reunion in 2003, with some of the previous winners. Left to right are Hakan Lindberg, Ove Andersson, Pat Moss, Erik Carlsson, the President and the Secretary of the Automobile and Touring Club of Greece, Paddy, Michèle Mouton, and Bjorn Waldegaard. (Paddy Hopkirk)

Above: The Hopkirk family reunion weekend in October 2003, organised by Paddy's brother Eric, at the Brown Trout Inn at Aghadowey in Northern Ireland. (Paddy Hopkirk)

Right: Paddy at home with his regular Sunday tennis group. Left to right are Barry Dinan, David White, Paul Hunnings, John Smith and Paddy. (Paddy Hopkirk)

Above: Paddy meets the Duke of Edinburgh at the opening of the Ulster Motor Show in Belfast in 1991. (Paddy Hopkirk)

Left: Paddy outside his 16th century home in the Chilterns, together with '6 EMO' and a new BMW MINI. (Paddy Hopkirk)

Below: Paddy receiving a Hall of Fame Award from swimmer Sharron Davies, at the Belfast Telegraph *Sports Awards ceremony in January 2005. (Phil Smyth)*

Left: Happy Birthday – Patrick and William arranged the present of a lifetime for the 'old man' on his 70th birthday. (Paddy Hopkirk)

Below: Fathers and sons – (from the left) Sir Anthony Bamford, Paddy, Jo Bamford and William Hopkirk outside the JCB plant with the Bamford Collection's MGB, which Paddy drove in the 1966 Sebring 12-Hour Race. (JCB)

Opposite: Paddy on a forest stage during the 1970 Scottish Rally, on his way to second overall in the former World Cup Rally Mini 1275GT; this was the last event for Paddy before the closure of the Competitions Department. (Esler Crawford)

Chapter 10

Paddy in business

The entrepreneur

Early days

One of Paddy's first involvements with the accessory industry was in 1956, when Dublin firm Auto Components featured a photo of Paddy in an advertisement endorsing Doduco replacement ignition points.

It was while working for Irish Tar Distillers that the first opportunity to go into business on his own came about, and with it the renting in 1957 of a little office and storeroom in Belfast, at 50 Gloucester Street. Supposedly Joseph Dunlop had invented the pneumatic tyre in the premises and there was a large hook in the ceiling from which he was said to have suspended his moulds down the

stairwell. Paddy called the business Paddy Hopkirk Ltd, and it made its first money selling a tyre-repair system.

"In Dublin I'd met this chap Albert Luykx, a Belgian, who was the concessionaire for Tip Top in Ireland and he asked me if I would be interested in becoming the Tip Top distributor for Northern Ireland. I went over to Munich and met the Grüber family, and Otto Grüber took a real liking to me. I went to the Tip Top factory in Poing and learned how to fit these patches to the inner tubes using their unique self-vulcanising process. To demonstrate the patches you would put a patch over a hole in a round piece of tube rubber and then you would fix the rubber membrane in a clamp

Paddy with his good friends and fellow competitors Robert Woodside and Dr Thomson Glasa at the opening of his new Belfast premises. (Paddy Hopkirk)

arrangement. Compressed air was pumped into the tube until it was blown up into a sphere about ten times its normal size to demonstrate how the patch stayed in place – it was very impressive.

"I used to go out in my car travelling round all the garages in the area selling the product. It sold well and eventually I had to hire some reps to help expand the business. My fleet soon included two Standard vans, a Ford 5cwt van and a VW pick-up, all sign-written with the Tip Top name and advertising my exclusive agency for Northern Ireland. I did a good marketing job for them, but how much money it brought in for me I am not sure.

"I also started selling Bardahl's oil-treatment products after seeing their demonstration of how this wonder anti-friction oil worked. Electrical products by Remax were popular and I took on selling their products as well. "But I wanted to expand the business and get into selling accessories, so I came over to London and saw rally driver John Sprinzel, who was selling Speedwell accessories. I remember my first visit to Speedwell, at their place in Finchley. They had this converted A35, and they took me round the block in it – round the neighbouring housing estate. The residents must have been really hacked off, with every hour or so someone coming round the corner sideways in an Austin A35! I was terribly impressed, and I became the sole

Taking on the agency for Tip Top led to an expansion of Paddy's transport fleet in Belfast. Nearest the camera are two Standard vans, then a Ford Thames 300E, and finally a split-screen VW pick-up. (Paddy Hopkirk)

Above: The front cover of the Paddy Hopkirk School of Motoring Ltd brochure. (Paddy Hopkirk)

Right: How many driving schools can publicise their motor sport successes? This is the centre spread of the Paddy Hopkirk School of Motoring brochure. (Paddy Hopkirk)

Above: Pat Moss, at the official opening of Paddy's Alfred Street shop in Belfast, tries on some driving gloves. (Paddy Hopkirk)

Above right: Champion rally-driver Erik Carlsson receives his pass certificate from Paddy for his first British driving licence, after instruction at the Hopkirk driving school; the car, naturally enough, is a Saab. (Paddy Hopkirk)

agent for Speedwell and Halda products in Belfast, selling anti-roll bar kits and so on for popular British cars such as the Morris Minor, Austin A35 and Austin-Healey Sprite, and Halda trip meters to the rally boys. It helped that I was friendly with Fergusons of Belfast, the Austin distributors, and I carried out Speedwell conversions on A35s and the new Austin-Healey Sprite for their customers.

"I suppose I must have made some money, and to cope with expansion I opened another shop, Paddy Hopkirk Auto Extras, in Sandy Row, behind the Opera House in Belfast. This was in a strongly Protestant district, and everyone was amazed that I opened a shop there in my name. I think I did it to show that I wasn't a bigot – and of course a well-known sportsman is always good to help bury the hatchet, when it comes to religion and all sorts of things. All the same, it did cause a few problems – especially when we had letters through the door saying 'Get Out You Fenian'! After about two years I closed the shop because it was too difficult to manage and not profitable."

Business continued to develop – even if Paddy cringes today at some of the products on offer. "I always remember the bug-deflectors we sold, to mount on the bonnet. They were terrible – they didn't work at all. And then there were those awful Peco exhaust-pipe trims..."

With or without the sales of such items, new premises soon had to be found, and Paddy

took over a reconstructed four-storey building at 12 Alfred Street, Belfast, inviting Pat Moss and Erik Carlsson to carry out the official opening ceremony in February 1961. Eric Hopkirk was now back in Belfast, and Paddy invited him to join the company. Eric said to Paddy he'd try it for six months and see how it went – and ended up working with his younger brother for over thirty years. Having Eric on board was a great help, says Paddy, enabling him to devote himself more fully to his rallying commitments. In 1962 Paddy opened the Paddy Hopkirk School of Motoring Ltd, located on the first floor of 12 Alfred Street, below the motor parts department. A trial driving course cost £4.19s.6d (£4.98), a concise course of ten lessons £9.17s.6d (£9.88), and a popular course of 16 lessons would set you back £15.15s.0d. (£15.75). The School was run by Dick Duffy and at one time Paddy had about a dozen cars on the school fleet. The driving school brochure included two pages of motor sport results achieved by Paddy between 1956 and 1962, with the slogan 'Do your test with the best'. There can't be many driving schools that use rally results achieved by their chief instructor to publicise the school! When Erik Carlsson needed a British driving licence, Paddy agreed to let him use the driving school to pass the British test, which was good publicity for the school and for Erik.

At the rear of the Alfred Street premises

Paddy had set up a workshop to fit conversion kits, seat belts, and so on. "This was when I'd started to do some Formula Junior racing, and I took on a mechanic who was a gearbox specialist, a chap called Neville Johnston who had been working for the Renault distributor in Belfast. He looked after the racing car between fitting conversions." In 1962, when Paddy joined the BMC team, he left the day-to-day running of his business interests in Northern Ireland to brother Eric and Neville Johnston.

The 'Toyo-something-or-the-other'

Soon another business was taken on board, as Paddy recounts. "After the 1964 Monte win I went off to Australia for BMC, after having a session at the Rob Slotemaker Skid School, where Timo, Rauno and myself were taught how to do 360-degree spins and that sort of thing. When I returned from Australia, I was met at Heathrow by Neville Johnston and we set off to go to the Motor Show at Earls Court. On the way we got talking, and Neville said 'Why don't we start selling cars?'. I said 'It's funny you should say that, because I've just seen this Japanese car in Australia called a Toyo-something-or-the-other. I had a drive of one and it seemed to be quite a reasonable effort'.

"And there, inside the show, outside the gents loo, was the cheapest, nastiest stand you could imagine, lit by one 40-watt bulb, and with a paper banner reading TOYOTA across it. It was the Pride and Clarke stand, and sitting on the stand was this maroon car – I think it was a Corona – just like the one I'd seen in Australia. I knew the car was better than the English thought it was, because I'd driven one, and I'd heard Australians talking about it – in fact I knew it was a good car probably before anyone else in England. I knew John Pride, so I had a chat with him. I said to him 'How many of these cars do I have to buy to get the agency for Northern Ireland?' He looked left and then right and said 'Well, if you just bought one...'

"So we bought the car off the stand. I knew Eric Knight of Lombard Banking, as I'd dealt with him when trying to get Lombard to sponsor the Circuit of Ireland. So I phoned Eric, explained what I wanted to do, and he loaned me £5000 without any security, but at no

Paddy modelling his driving gloves shortly after winning the 1964 Monte Carlo Rally. (Paddy Hopkirk)

doubt a high interest rate, to buy this Toyota and set up the agency."

Paddy decided to keep the car sales business separate, and formed Paddy Hopkirk Garages as the Toyota agency in Belfast, with Johnston – "a very good businessman" – running it. With Paddy driving for the BMC team the new enterprise caused a bit of a problem: "Sir George Harriman, chairman of BMC, became a little embarrassed to learn that my name was being associated with a Japanese product. He

Never one to miss a publicity shot, Paddy lines up team-mates Timo Makinen and Rauno Aaltonen on Moulton bicycles on his stand at the 1964 London Racing Car Show. (Paddy Hopkirk)

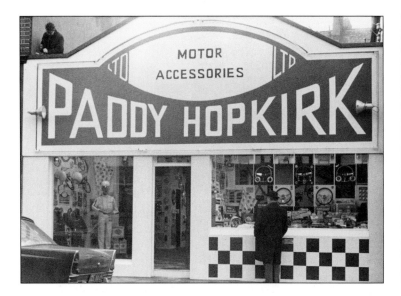

Above: Paddy's new shop in Lincoln Place, Dublin – difficult to miss, with such a frontage! (LAT)

Above right: The shop was opened by Paddy's friend – and lodger – top racing driver Jim Clark. (Paddy Hopkirk)

The famous rally-plate logo: it was John Cracknell's idea to use this. (Paddy Hopkirk)

asked me to change the name of the garage, which I did, to Neville Johnston Garages Ltd. I was on the board of Belfast Airport at this time, which meant almost weekly visits to Belfast, and this gave me the opportunity to see lots of Neville and visit the family too."

When discussing motor sport in Ireland, one tends to forget the political situation which existed in the country, on both sides of the border. During the height of the 'Troubles' in Northern Ireland, the garage premises were bombed two or three times. "I don't think it was a sectarian problem," says Paddy. "I worked out, all the same, that we were employing over 80 per cent Protestants at this time. I was involved in a predominantly Protestant business, the motor trade, although I was of course a Catholic. The IRA just chose targets which would get them publicity. But in those days the government compensated you, so it was quite profitable to get bombed sometimes!

"In about 1975 my shop in Alfred Street had a firebomb placed in it, the front of the building being blown out and there being a lot of fire damage. During

the night the British Army stood guard over the building which was now open. There were some of my rally finishing plaques on the wall inside, now blackened with soot and smoke, and one of the squaddies said to Dick Duffy 'Those are interesting' and Dick said to him 'Keep them!'.

"About four years later I received a letter from the CO of one of the regiments in Belfast, saying that a number of plaques had been found in the possession of one his men, and that he had no right to have them. I wrote back telling him that he did have the right to them, as he had been given them by Dick Duffy. The CO wrote back saying that it was against Army policy for the men to receive gifts while on duty and the plaques were all returned to me, which was quite nice."

About eight months after the fire, the business, now run by brother Eric, moved to new premises in York Street. This was also bombed, in the worst attack the company suffered, one of Eric's staff being shot dead during the raid.

"We'd had at least three break-ins prior to this attack, with apparent attempts to set fire to the place," says Eric. "I was in the York Street office when one of the girls ran in and said 'They've put a bomb in the shop'. As everyone immediately started to run out I heard a shot. I ran along the street towards the door that I thought the bombers had used, and found that Norman, a teenager working in our parts department, had been shot. We got him to hospital but tragically he died later that day. Later the bomb exploded, causing considerable damage."

Using the name

In 1965 Paddy joined forces with John Cracknell, who ran an accessory business in Peterborough called Carquip, with Roger Hawkins and Jim Lewin. The newly-formed company was called Paddy Hopkirk (Motor Accessories) Ltd, and was situated in Mayors Walk, Peterborough. "We started to market products with the Paddy Hopkirk name on them – it being John's idea to use a Monte Carlo rally plate as my trademark. I suppose the most famous product was the throttle-pedal extension for the Mini." Paddy also introduced racing overalls to the range of products, with the overalls being made by a factory in Belfast. Another successful line was Japanese-made ARI helmets. "Really I was trying to imitate Les Leston," confesses Paddy. "But Les was a great innovator. He commercialised fireproof overalls and go-faster driving gloves, and he invented the rally jacket – which I copied."

After many years of friendship and association in business with Neville Johnston, it was shattering news on 24th May 1975 for Paddy to learn that Neville had been killed while driving a Toyota on the Spelga Hill Climb, near Newry. His family took over the running of the Toyota business and Paddy eventually sold his majority shareholding to them.

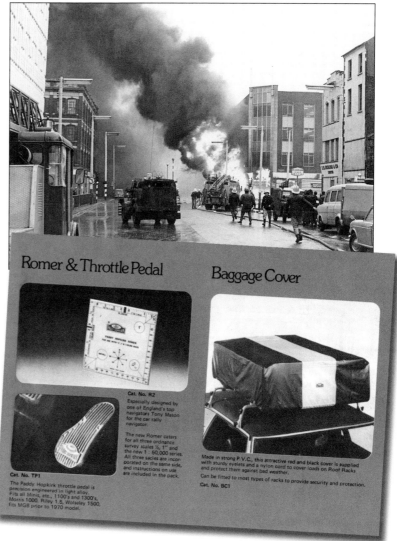

Into the big time: Mill Accessory Group

The next stage in the development of Paddy's business interests came in 1969 with the formation of the Mill Accessory Group. "I was working with John Cracknell in Peterborough and one day Bobby Longmuir, an Edinburgh-based rally-driver I knew, phoned me and asked if we could we have a meeting in London with Richard Grant, who made wheels in an old flour mill at Eaton Bray, near Dunstable. We decided to merge the companies and form a new company called the Mill Accessory Group Ltd and based at the Eaton Bray mill. The directors were Bobby Longmuir, Peter Riley, Richard Grant and myself."

Top: The Hopkirk premises in York Street, Belfast, in flames after an IRA bomb had gone off. (Century Newspapers)

Above: Part of the range from Paddy's catalogue, including the famous throttle pedal. (Paddy Hopkirk)

Left: The Duke of Kent pays a visit to Paddy's stand at the London Racing Car Show. (Fox Photos)

The team behind Mill Accessory Group pose for the camera. From the left are Peter Riley, Paddy, Richard Grant, and Bobby Longmuir. (LAT)

Former BMC rally-driver Peter Riley was then the Speedwell agent for the Midlands and Bobby Longmuir was the Speedwell agent in Scotland. "Wanting to expand, but not into wholesale, we first spoke to Les Leston but eventually decided we would discuss a merger with Paddy," recalls Riley. "After a day-long meeting finishing at four o'clock in the morning, and with the help of a very good Scottish accountant, we had thrashed out what I thought was an excellent agreement. We directors worked well together – it was a very harmonious partnership. Paddy wasn't very good at running the business side, but he excelled at PR and was a brave salesman, winning us some unbelievable contracts." Paddy doesn't dissent from this assessment. "That's very true," he says. "I wasn't good at running businesses. I was good at developing business, but running a business day-to-day needed someone with their feet more on the ground."

With the formation of Mill Accessories Group Paddy parted company with John Cracknell, who sold the Paddy Hopkirk name back to Mill Accessories. Cracknell reformed his company under the name Jaycessories and successfully relaunched the fireproof racing overalls under the Jaybrand name. Meanwhile, in 1982 brother Eric sold his share of Paddy Hopkirk Ltd and continued as Eric Hopkirk Ltd, with a warehouse in Mallusk on the outskirts of Belfast.

The alloy wheel business inherited from Richard Grant did not prove a success for Mill Accessories, despite having customers such as Morgan, and was sold to GKN. Paddy had some other irons in the fire, however: "I'd

come across the Valor petrol can, and we bought the production plant and moved it down to Eaton Bray to manufacture the can in our factory. I contacted the Vulcan company in Canada that made the key element, Explofoil, a honeycomb alloy foil. Put in a petrol can, the foil only took up about one per cent of the volume and when fuel cans were filled with this expanded foil they became explosion proof. I used to love demonstrating this feature. We had a piece of foil suited to the volume of a pint glass and I'd go into a bar and get a pint glass filled to within 1mm of the top. I would then say 'I bet you £10 I can get this cylindrical block of foil into the glass without spilling any.' It worked every time..."

Despite vigorous marketing and selling of these Explosafe cans, from places such as Halfords, they were not a commercial success: safety doesn't always sell. The cans were used quite a lot by the military, the marines and the US Coastguard, however, and are still marketed today.

Another chapter in Paddy's business dealings came about in 1973 when the Mill Accessory Group bought car-seat manufacturer Terry Hunter Ltd from the receivers. The company was one of the largest aftermarket seat suppliers in the country, but had run into trouble. The company was renamed Bilover Ltd, a registered name bought off the shelf at Companies House, and production was moved to Eaton Bray. Paddy found out later that Bil is the Swedish word for 'car', so the name literally meant 'car lover'. The seats were later sold under the Paddy Hopkirk name, as Paddy sought to develop them into a rival to the famous Recaro brand.

With the Bilover side of the business making seats and Mill Accessory Group producing wheels, petrol cans and later roof-racks, dog-guards and cycle-racks, Paddy now had a nicely integrated business. It was at this juncture that Tony Mason came into the picture. "Paddy had always been my hero, especially from the day he won the Monte. I first met him in 1970 at a Ford Rally Forum which I organised at Morecambe, where Stuart Turner brought along Paddy, John Surtees and Roger Clark. We had to push these Ford rally cars along to the end of the pier, fearing that the rotten boards might collapse at any moment. After the forum we all went along to Alfredo's restaurant for a meal, and I was delighted to be sitting alongside Paddy. When the steaks came, Paddy rejected his and I think it was only after the third steak arrived, accompanied by Alfredo waving a meat cleaver, that Paddy finally accepted his meal!"

In 1972 Tony joined the Ford rally team at Boreham as rally manager, to replace Bill Barnett. "One day I had a phone call from Paddy, who asked me if I would design a new map roamer for his accessory range. I felt very honoured to be asked and on the kitchen table came up with a new design. Paddy said 'You can have your name on it so long as it's smaller than mine'. This was my first business contact with Paddy."

In 1973 there was a change in the management structure of the Mill Accessory Group, when Richard Grant's share of the business was bought out and Richard moved on to form his own company making spoilers and air dams for the accessory market.

It was around this time that the petrol crisis threw motor sport in turmoil, with events being cancelled all over the place. What with short time in the motor industry, jobs at Boreham didn't look too secure, and Tony Mason was unsure what the future would hold. So when in 1975 he had a call from Paddy asking him if they could meet up in London to talk about things, he was naturally enough interested.

"I met Paddy, who was accompanied by Bobby Longmuir, and after some chat they asked me if I would be prepared to join them

as export manager. I had been discussing a move with my wife, who hated Essex, and I eventually decided to join Mill Accessory Group.

"I really hated selling, but I enjoyed working with Paddy, who was a very encouraging and generous employer. For example he would take his staff to Christmas parties at places like the Talk of the Town. I respected Paddy as a driver and never had an argument with him when I was with Mill Accessory Group. I worked there until 1979, travelling all over Europe and with several trips worldwide, probably multiplying their export sales ten times. Of course Paddy was very much into manufacturing his own products such as dog guards – metal-bashing, as he put it! – but he did import some accessories such as Fiamm air horns. Paddy made an advertising cassette tape describing the virtues of what he said were the best air horns in Europe.

"I made no end of contacts and received various offers from competitors in the accessory field. I decided to have a go at running my own business, and an offer from Ken Harris, who had some money to invest, brought about the formation of my company, which we called Tonken. Paddy was very supportive when I told him I was leaving and I still have the barometer I was presented with when I left Mill Accessory Group."

During the 1970s Paddy collaborated with artist Sydney Jordan and Porsche enthusiast Nick Faure on this Sunday Mirror *cartoon strip on better driving. Jenny was very much part of the strip's story lines.* (Sunday Mirror)

Changing gear: Paddy Hopkirk Ltd

The Mill Accessory Group continued to prosper and then, in 1981, Peter Riley decided to move on, and the name of the company was changed to Mill Automotive Group. "Partly due to the ill-health of my parents, I decided that I had probably done enough with the business and the directors bought me out. It was a very amicable parting and I was retained on a seven-year consultancy." Paddy later bought out Bobby Longmuir and changed the name of the business to Paddy Hopkirk Ltd, moving to new premises in Leighton Buzzard in 1989. Manufacturing was still an important part of the business, and alongside roof-racks the company introduced a newly-fashionable product, popularised by the American-led boom in mountain-biking: strap-on cycle racks. "I actually introduced strap-on cycle racks to Europe, I'd say," claims Paddy. "I brought some back from the US, and copied them. We were very big in these – and Paddy Hopkirk racks are still a strong seller". Meanwhile, at the beginning of the 1990s Eric Hopkirk sold his business.

Another string to Paddy's bow was a deal to sell MPA helmets. MPA was based in the small town of Agordo, a few miles north-west of Belluno in Italy. Paddy negotiated a contract with the company and decided to call the helmet the Agordo helmet in England. This was very good business, with sales of about 50,000 helmets a year at its peak, representing 18 per cent of the UK market – although Paddy had some trouble getting the Italians to meet all the BSI requirements demanded by UK regulations.

Profitable or not, there was one aspect of helmet sales Paddy didn't like. "I was receiving letters from people saying, for example, 'My son died in an accident while wearing one of your helmets.' They didn't necessarily blame the helmet, but I didn't like the idea of people dying in our products. Then the boss of the Agordo factory was killed in a car crash and his son came over and worked at our factory and stayed in my house in London.

"It all came to an end when we were on a visit to the factory in Italy. At dinner the son's aunt said to Bobby and myself 'We've had an approach from a motorcycle shop in England who thinks it can sell more helmets than you'. We said 'You must be joking – how can one shop expect to sell more than 50,000 helmets a year?'. We were so insulted by this stupid proposal, and didn't trust the new management, that we told them what they could do with their helmets and that was that. Incidentally, I have never seen one of their helmets in this country since."

Crisis: selling the business

With the changes taking place in car design and with more and more manufacturers fitting built-in roof-racks, it was clear, what with all the EU regulations, that considerable investment would be required by Paddy Hopkirk Ltd if it were to continue in the roof-rack business. Indeed, by the early 1990s the company was in some difficulty, and in 1994 it was forced to go into administration. Paddy says he had been the victim of bad financial advice – "Don't talk to me about it!" – and this seemed the only solution.

"I realised that without going into administration – and without investing some of my own money – we were going to be in a difficult financial position. The bank gave me a bit of a breathing space, giving me time to sell the business as an alternative to going bust as a result of creditors foreclosing. I brought in a company from Manchester called Leonard Curtis, and we reluctantly went into administration. We got the bank to agree to this only on the understanding that I put money in, on a temporary basis. This I did – it was risky, but I put in another £100,000 or something of that order. That allowed us a three-month breathing space in which we had to sell the company – and if we hadn't sold it we'd have certainly been in big trouble.

"But when the business was advertised in the *Financial Times* we had 79 enquiries, and 12 bidders. I felt more comfortable about selling to the Mont Blanc group because I felt it would be good for the continuation of the company, and a deal was completed in 1995 – with my leasing the building, which I owned, to the new company. Everyone was paid 100-per-cent, and I don't owe anyone any money. Most of the creditors are still supplying the current owners.

"I'd like to make that point, because so many people go bankrupt, start again, do a deal with the receiver, and come up smelling of roses. I'm not in that game. Every creditor got paid in full. I've always been very straight and honest in my business dealings – my reputation in that respect is very important to me."

After the sale the Paddy Hopkirk name was licensed for use on many products – as it is to this day – but a few years later Mont Blanc was bought by Jack Products of Detroit, the world's largest manufacturer of roof-systems. Jack Products are part of Citicorp, and supply most of the world's vehicle manufacturers.

Re-birth – and Smarter Direct

Now without premises, but with space at home at Penn, Paddy formed a new company. "I set up a sub-contracting sales company called Smarter Direct, formed with friends who had been agents for me in Europe. We had a European group of agents – or representatives, to use a word I prefer. In America if you're selling stuff these days you don't use salesmen of your own – you use a company of reps and and pay them fees or commission. We were trying to do that in Europe, and we did it very successfully. But the other guys weren't really pulling their weight, so I decided to go my own way in this country, and set up Smarter Direct Ltd.

"So now I represent a few big companies who trust me and my reputation. We sell their products and they deliver direct and get paid direct by the customer. As their reps, we get paid a fee. What we're doing is placing product, managing the accounts, and helping with marketing and the introduction of new products. So I'm still really doing the same thing, but it's not my products, and I don't have to employ 150 or so people."

Products that were marketed by Paddy Hopkirk Ltd

Spot lamp covers
Bonnet safety pins
Blind-spot mirror
Dog guards
Waterproof ignition kit
Motorcycle helmet lock
Screen aerial
T-bar gearlever knob

Tow ball boot
Window aerial
Explosafe petrol can
Bicycle rack
Ski racks/holders
Roof racks
Agordo helmets
Fiamm air horns

Rubber safety hooks
Door mirror
DIY wheel balancer
Ladder/boat racks

Paddy with his successful fuel can.
(The Times)

Chapter 11

Australia again

1977

To mark its 30th anniversary, Singapore Airlines decided to sponsor a long-distance car rally. To take place in 1977, it was billed as being the longest rally in history, and was to cover 30,000km or roughly 18,600 miles, with 30 control points, all this in 30 days.

A friend of Paddy, former racing driver Michael Taylor, had tried to get Citroën in France to provide him with a car, but in the end Patrick Vanson, who was driving for Citroën Australia, persuaded the Australian side of the firm to fund a CX 2400 in full. This was provided that he could lure Paddy out of retirement. After a lot of negotiation, Paddy agreed, and a deal was struck which allowed Paddy to have his company logo all over the car.

Part of the deal was they should take driver/mechanic Bob Riley, an Aussie, as third crew member. "Bob Riley is coming with us because he only weighs eight stone, and we want to keep the weight down," Paddy joked at the time.

The final line-up for the Total Citroën Australia team of CXs would be Paddy, Patrick Vanson, Jim Reddiex and Claude Laurent. The cars were prepared in the Brisbane workshop of Citroën dealer Jim Reddiex, and shipped to France in June.

Part of his preparation saw Paddy down in an old chalk-pit near Maidstone at the Ford Rally School, where Andy Dawson and Will Sparrow were the instructors. "We put him through our course in a Ford Mexico and then did some driving in the Citroën CX which Paddy had come down in. It was just a refresher course really, and Paddy was a good pupil," remembers Andy Dawson. Paddy was keen to increase his fitness level and took up running in Holland Park and using exercise machines, resulting in the loss of about one stone in weight before the start.

Back to school: instructor Andy Dawson (left) with Paddy and Michael Taylor at the Ford Rally School before the 1977 London-to-Sydney. (LAT)

A touch of adventure: out on recce

Part of the preparation for the event was carrying out recces in some of the more exotic places through which the rally was to pass, as Paddy recalls. "I remember going out to Iran to do a recce in a local hire car near Tehran, and returning the hire car in a terrible state with the wheels pointing in different directions and with shredded tyres.

"We went out during darkness on the Yaz-to-Tabaz road, practising in the middle of the night, flat-out, and every time we covered this piece of road a busload of Iranians came along in the opposite direction at three or four o'clock in the morning, returning from a prayer meeting.

"This was the same area that the US military used as a rendezvous point during the subsequent Tehran hostage crisis. If the CIA had asked us, we could have told them that at 04.00hrs each day this bus would come along. Apparently it was the arrival of this very bus during the dust storm caused by the helicopters landing that led to the confusion in which the US Special Forces guys had to arrest the people on the bus to maintain secrecy – thereby compromising their mission. The CIA hadn't done its research properly..."

Paddy also did a recce in Malaysia. "We rented one of the old Citroën DS models. We knew that one of the stages was in a rubber plantation, but we didn't know exactly which one. After calling at several, only to be told that they didn't know anything about a rally coming through, we were ready to give up when we came to this one and found the plantation office. The girl there said 'The manager

Paddy with Bob Riley (right) and Michael Taylor, receiving a good send-off from the Mill Accessory Group workforce at Eaton Bray, before the start of the 1977 Singapore Airlines London-to-Sydney Rally – plenty of publicity for the company is in evidence on the Citroën. (Echo & Post Ltd)

*Helmets on and full
lock, on a typical
Acropolis special
stage in Greece.
(Hugh Bishop)*

*Opposite: Some of
the rigours of the
Yugoslavian 'outback'
– no need to go to
Australia for such
conditions...
(Hugh Bishop)*

is busy at the moment. What's your name?'.
From the next office the manager obviously
overhead the conversation and I heard this
voice say 'Is that *the* Paddy Hopkirk?'. He was
Scottish and I said yes, the rally was coming
through his plantation. He took us up in his
aeroplane to see it from the air and then showed
us the stages – which we then practised, making
lots of notes. Unfortunately the German
Mercedez-Benz team also found out where he
was, so I wasn't the only one to have notes."

Paddy was keen to learn something about
the Citroën's ingenious hydraulics and
attended a three-day service briefing given by
Paul Buckett at the Citroën Service School in
Slough. "I was surprised at how eager Paddy
was to learn about the mechanicals of the car,
possibly because I had a pre-conceived idea
about professional rally drivers," recalls
Buckett. "He was certainly a quick learner. I
was amused when Paddy jokingly said, as I
described the steering system, 'I was just getting to grips with the suspension. How do you
expect me to understand the working of that
'whirly-gig thing' in the steering?'...."

Marlène Cotton, Citroën's competition
manager at the time, has always made a point
of how small her budget was, and the London-
to-Sydney was no exception: it was estimated
that the Mercedes team budget was around a
million dollars, compared with Citroën's
spending of about 120,000 dollars. "The
budget was too low," comments Paddy. "We
ran out of servicing in Australia. But the CX
was a bloody good car, because it went on for
so long without proper servicing. All we had
was a plane, to drop parts when needed".

Early misfortunes...

The European leg started near Covent
Garden, crossing the Channel on the
Sheerness-to-Vlissingen ferry. In Frankfurt,
Bob Riley cut his finger slicing bread and was
the first team casualty. Then during his turn at
the wheel on the section after the Mont Blanc
tunnel he was stopped by police for speeding,
only being sent on his way when the police
gave up the struggle to understand his
Australian-accented English. Finally, at a filling station outside Milan he lost his jacket
with 500 dollars in the pocket, it being stolen
from the car at the filling station. From
Europe the rally moved into Asia, passing
through Istanbul and Ankara to reach
Teheran. Both Paddy and Michael became
alarmed at some of Riley's driving in Turkey
and from then on kept him from behind the
wheel as far as possible. By this stage the
unfortunate Riley seemed to have become a
bit of a liability, but he was to prove his worth
when on his home territory. "He was a liability as a driver, but certainly not as a co-driver,"
says Paddy. "He was a very good co-driver,
and a really nice guy."

Regardless of poor Bob Riley's misfortunes,
Michael Taylor got on well with Paddy in the
car, after almost falling out on the first day.
"Paddy shouted at me to stop dithering about
while I was navigating, and I said I would
throw the maps out of the window if he
continued. I said 'You're the works driver, you
read the maps'. Then he confided in me that
when with British Leyland he didn't have to
map-read."

Repairs being carried out to the holed sump on the Flinders ranges in Australia, following a heavy landing after a 'yump'. (Paddy Hopkirk)

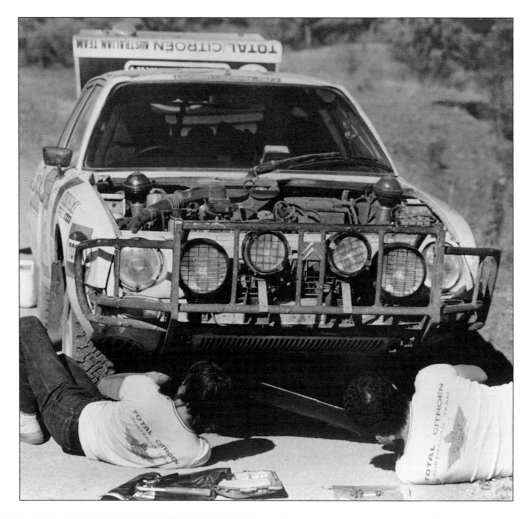

Australian dust does not deter this photographer, as Paddy and his crew get nearer to the finish of the rally. (Paddy Hopkirk)

Despite the car intercom packing up in Iran, Paddy – described in *Asia Magazine* as a flamboyant driver and a 'quick-witted, cigar-chewing, wise-cracking Irishman' – was lying fifth overall when they arrived at Bombay. After Madras the cars were transported by ferry to Penang, with the crews flying out. The competitors now faced 680 miles through Malaysia, but with some competitors getting lost on the special stage in the rubber planta-tion – although not Paddy, needless to say, after his earlier recce – there were late arrivals in the parc fermé at Singapore. There were several protests, resulting in Zasada (Porsche) being demoted to second overall, behind Tony Fowkes (Mercedes), with Andrew Cowan (Mercedes) third, Kling (Mercedes) fourth, and Paddy fifth.

The restart was at RAAF Butterworth, on 6 September, with the route finishing in the Far East in Singapore, with Paddy still lying fifth overall.

...and resourcefulness isn't enough in Australia

Australia now beckoned, complete with a route change and an estimated 4002 farm gates. Competitors suffered heavy rain in Western Australia and at the service point at Menzies the CX's gearbox filler plug was mislaid, Paddy having to borrow one from a private Citroën owner. On the 225km section over the Flinders Ranges to Adelaide, Paddy hit a rock, splitting the sump. While Bob Riley carried out repairs, Michael Taylor went back to a farm they had just passed, found it deserted and proceeded to drain the sumps of two vehicles parked there, leaving the sump plugs on the bonnets in the hope the farmer would find them when he returned. The delay resulted in Paddy finishing the section 31 minutes behind the Tony Fowkes Mercedes.

It was hot and sticky in the wilds of Australia, recalls Paddy. "I remember coming to a control point and there were a lot of aborigines sitting about and there was one old boy with flies all around his nose. I was very hot and dusty and I was dying for a wash. One of them showed me into his hut and there was an old rusty tank there with a lever. I stood under this and I had this brown water running down over me and it was like travelling first class again – it was so wonderful to feel that cooling water!"

In New South Wales, a 100km error in the route instructions from Menindee to Warrigate became the subject of more controversy. The instructions said 'In 27kms T-junction – turn left' when it should have read '127kms turn left'. Peter O'Gorman, navigating the Fowkes Mercedes, spotted the error and radioed his other team-mates, but lost 63 minutes on this very rough section which had many closed gates. Bob Riley did not spot the error but with his local knowledge navigated Paddy along a more or less parallel road, arriving at Warrigate losing only one minute. The organisers scrubbed this section when the route-note error was highlighted. A protest from the Citroën team against the cancellation of penalties on this section was perhaps unsurprisingly rejected, as Andrew Cowan recalls.

"We followed the route instructions, but Bob Riley, who knew the area, took Paddy on the road on the other side of the river. We lost time because the control was closed and the

marshals had left by the time we arrived. As Paddy had been about the same amount of minutes behind us, he was now in the lead. However, we protested, and the section was cancelled partly because of the mistake in the road book but mainly because the control was closed. The Citroën team protested, but the result was not changed."

Massive crowds near the Sydney Opera House welcome Paddy's Citroën, which finished third overall. (Paddy Hopkirk)

A good advert for dieting – a thin-looking crew near the end of the rally. (Paddy Hopkirk)

William Hopkirk

William was born in Paddington in July 1973, and is the youngest of Paddy's three children. When he was nine years old, William went to school at Worth Abbey in Sussex. He continued his Sixth Form schooling at Uppingham School where he won an Army scholarship to Manchester University. He was a successful participant in all sports, and reached national level at the triple jump.

Upon leaving Uppingham, William spent a 'gap year' hitch-hiking round the four islands of Japan. He had had an interest in Japan from the age of nine after seeing *Shogun* and reading the book, and found a BBC language course very useful during this period.

In 1992 William went up to Manchester to read Russian and Soviet Studies, spending the third year of the four-year course at the University of Kiev learning the language. This was all in preparation for entry to the Royal Military Academy at Sandhurst where the one-year officer-training course ended with William passing out as a 2nd Lieutenant. In 1998 he was posted to the Irish Guards, stationed at Munster in Germany. A period as an infantry training instructor at Catterick and a spell on ceremonial duties at Wellington Barracks, London, followed and then William completed a course to become a Russian interpreter.

This resulted in a posting with the UN to Georgia as a weapons inspector and observer. In 2003 he left the Irish Guards for 'Civvy Street' – having acquired a PADI deep-sea-diving instructor's qualification along the way. Until recently he worked in Russia as business manager for the worldwide JCB company.

William was always aware of his father's involvement in motor sport although Paddy had retired from professional rallying three years before he was born. "There were always photos around the house and visits from many friends of the family who had been or were still involved in rallying or racing. I remember Dad coming to Worth Abbey to give a talk on rallying and his arrival with an Audi Quattro was the talk of the school for months.

"One of my first memories of his successful career was Dad's win in the 1990 Pirelli Classic Marathon in his own Mini and then in 1994 all the publicity around his entry in the 1994 Monte Carlo rally to commemorate his win in 1964. The birthday party given by BMW at the Mini factory at Cowley was great. I was really shocked and almost unbelieving at the queues of Mini club people waiting patiently for autographs during the evening. It was quite moving."

So the Cowan Mercedes – backed up by a superb support team – retained the lead. Typical of the thoroughness of the German effort, Mercedes had Unimog 4x4 trucks at hand in the Australian desert, to pull out their cars if they became stuck. "Yes, I suppose it was cheating," says Paddy. "But we used one of the Unimogs ourselves. I think we bribed the driver. Mercedes had gone through, and we got a bit stuck, so we bribed the guy to get us out. So we weren't going to protest."

There was more controversy at the Durikai control. The start marshal retained the road-book of Tony Fowkes, in a Mercedes, but Tony's co-driver, Peter O'Gorman, assumed it would be returned at the finish control which

was close to the start control. On arrival at the finish control the roadbook was not there, so Mercedes Team Manager Eric Waxenburger set off down the road to retrieve the roadbook from the start control. When he returned with the missing document, Tony was able to continue, but with no delay allowance offered. However, they made up enough time on the next section to avoid a penalty.

The Citroën team protested about this incident and the stewards imposed a 30-minute penalty, but this did not affect the overall positions. Despite all the problems, the Total Citroën Australian Team won the team prize and Paddy, Michael and Bob were placed third overall in the general classification.

Enough is enough

"There seemed to be an awful lot of arguments with the organisers on the rally," says Paddy. "For three days after the finish, crews and the organisers argued over the results, while we recovered. Jenny and Michael's fiancée Elaine flew out to Australia to meet us. They were late arriving and the only hotel they could find was a motel at Pokolbin with this flashing red light pronouncing 'A Home Away from Home'. It was a bit primitive and the girls thought it was dreadful, but we were knackered and it had nice towels and hot water, and once again it felt like we were in Claridges."

Exhausted or not after the experience, Michael Taylor reckons today that he picked the right driver: "I'd done the first London-to-Sydney Marathon with Innes Ireland and the London–Sahara Rally with Stirling Moss. They couldn't hold a candle to Paddy off-road, and his ability to conserve the car was magical. I can't say enough about his skills!"

But if the rally had been a memorable event, Paddy was glad it was over, as he told the *Belfast Telegraph*: "It was lovely when it stopped," he was quoted as saying. "You can take it that I have definitely retired now. I never want to drive in another rally again." Today he continues to believe that the organisation left a lot to be desired. "There were gaping loopholes in the regulations. Most of the trouble centred around the Mercedes team. On the stage to Brisbane I dropped one minute, but Cowan and Fowkes were over one hour behind. That put me in the lead but they accused me of taking a short cut. The Germans were very manipulative at getting that section taken out."

Reservations about the organisation or not, Paddy retains a fond memory of the CX, Citroën's long-awaited replacement for the legendary DS. "The car was marvellous – the handling was terrific and the ride over the corrugations was fantastic. Over some of the stages we were really able to wind it up. I loved driving it – it was so safe. I don't think I scared myself in it once. We lost one of the gears near the end but we knew that the gearbox was the weak link on the car. I hadn't wanted to use a five-speed gearbox – I wanted to use the four-speeder, which was more reliable, but they said the 'five' would be alright. And sure enough we had trouble with fifth – the 'box just had a few too many cogs in it."

This event was a good exercise for the Mill Accessory Group, resulting in considerable publicity for Paddy Hopkirk products, the logo for which was more than prominently displayed on the bonnet of Paddy's car.

Paddy and the 2CV

Although the Citroën 2CV was the antithesis of the compact, nimble little Mini, Paddy confesses to a soft spot for the eccentric small Citroën. This fondness goes back to his BMC rallying days.

"I love 2CVs! I think it all goes back to when I was practising with Ron Crellin one year for the Monte. We were coming down one night from the mountains after practising some bloody col all day. It started to really snow. We thought 'God! Hope we get down alright'. So we decided we'd try to catch up with some of the others, because we'd been out on our own. We saw these tail-lights ahead. 'Ah, it must be the Germans or the Scandinavians. Or maybe it's Ove', I said. 'Let's try to catch them up, and we'll have dinner together'. I tried to catch these lights up, and I couldn't. Eventually we got a bit of straight and I passed them. It was two nuns in a 2CV...

"I've always been fascinated by the 2CV, and we've had about nine of them. The kids all learnt to drive in them. Slow cars teach you a lot about driving, because you've got to keep them wound up. I've never seen one turn over, either – although you could get them to go up onto three wheels. They're terribly dangerous cars, all the same, because in an accident there's not a lot around you. But partly because of that I think they make you a good driver.

"The gearbox was lovely. I adored that push-pull-twist gearlever. You had to get it right. If you grabbed it with your hand it didn't work. But if you used your fingers gently on it, it was wonderful.

"They were rust-buckets, though. They rusted awfully, even when they were new. I remember one of my sons thought it great fun going flat-out over speed humps. He went flat-out over one and came back with his chassis bent..."

Chapter 12

Historic rallying

1982–1994

By the beginning of the 1980s the popularity of historic rallies was increasing and to celebrate the 50th anniversary of the RAC Rally, the RAC, with sponsorship from Lombard, decided to run an event in April 1982 called the RAC Golden Fifty Rally. Paddy and Brian Culcheth were among the 'golden oldies' invited to take part, and were entered in the Mini in which Timo Makinen had won the 1965 Monte Carlo Rally, with sponsorship from Unipart. The car was prepared by Austin Rover Motorsport at Cowley, by two of the Abingdon mechanics, Garry Wiffen and Dave Hart, at an estimated cost of £7000.

Success in the 1982 'Golden Fifty'

The rally started from Stratford-upon-Avon with the first test at Silverstone, where Paddy was fastest in the driving test – Brian having agreed with Paddy that he would drive the stages and hill climbs and Paddy would be behind the wheel on the circuits and driving tests. Lunch was at Belvoir Castle, with another fastest time, followed by a stage and then there was a run to the Jaguar factory for another driving test. Saturday morning took the cars on a long run to Oulton Park. At Weston Park, the weather had brightened up for the stage, although some of the potholes caused a bit of damage. A run up Shelsley Walsh was followed by the finish at Ragley Hall in front of a big crowd. Paddy and Brian were declared the winners, the prizes being presented by Ray Morley, who had participated in the 1932 RAC Rally in a 1927 AC Montlhéry Sports.

"We're really pleased to have won the event," Paddy told the press. "We both needed that win – it's our first RAC win. We hope now we can go for a real works drive! I just wish they'd print the roadbook in larger print, as I can't read it without my bi-focals..."

As for Brian Culcheth, he says he had a great time, and got on well with his one-time rival. "Paddy was quickest on all the driving tests and on all the circuits, and I think we were fastest on all the stages as well. I was disappointed that we were not fastest at Donington, where a bloke in a Morgan V8 beat me by a second. I had an excellent relationship with Paddy."

The 'Coppa' – in a Lancia

The next time Paddy was lured out of retirement was for a drive on the 1986 Coppa delle Alpi in a red left-hand-drive Lancia Fulvia HF 1.6 owned by Robs Lamplough. This winter event, to celebrate the 50th anniversary of the 1936 Alpine Rally, ran from Sestriere to Cortina, via Madonna di Campiglio. Lamplough, entered in only his second rally, asked Paddy if he would like to do the event. The Lancia was already down in Italy being prepared by specialist tuners Carlo Facetti and it turned out to be a difficult event, as Lamplough recalls.

"There was a lot of snow and we had some additional tyres fitted with studs. It was a great laugh, and we had a splendid time. Paddy – in the entry list as 'Toddy' Hopkirk – agreed to do the rally bits, with me doing the ice races. We arrived at the finish with all the studs pulled out of the tyres and a puncture. I remember driving in torrential rain alongside this lake with Paddy shouting 'Be careful! Be careful!' and me running up the kerb, luckily without hitting anything. In an amazing coincidence, three years later, not on a rally, I went up the kerb on exactly the same piece of road!"

Paddy remember that there was a lot of snow.

"We had spiked tyres which I insisted we put on, but they were useless. Modern snow tyres would have been better. They are so good – they really are amazing, and give better grip than we managed in the old days with spikes. It was a funny event, with a lot of regularities and secret controls. I did most of the driving but we made a 'horlicks' of it! I think part of the problem was that we weren't properly prepared – we had problems with stupid things, such as the windows steaming up.

"But the Lancia was very good – I was surprised by it. It was just like an engine with a front-wheel-drive transmission attached and not much in the way of a body – the body was so light. It was a wonderful-handling car, and as for the performance..."

In 1988 Paddy was inducted into the Texaco Hall of Fame. It was the same year that interest in historic rallying took another leap forward with the staging of the first Classic Marathon, the brainchild of Philip Young. His idea to run a week-long event over famous rally routes in the Alps and Dolomites attracted a good entry, with ex-works drivers Anne Hall and Mike Sutcliffe amongst the starters. The BBC sent out a film crew and a successful one-hour documentary attracted around six million viewers.

Brian Culcheth and Paddy were coaxed out of retirement to compete in the 1982 Lombard RAC Golden Fifty Rally. Here they are seen inspecting the ex-Makinen Mini that won the 1965 Monte Carlo Rally and which they would use to win the event. (Brian Culcheth)

Evan Green (centre) was a well-known TV presenter and PR man, and introduced the BMC team to Australia in 1964 after the Monte Carlo Rally. He was featured in a This Is Your Life *programme on Australian TV, and Brian Culcheth and Paddy were surprise guests from England on the show. (Paddy Hopkirk)*

Classic Marathon debut – and back to a Mini

Young approached a number of sponsors for the 1989 event, but it was Tom Northey of Pirelli who showed immediate enthusiasm for the event, resulting in the Pirelli Classic Marathon being launched at the Whitbread HQ in the Barbican with personalities from the world of rallying present, including Paddy, Stirling Moss, Roger Clark, Timo Makinen, and Ove Andersson. Young was keen to have a number of famous rally drivers in the event and Pirelli agreed to pay the 'superstars' a fee, plus expenses.

In Paddy's case one of the problems was to find a car. The owner of an ex-Abingdon 1275cc Mini-Cooper S, Guy Smith had met Paddy when he had called on him at his home to show him one of his cars and had enjoyed a long chat with him. "Out of the blue, Paddy phoned me four weeks before the Marathon and said 'Do you know anyone who would loan a suitable car for the Marathon?'. I had been restoring 'EBL 56C' over a six-year period but it had done only about 600 miles since I'd put it back on the road. I was extremely reluctant to loan the car, but Paddy and Alec Poole were very persuasive and made me an offer I couldn't refuse. Alec tried the car and decided it was what he wanted, and I took it over for Paddy to try in the lanes around his home.

"They wanted the diff ratio changed for the Alpine climbs and decided to have a 3.9 final drive fitted and the standard Cooper S camshaft changed for a '544' rally camshaft. Paddy also wanted the heated windscreen changed for a clear laminated type. The only thing we had to buy were some Cooper wheels because the old Minilites with the car were showing signs of corrosion, and the Minilite company wasn't operating at that time."

Paddy wanted ex-Abingdon engine wizard Cliff Humphries to look over the engine before the event. "Cliff was the genius of Abingdon engines. He wasn't just an engine-builder – he was truly responsible for these wonderful engines. He was a very academic mechanic, if you know what I mean. He was the academic strategist at Abingdon – a guy who thought before he answered your questions. He was a bloody good mechanic, but one of those mechanics who didn't have grease under their fingernails – he was very very neat. He looked more like a lawyer than a mechanic."

Alas, Humphries was too busy, so it was decided to send the engine to Richard Longman, the successful Mini racer and respected ex-Downton tuner. "I refused to let the car go on the event until the rebuilt engine had been run-in ready to be tuned on the rolling-road," says Smith. "I spent many a long night doing the miles, and when the car was ready, about two or three days before the event, I took it over to Paddy's house. He had it for a couple of days to familiarise himself with it, and had some press photos taken. The next time I saw the car was at the start."

Guy Smith and his friend Chris Spennewyn – who also owned an ex-works Mini-Cooper S – took a week's holiday and scrounged an XR3i car from Budget to follow the rally and take some photos. Budget wanted a sticker on the Mini, but Paddy soon took it off. "We weren't an organised service team but we threw a few spares in the car, including two driveshafts which Chris happened to have in stock," says Smith. This was in fact in contravention of the regulations, which stated that organised service by non-competing persons was forbidden. As part of the official support team, the author managed to borrow two Sierra 4x4 estates from Ford Motorsport at Boreham, one being crewed with Den Green and the second car manned by former Abingdon mechanics Robin Vokins and Tommy Eales – Robin then being chief mechanic at Boreham.

A vast crowd gathered on Tower Bridge for the start of the 200-mile rally across six countries to Cortina d'Ampezzo. There were 130 starters, and the 'superstars' included Ove Andersson with Mike Greasley in a Toyota 2000 coupé, Timo Makinen and Paul Easter in an ex-works Austin-Healey 3000, registration '67 ARX', Roger Clark and Tony Mason in a Ford Lotus Cortina, and Stirling Moss and US journalist Jean Lindamood in an MGB. Paddy and Alec were seeded number two in the Mini.

The crews headed for Pegwell Bay for the first test, at the Hoverport. Paddy was fastest but managed to clip a cone, incurring a 20-second penalty. Guy Smith, meanwhile, had an unexpected spell of direct participation in the event. "On the ferry going out there was one very dejected competitor, Harvey Shand. He and his co-driver had had a row at the start and the co-driver had stormed off home, leaving Harvey without a navigator. Journalist Chris Harvey's wife sat in the car from Tower Bridge to Dover but could go no further. Harvey said 'Does anyone want to be a co-driver?' so I took it in turns with Chris to act as co-driver on alternate days!"

On the Nürburgring test Paddy was equal fastest with John Chatham in his Austin-Healey 3000, and by the time the rally arrived at Speyer he was up to fifth overall. John Chatham was now leading the rally by 19 seconds, from Henry Pearman in a Jaguar E-Type, with 'Piggy' Thompson third in a Ford Cortina, followed by the MGB of Tony Dron. The next test was on a section of the Hockenheim circuit, and here Timo Makinen scorched round in his Big Healey to make fastest time, six seconds faster than Paddy. Roger Clark lost about 30 seconds when his Cortina engine stalled. There was now quite a long route through Austria to the overnight halt at Merano, in Italy. Paddy was now up to fourth overall, with 106 cars booking in at the finish control.

Next day was the Stelvio test, with a bogey (set minimum) time of 16 minutes. Guy Smith was with Harvey Shand and he was dismayed to pass Paddy stopped near the bottom of the Stelvio with a broken driveshaft, losing over an hour. In the film of the event, Stirling Moss, who had been equipped with an in-car camera, is heard to say 'Oh, poor sod!' as he passed the stranded Paddy. Chris Spennewyn, in the hire car, was at the top of the climb waiting for the cars to come through, and heard that Paddy had stopped. As soon as the road was clear, he shot off down through the 48 hairpins to find him. Alec Poole then set about fitting a new driveshaft with Mini specialist Simon Wheeler, while the Pirelli 'management' crew of Bob Freeborough and Phil Cooper offered moral support. This delay caused Paddy to miss the Stelvio control, with a heavy penalty, dropping him from about 12th to 64th overall. Meanwhile, it was not until the Saturday that Philip Young found out

*Opposite: Out of
retirement again in
1990, Paddy – with
Alec Poole – attacks
a Belgian special
section in the Pirelli
Classic Marathon,
in the 1965 Mini-
Cooper S rebuilt
specially for
the event.
(Paddy Hopkirk)*

about the 'illegal' crew member and excluded Harvey Shand from the rally.

On arrival at Cortina the Henry Pearman E-Type was in the lead, with the Thompson Lotus Cortina second and Stirling Moss third. At the three-hour service session in Cortina, Alec Poole changed the other driveshaft on Paddy's car, as it was clear that new ones hadn't been fitted before the start. The last day was a run from Cortina into Yugoslavia and back to Cortina. There was a re-route caused by a landslide, but many crews missed the arrows and went through the rough. However, despite missing nine control points, Paddy and Alec were classified 72nd overall.

"The car was unmarked after the rally," says Smith. "In Yugoslavia Paddy handed me a broken inner door handle, and that was really the only other problem with the car. It had been very satisfying for me to have my car in the event with Paddy driving, particularly as the Mini-Cooper S had featured so prominently in his career with BMC."

Philip Young was less happy about the role Guy Smith had played. "We were a bit upset at the way the owner of Paddy's car shadowed him in a service crew role, getting round the very innocent regulations of the time," he said later. "But without this, Paddy would not have been rescued so quickly when the driveshaft failed, although to no avail in the end."

Gunning for a win – the 1990 Classic Marathon

The Classic Marathon was clearly going from strength to strength and for 1990 Philip Young retained sponsorship from Pirelli, who lined up five famous names from the past – Timo Makinen, Paddy Hopkirk, Ove Andersson, Roger Clark and Stirling Moss.

"Paddy and I decided that after our experience in 1989 we would have a serious go at winning the event, and we built what in effect was a new 1965 Mini (Paddy Hopkirk Replica No 1), with new mechanical parts," says Alec Poole. "The car was built by Simon Wheeler under my supervision. I found the registration number '6 EMO', which was close to that on one of Paddy's works cars." Before the event, Guy Smith, who had loaned Paddy his ex-works car in 1989, attended the Millbrook test track with his car while Paddy and Alec in their freshly-finished Mini were being filmed

by the BBC. "I think Alec was a bit miffed that 'EBL' managed to keep up with their newly-completed car," says Guy.

118 cars started from Tower Bridge, with Paddy's car seeded second, soon followed by 60-year-old Stirling Moss driving an MGB prepared by Brown & Gammons and carrying the number '7', his favourite competition number. After a test at the Lydden circuit, the competitors crossed to France and journeyed into Belgium. At Trier, Paddy and Alec found themselves at the top of the leader board, 19 seconds in front of old team-mate John Handley, also in a Mini-Cooper S. The next stage was from Trier to Merano in Italy, and at the end of this day Paddy and Alec still held the lead, 24 seconds in front of Stirling Moss, despite having problems with the brakes.

"Paddy was much more relaxed than I recall him back in 1965, when I was doing a spell in the Competitions Department at Abingdon, during my apprenticeship," recalls Alec Poole. "Then he seemed to have an almost aggressive attitude – whether this was anything to do with having to compete against the two 'Flying Finns' I don't know. He would come into the workshop when I was there, as a mere apprentice, and quietly ask me 'What is the latest?' or 'What's going on?' – almost as if he were trying to find out if he was missing out on something."

Paddy confirms that this was how it was back in those days. "You were under terrible pressure. If you have two team-mates who are faster than you, it keeps you on your toes – but it probably doesn't bring out the best in you. Maybe it did so in terms of my driving, but not necessarily in terms of how I was as a person. I'm sure that I was often sniffing around to see if the Finns had something better than me on their cars. Rauno in particular had a good feel for the mechanicals of a car. He was a disciplined and meticulous man, and worked things out – why something should be an inch shorter, or an inch longer. If he couldn't explain exactly what he meant, he'd make up a story to explain – he was very good like that at describing why he wanted something a particular way."

Paddy and Alec held their lead despite hitting a high kerb and bending the steering, and despite an oil leak. On the final day there was first the Giau Test in the wet and then the final test up the Tre Cime Hill Climb. There were heavy rolling clouds towards the top of the mountain, and this affected many drivers' times and resulted in Ron Gammons in his MGB just beating Stirling Moss into third

place. However Paddy and Alec retained their lead, finishing first overall – a popular win, without a doubt. Not that the duo hadn't worked hard for their victory: "It was dog-eat-dog," says Paddy. "Gammons and Moss weren't hanging around in their MGs, and uphill the Mini isn't very good – it's not an uphill car, and going up something like the Stelvio it's pretty awful. On those hairpins a rear-wheel-drive car is much better. So it was a good win on which to go out."

After the event, Paddy kept '6 EMO' and it is now carefully stored so he can use it for promotions or for showing off to his grandchildren. Plans to capitalise on the win by selling 'Paddy Hopkirk' replicas assembled by Simon Wheeler alas came unstuck as a result of the early-'90s recession, and only two further cars left Wheeler's works.

South African interlude

In 1992 great MG enthusiast Norman Ewing invited Paddy over to South Africa as part of the celebrations to commemorate 30 years of the MGB. The idea was that Paddy would be part of the MG Car Club team competing in the Pirelli Classic Marathon. Ewing arranged some sponsorship with South African Airways and Paddy and Jenny were flown down courtesy of the airline, while the team was kitted out in SAA t-shirts and the cars adorned with SAA stickers.

"I had promised SAA some TV cover and without the knowledge of the SAA top-dogs we staged a mock arrival at Jan Smuts Airport, Johannesburg," recalls Ewing. "We smuggled in 36 MGs, telling the security people it had been agreed at HQ. Paddy was interviewed by the TV people on the steps of what was really a stationary training 'jumbo'. It was spectacular, as it appeared that the MGs were all under the wing of the 'jumbo' on the runway. When the SAA boss saw the national news, his supper on his lap, he apparently stood bolt upright in disbelief, with inevitable results!"

Norman Ewing organised a race MGB from Chris Costas for Paddy to drive, shod with slicks and painted red with a white hardtop, running on racing fuel and with a very loud exhaust. "It damaged my hearing, that thing," says Paddy. "It was a racing car, running on methanol, with an exhaust pipe about a foot in diameter. It was quite some beast." Unfortunately, the MG only did about 8mpg and the fuel gauge was faulty, so perhaps

Opposite: Paddy and Alec Poole with their winners' garlands at the finish of the 1990 Pirelli Classic Marathon in Cortina d'Ampezzo, Italy. On the left are Stirling Moss and Chuck Shields and on the right Ron Gammons and Paul Easter. (Paddy Hopkirk)

Paddy and Alec Poole after returning home with the spoils, outside the new Mill Automotive Group factory at Leighton Buzzard. (Paddy Hopkirk)

unsurprisingly the car ran out of fuel soon after the start. This resulted in the car finishing down the field overall. However, the special stages at Witbank and Middelburg were absolutely spectacular, with the Hopkirk magic shining through. Peter Gough in a Porsche and Bob Olthoff in an AC Cobra put in great drives, but Paddy won the special stages – enabling him to finish second in Class C with co-driver Eddie Fee, with the MG team winning the team prize.

The event ended with a Pirelli dinner at which Juan Manuel Fangio was guest of honour. Norman Ewing had done the programme and had given Paddy the job of replying to the guest of honour, without his knowledge. "The look on Paddy's face as he read the menu and realised that he was to reply is a memory which will live with me forever. But he got up and with that wonderful silver Irish tongue gave the speech of the evening – so good that I told him he should give up driving!"

Norman had arranged for Paddy and Jenny to stay with MG Car Club member Esra Martins and as Norman was driving them in his BMW to Bapsfontein they stopped in the little town of Belfast so that Paddy could have his photo taken with the town sign.

After a breakfast stop, recalls Ewing, Paddy asked if he could drive, and if there were any twisty bits coming up. "I am proud of the fact that I have been an advanced driving instructor, but this was just incredible. I learnt there and then what 'driving on the limit' was really like, as Paddy hurtled the car along this sandy road! He was without doubt the most approachable and frankly loveable of all the motoring greats I invited to South Africa."

The South African trip was to be Paddy's last sortie into the world of historic motor sport – but there was to be one further event in which he was to participate that was certainly historic, even if it didn't involve a classic car.

Back to Monte Carlo

John Brigden and Jeremy Coulter, themselves successful competitors in Minis, came up with the idea of running a Mini in the 1994 Monte Carlo Rally, to commemorate the 30th anniversary of the 1964 Hopkirk win. They formed a company called Brigden Coulter Motorsport Ltd for what they called 'Project Mini Monte Carlo'.

Paddy was contacted and almost straightaway said he would drive the car for a small fee plus expenses. When Coulter and Bridgen contacted Rover, it was immediately obvious that the company had not given any thought to commemorating the Monte win. However, through Rover Group PR man Kevin Jones they were put in touch with Michael Kennedy, head of Rover PR/Marketing.

Matters of money – and some skullduggery

Brigden had calculated that his budget would be in the region of £140,000. Rover agreed to provide some money and with good Japanese sales of the Mini, Rover Japan was approached and said they were very keen to support the project. They in turn started to organise further sponsorship and contacted British Aerospace, with the net result that a verbal agreement for about £65,000 was confirmed.

Coulter meanwhile went to see Chris Belton of Roversport, (Rover's in-house competition arm) who was adamant that one thing Rover would not do was homologate the Mini. However Wynn Mitchell, chief engineer at Tony Pond Racing, agreed to compile the homologation forms, taking all the photos for the forms and obtaining technical information and drawings.

Things took a turn for the worse when Rover Japan were advised by an unidentified person that the Brigden/Coulter organisation was not up to the job, and that sponsorship should be diverted to a car being prepared by Mini parts specialist Minisport for Timo Makinen.

Sponsorship was indeed switched to the Makinen car, but by now Brigden/Coulter had spent money in the belief that British Aerospace was as good as its word. Rover became very unhelpful at this point, and withdrew all of their support, although the enthusiasm of Kevin Jones kept the project afloat.

"I believe that British Aerospace left it as late as possible to pull out, in the hope that we would not be able to continue," says Brigden. "With the rug pulled from under our feet, I contacted Norri Yamagata of Sanwa Trading (approved importers of classic car parts to Japan), and obtained some help from them, although relations between Sanwa and Rover Japan were not good. This sponsorship came with additional strings for each payment, which in the end left us owing Rover around £50,000".

Meanwhile, Paddy's former BMC partner Ron Crellin had been enlisted as co-driver. "Paddy contacted me out of the blue and said 'Would you like to do the 1994 Monte?'. There was a launch at the Motor Show with a car, and Prince Michael came. We were paid a small fee and we had a recce car, a green Cooper. We went down to the South of France before Christmas to do a recce."

The Automobile Club de Monaco allowed the car to run with competition number '37', the number on 1964's winning car, and Kevin Jones of Rover found that the registration 'L33 EJB' was available. This was duly acquired – a brilliant move.

Preparing the car

John Brigden wanted the car to look different, and designed a lamp pod for the car which was produced by Mini specialist Mini Machine. An industrial unit at Canterbury was used for preparation of the car, with support from Rover dealer Barretts of Canterbury. Brigden found he was unable to spend enough time supervising the build-up but was able to get Gerry Brown, proprietor of Merton Motorsport, to come in to act as workshop manager. There were now three cars to be prepared, and so his input was invaluable: Brigden Coulter Motorsport had been asked to build replica cars for the Monte for two private competitors, Philippe Chevalier and Philippe Camandona. Money from this would supplement the very tight budget for the Hopkirk car.

The two customer cars were rushed out, resulting in the Hopkirk car being a real last-minute job. There was a problem finding suitable 12in tyres and so the decision was made to run on 13in wheels. Studded regular 13in tyres would not fit under the wheel-arches but with help from John Haugland of Dunlop in Norway some special low-profile studded tyres were arranged. Dunlop was especially helpful, supplying most of its tyres free of charge and providing on-event service. "I was nervous at first about the new tyres and the big 13in wheels," says Paddy. "The car held the road a lot better, so if you were going flat-out and you hit a bit of gravel there was more chance of flying off the road. But the centrifugal force was much greater with the higher speed than in the old days, and I was nervous about hurting myself if I did lose it."

Special driveshafts and CV joints were obtained and all the suspension bushes were hand-made. For Paddy, though, modernising the Mini could go only so far. "I was almost forced to have a five-speed gearbox in the Mini. I questioned whether it had been properly tested and was told it was race-proven. I said 'That's a different type of testing – no thanks. I want only rally-proven products, please.' So we stuck to the four speed 'box...

"I was also terrified of the electronics, so I made them put another ECU on top of the normal one. I said 'I'm not having that thing running my life', and so the car was equipped so that if something went wrong I only had to plug in the reserve unit. "

Tony Mason was with the BBC's *Top Gear* and at a chance meeting with Paddy he found out that he was doing the Monte in a Mini. "I supposed he meant one of the historic Montes. No, said Paddy, it was the real thing, to commemorate the 30th anniversary of his win. My producer was one of the old school and he was

so delighted with the news that the BBC decided to cover the event for *Top Gear*. I remember filming at Millbrook with Paddy, for the programme introduction, and was amazed at how quick and accurate he was in the Mini. I had at last achieved my ambition, after 40 years, of sitting next to my hero!"

The car was finished at the eleventh hour, as perhaps was only to be expected; meanwhile the organisational infrastructure was put in place. John Brigden was team manager, with Gerry Brown and rally co-driver and service co-ordinator Simon Warner doing the on-event supervision. Rob Arthur of Mitsubishi Ralliart helped compile the service schedule, and provided colour copies of the service maps.

The service vehicle fleet comprised a Range Rover, three Discoveries, two Sherpa vans, a Land-Rover for the Weber engine management crew, and a Subaru from Barretts of Canterbury. Bill Richards, the engine builder, travelled in one of the Sherpa vans and spent most of the event worrying about the valves and valvegear on the tweaky 110bhp engine he had built. The author and Den Green were asked to man one of the Discovery chase cars: for some reason, John Brigden wanted 'wrinklies' from the 1964 event on board.

The chosen start was Bad Homburg, mainly because John Brigden had a number of contacts in Rover Germany and they were keen to offer support to the team and provide

Paddy and Ron Crellin crossing the Col de Turini during their 40th anniversary publicity run in the 1994 Monte Carlo Rally in their injection Mini-Cooper, registered 'L33 EJB'. (Robert Young)

pre-event publicity. Rover Germany also provided roughly £2000 in funds, which paid for things such as hotels. Paddy never thought he was going to post a good result against the modern pack. "I did it purely as a fun and publicity thing. It was paid for, and it was probably going to be my last fling ever. But I practised for six weeks before the rally – and I just got better and better! I couldn't see in the dark as well as I used to, though..."

All in vain – thanks to a fanbelt

Soon after the start, Gerry Brown in his Discovery passed a car stopped on the motorway only to realise as he passed that it was Paddy and Ron in the Mini. The car was overheating seriously owing to the switch for the electric cooling fan being set in the wrong position. This was sorted and the mechanical fan blades were refitted to the engine as a precaution. This was a scare that could have so easily put the car out of the event within hours of the start.

At the main service point at Valence only routine servicing was required before the start of the rally proper. At the service point near Gap there was a minor panic when the car would not start. Eventually it was discovered that the plug connecting the speed sensor to the ECU had been knocked by a jack during a wheel change, and this was soon put right.

"There was only real snow on one stage, the Sisteron, and we hadn't recce'd that one because it had been closed by snow," says Crellin. "We had a gentle 'off' and had to be pushed back on – we weren't on studs".

Paddy remembers how somewhere near Colmar he came over a hill to find the rally all stopped in a queue, and the gendarmes breathalising everybody. "The only thing was that we were in a right-hand-drive car and they breathalised Ron without realising he didn't have a steering wheel in front of him – but he was clear anyway!"

On the mountain circuit the fanbelt failed and Paddy played mechanic and set to and changed the belt. While doing this the BBC film crew arrived with Tony Mason. Unfortunately, the replacement belt was the wrong size and before long a flat battery caused the Mini's retirement, the car being towed into Monte Carlo. "They wanted me to have an extra-big alternator, and I'd said 'no',

Monte Carlo Rally timetable, 1994

Thurs 20 January:	Rally car to Bad Homburg
Sat 22 January:	Scrutineering and start Concentration Run at 1800hrs
Sun 23 January:	Cars arrive Valence at 1800hrs
Mon 24 January:	Valence to Valence leg
Tues 25 January:	Valence to Gap leg
Wed 26 January:	Gap to Monaco leg
Wed 26 January – Thurs 27 January:	Mountain Circuit – start 2200hrs and finish 1030hrs

but eventually they persuaded me – and this eventually caused the fanbelt failure," says Paddy. "I always said I would prefer some lights for a long time instead of lots of lights for a short time. The thing was using so much power that the fanbelt couldn't cope."

Despite this ignominious end to the team's efforts, Paddy and Ron were classified 60th overall and fourth in class. "I'd very much enjoyed myself, and I didn't regret for a moment doing the event. It wasn't too hard work, our performance was reasonable, and I don't think I made an ass of myself," says Paddy. "I was just sad about the fanbelt incident on the last night. "

At the finish the car and crew had the honour of being invited to the royal palace in convoy with the first three finishers in general classification, with Paddy receiving a watch from Prince Rainier. "When Rainier gave Ron and myself the gold watches outside the palace he said 'Welcome back'. I said 'Does this mean you don't want to see us again? Is it the final goodbye?'..."

When the dust settled, Brigden Coulter Motorsport found that they were £20,000 in the red and it was about a year before Rover very grudgingly paid £10,000 in final settlement.

The project received tremendous publicity on BBC's *Top Gear* and Coulter and Brigden estimated from press cuttings after the rally that coverage had amounted to between £1m and £2m in free advertising. A touch of gratitude from Rover might have been appropriate...

Chapter 13

The BMW connection

A new Mini

It is interesting to observe that at the 1999 Ecurie Cod Fillet reunion of former rally drivers and co-drivers a ballot was held asking members to vote for their top ten most important milestones in British motor sport. They were invited to choose from a list of twenty events, drawn up by a panel. The results were first the 1955 Mille Miglia victory of Stirling Moss and Denis Jenkinson, second the 1964 Monte Carlo win by Paddy Hopkirk and Henry Liddon, and third-equal the Indianapolis 500 victory of 1965 for Jim Clark and Colin McRae's 1995 World Rally Championship win. So, 35 years after his Monte win, Paddy was still up there with the greats.

The year 2000 saw many celebrations and the Historic Rally Car Register, the leading club devoted to historic rallying in the UK, organised a 'Car of the Millennium' poll. At the annual HRCR dinner-dance, which Paddy attended along with his Monte-winning Mini-Cooper S, the result was announced: the Mini came out the clear winner. Perhaps it is no surprise, then, that in 2002 Paddy was invited to become president of the club, a post which he was delighted to accept; he remains president today.

Paddy tries to amuse the audience during the Monte Carlo Rally 40th anniversary celebration party given for him at the new BMW MINI plant at Cowley. (Paddy Hopkirk)

Paddy on Jenny – "My tower of strength"

"Jenny was a highly-qualified PA in a top London advertising agency when we got married in 1967 – which is now 38 years ago. When Kate arrived, Jenny gave up all that and became a perfect mother and housewife. She carried on supporting me when Patrick and William arrived. The Hopkirk family unit is a sound one, and all the time I was running around rallying or on business she was always there to keep the family standards as they should be.

She is a good looker, a qualified tennis teacher, and a gourmet cook (which is just as well, as I can hardly boil an egg!); she loves entertaining, is good fun, and has loads of nice girl friends. Yet she seems to find more and more time for her charities, helping people and of course still bringing up the family and grandchildren, which is a never-ending job. I am lucky to have made such a good choice, and although I am not well known for saying it, I suppose I must love her very much."

Family Christmas in 2001. From the left are Kate's husband Hugh, Kate, Patrick, Paddy, Jenny, first grandchild Molly, and William. (Paddy Hopkirk)

Towards a new Mini...

Mini fans the world over were now becoming aware that production of the Mini would soon end, and that Rover, since 1994 owned by BMW, would be bringing out a new car carrying the famous name. Paddy, as he recalls, was in on the ground floor.

"I suppose I first became involved in the new Mini in 1997, when the combined Rover and BMW engineering teams produced a concept car called ACV 30. This was one of a number of concept vehicles, and BMW decided to cash in on the 30th anniversary of Rauno winning the Monte Carlo Rally by holding a publicity stunt in Monte Carlo.

"I was invited, together with Timo and Rauno, and along with the winning cars from 1964, 1965 and 1967. Heading the parade in the wet around the GP circuit was the Anniversary Concept Vehicle, as they called the ACV 30. The publicity gained by the event was priceless, with pictures appearing all over the world of a car which many took to be the

Chicago Motor Show 2004 – Paddy with the Limited Edition (1000) MINI Cooper S, sold exclusively in the USA and bearing 1964 Monte Carlo numbers and rally plates plus Paddy Hopkirk signed plaque. (Paddy Hopkirk)

prototype of the new Mini – although it had actually been planned as a styling exercise for a possible Mini coupé.

"I became involved with BMW because it was finally decided that it wanted to build a link with the original Mini. When it first wanted to bring the enthusiasm for the old Mini over to the new Mini, BMW had been worried about quality and safety issues with the old model. It didn't want to be associated too closely with the old car, because it leaked and smelt of petrol and was unreliable – all that sort of stuff. Eventually, though, the strategists said 'Hey, without this we'll just have another small car. Why don't we latch onto the old Mini?'. They had realised they needed to evoke this heritage. People say it's a pity the British didn't do it. But they wouldn't have done – they didn't have the resources."

Paddy was to find himself an integral part of the marketing for the new car, after hitting it off well with Dr. Herbert Diess, the managing director at Plant Oxford at Cowley. "At a seminar held in Oxford by the Mini Cooper Register, where I was on stage with Ron Crellin, Dr. Herbert Diess was in the audience – incognito. I met him and got on very well with him. "

...and goodbye to the classic original

In the meantime MG Rover, as it had become, following the severance from BMW, finally ended production of the original Mini. On 4 October 2000 a special press event was held at Longbridge. This was to celebrate the manufacture of the last Issigonis-designed Mini, alongside the production of the first Rover 75 at Longbridge – assembly of the 75 having been transferred to Longbridge to make space for production of the new MINI at Cowley.

A large gathering of press assembled in the old Austin exhibition hall, where there was a display of various examples of the Mini with Paddy, Stuart Turner and Issigonis right-hand man Jack Daniels amongst the VIPs in attendance. After coffee and biscuits, all the guests were taken by coach to the end of the assembly line, where special doors had been erected. After a brief presentation by MG Rover's Kevin Howe, the doors were dramatically opened and the last Mini, driven by sixties pop star Lulu, appeared alongside a new Rover 75 on the adjacent track. It was quite a nostalgic occasion – Lulu was a real star guest.

Home life

Although he has scaled down his business life, Paddy remains very active. He has played tennis with a group of good friends every Sunday morning for the last 15 years, on the court at home, the game always ending with a coffee and often a glass of something while catching up with the events of the week. Skiing, a long-time passion, has taken a back seat while Jenny recovers from a back operation, but the couple hope to be back on the slopes soon. Meanwhile Paddy is persevering at learning golf, and enjoys his swimming pool, although he doesn't claim to be a particularly good swimmer. For quite a few years he also had a work-out class in the barn on Monday evenings with five pals. Another way he keeps fit is by walking the dogs every day for a good 50 minutes – he and Jenny have a warm-hearted nine-year-old Flatcoat retriever and a lively family of three Lucas terriers, as well as two family cats, Beaver and Muff, who earn their keep as mousers.

More leisurely pursuits include playing snooker and a poker evening every six weeks or so with the boys. Much to Jenny's disappointment, Paddy gave up playing bridge in favour of poker!

The house, dating from the 16th century, naturally takes up a fair amount of Paddy's leisure time: he enjoys DIY and has a particular love of gadgets. Thus the barn door and five-bar gate are automatic, and sensor lights are set up around the house. Despite an inevitable affinity with wheeled garden machinery, this enthusiasm doesn't extend quite as far as it might when it comes to gardening, though, says Jenny. "He doesn't exactly garden, but he sits on the tractor cutting the long grass, and is known to hack back overgrown greenery indiscriminately, much to the distress of his wife!"

Away from house and garden, Paddy is a patron of Wheelpower, the British body representing wheelchair sport, and he helps out from time to time with

BEN, the motor industry benevolent fund. He has been a life member of the BRDC – the British Racing Drivers Club – since 1965 and was a director for nine years. Another motoring involvement is helping Rally Ireland to pitch for Ireland to be used for a World Rally Championship event.

Charity work recently undertaken has included appearing with a gaggle of '60s celebs at the Chelsea Flower Show, in a reproduction of a 1960s garden and garage, complete – of course – with a Mini of the period. As well as welcoming the Penn Carers group for tea and meetings at home four times a year for the past ten years, Paddy has also supported Jenny's charities wholeheartedly. These include the RNLI, with which Jenny has been associated for 25 years, and the NSPCC. He has not been heard to complain too vigorously, either, about being enrolled to run the bar at the Ladies Tennis Final Summer Lunch for the past 19 years. These public appearances have now taken on a new twist, with Jenny's appointment as High Sheriff of Buckinghamshire: while his wife enjoys the limelight, Paddy is happy to play the self-effacing loyal consort...

Being very much involved still with the lives of their three children and two grand-daughters, and with a hectic social life in Penn and in London, Paddy and Jenny still seize every opportunity for travel that they can – whether for business, pleasure or in connection with motor-sport pursuits. Paddy in particular attends many motor club dinners and annual trade shows, in places as far apart as Las Vegas, Frankfurt, and – this year – Shanghai. Wherever possible they try to mix work with relaxation, and en route to help launch the new MINI in San Francisco they travelled through South America, white-water rafting, swinging through the trees in the jungle, and missing a much anticipated visit to Machu Picchu as a result of being stranded on a train due to a landslide.

Sales of the new 'BMW' MINI began in July 2001, and Paddy was present at a Mini party at the Randolph Hotel in Oxford. "There was a new MINI under wraps and Dr Herbert Diess, supported by MINI brand manager Trevor Houghton-Berry, made a wonderful, charismatic speech about the car and the history of the old Mini. Most of the Mini club people present were rather anti-German and anti-BMW. He said 'I'm German, and I did actually work at Longbridge', and I think the audience really warmed to him as a result of what he had to say. The car was then unveiled and the Mini people didn't really go 'Wow! What a wonderful car'. However, after a few more drinks one of the wives opened the door of the new car and within thirty minutes you couldn't get them out of the car. They were hooked!"

Ambassador for BMW

As a result of meeting Dr Herbert Diess at that Mini Cooper Register seminar, Paddy was offered a contract by BMW to appear and speak at press launches and so on, and has been busy doing this ever since. "I act as an ambassador for BMW, if you like," says Paddy. "I'm employed by them on a freelance basis, and I'm an ambassador for the new MINI. I think I've sold a lot of cars for them. I drive one myself, and love it – it's a beautiful little car."

It was during September 2000 that Paddy was lured over to Belfast for a dinner – by Paul Buckett, who had been involved with Paddy in the preparations for 1977 London-to-Sydney Marathon. At the dinner, Paddy was presented with the W A McMaster award for motorsport achievements by Ulstermen.

In 2001 a further honour was bestowed on Paddy. It was the centenary of the Royal Irish Automobile Club, and An Post, the Irish General Post Office, issued a set of four stamps depicting various aspects of Irish motor sport. One of these stamps showed a picture of the Monte-winning car of 1964. The three other stamps were of Rosemary Smith in a Tulip Rally Hillman Imp, a 1929 Mercedes SSK in the Irish Grand Prix at Phoenix Park, and Damon Hill winning the 1998 Belgium Grand Prix in Jordan. A very select group!

With this commitment to BMW, it was appropriate that with their new showroom ready for operation, Sytner MINI should ask Paddy to open its new premises at Gerrards Cross in July 2001. As Paddy lives just down the road at Penn, he didn't have to travel far....

Despite initially blowing hot and cold about using the old Mini successes to promote their new baby, on 24 January 2004, BMW organised a party at the production plant at Cowley to celebrate the 40th anniversary of the 1964 Monte win. Members of Mini clubs from all over the country were invited, making up a total of approximately 180 people, together with Paddy and Jenny and their three children, Kate, Patrick and William.

When all the guests had arrived, they were guided into a small lecture theatre where Trevor Houghton-Berry greeted Paddy and all the guests. A short film was then shown with some rare archive footage taken on the 1964 Monte. When this ended, Houghton-Berry introduced Paddy, who then entertained the audience with an amusing speech.

An excellent meal was served, culminating in a chocolate dessert on which was displayed a small red-and-white MINI, so everyone had a souvenir to take home. Red and white wine was served with the meal, the label on the bottles showing a Michael Turner painting of the '64 Monte Mini in the snow with the caption 'Celebrate with MINI and Paddy Hopkirk – Monte Carlo 40th Anniversary'.

The actual 1964 Monte car was on display, together with the 1965 Monte-winning Mini, as well as a selection of new MINIs in various specifications and colours. Music was played by strolling players called the Cosmic Sausages.

In February 2004 there was a big BMW press event in Monte Carlo with Paddy, Timo Makinen and Rauno Aaltonen in attendance. Three flights each brought 40 journalists down to Monte Carlo where they were given the opportunity of driving the old Mini and new MINI up and down the Turini. In the evening dinner with the superstars and interviews and photo opportunities laid on.

To Mini enthusiasts in Europe, it may seem strange that a limited edition MINI Cooper called the Paddy Hopkirk model should be launched in North America. However, on 1 April 2004 BMW launched the model – complete with the number '37' on the doors, mock Monte Carlo Rally plates, twin spot lamps, a red-and-white colour scheme, a special fuel filler, and a silver plaque by the gearlever signed by Paddy listing the car as a limited-edition model. All these special modifications were added to the standard model upon arrival in the States.

Having a special-edition MINI named after you might be nothing more than a marketing stunt, but it is a powerful tribute to the enduring reputation of Paddy Hopkirk. Aged 72 at the time of this book's publication, Paddy is however no washed-up relic from the glory-days of the 1960s.

Of his contemporaries in rallying some are dead, including one who sadly committed suicide, and others have fallen into ill-health or alcoholism, or into unfortunate brushes with the law. In contrast the cheeky-chappy Ulsterman the media so loved has built a second career as a successful businessman, takes care to remain physically fit, and has a happy family life centred around the same lady that he married in his rallying heyday – all this from a base in a delightful sixteenth-century home restored and furnished in meticulous good taste.

It might seem like a long journey from those carefree days in Northern Ireland, fooling around with his brothers in a motorised bathchair, but Paddy Hopkirk has made that journey with his feet firmly on the ground. He has worked for his success – and made his success work for him.

Family group at the BMW Mini party at Cowley. Left to right are Paddy, Jenny, Kate's husband Hugh, Patrick, Kate and William. (Paddy Hopkirk)

Appendix I

Paddy Hopkirk rally and race record

Event	Car	Reg.	No.	Co-driver	Result
1952					
DUMC & LCC, Fernhill	VW Beetle	-	-	-	-
1953					
DUMC & LCC Night Trial	-	-	-	-	Saloon Award
Circuit of Ireland	VW Beetle	EI 7576	58	-	-
Trial 1000 Miles	-	-	-	-	-
Cairncastle Hill Climb	VW Beetle	EI 7576	7	-	-
Stepaside Hill Climb	VW Beetle	ZO 19—	4	-	5th overall
St Patrick's Day Trial	VW Beetle	-	-	-	-
1954					
DUMC & LCC Grafton Trial	-	-	-	-	2nd in class
DUMC & LCC Clontarf Autocross	-	-	-	-	2nd in Saloon handicap
Ulster AC Night Trial	VW Beetle				7th overall
Circuit of Ireland	VW Beetle	PZ 6160	78	-	2nd in class
Dublin University Rally	VW Beetle	ZU 4484	7	-	-
MG CC Trial	VW Beetle	ZU 4486	10	-	1st overall
Cork 20 Trial	VW Beetle	-	-	J.Garvey	5th overall
MGCC Night Trial	VW Beetle	-	-	-	2nd overall, 1st Saloon
1955					
Grafton Trial	VW Beetle	-	-	-	1st Saloon
St Patrick's Day Trial	VW Beetle	-	-	J.Garvey	1st overall
Circuit of Ireland	VW Beetle	PZ 6149	121	J.Garvey	1st in class, 8th overall
Dublin University Rally	VW Beetle	-	13		-
Circuit of Munster	Triumph TR2	-	-	-	-
MG CC Trial	VW Beetle	ERI 152	13	J.Garvey	-
Stepaside Hill Climb	Triumph TR2	PRI 222	22	-	1st in class
Sligo Trial	VW Beetle	ERI 152	-	-	-
Phoenix Park Race Meeting	Triumph TR2	PRI 222	19	-	1st in Heat 2
Baird Memorial Race, Kirkistown	Triumph TR2	PRI 222	9	-	-
Leinster Trophy	Triumph TR2	-	15	-	4th overall
Craigantlet Hill Climb	Triumph TR2	-	-	-	2nd in class
MGCC Night Trial	Triumph TR2	-	-	J.Garvey	1st overall
Irish 900 Mile Rally	Triumph TR2	-	-	J.Garvey	1st overall
Circuit of Clare Trial	Triumph TR2	PRI 222	27	-	1st overall
Cork 20	Triumph TR2	-	-	J.Garvey	3rd overall

Hewison Trophy: Paddy Hopkirk/John Garvey – Winners

Event	Car	Reg.	No.	Co-driver	Result

1956

Event	Car	Reg.	No.	Co-driver	Result
RAC Rally	Standard 10	PRW 534	25	J.Garvey	Finisher
Dublin University MCC & LC Winter Rally	Triumph TR2	-	-	-	1st Open class
Munster 20-hour Navigation Trial	VW Beetle	-	-	-	3rd overall, Conway Cup (Team Award)
Kilkenny Winter Trial	Triumph TR2	-	-	-	15th overall, 3rd in class
Connaught Winter Trial	Triumph TR2	-	-	-	4th overall, 1st Sports Car
MGCC Winter Trial	Triumph TR2	-	-	-	5th overall, 2nd in class
Dublin University Rally	Triumph TR2	-	-	-	8th overall, 2nd in class
Henderson Cup Trial	Triumph TR2				5th overall, Sports Car Award
IMRC Winter Cup Trial	Standard	-	-	-	12th overall
Circuit of Ireland	Triumph TR2	PRI 222	159	-	-
Circuit of Munster	Triumph TR2	-	-	-	13th overall
Tulip Rally	Standard 8	SHP 876	201	J.Garvey	3rd overall, 3rd in class, Team Prize
Cranfield Race Meeting	Triumph TR2	PRI 222	27	-	3rd, scratch race; 1st, A-Healey v TR race
IMRC Enniskerry Hill Climb	Triumph TR2	-	41	-	3rd in class (Open h/cap) 5th in class (Open Scratch)
Dungarvan Hill Climb	Triumph TR2	-	-	-	FTD (equal) 1st in class (h/cap class) 1st in class (Scratch class)
Midnight Sun Rally	Triumph TR3	SRW 991	-	W.Cave	5th Series Sports Car Class
Alpine Rally	Triumph TR3	SRW 991	408	W.Cave	13th overall, 2nd in class Coupe des Alpes
Knock MC & CC Night Trial	Triumph TR3	-	-	-	1st in class, Team Prize
Circuit of Clare	Triumph TR2	PRI 222	30	J.Garvey	1st overall
Craigantlet Hill Climb	Ford Anglia	ZF 6122	-	-	3rd in class
Cork 20	VW Beetle	-	-	J.Garvey	1st overall, Conway Cup
IMRC Autumn Trial	Ford Anglia	-	-	J.Garvey	1st overall
Kilkenny Trial	Ford Anglia	-	-	J.Garvey	2nd overall
VW O'Flaherty Trial	VW Beetle	-	-	C.Brady	1st overall
Connaught Winter Trial	Ford Anglia	-	-	-	1st overall

1956 Hewison Memorial Trophy – P. Hopkirk winner

1957

Event	Car	Reg.	No.	Co-driver	Result
Irish MRC Trial	Ford Anglia	ZF 6122	-	J.Garvey	2nd class Award
Irish MRC Baldonnel Tests	Ford Anglia	ZF 6122	-	J.Garvey	1st in class
Ulster AC Easter Rally for Motors	Ford Anglia	ZF 6122	-	J.Garvey	1st overall
MEC Conducted Trial	Ford Anglia	-	-	J.Garvey	1st Saloon
Knock MC & CC Night Trial	Ford Anglia	ZF 6122	-	J.Garvey	2nd overall, 1st in class
Kilkenny Vigzol Cup	Ford Anglia	-	-	-	Vigzol Cup
Tulip Rally	Triumph TR3	TRW 737	19	J.Garvey	20th overall, 3rd in class
Circuit of Down	Ford Anglia	-	-	J.Garvey	4th overall, Scratch Award
Circuit of Munster	Ford Anglia	-	-	A.Jolley	2nd overall, Team Award
Kirkistown Race Meeting	Ford Anglia	ZW 3113	-	-	3rd, Saloon H/Cap Race
Craigantlet Hill Climb	Ford Anglia	-	-	-	3rd in class
Lisdoonvarna Hill Climb	Ford Anglia	-	-	-	1st, over 1-litre Saloon Scratch
Midnight Sun Rally	Standard V/Junior	TRW 599	77	J.Garvey	22nd overall
Circuit of Clare	Ford Anglia	-	-	-	1st overall, 1st in class
Kilkenny Winter Trial	Ford Anglia	-	-	-	1st overall
Holt Cup Trial	Ford Anglia	-	-	-	3rd overall
Connaught Winter Trial	Ford Anglia	-	-	-	1st overall
Cork 20 Rally	VW Beetle	-	-	J.Scott	1st overall, Team Award

Hewison Trophy (abandoned after 5 events owing to Suez crisis) – P.Hopkirk Special Award
Newry Trio – 3 events (reduced by Suez) – P. Hopkirk 4th overall

1958

Event	Car	Reg.	No.	Co-driver	Result
IMRC Winter Cup Trial	Ford Anglia	-	-	-	16th overall
Monte Carlo Rally	Triumph TR3A	VRW 220	329	J.Scott	Retd – OTL
Corkscrew Hill Climb	A35 Speedwell	WZ 7222	-	-	1st in class
RAC Rally	Std Pennant	VWK 284	133	J.Scott	Finisher
Cairncastle Hill Climb	A35 Speedwell	WZ 7222	-	-	1st, Saloon H/cap
Enniskerry Hill Climb	A35 Speedwell	WZ 7222	-	-	-

Event	Car	Reg.	No.	Co-driver	Result
1958 continued					
Spelga Hill Climb	A35 Speedwell	WZ 7222	6	-	1st, Production Saloon class
Syonfin Hill Climb	A35 Speedwell	WZ 7222			1st, Saloon H/cap; 1st, H/cap overall
Kirkistown Race Meeting	A35 Speedwell	WZ 7222	-	-	1st, Saloon H/cap
Circuit of Ireland	Triumph TR3A	VRW 220	1	J.Scott	1st overall, 1st in Class, Team Prize
Alpine Rally	Triumph TR3A	VRW 220	401	J.Scott	Retd – engine
Circuit of Down Trial	A35 Speedwell	WZ 7222	-	-	1st overall, Scratch Award
McMullan & Holt Cups	A35 Speedwell	WZ 7222	-	-	3rd overall
Lisdoonvarna Hill Climb	A35 Speedwell	WZ 7222	2	-	1st, 1000cc; Scratch 3rd, Unlimited H/Cap
Kirkistown Race Meeting (May)	A35 Speedwell	WZ 7222	-	-	3rd overall; 3rd, Saloon H/cap
Long Kesh Race Meeting (June)	A35 Speedwell	WZ 7222	-	-	1st, H/Cap Final
Craigantlet Hill Climb (Aug)	A35 Speedwell	WZ 7222	2	-	1st, 1000cc H/cap class 3rd, overall H/cap
Knockagh Hill Climb (Sept)	A35 Speedwell	WZ 7222	4	-	1st, 1000cc Saloon class
Circuit of Clare	Ford Anglia	-	-	-	7th overall
Cranfield Race Mtg	A35 Speedwell	WZ 7222	-	-	1st Gen H/cap Final
Kirkistown Race Meeting	A35 Speedwell	WZ 7222	-	-	Hutchinson Trophy, 5th overall
Cork 20 Rally	VW Beetle	-	-	-	3rd overall, Conway Cup
Connaught Winter Trial	A35 Speedwell	WZ 7222	-	-	1st overall
MGCC Winter Trial	Ford Anglia	-	-	-	4th overall

The Newry Club Shield – P. Hopkirk 3rd overall

Event	Car	Reg.	No.	Co-driver	Result
1959					
Dungarvan Hill Climb	AH Sprite	WZ 9303	28	-	-
Monte Carlo Rally	Riley 1.5	-	116	Les Leston	82nd overall, 2nd in class
Dungarvan Hill Climb	A35 Speedwell	-	-	-	2nd, Allcomers H/cap
Dunboyne	AH Sprite	WZ 9303	34	-	-
Enniskerry Hill Climb	AH Sprite	WZ 9303	-	-	2nd, Open Car H/cap 1st in class, Premier Award
Coronation Safari Rally	Hillman Husky	KGD 835	30	R.Dalton	Retd – engine
Circuit of Munster	AH Sprite	-	-	-	1st overall
Long Kesh Race Meeting	Speedwell Sprite	-	-	-	1st, h/cap for Prod Sports Cars 1st, h/cap for all cars
Alpine Rally	Sunbeam Rapier	VRW 507	62	J.Scott	3rd overall, 1st in class
MEC Toastal Rally	AH Sprite	-	-	-	Toastal Shield
Liège–Rome–Liège Rally	Sunbeam Rapier	VRW 507	59	C.Vard	Retd
Knockagh Hill Climb	A-Healey Sprite	-	-	-	1st, class up to 1300cc
Ken Wharton Trophy D/Tests	AH Sprite	-	-	-	Captain of winning Ulster team
Kirkistown Race Meeting	AH Sprite	WZ 9303	28	-	1st in class
RAC Rally	Sunbeam Rapier	VRW 507	86	J.Scott	Retd – axle

Event	Car	Reg.	No.	Co-driver	Result
1960					
Monte Carlo Rally	Sunbeam Rapier	YWK 3	62	J.Scott	Retd – accident
Pre-Circuit Navigation Event	AH Sprite	WZ 9303	-	J.Scott	1st overall
UAC Winter Rally	Trokart	-	-	-	2nd in class
MGCC Irish Centre Midland Circuit Trial	Austin Mini	-	-	-	1st in class
East African Safari	Sunbeam Rapier	-	85	K.Mandeville	Retd – diff
MG Midland Circuit	Austin Mini	-	-	-	1st in class
Dunboyne Race Mtg	AH Sprite	2222 AZ	7	-	5th overall Holmpatrick Trophy
Kirkistown Race Meeting	AH Sprite	2222 AZ	48	-	1st, Memorial Trophy; 1st, A-Healey race
Baird Memorial	-	-	-	-	-
Knock All-Night Rally	AH Sprite	2222 AZ	60	-	-
DU MC&LCC Grafton Cup	AH Sprite	-	-	-	2nd overall
Castlemaine Hill Climb	AH Sprite	-	-	-	3rd in class, up to 1250cc
Phoenix Park Race Meeting	AH Sprite	2222 AZ	32	-	1st Heat 2, Open H/cap
Gran Canaria Rally	Sunbeam Rapier	YVC 431	16	L.Garrard	6th overall, 1st in class
Tulip Rally	Sunbeam Rapier	YWK 2	116	J.Scott	Retd – OTL
Knockagh Hill Climb	AH Sprite	2222AZ	-	-	1st, sports car to 1000cc; 1st, up to 1300cc class
British GP Silverstone Trg Car Race	Sunbeam Rapier	YWK 3	12	-	1st in class
Alpine Rally	Sunbeam Rapier	YWK 3	33	J.Scott	10th overall, 6th Trg Cat, 2nd in class
Craigantlet Hill Climb	AH Sprite	2222 AZ	-	-	1st in class to 1000cc

Event	Car	Reg.	No.	Co-driver	Result
1960 continued					
Riverside GP Compact Car Race	Sunbeam Rapier	-	75	-	Retd – lost wheel
Ken Wharton Mem Driving Tests	AH Sprite	2222 AZ	-	-	1st in class, NI team Prize
1961					
Monte Carlo Rally	Sunbeam Rapier	YWK 3	45	J.Scott	13th overall, 2nd in class
Sebring 12-hr Race	Sunbeam Alpine	-	40	P.Jopp	4th in class
Enniskerry Hill Climb	FJ Elva	-	-	-	2nd, Allcomers scratch 2nd, racing car scratch
Circuit of Ireland	Sunbeam Rapier	YWK 4	75	J.Scott	1st overall, Team Prize
Dungarvan Hill Climb	FJ Elva	-	-	-	2nd in class A
Le Mans 24-hr Race	Sunbeam Alpine	3001 RW	35	P.Jopp	Disqualified
Farnanes Hill Climb	FJ Elva	-	-	-	FTD
Alpine Rally	Sunbeam Rapier	YVC 431	33	J.Scott	3rd overall, 1st in Group 1 Team Prize Gatsonides Cup
Knockagh Hill Climb	Lotus 18 FJ	-	-	-	1st F/Junior
	Sunbeam Alpine				1st in GT 1000-1600cc class
Dunboyne Trophy Race	Sunbeam Alpine	-	57	-	Retd – radiator
Tour de France	Sunbeam		73	J.Scott	Retd
Kirkistown Race Meeting	Sunbeam Alpine	-	-	-	1st in MGA/Sunbeam race
	FJ Elva	-	-	-	3rd, F/Libre race
Rhodes Cup Trial	Sunbeam Alpine	-	26	-	1st in class
RAC Rally	Sunbeam Rapier	5192 RW	9	J.Scott	4th overall, 2nd in class, Team Prize
Ken Wharton Mem Driving Tests	-	-	-	-	1st overall, Team Prize
1962					
Monte Carlo Rally	Sunbeam Rapier	5192 RW	155	J.Scott	3rd overall
Circuit of Ireland	Sunbeam Rapier	YH...88	70	J.Scott	1st overall
Phoenix Park Race Meeting	Hillman Minx	HOP 750	3	-	1st, Saloon h/cap
	Lotus 18 FJ		4	-	
Enniskerry Hill Climb	Hillman Minx	HOP 750	-	-	1st, Scratch over 1000cc
Le Mans 24-hr Race	Sunbeam Alpine	9203 RW	33	P.Jopp	Retd – engine
Dunboyne Race Meeting	Lotus 18 FJ	-	20	-	3rd overall FJ race
	MGA T/Cam	-	31	-	Not placed (Leinster Trophy)
	MGA T/Cam	-	41	-	Not placed (Holmpatrick Trophy)
Kirkistown Race Meeting	Lotus 18 FJ	-	15	-	-
Tostal Trial	Hillman Minx	HOP 750	-	-	1st in class
Acropolis Rally	Sunbeam Rapier	-	-	J.Scott	Retd – engine
Liège–Sofia–Liège Rally	A-Healey 3000	57 ARX	12	J.Scott	Retd – suspn
London Rally	Morris 1100	577 BRX	22	J.Scott	Retd – clutch
Knockagh Hill Climb	Elva FJ	-	45	-	-
Brands 6-hr Race	Riley 1.5	VUV 390	21	A.Hutcheson	Retd – lost wheel
Enniskerry Hill Climb	Elva FJ	-	61	-	-
RAC Rally	A-Healey 3000	67 ARX	19	J.Scott	2nd overall, 1st in class
Go-As-You-Please Rally	A-Healey Sprite	-	-	-	1st overall
1963					
Monte Carlo Rally	Mini-Cooper	407 ARX	66	J.Scott	6th overall, 2nd in class
BBC Grandstand Autobog, Brands	Mini-Cooper	407 ARX		-	2nd overall
Lombank Trophy Meeting, Snetterton	Mini-Cooper	-	66	-	Not placed
Sebring 12-hr Race	A-Healey 3000	54 FAC	34	D.Morley	26th overall; 4th, Prot. class
Aintree 200 Race Meeting	Mini-Cooper	-	-	-	3rd in class
Oulton Park Race Meeting	Mini-Cooper	-	128	-	3rd in class
Easter Mon, St Mary Trophy, Goodwood	Mini-Cooper	-	94	-	Not placed
Int. Trophy, Silverstone	Cooper S 1071	-	18	-	2nd in class
Tulip Rally	Mini-Cooper	17 CRX	130	H.Liddon	2nd overall, 1st in class
Crystal Palace Small Car Trophy	Mini-Cooper	-	-	-	2nd overall
Le Mans 24-hr Race	MGB	7 DBL	31	A.Hutcheson	12th overall, 1st in class
Alpine Rally	A-Healey 3000	XJB 877	5	J.Scott	Retd – accident
RAC British GP – Touring Car Race	Cooper S 1071	-	7	-	2nd in class, Lap rcd 2m 01s 87.08 mph
Int. 6-hr Touring Car Race, Brands Hatch	Cooper S 1071	-	-	J.Whitmore	6th overall, 1st in class; 2nd, Index of Price
Mallory Park Race Meeting	Cooper S 1071	-	64	-	1st overall, Molyslip Trophy

Event	Car	Reg.	No.	Co-driver	Result

1963 continued

Event	Car	Reg.	No.	Co-driver	Result
Phoenix Park Race Meeting	Cooper S 1071	-	-	-	Retd – fuel pipe
August Bank Hol Meeting, B/Hatch	Cooper S 1071	-	-	-	3rd, Molyslip Trophy A; 3rd, Trophy B
Liège-Sofia-Liège Rally	A-Healey 3000	XJB 877	120	H.Liddon	6th overall, 1st in class
Tour de France	Cooper S 1071	33 EJB	38	H.Liddon	3rd overall
RAC Rally	Cooper S 1071	8 EMO	21	H.Liddon	4th overall, 2nd in class

1963 British Touring Car Championship – P. Hopkirk 6th overall

1964

Event	Car	Reg.	No.	Co-driver	Result
Monte Carlo Rally	Cooper S 1071	33 EJB	37	H.Liddon	1st overall, Team Prize
BBC TV Grandstand Prescott Hill Climb	Cooper S 1071	569 FMO	-	-	12th overall
Sebring 12-hr Race	A-Healey 3000	767 KNX	33	G.Clark	Retd – accident
Targa Florio	A-Healey Sprite	693 LAC	192	T.Wisdom	Retd – diff
Int Trophy Meeting, Silverstone	Cooper S 1275	-	8	-	1st in class
Int. Race Meeting, Snetterton	Cooper S 1275	-	87	-	2nd in class
Austrian Alpine Rally	A-Healey 3000	ARX 91B	2	H.Liddon	1st overall
Acropolis Rally	Cooper S 1275	AJB 55B	67	H.Liddon	Retd – battery cable
6-hr Int Touring Car Race, Brands Hatch	Cooper S 1275	-	-	-	Retd – clutch
Le Mans 24-hr Race	MGB	BMO 541B	37	A.Hedges	19th overall, 2nd in class; *Motor* Trophy
Aintree 200 Race Meeting	Cooper S 1275	-	-	-	2nd in class
GP of Europe, Brands Hatch Race	Cooper S 1275	-	74	-	12th overall, 4th in class
Alpine Rally	Cooper S 1275	AJB 44B	18	H.Liddon	Retd – suspension
Guards Trophy Meeting, B/Hatch	Cooper S 1275	-	-	-	DNS – fan belt
Spa-Sofia-Liège Rally	A-Healey 3000	BRX 852B	29	H.Liddon	Retd – gearbox
Spa 24-hr Touring Car Race	Cooper S 970	-	534	J.Vernaeve	1st in 851-1000cc class
Tour de France	Cooper S 1275	AJB 44B	19	H.Liddon	Retd
Knockagh Hill Climb	Cooper S 1071	288 JOB	-	-	1st in class
Mid-Antrim MC Driving Tests	Cooper S 1275	288 JOB	-	-	1st overall
RAC Rally	Cooper S 1275	CRX 90B	1	H.Liddon	Retd – accident

1965

Event	Car	Reg.	No.	Co-driver	Result
Monte Carlo Rally	Cooper S 1275	CRX 91B	56	H.Liddon	26th overall, 1st in class
Swedish Rally	Cooper S 1275	AJB 33B	28	H.Liddon	Retd – gearbox
Sebring 12-hr Race	Midget coupé	-	62	T.Makinen	18th overall, 2nd in class
Sebring 3-Hour Touring Car Race	Cooper S 1275	-	-	W.Banks	7th overall
Circuit of Ireland	Cooper S 1275	CRX 89B	2	T.Harryman	1st overall
Luxembourg Slalom	Cooper S 1275	CRX 89B	66	-	7th overall, 1st in class
Targa Florio	Midget coupé	771 BJB	44	A.Hedges	11th overall, 2nd in class
Guards 1000 Race, Brands Hatch	A-Healey 3000	ARX 91B	8	R.Mac	4th overall, 2nd in class
Le Mans 24-hr Race	MGB	DRX 255C	39	A.Hedges	11th overall, 2nd in class
Scottish Rally	Cooper S 1275	CRX 89B	3	H.Liddon	Retd – final drive
Nordrhein/Westfalen Rally	Cooper S 1275	DJB 92B	58	H.Liddon	6th overall, 1st in class
Alpine Rally	Cooper S 1275	EBL 56C	60	H.Liddon	4th in category, 2nd in class
Bridgehampton 500	MGB	BRX 853B	48	-	4th overall, 2nd in GT class
London Rally	Cooper S 1275	JBL 495D	6	H.Liddon	Retd – water pump
1000 Lakes Rally	Cooper S 1275	EBL 56C	22	K.Ruutsalo	6th overall
Ilford Films Trophy, Brands Hatch	Cooper S 1275	-	-	-	Retd
Six-hr Race, Sandown, Melbourne	Cooper S 1275	-	60	J.Fitzpatrick	5th overall
Armstrong 500, Bathurst	Cooper S 1275	-	30C	T.Makinen	3rd in class
RAC Rally	Cooper S 1275	EBL 56C	8	H.Liddon	13th overall, 2nd in class

1966

Event	Car	Reg.	No.	Co-driver	Result
Monte Carlo Rally	Cooper S 1275	GRX 5D	230	H.Liddon	3rd overall (Disqualified)
Rally of the Flowers	Cooper S 1275	GRX 309D	50	R.Crellin	15th overall, 6th in class
Sebring 12-hr Race	MGB 2-litre	8 DBL	44	A.Hedges	Retd – conrod
Sebring 4-hr Race	Cooper S 1275	-	-	P.Manton	Retd – timing chain
European Touring Car Ch'ship, Monza	Cooper S 970	-	-	-	5th in class
Circuit of Ireland	Cooper S 1275	GRX 55D	1	T.Harryman	Retd – accident
Le Mans 24-hr Race	A-Healey Sprite	-	49	A.Hedges	Retd – engine
European Touring Car Ch'ship, Aspern	Cooper S 970	-	-	-	3rd in class
Austrian Alpine Rally	Cooper S 1275	DJB 92B	58	R.Crellin	1st overall
European Touring Car Ch'ship Race	Cooper S 970	-	-	-	3rd in class
Acropolis Rally	Cooper S 1275	GRX 311D	67	R.Crellin	3rd overall, 1st in class

Event	Car	Reg.	No.	Co-driver	Result
1966 continued					
Geneva Rally	Cooper S 1275	JBL 495D	50	T.Harryman	Retd – gearbox
London Rally	Cooper S 1275	JBL 495D	6	R.Crellin	Retd
European Touring Car Ch'ship (500 Kms), Snetterton	Cooper S 970	-	-	A.Hedges	10th overall, 4th in class
German Rally	Cooper S 1275	GRX 311D	42	C.Nash	Retd – engine
European Touring Car Ch'ship 6-hr Race, Nürburgring	Cooper S 970	-	-	J.Rhodes	3rd in class
Alpine Rally	Cooper S 1275	GRX 311D	67	R.Crellin	Retd – transmission
Guards Trophy Race, B/Hatch	Cooper S 1275	-	-	-	3rd in class
Gallaher 500, Bathurst	Cooper S 1275	-	28C	B.Foley	Retd – engine
Southern Cross Rally	Cooper S 1275	-	-	G.Chapman	10th overall
Shenstone Rally	Cooper S 1275	-	1	R.Harper	1st overall
Motor Show 200 Meeting, B/Hatch	Cooper S 1275	-	-	-	4th in class
RAC Rally	Cooper S 1275	JMO 969D	10	R.Crellin	Retd – d/shaft
1967					
Monte Carlo Rally	Cooper S 1275	LBL 666D	205	R.Crellin	6th overall, 5th in class
Rally of Flowers	Cooper S 1275	LBL 590E	67	R.Crellin	2nd overall, 2nd in class
Circuit of Ireland	Cooper S 1275	GRX 5D	1	T.Harryman	1st overall
Sebring 3-hr Race	Cooper S 1275	GRX 309D	48	J.Rhodes	1st in class
Sebring 12-hr Race	MGB GT	LBL 591E	30	A.Hedges	3rd in category, 1st in class
Acropolis Rally	Cooper S 1275	LRX 830E	89	R.Crellin	1st overall
Targa Florio	MGB GTS	MBL 546E	230	T.Makinen	9th overall, 3rd in Sports Prototype class over 2000cc
Alpine Rally	Cooper S 1275	LRX 827E	107	R.Crellin	1st overall
Gallaher 500, Mt Panorama	Cooper S 1275	-	28C	B.Foley	4th in class
Southern Cross Rally	Cooper S 1275	LRX 828E	14	G.Chapman	Retd
Tour de Corse	Cooper S 1275	GRX 5D	79	R.Crellin	Retd – fan belt
World of Sport Rallycross, Lydden	Cooper S 1275	-	1	-	2nd overall
World of Sport Int Rallycross Trophy	Cooper S 1275	-	7	-	2nd overall
1968					
Monte Carlo Rally	Cooper S 1275	ORX 777F	87	R.Crellin	5th overall, 3rd in category
Sebring 12-hr Race	MGC GT S	MBL 546E	44	A.Hedges	10th overall, 1st in class
Circuit of Ireland	Cooper S 1275	JMO 969D	1	T.Harryman	Retd – diff
Canadian Shell 4000 Rally	Cooper S 1275	GRX 5D	119	M.Kerry	Disqualified
Targa Florio	MGB GT	LBL 591E	130	A.Hedges	12th overall, 2nd in category
TAP Rally	Cooper S 1275	LBL 606D	71	A.Nash	2nd overall, 2nd in class
London-to-Sydney Marathon	BMC 1800	SMO 226G	51	A.Nash/A.Poole	2nd overall
1969					
BBC TV Rallycross, Lydden Hill	BMC 1300 inj	-	66	-	6th overall
Sebring 12-hr Race	MGC GT S	RMO 699F	35	A.Hedges	15th overall 9th, Prototype category
Circuit of Ireland	Cooper S 1275	GRX 311D	2	A.Nash	2nd overall
Austrian Alpine Rally	Triumph 2.5PI	UJB 643G	11	A.Nash	Retd – clutch
Brands Hatch 6-hr Race	Cooper S 1275	GRX 310D		J.Rhodes	7th overall, 3rd in class
Tour de France	Cooper S 1275	OBL 45F	57	A.Nash	14th overall, 1st in class
RAC Rally	Triumph 2.5PI	VBL 197H	8	A.Nash	15th overall, 2nd in class
1970					
London-to-Mexico World Cup Rally	Triumph 2.5PI	XJB 302H	98	A.Nash/N.Johnston	4th overall, 2nd in class
Scottish Rally	Mini 1275GT	XJB 308H	14	A.Nash	2nd overall, 1st in class
1977-94					
1977 London-to-Sydney Marathon	Citroën CX2400	PJM 515R	45	M.Taylor/R.Riley	3rd overall
1982 RAC Golden 50	Cooper S 1275	AJB 44B	39	B.Culcheth	1st overall
1986 Coppa delle Alpi	Lancia Fulvia	319792	125	R.Lamplough	Retd
1989 Pirelli Classic Marathon	Cooper S 1275	EBL 56C	2	A.Poole	72nd overall
1990 Pirelli Classic Marathon	Cooper S 1275	6 EMO	2	A.Poole	1st overall
1992 Pirelli Classic Rally, South Africa	MGB	RLF 488T	6	Eddie Fee	2nd overall
1994 Monte Carlo Rally	Cooper 1.3i	L33 EJB	37	R.Crellin	60th overall, 4th in class

More about the 1964 Monte Carlo Rally

Special Stage Positions

Position	Stage 1	Stage 2	Stage 3	Stage 4	Stage 5
1.	Ljungfeldt	Ljungfeldt	Ljungfeldt	Hopkirk	Ljungfeldt
2.	Hopkirk	Trana	Böhringer	Morley	Carlsson
3.	Böhringer	Makinen	Makinen	Schlesser	Hopkirk
4.	Trana	Böhringer	Trana	Hopkirk	Skogh
5.	Makinen	Makinen	Carlsson	Böhringer	Pat Carlsson

Total Special Stage Times on Scratch

Position	Driver	Car	Time
1.	Ljungfeldt	Ford Falcon	105.52
2.	Hopkirk	Mini-Cooper	107.14
3.	Trana	Volvo	108.27
4.	Böhringer	Mercedes	108.41
5.	Morley	MGB	109.23
6.	Skogh	Volvo	110.01
7.	E.Carlsson	Saab	110.20
8.	Makinen	Mini-Cooper	110.25
9.	Pat Carlsson	Saab	111.07
10.	Aaltonen	Mini-Cooper	111.17

Overall Points after the Special Stages (including Coefficient)

Position	Driver	Car	Points	Coefficient
1.	Hopkirk/Liddon	Mini-Cooper	2152.17	(0.3345)
2.	Carlsson/Palm	Saab	2183.27	(0.3298)
3.	Carlsson/Wirth	Saab	2198.77	(0.3298)
4.	Makinen/Vanson	Mini-Cooper	2216.06	(0.3345)
5.	Ljungfeldt/Sager	Ford Falcon	2216.21	(0.3489)
6.	Trana/Lindstrom	Volvo	2223.44	(0.3417)
7.	Aaltonen/Ambrose	Mini Cooper	2233.45	(0.3345)
8.	Skogh/Berggren	Volvo	2255.56	(0.3417)
9.	Böhringer/Kaiser	Mercedes	2258.22	(0.3463)
10.	Toivonen/Jarvi	Volkswagen	2283.81	(0.3396)

GP Circuit Test Times – 3 Laps of 1.9 miles

Position	Driver	Car	Time
1.	Bo Ljungfeldt	Ford Falcon	5m 50.3secs
2.	Jo Schlesser	Ford Falcon	5m 53.9secs
3.	Günther Klass	Porsche Carrera	6m 2.7secs
4.	Graham Hill	Ford Falcon	6m 13.4secs
5.	Peter Jopp	Ford Falcon	6m 14.0secs
6.	Paddy Hopkirk	Mini-Cooper	6m 24.1secs
7.	Erik Carlsson	Saab 96	6m 30.5secs
8.	Pat Carlsson	Saab 96	6m 38.2secs
9.	Eugen Böhringer	Mercedes 300SE	6m 3.7secs
10.	Henry Taylor	Ford Cortina GT	6m 10.1secs

Final Results (after the 3 lap GP Circuit Test)

Position	Driver	Car	Points
1.	P.Hopkirk/H.Liddon	Mini-Cooper S 1071	2536.27
2.	B.Ljungfeldt/F.Sager	Ford Falcon 4.7-litre	2566.71
3.	E.Carlsson/G.Palm	Saab 96	2573.17
4.	T.Makinen/P.Vanson	Mini-Cooper S 1071	2593.86
5.	P.Carlsson/U.Wirth	Saab 96	2596.97
6.	T.Trana/S.Lindstrom	Volvo 122	2609.74
7.	R.Aaltonen/J.Ambrose	Mini Cooper S 1071	2619.55
8.	C.Skogh/L.Berggren	Volvo 122	2255.56
9.	E.Böhringer/K.Kaiser	Mercedes 300SE	2258.2
10.	P.Toivonen/A.Jarvi	Volkswagen 1500	2283.81

Mini-Cooper 'S' (1071cc), Monte Carlo Rally 1964

Brief specification of the winning car:

RAF-type sumpguard with alloy extensions
Oil cooler
10.5-to-1 compression ratio
Flat-top pistons
Champion N4 plugs
4.133-to-1 differential ratio
Twin 1½-inch SU carburettors
   with MME needles
Competition dampers
Four-bladed fan
28-amp dynamo
Two-speed wiper motor
Iodine headlamp bulbs dipping
   to fog lamps
2 x Lucas 700 fog lamps
1 x Lucas 576 long-range lamp
Roof lamp
Reversing lamp

Flexible navigator's lamp
Special dashboard
Headlamp washers
Accelerator pedal adapted for heel-and-toe
Fly-off handbrake
Electric rev counter
Stowage for two spare wheels
Ferodo DS11 front pads and VG95 rear shoes
All hydraulic pipes protected
Competition exhaust system
Wood rim steering wheel
Extension to steering column rake brackets
Heated windscreen
Perspex side and rear windows
Perspex heat shield inside front screen
Special heater unit
Passenger grab handle above door
Twin petrol tanks
Twin petrol pumps
Special Microcell seats, passenger's reclining

Index